# A MAN OF HIS WORD

©2011 MICHAEL ARCHER

Published by Hellgate Press

(An imprint of L&R Publishing, LLC)

All rights reserved. No part of this publication may be reproduced used in any form or by any means, graphic, electronic or mechanical, including photocopying, recording, taping, or information and retrieval systems without written permission of the publisher.

Hellgate Press
PO Box 3531
Ashland, OR 97520
www.hellgatepress.com

*Editing*: Harley B. Patrick
*Cover design*: L. Redding

*Cover photo, and all photos unless otherwise specified, courtesy of the Raggio Collection.*

*Back cover photo courtesy of Bob Cook.*

Library of Congress Cataloging-in-Publication Data
Archer, Michael, 1952-
A man of his word : the life & times of Nevada's Senator William J. Raggio / Michael Archer ; foreword by Richard Bryan. -- 1st ed.
p. cm.
ISBN 978-1-55571-680-6
1. Raggio, William John, 1926- 2. Legislators--Nevada--Biography. 3. Politicians--Nevada--Biography. 4. Public prosecutors--Nevada--Biography. 5. Nevada. Legislature. Senate--Biography. 6. Nevada--Politics and government. I. Title.
F845.25.R34A84 2011
328.73'092--dc22
[B]
2011008162

Printed and bound in the United States of America
First edition 10 9 8 7 6 5 4 3 2

G000095620

# A MAN OF

## THE LIFE & TIMES
## SENATOR WILLIA

Michael A

*Foreword by Richard*
*Former U.S. Senator and Gove*

HELLGATE PRESS    ASHLAND,

*To Becky, my loving wife and friend,*
*for all your encouragement and wisdom.*

# ❖ CONTENTS ❖

# A MAN OF HIS WORD

## THE LIFE & TIMES OF NEVADA'S SENATOR WILLIAM J. RAGGIO

### Michael Archer

# INTRODUCTION

I must acknowledge that I initially resisted the idea of a book written about my life. My career, though long, didn't rise to the heights of national or international importance, but rather was confined primarily to my native and beloved state of Nevada.

I guess I still question why anyone would want to read about my exploits; there are so many more interesting personages out there than I. But, so many friends insisted, as did my beautiful and supportive wife, Dale, that I acquiesced to participate in this book.

I agreed to do so if Michael Archer would agree to do the research and author the book. He is an outstanding writer who I knew as a member of our legislative staff and who had written a book entitled *A Patch of Ground* about his service as a marine in the Vietnam War. His style and prose are excellent and I commend him for his efforts in making my rather dull story interesting reading.

When I stopped to count the years during which I was engaged in public service in our state, I was amazed when I realized it was more than fifty-six years; that must be some kind of a record! This includes six and a half years as an assistant district attorney, twelve years as the elected district attorney of Washoe County (three terms) and thirty-eight years as an elected state senator (ten terms) from Washoe County.

Obviously, a book covering that long a period of time will have some omissions. Frankly, it's tough to remember everything that ever happened to oneself, and memories do grow dimmer as the years go by.

There were persons who played important roles in my life that have not been included in this book, most of them now deceased. In addition to my own family, including my two daughters, Leslie and Tracy, and the memory of my son Mark who died unexpectedly in 2004, I am blessed with six grandchildren of whom I am exceedingly proud: Jennifer Righetti Santos; Michael Righetti, J.D.; Jonathan "Jolly" Righetti, B.A.; Meghan Righetti, B.A.; Sommer Fernandes; Anthony Woodring; and a new great-grandson, Julian.

My high school chums included John Webster Brown (a noted civil engineer), George Siri (Annapolis graduate and Reno businessman), Bill Teipner (noted orthopedic surgeon), Mel Rovetti (florist-deceased), Bob Uecker (best man at my first marriage, deceased) and Dick Munn (best friend and hunting partner, deceased ). I met Dick Lee while in the service (he and his brother, Jennings, founded Lee Bros., a Reno car establishment still in existence). All of these individuals were a large and important part of my early years.

During my years as district attorney I had the opportunity to be associated with many dedicated law enforcement personnel whom I would like to remember: former Reno police chiefs Ted Berrum, Clayton Phillips, Elmer Briscoe; assistant police chief Bill Brodhead; Sparks police chiefs Bob Galli and Tommy Hill; Washoe County sheriffs Ray Root, George Lothrop, Dick O'Boyle, C.W. "Bud" Young, Vince Sweeney; chief investigators Bill Driscoll and Dallas Seevers; and chief of the Nevada Highway Patrol, Jim Lambert, among others. As chief law enforcement officer of the county, I had a close working relationship with all of them and their staffs.

I enjoyed a close friendship with many fine jurists whom I admired and respected, including judges Grant Bowen, A.J. Maestretti, Gordon Rice, Clel Georgetta, Harold Taber, Tom Craven, John Barrett, Bill Forman and three of my ex deputies, Emile Gezelin, John Gabrielli and Jack Mathews. I also admired supreme court justices Frank McNamee, Milton Badt, Miles Pike, Gordon Thompson, John Mowbray and Cameron Batjer, and others. I tried a number of cases before all of them—usually successful, I might add!

As district attorney, I created the Nevada District Attorney's Association, serving as its initial president, and it continues until this day. I enjoyed the support of some fellow DA's including George Dickerson, Ted Marshall, George Foley and Jack Cherry of Clark County; Bob Moore of Storey County; Ted Stokes of Ormsby County; Doc Ballinger of Pershing County; Joe McDaniel of Elko County; and Howard McKibbon of Douglas county. All were dedicated professionals.

In my career as a lawyer, I've been fortunate to have been associated with some of the finest members of the state bar, including Clint Wooster, Mike Lindell, Al Pagni, Dave Guinan, Lee Walker, Rennie Ashelman, Skip Avansino, Louis Wiener, J. Charles Thompson, Dave Goldwater, John Sande III, Michael Alonso, Ann Morgan, Gary Goodheart, Joe Brown and Jim Wadhams, among others, all of whom put up with my eccentric practice habits.

I would be remiss if I did not mention the loyal and dedicated secretaries and executive assistants who worked with me for long periods of time in my law practice, including Fern Gwen Davis, Rynell Butler, Lee Eakes, Dorothy Roberts, Lucille Hill, Dorothy Souza, Mildred Row and several others. I could not have functioned without their assistance.

I have also appreciated the opportunity to serve on a number of boards over the years, both for profit and non profit, including the Salvation Army; Washoe County School District Education Foundation (Now Education Alliance); the American Legislative Exchange Council (ALEC); Las Vegas Sands Corporation and Archon Corporation, headed by my close friend, Paul Lowden; Sierra Health Services (now United Health Care), and their able chairman of the board Dr. Anthony Marlon; and the E.L. Wiegand Foundation, the latter under the leadership of Skip and Kristen Avansino with the opportunity to participate in some meaningful contributions.

As a state senator for over thirty-eight years, I served with many colleagues for whom I had great respect. I can't begin to name all of them, nor are they all referenced in this book. I benefited from my association with all of them, great law makers such as Mahlon Brown (Clark), Jim Gibson (Clark), Floyd Lamb (Lincoln/Clark), Snowy Monroe (Elko),

Coe Swobe (Washoe), Cliff Young (Washoe), Spike Wilson (Washoe), Carl Dodge (Churchill), Rick Blakemore (Mineral), Richard Bryan (Clark), Archie Pozzi (Ormsby), Lawrence Jacobson (Douglas), Margie Foote (Washoe), Mel Close (Clark) Norm Glaser (Elko), Jean Ford (Clark), Don Ashworth and Keith Ashworth (Clark), Bob Ryan (Clark), Bob Robinson (Clark), Nick Horn (Clark), Jim Bilbray (Clark), Jack Regan (Clark), Ray Rawson (Clark), Sue Lowden (Clark), Mark James (Clark), Ann O'Connell (Clark), Joe Neal (Clark), Sue Wagner (Washoe), and more recently Dennis Nolan (Clark), Dina Titus (Clark), Dean Rhoads (Elko), Bob Coffin (Clark), Bernice Mathews (Washoe), Terry Care (Clark), Mark Amodei (Carson), Steven Horsford (Clark) and especially Randolph Townsend (Washoe), who really was my loyal aid-de-camp during my years as leader. There were so many others, whom I have failed to mention, but all of these were examples of the dedicated men and women who helped preserve the dignity and high purpose of the Nevada State Senate, an institution I revere.

I had the privilege of serving with nine lieutenant governors in their capacity as presidents of the state senate, including Harry Reid (now our senior U.S. Senator), Bob Rose (who became a justice of the supreme court), Myron Leavitt (also a justice), Bob Cashell (now mayor of Reno), Bob Miller (later our governor), Sue Wagner, Lonnie Hammargren, Lorraine Hunt and Brian Krolicki. Each had his or her own style, but all presided with fairness and helped to maintain the dignity and decorum of the senate. I have been proud to call each of them a friend.

The Nevada legislature, although we are one of the smaller states and only meet bi-annually, has one of the finest staffs of any legislature body. It has had some fine and talented attorneys who have served as legislative counsel, including Russ McDonald and Frank Daykin, both of whom had instant recall and served before modern technology, as did Lorne Malkiewich (now director of the LCB) and Brenda Erdoes, the latter lady whom I would rate as an outstanding lawyer and without peer. This job has grown immensely and Brenda handles it with great proficiency, unique skill and competent administrative ability. She, at all times, keeps her cool, and resists when legislators, and others, try to lean on her to abandon her firm non-partisan posture and issue "favorable" opinions. Brenda runs an extremely dedicated and efficient legal division.

As chair of the Senate Committee on Finance, I was fortunate to have the assistance of a highly competent staff from the Fiscal Division over the years, including Ron Sparks, Bill Bible, Dan Miles, Gary Ghiggeri, Bob Guernsey, Mark Stevens, Brian Burke, Steve Abba, Jeanne Botts, Pepper Sturm, Mindy Martini, Russell Guindon, and many others. These folks worked long hours to aid us in understanding difficult budget issues—we could never have completed our work without them.

Don Williams in research, and Paul Townsend in audit, head very competent divisions which provide extremely valuable services to an ever changing array of legislators, all directed by Lorne Malkiewich, who is also firm and competent, but somehow manages to make every legislator feel important. I would be remiss if I failed to mention former directors Art Palmer and John Crossley, as well as Andy Grose, Bob Erickson and Fred Welden, the latter three of research, all of whom played significant roles.

I've also had the good fortune to serve with three outstanding secretaries of the senate and their very competent and dedicated staffs: Leola Armstrong, Jan Thomas and Claire Clift; my gratitude to each of them. The senate would not have functioned without their direction.

I never had the opportunity to serve in the assembly, the "lower house," but always worked closely with its leadership, including some very able and dedicated speakers including Paul May, Jack Vergiels, Keith Ashworth, Bob Barengo, Bill Bilyeu, Lynn Hettrick, Richard Perkins, Barbara Buckley and, of course the longest serving speaker, Joe Dini. The latter and I enjoyed a close relationship, especially since we were both of Italian descent and represented the northern interests. And I can't fail to mention (the late) Marvin Sedway and "Moose" Arberry, who chaired the Assembly Committee on Ways and Means during the twenty years I served as chair of the Senate Committee on Finance. Together, we were able to work through a lot of difficult matters and enjoyed the respect of one another.

Interaction with the media is an integral part of public service, though it can often be disturbing. I have always looked forward to the daily newspapers, but unfortunately the print media is in decline and is being replaced by technology, including web sites where cowardly anonymous bloggers are permitted to vent their spleens! Truly unfortunate!

Over the years I would divide the media into two camps: the straight-forward reporters who are objective and strive to be fair and accurate, and the "slanters," who develop a personal bias and have the story written their way even before they call you for "your side."

Among the former, I would mention Paul Leonard (Editor, *Nevada State Journal*); Charles Radebaugh (*San Francisco Chronicle*); Herb Caen (*San Francisco Chronicle*); Walt McKenzie (*Reno Evening Gazette*); Ed Montgomery (*S.F. Examiner*); Frank McCulloch (*Nevada State Journal*); Rollan Melton and Warren Lerude (Reno newspapers); Frank Johnson (*Nevada State Journal*); Joe Midmore (*Reno Evening Gazette*); Russ Nielsen (UPI); Brian Greenspun and Cy Ryan (*Las Vegas Sun*); Geoff Dornan (*Nevada Appeal*); Guy Shipler, (*Time*); Dennis Myers (*Reno News & Review*); Ed Vogel, Sean Whaley, Laura Myers and Jayne Ann Morrison (*Las Vegas Review Journal*); Ray Hagar and Guy Clifton (*Reno Gazette-Journal*); Steve Sebelius (*Las Vegas City Life*); and David McGrath-Schwartz (*Las Vegas Sun*). They have been a credit to the journalistic profession.

I would also mention Jon Ralston and Sam Shad in this group. Their television programs are always well presented and they attempt to air all sides of an issue.

Lastly, the lobbyists with whom I have come in contact over the thirty-eight years I served in the senate, both those who are paid and unpaid. There have been hundreds, some great, some mediocre, some bad. To the average citizen the term "lobbyist" is in disfavor, but be assured that they play an important role in the legislative process, furnishing important information on bills and issues. The good ones never misinform you and are willing to tell you all sides of the issue.

Some of the great one's were people like George Vargas, Bob Guinn,

Wallie Warren, Jim Joyce, Harvey Whittemore, Jon Sasser, Greg Ferraro, Billy Vassiliadis, Mary Henderson, Tina Nappe, John Pappageorge, Pete Ernaut, Richard Bunker, Sam McMullen, Jan Gilbert, Irene Porter, Joe Guild, Randy Brown, Jeanette Belz, Judy Stokey, Bebe Adams, Mike Hillerby, Fred Hillerby, John Madole, Rennie Ashelman and certainly others too numerous to mention.

So this is an attempt to reflect on over fifty-six years of public service and over eighty-four years of life which the good lord has given me. There are very few things I would have done differently, even now knowing the consequences, but I have always tried to keep my word on things that I believed. I am honored and privileged to have had the sustained support of my constituents, and must acknowledge that it's been a great ride.

BILL RAGGIO
January 1, 2011
Reno, Nevada

I first came to know Senator Bill Raggio in January 2003 when, as a new senate attaché, I was assigned to the Committee on Finance. I was immediately impressed by his wisdom, humor and élan. In each succeeding session of the Nevada legislature, I grew more respectful of his talent, particularly his knack for cutting through what appeared to be an unfathomable amount of data and extracting the essence of an issue.

I was honored when Senator Raggio asked me to write his life story. Yet, there was also some anxiety. I questioned whether anyone's skills would be adequate to the task of capturing the life of someone whose dynamic nature and tireless dedication to public service seemed to fill every waking moment of the last sixty years.

Underlying that concern was my long-standing skepticism about politics and politicians. I wondered if such suspicion would cloud my perspective. Worse, that exploring the life of such a significant political figure as Bill Raggio might somehow amplify my distrust of the political process. "No man is a hero to his own valet," wrote 16th century French Renaissance essayist Michel de Montaigne, while suffering through his own "skeptical crisis."

Nearly three years of research went into this project, including hundreds of hours poring over books, periodicals, government records and newspapers. I also conducted scores of interviews with family members, schoolmates, friends, professional colleagues and fellow legislators.

This process, along with my continuing work at the legislature each session, taught me that the majority of legislators, from both political parties, are decent, hardworking individuals deserving of the public trust. Yet despite this, they are often unappreciated, and occasionally insulted, for the sacrifices they make in time away from their families, and their livelihoods, in order to do the work of the people.

For many years, Bill Raggio has been recognized as the most skilled and knowledgeable of these lawmakers and is widely admired for his prodigious intellect, extraordinary retention and keen political instincts, even among those who do not share his political philosophy.

Bill is a person of intense loyalty and (often-anonymous) compassion. In the course of my research, I came across scores of notes and letters thanking Senator Raggio for some act of kindness or generosity. It would be impossible to count the number of flowers and cards, calls of encouragement or congratulations, visits to sick beds, words of condolence, or eulogies, Bill provided over the years; nor imagine where, among the demands of his personal and professional life, he found the time and the energy to be there for so many people.

He is also a person of honor. In what I found to be a remarkable illustration of consistency, nearly everyone I interviewed for this book voiced the identical phrase in describing him—"A man of his word." Each of those utterances seemed tinged with a longing for a time past; when to have been otherwise, would have been a disgrace.

Bill Raggio has guided the state senate with a willingness to listen and consider the needs and opinions of others. His charm, patience and sense of fairness, balanced, when he felt it necessary, with an intimidating presence and an occasional calculated fit of temper, has steered colleagues to acceptable compromises and kept that governing body functioning for decades.

My early concern that a thorough study of his life would lead me to greater skepticism of the political process could not have been more unwarranted. In fact, there were times I had to shake my head in amazement at his courage in the face of both physical danger, as a district attorney, and weighty matters of conscience, as a lawmaker.

I hope the example set by Bill Raggio throughout his life helps inspire others to recognize that integrity, courage and compassion are not merely worthy and attainable virtues, but are essential to the healthy governance of Nevada and our nation.

When Bill Raggio came to the Nevada State Legislature as a newly elected senator from Washoe County, he was already an established political figure. As a deputy district attorney, and later, as the District Attorney of Washoe County, Bill frequently graced the front pages of Nevada's newspapers and achieved some national notoriety with his high profile criminal prosecutions and the celebrated torching of Joe Conforte's brothel.

Occasionally, his stand on issues would lead to public clashes with the Governor's Office and the Nevada Supreme Court. But, Bill was highly respected by his fellow prosecutors across the country, best illustrated by his being honored as the Outstanding Prosecutor in the United States in 1964 and later being the first Nevadan elected as president of the National District Attorneys' Association.

I joined Bill Raggio in the legislature, as a newly elected state senator, in January of 1973. Although I had met him on a number of occasions prior to our state senate service, I did not know him well. My expectation was that he would continue to be the personification of a fire-and-brimstone prosecutor and that his legislative interests would be confined primarily to law enforcement issues. I could not have been more wrong.

Though Democrats held a fourteen-to-six majority in the state senate at that time, Raggio, a Republican, was immediately welcomed into the "bosom of the lodge" where the key decisions were made. The Nevada Legislature was then a collegial body. There was no personal acrimony between its members and, if there were party caucuses in the senate, they were few and far between.

In just over a decade, Raggio would become the senate majority floor leader and chair of the Senate Committee on Finance—positions he would hold until the Democrats regained control of the Senate in 2008. His longevity in these legislative positions is all the more remarkable because of the dramatic political power shift to Clark County during his tenure. The year Raggio came to the senate, Clark County had eleven state senators and the rest of the state had nine. Following the 2000 decennial census, that margin would grow to fifteen to six.

How did he do it? Bill Raggio is smart, hard working and plays the political game like an accomplished chess player—always several moves ahead of his adversaries. No one understands the legislative process better and no one plays his legislative cards closer to his vest. In his thirty-eight years in Carson City, Bill became acknowledged by all as the "Master of the Senate."

Bill Raggio is a product of the old school of Nevada politics, a conservative by philosophical orientation—but no ideologue—with a clear eye on his objective. He is a pragmatist who recognizes that compromise is not an act of betrayal or surrender, but the only way in the legislative process to achieve results for his constituents. Although what was best for the state of Nevada was always his guiding star—no one benefited more from his legislative craft than Washoe County and the University of Nevada, Reno.

Travelers arriving at the Reno airport are greeted with a bust of the senator—proclaiming him as the father of the Washoe County Airport Authority. On the University of Nevada campus, students are reminded daily of the senator's strong commitment to higher education by the looming presence of the William J. Raggio College of Education Building. In Clark County, his contribution as an outstanding role model for those entering the legal profession is seen in his name on the largest classroom facility at UNLV's Boyd School of Law. No legislator in the annals of Nevada history has left a larger footprint on the political landscape of Nevada.

Mike Archer, in his carefully researched and very readable book, informs the reader of Raggio's deep family roots in Nevada; the events in his life that formed his character; and the triumphs, and defeats, of his nearly six decades of public service. In recounting the remarkable life of Nevada's longest serving state legislator, Archer also provides valuable insight into the changes that have occurred in Nevada from mid-twentieth century to the present.

*A Man of His Word* is a must read for scholars of Nevada history and is a book every Nevadan will love.

SENATOR RICHARD H. BRYAN
January 19, 2011

On election night, November 3, 1970, Bill Raggio sat back in a red leather reading-chair in the living room of his home, surrounded by family and friends, watching the returns on television. The capable and eloquent forty-four year old Republican District Attorney of Washoe County had challenged incumbent Howard Cannon for his seat in the United States Senate.

Televised vote tabulations indicated Bill was doing well throughout most of the state, yet was being soundly defeated in populous Clark County. This had been predicted in pre-election polls, so he was not surprised. He was, however, angry.

What angered Bill was that he had never really wanted to run for the U.S. Senate. Instead, he had set his sights on the governorship and all indications were that 1970 would be a promising year for him to make that run. Early polls showed Bill to be a twenty-point favorite over any Democratic challenger. It would take a stroke of exceedingly bad luck to prevent him from becoming Nevada's next governor. Yet, just such misfortune occurred when President Richard M. Nixon decided to take a personal interest in Bill Raggio's political career.

A Democratic majority in the U.S. Senate had recently handed the president two humiliating defeats on his Supreme Court nominations. In addition, they had challenged his prerogative to invade Cambodia and barely permitted him a victory on his anti-ballistic missile program.

To remedy this situation, Nixon decided to create a line-up of nine handpicked, candidates to recapture a Republican majority. All were attractive, articulate and energetic young men from key states. Besides, Bill Raggio, this group included, among others, Minnesota's Clark MacGregor, William V. Roth, Jr. of Delaware, Tennessee's William Brock III and George Herbert Walker Bush from Texas.

Bill came under intense pressure from both state and national Republican Party leaders, including a personal telephone call from Vice President Spiro T. Agnew on the president's behalf. He was eventually persuaded to belay his dream of the governorship and run for the U.S. Senate.

Loyal to his party, even in the face of a decision he knew to be misguided, Bill ran a hard campaign. Despite being saddled with the political fallout from the president's unpopular decision to invade Cambodia, the subsequent national shock of the Kent State shootings; a faltering economy and political blundering on the part of fellow Nevada Republicans, Bill worked to articulate the concerns of enough conservative Democrats to overcome the huge disadvantage in voter registration.

Yet, in the end, Nixon would betray Bill for the sake of political expediency—helping Democratic Senator Cannon's reelection. In 1996, Bill would say, "It turned out to be the biggest mistake of my political life… The White House pulled the rug out from under me, even though they had persuaded me to run."[1]

Raggio had built his reputation on audacity and brilliant prosecutorial skills. Highly respected and nationally recognized for his ability and sense of duty to the public he served, Bill had been honored by his peers as the Outstanding Prosecutor in the United States for 1964. He was subsequently elected president of the National District Attorneys Association.

As a fledging district attorney, Bill was appalled by rampant corruption in the Reno Police Department and City Council, eventually exposing individuals who were "in the pocket" of popular vice-kingpin Joe Conforte. Surrounding himself with a bright and dedicated young staff, Bill sent the previously "untouchable" Conforte to prison and drove crooked city and police officials out of office. His devotion to public safety brought threats, often from violent criminals, against himself and his family.

A smear campaign, orchestrated by Conforte minions, nearly cost Bill reelection. Yet, his determination to do what was right, won over the trust and admiration of the electorate and, by his third term, he was running unopposed. In 1970, when he made his run for the U.S. Senate, Bill Raggio was widely respected for his guts and integrity—even by those who did not share his political views.

As he sat in his living room that November evening watching news of his defeat on the television, Bill's disappointment was magnified by the awareness that he may have missed his one real opportunity to become governor—the only high office to which he had truly aspired.

Yet, such thoughts were quickly overshadowed by a more immediate concern. He had a wife, three children, and had recently given up his long-time position as Washoe County District Attorney to campaign for the senate. For the first time in his adult life, Bill Raggio was without a job.

Speaking about it nearly four decades later, Bill could still taste the despair, "As prosecutor for over eighteen years, I had been active from morning until late into the night. I now had all this experience, knowledge and ability, but I was doing nothing. I felt completely useless."

However, being "useless" was not in his nature or his upbringing. Over the next several months, Bill weighed his options. When he finally decided to move on, it would be in a direction that would influence the course of history and shape the lives of generations of Nevadans in ways few could then imagine.

# CHAPTER ONE

# Avansino

William John Raggio, Jr. is a fourth-generation Nevadan. His maternal great-grandfather Giobaptisto "Giobata" Avansino arrived in America from Genoa, Italy in 1862.

In densely populated New York City, the lean, brown-haired, twenty-year-old Avansino found competition for jobs intense. In due course, he found passage on a steamer bound for San Francisco, a perilous 15,000-mile journey around "The Horn" of South America.

Upon his arrival, young Giobata met Mike Perazzo, a friend from Genoa. The two soon headed for the goldfields of the Sierra Nevada. Although the Gold Rush of 1849 had long abated, quantities of the precious metal remained locked in steep hillsides and icy streams for those willing to work hard to extract it. Giobata and Mike staked a claim near Placerville, California.

During the winter months, Giobata would take his share of the gold and return to San Francisco for its more temperate climate and the sizable enclave of fellow compatriots from his native Liguria. The coastal waters of northern California already hosted an armada of graceful sailing feluccas, and along San Francisco's North Beach, whose name was already synonymous with the city's thriving Italian enclave, immigrant fishermen huddled in small groups, mending their nets and telling stories of home. One enterprising émigré, Domenico Ghirardelli, provided employment for many new arrivals at his chocolate factory; then located at the corner of Broadway and Battery Streets.

On August 28, 1869, Giobata became a citizen of the United States.*

His son, John Avansino, would later tell of how his father was paid $30 by a functionary of the Democratic Party in El Dorado County, California, to become naturalized, and then vote for a local party candidate. Honoring that agreement far beyond its intended provisos, the Avansino family would remain Democrat for the next 140 years.

As the mining claim grew less profitable, Giobata took work as a laborer constructing roadways through the Sierra Nevada. One such project was the Strawberry Grade, today a steep stretch of U.S. Highway 50 between Placerville and South Lake Tahoe, California.

Perazzo did not join Giobata on the labor gangs, but instead set out to find his fortune in the booming silver mines of Nevada, 100 miles to the east. He quickly recognized the profitability of providing agricultural products to the mining communities of The Comstock, where close to 25,000 people, about half the state's population, now resided. At Perazzo's suggestion, Giobata soon joined his friend in the newly created county called Washoe.

---

*At that time, the naturalization process consisted of being present in the U.S., paying a fee and, if necessary, renouncing allegiance to one's previous head of state; in Giobata's case, the king of Italy.

# CHAPTER TWO

# The Washoe

G iobata Avansino arrived in Washoe County in 1867, just three years after Nevada had been admitted to the Union as the 36th State. He quickly found work as a laborer on a major irrigation project called the Steamboat Ditch.

Because early Italian immigrants had a reputation for diligence and sobriety, Giobata had no problem finding additional employment on ranches throughout the Truckee Meadows. He was relatively well compensated for time, receiving $1 per day, free meals and a place to sleep in the barn. More importantly, the young man was learning how to ranch.

Despite the quick money to be made in the still-booming mines just a few miles to the east in Virginia City, Giobata saw his future in agriculture and, by dint of hard work and a frugal lifestyle, was able to save most of his daily dollar.

During this time, Virginia City newspaperman Samuel L. Clemens, aka Mark Twain, also noticed the agricultural abundance of the valleys surrounding The Comstock. In his book *Roughing It*, Twain would wryly comment about how the legislature in Carson City responded to such fecundity, a comment made even more amusing because Giobata's great-grandson, Bill Raggio, would someday exercise such influence within that body:

> They had got to raising pumpkins and potatoes in Washoe Valley, and of course, one of the first achievements of the legislature

was to institute a ten-thousand-dollar Agricultural Fair to show off forty dollars worth of those pumpkins in.[1]

Among most Italian immigrants, it was a dream that once they had secured their fortune, they would return to Italy and live out their days in relative luxury. Some did, but most adopted the new land as their home and, with time, the yearning to return to the old country diminished. Yet family ties remained strong, and the need to find a suitable mate, and mother for one's children, usually required at least one return visit to Italy.

Giobata had left a fiancé, Benedetta Colta, behind in Genoa. Because the cost of his transportation back to Italy would further delay his ability to purchase a farm, he asked his trusted friend Mike Perazzo, who was planning his own return visit to Liguria, to escort her back to Nevada.

In early 1875, Perazzo returned with the bride-to-be. Giobata and the petite, rosy-cheeked twenty-five-year old Benedetta were married on May 18th of that year. In 1881, they purchased the eighty-eight-acre William Warner Ranch, about seven miles south of Reno, near a small train station on the Virginia & Truckee Railroad called Huffakers.

Benedetta quickly earned a reputation for her kindness. She was a capable nurse and a discerning and accessible midwife—valuable qualities at a time where the services of a physician were not always available. She was also courageous, once saving Giobata's ranching partner, Angelo Ferretto, from being trampled to death by a team of panicking horses. Benedetta, "leapt in front of the horses, waving her hands and shouting," until they came to a stop just short of running her down.[2]

As with most pioneer women, Benedetta could also improvise. Neighbors would later recall in amazement examples of her ingenuity; how she hand-carded natural wool and spun her own yarn, or, how she once fashioned a loom from switches off a cottonwood tree in order to make clothing. Benedetta even made mattress ticking from the down of pussy willows and bits of wool left by lambs who clumsily stuck themselves on the barbed wire fences around the ranch.

The Avansinos eventually produced nine children, two of whom died in infancy of diphtheria. A daughter, Angelina, would become Bill Raggio's grandmother and an important influence in his life.

In 1903, forty-two years after Giobata Avansino arrived in America, he and Benedetta revisited their families in Italy. The sixty-two-year old Giobata celebrated as if, after a lifetime of self-restraint, he was at last free for one, long, memorable evening: "He danced the old dances when he was there. The party went on all through the night with a meal at midnight, and then more dancing…until 4:00 a.m."[3]

# CHAPTER THREE

# Ben Raggio

In January 1865, a newborn baby boy was deposited anonymously on the steps of a church orphanage in Genoa, Italy. Having no hint of the infant's origin, the rector chose for him the name Beniamino (Benjamin) Augusto Raggio. The name Raggio, which means, "ray" (as in a "ray of light"), was most likely chosen in honor of the aristocratic Genoese family that had controlled the city's commerce and politics for centuries.

At age fifteen, with no family, and thus no opportunity for social or economic advancement in the culture of 19th century Italy, Benjamin Raggio struck out on his own. Carrying few worldly possessions, and his only point-of-reference being the memorized name of a family who might assist him upon his arrival in New York City, young Raggio found work on a freighter in exchange for fare to the United States.

After several weeks at sea, and for the second time in his short life, the slender and solemn young man found himself seeking shelter, this time on a doorstep of strangers in Staten Island. The Comoforo family, to whom he had been referred, was not expecting him, but took him in. Young Raggio, though barely in his teens, and not yet fluent in English, was soon expected to compete for whatever jobs he could find on the teeming streets of 1880 New York City.

His stay with the Comoforos in New York City was the first family life young Benjamin had ever experienced, one he recalled with contentment and appreciation a half century later, in October 1930, when Ludwig Comoforo and his daughter, Ernestine, came west to visit Ben

Raggio in Reno. A notice of their arrival was posted on the social page of the *Reno Evening Gazette*, in which the "orphan" Ben Raggio referred to Ludwig as "his brother."[1]

By the end of 1881, sixteen-year-old Ben had somehow transported himself across the continent to Nevada. He found jobs where he could, often on various ranches throughout the Truckee Meadows, saving his money in hopes of one day owning his own ranch.

He eventually was able to purchase a small farm in the Villa Roma area of Washoe County. Later, in November 1889, Ben sold that property and paid $5,400 for what the deed describes as "40 acres, more or less" of agricultural property northeast of Reno, previously known as the English Mill Ranch. The deal included four horses, harnesses and several buildings. Ben Raggio, now twenty-four, with an impressive handle bar mustache and broad shouldered from years of hard work, began raising alfalfa and cattle.

The following year he married Angelina Avansino, daughter of Giobata and Benedetta. Ben was twenty-six, she sixteen—not an uncommon age for a bride in the 19th century. Angelina was a handsome woman, with warm eyes and a head full of short of auburn-colored, spiral curls. Raggio had known the Avansino family since moving to Nevada eight years earlier.

The Nevada state fair grounds were adjacent to the English Mill Ranch and Ben was soon receiving praise for his award winning vegetables. He received first prize for producing the best green peppers and celery in 1894 and the following year received ribbons for "the largest pumpkin" and a "mammoth squash."[2]

Ranch life, however, was not just about impressive gourds and blue ribbons. It was a tough existence and often every bit the image of the recently tamed frontier. On June 18, 1901, the *Reno Evening Gazette* reported:

> B. Raggio was brought into town last evening in a very badly used up condition. It seems that he had some trouble with an employee by the name of B. Rosasco, the results of which was

the discharge of the latter. Words followed and suddenly Rosasco commenced belaboring Raggio over the head with a club and wound up by biting a good-sized piece out of Raggio's cheek. The latter's wound was dressed here and a warrant issued for Rosasco's arrest.[3]

Over the next several years, Ben would engage in numerous real estate transactions, not only expanding the size of his ranch, but also buying and selling property in the towns of Reno, Sparks and Glendale.

In March 1906, he sold five acres in Sparks for $400 to Roman Catholic Bishop Thomas Grace of Sacramento for use as a cemetery. Along with neighboring rancher, P. J. Kelly, Ben would later that year again become involved in disposition of the dead, though this time attending a city council meeting and requesting that a crematory in northwest Reno be shut down because it was blowing "obnoxious fumes" in the direction of their ranches, "injuring the health of the residents."

As with their financial investments, Benjamin and Angelina's family was growing as well. A son, William John Raggio, was born on April 30, 1895 and a daughter, Florence, followed in 1897. Daughter, Carmel, was born in 1900 and twins Edith and Ethel in 1904. The youngest child, Benjamin, Jr., was born in 1907.

On August 15, 1905, twenty-month-old Edith Raggio would die tragically from an accidental poisoning. While sitting beside her mother, who was using gasoline to clean her husband's work clothes, the child suddenly picked up the saucer containing the fluid and gulped it down. A doctor was immediately summoned to the ranch, but little Edith was beyond help, dying within two hours.

The child's terrible death seemed a prelude to a decade-long run of misfortune. On the afternoon of June 12, 1908, a woman appeared at Ben Raggio's ranch house door to advise him there was a dead man on the road near his house. The encounter became even more bizarre when she subsequently asked Ben if he would assist her in lifting the heavy corpse into her buggy. Raggio followed her the quarter mile to the scene.

Upon examining the dead man, and seeing that he had been shot in the back, Ben refused to help her and instead returned to his house and telephoned the police.

The woman, Alice Winters, was the wife of George Winters, of a prosperous northern Nevada family of ranchers and politicians. Mrs. Winters had been traveling in the buggy along the county road between Reno and Sparks in the company of the man, James Baty, when, according to Mrs. Winters, Baty suddenly attempted to kill her by strangulation. Mrs. Winters promptly drew her pistol from her purse and shot Baty in self-defense. The Washoe County prosecutor thought otherwise and charged her with murder.

Despite the prosecuting attorney's compelling argument that it would have been virtually impossible for her to inflict a gunshot wound to the victim's back while being strangled as she described, the jury acquitted Alice Winter's after just three hours of deliberation. Ben Raggio, who was referred to in the local newspaper accounts simply as "an Italian," had been called as a witness in this sensational, and slightly salacious, trial.

A year later, on June 6, 1909, Ben's name appeared in the *Gazette* again, though now elevated from merely "an Italian" to "one of the wealthiest Italian ranchers in Washoe County."[4] However, that would be the only remotely amusing aspect of the event, as the news account records:

> Ben Raggio is the latest to receive a mysterious Mafia letter fairly bristling with awful threats. Raggio, one of the wealthiest Italian rancher's in Washoe County, who owns a large ranch on the English Mill Road near the state fairgrounds, last evening received through the mail a letter writ [sic] in Italian, and in that way was informed that he had better take $1500 within the next five days and place it in a hole in the side of the half mile post to the state fairgrounds race track or he would be killed and this property would be destroyed. The letter was written by the Black Hand.*

---

*"Black Hand" was the name by which the Sicilian Mafia was known at the time. The term comes from an initiation ceremony where an inductee swears to an oath written on a piece of paper that is then burned while being held by the initiate in the palm of his hands.

As with (previously sent) letters to Luis Avanzino and Manuel Capurro, this letter was written in Italian. Raggio was quite excited when seen by a *Gazette* man and declared that although he believed a member of the Black Hand had written the letter he would not give them the money demanded. "I will allow them to cut my body into shreds and burn all my property before I give them a cent," said Raggio. The letter was full of profanity and fearful threats.

Evidently, no further threats were made against these three men.

Early on Sunday morning, September 8, 1912, fifty-year-old Ben Raggio was alone in a corral on his ranch attempting to domesticate a spirited, young colt. Suddenly the animal bolted, slinging Ben with great force into a nearby fence and causing multiple injuries including a double fracture of his right leg. His calls for help eventually brought aid, and soon the family physician, Dr. St. Clair, was summoned.

Due to the severity of his injuries, and the subsequent infection of his damaged leg, Ben was bedridden and in excruciating pain for the next five months. In January 1913, with a gangrenous infection now threatening his life, the leg was amputated above the knee. After two-week convalescence in a local hospital, he returned home.

Raggio attempted to participate once again in the operation of the ranch, but soon discovered his new artificial leg resulted in near-constant pain when he moved about.

To complicate matters, in 1913 Ben would begin a lengthy feud with ranching neighbors Pietro Cassinelli and R.W. Williams over, what they described in a subsequent lawsuit as, "the inappropriate and destructive diversion of water" from an irrigation ditch. Cassinelli and Williams were asking total compensation of $7,000 for damages to ten acres of land; the loss of several hay, wheat and potato crops between 1911 and 1913; and the premature deaths of "numerous chickens."

Before the civil case came to court, Ben Raggio had the two men arrested on criminal charges of assault and battery. The complaint alleged the two men threw stones at his son, Bill, one striking him on the leg; however, a jury later determined no crime had been committed.

On June 17, 1915, moments before the start of the civil trial in the Washoe County Courthouse, a compromise was reached. The plaintiffs' claims were settled for $5,500.* Five days later, Ben Raggio deeded all his property to his wife Angelina, and son William, as compensation for their "love and affection." This would include the English Mill Ranch; a large piece of agricultural property along the north side of the Truckee River between Reno and Glendale; and a 12,000 square foot lot near the corner of Liberty and Granite Street in Reno.

Later that year, the Raggios sold the English Mill Ranch to Benedetto "Bert" Rosasco. This may have been the same "B. Rosasco" who, fifteen years earlier, struck Ben on the head with a club and bit "a good-sized piece out of his cheek." However, it would not be surprising to learn that a savvy businessman like Ben Raggio would not allow personal rancor to interfere with a good deal—a family trait that would serve his grandson well throughout his extraordinary legal and political careers.

Ben Raggio's neighbor, Carlo Maggiolo, a distant relative through his marriage to Angelina, also sold his ranch. Years before, Ben had asked Carlo to come to America and even helped him purchase property adjoining the English Mill Ranch. Maggiolo, a lifelong seaman, whose home port was Genoa, soon learned he did not like farming and so was relieved when Ben decided to sell.

The men formed a partnership and purchased two small hotels: the Walton and the Manning. Both establishments, two-story buildings each with fifty feet of frontage, were located on "The Plaza" (later Plaza Street), near the Central Pacific Railroad station, around which the greater part of Reno was still located.

---

*The equivalent of $121,000 in 2009.

# CHAPTER FOUR

# Reno

Reno had not even existed at the time of Benjamin Raggio's birth in 1865. Then, it consisted of a toll bridge spanning the Truckee River, a small inn, gristmill, kiln, livery stable and a few outbuildings. Locals called the place Lake's Crossing, after its owner Myron Lake. Lake used profits from his toll bridge, and other commercial enterprises, to acquire as much surrounding property as possible in hopes the location would be selected as a stop along the first transcontinental railroad line.

In December 1867, Lake wrote Charles Crocker, one of the "Big Four" principal investors in the Central Pacific, offering Crocker generous acreage if he would agree to locate a depot at Lake's Crossing. In his letter, Lake described the advantages to such a decision, such as its location at the axis of the north-south wagon road (later South Virginia Street) to Carson City and the east-west immigrant road (later Commercial Row). The site, Lake argued, would be perfect for, not only moving silver from the mills of The Comstock, but also delivering goods back up the mountain to thriving mining communities. Rapid development of the region as a ranching and farming center now produced surpluses that required accessibility to distant markets, all of which the transcontinental railroad would provide.

Most importantly, construction of a branch railroad line north from Carson City to Lake's Crossing was about to begin. Though the line would not be completed until 1872, it clinched the deal. In March of 1868, Myron Lake deeded 400 acres of right-of-way to Crocker, who then had the land surveyed and divided into lots for auction to home-builders two months later. As a token of his appreciation, Crocker gave 127 of those lots back to Lake.

As part of the agreement, the Central Pacific Railroad insisted the name of the new town be changed to something other than "Lake's Crossing." The prevailing opinion among railroad planners of the day was that a short name, without the extraneous ending of "City," would be easier to post on schedules and timetables and better heard by passengers when shouted out by a conductor above the clattering din of contemporary railroad cars.

At first, Crocker considered "Argenta," the Italian word for silver, in honor of the still-booming mines just to the southeast, and a name much preferred by the inhabitants of The Comstock. However, General Irvin McDowell, who headed the U.S. Army's Department of California, headquartered in San Francisco, and a social acquaintance of the Crocker family, asked that the new town be named in honor of the late Brigadier General Jesse Lee Reno.*

As a polite accommodation to General McDowell, Charles Crocker is said to have written the two names on pieces of paper and drew one from a hat. If Reno was named by a game of chance, it would be an ironic herald of the city's future.

The steel rails of the Central Pacific finally emerged from the high Sierras and into Reno in the spring of 1868. Fifteen hundred miles to the east, the Union Pacific Railroad had simultaneously been building westward from Omaha, Nebraska. The two railroads connected at Promontory Summit, Utah, just north of the Great Salt Lake, on May 10, 1869. Reno, and a hundred other such dots on the map, was now connected with the rest of the world like never before.

---

*McDowell, once commander of all Union forces during the Civil War until the Confederate victory at the First Battle of Bull Run, had been Jesse Reno's friend and commanding officer. General Reno was killed by a sniper's bullet at South Mountain, Maryland, in September 1862. Upon emigrating from France to America in 1770, Reno's ancestors "anglicized" the family name from its original spelling of "Renault." The pronunciation continued as "Rain-o" and would remain the standard pronunciation of the town until it gradually changed to "Ree-no" during the early 20th century.

In January 1920, national prohibition on the consumption of alcohol was accomplished by means of the Eighteenth Amendment to the U.S. Constitution. Though Nevada voted to ratify the amendment in 1919, the state's culture of hard-living miners and ranchers cast doubt upon the effectiveness of local compliance.

Douglas Alley, a block south of the train station, was the hub of the seamier elements in Reno society, with several illegal gambling establishments and saloons, called "speakeasies," due to the necessity of keeping them inconspicuous.

Four years earlier, Ben Raggio had purchased two buildings at 14 and 16 East Commercial Row. Each lot had twenty-five feet of frontage facing the railroad tracks. Both buildings also had entrances in the rear on Douglas Alley.

As a result of a November 1923 raid by prohibition enforcement officers, United States Attorney in Nevada, George Springmeyer, instituted abatement proceedings against an establishment called the 49er Club, at 15 Douglas Alley. *The Reno Evening Gazette* reported that the club's operators were listed on criminal warrant as "S. Lorenzi, G. Successi and B. Raggio."[1] After what can be assumed to have been an immediate and compelling visit by Ben Raggio, the *Gazette*, printed a clarification the following day, stating, "Ben Raggio simply owns the building and is not one of the operators."[2]

The question of whether a prudent property owner like Raggio would be oblivious to business activities occurring at one of his properties remains unanswered. What is known is that prohibition laws were often ignored by the public and "winked at" by local law enforcement. Yet, during 1923, several Reno businesses were raided by federal prohibition enforcement officers, including one of the city's most popular restaurants, Eli Francovich's Wine House, located next door to Ben Raggio's building at 16 East Commercial Row.

On December 21, 1923, Federal Court Judge E. S. Farrington ordered the entire building "placed under lock and key for 10 months" with court and law enforcement costs directed against "Sam Lorenzi and G. Successi, as lessees—and Ben Raggio, as owner."[3]

Despite this financial setback, Benjamin and Angelina lived comfortably on income from their hotels and other investments. The family moved to 135 Maple Street, where attractive homes along its magnificently tree-lined length were generally occupied by educators from the nearby University of Nevada. Maple Street had the reputation as being the most picturesque in Reno and Hollywood filmmakers were drawn to it as the setting for several major movies.*

Now retired, Ben Raggio became a fixture around downtown Reno. He dressed impeccably, never leaving the house unless wearing a well-tailored suit, tie and hat. Even the cane he required enhanced his gentlemanly appearance. Angelina's niece, Betty Melarkey, would remark years later that "Ben Raggio was a very classy guy."

His grandson Bill recalls that, from an early age, he had been proud of his grandfather's dignity and appearance and believes that it likely influenced his own penchant for impeccable grooming. Bill remembered his grandfather as a highly intelligent man, who spoke excellent English and possessed an aptitude for business and investment. It is unknown whether Ben had received any formal education, beyond that provided by the orphanage in Genoa. "He just never spoke of it," said Bill.

Angelina, in addition to running the household, now had taken over the operation of the family's businesses. She was also active in civic organizations, particularly the Women's Relief Corps. Though a native-born Nevadan, Angelina especially enjoyed participating in that organization's assistance to immigrants in preparing for U.S. citizenship. From 1923, until after the end of World War II, she rarely missed a naturalization ceremony held in Reno—where she distributed tiny American flags to each proud new citizen.

After Giobata Avansino's death in 1922 at the age of eighty, Angelina's brother John assumed responsibility for running the ranch near Huffakers.

---

*Including the 1944 film *Andy Hardy's Blonde Trouble,* starring Mickey Rooney, and *Margie* (1946) with Jeanne Crain. The homes were subsequently destroyed to make way for an expansion of U.S. Highway 80.

Years earlier, John Avansino had to drop out of elementary school in order to meet his responsibilities around the ranch. Despite that, his interests ran beyond agriculture, to music, art and literature. Angelina shared these interests and, despite their fifteen-year difference in age, they remained close throughout their lives. As such, the Raggio and Avansino families would share many wonderful times together.

Most Italian immigrants and their families of that era identified with the Democratic Party. Benjamin Raggio was an unabashed exception. On September 10, 1896, the Nevada State Journal listed him among newly admitted members of the McKinley and Hobart Club, a Republican political organization established to encourage "full and free discussion of the questions now agitating the public mind."

Chief among those questions were protective tariffs and the "Free Silver"* issue being extolled by the Democratic Party's presidential candidate, William Jennings Bryan. Bryan had eloquently made the case for Free Silver in his famous "Cross of Gold" speech at the Democratic Convention in Chicago just two months earlier. The McKinley and Hobart Club "resolved" during its meeting to challenge the local Bryan Club to a series of debates.[4]

The result of adopting this silver policy would have been a considerable increase in the money supply and inflation. Free Silver supporters believed inflation was an effective way of maintaining higher wages and honest interest rates. However, since the nation was in the throes of a long economic depression, the mood of the eastern banking centers were decidedly deflationary. A majority of Republicans felt the best engine to drive much-needed economic growth and regain national prosperity was a "sound money" policy of maintaining, or even increasing, the dollar's value. This policy rewarded those who had accumulated wealth and,

---

* Free Silver advocates wanted uncoined silver to be freely accepted and minted by the U.S. government in the same way as gold, at the rate of $1 per troy ounce (gold was then valued at $20 per troy ounce). The idea was particularly popular in western states like Nevada, where there were large silver reserves.

theoretically, would provide them with a strong incentive to produce and accumulate even more.

In 1896, Free Silver Republicans from western states, including Nevada, split from the mainstream Republican Party to form the short-lived Silver Republican Party. This party endorsed Democratic candidate William Jennings Bryan.

Though the McKinley-Hobart ticket won in the presidential election of 1896, Nevadans overwhelming voted for Bryan. Of the approximately 30,000 Nevadan's who cast ballots in that election, over 23,000 were for the Silver-Democrat candidate. Benjamin Raggio was not one of them.

Raggio continued to stay active in politics following the 1896 election. In July 1916, he was selected as a delegate to the Washoe County Republican convention, endorsing Judge Norcross for U.S. Senate. In January 1920, Ben represented Nevada Republicans at a San Francisco meeting with Will Hayes, Chairman of the Republican National Committee.

While grandson Bill recalled Ben as being an ardent Republican, he most remembered his grandfather for his loathing of President Franklin Delano Roosevelt. Roosevelt, whose term of office lasted nearly thirteen years, was the only president many young Americans knew. Like them, Bill grew up admiring FDR and could not imagine a world in which things could be otherwise. For that reason, he was as surprised by his grandfather's animosity.

While it is unlikely Ben blamed Roosevelt for the stock market crash of 1929 and the advent of the Great Depression, neither of which occurred on his watch, Benjamin did hold FDR personally responsible for problems arising from his attempt to fix things.

Shortly after Roosevelt's inauguration in March 1933, Angelina's mother, Benedetta Avansino, lost her entire life savings of $9,000 when her bank became insolvent and closed. A month later, the president took the nation off the gold standard, no longer honoring the government's promise to redeem paper money for gold, an economic philosophy abhorrent to Ben Raggio.

Yet, what may have been most galling to Ben Raggio occurred on

April 5, 1933, when Roosevelt signed Executive Order 6102, commanding citizens to turn their gold over to the government at a price of $20.67 per ounce.* As a good citizen, Benedetta dutifully complied. A year later, the president raised the price of gold to $35 per ounce. Benjamin saw this as a second swindling of his mother-in-law by the Roosevelt Administration.

Despite Benedetta's financial misfortune, the Avansinos remained loyal Democrats. While Benjamin's enmity toward FDR remained intense, Betty Melarkey, Benedetta's granddaughter, recalls that there were never any heated political discussions at family gatherings.

---

*Roosevelt based Order 6102 on the Trading with the Enemy Act of 1917, which gave him the power to prevent people from "hoarding gold" during a time of war. Though the United States was not at war in 1933, FDR claimed it was in an equally perilous "national emergency" and Congress and the courts did not resist.

# CHAPTER FIVE

# Wingfield

If Benjamin Raggio detested anyone more than President Franklin D. Roosevelt, it was Nevada banking mogul George Wingfield. During the first years of the 19th century, Wingfield, a young cowboy turned gambler, used his winnings to speculate in low-price mining stocks around the boomtown of Goldfield, Nevada. In 1906, George "struck it rich" when one of his investments, The Mohawk Mine, located a sizable vein of gold.

Wingfield and local banker, George Nixon, soon joined forces. With a $1 million loan from Wall Street financier Bernard Baruch, the two men incorporated their properties. In less than a year, Wingfield's share of the profits would be $6 million – built from an original investment of just $500.

When the precious minerals in Tonopah and Goldfield began to play out, Wingfield and Nixon moved to Reno, building enormous mansions along California Street on a bluff overlooking the Truckee River. The two men soon had a falling out and established separate banks and businesses.

Nixon became a U.S. senator, and when he died in 1912, George Wingfield was appointed by the Republican Party to succeed him. Wingfield declined the job, opting instead to establish himself as the principal economic and political force in the state. Eventually he would own twelve banks, a chain of gambling halls, numerous mines, a string of racehorses and Reno's two finest hotels, the Riverside and the Golden.

George Wingfield exercised enormous political influence over the state from his offices on the second floor of the Reno National Bank Building. While he directly controlled the state's Republican Party, his associates, attorneys William Woodburn and George Thatcher, controlled the Democratic Party from their offices in the same building. This arrangement was sometimes referred to as a "bi-partisan machine."

Not much escaped their attention. Elected officials called them before making appointments or casting votes in the state legislature—and even in the U.S. Congress.

The Stock Market Crash of 1929 signaled the end of such good times. Still a gambler, Wingfield ordered his twelve banks to continue to grubstake farmers and prospectors despite the higher debt structure and risk to his financial institutions. He lent millions to ranchers, taking mortgages on thousands of head of cattle.

Although, this made him a popular figure with many in the state, Wingfield's credit structure grew precariously top-heavy and the drought of 1930-31 toppled it. In November 1932, after a twelve-day long state bank holiday, none of Wingfield's banks reopened. *Time* magazine quoted a Reconstruction Finance Corporation bank examiner as saying, "It was the most honest failure I have ever seen."[1]

The examiner's words were no consolation to Ben Raggio who endured a substantial financial loss when the banks closed. Although a staunch Republican, Ben's resentment of those he thought to be unscrupulous— was decidedly bipartisan.

Benjamin and Angelina Raggio's oldest child, William, attended Reno High School and, after graduating in 1913, enrolled in the respected Heald's Business College in San Francisco. To help defray his expenses, Bill took employment as a teller in A.P. Giannini's Bank of Italy. Giannini, who like Raggio, was the son of a Genovesi immigrant, began the nation's first system of statewide branch banks, later changing the name to Bank of America.

Shortly after Bill returned to Reno, the United States declared war on

Germany. Four months later, in July 1917, the *Nevada State Journal* listed William John Raggio among the first names of those selected to meet Nevada's quota for the "new National Army."[2] William soon left by train for basic military instruction at American Lake, Washington.

On September 5, 1917, he was reassigned to Fort Douglas in Utah. Before he could be sent to the fighting in Europe, Bill was diagnosed with a hearing problem. He received a medical discharge from active duty. Always proud of his military service, Raggio become a life-long member of the American Legion.

Upon returning to Reno, William found employment at the Farmers and Merchants Bank. He and a friend, Eddie Questa, worked there together as tellers. They had known one another since their teens, through mutual family acquaintances in the Huffakers areas. The Questas, early pioneers in northern Nevada, had prospered in ranching and mining. Eddie would eventually become president of the First National Bank of Nevada and would be a central figure in the economic development of the state.

While working as a bank teller, Bill could not help noticing a pretty, petite, hazel-eyed young woman who made regular deposits there as bookkeeper for the Union Mill. Moreover, she could not help noticing him. Years later, she would tell her son how "very good looking" the young banker teller was and how she always made a point of going to his window. Her name was Clara Cardelli and the path leading her to William Raggio's teller window had been a circuitous and difficult one.

# CHAPTER SIX

# Cardelli

In 1870, as the civil war in Italy was finally drawing to a close, sixteen-year-old Tancredi Cardelli left his home in Ponte Buggianese, Tuscany and found work in a sugar mill in Marseille. Marseille was home to a large and active Italian expatriate community, often drawing to it those seeking refuge after finding themselves on the losing side of a revolutionary movement.

It is not known whether politics, economic distress, or some other reason drove young Tancredi there, but he would not stay long. By May 1871, in exchange for passage, Cardelli began work as a crewmember on a steamship bound for San Francisco. He arrived there, by way of "rounding the Horn," after ninety-five days at sea.

Of sinewy build, with a shock of sand-colored hair and inquiring, brown eyes, Tancredi Cardelli set out to strike-it-rich in the gold country of the western Sierra Nevada. Like almost all later arriving immigrants, he would soon learn the gold was no longer as plentiful as the legend promised.

In Jackson, California, he found work washing dishes in a mining camp, then moved on to the town of Bodie where he tried his hand at various jobs. Winter found him in Boca, California, located between Truckee and Reno, where Cardelli worked cutting blocks of ice from frozen ponds and hauling them by horse team to Truckee. There, packed into straw-insulated railroad boxcars, the frozen blocks were soon bound for the "ice boxes" of affluent San Franciscans.

In the spring of 1872, Tancredi moved to Virginia City where he found work driving an eight-horse team hauling lumber and supplies up the treacherous Geiger Grade toll road.

Like Giobata Avansino, now living less than a dozen miles to the west, Cardelli soon recognized that good money could be made in farming. He wrote his brother Leopoldo, still living in Tuscany, about the possibilities. Leopoldo immediately set out for the United States.

In 1875, Tancredi and Leopoldo Cardelli began buying land along the Carson River, a verdant ribbon meandering through an otherwise parched and rocky landscape, about six miles east of Virginia City. Despite the scarcity of arable land, the Cardelli brothers shrewdly purchased what was available, until the ranch covered nearly 12,000 acres. One-third of the spread was cultivated in alfalfa and potatoes and the remainder was used for grazing cattle. Tancredi became a U.S. citizen at the courthouse in Dayton, Nevada in 1885.

In early 1895, he returned to his village of Ponte Buggianese as a forty-one-year-old success story. There he met and subsequently married a slender and pretty, seventeen year-old by the name of Julia Carrara. He brought his bride home to the Cardelli ranch in the spring of 1896. Over the next five years, Julia would give birth to three daughters. Tetide, nicknamed "Teddy," born in 1896, followed by Clara on August 18, 1898. The third daughter, little Julia, would arrive in 1900.

A typhoid fever epidemic struck the following year. Julia Carrara Cardelli contracted the disease and died just a month after her 22nd birthday. She was buried in the Catholic Cemetery in Virginia City. A grieving Tancredi, unable to both operate the ranch and properly care for his three young daughters, sent the children to Ponte Buggianese to live with an aunt. Shortly after arriving in Italy, one-year-old Julia fell ill and died.

Late in 1903, Cardelli returned to Italy to bring Teddy and Clara home to Nevada. While there, he was introduced to Eugenia Quiriconi, a sturdy and serious twenty-nine-year-old widow and mother of two children. After a brief courtship, Tancredi and Eugenia were married. In the fall of 1904, the couple and their four children returned to the ranch.

Just six years of age, Clara was now considered one of the older children and was expected to help care for her younger siblings. Much to her chagrin, there would be no shortage of them. Tancredi Cardelli would eventually father nine children.

It required enormous effort and dedication to obtain an education in rural Nevada. In order for Clara and Teddy to go to elementary school, they had to drive a horse and buggy several miles to the tiny community of Sutro, this after completing their chores, which in Clara's case, included milking her favorite cow—and confidant—"Bossy." Clara and her sister Teddy had only one warm winter coat that fit them both. In cold weather, they would alternate school days based upon whose turn it was to wear the coat.

Eugenia, who did not appear to place a high priority on formal education for her stepdaughters, often kept the girls home from school to care for the ever-increasing number of children in the household. Teddy grew weary of trying to get an education under such difficult circumstances and stopped attending classes in her second year at Dayton High School. Clara, however, was determined to learn as much as she could and envisioned herself in a world beyond the Cardelli Ranch. Such independence and fearlessness were apparent early in her life. As an example, when her father bought the family's first automobile, intrepid fourteen-year-old Clara taught herself to operate it and soon became an excellent driver.

Clara's frustration with her stepmother grew as Eugenia clearly favored her own children over the two girls from Tancredi's previous marriage. "This was not a happy time in my mother's life," her son would later comment. Tancredi evidently recused himself from the issue. He was, by all accounts, a well-educated man with an encyclopedic knowledge of opera. It was common to hear him sing an entire operatic opus as he went about his labors on the ranch. Yet, if he understood Clara's desire to advance her education, he did not communicate it to her, or Eugenia.

Shortly after her twenty-first birthday, Clara left home and moved to Reno.

It is difficult for those not of her generation to grasp the implications of such a decision—or the courage it required. In 1919, when Clara moved away from home,  most women were not yet permitted to even vote.* Employment options were limited. Nevada was still very much influenced by a frontier mentality that often made it a formidable place for a young, single woman on her own. Certainly, Clara did not fail to recognize all this, and yet she still chose to follow her dream.

She found lodging at the Frandsen Apartments on Fourth Street and enrolled in Reno Business College where she trained as an accountant. To meet her expenses, she took employment caring for the children of Charles Mapes, whose father, George, had made the family fortune in ranching and banking. One of the children Clara looked after, one-year-old Charles Mapes Jr., would become best known for building one of Reno's most famous landmarks, The Mapes Hotel.

Clara's studies in accounting soon qualified her for a position as a bookkeeper for the Union Mill, where her eagerness to learn and strong work ethic made a positive impression on her employer Fred Pierson.

While employed by the Union Mill, she one day took the company's receipts to the bank and there met a handsome teller. On January 26, 1924, a short announcement appeared in the *Reno Evening Gazette*:

> Last Wednesday evening Miss Clara Cardelli became the bride of William J. Raggio in a simple ceremony performed by the Reverend P. J. Moran.  Mr. and Mrs. A. Capurro, sister and brother-in-law of the bridegroom, witnessed the ceremony after which a wedding supper was served in a downtown cafe.[1]

---

*In 1914, the Nevada Constitution was changed to permit women the right to vote in state and local elections. Yet it would not be until 1920 that the U.S. Constitution was amended to include that privilege.

# CHAPTER SEVEN

# "Little Billy" Raggio

William John Raggio, Jr. was born in Reno on October 30, 1926, just hours short of Nevada Day, in a small maternity cottage a few doors away from Bill and Clara's residence at 426½ Vine Street.

The nation was in a period of relative prosperity and security and Reno, the picturesque City of Trembling Leaves, was an almost idyllic place to live. An illustration of this time of innocence was evident in a society page story in the *Reno Evening Gazette* on November 1, 1928:

> Little Billy Raggio celebrated his second birthday yesterday afternoon at the home of his grandparents, Mr. and Mrs. Ben Raggio on Maple Street, where a number of playmates came to bid him greetings. Games were played, and later dainty refreshments were served. The table was beautifully decorated in Halloween colors. [1]

Little Billy's next birthday would, however, be the day following "Black Tuesday," October 29, 1929. By that afternoon, the Stock Market crashed beyond recovery. For most Americans, their safe and carefree world was about to unravel. Financial panic ensued. The nation and world plunged into an economic depression of unprecedented severity. It would require another fifteen years before America would once again achieve prosperity.

In 1930, William and Clara purchased a house from the Gardella family at 630 Surprise Valley Road.* This 780 square foot wood frame home, built in 1910, consisted of one bedroom, a living room, dining room, a single bathroom and kitchen. The kitchen contained a wood burning (later coal) cooking stove.

William, Sr. immediately built a small addition to the house as a bedroom for his wife and him; his son was assigned the old bedroom. Billy's bedroom had enough space for a bed and dresser, and, over the ensuing years, became filled with the bric-a-brac of boyhood. "I had my room fixed up with pictures and items I collected," Bill later recalled. "I started at an early age, pennants, souvenirs, rocks and little toy soldiers cast in lead. I had several toy trains and enjoyed building model airplanes. I was always a great collector of things, and am even now. I never throw anything away."

William, Sr., held a variety of jobs until 1932, when he began work as an independent contractor for the Sunshine Laundry Company. He purchased rights to a route, owned his own truck and kept his own business accounts.

The bundles of laundry were often large and heavy, but, William, six feet tall and muscular, relished the activity. Even after a hard week's work, he would spend hours chopping wood and digging in the garden.

In the early 1930s, little Billy looked forward to the days when his dad would take him along in his yellow panel truck with white lettering. William's engaging personality and perpetually playful smile, was a big part of his success. "My dad was a very energetic person." Bill would later recall. "He seemed to know everyone in town, and no matter where he went, everyone seemed to know his name."

Among his dad's favorite stops on the laundry route were the fraternity houses at the University of Nevada. He was particularly fond of the members of Alpha Tau Omega (ATO) and would often schedule his deliveries so he could eat lunch with them. Bill recalled once seeing a page

---

*Later changed to Valley Road, where the house still stands as of April 2009.

from his dad's business ledger showing how much money he was owed by the ATO members. William appeared to have a soft spot in his heart for the college kids. "If I collected all the money those guys owe me," he once told his son, "I'd be rich."

Young Bill would also recall the friendliness of people at the laundry, especially the women working all day at the hot pressing machines. His dad would often wheel him around the plant in a large canvas wash basket. After seven decades, Bill could still feel the damp laundry and the love.

When Bill was old enough, he began attending Orvis Ring Elementary School, where he excelled immediately. He gives credit for his early academic excellence to Helen Banta, Ethel Maguire, Valentine Olds and Grace Warner, for whom an elementary school in Reno was later named.

"Our teachers spent a lot of time with us and we were very respectful of them," Bill would later say. "In recent years, there has been much discussion about class size reduction. Some classes are now as low as sixteen students. In my elementary school, we had about thirty students in each class and never had any problems. In those days, we had to study and we had to pay attention. Because of the discipline then, class size was not an issue." Because of his high level of academic achievement, Bill skipped most of fourth grade, moving on to fifth.

He enjoyed all his subjects in school, particularly geography. From an early age, Bill loved drawing maps and imagined travel to exotic and faraway places (in later life, he would realize those boyhood dreams, traveling to nearly every corner of the world). He loved books and spent hours in the Washoe County Library. Bill had a special fondness for the stories of L. Frank Baum, author of the *The Wonderful Wizard of Oz*, eventually reading all thirteen sequels to the original. At home in the evenings, young Bill would join his parents in front of the radio listening to popular shows such as "Little Orphan Annie," "The Jack Benny Program" and "Fibber McGee and Molly."

Such was the uncomplicated pace of life in Reno, that when the school-children held their annual pet parade, nearly everyone in town came out to watch. Bill joined the other kids, pulling his colorfully, crepe-papered fox terrier, Mitzie, in a wagon behind him through the streets to the mirthful ovation of the crowd.

Despite the austerity the Great Depression imposed on many, the Raggios lived comfortably. Clara would always manage to take Bill, and usually one of his cousins, on a summer vacation. Many summers, they would rent a small housekeeping unit in Santa Cruz, California, staying for a month while Bill and his cousin, Lila Perondi, frolicked each day at the beach.

In 1935, William and Clara purchased a brand new black, Dodge coupe and decided to break it in by visiting southern Nevada and the newly completed engineering marvel, Hoover Dam. The family drove down state Highway 95 in the sweltering summer heat. The Dodge did not have air conditioning and, as with most cars along that route, a canvass water bag was strapped to the front grill in case the radiator overheated. It was young Bill's first introduction to Nevada from end to end.

Heading south, they passed the new Hawthorne Army Depot and on to declining Tonopah. Just twenty years before, Tonopah had been a thriving mining town supporting numerous businesses, banks, theaters, several churches, a school, two newspapers and more than thirty saloons. One of these saloons, The Northern, was owned by the legendary Wyatt Earp, who had established himself in town as a "persuader" in local politics.

About the same time Earp was setting up shop in Tonopah, the San Pedro, Los Angeles and Salt Lake City Railroad was connecting to a tiny, tent community about 200 miles to the south in the middle of the parched and rocky Mojave Desert. The place was called Las Vegas, the Spanish name for the lush meadows located near an unusually productive artesian spring.

Despite the arrival of the railroad, Las Vegas languished in virtual obscurity until the federal government decided to "electrify" the southwest by damming the Colorado River thirty-five miles away. The hydroelectric power it generated would eventually change the demographics of Cali-

fornia and Nevada in ways unimagined at the time. Yet in the summer of
1935, as the Raggio's black Dodge coupe passed through sleepy Las Vegas, it was, as Bill later remembered, "an unremarkable place."

Back at Orvis Ring Elementary School, Bill met Dick Munn. They
soon became best friends, playing baseball, going to movies and exploring
the town. At the time, almost every boy joined scouting, and when the
two reached the minimum age of twelve, they joined the Boy Scouts of
America, Troop Number 4.

Scout meetings were held in the basement of the Methodist Church in
Reno. Dick Curnow, a local silversmith, was the scoutmaster. Although
Curnow was a fine scoutmaster, the two boys soon changed to Troop
597. Those meetings were held in the basement of the Elks Club; then
located at the corner of Sierra and West First Streets in Reno.

The change to a new troop occurred primarily because of scoutmaster
Dave Barber, who had a reputation for passionate involvement in scouting,
providing the boys with strong encouragement to achieve. Barber worked
for a laundry, but dedicated nearly all his other waking hours to the troop.

Troop 597 spent as much time as possible outdoors, camping and
hiking in the mountains near Reno. On Nevada Day, the troop rode the
V&T Railroad to Carson City and marched in the parade. Bill could not
get enough of the stimulation and sense of accomplishment scouting
provided and rapidly moved through the ranks, earning numerous merit
badges and, in October 1940, the rank of Life Scout.

Bill's only regret was that he was not able to attend any national scout
jamborees. By the time he was old enough to go, the war in Europe had
begun and many such events were being curtailed as the country reluctantly prepared to become involved.

The troop disbanded in 1941, when Dave Barber joined the Navy after
the Japanese attack on Pearl Harbor. In 1945, Barber, the scoutmaster
who had given so much of his life to teach Bill and the others the importance of honor and sacrifice, was killed when a kamikaze aircraft struck
the destroyer he was aboard, just two months before the war ended.
Years later, Bill Raggio remembered Dave Barber as "the one I credit
for inspiring me to achieve what I did."[2]

# CHAPTER EIGHT

# Formative Years

In 1939, Bill began attending Northside Junior High School. The principal was Darrel Swope, who was later honored by having a Reno middle school named for him. Bill credits a number of Northside teachers with having an important influence on his life, including John Agrusa, Sessions "Buck" Wheeler, Nevada Pedroli and Inez McGillivry.

The attractive Miss McGillivry was a member of the Gamma Phi Beta sorority at the University of Nevada. Through her intercession, and in exchange for doing chores around the house, Bill was soon "adopted" as the sorority mascot. At Homecoming, he helped build the sorority's float and was once permitted to ride on it during the parade. As one might imagine, Bill's association with these college girls made him the envy of his junior high school chums.

During these years, Bill maintained high marks. In addition to the basic curriculum, he tried his hand at acting. At the annual PTA Harvest Festival in November 1940, Bill joined fellow aspiring thespians in performing a one-act play, *Willie's Lie Detector Test*, a strangely prophetic title given his later years as the county's chief prosecutor.

Bill also played on the basketball team and sold newspapers in front of the Golden Hotel, just around the corner from the saloons and gambling halls of Douglas Alley. Although too young to take an interest in famous, and infamous, guests passing in and out of the hotel each day, Bill was more fascinated by things like the sidewalk in front of the nearby Bank Club, where real silver dollars were imbedded in the concrete.

In addition to hawking newspapers on the corner, young Raggio had a regular subscription route on Sundays. He would deliver door-to-door, a choice of the town's local newspapers or the *San Francisco Examiner*. Once a month, the selections included the *Saturday Evening Post*. Bill would read these publications, often cover-to-cover, developing an early interest in local and world current events.

On May 23, 1940, he was elected student body president of Northside Junior High. "I suppose," Bill would later conclude, "that was when I was first bitten by the political bug." In January of the following year, the *Gazette* reported that Bill had performed admirably as "toastmaster" at the Northside Junior High School graduating class dinner, held in the school cafeteria.[1]

As was typical of households of that era, Bill's parents instilled strong values. He later recalled that if he did something he knew he should not be doing, or acted disrespectfully to his parents or teachers, "my dad would likely pick up a slat from the woodpile and swat me with it." His father was never excessive or abusive in this way, but was not reluctant to impart "a clear message."

Corporal punishment was then an accepted form of discipline at both home and school. Some teachers employed a wooden paddle to apply a stinging swat to one's bottom, or a ruler across the back of the hand. The kids rarely complained and swiftly learned there were unpleasant consequences associated with improper behavior. Bill remained a strong proponent of such behavior modification methods, saying, "We would have far fewer problems in our classrooms if there were more discipline and greater respect for authority."

While the Raggios were not particularly active church members, they did attend Catholic mass regularly, more so Clara than William, Sr. Clara insisted her son receive religious instruction in that faith at St. Thomas Aquinas Cathedral, then the only Catholic church in Reno.

The equilibrium provided by his father's judicious discipline and his mother's nurturing vitality was perfectly articulated in a simple yet sincere statement by their son years later: "I could not have had a better mother or father."

Once he began attending junior high school, Bill and his father did not share as many activities. William was busy with his laundry business and chores around the house. He also loved bowling and frequently spent his evenings in league competition. Young Bill was occupied with school and scouting.

Yet, his father did find time to teach Bill how to hunt native pheasants on the Avansino Ranch, buying his son a double-barreled 16-gauge shotgun when he was twelve-years-old. His parents took him fishing, and Bill vividly remembers the pride he felt upon catching his first trout at age eight, along the Truckee River near Verdi.

Clara, whose difficult childhood had molded her into a generous and compassionate woman and nurturing mother, was also a frugal housekeeper and a good cook. She cultivated an extensive vegetable garden and those items not eaten fresh, were canned for later use. Clara participated in the activities of several civic organizations, the most important to her being the American Legion Auxiliary. Both she and her husband were active in politics and were elected by their precinct to attend the Washoe County Republican Conventions in 1946 and 1948.

Clara's most important mission in life was in the formation of her son's character. From Bill's earliest days in school, she was active in the PTA and later participated in fundraising efforts for the boy scouts. She kept his day full with additional activities. When Bill was eight years old, Clara purchased a player piano for $35 and had him begin taking lessons. Bill disliked practicing on the piano and was delighted several years later when his mother bought him a trumpet, which he enjoyed playing and quickly mastered. Despite his reluctance to practice on the piano, those who knew him in his youth say he was a talented pianist.

In addition to music lessons, Clara encouraged her son to engage in athletic activities, such as skiing. Though recreational snow skiing was still in its infancy in the early 1940s, Bill and his friends would improvise as only kids can do.

A typical ski trip was later recalled by Fred Davis, a friend of Bill's since their high school days. "We would crowd eight to ten people in a car," Fred recalled, "along with our skis—which were over seven feet long—and drive up to Galena Creek. There, someone had previously parked an old Ford pickup truck about 100 feet up the slope and constructed a makeshift rope tow line to one of the truck's rear wheels. By siphoning enough gas from our car to keep the truck's engine running, we could repeatedly ski down the short incline…at least we thought we were skiing."

Around this time, the neighborhood on Surprise Valley Road began changing in a way that eventually made Clara want to move elsewhere. Because of their proximity to the railroad tracks, the Raggio home was regularly visited throughout the Depression by hobos looking for something to eat. Clara would often help them, but only on condition that they earn the meal by doing chores, such as chopping wood.

Today, the idea of handing an axe to a disheveled stranger appearing at one's back door would be frightening. However, in Reno of the 1930s, regardless of the widespread economic distress, people felt safe. The Raggios rarely thought to lock the front door of their house, even at night.

In 1941, as Bill was about to enter Reno High School, the family relocated to a comfortable two-bedroom brick home at 1226 Lander Street, in a new development called Arlington Heights.

Reno was an exciting place for a high school boy in the early 1940s. In addition to the recreational activities available in the nearby mountains, action in the downtown area was exhilarating to observe.

The main casinos were the Bank Club and Palace Club on Center Street, and the Fortune Club, on South Virginia Street. Bill's parents, like many residents of Reno at the time, did not gamble and considered the casinos to be a kind of novelty. Reno was one of the few places in the country where gambling was legal, and the excitement generated by the glow of neon and the clanking of real silver dollar payoffs dropping into metal slot machine bays, was the signature of this "Biggest Little City in The World."

Few high school students owned cars during the Depression and war years,* yet the town had several successful drive-in restaurants. The two

---

*Bill's schoolmate Fred Davis would later recall that of the approximately 400 students enrolled at Reno High School at that time, only about three owned a car.

most popular were Mel's and an enigmatically named establishment called Harvey's QneQ. There, for just fifteen cents, Bill recalls being served "the best hamburger I have ever eaten."

During the summer, high school kids would frequent Reno Hot Springs near the intersection of the Mt. Rose Highway and South Virginia Street, or swim in the huge outdoor pools at Lawton's Resort on the Truckee River, a few miles west of town.

Bill worked afternoons and Saturdays at the Washoe Market, first in the produce section and later as a sales clerk. He was also employed in the stock room of J.C. Penney's. In addition, Bill delivered flowers for the local florist shops. Knowing the purchase of a car was an unattainable goal, Bill, instead, spent most of his earnings on clothes and was always fashionably attired.

Besides working and keeping his grades up, young Raggio was active in school activities and was elected president of the popular TNT Club, which organized pep rallies for school athletic events. High school fraternities were popular then and Raggio was accepted by Delta Sigma, the most coveted of the three fraternities on campus. He would later become president of fraternity chapter.

The principal of Reno High School at the time was Earl Wooster, for whom a high school in Reno was later be named. Wooster was a tall, serious man who, because he was balding, would be dubbed by the students with the droll double-entendre, "The shining head of the faculty."

In his senior year, Bill Raggio would become student body president of Reno High School—but just for two days.

Surprisingly, everyone else in the school had forgotten the closing date for nominations and so Bill became president by default. Experiencing an immediate twinge of conscience, Bill went to Principal Wooster and asked that the election be reopened for the sake of fairness. "Wooster agreed to my request and reopened the election," Bill said years later. "I subsequently lost to my good friend Ernie Hall, who was a stellar athlete at the school. It was a lesson in politics I never forgot: Do not seek opposition."

Dorothy Brigman entered the 9th grade at Reno High School in 1943.

Dottie, as she was known, was a slender, attractive young woman, who immediately caught the eye of 11th grader, Bill Raggio.

She had been born Dorothy Broz on April 14, 1927 in Cleveland, Ohio to Charles and Irene Broz. Irene later divorced Charles to marry Dr. Lemuel R. "Doc" Brigman. Because Dr. Brigman was unable to obtain a divorce from his wife in Ohio, and Ohio did not recognize the legality of a Nevada divorce, Irene moved to Reno with her children, ten-year-old Dorothy and son Charles Broz Jr., and married Dr. Brigman. Dorothy was later adopted by him and took his surname.

Doc Brigman began practicing pediatric medicine in Reno in 1935 and immediately became a highly regarded physician. A well-liked and gregarious couple, Doc and Irene also owned a popular local tavern called Daugherty's at the corner of Mount Rose Street and South Virginia.*

While Bill had several girl friends in high school, Dottie was the only one to whom he gave his fraternity pin. Before long, they were going steady. Dottie would often ride around town with Bill in his florist delivery truck, and on occasion Bill's father would allow him to use the family's Dodge to take her out on dates and to dances. Dorothy was an accomplished pianist and soon Bill and three of his chums formed a musical group with the snappy name "Four Dashes and a Dot."

During his summer months in high school, Bill and his friends were employed by the Civilian Conservation Corps and lived in camps north of Reno. In 1942, they were assigned to a camp at the Canyon Dam near Quincy, California. The boys received the, then, handsome sum of $90 a month, in addition to room and board. While the pay and food were good, the work, clearing undergrowth from the forest floors or repetitiously painting the camp buildings, was tedious.

The only hope for excitement came in the knowledge that they might be called upon to fight a forest fire. Fred Davis later said, "We all prayed for lightening." As if in answer to their prayers, lightening soon sparked

---

*Doc Brigman had been a NCAA record holder as a fullback on the Kenyon College football team. Upon completing medical school, he joined the army and served along the Mexican border during the Pershing Expedition against Pancho Villa. Brigman would go on to become a member of the Washoe Medical Center and St. Mary's Hospital staff. In 1951, he was appointed by Governor Charles Russell as the first Director of the Nevada State Department of Health.

a forest fire south of Reno, near Walker, California. The boy's were given axes and scythes, put aboard U.S. Forest Service trucks and, without any formal training on how to stop a forest fire, were driven to the blaze. Fortunately, there were no serious injuries, though the situation became quite dangerous at one point when the wind shifted and the teenagers were forced to dash back to the trucks, narrowly escaping being trapped by the flames.*

During the return trip, the trucks stopped in Reno and the boys were allowed to spend the night with their families. The next morning, Doc Brigman permitted Dottie to use his flashy, new, bright-red Plymouth convertible to drive them back to Canyon Dam. Delighted at not being crammed in the back of the government truck with other boys, and quite satisfied with themselves and their recent flirtation with danger, they all lit the cigars that one of them had brought along and cruised happily up Highway 395 with the sun and wind on their faces and glowing cigars clenched in their teeth—even Dottie's.

Bill spent part of the summer of 1943 at the Herlong Ammunition Dump, about fifty miles north of Reno, pulling nails from dunning (the wood frames which encased bombs when they were being transported). The boys lived in barracks, four to a room, and took their meals in the civilian mess hall. Bill took the job because the pay was better than he would receive for his usual combined summer employment in Reno.

As Bill's senior year approached, he continued to maintain high grades and genuinely loved learning. Certain teachers had a lasting impact on him, including Helen "Peaches" Aldaz, David Finch, (mathematics) Al Alegre (French), Dr. Ed Strong (chemistry) and, most particularly, his civics teacher, and noted Nevada historian, Dr. Effie Mona Mack, for whom the social science building at the University of Nevada was later named.

His grandparents, Ben and Angelina, were also an important source of encouragement for Bill and he often walked from the campus to their house on Maple Street for lunch. On Christmas Day 1942, shortly after

---

*On July 29, 1939, five young Civilian Conservation Corps workers were burned to death while fighting an 8,000-acre range fire near Orovada, Nevada.

the family finished their holiday meal, Benjamin Raggio, the seventy-seven-year-old patriarch of the family, collapsed and died of a heart attack. An orphan who came to the United States penniless at the age of fifteen, Ben had truly lived the American dream. His work ethic and courage of conviction were an inspiration to many; none more so than his grandson Bill.

His grandparents had continuously reinforced the importance of a good education to Bill's future success, though they never specifically discussed what he might do later in life. At that time, "later in life" for a healthy, young man like Bill, meant only one thing—joining the military and going to war.

# CHAPTER NINE

# On His Own

Though the war was fought far from U.S. shores, it personally affected nearly everyone. Before it was over, nearly 300,000 Americans would be killed and 700,000 wounded. Northern Nevada was not spared its share of the national grief.

Bill's uncle, Ben Raggio, Jr., would be in the thick of the fighting in Italy and later in Belgium and Germany. A cousin, John Raffetto, Jr., was held in a German prisoner of war camp after being captured in battle. Both would safely return to the United States, however, a number of Bill's classmates never came back.

Bill entered Reno High School in January 1941, eleven months before the Japanese attack on Pearl Harbor. Yet for those who paid attention to world events, it was clear the hostilities in Europe, Asia and North Africa would inevitably pull the United States into the conflict. A peacetime draft was begun in 1940 and Reno High required all physically fit boys to enroll in the Reserve Officer Training Corps (ROTC) program. Bill took ROTC classes for three years and wryly recalled, "I was not what one might call a sterling military candidate. However, in my senior year I received an officer's commission as second lieutenant. My assignment was to conduct court-martials. Technically, that was my first job as a prosecutor."

After completing a competitive military placement examination, Bill was selected for the Naval Officer Training Program. However, because he had been put forward a grade while in elementary school, Bill graduated from high school in January 1944 at the age of seventeen, too young for immediate military service. Nearly all his friends were eighteen and had quickly departed town for active military duty.

Bill decided to use the time before his departure attending the University of Nevada for one semester. There, he took courses in logic, advanced mathematics, trigonometry, political science and economics. During this time, he joined the Alpha Tau Omega fraternity. Bill had no doubt about which fraternity he would choose, largely the result of his fond boyhood memories of riding along with his dad on his laundry route and sharing lunch there with the Tau brothers.

In June 1944, Bill received orders to proceed by train to Ruston, Louisiana, where his Naval Officers Training Program training would be held on the campus of Louisiana Polytechnic Institute. He had never been far from home and did not even know where Ruston was. He quickly consulted an atlas and learned that it was a small town between Shreveport and Monroe, in the northern part of the state.

Bill exchanged poignant goodbyes with Dottie, his parents, grandmother Angelina and others, who assembled that morning on the platform of Reno's Southern Pacific Railroad depot to see him off. As the train chugged eastward out of the station, he sensed the significance of that moment. For the first time in his life, he was entirely on his own.

Several days later, Bill arrived in Ruston. Having lived his whole life in the dry, high desert climate of Nevada, the oppressive combination of heat and humidity overwhelmed him as he stepped from the train. Bill proceeded to the Louisiana Tech campus, where the Navy utilized a series of dormitories and an administration building to conduct officer's candidate school. Upon receiving his uniform and seeing the insignia of apprentice seaman, the lowest possible grade in the Navy, Bill realized he was a long way from becoming an officer.

Prior to the successful invasion of Normandy, which was underway at the time Bill arrived in Ruston, most Americans believed the outcome of the war was still in doubt. Consequently, Bill found himself in an accelerated program, which allowed little free time. The curriculum included regular university-level course work and military classes in seamanship, navigation and officer development. Because he had already taken some college courses, he was allowed a few electives. As one would expect in military environment, life outside the classroom was regimented and included marching, physical training and maintaining equipment.

While he did not consider himself an outstanding officer candidate, Bill was a good one. An incentive to keep up with the program was knowing that if he did not maintain high grades and exceptional military bearing, he would flunk out and be sent to regular Navy boot camp; serving out the remainder of his obligation as an enlisted man. While some candidates did "wash-out," most quickly adjusted to military life, toughened by the discipline they had been exposed to at home and school, and the rigors of the Great Depression.

What Bill most vividly recalled about living in northern Louisiana, beside the ever-present rain and pervasive heat and humidity, was the difference in culture from where he had been raised. "I had never been exposed to anything like it," Bill later said. "It was shocking to see the 'Colored only' signs on the public drinking fountains and restrooms. When I first walked into Ruston, black people walked off the sidewalk into the street to let me pass. That appalling image stayed with me my entire life and was the basis for my wanting to be part of eradicating segregation in this country."

Bill's home state of Nevada had also witnessed shameful episodes of racial intolerance, although most had occurred before Bill was born. Chinese immigrants, who had been instrumental in the development of the state, were most often the target of such discrimination and would eventually be systematically driven from every town in Nevada, forfeiting their property and possessions.*

Though not as extreme as the animosity toward the Chinese, all immigrant groups coming to Nevada were initially unwelcome. All would be

---

* On the night of October 30, 1908, precisely eighteen years before Bill's birth, the Reno City Health Department ordered Chinatown destroyed. Given no warning of the grand jury-sanctioned decision to level their homes, about 150 Chinatown residents were caught by surprise and thrown out into the snow with only the personal possessions they could carry.

the victims of violence because of their perceived threat to economic security of those who had arrived earlier. In some cases, as with the Basques, deadly "range wars" ensued. Nevertheless, in each instance, relative harmony eventually prevailed.

Non-immigrants had always been subject to the worst forms of discrimination. It was not until 1917, that the enforced isolation of Native Americans on remote reservations ended. In that year, the federal government acquired twenty acres south of the Truckee River and founded the Reno-Sparks Indian colony. This allowed Native Americans, for the first time, to have homes in the city. Most were initially employed as low paid laborers or domestics. Some speculated the move was intended to fill the void left by increasingly severe immigration restrictions and the earlier exodus of Reno's Chinese population.

Another non-immigrant group, African Americans, made their way to Nevada during the silver boom of the 1860s, though in relatively small numbers. The census of 1860 indicated there were less than fifty blacks in the state, and by 1900 only 134. It would not be until the construction of Hoover Dam and the beginning of World War II, that significant numbers of African-Americans began to arrive. Most settled in the "Westside" area of Las Vegas.

During the time Bill Raggio was growing up, Nevada, encouraged separation of the races. Casinos, businesses and even churches were segregated. The Reno train station had a separate waiting area for blacks. Yet in Reno, there were so few black residents that such discrimination was barely perceptible to most white residents. John and Edwina Hamlet, and their daughter, were a black family who lived across the street from the Raggio's on Surprise Valley Road. Clara and Edwina became friends and would often share surplus vegetables from each other's gardens. There was never talk of race in the Raggio home and, because he was oblivious to the segregation that did exist in Nevada, Bill's cultural awakening in Louisiana was profound.

Raggio quickly learned that not all prejudice was directed towards blacks. As a Catholic, he frequently heard disparaging remarks about his faith from both locals and those in his military unit. When attending mass in the tiny, inconspicuous, wood frame building that housed the only Catholic church in town, Bill would have to be very careful, in order to avoid reprisals from those affiliated with the more predominant Christian congregations in the region. When granted a rare weekend pass, Bill visited the surrounding states of Arkansas and Texas, and learned that Louisianans were not alone in their institutionalized intolerance.

After the equivalent of three college semesters, Bill transferred from Louisiana Tech to the University of Oklahoma. He was allowed a few days of leave in Reno before he reported in at the Norman campus in July 1945. No longer a lowly apprentice seaman, Bill and his classmates now wore Navy midshipman's uniforms and lived in better dormitories.

By the time of his arrival there, the war in Europe had ended, though fighting against the Japanese in the Western Pacific remained intense. A month later, after the U.S. detonated nuclear weapons over Hiroshima and Nagasaki, Japan surrendered. Bill and his fellow midshipmen, though fully prepared to enter the fight, were nonetheless relieved that the war had finally ended.

Bill's friend, John Webster "Web" Brown, was attending another naval officers training program in Norman. He met Bill, and their mutual friend, Bob Hildebrand, in Dallas, Texas to watch a Southern Methodist University football game and do some sightseeing.

When asked in 2008 to describe Bill's personality and character during that time in his life, Brown said:

> He always had great resolve, that is to say, he was never "wishy-washy." Bill always thought before he opened his mouth and was equipped for this level of maturity by his upbringing and because of the war, which went on through so much of our adolescence. We were all more serious about life and Bill focused on being prepared. It was all part of what built his character.

Despite the war now being over, the men were required to complete their military obligations. After three semesters at the University of Oklahoma, Bill was given an option to become an officer in the Marine Corps, rather than the Navy. He chose the marines. In June 1946, Bill was commissioned as a second lieutenant in the United States Marine Corps Reserve and sent to Parris Island, South Carolina for basic training.

At that time, officers went through the same boot camp as enlisted men, though in a platoon consisting entirely of second lieutenants. Marine boot camp is notoriously tough, and Bill surely wished at times—while engaged in the endless physical training, marches through the mosquito-infested swamps and unending verbal abuse and indignities heaped upon him by battle-hardened drill instructors—that he had chosen the Navy commission.

After completing boot camp, that grueling initiation rite of becoming a Marine, Bill was transferred to Officers' Basic School in Quantico, Virginia. Though it provided a bit more dignity than he had experienced in boot camp, basic school was just as intense.

"Marine Corps boot camp and basic school were tough, both physically and mentally," Bill recalls. "I was probably in the best shape I've ever been in my life by the time I had completed all that training and received my commission in the Marine Corps. I was pretty skinny, six feet tall and 144 pounds, but in great physical condition."

His grades in basic school were average and he completed all the other requirements, such as qualifying with a variety of weapons. Now that the war was over, Web Brown noticed Bill had lost some of his motivation. Bill would later euphemistically remark, "I didn't set any records."

Lieutenant Raggio utilized his weekend liberty passes to see more of the countryside. As he had done when stationed in Louisiana and Oklahoma, Bill hitchhiked everywhere. In those days, a military man, particularly one in uniform, had no problem getting a ride. Consequently, he saw a great deal of the country and talked to many people he otherwise would not have met, later saying the experience was probably the most important thing he came away with from his time in the military. "Having the opportunity to study the differences between the inhabitants of our country," Bill later remarked, "taught me invaluable lessons in how to get along with people from diverse cultures and circumstances."

In December 1946, as part of extensive military downsizing, Lt. Raggio was given the option to be discharged from active duty. Since he had been commissioned at the age of nineteen, Bill flirted with the idea of a bright future in the Marine Corps and then retiring, with twenty years of service, before the age of forty. Yet, Bill recognized that he had lost much of his enthusiasm for military life now that the war was over, and so decided to return home to Dottie and his family and finish his education. He arrived back in Reno just before Christmas and reentered the University of Nevada in January 1947.

Dottie and Bill had corresponded often while he was away and he looked forward to her letters. He had dated casually in the years he was away, and, near the end of his military service, they broke up. Dottie began going steady with another. Yet, after Bill returned to Reno, they quickly resumed an exclusive relationship.

The University of Nevada had changed considerably since Bill last attended there in 1944. Classes were larger and there were more faculty members. Though many students were still coming to campus directly from high school, a large number were returning from military service. Earlier hazing traditions would have required all male freshmen to wear a small skullcap called a "dink." If a freshman were caught not wearing his "dink," he would be thrown into a pond on campus called Manzanita Lake.

It soon became apparent that no one was going to insist war veterans wear "dinks." Other hazing practices, such as requiring new students re-paint the big letter "N" on the side of Peavine Mountain, were also made obsolete by this new breed of lower classmen.

Despite the G.I. Bill educational payments, almost all veterans were required to hold jobs in addition to attending classes. Bill was no exception, working part time throughout his college years and living with his parents to save money. He chose political science as his major, with a minor in economics, and credits three professors, in particular, for making a lasting impact on his life: Dr. Robert Gorrell in English, M. Beasley in advanced mathematics and Professor C.C. Hicks in political science.

Because he had wisely earned transferable credits while at Louisiana Tech and Oklahoma, Bill was able to complete his baccalaureate program in two years. The dark forces of totalitarianism had recently been defeated in battle and the cause of freedom now seemed ordained. Bill, like his peers, felt a sense of optimism and anticipation unlike any generation before.

On June 7, 1948, Industrialist Henry J. Kaiser gave the commencement address and Nevada Supreme Court Associate Justice Milton Badt administered the "Civic Oath," by which the graduates pledged loyalty to the ideals of liberty, equality and justice. The oath ended on the hopeful note that "This, my generation, shall bequeath an even better and nobler civilization than came to it."

# CHAPTER TEN

# Learning the Law

In early 1948, after an evening of dinner and dancing, Bill and Dottie parked on Windy Hill, a popular after-date location south of Reno. There he slipped an engagement ring on her finger and proposed. She accepted. Because of Dottie's popularity, a round of wedding showers ensued. Bill's future father-in-law, Doc Brigman, threw a stag party for him just prior to the wedding.

On August 15, 1948, Bill and Dottie were married at St. Thomas Aquinas Cathedral in Reno. They were an eye-catching couple; the handsome groom in his white tuxedo jacket and black trousers and the lithesome, radiant bride, elegantly draped in lace. Monsignor Patrick J. Connors, pastor of our Lady of Snow's Church, performed the service at the cathedral because his building was too small for the number of invited guests. It would be one of the largest weddings ever held in Reno.

The reception was held at the Twentieth Century Club just around the block from the church. As a prank, Web Brown and two of the groom's other close friends, Bill Teipner and Mel Rovetti, abducted Dottie from the reception and drove her away. Once Bill Raggio learned of this, he commandeered a car and raced after them. Brown remembers Dottie's charming nonchalance during the entire escapade, looking back over her shoulder and saying, "Hurry up! He's catching up with us." They all finally returned to the reception about a half an hour later.

The newlyweds honeymooned in the Monterey Bay area and then moved on to San Francisco where Bill would begin attending the University of California's Hastings School of Law.

Dottie's good friend and bridesmaid, Eleanor Norris,[1] helped with apartment hunting and eventually the newlyweds decided on a one-bedroom place on Nob Hill at 1225 Taylor Street for $74.75 a month. The apartment had a small kitchen and two guest rooms containing Murphy beds, which folded into the walls to maximize living space. Housing was at a premium in those post-war years, and rent control gave landlords little incentive to fix things up. Yet, they loved it.

The apartment was often filled with guests. Angelina, Bill's now-widowed grandmother, would visit frequently, as would their friends coming from Reno to enjoy "The City" and its famed nightclubs and restaurants. "Three or four of us guys would often go visit them in their apartment and sleep on the floor or couches," Web Brown later recalled. "We nicknamed the place 'The Reno Apartments.' Dottie was always a very gracious hostess."

Dorothy, who had been attending the University of Nevada and was a member of the Kappa Alpha Theta sorority, chose not to complete her degree in order to move with her new husband to San Francisco. Having worked during high school as a salesperson for the upscale woman's clothing store, Joseph Magnin's, in Reno, she easily found employment in San Francisco at another fine clothier, Hale's Grant Avenue, riding the cable car to and from work each day.

Because the intensity of the law school curriculum required long hours of study, Bill did not work, except during the summer months. The small amount of "mustering out pay" Raggio had received from the Marine Corps was set aside for law school tuition and he qualified for educational funding under the G.I. Bill. In addition, his grandmother Angelina provided a monthly stipend.

Bill was also awarded the Hastings' Nevada Scholarship, established by William Clark Sanford, a newspaper publisher and member of the Nevada bar, who had previously graduated from the law school. This award helped defray the cost of Bill's second year tuition. By the end of each month, he and Dottie were nearly out of money and had to find places where, as he later said, "they could eat for a buck." Though this might sound like a hardship to some, it was not for them. Being young, living in a romantic and exciting city, working together toward a bright future, they considered such minor inconveniences to be fun. Bill would fondly recall it as being "the best three years of our lives."

The wartime call to arms had deprived American universities of educators, and Hastings College had to vie with more prestigious law schools for the services of those left available. Hastings' Dean, David Ellington Snodgrass, remedied this situation by hiring a group of eminent scholars and jurists, most of whom were involuntarily retired from the nation's top law schools upon reaching the age of sixty-five. They would become known as the Sixty-Five Club. *Newsweek* magazine later described the spectacular results of the school, and quoted the former dean of the Harvard Law School, Roscoe Pound, as saying of Hastings, "I am inclined to think it has the strongest law faculty in the nation."[2]

The eccentric Dean Snodgrass was remembered for his trademark threadbare jacket and green visor. His wit was variously described by Newsweek as "trenchant" and "caustic." A visitor to the college once found him sweeping the hall and, mistaking him for the janitor, asked directions to the dean's office. Snodgrass obligingly led him there and then returned to his sweeping.

In the transition from military to civilian life, where students were often married and had to work, few were able to maintain the near-perfect grade point averages required for admittance to more prestigious law schools. Dean Snodgrass decided to allow many such applicants the opportunity to enter Hastings, even without an entrance examination. Snodgrass was betting on the discipline and maturity of returning veterans to compensate for less-than-stellar undergraduate grades. In return for this opportunity, law students would be expected to work hard. Bill recalled the dean speaking to his first-year class of 440 students during their orientation session. "Look to the left and to the right," Snodgrass admonished them. "Only one of you is going to be here in the end." His prediction came true—only 140 of them graduated.

It was in this high pressure and unconventional environment that twenty-two-year-old Bill Raggio now found himself—and he excelled. By the end of his first year, he was maintaining a straight "A" average. Although he enjoyed all his classes, he was particularly fond of real property law and received an "A+" on that final examination. In addition, Bill was made a member of the Thurston Honor Society, forerunner of the Order of Coif, and was accepted into the Phi Alpha Delta law fraternity, whose distinguished membership included four U.S. Presidents, Taft, Wilson, Harding and Truman.[3]

The demands of law school were intense. Each course had only one test, a final examination. If a student did not pass that examination, he or she failed the course. The school had a strict policy of not allowing make-up examinations for any reason. A student who missed an examination would be required to take the class again the following year, or was often asked not to return.* The examination period lasted two weeks.

At the end of Bill's second year, he had done well and breezed through the first week of examinations. He was looking forward to completing his final week of tests before a well-deserved respite from his studies. Tragically, things did not go as planned. On Sunday night, May 21, 1950, Bill received a call from his Uncle Ben informing him that his dad had died. William, Sr., had been preparing for bed at the family home on Lander Street that evening and collapsed from either an embolism or massive heart attack. The robust fifty-five year-old, who his son remembered as "never having been sick a day in his life," was now gone.

Despite his shock and grief, Bill was conscious that if he missed the examinations scheduled to begin the following day, his entire second year of law school would have been for nothing. With his father's funeral planned for Tuesday in Reno, 250 miles away, Bill would have to find

---

*In a 2008 interview, former Nevada governor and U.S. Senator Richard Bryan, a Hastings graduate, had a different perspective: "I did not like the way Dean Snodgrass operated at Hastings. While they would let anyone into the school, they then worked very hard to flunk people out. This might be considered OK in the first and second year of law school, but oftentimes they would flunk a person out of their third year of law school and it was not uncommon for a person to be ready to graduate and find out the day before that they had flunked. I think that was unfair."

someone at Hastings with the authority to override the institution's policy on makeup examinations—and then convince them to do so in his case.

To complicate matters, one of Dean Snodgrass' eccentricities was that he did not allow students to speak to him outside of the classroom. Although he had been Bill's first year professor on contract law, Snodgrass was now unapproachable. So Bill located an associate dean, Arthur Sammis, who finally agreed to let him take the examinations as soon as he returned to San Francisco from the funeral. The conditions he set for this unusual circumstance were that Bill would be required to complete the tests alone in Sammis' home. The professor also insisted Bill sign an affidavit confirming that had not talked to anyone about the examinations. With that matter settled, Bill and Dottie hurried to Reno to comfort Clara and help with the funeral arrangements.

Taking his makeup examination in San Francisco, just hours after his dad's funeral, was one of the most difficult things Bill Raggio would ever do in his life. Leaving his anguished mother, trying to pull himself out of his own shock and sorrow, all the while preparing for complex examination problems, required enormous self-discipline. Bill's grades on the makeup tests were not perfect, denying him the straight "A" average he had originally set as his goal for law school. Yet, the experience, painful as it was, undoubtedly made him tougher and more determined than ever.

After completing his chaotic second year at Hastings, Bill and Dottie returned to Reno for the summer, staying with his mother on Lander Street. Clara had proved to be resilient after the sudden death of her husband. She soon assumed sole responsibility for running the Manning Hotel, where she had already been doing the bookkeeping. Bill and Dottie kept the apartment on Taylor Street in anticipation of returning there for Bill's third and final year of law school. He resumed his work part time at the Glen Turner florist shop in downtown Reno. Bill also found part time employment at Jacob's, a men's clothier, where the employee discount allowed him to continue to dress in style.

Bill graduated from Hastings in 1951. He immediately enrolled at

Boalt Hall, the law school at the University of California in Berkeley, to work on his master's degree. The couple moved into an apartment in Berkeley and Dottie began work at Hale's Department Store in nearby Oakland.

Bill stood for the Nevada bar examination that year along with just nine others (only five would pass). Though he had received job offers from law firms in California, Bill decided to practice in Reno so he could be close to his recently widowed mother. Consequently, he did not take the California bar examination. After just one semester at Boalt, Bill learned he had been admitted to the Nevada bar. Anxious to settle down and begin his career, he excitedly phoned Dottie at work with the news: "Honey, you can quit your job, we are going home to Reno."

# CHAPTER ELEVEN

# Ernest Brown

The person who had the greatest influence on Bill Raggio's decision to become a lawyer was Ernest S. Brown, father of his childhood friend, Web Brown. The Brown family lived on West Street, just around the corner from the Maple Street home of Bill's grandparents. One of Bill's most vivid boyhood memories was of looking out the front window of his grandparent's home as the dignified and perfectly attired Ernest Brown walked by on the way to and from his office in downtown Reno.

Brown was man of high principles and self-determination. Without the financial means to attend law school, he had enrolled in the LaSalle University Correspondence Law School program and swiftly mastered the subject, passing the Nevada bar examination after just one year of study. Those who observed him arguing cases in district courts, before the Ninth Circuit Court of Appeals or the Nevada Supreme Court, marveled at his profound grasp of the law despite an absence of formalized law school training.

In 1933, Brown, a Republican, was elected to the state assembly where he served one term. He was subsequently elected to the position of District Attorney of Washoe County just as the Wingfield bi-partisan political machine was collapsing. He would soon set the standard for personal integrity and intolerance of corruption.

Ernest was fearless, as well. In October 1938, construction of U.S. Highway 40 over the Sierra Nevada Mountains from California was a major public works project, employing hundreds of workers. Each segment of the highway project was awarded by the federal government to a private contractor, with the Isbell Construction Company receiving the assignment of building the stretch of highway from Verdi to Lawton Springs, just west of Reno. The Congress of Industrial Organizations (CIO), an aggressive labor organization founded just three years earlier, was threatening to picket the Isbell project because the company refused to sign an operating contract with the new union.

District Attorney Brown decided the CIO had no jurisdiction at the Nevada construction site and, along with Washoe County Sheriff Ray Root, a posse of armed deputies and about 100 axe handle-wielding citizens from Reno, set out to stop the 150 union members as they were entering the state.

Near the town of Verdi, Brown, cradling a rifle in his arms, ordered the group to turn back to California voluntarily, or they would be forcibly driven out. Tense moments ensued as labor leaders tried unsuccessfully to negotiate with the DA. A hotheaded, young union member suddenly attempted to force his way through the blockade. Brown rendered him unconscious with the butt of his rifle, later explaining his action to be the result of the man having "used insulting language." With that, the contingent of would-be-picketers boarded their trucks and returned to California.

The following day, the *Reno Evening Gazette* reported the confrontation:

> District Attorney Brown failed to see the peaceful character of this invasion. One hundred and fifty marching into this state did not appear to them to resemble a peaceful movement. This afternoon they ordered them back into California from whence most of them came. These two Washoe county officers (Brown and Root) took these steps to preserve the peace and to prevent possible bloodshed.[1]

The standoff resulted in huge local popularity for Ernest Brown. Two future Washoe County district attorneys, Jack Streeter and Bill Raggio, would later remember how impressed they were as kids hearing of Brown's courage that day.

Yet, public acclaim almost assuredly did not factor into his decision. Just two years earlier, DA Brown had faced significant public condemnation in his of pursuit of justice, while protecting the rights of a local black man by the name of Jack Danvers.

One evening in June 1936, Danvers was allegedly spotted by two Reno police officers on the porch of Ben Raggio's Maple Street residence attempting to break into the home. The officers chased Danvers from the property and shot him several times in the back. He was taken to a local hospital where he survived his wounds and was subsequently transported to jail.

Police knew Danvers to be a partner in a nightclub on Douglas Alley that catered to black locals and tourists. A police search of his business and apartment reportedly turned up a number of stolen items. During his interrogation, Danvers was said to have confessed not only to the attempted break-in of the Raggio residence, but also to several other burglaries in the neighborhood.

In light of such damning evidence, it appeared Jack Danvers would be incarcerated for a very long time. Yet, on September 2, 1936, the *Reno Evening Gazette* reported that had been released by order of the district attorney. The following day, a front-page headline in the *Nevada State Journal* read, "Release of Jack Danvers Draws Protest":

> The release of Jack Danvers, 30-year-old Negro, who was arrested June 15 on a first-degree burglary charge yesterday brought a storm of protesters to the Reno Police Department. Police officers were silent regarding the affair. Ernest Brown's only comment was that "there was insufficient evidence to hold Danvers."[2]

The news account went on to remind readers of Danvers' confession and the stolen property that officers found in his possession. Reno Chief of Police Lou Gammel responded to the public outcry by asking for a meeting with the DA that afternoon. There is no record of what was discussed, or any further news report about the case. It may never be known exactly what happened. However, in 2008, Web Brown spoke of his father's respect for the law, saying Ernest would not have thought twice about facing public disapproval in order to protect the rights of Jack Danvers. His father's commitment to enforcing the law, Web explained, often resulted in threats against the DA and his family. During one particularly bad period, Ernest Brown asked federal narcotics officers to take Web to a rifle and pistol range and teach him "to shoot straight" for his own protection.

When America went to war in 1941, Ernest Brown, at age thirty-eight, well beyond draft age, resigned his position as DA and entered the Army at his reservist rank of major. By the end of the war, he had risen to the rank of colonel, and upon his release from active duty, Brown returned to Reno to practice law.

During the summer of 1950, after completing his second year of law school, Bill Raggio interned, part time, at Ernest Brown's law office. Bill was thrilled at this opportunity to learn the practice of law from his boyhood hero. He would help by doing research, prepare pleadings and sundry other office tasks that were not taught in law school.

"Ernest Brown was my first mentor in the practice of law," Bill would later say. "He took the time almost every day to discuss cases and explain things to me. This was great experience for a second year law student. He was of that old style and very forthright. I admired these qualities and they later became part of my style as a district attorney."

Bill most enjoyed the days when he was invited to join Brown in the courtroom. He once helped prepare a case to be tried before Judge William McKnight in the Washoe County Courthouse. Morley Griswold, who had been governor of Nevada sixteen years earlier, was the opposing counsel. After two days of deliberation, the judge ruled in favor of Griswold's client. The attorney then rose and began a long, florid speech praising the decision and the work of the court.

Brown quickly popped up from his chair, interrupting Griswold, and asked the judge if court was in recess. Judge McKnight replied that the ruling had been made and so the proceeding was technically over. With that, Brown collected his belongings and walked out, his way of showing displeasure with the decision. Startled for a moment, his young intern, Bill Raggio, quickly recovered his wits and scuttled out of the room behind his irritated mentor.

"Ernest Brown was a person who said what he thought, and said it well," Bill later remarked. "As with most attorneys in those days, he never spoke ill of other lawyers or judges. He was highly dedicated to the practice of law and extremely ethical."

Bill Raggio could not have had a finer role model.

In the summer of 1952, after having been admitted to the state bar, and back living in Reno, Bill set out to practice the law. He secretly hoped to become a partner of his idol Ernest Brown, but Brown preferred practicing alone and did not ask. Therefore, Bill did what nearly all Nevada lawyers did during those days in order to pay the bills—he hung out a shingle and took divorce cases.

# CHAPTER TWELVE

# Practicing the Law

Nevada's liberal divorce law was established during the first session of the territorial legislature in 1861 and remained essentially the same for decades. The original intent, of what many at the time considered an immoral code, had to do with the peculiar "boom and bust" cycle of the state's economy. Given the mercurial nature of the mining business, towns would spring up while the ore deposits were rich and then disappear once the mineral played out.

As mineworkers moved from place to place in search of employment, women and children were often abandoned. Left to fend for themselves, these women did not know whether they would be reunited again with their husbands when times improved, or, in such a precarious environment, whether the absent spouse was even still alive. Thus, the legislature provided a pragmatic option to cope with the uncertainty of frontier life.

Other states had far less flexible divorce laws. Some did not grant divorce at all, while others had minimum residency requirements of at least one year. New York had a long residency requirement and granted a divorce only in cases where adultery was proven in open court. Such embarrassing public exposure of one's personal life prevented many, even the wealthiest Knickerbockers, from pursuing the option.

The floodgate of those seeking a Nevada divorce did not open until 1906, when the wife of William Corey, president of the United States Steel Corporation, came to Reno for what became a scandalous and much publicized event.

Soon, titillating accounts of other high profile divorce cases were filling newspapers across the country. The name Reno became synonymous with a "quickie divorce," euphemistically referred to as "The Cure." Locals took undisguised pride in thumbing their noses at social convention and in the town's reputation as "Sin City." As an example, in September 1917 the *Nevada State Journal* proudly proclaimed that six divorces had been granted the day before; lamenting that "if the court reporter had not gotten ill and gone home at 3 p.m.," the judge would have likely granted a seventh one—breaking the single-day record.[1]

By 1927, the divorce business in Nevada had become so profitable, legislators lowered the residency requirement to a mere three months. Over the next decade, more than 30,000 divorces were granted at the Washoe County Courthouse, and Reno became known as the "Divorce Capital of the World."

In 1931, facing the consequences of economic depression and drought, Nevada effectively drove other states out of the migratory divorce business by reducing the residency requirement to six weeks. The results of this change were astounding. Hotels, boardinghouses and "divorce ranches" multiplied, providing accommodations for divorce seekers six weeks at a time, and there appeared to be no shortage of them. As a result, Nevada's business community came through the Great Depression in much better condition than that of other states.

Traditions peculiar to a Reno divorce were created and widely publicized. One of the most celebrated was that of newly granted divorcees throwing their wedding rings off the Virginia Street Bridge into in the Truckee River. Bill Raggio later tried to capitalize on this custom when, as a boy scout leader, he would organize outings for his scouts to wade into the Truckee River below the bridge to fish out these rings in an effort to help fund scouting projects, though they rarely found anything of value.

Even citizens, who did not directly reap the financial benefits of the divorce trade, still enjoyed its great entertainment value. Local newspapers of the 1920s-1930s were filled each day with lurid accounts of extra marital affairs exposed in court, or darkly humorous circumstances that brought a marriage to its end. It was local lawyers, however, who benefited most directly from the divorce trade and in 1952, when twenty-five-year-old Bill Raggio first began practicing law, it was thriving.

Bill rented a small office in the American Bankers Trust Building at the corner of Sierra and West First Streets along with another lawyer, Dale Murphy. The two attorneys then hired a secretary and put an "open for business" announcement in the local newspaper. Unable to afford books, Bill spent long hours in the law library of the Washoe County courthouse.

Typically, Raggio would charge $150, plus costs, to handle a divorce case. Competition was fierce and some attorneys in town sought to undercut that price by increasing their volume. Bill took on other matters for less financial gain. Relatives came for legal advice or the drawing up of leases and contracts and, because they were "family," did not expect to pay for the service. Bill once received a model sailboat in lieu of payment, and occasionally would get a sack of potatoes or some onions as compensation.

Bill had many clients from whom he never received payment. At times, he even wondered why someone should pay him for what he did. "It was fun," he later recalled. "I felt the value of what I was learning from the services I was providing was greater than what the client was getting in return. Despite the fact that I had gone to law school, it seemed as if they were providing me with an education."

Bill typically arrived at the office before 8:00 a.m. and took his lunch at the nearby Elks' Club, where many of Reno's professional people met. He would be home by 5:00 p.m. for dinner and very often return to the office to prepare for upcoming cases. In 2009, he would fondly recall those early days:

> There used to be a saying that "the law is a jealous mistress," and as a new lawyer in those days, I learned that rule to be true. I spent a lot of time in the office and the law library and expected very little in return. You hoped to make a living, but didn't expect

much money. It was a challenge and a real profession. Like most other lawyers in those days, I so much enjoyed practicing the law that I could not wait to get to the office in the morning.

On weekends, Bill would try not go to the office. Instead, he and Dottie would do yard work and then spend Sunday relaxing at nearby Lake Tahoe. Bill also enjoyed fishing with his Uncle Ben and, in season, bird hunting.

Cases soon began to come in "off the street," largely because of name recognition from his family's long presence in the area. Other attorneys would often send over legal matters to help the young attorney, or because they did not want to be bothered with a matter. John Sinai, a prominent lawyer in town, gave Bill several, providing the young lawyer with valuable experience.

One such case, involved a young girl who had fallen off a city bus. Bill met with the insurance company representative, who, upon seeing how young and inexperienced Bill was, became condescending. He tried to intimidate Bill into accepting a lower settlement by threatening to "take this one to court."

Though Bill had virtually no courtroom experience up to that point, he countered with a convincing, "OK. See you in court!" The company settled for $25,000, a great deal of money in the 1950s. This was Bill's first contingency fee and helped cover his household expenses for the rest of the year. "I would not do much personal injury work during my legal career," he later said. "So this settlement may well have been my largest."

In 1952, Bill was admitted to practice before the U.S. District Court. At that time, the federal bench in Nevada consisted of one judge, John Ross. Judge Ross was known for his gruffness, especially if an attorney appeared in his court ill at ease, or unprepared. It was customary that a newly admitted attorney be appointed to defend an indigent client. Bill was selected to defend a man charged with the violation of the Dyer Act, taking a stolen car across a state lines. Bill's knowledge of criminal law consisted entirely of a single, first year, law school course. He did not know much about procedure or plea, and would later recall, "My client finally convinced me that he was caught red-handed and wanted to plead guilty. In retrospect, I think he took one look at this rather green, newly admitted attorney and decided he stood a far better chance with Judge Ross than he did with me."

It was during that time that Peter Echeverria* asked Bill to assist him in a murder trial. Echeverria had recently left the Woodburn firm in Reno and was hoping to make a reputation by winning a high-profile case. This one was made to order, with the elements of Old West justice and salaciousness the public had come to expect from a good Nevada story. Bill had not yet been involved in a criminal trial and, though he would be paid nothing, jumped at the opportunity to get the experience.

On trial for his life was local mineworker, Ray Milland, who had been charged with murdering a prostitute at Taxine's brothel in Tonopah. Although there were no eyewitnesses to the crime, Milland was accused of being the killer by a local hoodlum, Bonny Ornelles. Even before the trial began, it was apparent to most of the townspeople, as well as both defense attorneys, that the more-aggressive Ornelles had committed the murder. The meek Mr. Milland, self-admittedly a customer of the brothel that day, was clearly a victim of circumstance.

In preparation for the case, Peter and Bill spent several days interviewing witnesses. Whether out of loyalty to Ornelles, or for reasons that were more personal, it was soon evident that their stories were largely contrived.

The trial took place in the old Tonopah courthouse before Judge William Hatton. While Echeverria handled most of the courtroom work,

*Peter Echeverria would have a distinguished thirty-year legal career in Nevada, and, as one of the finest trial lawyers in the country, later served as a National President of the American Board of Trial Advocates. He was a founding member of the Nevada Trial Lawyers Association and received their Lifetime Achievement Award in June 1999. Peter also served in the Nevada Senate, elected in 1959 as the first senator of Basque heritage, and later was head of the Nevada Gaming Commission. His reputation was impeccable.

he did allow his young assistant to cross-examine several witnesses. Bill was enthralled by the process and would later describe the principals as "colorful local characters, most of whom had few aspirations in life other than hanging around a brothel."

One in particular, Billy Gallagher, tried to hide the fact that he was employed by the brothel as an errand boy. Under repeated questioning, Gallagher insisted that he did not work for Taxine's, but rather did odd jobs around town. When Raggio then asked what kind of "odd jobs" he performed, Gallagher replied, "I mow lawns." With that, the courtroom audience and jurors broke into uproarious laughter because, at the time, there was not a square inch of lawn in all of dusty Tonopah.

Milland was promptly acquitted.

Bill Raggio now had not only an extremely interesting criminal trial "under his belt," but also a proper and popular verdict. Bonny Ornelles, the likely killer, was never charged with the crime. Bill believed he died some time later "of something other than natural causes."

Though stimulated by what he had experienced during the Tonopah murder trial, Bill was still looking for his professional niche. His strongest subject at Hastings had been real property law. He gravitated toward this because of his innate mathematical skills. He enjoyed drawing diagrams and illustrations. However, in the early 1950s, most attorneys in Nevada did not have the luxury of specializing in a single facet of the law. In order to make a living, lawyers had to be competent in a broad range of legal skills.

In 2009, Bill would say, "At this time, I only wanted to further my law practice, and I was doing pretty well. In Reno, you were always assured of getting some nasty divorce cases to cover your overhead—although I never wanted to be a divorce lawyer. I had also decided that I was really not suited for criminal law."

The Milland murder trial had been Bill's first criminal defense case and awakened him to certain realities with regard to a thorny facet of the legal profession.

"It is not the goal of the prosecuting attorney and defense attorneys simply to win the case. The goal is to make sure that due process is followed and the individual's rights are fully protected in the course of the trial. In criminal cases, justice is not always served.

A truly professional attorney will feel obligated to make sure that proper procedures are followed—even if they believe, or know, their client committed the crime. A person may, as an example, have killed somebody, but in self-defense; or it might have been justifiable; or it could even require an insanity defense. Whether someone is guilty of an act is not always black-and-white. They may have committed the act, but are not necessarily guilty of the crime for which they have been charged."

Ironically, the more dedicated a criminal defense lawyer is to these principles, the more he, or she, is perceived by many outside the legal profession as being unprincipled—the root of all darkly cynical "lawyer jokes."

"The innocence or guilt of defendants in the few criminal cases I defended," Bill would later say, "was so indisputable that I was never put in a position of moral ambivalence."

The reason Bill represented so few criminal defendants in his career was because would spend the next eighteen years trying cases from the opposing side, as a prosecuting attorney. He would go on to become one of the mostly highly respected prosecutors in the nation, an interesting outcome for someone who once felt he was "really not suited for criminal law."

# CHAPTER THIRTEEN

# Deputy District Attorney

In August 1952, Bill received a phone call from Washoe County District Attorney Jack Streeter asking him to consider a position as deputy district attorney. Though Bill had never met Streeter, he, like most Nevadans, knew of him.*

"I called Bill and asked that he come to my office for an interview," Streeter would say in 2008. "During that interview, I sensed his brilliance and felt he would make an able deputy district attorney." Streeter offered Bill a salary of $325 a month. After discussing it with Dottie, Bill accepted the position.

While, the relatively low amount of starting salary would have prevented Bill from taking the job, it was customary at the time for members of the district attorney's office to engage in private law practice during off-duty hours. As such, Bill was able to supplement his income by handling about fifty divorce cases during his first year. The Raggios would soon need all of that additional income, because in the fall of 1952, Bill

---

*Jack Streeter was raised in Sparks, Nevada and attended the University of Nevada, where he participated in ROTC and won the Pacific Coast Golden Glove boxing championship in the light-heavyweight division. Upon graduation in 1943, Streeter went to Army Officers' Candidate School, and almost exactly one year later, on June 6, 1944, led his platoon ashore at Omaha Beach under murderous German gunfire. Streeter would be wounded at least five times as he fought his way across Western Europe. By the time the German army surrendered in April 1945, Jack Streeter was (and remains) Nevada's most decorated warrior.

Upon his return, Streeter attended Hastings Law School, graduating in 1948 (the same year Bill Raggio began attending there), and was admitted to the Nevada Bar. Jack was subsequently elected district attorney in 1950, running as a Democrat, and would go on to write several significant journal articles and books, including the groundbreaking *The Fourth Degree: The Lie Detector*, which he coauthored with famed attorney Melvin Belli.

and Dottie learned they were expecting a child. Daughter Leslie Ann was born the following year.

The little house in which they were residing on Hoyt Street, owned by Dottie's parents, would no longer be large enough, and so they purchased a new, 1,513 square foot, two bedroom, one bath home at 795 Robin Street. They were able to come up with the small down payment and a G.I. housing loan accounted for the remainder of the $19,500 sale price. The monthly mortgage payment was less than $100 a month.

Bill reported for work at the Washoe County District Attorney's Office in August 1952. At that time, there were only three deputy district attorneys in the office. He would be replacing one of them, John Bartlett, who had decided to return to full time private practice.

Some in the community thought Jack Streeter's style trampled the civil liberties of certain individuals, yet as Bill was to point out later, "Even though the rights available to criminal suspects were much different in the early 1950s, I never saw Streeter abuse his authority…that is not to say Jack would take any back talk from people."

Bill was immediately impressed with Streeter's style:

> Jack was a tall, dashing, flamboyant figure with great credentials. He had a very direct manner and made it clear that people were going to comply with the law. He was not inclined to back down, or to "suffer fools lightly." Like Ernest Brown, Jack would become an important mentor in my career. I like to think some of his style and toughness rubbed off on me, particularly in the way I conducted myself as a prosecutor in court.

When Bill Raggio accepted the job as deputy district attorney, he envisioned spending a year or two there to get some experience and then return to the practice of law. However, he soon became "caught up in the prosecutorial field." With Streeter's style as a guide, Bill began to forge close relationships with law enforcement officers, often riding along on patrol or accompanying them to crime scene investigations. He became a passionate believer that the administration of criminal justice was important—and set as his goal to become the best prosecuting attorney possible.

Just a few days into his new job, Bill was required to make a trip to San Francisco. When he requested time off, Streeter not only granted it, but also suggested Bill drive the new, red convertible on which he had just taken delivery. The car had been dropped off that morning in a parking lot adjacent to the courthouse by an employee of the dealership and so Jack had not even had a chance to see it. Gratefully accepting the offer, and leaving the keys to his old Pontiac, twenty-six-year-old Bill Raggio was soon cruising contentedly west on Highway 40, ensconced behind the steering wheel of his boss' luxurious new car—until a deer stepped out on to the roadway.

Bill was aware of Streeter's reputation for toughness, and was not sure how he would explain that the new car his boss had just purchased, but had never even seen, was now "totaled." Even as the phone on the DA's desk was ringing, Bill was not sure how he would break the news. When Jack Streeter answered, Bill found himself improvising: "Say Jack, I just wanted to let you know that you won't have to take your car in for its initial 1,000-mile maintenance." Over fifty years later, when Jack Streeter told this story, he shook his head as if still slightly incredulous at young Raggio's *chutzpah* that day.

As the new guy, Bill was initially assigned work that more experienced deputy district attorneys did not want, such as traffic cases. Yet, not long after he moved in, Bill recalled, "Mr. Streeter came in with a very thick file—about two feet high—and put it on my desk." Streeter wanted Bill to retry an arson case that he had personally tried earlier, which had resulted in a mistrial due to lack of jury unanimity on a verdict.

The case involved a man by the name of O'Brien who had been charged with setting fire to the Modern Music Center at the corner of California and South Virginia Streets. The Reno Fire Department had done an excellent job investigating the case and arson charges were filed. O'Brien was defended by the renowned and highly respected attorney Harlan L.

Heward, who had once been a deputy district attorney under previous Washoe County district attorney, Harold O. Taber.

Bill would join his new colleague, Emile Gezelin, in prosecuting the case. Gezelin and Streeter had been a classmates at Hastings and, in 1950, after his election to the office of Washoe County District Attorney, Jack Streeter asked Emile to join him as his deputy district attorney. Streeter would later say, "Emile was very successful because had been a school-teacher before going to law school and handled juries in much the same way as a schoolteacher would instruct a class. I greatly respected him."

Bill would also come to respect Emile's skill and integrity, and the two would remain life-long friends. "Emile," Bill would later say, "was one of the more important people in my life and my professional career."*

Raggio and Gezelin knew that arson was one of the most difficult crimes to prove. Not only is it necessary to show the fire was deliberately set, but also that the defendant could have been present at the time. The accused had already escaped conviction once because of disagreement by the jurors. The two young deputy district attorneys needed something to grab the jury's attention this time, and that something was called "demonstrative evidence."

Prior to World War II, there had not been a great deal of imagination in preparing court cases. Besides a blackboard for charting or diagramming, little other equipment was used. However, life had become more complex and post-war prosperity was bringing higher expectations from the public. Those entering the legal arena at the time recognized something more had to be done to hold the focus of jurors and keep them from becoming bored. A court case now not only had to present compelling testimony and evidence, it also had to be interesting—perhaps even entertaining.

---

* Bill Raggio had grown up just around the corner from Emile Gezlin and years later, at a testimonial dinner for Bill, Gezelin humorously recalled, "Even on a tricycle, Bill was the meanest kid in the neighborhood."[1]

Gezelin began his professional life as a teacher in eastern Nevada and later went on to become Deputy State Superintendent of Schools for Nevada. With a growing family to support, he decided to seek a law degree and, after being accepted to Hastings, he and his family moved to San Francisco. Bill Raggio admired the courage and determination it took for Emile to change careers so relatively late in life.

For this case, Bill and Emile created an exhibit showing how flammable liquid could be poured on wood and how it charred. They then burned this exhibit in the courtroom while an expert witness, Reno Fire Department Investigator Johnnie Patton, explained to the jurors what they were observing. This may sound tame compared to some modern courtroom theatrics, but it was revolutionary at the time. In fact, it was the first use of such demonstrative evidence in a Washoe County courtroom. "We did not invent this idea," Bill would later say, "Although we were one of the first to employ it in Nevada. Melvin Belli had begun doing it and we were following the trend."[1]

Their effort and imagination paid off, and this time O'Brien was convicted. Bill Raggio had won his first jury trial as a prosecutor, later saying, "When I walked into that first jury trial as a deputy DA, I was scared to death. We learned nearly nothing about criminal law in law school. What I knew then would fit into a thimble."

As the 1954 election approached, Jack Streeter decided not to run again for district attorney. His choice to return to the private practice hinged on several factors, but was primarily due to the enormous demands of job. In 2008 Streeter recalled having routinely worked seven days a week, often 18 hours a day. In addition to administering the operation of the office, he did his own investigations. Then, Washoe County did not have a crime lab and so fingerprints and other laboratory work had to be sent to the FBI in Washington, D.C. "This was a slow, labor-intensive and frustrating process," he said.

Two candidates announced their intention to run for the office. One was Reno City Attorney Sam B. Francovich* and the other was Deputy District Attorney Dyer Jensen. Before joining the district attorney's office, Jensen had graduated summa cum laude from the Georgetown University School of Law. Such impressive academic credentials and

---

*Sam Francovich, a decorated World War II naval aviator, hailed from one of Reno's earliest settler families. Instead of going into the restaurant business as had his father and grandfather, Sam chose to attend law school and practice in Nevada. He was elected Reno city attorney in 1950.

prestigious associations certainly would have seemed to make him an ideal candidate for the job. Jack Streeter, however, had doubts about whether Jensen possessed the decisiveness and "toughness" for the job.

Early in the election year, Streeter decided to let Jensen prosecute a high profile murder case in order to provide him with positive media exposure in his race against Francovich. Two ex-convicts, Frank Pedrini and LeRoy Linden had robbed and strangled a man to death near Mustang, east of Reno. Their victim, Clarence Dodd, picked the two men up while they were hitchhiking near Winnemucca. Dodd generously treated them to breakfast at a Lovelock diner shortly before they killed him. The public demanded justice in what the press labeled the "The Good Samaritan Murder."

Pedrini and Linden later confessed to being present when Dodd was killed, though the stories conflicted as to their individual degree of participation in the crime. Jensen told Streeter that he was going to allow Linden to plead to a lesser crime in return for his testimony against Pedrini. Streeter insisted both men deserved to be executed. When Jensen balked, Jack removed him from the case and personally took over the prosecution.

He immediately visited the forty-six-year-old Pedrini in San Quentin Prison, where he was serving time for parole violation, and found him terminally ill with cancer. When Pedrini learned that Linden was prepared to testify against him in exchange for leniency, he confessed to the murder and implicated Linden. The two killers were subsequently convicted of first-degree murder and sentenced to die in Nevada's gas chamber. The vengeful Pedrini requested that the two be executed together— so he could watch Linden die. The request was granted and the sentences were carried out on July 15, 1954. Jack Streeter believes "it was the only double-gassing execution in U.S. history."

Among the witnesses, attending this unusual execution was Deputy District Attorney Bill Raggio, who later described the event, saying he went because he was curious to see what it would be like. "The two did not struggle too much; inhaling a few times in jerking upward motions and then their heads slumped forward," he recalled. "It is sobering to watch someone executed. I would go on to try nine capital cases in my career, all successfully. Because I had attended this execution, I knew first-hand the gravity of the penalty I was seeking."

Despite the absence of an endorsement from Jack Streeter, Dyer Jensen won the race for district attorney in a close election. Bill campaigned for his new boss and years later spoke of his mixed feelings about the election saying the Francovich and Raggio families had been close for many years and so it seemed as if Bill was pitting himself against his friend, Sam. However, he felt a loyalty to Dyer Jensen because he worked with him. "This was the first time I was ever actively involved in any kind of political campaign," Bill would later say. "Partisan politics did not even cross my mind because it never occurred to me then that I might ever be running in an election."

Bill's absence of political partisanship can be seen in his early voting record. He first voted in a presidential election in 1948, choosing the incumbent President Harry Truman over Republican challenger Thomas Dewey. In 1952, although impressed with oratorical ability of the Democratic candidate Adlai Stevenson, Bill voted for General Dwight D. Eisenhower.

Although a registered Republican, Bill did not heavily identify with either party at that time. "I believed that the Republican Party represented free enterprise and other ideals I embraced," Bill said in 2009. "But my parents and grandparents had been Republicans, so it was not a difficult choice to make."

# CHAPTER FOURTEEN

# McCarran

The election of 1954 was a turning point in the history of Nevada politics. Just thirty-six days before the election, U.S. Senator Patrick McCarran died of a heart attack in Hawthorne, Nevada, while campaigning for fellow Democratic Party candidates. During his twenty-two years in office, McCarran had become one of the most influential senators in U.S. history and the most powerful politician in Nevada history.

McCarran was born in 1876 on the family sheep ranch along the Truckee River, fifteen miles east of Reno. His father had fled to America at the age of fourteen, after much of his family starved to death during the Great Irish Potato Famine.

Because Patrick was required to help his father on the ranch, he did not graduate from Reno High School until he was twenty-one. He then attended the University of Nevada where he excelled at debate and wrote for the school newspaper. After studying the law at home, McCarran was admitted to the Nevada bar in 1905. His first trial experience was successfully defending his father, a cantankerous old man, who had cut down telephone poles he believed were inappropriately placed on his property.*

By age thirty, Patrick McCarran had been both a state assembly member and the District Attorney of Nye County. Yet, he was viewed as a

---

*McCarran became a brilliant defense lawyer, though not a successful prosecutor. In 1906, he earned the ire of politically powerful George Wingfield, by representing Wingfield's common law wife, Mae, during their bitter and humiliating divorce action. He further alienated Wingfield and other mine owners by criticizing a decision by Nevada Governor Sparks to call in federal troops to break up a labor strike in Tonapah. For this, McCarran earned a reputation as a dangerous radical.

stubborn and uncooperative flop, even within the Democratic Party. Between 1902 and 1932, he ran for eight political offices, winning only three. On two other occasions, he was prevented from running by his own party. The highest state office McCarran attained during this period was that of Justice of the Nevada Supreme Court, from 1913 to 1918—a position often held at the end of a career.

After leaving the court, McCarran kept himself in the public eye by finding sensational divorce cases. The most famous of these was for Hollywood silent film star, Mary Pickford. Pickford was anxious to marry film star, Douglas Fairbanks. McCarran found a loophole in Nevada's divorce law, later closed by the state legislature, which allowed Miss Pickford to meet her six-month residency requirement in just sixteen days.

In 1932, at the age of fifty-six, McCarran ran against Republican incumbent Tasker Oddie for his seat in the U.S. Senate. Oddie was hugely popular and had an enormous campaign fund. Because no one else wanted to suffer the humiliation of being trounced by such a formidable opponent, the Democratic Party happily allowed its political maverick to run—though offering McCarran next to nothing in financial support.

Shortly before the election, a chain of banks owned by George Wingfield failed, going down with the savings of thousands of Nevadans and a significant amount of funds required to operate the state government. Because Oddie was closely associated with Wingfield, he was held responsible.

McCarran's campaign was also helped by the "coattail effect" of a landslide victory by Franklin D. Roosevelt in the presidential election. He won the election and would serve in the U.S. Senate for the next twenty-four years. Pat McCarran presided over what would be the last of the old time political machines in the state, one secondarily loyal to the Democratic party—but primarily loyal to him.*

By the mid 1950s, McCarran's political power began to wane. The

*Senator McCarran hired numerous part-time staffers, allowing young Nevadan's the opportunity to attend Washington-area law schools while in his employ. Some of them, like Grant Sawyer, Jon Collins and Harvey Dickerson became the next generation of state leaders. McCarran benefited from the research and analysis produced by these bright, young minds, as well as their loyalty to him. The senator could be unforgiving of those who opposed him — particularly those in his own party.

population of Nevada had grown from about 90,000 when he was elected in 1932, to approximately 200,000. McCarran's early constituency, one he carefully cultivated and knew nearly on first-name basis, had been thinned by waves of new arrivals, especially in the Las Vegas area. The senator did not fully comprehend the impact of such growth, nor was he used to being criticized by the press in a state he largely controlled.

When one of those new arrivals, *Las Vegas Sun* publisher Herman "Hank" Greenspun, began writing unfavorable editorials about him in early 1952, McCarran reacted by ordering the owners of several major casinos to withdraw their advertising from the *Sun*. Greenspun sued, and McCarran settled out of court. Casino owners rushed to provide the settlement money for the senator, but the cost to McCarran's political prestige was enormous.

Though his reputation had been tarnished by the time he died in 1954,* Patrick McCarran was not forgotten by the constituency who had made him. Robert Laxalt described the send off:

> His funeral in Reno was attended not only by men of high station and great wealth, but by hundreds of his little people—prospectors, sheepherders, buckaroos and working men. The smell of mothballs was everywhere.[1]

Governor Charles Russell, a Republican, appointed Ernest S. Brown to serve out McCarran's unexpired senate. Brown immediately announced he would run as Republican candidate for the seat in the coming election —just thirty-three days hence. His opponent was former state attorney general Alan Bible who had been groomed over the preceding decade to be McCarran's successor. Brown had little time to make the kind of po-

---

*By the 1950s, McCarran's fear of communist infiltrators, especially into positions of power in the government, universities, media and entertainment industries, led him into an ill-advised alliance with the "Red-hunter" Senator Joseph McCarthy of Wisconsin. It was an association that would permanently stain McCarran's image, particularly after McCarthy was humiliated and discredited during the 1954 Army-McCarthy hearings, and subsequently censured by the senate.

litical connections necessary to win a statewide race. Running against a McCarran protégé, and a three-to-two Democratic Party edge in voter registration, Ernest Brown lost resoundingly.

Instead of serving out his term, Brown voluntarily resigned his seat in the U.S. Senate. This allowed Senator-elect Bible to be seated in the current Congressional session, thus taking important seniority for committee appointments into the following one. Bill Raggio's role model and mentor had once again displayed a degree of dignity and decency few possessed. Putting aside pride and political partisanship, Ernest Brown did what he knew would be best for all the people of Nevada.

While Bill Raggio had relatively little contact with Patrick McCarran, he would occasionally join him for coffee at the Riverside Hotel when the senator was back from Washington, D.C., and always found him to be "a pleasant and extraordinarily interesting person." Nevertheless, with McCarran's passing went the last vestige of old-time "machine politics" in the state. Post-war prosperity and a flood of recent arrivals to Nevada created a need for new politics and new politicians, a world Bill Raggio, and his generation of bright, young attorneys, was about to inherit.

Dyer Jensen was sworn in as district attorney in January 1955. Because he was a less dynamic leader than his predecessor, Jensen delegated more assignments. Bill was soon trying an increasing number of criminal cases. The most notable of those involved defendant Robert Fox. Fox had shot and killed his wife and then, in a bungled suicide attempt, damaged his frontal lobe and shot out an eye.

The trial was noteworthy as it was one of the few times in Nevada where the so-called "insanity defense" was used. To help clarify this complex issue, most courts relied on the McNaughton Rule,[2] a common law principle that does not allow a criminal act to be excused if the defendant knew the nature and quality of the act, and knew it was wrong. Robert Fox's defense counsel was Bert Goldwater, who Bill knew to be one of the best trial attorneys in Nevada.

This was the first opportunity Bill had to examine and cross-examine psychiatrists in court, a talent for which he would later become widely admired. He would recall the Fox case as "one of the principal experiences of my trial attorney career. I learned a lot, not only from what we did, but also from what the defense put forth. Because of it, I became conversant in the parlance, terminology and workings of psychiatrists and the evaluations that they utilized in these kinds of cases."

Both sides used several psychiatrists in court. One was Dr. Rudolph Toller, the Director of the State Psychiatric Hospital in Stockton, California. "He was a brilliant guy and very good witness who I would use often through my career," Bill recalled. Adding, "Perhaps I shouldn't say this, but he was one of the few psychiatrists I've ever known that acted like they didn't need one themselves."

"I really enjoyed cross-examining psychiatrists," he continued. "The McNaughton Rule allowed me a trial tactic where I would get the defense's expert witnesses so far out on a limb with what they were saying; they could no longer defend their position. The testimony would ultimately fall apart when I asked one final question: 'Would this defendant have committed the act if there had been a police officer standing there?'"

If the answer was "no," Bill said, then the defendant knew the nature and quality of his action, and that it was wrong. The psychiatrist would usually pronounce a diagnosis. Bill would then pick up the Diagnostic and Statistical Manual of Mental Disorders and read each element of the diagnosis aloud, asking if they all applied. "They almost never did," Bill stated. "As I said, I loved cross-examining psychiatrists."

The effectiveness of Raggio's cross-examination was borne out a few days later when Robert Fox was found guilty of first-degree murder and sentenced to death. For years thereafter, *State v. Fox* was cited as precedent in criminal cases across the country where the insanity defense was being employed.[3]

With the exception of an occasional homicide case, most of Bill's years as a deputy district attorney were devoted to civil actions and "run-of-the-mill" crimes. Under the less aggressive Jensen, Bill and Emile chafed at the routine and soon their pursuit of more interesting casework would find them in trouble with their boss.

While still in office, Jack Streeter had purchased flashy, gold badges for the deputy district attorneys and encouraged them to be active in the fight against crime. So when Bill and Emile received a tip one evening that a brothel was operating at the north end of Sutro Street in Reno, they decided to pay the place a visit and perhaps close it down. After arriving at the address and knocking on the door, a kindly middle aged, black woman by the name of Gurtha Jamar answered. The men flashed their badges and asked to enter. Gurtha reluctantly allowed them in.

As Bill recalled, "It turned out we had picked a very unfortunate night to do this, because there was a large contingent of Reno police officers and other city employees visiting at the time and were, for the most part, pretty well inebriated."

The two men then instructed Gurtha to close the house down. As Bill would later say, "Emile and I were idealistic and dedicated enough to believe that if it was against the law in this county to operate a brothel, it should not be operating. I know we upset a lot of people that night."

Indeed, they did. Dyer Jensen was furious that the two had failed to get his permission before going out to investigate. Washoe County Sheriff Charles W. "Bud" Young, while not rebuking them, made it clear he was not happy they had acted without informing him.

Reno Chief of Police, L.R. "Pinky" Greeson came to Bill the next day and wanted to know if one of his captains had been at the brothel. The man, was a rival of Greeson's within the department and had a loyal following.

Bill had seen the captain at the brothel that night, but believed the police chief wanted the information only as an excuse to have the city council fire the man. Confronted with this dilemma, Raggio tactfully responded, "I'm not going to tell you who was there, because I don't want to get half the police department in trouble." The chief decided not to pursue the subject further.

Though he had protected him, and likely saved his job, the captain would remain cool to Bill for the rest of his life. Evidently, he felt Bill might use the information at some point in the future to pressure or embarrass him.

Bill and Emile chose not to press charges against any of the brothels' patrons, or even file a report. Several reputations were saved as a result. While the house on Sutro Street remained closed, Bill suspected Gurtha Jamar opened for business again elsewhere. This gentle madam never held it against him for interrupting her business and became an avid supporter of Bill's whenever he ran for office.

# CHAPTER FIFTEEN

# Prostitution in Nevada

Nevada is often identified for its libertarian acceptance of what other states consider to be criminal, and none captivates the curiosity of the public more than legalized prostitution.

From the time of the Territorial Legislature in 1861, regulation of brothel prostitution had been a matter of local option. Local ordinances defined areas where "houses of ill fame" could operate. In 1871, a bill was introduced in the state legislature making brothel prostitution legal throughout Nevada. It called for licenses to be issued and mandated regular health examinations to detect venereal diseases. Easily passing in the assembly, the bill was indefinitely postponed in the senate.

In the 20th century, the cities of Reno, Sparks and Las Vegas, chose to become incorporated. As State Archivist Guy Rocha later observed, "The incorporation language…gave the City Council the power "to license, regulate, prohibit or prescribe the location of saloons or barrooms, houses of ill-fame, hurdy-gurdy houses, or dance houses or houses that have special attractions such as music."[1]

Reno confined its legal brothels to "The Stockade," along the Truckee River, just east of town. In Las Vegas, an area of the downtown, called "Block 16," was designated as the red-light district. Where towns did not incorporate as cities, the state legislature approved the Town Board Act of 1881 by which county commissioners regulated brothel prostitution. The sheriff and the district attorney were responsible for enforcing the local ordinances.

In 1912, a statute was added to Nevada law that outlawed brothels "on any business thoroughfare or main street, or within 400 yards of a school, or any church edifice, building or structure, erected for and used for devotional services or religious worship in the State of Nevada." The state law took precedence over a local ordinance. Communities dealt with the new statue in different ways. Residents of Searchlight, Nevada, when confronted with the dilemma of finding their brothel located within 400 yards of a school—moved the school!

There is no better example of this laissez faire attitude then in the 1923 mayoral election in Reno. Incumbent H.E. Stewart ran for reelection promising to enforce prohibition laws and public morality. Supported by reform groups such as "The Red Light Abatement Movement," Stewart's campaign slogan was "Reno Beautiful, Not Reno Notorious." The election was considered a referendum on whether the public would stand against institutionalized vice, or allow Reno to become a "wide open city."

Opposing Stewart was E.E. Roberts, a divorce lawyer who had been Nevada's sole Congressional representative from 1911 to 1919. Roberts, a maverick Republican, who, while  generally eschewing progressive era reforms, had stood against his party and voted in opposition to the nation's participation in World War I.

The local press believed Stewart would win handily and the *Nevada State Journal* wrote that his opponent, Roberts, had a reputation for frontier ethics and was out of step with public opinion. Roberts welcomed that description, saying, "I don't believe in prohibition or any kind of reform that takes from any man or woman the right to find happiness in their own way.  I would repeal all blue laws; I would make Reno the playground of the world."[2] On Election Day, Roberts shocked reform organizations and religious leaders by receiving four times as many votes as his opponent.✷

---

✷After finding him good to his campaign pledges of not enforcing prohibition and other blue laws, the Wingfield political machine openly supported Roberts for reelection in 1927. During the 1931 election campaign, while Prohibition was still in effect, the colorful mayor advocated placing open barrels of whiskey on every street corner—with ladles for all to use. Roberts, who gained the reputation as "the nation's most permissive mayor," died in 1933 near the end of his third term.

In October 1937, the Nevada State Board of Health adopted rules and regulations requiring that prostitutes have weekly medical exams for gonorrhea and a monthly blood test for syphilis; a policy which was aggressively enforced. The advent of World War II brought with it a presidential executive order to suppress all prostitution near military bases and installations. "Block 16" was closed in 1942, following a failed appeal to the Nevada Supreme Court.

Following World War II, the regulation of brothel prostitution was returned to the state once again as a local option.[3] Carson City and nearby Douglas County chose not to exercise that option. Due to increasing population and the newfound "respectability" of gaming in the post-war era, cities like Reno and Las Vegas found a return to regulated brothel prostitution an image—and a diversion of potential gaming dollars—they no longer wished to cultivate.

# CHAPTER SIXTEEN

# District Attorney Raggio

As the 1958 election approached, Dyer Jensen was having a difficult time deciding whether to run for reelection, or for the position of district court judge. Bill Raggio had already decided to run for DA and so became increasingly irritated with Jensen's lingering indecision.

Finally, Bill met with his boss to force the issue. He told Jensen that he intended to run for district attorney and that he was annoyed by the DA's reluctance to make up his mind. Bill further advised Jensen that if he did decide to run for reelection, Bill was prepared to resign as deputy district attorney in order to campaign for the job. Years later Bill would recall, "It was not an amicable meeting and left our working relationship a bit strained. However, after he made up his mind to run for district court judge, it was no longer a problem."

During his six and a half years in the DA's office, Bill had come to enjoy the work, especially participating in criminal trials. Initially concerned that other, more senior, deputy DAs were also going to seek the position, he was soon relieved to learn that not only were none of them thinking of running, but all enthusiastically endorsed his candidacy.

"This was my first run for elective office," Bill later stated, "and though I ran as a Republican, the party had no influence on my decision. Political parties were not that involved in the local races and provided little or no funding. My campaign was decidedly apolitical."

As a formality, Bill sent a letter to the chair of the state Republican Party advising him of the decision. In his letter, the thirty-one-year-old Raggio informed them that he was not seeking the office as "a political endeavor," but rather because of his "earnest zeal to continue in prosecution and act as a legal adviser to our county agencies."

Emile Gezelin and Edwin Mulcahy, another fellow deputy district attorney, were soon working hard for Bill's election. None of them had any experience in running a campaign and received little advice along the way. However, the population of Washoe County was relatively small and, because television was not as important to the political process as it later became, it required relatively little money to run a campaign. They paid for some newspaper ads and took cardboard posters around to businesses asking that they be prominently displayed. What financial contributions did arrive usually came from Bill's family, friends and a few businesses. Bill used some personal funds, but with a family to support, those were limited.

There were few fundraisers. Raggio gave speeches to gatherings and service club meetings. He went door-to-door throughout the community and, because his family had been in the area for generations, he was already known to many. He had also acquired a reputation in his six years as a deputy district attorney. He later spoke of any advantage he felt he had:

> My experience as a prosecutor was the biggest difference. Some people say I was a tough guy. I don't think I came across as a tough guy. I think I came across as a tough prosecutor. We worked hard on our cases and I enjoyed the trial work. I developed some good techniques in trying cases. I had two excellent role models in Ernest Brown and Jack Streeter, both no-nonsense men. If they felt they were right, they did what was necessary. I like to think I developed that kind of reputation.

Bill's opponent was attorney Murray Dolan, a Democrat from Sparks. With few exceptions, Democrats swept Congressional and state house races across the United States on Election Day, 1958. Bucking that trend, Bill was easily elected as Washoe County District Attorney—and the organization would never be the same.

Upon taking his oath of office in January 1959, Bill set out to restructure and modernize the operation of the office. Despite the rapidly increasing number of cases, the office had only four deputy district attorneys. Workloads were not being controlled in an orderly fashion and there were few administrative staff members in support of the prosecutors.

Bill created a criminal division and a civil division. In time, he would also form an appellate division and separate divisions to handle welfare, hospital and non-support issues. He selected Emile Gezelin as his Chief Deputy District Attorney and, over the next year, appointed as deputy district attorneys such gifted young lawyers as Eric Richards, Drake De-Lanoy, Herbert "Rick" Ahlswede, Jack Mathews and John Gabrielli.

Instead of relying entirely on law enforcement agencies for investigative work, Bill decided to add an investigator to his staff, appointing Roger Corbett, a former teacher and retired Washoe County school superintendent. Bill instinctively understood there might be some resentment on the part of law enforcement regarding the change and so selected Corbett as much for his intellect as his personality. "Roger was the kind of person I knew wouldn't step on toes," Bill said, "and would maintain a good working relationship with all the local law enforcement agencies."

Later, Raggio would hire additional investigators with more law enforcement experience, such as Russell Schooley, John Peevers, Bob Canfield and Bob Black. These men formed the county's first Law Enforcement Intelligence Unit (LEIU). Having such a unit in a county DA's office was uncommon at the time, yet due to the diligence and hard work of the staff, the LEIU was soon recognized as a credible, reliable and trustworthy entity. Accordingly, Washoe County was one of the few district attorney offices in the nation to develop a good relationship with the FBI; one based on mutual trust. Such a bond was frequently absent in relationships between the FBI and local police agencies, a situation often arising from traditional jurisdictional jealousies and lack of shared respect.

Bill showed his foresight and innovation in other ways as well. Early in his tenure, when drug use was still negligible in the United States, he anticipated the impending crisis and associated increase in other crimes.

Hoping to lessen its impact on the community through education, Bill spent hours addressing service clubs and other gatherings, explaining the nature of drugs and displaying drug paraphernalia. "My goal was to impress upon them what a serious problem this was going to be. Unfortunately, it all came to pass," he said.

Juvenile crimes, including robbery and murder were also on the increase. Raggio attempted to enforce a curfew on those under age eighteen, though it created a vocal protest from many in the community.

In 1960, he took an inventive and practical approach to the problem of juvenile delinquency, forming an organization called the District Attorney's Reaction Team, or D.A.R.T. Bill's hope was to "encourage the stern, firm treatment on the part of law enforcement and others concerned with repeated offenders and to assist in providing recreational facilities for idle and dissolute youth."

Despite his growing reputation as an imaginative and resourceful young district attorney, it would be a series of sensational trials in the early 1960s that would catapult Bill Raggio into the national consciousness as one of America's toughest and most competent prosecuting attorneys.

# CHAPTER SEVENTEEN

# Conforte

B ill Raggio will probably be most remembered for his feud with America's legendary pimp, Joe Conforte. Born in Augusta, Sicily on February 6, 1926, Conforte immigrated with his family to the United States in 1937, settling in Dorchester, Massachusetts. He was drafted into the U.S. Army late in World War II and naturalized as a citizen while stationed at Fort Riley, Kansas. Upon being discharged, Conforte took up residence in Oakland, California, where he drove a cab and learned the profitability of procuring customers for local prostitutes. He soon moved into operating his own brothel, but after several run-ins with the Oakland police, Conforte decided to move his operation to Nevada. In October 1955, he opened the Triangle River Ranch (later the Triangle Ranch) brothel, near the small town of Wadsworth, about thirty miles east of Reno.

The name Triangle Ranch appears to have stemmed from its geographical location at a point where Lyon, Storey and Washoe Counties converge. Here, Conforte could quickly move his operation a few hundred yards into an adjacent county, depending upon the degree of pressure a particular sheriff might be exerting on him. The Triangle Ranch was also only a short distance from Churchill County, where Joe met a brothel madam, Sally Jesse Burgess, who would soon become his business partner and wife.

Before Bill Raggio's predecessor, Jack Streeter, left office, he had made it clear to Joe Conforte that he was not welcome in Washoe County.

However, during the term of Dyer Jensen, Conforte became more brazen in his compulsive need to flaunt his affluence. The squat, raspy-voiced Conforte, bejeweled, and occasionally wearing a mink coat, would often drive to Reno in his expensive convertible, always accompanied by two or three prostitutes from The Triangle Ranch. With his black hair carefully combed back across his pate and a shirt pocket overstuffed with expensive Cuban cigars, Conforte would spend hours in the Riverside Hotel, located literally next door to the district attorney's office, spending large amounts of money, often tipping card dealers and busboys with hundred dollar bills.

Bill was particularly annoyed by reports Conforte was ingratiating himself with police officers and deputy sheriffs by routinely handing out cigars with $20 bills wrapped around them—a generous amount of money in the mid-1950s. He later said, "He [Conforte] thought he was bigger than the law, and so it became a test of who was going to run the county—him or the district attorney. That is how it grew into what you might call a 'contest of wills.' If he had been a guy running a brothel in another county, who didn't do all that, he probably would not have been bothered by the authorities. However, his presence was a violation of the law because he was obviously a pimp."

Bill first met Conforte in June 1959. During that meeting, he advised Conforte that, henceforth, he would be arrested for vagrancy each time he entered Washoe County. The basis for such actions was a provision in the Criminal Practice Act of 1911, defining a "vagrant" as, among other things, "a pimp, panderer or procurer or live in or about houses of prostitution." The crime was a misdemeanor, resulting in a fine and jail time for repeated violations.

Bill carefully explained the vagrancy provision to Conforte and reiterated it would be strictly enforced. Conforte turned imploringly to Washoe County Sheriff Bud Young, who also attended the meeting. "Joe, I can't help you," said the Sheriff. Young then began to set conditions under which Conforte might be allowed into the county "on legitimate business." Bill, however, was the one setting the rules that day and later described what happened next:

> I made it clear to him [Conforte] that he was not to be in Washoe County. He was not to operate in Washoe County and he was not to come into Washoe County. Nothing in particular provoked me to tell him this. It was not a personal vendetta. He had been told years before by Jack Streeter that he was not wanted here and was in violation of the law.

> I subsequently put out an order that he be arrested when he showed up, though that was often complicated because many members of the law enforcement community considered him a friend and refused.

Yet, some peace officers were more than willing to arrest Conforte and over the next year he was taken into custody for vagrancy several times in Lyon and Clark counties, later claiming to have been "harassed" by the Las Vegas police. When arrested for vagrancy in Washoe County, Conforte's booking card showed him to be 5' 7" tall and weighing 150. He amusingly listed his occupation as "Rancher."

He frequently failed to appear in court on such misdemeanor charges and, when he did, would often act belligerent and sometimes angrily storm out of the courtroom during the proceedings. As a result, he found himself facing additional charges of contempt of court.

District Attorney Raggio would not back down. "I was sitting in the Riverside Hotel one evening with my wife and some friends and Conforte came in," Raggio recalled. "He had been arrested and charged with vagrancy earlier that day, yet seemed to want to flaunt the fact that he was free, as if indicating to me, 'I dare you to pick me up.'"

Raggio had him arrested for a second time—in the same day.

This was the final indignity for Joe Conforte, a man not to be pushed without pushing back. He became consumed by one goal—to humiliate Bill Raggio and destroy his career. Raggio knew that Conforte would not allow this kind of treatment to continue without some form of retaliation, and he soon received warnings from two different informants that

"Conforte was going to do something to get me."

On a Friday, November 13, 1959, an attractive young woman came to Bill Raggio's office to seek assistance in obtaining a divorce. Because it was still customary at the time for attorneys to maintain a private law practice in addition to their civil service or elective positions, it was not unusual for a client to walk in off the street seeking legal services. However, this "Friday the 13th" encounter was about to snowball into an international news sensation.

The shapely, brown-haired woman introduced herself as Val Newton, but provided Bill with few other details about herself or her marriage, except to say that she was twenty-two-years-old and staying at the nearby Riverside Hotel. Bill advised her that he would begin preparing the necessary paperwork and contact her later.

The following day, while working in his office, Bill received a telephone call from Newton. "I need to see you." She anxiously intoned. "Can you come over to the hotel?" Bill walked the short distance to the Riverside and found the woman sitting in the cocktail lounge. "It was the early afternoon and there was something about the way our conversation was going that roused my suspicion," Bill recalled. "We ordered drinks and began talking. Soon she said that she was feeling ill and asked me to help her to her room. It was then that the proverbial 'light bulb' went on in my head."

Sensing something was not right, Bill excused himself and went to speak with Harry Spencer, a friend and public relations representative for the hotel, who was nearby. Spencer would later testify in court that the now-suspicious DA asked him to check out the woman's room for anything suspicious, including possible surreptitious recording devices. He obtained a room key from a bellman and, after a thorough inspection, found nothing suspicious.

By prearrangement, Spencer was waiting outside her hotel room door when Bill and the woman arrived ten minutes later. The two men joined her in the room, chatted for about a half hour and left together. Though Bill knew through informants about Conforte's threats to "get him," and the woman's behavior made him wary, he did not immediately associate the two. When she did not follow up with him about filing for her divorce, it only furthered Bill's suspicions that something was wrong.

Those suspicions were validated a few days later when Reno attorney Frank Peterson, who represented Joe Conforte, called Bill to ask if he would meet face-to-face with his client. When Bill suggested the meeting take place at the district attorney's office, Peterson replied that Conforte had expressly stated he would not meet there.

Bill agreed to a meeting at Peterson's office and then immediately contacted district court Judge Grant Bowen to obtain a court order to have the conversation "bugged." Once the order was granted, Bill began developing a plan to incriminate Conforte with his own words, because, as Bill later remarked, "He [Conforte] never knew when to keep his mouth shut."

Because Conforte's influence extended well up into the ranks of the police department and sheriff's office, with some officers displaying open resentment about the DA's treatment of the brothel owner, Bill did not know whom to trust.

He decided on Harold K. "Hal" Lipset, a private investigator from San Francisco. Lipset was already a legendary figure in criminal investigation and an icon among the many young, innovative, post-war attorneys trained in San Francisco law schools. In Washoe County, DA Jack Streeter, a Hastings graduate like Bill, had previously utilized Hal's services.*

Hal Lipset would work with Bill on many occasions over the ensuing

---

*Hal Lipset was born in New Jersey and attended the University of California at Berkeley, before enlisting in the Army in 1941. He saw combat action in Europe, was promoted to captain and later attended military criminal investigation school. Hal used these skills to begin his private investigation business in San Francisco. With the introduction of the transistor in the 1950s, Lipset pioneered electronic surveillance. In 1968 he testified about eavesdropping before a U.S. Senate subcommittee demonstrating perhaps his most ingenious bugging device—a fake green martini olive, featuring a "pimento" microphone and a "toothpick" antenna.

Ironically, Hal's martini olive presentation was so compelling, it resulted in a federal law curbing the use of wiretaps and recordings without a court order. Much to Lipset's dismay, California, where he did most of his business, banned private recordings unless all participants consented. Yet, Lipset's reputation was such that in 1973 he was appointed chief investigator for the Senate Watergate Committee.

years, but none would be more critical to the DA's reputation and career than the bugs he placed, unbeknownst to Frank Peterson, in the attorney's office on November 18, 1959.

Lipset favored two types of recording devices: a wire recorder, with a line leading from a hidden microphone back to a tape recorder, and a wireless, or radio, microphone. Because it would be critical to obtain a clear record of Conforte's demands, Lipset decided to use both. Once Frank Peterson acceded to the court order by allowing his office to be bugged, Lipset went to work, hiding the two microphones in strategic locations and then settling himself into an upstairs room to monitor the equipment along with his recording engineer, Ralph Bersche.

When Conforte arrived at the office, he and Raggio immediately frisked one another other to see if either was wearing a recording device. They found none, but Conforte continued to appear apprehensive about the possibility. However, as the conversation evolved, he gradually became more relaxed and talkative. As was his style, Conforte's language was peppered with expletives and vulgarities.

He finally divulged to Bill that he had arranged to have the woman meet with him. Despite her claim to be twenty-two years old, she was only seventeen. Because Bill had purchased her liquor, Conforte continued, his career was over. For good measure, he would be facing a charge of statutory rape, because she was prepared to allege Bill had sex with her at the Riverside.

Conforte then changed his story, apparently trying to ingratiate himself with the DA, by explaining that this current meeting with Bill was not his idea, but rather a favor to the girl's mother who had come to him with details of Bill's "crimes." He was meeting with Bill as a Good Samaritan "to try and arrange things."

Bill pointed out that he did not have sex with the woman, to which Conforte replied, "Yes, I know that, but it's your word against hers, and they're going to believe her." Bill then asked what Conforte wanted. He replied that the vagrancy charges be dropped and that Bill make a public apology, in court, for the way had treated him.

Emboldened by what he perceived as the DA's acquiescence, Conforte then demanded dismissal of charges against a local physician, Dr. William J. Bryan. The doctor was employed by Conforte to examine prostitutes at his brothels for venereal disease. Bryan had recently been convicted of providing liquor to a teenage girl. "He is a friend of mine," Conforte said. "And I help my friends."*

Bill then explained that it would be impossible to change the charges against Dr. Bryan, because the case was already on appeal to the Nevada Supreme Court. He then changed the subject, asking Conforte who was going to file the charges against him for his alleged liquor violation and statutory rape.

Conforte replied that the state attorney general, Roger Foley, would be taking the action. "Roger would love to do it," he said. "It would make him governor. He wants to be governor." Bill then asked, "Do you mean you have Roger Foley in your pocket too?" Conforte then explained that Roger would comply because Joe had incriminating information about his brother, George Foley, the Clark County district attorney.

Bill then inquired what assurances he had that the matter would be forgotten if the vagrancy charges were dropped. Conforte assured him it would be done, saying, "All I want is to be left alone. I want to be friends. I want to be treated like a human being."

The entire conversation lasted about thirty minutes and now Bill finally knew the details of the plot to ensnare him. Once Conforte left the office, Bill raced upstairs to where Hal and Ralph were running the taping devices. He was anxious to confirm that the entire conversation had been clearly recorded. Bill knew Conforte's influence in the town was pervasive. By liberally spreading money and favors, he had cultivated a kind of Robin Hood image. Prostitution was winked at by many in the state

---

*Dr. William J. Bryan was extradited from California to Reno in June 1961 and tried (just days before the Conforte trial) on charges of contributing to the delinquency of a minor by giving liquor to an underage female employee in May 1959. After months of appeals, which eventually came before the Nevada Supreme Court, he entered into an agreement with Washoe County DA Raggio to leave Nevada and never come back. Dr. Bryan moved to Los Angeles where he opened a chain of sexual therapy schools. He later testified at the trial of Charles Manson.

as a ribald joke, a victimless and non-violent crime. Many sympathized with Joe and viewed the DA as vindictive and heavy-handed.

"People would have believed this guy [Conforte]," Bill would later say. "He was popular; everybody thought he was a colorful figure. It was important to have the tape because then there was no question about who was telling the truth or about his effort to trap and extort me."

Bill was greatly relieved when Ralph played back a clear and complete recording of the conversation. Because he did not know exactly whom he could trust, the DA decided to have both the location of the tape— and its very existence—kept secret until the trial.

Now, better understanding the specifics of this attempted "set up," Bill informed Dottie. He knew it would be several months between Conforte's arrest and the start of his trial; months in which those who disliked him would spread slander. When the accusations and innuendo came, it was going to be difficult on Dottie and his family.

Bill too endured "a lot of heat; a lot of criticism." Most exasperating, however, was that while he and his family were suffering such insults, tape recorded evidence vindicating him had to be kept hidden until the trial.

"When I look back on it," Bill later said, "and see how difficult it made things by not having the full trust of the law enforcement agencies, I wonder if I would choose to go through it again."

After leaving Frank Peterson's office, Bill immediately issued a warrant for the arrest of Joe Conforte on the charge of "extortion by threat." Bill then delivered a public announcement detailing the events of the last week. His statement concluded with a blunt rebuke, tinged with fury: "I will not be intimidated. I feel that it is my duty to see that scum and filth do not influence the actions of public officers."

Joe Conforte was arrested three days later by criminal investigator Roger Corbett and two Washoe County deputy sheriffs at a Conforte brothel in Lyon County, just east of Carson City. He was transported by them back to Washoe County where he was booked. Bail was set at $50,000.

Conforte was indignant, telling the local press, "This is all illegal. I'm a businessman minding my own business. I don't bother nobody." Regarding the district attorney's statement detailing the charges against him, Conforte was glib: "He [Raggio] ought to be writing for a movie company. This is a bum rap."[1]

Before his extortion trial began, Conforte would face the vagrancy charges in Washoe County. On February 6, 1960, Raggio personally prosecuted the case. He informed the jury of ten women and two men that as the owner of several brothels, including the Triangle Ranch in Wadsworth, Conforte met the definition of a vagrant because he was a "dissolute male, a pimp and panderer of loose morals."

Assisting Frank Peterson in Conforte's defense was Las Vegas attorney Madison Graves, who had successfully defended him on vagrancy charges in that city earlier in the year. Graves explained that it was uncommon to have jury trials in vagrancy cases, but that Conforte "believes he is innocent as a matter of principle, and that's what we're fighting for."

During the trial, Conforte twice interrupted the proceedings to object to Raggio's reference to him as "a pimp." The presiding judge, Justice of the Peace William R. Beemer, silenced him each time with sharp raps of his gavel and stern warnings to desist. Later, Joe angrily told reporters, "I am not a pimp. They beat their woman and treat them badly. I'm a businessman."[2]

In his final argument, Bill told the jurors that Conforte's very presence in this community is a criminal act under the vagrancy law. "I can't fathom how much more loose one can be in morals and conduct than this defendant," he added. The jury agreed and the judge sentenced the defendant to ninety days in jail and a $300 fine. Conforte's attorney, Frank Peterson, immediately notified Beemer that he was appealing the decision.

Conforte's extortion trial would not begin until June 27, 1960; however, the sensational series of events leading up to it had become headline news. Newspaper and magazine stories across the country and abroad, captivated readers as one salacious detail after another unfolded. While this would do nothing to change the preconceived image of Nevada as the "Sin State," William J. Raggio's reputation as a tough and talented DA would be imprinted on the national consciousness, marking the beginning of a storied career.

To those who lived in Nevada during Bill Raggio's tenure as DA, the mention of his name invariably results in some variation of a story about his burning down a brothel. Bill admits his participation, but as minimal, "a spectator." However, given his bitter feud with Conforte, and his reputation as a tenacious law enforcement official, Bill's presence at that celebrated conflagration forever labeled him as the perpetrator.

The Triangle Ranch brothel consisted of a number of buildings, positioned several hundred yards from each other, but in different counties. The furnishings and fixtures would be moved periodically from one site to the next, as pressure from law enforcement in one county, or the other, increased. By late 1959, a long wooden building, painted in two shades of green, was open for business just inside Storey County, about 100 yards from the Washoe County line.

This had gotten the attention of Storey County District Attorney Robert Moore, who had been putting pressure on county commissioners to take action against Conforte. Several of the commissioners were influenced by the brothel owner's largess and resisted Moore's request.

The issue came to a head in December 1959 when University of Nevada student Dudley Nicols was shot in the foot after he refused to leave the premises. Moore quickly filed a complaint against Joe Conforte and called Sally Burgess in for questioning as the possible shooter. Moore again went to the Storey County Commission about the brothel, arguing that they should order it closed "once and for all."

On March 18, after consulting with his friend and fellow DA, Bill Raggio, Moore obtained an order signed by First Judicial District Court Judge Richard Hanna to have the building destroyed because it was "unlawfully used for the purpose of maintaining a house of prostitution." It was further stipulated that Joe Conforte was to pay for the cost of demolition, which the DA estimated at the time to be "in excess of $100."

Robert Moore decided to have the building burned and asked Raggio to witness the event and provide fire protection should the blaze inadvertently spread. They would carry out the court order on the afternoon of March 23. Because a number of law enforcement officers in both Storey and Washoe County were sympathetic to Conforte, the plan was to be kept confidential, lest he be tipped off and get there in advance to remove potentially incriminating evidence.

In 2008, former Washoe County Fire Chief Bill Farr recalled the events of that day. He received a call from Bill about 11:30 a.m., asking that he meet him in Sparks and bring one of his fire engines. "I was waiting there when about four or five cars pulled up." Farr recalled:

> Bill was in one, but would not tell me yet what was going on; he simply asked me to follow him out the canyon. I told him I would not go any further until I knew why I was taking the engine out there and so he explained the situation to me. We followed him out to the brothel, but parked the engine just on the Washoe County side of the line. We were so close to the building, which was technically inside Storey County, that our hose reached from the engine all the way there.

The Washoe County contingent arrived at the Triangle Ranch about 2:00 p.m. and found Moore, Storey County Sheriff Cecil Morrison and several deputy sheriffs, including one from nearby Lyon County, already waiting. A gated, seven-foot high, barbed wire-crowned, cyclone fence surrounded the building. One Storey County deputy sheriff quickly produced a bolt cutter and removed the lock. Upon ringing the doorbell, two maids answered. They were the only occupants of the building and claimed to be new employees who did not know the purpose for which the place was used.

Moore, Morrison and Raggio began a search of the premises. In the master bedroom, used by Joe Conforte and his wife, Sally Burgess, they found a blackjack-type bludgeon, rifle, pistol and ornamental knife, as well as a collection of pornographic films and photographs. The closet contained a large assortment of costumes, or "trick outfits," as well the couple's regular clothing and shoes.

Farr was asked to inspect the building to determine the best location to start a fire. He found electrical wires on the roof, and, upon closer inspection, realized that they went through into each of the rooms used by the girls to a microphone hidden in ceiling light fixtures. "The other end of the wires appeared to have been connected to a control box in Conforte's master bedroom closet," he observed. "It is my belief the wiring system was not used, as Joe Conforte later claimed, as a safety measure for the girls to use if they needed help, but rather to eavesdrop on patrons in order to extort them."

The master bedroom also contained personal belongings and photographs of Conforte and Burgess. Above the king-size bed was a large painting of a nude woman done on black velvet. By 3:15 p.m., when the fire was started, the maids had removed nearly all the items from the master bedroom, which were carried to another brothel building 500 meters to the east, in Lyon County by a willing group of brothel patrons and onlookers. However, they had left behind the biggest prize of the day for law enforcement—a locked safe found hidden in a hollowed-out phonograph.

Bill Raggio was on hand later when the safe was opened. Inside was a small bundle, which contained, among other items, a set of identification "dog tags" belonging to a U.S. Army general who had evidently visited the brothel. The bundle also contained cancelled checks showing Conforte's contributions to the Grant Sawyer for Governor campaign and the campaign to elect Ray Peterson as Washoe County Commissioner. In addition, there were several personal checks that the Churchill County district attorney had passed at several business locations, but which had been returned for insufficient funds. Conforte had subsequently issued payment to cover them. There is only one reason Bill Raggio could think of as to why Conforte would have kept these items, and that was "to use them to blackmail these people in the future."

In the rooms where the prostitutes worked, police found health certificates verifying that the women were free of infectious and communicable diseases at the time of the examination. The most recent certificates had been signed and dated by Dr. Bryan about a month earlier.

By this time, Bill Farr was ready to start the fire. He had located a closet vented in the ceiling, which would be ideal. Farr placed flammable material in the closet, but because he had no jurisdiction there, let Storey County Sheriff Morrison light the fire. The building was soon engulfed in flames.

In a 2008 interview, Bill Farr would say, "Officially, the Washoe County Fire Department had been asked there to prevent any damage from flames traveling across the county line. Of course, the real reason we were there was to assist in burning the building down. I had been trained to stop fires, not start them. The irony was not lost on me even as I was going about my business that afternoon."

A number of people had come from the nearby towns of Fernley and Wadsworth to watch. Many of them were angrily swearing and shouting derogatory names at the law enforcement officials. All the while, cars were coming down the road bringing customers to the other brothel, in clear view of what was going on just a few hundred yards away in Storey County.

Farr would then offer up one of the more amusing anecdotes of the day:

> Soon, a very nice convertible drove up near us and stopped. Two beautiful ladies stepped out of the car; one in a lavender jumpsuit the other in a bright pink jumpsuit. I turned to a Storey County Deputy Sheriff standing nearby and commented, "There are two girls who won't be working tonight," to which he snapped back, "Your damn right they won't—one of them is my wife!" I was relieved when he and I met sometime later, that there were no hard feelings about my remark.

No one expected Joe Conforte to attend what one Storey County official referred to as his "housewarming." In addition to a warrant for his arrest in Las Vegas on a "disorderly persons" charge, Conforte was being sought by Storey County authorities to serve a twenty-five-day jail sentence for being in contempt of a 1957 court order to abate his prostitution operations. This was all in addition to his being out on bail pending a pair of trials in Washoe County for vagrancy and extortion.

The fire was extinguished about 5:30 p.m., after 1,800 gallons of water, pumped from the nearby Truckee River, was poured over the charred remains.*

For Bill Raggio, though technically a spectator, the Triangle Ranch fire would become the source of both admiration and vilification. While most Nevadans were generally conservative when it came to enforcement of the law and punishment of lawbreakers, they also disliked government intrusion into their lives. Destruction of private property—anyone's private property—by a government entity was not soon forgotten. This was particularly true of rural Nevadans and may have had an adverse affect on Bill Raggio's campaigns for statewide office a decade later.

Despite the incriminating tape recordings of Joe Conforte's extortion demands, Bill did not feel completely comfortable about winning a conviction. He knew he was disliked by many within the police department, city council and the community-at-large for his treatment of Conforte. He recognized the importance of finding the woman who had attempted to entrap him, before Conforte exerted his influence upon her to commit perjury.

By then, Bill had learned the identity of "Mrs. Newton" to be Jacqueline "Jackie" Hitson, the seventeen-year-old sister of Conforte prostitute, Elsie Hitson. Jackie Hitson had seemingly disappeared and so once again, Bill called upon the services of private investigator Hal Lipset.

---

Sally Burgess, aka Eleanor Anderson, claimed ownership of the building and sued Moore, Raggio, et al, for $50,000. In January 1962, District Court Judge Thomas O. Craven ruled that the burning had been illegal. On May 2, 1962, the trial venue was changed from Storey to Elko County. The civil case was eventually dropped.

Hal quickly located Hitson's mother in southern California. From her, he learned Jackie had lived briefly in Seattle, Washington, but was now somewhere in San Francisco. Because San Francisco was Lipset's base of operations, it did not take him long to discover Jackie was residing in an apartment at 213 Ashbury Street and was being guarded by her sister Elsie and Joanne Johnson, also a prostitute working for Joe Conforte.

On May 7, 1960, Hal Lipset waited outside the Ashbury Street apartment until Elsie left the premises. He then knocked on the door. When Joanne Johnson opened it, Lipset pushed past her and confronted Jackie Hitson. Jackie agreed to leave with him, despite protests by Johnson.

There is no way of gauging the level of Conforte's rage when he learned that Bill Raggio's investigator had personally snatched his "star witness." However, Joanne Johnson was walking on crutches when she appeared as a defense witness during Conforte's trial the following month, the result of a broken ankle. She would state, under oath, the injury was not sustained when Conforte pushed her down a flight stairs on Ashbury Street, but rather, from "accidently" falling down them on her own.

Hal Lipset took Jacquelyn Hitson to his office, where her handwritten and taped confession, revealed a sad and complex story.

She and her sister Elsie, four years her senior, were raised by their mother and stepfather in southern California until Elsie began attending high school. Elsie was then sent to live with her biological father in Sacramento, whom she eventually had charged with incest. He was convicted and sent to prison.

Elsie turned to prostitution at age sixteen, and a year later drifted into Conforte's employ at a Nevada brothel. She then introduced Jackie to Joe Conforte, who immediately offered to "turn her out" as a prostitute. Jackie refused.

In late 1959, after Conforte's third arrest for vagrancy in Washoe County, he and Elsie drove to Escondido, California, where Jackie, after having dropped out of high school in her junior year, was now working as a carhop. Conforte asked her to help him with a "special job." "I'm going to get Raggio out of office," he told her, "if it's the last thing I do." Jackie agreed to help, based on a promise by Conforte that "he would help me finish my education and get a good job."

Conforte had initially planned to have Elsie act as the bait to get Bill into a compromising position. However, she was, at the time, free on bail pending appeal on a contempt of court order for refusing to answer questions about Mann Act violations before a federal grand jury in Sacramento. Therefore, Conforte and Elsie prevailed upon Jackie to act as the femme fatale.

"At first I was just supposed to have Mr. Raggio buy me a drink," Jackie would later state in court. "Because I was only seventeen, it was enough to get him in trouble. Then Joe decided that wouldn't be enough, and I was supposed to be in bed with him." She attempted to entice the DA to her room alone, but "he came with another man," and, after a brief conversation, they left.

Conforte, now obsessed with the possibility of being secretly recorded, did not allow Jackie to call him after the meeting with Bill at the Riverside. When he finally contacted her two days later, Jackie explained to Conforte what had happened and admitted she had not enticed Bill into bed. She later recalled, "Joe said, 'that's not enough,' and told me I'd have to change my story to say we had been intimate." At her sister's urging, Jackie agreed to go along with the story. As a result, Conforte met with Bill and made his extortion demands.

Joe Conforte knew Bill would make every effort to locate Jackie, so she was sent to live with one of his prostitutes in Seattle. There, she was introduced to "sex and dope parties" and was soon pregnant. Jackie did not know until later that her becoming pregnant was part of Conforte and Elsie's plan to incriminate Bill further—by claiming that he was the father.

From Seattle, Jackie took several car trips with Conforte and later admitted being intimate with him during these trips. When Jackie told Elsie of this, the sister went into a jealous rage. According to Jackie, "Joe came in and was so mad at Elsie he took her right back to Wadsworth [The Triangle Ranch brothel] and put her to work."

Conforte then seemed to have had second thoughts about accusing Bill of impregnating Jackie, and, for a time, drove her to several places in both northern and southern California in a fruitless attempt to obtain an abortion. Jackie had been living in the Ashbury Street apartment for several months before Hal Lipset and Bill Raggio knocked on the door.

The search for Jackie Hitson drew the attention of the media. Celebrated *San Francisco Chronicle* columnist Herb Caen quipped on March 9, 1960:

> This represents a complete breakdown in intelligence, but I do not know what District Attorney Bill Raggio of Washoe County, Nevada was discussing so earnestly with private eye Hal Lipset for two hours at Paoli's the other night. Except that it wasn't the soup.[3]

On April 3, 1960, Caen again observed:

> Bill Raggio, the Reno district attorney, and private eye Hal Lipset have been snooping secretly around town trying to nail the prostitute involved in the recent Reno attempt to frame Raggio in a so-called sex trap. William J. Raggio wants her to testify against the guy, who is already under arrest, who arranged the hoax.[4]

Jacqueline Hitson would stay secluded in Reno at the home of investigator Roger Corbett, and his wife, until the trial. Jackie called her sister a few days later, saying, "I'm okay and you can tell Joe to go to hell." She was also allowed to call her mother regularly, though on condition she did not divulge her location. During one such call, her mother advised Jackie that a week after her "escape," Elsie  and Conforte were married in Mexico because, "Joe believes a wife cannot testify against her husband in a matter of this sort."*

On June 15, 1960, Elsie Hitson, through attorney Emmett Haggerty, filed suit in San Francisco Superior Court claiming that her sister Jackie

---

*Conforte had been married to Sally Burgess since 1955. Evidence presented later at his trial would show Conforte and Elsie Hitson merely signed an application form for a Mexican marriage.

had been "kidnapped by force and violence and removed" from her Ashbury Street apartment. Haggerty requested that Raggio and Lipset be ordered to show cause why they should not produce Jacqueline in court.

During the proceeding, Elsie scurrilously accused Bill Raggio of hiding
Jackie to cover up the fact that he was the father of her unborn child.
Raggio heatedly responded that Elsie was a prostitute and "a constant
companion of Joe Conforte, and this is just Conforte's way of reaching
for slime in an effort to keep out of jail."

Superior Court Judge Clarence W. Morris pointed out that despite the
claim of kidnapping being made by Elsie, the San Francisco district attorney's office had filed no criminal charges against Lipset and Raggio.
Consequently, the judge refused to issue the order.*

The extortion trial of Joe Conforte opened in district court on Monday,
June 27, 1960. Because Bill was a material witness, he could not be involved in the prosecution. To avoid even the slightest appearance of impropriety, it was determined that his subordinates should not be involved
either. Instead, former Washoe County District Attorney Harold O. Taber,
and former deputy district attorney John Bartlett, would act as the prosecuting attorneys. The presiding judge, Jon Collins, was from White
Pine County.

Joe Conforte was represented by attorney Gordon Rice. Rice had
begun his law career as partner of the celebrated Patrick McCarran. He
would later go on to become a district court judge in Washoe County.
He was, Bill, would later state, "a very good trial attorney with years of
experience in high profile criminal cases."

By the end of the first day, a jury of eight women and four men were
impaneled. They would be kept sequestered throughout the trial to avoid
the possibility of being influenced from outside the courtroom.

The following morning, over 100 spectators and news reporters jammed

---

*Bill would later sue the *San Francisco News-Call Bulletin* for libel. The suit charged the newspaper with damaging his reputation by publishing Elsie's accusation that he had fathered the child
of then-eighteen-year-old Jacqueline Hitson. Bill won the case and was awarded $15,000.

the courtroom to hear Bill testify—and they would not be disappointed. Rice took over on cross-examination shortly before noon and appeared to be trying to show that the DA was harassing his client. Bill admitted having had Conforte arrested twice in one day on vagrancy charges, but denied harassment.

Rice also sought to show that the DA had ordered Conforte to be "unwelcome" at downtown Reno casinos and hotels. Bill responded by saying this was a joint effort, and named former Reno Police Chief William Gregory and City Attorney Roy Torvinen as cooperators in the move to keep Conforte out of town. Bill denied giving any explicit instructions to anyone to keep Conforte out.

Special prosecutor Taber objected to questioning about a Conforte blockade, but Rice argued that he was attempting to "show a deep-seated feeling against Joe Conforte by the witness." The judge allowed this and Rice continued testing Bill's credibility for the next two hours.

Late in the afternoon, Bill dropped what newspaper headlines later that evening described as a "bombshell," revealing the existence of tape recordings from his meeting with Conforte the previous November. The defendant was observed by those in the courtroom to appear "astounded" at that information, slowly rubbing his hand over his face several times in a gesture of dismay. Judge Collins immediately recessed the trial while the defense counsel and the jurors listened to Conforte's string of supercilious, vulgarity-laced threats pouring from the speaker on the tape player.

On June 28, Jacqueline Hitson took the witness stand wearing a navy blue maternity dress. She appeared unnerved during the intense examination and cross-examination that lasted more than three hours. Jackie was on the verge of tears when defense counsel Gordon Rice pressed to know the names of friends she stayed with more than a year ago, in an attempt to test her memory and establish her credibility as a witness. Yet, according to a reporter for the *San Francisco Examiner*, Rice "failed to shake Jacqueline's story."[5]

On the morning of June 30, Elsie Hitson was called to the stand wearing an aqua blue, linen suit, white hat and matching gold religious crosses on her necklace and bracelet. The twenty-two-year-old prostitute testified that she had concealed herself in a closet at the Riverside Hotel the previous November and had listened while her teenage sister met with Bill Raggio.

Answering questions put to her by Gordon Rice, Elsie refuted earlier testimony by both Bill and her sister, Jackie Hitson, that there had been no sexual advances made by either Raggio or Harry Spencer. Elsie also denied the prosecution's contention that Joe Conforte had masterminded the plot against Raggio.

She stated several times that she, alone, had planned to "frame" the district attorney. Her alleged motive was revenge for Bill having had her subpoenaed the previous year by a federal grand jury in Sacramento during an investigation of sex slave traffic in California, Nevada and Arizona.

Conforte, Elsie insisted, had been unaware of her plan to have her under-age sister lure Bill into buying drinks for her. She went on to claim the plan worked too well: "Jackie came back to the hotel room pretty drunk and told me she and Raggio had about ten drinks at the bar and more in his office." Elsie then testified that a knock on the door caused her to hide in the closet. Raggio and Spencer entered the room and flipped a coin to see who would stay with the girl. Harry lost the toss and left. Elsie added that when she told Conforte what had happened, he told her he would talk to Raggio and "try to work things out."

According a news report, Elsie "floundered badly" under cross-examination.[6] She could not explain why she allowed her younger to sister be seduced just a few feet away. She admitted that she had lied under oath less than a month before. Moreover, she could not explain why she had testified earlier in the day that she had "very few dealings with Joe Conforte," and yet the two had recently signed a license form to obtain a Mexican marriage.

On July 1, before another packed courtroom, Joe Conforte took the witness stand in his own defense. Ed Montgomery, University of Nevada graduate and journalist for the *San Francisco Examiner*, described the occasion with precision and humor, saying the witness used a string of "hard-boiled homilies" to explain why the jurors should not find him guilty. "It's like I'm a neighbor," said Conforte, "and I go next door and borrow some salt, and I say, thanks for the salt, do you need any pepper?"[7]

It was a big misunderstanding, Montgomery mockingly wrote, "back scratching—not extortion is what Conforte had in mind when he promised to extricate the district attorney from the lurid sex trap." In what the reporter then described as *patois* borrowed from Nathan Detroit, Conforte let loose with more similes:

"It's like you got shoes on. You got shoes on, and one doesn't fit. It hurts your foot. Now I got shoes, and one shoe hurts my foot, so we trade shoes and we're both happy...It's like a man tells you that you have an ugly face. You tell him to go back and look at his own."

Conforte then addressed the jury about the tape recording of his meeting with Bill Raggio:

> I want, first of all, ladies and gentlemen, to apologize to you for swearing at you. It was just a case of I simply say, will you do me a favor and I can do you one. Just man-to-man talk, that's all. If I'd wanted to extort him, why would I see him personally? My lawyer could've accomplished ten times as much. I wouldn't have even had to see him.

Conforte spent another four hours on the witness stand under direct examination. When he felt he had completed a particular portion of his testimony, he would say to his attorney, "You got that? Okay." He would then command Gordon Rice to "Gimme a lead." Rice would follow up with a new question and Conforte would take off on another streetwise dissertation. At times, the judge had to bang his gavel for order to quell the spectator's laughter.

In contrast, his cross-examination by the prosecution lasted only ten minutes. One of those questions asked was whether Conforte had used aliases in the past. "Yes, I have," he said. "But not from shame. It was so people wouldn't borrow money from me." He also conceded that he could not vouch for the veracity of the star defense witness, Elsie Hitson.

While many in the courtroom found Conforte's ramblings amusing, his attorney Gordon Rice did not. On several occasions, Rice took the unusual step of reprimanding his client for making speeches to the jury. At one point, Conforte asked for time to refer to his notes and then asked Rice if he was permitted to talk about the tape recording. Rice replied, with barely concealed exasperation, "You have been anyway."

Conforte would claim he first met Bill Raggio in early 1958 when he came to the Washoe County District Attorney's Office in Reno to assist one of his Triangle Ranch girls in straightening out a civil problem. At that time, Conforte stated, Bill confided in him that he planned to run for district attorney against Dyer Jensen. "He asked me to help him get votes," Conforte testified, "but wouldn't take any money for his campaign."

He claimed to have also helped DA Raggio with information on "dope peddlers" and convinced Max Kirchner, a local hoodlum who had been threatening Bill, to leave town. For this, Conforte maintained, Bill thanked him effusively and made the rather improbable pledge: "I owe you a favor." Conforte believed he and Bill "were friends," until June 1959 when he met with him and other law enforcement officers in Bill's office: "His [Raggio's] attitude changed completely...No more 'Joe'...it was now 'Mr. Conforte.'"

Due to the length of Conforte's testimony, the trial recessed for dinner and then resumed into the evening. Bill Raggio was called again to the stand as a rebuttal witness and vehemently denied Conforte's claim of friendship. As for his political support, Bill fumed: "It's an absolute lie. I wouldn't solicit his support and I'd be ashamed to receive it." Regarding the Max Kirchner incident, Bill stated he never requested the man be run out of town and there was no "favor" involved; though he did agree Kirchner's departure was a case of "good riddance."

The final witnesses, including Harry Spencer and a waitress from the cocktail lounge in the Riverside Hotel, corroborated both Bill's and

Jackie Hitson's accounts of what had occurred on November 14, 1959.

Joe Conforte's compulsion to be the center of attention, a "big wheel," as Bill would later observe, was not only what brought him to be charged with the crime of extortion, but what was about to seal his fate.

On the morning of July 2, the trial came to an abrupt end when Gordon Rice astonished everyone by stating that, at his client's request, he was waving his closing argument. Rice thanked the jurors for their efforts and said he was sorry they had been required to spend the week sequestered during the trial. He was confident the jury could decide "its own interpretation of the evidence without the necessity of an argument."

Just prior to Rice's surprise move, special prosecutor Taber had, in his closing statement, argued that Conforte had made "cunning threats" and was "calculating and cagey...Elsie is taking it on the chin for Joe... she is a slave, loyal to her master." Taber went on to describe how Elsie's story of personally plotting the Raggio frame-up and then listening from the closet to the seduction of her younger sister was "the incredible testimony of a pitiful creature."

He asked the jurors to weigh the statements repeated on the tape and decide for themselves whether this was a "casual conversation," as Conforte called it under oath, or extortion. "Law enforcement and public duty hang in the balance," Taber warned the jurors.

Jury deliberations began at 11:30 a.m. After asking for numerous replays of the tape recording, they reached a verdict by late afternoon. Conforte was found guilty of extortion.

Bill Raggio, who Judge Collins had excluded from attending the trial except to testify, appeared in the courtroom shortly after 5:00 p.m., as the verdict was about to be read. Dorothy Raggio, who had sat in the front row each day of the trial, was near tears as she and her husband embraced after the jury announced their decision.

Nearby, Jackie Hitson smiled with relief after hearing the decision and joined the district attorney and his wife in enthusiastic congratulations and a warm display of emotion. As Dottie affectionately hugged the young woman, Jackie tearfully told her, "I'm so sorry I did this to your husband."

Joe Conforte, who appeared weary from the long trial, was taken to the Washoe County jail until sentence was to be imposed the following Monday morning. Before the jury retired, Bill was given consent by the judge, over Gordon Rice's strenuous objections, to address them:

> Ladies and Gentlemen: as district attorney, I want to thank each of you for your conscientious approach to this most difficult matter. As an individual, I want to tell you that as representatives of the community you have, in some measure, justified the ridicule, embarrassment and abuse to which I have had to subject my family and friends in order to fulfill the oath, which I took when I assumed this office. I know I can never heal some of the wounds, which they quietly suffered on my behalf, until this vindication. You have also restored my faith in the basic structure of our community. For these things, I am most grateful.[9]

It had been difficult for Dottie, and not just as the result of the rumors and innuendo to which she was subjected by those who wished her husband ill. The Raggio's seven-year-old daughter Leslie was now in school and concerns about her safety was paramount. Despite the fact that the school was only a block away, Leslie was usually driven there and back. She was not allowed to play outside without someone watching her. Throughout the night, a police guard sat in an unmarked vehicle near their Robin Street home. The kind-hearted Dottie would feel sorry for them having to spend all night there and would often bring sandwiches or soup to the car; jeopardizing the clandestine facet of the stakeout.

On July 5, the *Nevada State Journal* disclosed that, prior to the trial, Bill had voluntarily taken lie detector tests about his encounter with Jackie Hitson. Though inadmissible in court, polygraph expert Jack L. Williams, concluded that, "based upon three examinations consisting of nine charts, Mr. William J. Raggio, District Attorney of Washoe County, is not attempting a deception in his answers to questions asked him by this examiner."[10]

A few days after the trial ended, Nevada Attorney General Roger Foley issued a statement in which he defended himself and his brother George, District Attorney of Clark County, against the allegations made by Joe Conforte on the November 18 tape recording. Foley denied that he and his brother knew Conforte on more than a "casual" basis. The attorney general stated that he would not "honor with a reply" questions asked by reporters about Conforte's claim that Roger would be happy to assist him undo Bill's career in order to further his own political aspirations.

Foley then ended the press conference by accusing the Washoe County District Attorney's Office of possible "misuse" of special funds for the trial. He called for an immediate investigation, by either the Washoe County Commission or the Washoe County Grand Jury.

This issue was quickly defused when court-appointed special prosecuting attorneys Bartlett and Taber issued a joint statement saying, "We neither expect, nor will accept, any compensation. We consider it a duty as officers of the court. It was a privilege for both of us to render assistance to such a courageous public official as William Raggio."

On July 12, 1960, Judge Jon Collins sentenced thirty-three-year-old Joe Conforte to three to five years in the Nevada State Prison. Conforte stood with his hands clasped behind him as Collins declared, "Nevada is one of the most liberal of states in allowing free choice of occupations, but this should not the construed as weakness. Nevada must be quick to guard against extortion of public officials."

He then ordered a stay of sentence until September 1 to enable Conforte to appeal the verdict to the Nevada Supreme Court. Bail was set at $50,000. As court adjourned, Conforte turned to his seventy-four-year-old father, Augustino, who, like Dottie Raggio, had spent every day in court, and remarked, "I'll see you later; if I get out." Ironically, he had now received a sentence much heftier than that of the vagrancy counts he was trying to avoid by extorting Bill Raggio.

The *Chronicle's* Herb Caen would continue to snipe at Conforte. The day after his sentencing, he wrote:

The news is all bad this week for Joe Conforte the Nevada baby giant panderer. First he gets nailed for three to five years on an extortion wrapped in Reno. Second he can't raise bail and is stuck in jail. Then a couple of nights ago, his number one girl-friend Sally Burgess cracks up his shiny Cadillac in the crash near Dayton, Nevada and is in the hospital. Besides which, Sally was not alone. There was a fellow with her.[11]

On September 21, 1960, Caen penned:

Joe Conforte, the Nevada baby giant panderer must be feeling even more bitter than usual today. His elaborate plot to frame the Reno District Attorney Bill Raggio backfired and he was nailed for extortion. And now comes the news about Jackie Hit-son, the young prostitute who Conforte charged was seduced and made pregnant by Raggio. Jackie who has been hiding out in LA just had a 7-pound baby girl—almost 11 months after the alleged seduction. So long, Joe.[12]

On May 19, 1961, just days prior to Joe Conforte's appeal being heard by the Nevada Supreme Court, nineteen-year-old Jackie Hitson, now married and known as Jackie Pearson, appeared at the office of state attorney general Roger Foley in Carson City. Mrs. Pearson signed an affidavit claiming her testimony during the Conforte extortion trial the year before was untrue and had been coerced by DA Raggio to save his reputation. Foley suggested she take the statement to the Washoe County grand jury. The grand jury acted swiftly, taking testimony throughout the night.

The following day Bill Raggio issued a statement explaining that for the previous few months Jackie Pearson had been consorting with Joe Conforte and her sister Elsie. "We have known that they have been con-sistently pressuring her to change her story," Bill said.

Bill said an investigation revealed that Conforte had transported Mrs. Pearson and her sister to the Nevada state line the previous day and awaited their return to Truckee while they used his automobile. This was an apparent effort on Conforte's part to continue to smear the district attorney's office for the purpose of deterring its actions in enforcing criminal laws against him. "It was likewise timed," Bill continued, "to coincide with the appeal of his conviction to be heard next week in the Supreme Court of Nevada…I subpoenaed her for immediate appearance before the grand jury…and advised the grand jury then I would not participate in the presentation of this matter to them."

An indictment was quickly returned by the grand jury charging Jackie Pearson with perjury. She was immediately brought before District Court Judge Grant Bowen and ordered her held in lieu of $15,000 bail. Jackie Pearson would eventually plead guilty to charge of lying to a grand jury and was granted probation.

Years later, Bill Raggio would reflect on his rocky relationship with the Nevada attorney general concerning the Conforte case. "There was no long-standing feud between Roger and me," Bill said. "We had our differences about such things as the state policy on early parole. However, I never fully understood why he seemed to take Jackie Hitson's side in this situation and assisted her in getting the affidavit directly to the Washoe County grand jury. He was a Democrat and I was a Republican, so perhaps he saw me as a potential threat to his position."

Five weeks later, the Nevada Supreme Court handed down its decision affirming Joe Conforte's conviction for extortion and he was sent to the Nevada State Prison in Carson City. There Conforte used his penchant for manipulation to make the twenty-two months he would eventually serve, reasonably comfortable. He was allowed special privileges.

A photograph in the *Reno Evening Gazette* showed him lounging near the prison casino, called "The Bullpen," smoking a long Cuban cigar, ensconced in an alpaca sweater, polo shirt and tailored slacks—while all the others around him wore prison denim.

"A guy like me," Conforte would later say, "goes to prison and you have it about as good as you can get because I had so much juice."[13] He claimed that he not only ran the prison casino, but also had a cook, a maid and, for $3 a week, "a guy to fan me while I played bridge."

Bill Raggio knew of this preferential treatment and recalls:

> Longtime Warden Jack Fogliani was an amiable individual with absolutely no training to run a prison. The only inmate rehabilitation program was a gaming facility called "The Bullpen" in which specially designed "prison money" was used. Conforte ran the operation. It was rumored, and pretty well established to my satisfaction, that on at least one occasion while a prisoner there, Conforte was allowed to attend an evening floorshow at Harrah's Lake Tahoe.

Immediately upon his release from Nevada State Prison, Joe Conforte was arrested on charges of federal income tax evasion. He eventually pled guilty and was sent to McNeil Island, Washington, for nearly three years. There, he enjoyed none of the pleasantries accorded him in the Nevada penitentiary.

Evidence found in the safe removed from the Triangle Ranch was a significant part of the government's case against him. Before deciding on his plea, Conforte's attorneys argued that the contents of the safe should be ruled inadmissible, because it was illegally obtained when authorities broke into and subsequently burned down his dwelling.

However, during an earlier civil suit filed by his wife, Sally Burgess, against Bill Raggio and others for destruction of the building, Conforte had provided a sworn statement that he had no ownership interest in the structure. As such, the court ruled that the evidence found in the safe could be used. Ironically, Conforte's earlier attempt to distance himself from state charges, ended up helping convict him of a federal crime.

Upon his release from federal prison in December 1965, Conforte and Sally began reclaiming control of Nevada's brothel industry. Rather than return to distant Wadsworth, they set their sights on an area just eight miles east of Reno, near the tiny community of Lockwood, in Storey County.

While Conforte was incarcerated, a competitor, Richard Bennett, had rented a corner of the Peri Ranch along the Truckee River and set up a brothel enclosure containing several mobile homes, which he named the Mustang Bridge Ranch.

Conforte quickly saw how profitable the operation was and, after a series of anonymous threats, mysterious fires and the bombing of the bridge leading to the compound, Bennett "voluntarily" sold the brothel to Conforte and Burgess for an undisclosed amount.

Conforte set about protecting his business from future incidents like the Triangle Ranch fire. In addition to his usual technique of ingratiating himself with local government officials and police, Conforte sought political power. Realizing there were less than 500 voters in all of Storey County, Conforte enlarged the little community of Lockwood by bringing in singlewide trailers and charging the new tenants low rent in return for their voting as he told them.

In this way, he gained such influence that he was able to persuade county officials to introduce the nation's first brothel-licensing ordinance, which went into effect on January 1, 1971. The Nevada Supreme Court upheld Storey County's right to legalize prostitution.[14]

Months after Conforte was released from federal prison, he and Bill Raggio met on a flight from Las Vegas to Reno. Bill recalled that as they were waiting to deplane, another passenger asked for Conforte's opinion on the possibility of brothel prostitution being legalized in Clark County. As Conforte was about to answer, he noticed Bill standing nearby in the aisle and shouted, "Hey Bill, do you think I should say something about this?"

"I'm going to give you some free advice," Bill replied. "Keep your mouth shut."

Conforte laughed and said, "Hey Bill, why don't you be my attorney, you're the best in the state."

"Joe," Raggio replied, "you don't have enough money to pay me to be your attorney."

Several years later the *Gazette* posted side-by-side comments by these two men, colorfully capturing the style and tone of their long and contentious relationship:

"I don't have any personal feelings about this guy." *-State Senator Bill Raggio, Reno*

"If he said that, he's full of s***!" *-Joe Conforte* [15]

# CHAPTER EIGHTEEN

# Organized Crime

B ill Raggio's comment about it not being "personal" gives hint to perhaps his greater goal, sending a message to others in the underworld that they were not welcome in northern Nevada, as they sometimes appeared to be in the south.

During a June 2008 interview, Paul Laxalt, former Nevada governor, U.S. senator and long-time Raggio friend, would observe, "Even though he took a lot of kidding about burning down that whorehouse, it was a real ballsy thing that Bill did in taking on the mob in Reno."

During the time of his extortion trial, Conforte's closest associate was Joseph L. Campo. Campo listed his occupation as an international labor organizer for the American Newspaper Guild. He was best known around Reno for his involvement in a failed 1959 newspaper strike, which cost Campo his job. Six years earlier, during the American Newspaper Guild's labor organizing campaign in southern California, the *Los Angeles Examiner* referred to "international representative Joseph L. Campo" as "an ex-jailbird."[1] Though adding no details in support of the claim, the implication was that labor unions of the day were often controlled by hoodlums.

In June 1960, it was Joseph Campo who used his connections in the newspaper business to plant the story in the *San Francisco News-Call Bulletin* accusing Bill Raggio of kidnapping eighteen-year-old Jacqueline from her sister's San Francisco apartment in order to hide the fact that he was the father of her unborn child. Campo would later make the same claims during his testimony at Joe Conforte's extortion trial.*

Conforte's association with members of organized crime had been largely rumor until March 21, 1976. On that day, investigative reporters for the *Nevada State Journal* broke a story describing a November 1974 meeting at the Canyon Country Club in Palm Springs, California, between Joe Conforte and John "Frank Joseph" Simone, identified by the U.S. Justice Department as a captain in the Angelo Bruno (Annaloro) organized crime family of Philadelphia. The country club, it was reported, had been under constant FBI surveillance because it was a well-known vacation spot for many of the nation's leading organized crime figures.[2]

The story further indicated that Conforte and Simone discussed building a hotel-casino on Conforte's property adjacent to the newly constructed Wild Creek Golf course in Sparks. Conforte had recently sold the land for the golf course to the Reno-Sparks Convention Authority.

Conforte, who was in Augusto, Sicily "for religious reasons" at the time the story broke, emphatically denied during a telephone conversation with a reporter that such a meeting had ever taken place. "I haven't been to Palm Springs in six years…Hey, I don't have anything to do with these Mafias (*sic*). Everybody always wants to say I'm with the Mafias (*sic*). I'm not a Mafia (*sic*)."[3]

Conforte conceded that he would like to see a large casino on his property in Sparks because "there'd be nothing better for the community." When asked about a recent Washoe County grand jury report accusing him of inappropriately influencing local government officials and asso-

---

*By 1959, Campo was making monthly payments to Joe Conforte for the purchase of a service station, restaurant-bar and brothel at Montgomery Pass on a remote stretch of Highway 6 about sixty miles west of Tonopah. Campo requested a license from the Nevada Gaming Commission to operate slot machines at the site. In April 1960, the commission gave him the option of withdrawing his application, in lieu of them making public the results of their investigation. He accepted their offer and withdrew.

In September 1960, just two months after testifying for the defense at Joe Conforte's extortion trial, the forty-five-year-old Campo was shot and killed by his common law wife near Dayton, Nevada. A subsequent police investigation determined she had fired in self-defense and no charges were filed.

ciating with underworld figures, Joe angrily responded that the jurors placed those comments in the report at the request of Washoe County Sheriff Bob Galli, to justify the continuing existence of his organized crime unit. "Organized crime does not exist [in Washoe County]," Conforte added, "and has not existed since I've been around… and it will not exist as long as I'm alive."

Despite his contention that organized crime did not exist in the northern Nevada, it had long remained a question of just how pervasive mob influence was in the Reno and Lake Tahoe area.

Early in the 20th century, James "Cinch" McKay and William "Curley" Graham made their way to Reno from the declining boomtowns of Goldfield and Tonopah. By the early 1920s, the two men were operating several illegal gambling establishments including the Cal-Neva Lodge at Lake Tahoe, Willows Roadhouse, Rex Club and the Bank Club. Under the protective umbrella of the Wingfield political machine, and lax law enforcement, Graham and McKay were soon providing Prohibition–era customers with "bootleg" liquor they smuggled into Nevada from the San Francisco Bay Area.

They also operated the large brothel east of Reno called "The Stockade."* Profits from that enterprise, as well as gambling, illegal liquor and narcotics trade, were rumored to have reached Wingfield, and others, in the highest level of Reno society. The Capone organization in Chicago was believed to own a percentage of the business.

In 1934, *Fortune* magazine referred to the five who "Rule Reno" as "Wingfield, Woodburn and Thatcher, as well as business associates Bill Graham and Jim McKay."[4] These two partners occasionally harbored

---

*The Stockade was surrounded by a high wooden fence, and contained a large dance hall and saloon. A series of small rooms, or "cribs," running the length of the enclosure were used by the prostitutes in around-the-clock, eight-hour shifts. Centralizing the town's prostitutes in one location had been the brainchild of Reno's unconventional Mayor Roberts in 1923 to appease reform-minded citizen groups by "putting prostitutes out of sight, but not out of business." It is estimated that several hundred prostitutes worked there in its heyday. The only entrance into the Stockade was guarded by an on-duty Reno police officer, usually one of the largest of the force, to discourage trouble from the patrons.

infamous criminals, like the FBI's Public Enemy Number One, Baby Face Nelson. Tex Harris, a business associate of Graham and McKay, would spend a year in federal prison after being convicted of conspiring to harbor Nelson in Reno.

Bill Raggio was a young boy at this time, but later observed:

> If there was a "criminal element" that was known to exist here, it was probably Bill Graham and James McKay. My parents and everybody talked about McKay and Graham. I never did know exactly what their involvement was, but they became kind of characters in town. Locals seemed to be more impressed by the grand buffet they offered at their primary establishments the Bank Club and the Palace Club.

"Cinch" McKay also had a knack for sports and horseracing. In 1931, he and Graham, in partnership with the great heavyweight-boxing champion Jack Dempsey, produced a prizefight between American boxer Max Baer and Paulino "The Bouncing Basque" Uzudun. With superb marketing savvy, the partners capitalized not only on the presence of the famous Dempsey, who acted as the referee, but a fan base comprised of Basque immigrants, who were rapidly becoming a significant segment of the northern Nevada population. The bout drew an audience of 23,000. After twenty rounds, the Bouncing Basque defeated the favored Baer (who would later go on to become world heavyweight champion).

It was also in 1931 that Nevada Governor Fred Balzer signed a bill legalizing commercial gambling. With the mining industry in decline, neither agriculture nor the state's limited commerce was capable of creating new jobs or tax revenue. The measure, intended to bring in outside dollars, further stigmatized Nevada as "The Sin State'" and risked keeping all but the most undesirable elements away.

Initially gaming revenue was disappointing, but soon tourism began to increase and a more "mainstream" customer base developed. Nevada lawmakers had correctly judged the mood of the nation in the wake of Prohibition.

Despite casino gambling and the sale of alcohol now being legal in Nevada, Graham and McKay continued to profit from illegal activity. While local law enforcement authorities made little effort to curtail this, the FBI investigated the partners relentlessly.

In 1934, the U.S. government brought charges against the two men for mail fraud and conspiracy. The first trial ended with a hung jury after the government's key witness, Roy Frisch, a forty-five-year-old cashier at the Riverside Bank, owned by George Wingfield, disappeared after attending a movie in Reno on the evening before he was to testify.

The government managed to protect their witnesses at a subsequent trial of Graham and McKay, which was held in New York City. The two were convicted of using the mail to commit fraud while engaging in a $2.5 million horseracing swindle. They were sentenced on February 17, 1938 and served nine years in the federal penitentiary at Leavenworth, Kansas.*

With Graham and McKay now out of the picture, a host of new operators began to appear in Reno; men unassociated with organized crime and intent upon making gaming a respectable form of entertainment.

Among them was Raymond "Pappy" Smith, a former carnival barker, who came to Reno in 1935. Smith's innovations would revolutionize the gaming business. He was the first to hire women dealers, develop a casino surveillance system to catch cheaters and offer his customers credit. His advertising idea of having "Harold's Club or Bust" signs appear throughout the United States (and eventually around the world) created phenomenal product recognition—without ever mentioning the nature of the business.

Pappy's Harold's Club (named for his son) boasted one of the great gun collections of all times and, in his shirtsleeves, bolo tie and bright red suspenders, he was loved by both customers and employees. Smith

---

*At the request of Nevada Senator Patrick McCarran, Graham and McKay received pardons from President Harry S. Truman in 1945. They resumed running the Bank Club. McKay died in 1962 and Graham in 1965.

was a generous benefactor in the community and sponsored hundreds of scholarships to help high school students attend the University of Nevada.

The only person to match Pappy Smith in the development of casino gambling was William F. "Bill" Harrah.

Harrah, who got his start in the card parlors of Venice, California, came to Reno in 1937 and opened his Club Tango (a form of Bingo) in Reno. Though it closed two weeks later, he had learned a valuable lesson: Being closer to the action was vital to success in the casino business. So he began searching for a site in the central business area to reopen.

In July 1938, after finding an excellent location, he returned to Reno and opened his new club, Harrah's Plaza Tango, at 14 East Commercial Row. The building was owned by Ben Raggio, and the two men worked out an acceptable lease agreement.

This time Bill Harrah found success, and through a series of wise and innovative business decisions, his fifty feet of street frontage in a modest building owned by Ben Raggio developed into Harrah's Entertainment— the largest gaming company in the world.

Harrah would not forget that connection and years later told Bill Raggio, "Your grandfather helped me get my start in this business."

"When I was DA," Raggio later recalled, "Bill Harrah had an interest in what was going on in the community and would call often. He never really ever wanted anything. He just wanted to be informed and kept up-to-date. Even when I was later in the state senate, he would contact me."

Of Harrah's impact on the gaming industry, Raggio said that while Harrah was not a very outgoing individual, he had great vision. He was the first one to upgrade the casino hotel properties to emphasis quality, and invested a great deal of money effort in having his hotel rooms more exquisite than any had been before.

"Bill Harrah represented what was clean about the gaming business," Raggio said. "He did not have any real connections with the illegal gamblers. He ran a good operation and kept good people around him like Bob Ring, Rome Andreotti, Maurice Shepherd and Lloyd Dyer."

* * *

Not all those arriving in Reno to enter the gaming business were free of mob associations. During the summer of 1950, Virgil W. Peterson, a former FBI special agent, now Operating Director of the Chicago Crime Commission, described the situation in Nevada to members of the United States Senate Special Committee to Investigate Organized Crime in Interstate Commerce, the so-called Kefauver Committee.[5]

Peterson identified Riverside Hotel and Casino owners Mert and Lou Wertheimer as having been operators of an illegal gambling enterprise in Michigan known as the Chesterfield Syndicate. Prior to that, the Wertheimer brothers were partners in an elegant casino called the Colonial Inn in Hallandale, Florida. There, the report continued, they associated with some of the nation's most notorious gangsters including Meyer and Jake Lansky, both of whom were members of the Frank Costello crime family of New York.

Peterson also identified Lincoln "Fitz" Fitzgerald and Daniel Sullivan, as having been powerful members of the Michigan underworld. The two had moved to Reno years earlier and opened the Nevada Club on South Virginia Street in 1946.

Reputedly an accountant for Detroit's Purple Gang, "Fitz," along with Sullivan, were extradited to Michigan in August 1948 where they were tried on charges of illegal gambling and bribery-of-public-officials. The bribery charges were later dropped, but the two were found guilty of the other charges and fined $52,000. After paying the fine, they then returned to Reno to resume their Nevada Club operation.

Just before midnight on the evening of November 18, 1949, as Fitzgerald was in the driveway of his home preparing to leave for his casino, an assailant approached him from behind and fired blasts from a double-barreled shotgun into his back. Remarkably, Fitzgerald survived the attack.

Reno Police Chief "Pinky" Greeson was convinced that robbery was not a motive in the attack. Fitzgerald was well known for carrying large amounts of money and paid his employees in cash. Yet no cash was missing. Greeson speculated that local club owners, Graham and McKay, might have had a motive in the shooting. The chief also acknowledged to reporters that his office was pursuing allegations from underworld sources of Fitzgerald engaging in secret meetings with shadowy racing wire service figures in the preceding few weeks.[6]

The most persistent rumor following the attack was that it had been a mob "hit" resulting from a falling out with his old bosses in the Purple Gang; an estrangement likely caused by Fitzgerald's efforts to keep them out of his casino business in Reno.

Hospitalized for six months and left with a limp and permanent fear for his life, Fitzgerald hired bodyguards and moved with his wife into a specially designed, steel-encased apartment on the second floor of the Nevada Club. His assailant was never identified and Fitzgerald, who told police he had no idea who would want to hurt him, subsequently asked the authorities to close the investigation into the shooting. In 1974, he moved his Nevada Club operation across the street and named the new hotel casino Fitzgerald's. He died of natural causes in 1981.

Most in Reno wanted to believe this kind of violence was particular to large eastern cities, or Las Vegas. However, the Fitzgerald shooting had come in wake of another attack on a casino owner, just sixty miles to the south, and was creating anxiety within the community that organized crime had arrived.

In 1946, Harry Sherwood took over ownership of the Tahoe Village Resort and Casino in Stateline, Nevada. Sherwood had spent time in federal prison for a 1936 robbery and later operated a gambling boat in international waters off Los Angeles. Before taking over the Tahoe Village, he ran several small bars in San Francisco and Reno.

His plan was to turn the Tahoe Village into an elegant resort for high rollers, much as Benjamin "Bugsy" Siegel was envisioning for The Flamingo in Las Vegas 400 miles to south. Like Bugsy, cost estimate overruns and the failure of high rollers to flock to the resort, ran him afoul of his business partners.

On September 20, 1947, just three months after Siegel was murdered in Los Angeles, Sherwood was shot and seriously wounded in the manager's office of the Tahoe Village. While no one was ever apprehended in the shooting of Bugsy Siegel, Ormsby County Sheriff Howard Hoffman soon picked up a suspect in the Tahoe Village shooting, Sherwood's business partner, Louis R. Strauss.

Further investigation revealed that the suspect went by the moniker "Russian Louie," and had grown up in the tough Williamsburg district of Brooklyn with Meyer Lansky and Bugsy Siegel. Strauss was closely tied to Lansky's criminal enterprises, which dominated illegal gambling throughout most of the United States, as well as legal gambling in Nevada and Cuba.

When Sherwood died from complications of surgery to remove the bullet, Strauss was incarcerated in the Douglas County jail. A preliminary hearing was held in the dining room of the Glenbrook Inn at Lake Tahoe, the only location in Douglas County large enough to accommodate the crowds of curious onlookers. Russian Louie pled self-defense and none of the witnesses would testify that they saw him pull the trigger. The case was ruled "justifiable homicide" and Strauss was released.[7]

\* \* \*

It was not until the 1940s that anyone dominated gaming in Las Vegas the way McKay and Graham had in Reno. Virgil Peterson's testimony to the Kefauver Committee relates how members of the notorious Frank Costello mob became firmly entrenched there through Bugsy Siegel. Siegel, who made a reputation as a hit man in the "enforcement" branch of the New York-based Costello organization, was sent to southern California to protect their financial interests in the film and music industry. Handsome and flamboyant, Siegel's association with Hollywood celebrities soon made him the most visible gangster in the country.

In 1946, Siegel was ordered by Meyer Lansky to oversee the construction and operation of the Flamingo, a sprawling hotel casino west of downtown Las Vegas. Mismanagement of construction funds and a disappointing opening in December 1946 gained the resentment of underworld investors. In June 1947, Siegel was shot and killed in gangland fashion as he sat on a couch at his girlfriend's home in Beverly Hills.

After Siegel's murder, a new breed of managers made the Flamingo profitable. Men like Gus Greenbaum, Moe Sedway and Davie Berman, though still connected to the mob and with criminal records for violent crimes, were all experienced casino operators and good businessmen. One previous business practice they continued was the routine underreporting of proceeds. This "skim" was sent to Lansky and other eastern investors. Over the next twenty years, almost every hotel-casino in Las Vegas would engage in skimming to some degree.

The Kefauver Committee hearings were broadcast live on television and fascinated the American public. They introduced millions of viewers to the existence of a violent, highly organized and secretive criminal association. Over seventy local crime commissions were established in cities across America. Ironically, while the committee's findings tarnished the reputation of Nevada, it helped the state as well, because earlier proposals to legalize gambling in Arizona, California, Massachusetts and Montana, were now defeated.

The Kefauver hearings made it evident that Nevada's system for oversight of gaming was inadequate. Kefauver personally introduced a bill in the senate to apply a 10% federal tax to Nevada casino earnings. Such a tax would have devastated the gaming industry and, with it, the economy of state. The senate vote was close, and only the vigorous intervention of Nevada's powerful Senator Patrick McCarran prevented it from passing. Paradoxically, McCarran had long objected to Nevada's growing dependency on gaming revenues, but had no choice other than defend the industry to keep the state's economy from collapsing.

About this time, an investigative report by the *Las Vegas Sun* uncovered widespread corruption among public officials, and taped evidence that Clark County Commissioner Rodney Colton, Sheriff Glen Jones and Lieutenant Governor Clifford Jones had financial arrangements with organized crime figures.[8]

A combination of Kefauver hearing revelations, Congressional action to assess a punitive tax on the industry and the subsequent exposé of corrupt public officials, forced Nevadans to demand reform. By 1955, the legislature established the Nevada Gaming Control Board within the Nevada Tax Commission. The purpose was to eliminate "undesirables" in Nevada gaming and to provide regulations for the licensing and operation of the industry.

Under these new regulations, licenses, which previously had been awarded by local governments, could now be granted only by the Gaming Control Board. More importantly, the Board could revoke a license at any time, a power necessary to keep those who already held licenses in compliance with the law and regulations. The relationship between casino operators and the new regulatory authority was immediately strained. Those who had previously operated outside the law before coming to Nevada were particularly resistant.[9]

Reno city planners were concerned with what they were seeing in Las Vegas, particularly with problems resulting from the rapid growth in population. By the 1950s, the Reno City Council enacted a zoning ordinance to limit the expansion of gaming establishments in the city. It came to be known as the "Red Line," initially encompassing five blocks in the central business district.*

Like nearly everyone else in Reno, Bill Raggio knew that some casino operators had been associated with the underworld. "Mert and Lou Wertheimer and Ruby Mathis were the operators of the Riverside Hotel and Casino." Bill later said. "I knew they had come from Detroit and were referenced as having been members of the Purple Gang. They may have been criminals in other states because they engaged in illegal gambling, but they were not considered criminals in Nevada. It was understood that whatever they did, in wherever they came from before, when they were here they complied with the law."

---

*The "Red Line" expanded from five to twelve city blocks by the 1970s; yet, still effectively controlled the city's growth. In the 1980s, this zoning restriction was finally lifted, creating an immediate casino construction boom and with it an unparalleled growth in population.

Eastern mob affiliated syndicates had by now mostly by-passed northern Nevada and were concentrating on Las Vegas. Soon the "sawdust joints" of downtown were being overshadowed by the dazzling new "carpet joints" of the Strip. While northern Nevada, particularly clubs in Reno, was drawing a more working-class clientele, the Vegas Strip was attracting a broad spectrum of customers from the huge southern California population centers, just a few hours' drive to the west.

Expansion on "The Strip" required millions of dollars; but credit was not forthcoming for a relatively new industry managed by some with criminal afflictions. Decisions for new hotel and casinos, often with outlandish themes, precluded traditional avenues of investment. Other sources of capital were needed. This often occurred through partnerships and the selling of ownership "points" in the casino, or through such allegedly mob-tainted sources as the Teamsters Central States Pension Fund.[10] In Las Vegas, with the exception of Nevada National Bank (later Valley Bank), financial institutions were not interested in loaning money for new casinos, and when they did, they charged exorbitant interest.[11]

While some organized crime figures, most notably Chicago crime boss Sam Giancana, would make their presence felt in northern Nevada into the 1960s, the gaming industry there was spared more widespread mob influence for several reasons. In addition to the Red Line, which helped rein in casino expansion, such gaming pioneers as Bill Harrah and Pappy Smith (and perhaps, Fitzgerald and the Wertheimer brothers) resisted further infiltration. Winter weather and geography, especially at Lake Tahoe, may also have been seen as a deterrent to higher profits. The climate in Las Vegas made it a year-round destination.

Bill Raggio remains skeptical about the commonly held image of a national criminal syndicate. "I'm reluctant to refer to it by the term 'mob,'" he said in a 2008 interview, "because even that gives it credit for being much more organized than it really was."

However, as Washoe County District Attorney, Bill Raggio remained vigilant: "When I was in the district attorney's office, we knew they had backgrounds, but we never had evidence that they were operating improperly in Reno. I can assure you that if they were doing something il-legal, as a prosecutor, I would have gone after them."

If there were extraordinary activities in, say, the casino counting rooms, Bill added, the jurisdiction to determine if a crime had been committed was with the State Gaming Control Board. Yet, if a crime was committed in a casino, or involving a casino, the police would investigate and the district attorney would prosecute. There were many such crimes, and often investigators for the Gaming Control Board would bring cheating customers to the DA's office for prosecution.

"There have been stories over the years that casinos routinely dealt with these situations themselves, such as taking cheaters out of the clubs and breaking their fingers," Bill said. "If such activity took place, I did not know about it; nor do I recall any such victims coming to us to complain. During my time as the DA, I would have taken a very dim view of that."

He added:

> There has always been a kind of controlled-growth attitude in northern Nevada and I think that deterred many potential in-vestors. As it turned out, maybe that was a good thing. I'm glad Bugsy Siegel decided to go Las Vegas instead of Reno.

# CHAPTER NINETEEN

# Corruption

While the drama of the Conforte trial gained national attention for the young district attorney of Washoe County, it was but one of several serious issues Bill faced in his first few years in office. Among the most daunting of these was his effort to clean up rampant corruption in the Reno Police Department and City Council.

Raggio's relationship with several in the police department had been chilly since the time, years before, when he and Emile Gezelin had raided Gurtha Jamar's brothel and found high-ranking members of the Reno police and city government there.

Despite the hostility, Bill recognized the need for good relations with law enforcement agencies and for better coordination between the Reno Police Department and the Washoe County Sheriff's Office. These two agencies traditionally vied over jurisdictional control. As an incentive to force them into a more efficient relationship, Bill regularly reminded them that he had control over all their criminal cases; the implication being that he had the power to decide which cases would be prosecuted, and when.

Not surprisingly, the police agencies were soon working well together. In addition, Bill worked hard to cement personal relationships with law enforcement at all levels, often riding on patrol with deputies or walking a beat with police officers. He had several police radios installed in his own car, so he could rapidly communicate with law enforcement agencies, including the Nevada Highway Patrol.

Bill later recalled how things began to unravel: "In 1959, Bud Baker was elected mayor and along with him a city council of questionable integrity. Because Police Chief Ted Berrum would not acquiesce to their demands to act inappropriately, this new administration fired him."

The council replaced Berrum with William Gregory, a detective sergeant on the police force whose primary duty had been collecting bad checks for casinos and other businesses.

"Although a nice man," Bill continued, "Gregory was completely unqualified for the job, having little true police experience and no management skills. Consequently, the department was soon disorganized and mismanaged."

By 1960, DA Raggio had become increasingly concerned about the deterioration of effectiveness and morale within the Reno Police Department—then news broke which shocked the community.

On the evening of May 4, 1960, a woman walking past a downtown business noticed two uniformed Reno police officers taking merchandise from the back door and loading into their patrol vehicle. She reported this to Reno Chief of Police William Gregory. Before official action was taken, rumors quickly spread throughout the community. The *Reno Evening Gazette* ran a photo of Chief Gregory, beneath which was the caption "Crumbs in the Cupboard."[1]

The events set in motion by these "crumbs" would soon topple the chief and several other high ranking police officers, expose a corrupt city council and, in the end, bring about sweeping changes in the way the citizens of Reno were to be protected and governed. "It became an immediate cause célèbre in the community," Bill said. "As district attorney, I decided it was time the Reno Police Department was cleaned up."

Things had gotten so bad there was a joke going around the community that when a local citizen was stopped by a Reno police officer for a traffic violation and handed the ticket he or she would exclaim, "Am I ever relieved! I thought you were going to rob me."

Then, in an even more blatant mockery of the public trust, word came that some officers were burglarizing the homes of people who had notified them that they would be away on vacation. "Nothing smells worse than corrupted law enforcement," Raggio told the press.

In a 2008 interview, Bill recalled, "The city council was composed of some nefarious people, like Charlie Cowen, Dick Dimond, Joe Mastroianni and John Marshall. Marshall particularly lacked scruples and had a friend in the police department who he socialized with by the name of Bob Taelour."

A crafty, intelligent man, Taelour knew that with his friend Marshall running things on the city council, he could become influential in running the police department. "Taelour," said Bill, "became the de facto chief, despite not formally holding a position of rank higher than patrolman."

The DA called for a meeting at Reno Police Department headquarters with the Chief William Gregory and the city council members. He advised them that the police department had a bad image and needed to do something to restore public confidence. Bill demanded they show the public that every effort was being made to ferret out the bad officers and suggested that all 109 members of the police department undergo a polygraph test.*

Bill later recalled how the issue came to a head:

> The city councilmen had stalled the investigation to that point and now told me they would not consider my suggestions. That, in effect, they were going to sweep the whole scandal under the rug. When I told them I would undertake a complete investigation of the police department, Councilman Marshall smugly remarked, "Take your best shot," meaning go ahead and try. He did not realize that the district attorney had the right to impanel a grand jury and to use it to investigate them.

---

*The Police Officers' Protective Association, which represented 109 members of the force, also insisted that all its members be given a polygraph test, not just the night shift employees as recommended by the city council, in order to help clear the reputations of the vast majority of honest officers.

Grand juries had been widely used in the United States throughout the 19th century. By the mid 20th century, however, most counties across the country had replaced them with a preliminary hearing process by which a judge weighs evidence concerning alleged offenses. Washoe County had used the grand juries very sparingly in the past, but Bill knew they were permissible and was prepared to proceed. Paul Laxalt would later recall how impressed he was by the breadth of the young DA's knowledge of the law: "Bill used the grand jury better than anyone I've ever known and was highly respected for that."

Shortly after Councilman Marshall challenged him to pursue an independent investigation of the police department, Bill took action. He had the district court impanel a seventeen-member grand jury and undertook to present them with all the evidence, not only about the burglaries, but also about other problems within the police department.

Bill called numerous witnesses and the process went on for weeks. Eventually, the grand jury produced a scathing report covering the inefficiencies, ineptness and failings of the Reno Police Department. "I had a least two grand juries and each were impanelled for about three years." Bill recalled. "They did more to stamp out problems in this community than anybody realizes."[2]

In their report, the grand jury recommended Chief William Gregory be returned to his former position as detective sergeant and that he should "be immediately replaced by a qualified administrator." The jury tried to soften the bluntness of their action by accusing the city council of doing Gregory "a great disservice" by appointing him as chief of police. The report further recommended that the city council stop interfering in police affairs and allow city manager, C.B. Kinnison, to manage the city.

The jury generally approved of the way the department was organized. However, they noted that blatant favoritism in the promotions of under-qualified people into positions of authority during Chief Gregory's administration had created serious morale problems.

The report charged that the chief of police, and ranking members of the city council, had condoned a "loose effort" to eliminate prostitution within the city. The most egregious of these charges came about after Councilman Charles Cowen sought police protection for a prostitute and Chief Gregory passed the order along to his vice squad.

Local narcotics traffic has been on the increase since Gregory took over as chief, the report continued, and "no real measures have been taken by the police department to combat this menace." With regard to the burglary ring within the department, the grand jury blamed a lack of training and a patrol division with "complete disregard for the chain of command and a lack of supervision."

William Gregory was dismissed. Instead of returning to duty as detective sergeant, he resigned from the force. Seven police officers were charged and prosecuted for the burglary of homes and businesses. Several others were fired, suspended or demoted for other violations. "The force had many dedicated officers," Bill later said. "Bill Brodhead was the assistant chief and a fine example of a police officer, as well as a nationally recognized polygraph examiner."

The city council members set about finding a "suitable" replacement for Chief Gregory. They decided upon a deputy sheriff from San Joaquin County in California. His name was Elmer Briscoe. After hiring him, Councilman Marshall warned Briscoe that District Attorney Raggio could not be trusted and the new chief should avoid him as much as possible. For the next first few months, Raggio and Briscoe had little contact.

However, much to the chagrin of the city council, Briscoe soon proved to be a person of high ethical standards and intelligence. His father had been a police officer killed in the line of duty and Elmer's dedication to the profession of law enforcement was beyond reproach. In an effort to undermine efforts by Briscoe to improve morale, Councilman Marshall continued to interfere directly with the administration of the police department through his friend, Patrolman Bob Taelour.

In early 1961, Marshall disbanded the vice unit, created the year before in the wake of the grand jury report, by reassigning the two officers to another unit. The *Reno Evening Gazette* described events leading up to that action:

It is known that Councilman Marshall conferred with Joe Conforte, known vice figure [who was at the time out on bail pending an appeal on his extortion conviction], the evening prior to his action at Mr. Marshall's home at which time Conforte produced information adverse to the existence of the unit. Conforte had made statements the prior evening to members of the [vice] unit that he could get them "kicked off" the squad insofar as Councilman Marshall was concerned.[3]

The unit later was reactivated.

A few weeks after the councilman's action, DA Raggio had John Marshall indicted for perjuring himself before the grand jury. Shortly thereafter, Chief Briscoe dismissed Patrolman Robert Taelour "for the good of the force."

"It did not take Chief Briscoe long to figure out what was going on," Bill later recalled. "We eventually became good friends, as did our wives, and we worked together very effectively over the many years he was chief of police—I think for the betterment of local law enforcement. Chief Briscoe was probably the most highly principled person I have ever met."

When C.B. Kinnison moved from city manager to county manager in 1960, the Reno City Council selected as his replacement, Joseph H. Lattimore. Lattimore was a person they felt would be compliant to their demands. This was important, because under the city charter it was the responsibility of the city manager to fire the chief of police. Now realizing Chief Briscoe was not going to do their bidding, the city council pressured the new city manager to fire him. Lattimore refused. The City Council then decided to fire Lattimore for not firing Chief Briscoe. However, it took a majority of four votes of the seven council members to do so.

Bill Raggio later described the bizarre standoff that ensued:

Whenever they [the city council] would try to fire Joe Lattimore, I would subpoena some of them. There were always a few of them, like Charlie Cowen and Joe Mastroianni, who I knew were very reluctant to come before the grand jury. Whenever they were getting close to enough votes to fire Lattimore, I would issue subpoenas and bring them all before the grand jury. I must have done that six different times. It was a miserable situation for them and consequently they never were able to muster enough votes to fire Joe Lattimore. And to his credit, Joe would never fire Elmer Briscoe.[4]

Joe Lattimore turned out to be a highly principled and honest person. The city council had picked him as a patsy and he turned out to be their undoing. We laughed about that irony for years.

During this period of the early 1960s, the Reno City Council was deciding where to locate a new convention center. Public interest was high and several locations were in the running, including three downtown sites. However, the city council decided on the purchase of a thirty-four-acre parcel at the intersection of South Virginia and Kietzke Lane, about three miles south of downtown Reno. Most in the community were outraged that the convention center would be located so far from downtown businesses and were not assuaged by a simultaneous decision to locate the 700-seat Pioneer Theater in downtown Reno for smaller events.

The land for the proposed convention center site, was owned by Harold's Club and selling for $1.2 million. Outgoing State Attorney General Charles Springer called for a grand jury investigation into possible "kickbacks."

Bill later said that he suspected the "fix was in." The manager of Harold's at the time was Guy Lent. During the course of the grand jury investigation, evidence was heard, though not enough to bring an indictment, that Lent had promised $25,000 to each council member who voted for the purchase of that land for the convention center.

Yet, it was fate, rather than the grand jury system, which dispensed justice in this situation. As Bill later recalled:

What we heard before the grand jury was that the corrupt council members asked that Lent hold their share of the money until they were out of the public eye, so they could avoid a potential federal investigation for income tax evasion. They were smart fellows, and in this instance showed surprising self-restraint; though, as fate would have it, Guy Lent subsequently died and they evidently never collected the money. In retrospect, and somewhat ironically considering they were acting primarily out of self-interest, they selected a good location for the convention center.

Continuing allegations of corruption compelled the grand jury to recommend a recall election for the mayor and three city council members.

At a public meeting in January 1962, Bill Raggio and his former mentor, Peter Echeverria, debated the appropriateness of such an election.

Echeverria contended that these problems could be better identified and corrected by a newly established commission to investigate the council's interference in police department matters, of which he had been appointed a member. He went on to charge that Bill Raggio was unduly influencing the grand jury in his direction. "If you took the twelve apostles," said Ecvheverria, "and left them with one attorney for two years, they would all think alike."

Raggio countered that "the city deserves a better say" during the eighteen months remaining for the present city administration, and that a recall election was the most effective way to that end. Closing with his signature directness, Bill told the audience, "It is the remedy for incompetence and maladministration in governments."

The mayor and city council members survived the recall movement, but were all voted out of office the following year in regular election.

For Bill Raggio, 1960 must have seemed a blur of activity. In addition to the exhausting preparation for the extortion trial of Joe Conforte, and the complicated legal maneuverings in breaking up corruption within the Reno Police Department and City Council, Bill Raggio was simultaneously working hard to see that a remorseless young killer paid for his crime.

# CHAPTER TWENTY

# Thayne Archibald

On August 28, 1959, twenty-year-old Thayne Archibald, a baby-faced, 5' 8", 120-pound, drifter, executed seventeen-year-old Larry Waters alongside the Truckee River east of Reno. Archibald had earlier kidnapped the high school honor student during the robbery of a Livermore, California service station where Waters worked.

Captured a month later in Baker, Oregon, Archibald confessed to local police. After his extradition to Reno, a psychiatric examination was ordered by the District Attorney. The prisoner was subsequently determined to be competent to stand trial.

Archibald, who Bill Raggio would later describe as "con wise," had already learned the nuances of the legal system from having served terms of confinement in a Utah youth reformatory and the Oregon State Penitentiary.

He chose to act as his own attorney and immediately pled guilty. District Court Judge Clel Georgetta denied Archibald's plea and appointed Edwin Mulcahy and John Squire Drendel as legal counsel.

While awaiting trial, Archibald nearly escaped twice from the antiquated Washoe County jail, one of the oldest buildings in the city. Each escape was attempted by sawing through cell bars with a hacksaw blade. Sheriff Bud Young suspected that "trustee" inmates had picked up the blades from an area of the building that was being demolished to make way for a new, more secure facility—and passed them along to Archibald.

On January 22, 1960, Archibald changed his plea to not guilty and asked for a change of venue, which was subsequently denied. In early

April 1960, the manipulative young killer would again change his plea back to guilty and receive new counsel—Robert Leland, Alex Garroway and, later, Reynar Kjeldson.

By this time, Judge Georgetta no longer objected to Archibald's plea. Under recently enacted legislation, his degree of guilt and sentence would be determined by a three-judge panel. The Nevada Supreme Court was charged with appointing two of the three judges from outside the local jurisdiction. Such a tribunal was intended to promote equitable sentencing in capital crime cases throughout the state.

The Supreme Court quickly appointed District Court Judges Jon Collins, Peter Breen, and Richard Hanna to preside over a hearing that would not only determine Archibald's fate, but also make Nevada judicial history. The new statute had not set out detailed rules for handling the situation. Therefore, prior to the hearing, defense attorneys, the prosecutor and judges met at the Washoe County courthouse to establish procedures for the first test of the statute.

Among the problems confronting them, was whether there should be, in essence, two hearings—one deciding the degree of guilt and the other to determine the penalty. This was complicated by other issues, such as whether arguments regarding the degree of guilt, and the sentencing information, should be allowed in the same hearing.

When the hearing finally began, Thayne Archibald, neatly dressed in an open-collared white shirt, gray jacket and black slacks, appeared calm as he sat next to his attorneys, winking and smiling to some in the audience and joking with nearby guards.[1]

The prosecution would be handled personally by District Attorney Raggio, with Herbert "Rick" Ahlswede as his assistant. Bill began the state's case by referring to the "unique tribunal prescribed by the rules of the state." He would request a verdict of first-degree murder and would not be hesitant in asking for the ultimate sentence, which in Nevada was death in the gas chamber. During the course of the hearing, Bill said he would prove to the jurists that Archibald "calmly, coolly and deliberately executed the boy without thought of compassion or remorse." Further, "that Archibald left his home in Roy, Utah on August 25, 1959, traveled to Elko where he purchased a .25 caliber automatic pistol which he used two days later to "snuff out the life of an unsuspecting seventeen-year-old boy."

Bill then began presenting evidence of previous crimes committed by Archibald to which defense attorney Garroway objected. Judge Collins ruled on the objection, ordering that the prosecution could introduce all evidence associated with the murder, but could not touch on other crimes.

Dr. John Callister, who performed the autopsy on the victim, took the stand and testified the bullets that killed Larry Waters were both fired from a distance of about eighteen inches. Archibald originally stated that he had, "in a panic," fired at the victim from a greater distance, as Waters ran up an embankment while trying to escape.

Bill would later describe how evidence, including two bullet cases left beside the body, indicated that Archibald had fired a single shot into the back of the Waters head from a distance of about eighteen inches and then "having killed him, stretched him out and delivered the *coup de grâce*."[2]

Testimony as to Archibald's psychiatric state was presented by Dr. Raymond Brown of Carson City and Dr. Rudolph B. Toller, of the California State Mental Hospital in Stockton, California. Both had examined him and concluded he was neither "legally nor mentally insane." While Dr. Brown was of the opinion that the young man would respond to therapy "if treated with understanding and dignity," Dr. Toller declared that Archibald had the capacity to premeditate, "to form intent to kill, and to kill." Toller said the slayer's actions at the scene of the crime "were not those of a person in panic."[3]

While questioning Archibald on the witness stand, DA Raggio deftly cracked the accused killer's veneer of nonchalance. Archibald was soon angrily matching retorts with the DA, but, more importantly, involving himself in a mass of conflicting statements. Each time his testimony deviated even slightly from his previous answers, Raggio would pounce, scornfully destroying its authenticity. Archibald became so confused and dispirited by Raggio's merciless cross-examination that he was soon reduced to muddled replies about not being able to remember.

The DA introduced into evidence a letter written by Thayne Archibald to Bill Raggio in September 1959, while he was waiting trial in the Washoe County Jail. In it, the slayer expressed his anger at Raggio for not allowing him to write a book titled *A Teenage Desire*. The letter went on to become a written admission of premeditated murder in which Archibald stated he had intended to seek a ransom for the return of Larry Waters and "planned it to the split second." The letter contained a reluctant admission that he "made one mistake, not getting rid of the gun and the cartridges near the body."[4]

On April 16, 1960, the three jurists unanimously ruled that Thayne Archibald had committed first-degree murder and should be executed for his crime. On June 8, 1960, DA Raggio successfully argued against an appeal by the condemned man before the Nevada Supreme Court. Though Archibald had admitted his guilt, he was asking for mercy from the court, insisting that he "was not a criminal, but a youth wounded by an unhappy background." His attorney, Alex Garroway, in a desperate effort to save his client's life, argued that he had not been a skilled enough attorney to handle such a hearing, thus denying Archibald proper representation. The court decided otherwise and upheld the death sentence.

On July 1, Archibald made a similar plea to the State Board of Pardons.* Prison psychiatrist Dr. E. Wesley Hiler testified before the board that Archibald was already reforming in prison and could be rehabilitated if his death sentence was reduced to life imprisonment. Hiler went on to describe the condemned man as "full of love." A similar depiction of Archibald was provided by Kenneth Smith, a Truckee, California laundry operator and part-time preacher, who stated the condemned man was "a lovable individual, a sweet person."

"Would you say he was lovable when he killed that boy?" board member and Nevada Supreme Court Chief Justice Milton Badt asked. "Yes sir, he was lovable then," Smith replied.

While the state did not send a representative to the hearing, two letters

---

*At the time, the Nevada Pardons Board was comprised of the three Supreme Court justices along with State Attorney General Roger Foley and Governor Grant Sawyer. The governor's power to commute a sentence could only be exercised in conjunction with the Pardons Board.

were presented. One was from Judge Jon Collins, who had been on Archibald's sentencing tribunal in June. In it, Collins stated that the sentencing panel had considered every factor thoroughly and unanimously recommended against commutation.

The other letter, from District Attorney Raggio, "sincerely recommended" that the execution be carried out. "This was one of the most brutal slayings ever perpetrated on a young victim," he wrote. "If the death penalty ever had any place, it is in this case." The pardons board decision was to let the sentence stand. Just before his execution, Thayne Archibald blamed his predicament on "that stiff collared, smooth talking DA." He was referring to Bill Raggio.

On the evening of August 22, 1961 after a visit to his cell by his parents and brother, Thayne Archibald ate his last meal of chicken, vegetable soup and cherry pie, prepared in the kitchen of Warden Fogliani's house. At 6:00 a.m. the following morning, he was led into the glass walled chamber. Cyanide pellets were activated in a bucket of acid beneath the chair to which he was strapped. Sixteen minutes later, the medical officer pronounced him dead.

Arthur Waters, father of the affable, seventeen-year honor student whose bright future was snuffed out by Thayne Archibald two years before, had been denied a request to witness the execution. Nevertheless, he drove from Livermore to Carson City. Arthur parked his car outside the prison as the dawn execution approached, but was ordered by prison authorities to move on.

Later, when informed that it was all over, Mr. Waters said simply, "That's all I wanted to know. Justice has been served. I'm glad it's all over."[5] He then turned his car toward the west and began the long, lonely drive home.

The Archibald case had a profound effect on Bill Raggio's professional life, crystallizing his sense of responsibility to the victims of crime—especially those tragic figures, like Arthur Waters, who trusted him to put some meaning back into their shattered lives.

This became an almost sacred mission to Bill, one in which he became eminently proficient. His sense of fairness and accountability allowed him no reluctance in asking for a death sentence, or for still believing in its effectiveness fifty years later:

> I do think there are some cases that are so heinous that the person forfeits their right to live in society. Sending them to prison, even carrying a sentence of life without the possibility of parole, does not always ensure that will happen. While such a sentence precludes them from ever going before the parole board, they can avail themselves to the pardons board or receive a commutation of sentence and be released. This does happen. I disagree with those who say the death penalty is never a deterrent. When I was a prosecutor, I had several criminal offenders tell me that the existence of capital punishment deterred them from killing someone they were physically assaulting.

He never wavered in the pursuit of justice, and over the next three years would personally prosecute some of the most savage crimes ever committed in Nevada.

# CHAPTER TWENTY-ONE

# Robert "Sandman" Williams

On Thanksgiving Eve, November 23, 1960, just a few months after conclusion of the sensational Conforte and Archibald cases, the relative tranquility of the Washoe County Courthouse was rocked again— this time by gunshots.

A contentious civil case had gone badly and fifty-two-year-old Robert Williams pulled a .38 caliber automatic pistol from his jacket and shot opposing counsel. Williams, known locally as the "Sandman," owned a small gravel pit in Reno that he operated by himself, using antiquated machinery to load sand and gravel onto his old truck, and delivering it around town. The Sandman lived at the pit in a shanty with no indoor plumbing. Reclusive and unwashed, he frequently exhibited erratic, often explosive, behavior.

His estranged wife, Joyce, and her mother each were asking for a one-third interest in the gravel pit business. Williams disagreed, and the civil proceeding on November 23 was to adjudicate that matter.

Williams had already received a continuance in the case, alleging through attorney Sam Francovich,* that he was hospitalized for a heart condition. Judge Collins ordered the bailiff go to Washoe Medical Center to check the veracity of this claim. Williams was indeed an inpatient at the time. Anxious to settle this case so he could return to Ely to meet his

---

\*Lillian Francovich would later say of her husband: "Many people came to Sam and he felt obligated to help, regardless of their ability to pay…There were very few cases he would turn down, because he had a big heart."

judicial responsibilities there, Judge Collins ordered Williams to be in court the following day.

Robert Williams appeared as scheduled, however, toward the end of the court proceeding he claimed to be experiencing severe chest pains and went into the hallway. Attorney Francovich asked the judge for a continuance until after Thanksgiving. Collins denied it saying, "We are going to finish this case today," and ordered the defendant back into the small temporary courtroom that was being used to hear the case.

Williams returned and minutes later pulled a gun from his clothing and shot the two attorneys representing Joyce Williams. Before Sam Francovich could wrestle the gun from his client, Eli Liverato, thirty-four-year-old father of three children, was dead. Edwin Mulcahy was seriously wounded and a third victim received a grazing wound.

Williams, questioned shortly after the shooting, claimed having no memory of the event. District Attorney Raggio immediately issued a complaint charging him with the murder of Eli Liverato.

Ed Mulcahy, an assistant district attorney, was in court that day as a private attorney representing Mrs. Williams. He and Bill Raggio had been co-workers and friends since Bill's early days as assistant district attorney. A few days after the shooting, while Bill was visiting his wounded friend in the intensive care unit of Washoe Medical Center, Ed whispered to him, "Let's get this guy [Williams]."

"I will," Bill promised solemnly.

Edwin Mulcahy died a few hours later.

The public outrage against Williams for the murder of these two popular family men was intense. Special arrangements were made to incarcerate him at the Nevada State Prison in Carson City while awaiting trial. Because the deaths had personally affected so many in the community, it proved difficult to find an attorney who would represent him. Within a few days of the shooting, major law firms bearing the names of twenty-three lawyers were listed as attorneys for plaintiffs in civil cases against Williams—thus precluding them from being appointed to act in his defense. Sam Francovich was excluded because he would be called as a witness.

In his 2004 oral history, then-Las Vegas attorney Harry E. Claiborne recalled being contacted by Nevada Supreme Court Justice Milton Badt. Badt was "very upset" that Robert Williams had been unable to obtain adequate defense counsel.

Claiborne told Judge Badt, "I will defend him, but if there is that much prejudice, I suggest they bring in a visiting judge from somewhere." As it turned out, Judge Merwyn Brown of Winnemucca was brought in to hear the case.

Due to previous contacts that had not gone well, neither Claiborne nor Judge Brown were great admirers of the other. "I was flabbergasted when Judge Brown was appointed," Claiborne later stated. "He was not a very knowledgeable judge…and knew less about the rules of evidence than probably any judge in the state. I was constantly frustrated by his rulings."

Claiborne would later say that the Williams case was the most difficult he ever tried, largely because Bill Raggio chose to handle the prosecution personally: "Bill Raggio is honest, and the best goddamn prosecutor the state ever had. I guarantee."[1]

The trial of Robert "Sandman" Williams for the murder of Eli Liverato began June 28, 1961. There was initially some difficulty seating jurors due to the prejudicial nature of crime. Eventually, eleven men and one woman were empanelled. The case hinged upon the application of the "McNaughton Rule," by which a mentally ill person can be found guilty of a crime if it could be established that he or she knew the nature and quality of the act and that it was wrong.

Bill Raggio understood the nuances of this legal standard as well, or better, than any prosecuting attorney in the country. Despite his recent promise to a dying friend, Bill's zealous persecution of this case was not the result of vendetta. Rather it was in his unwavering belief that Williams had premeditated his act and knew "right from wrong" when he was pulling the trigger. As such, the most important testimony would be that of the psychiatrists.

Defense attorney Claiborne, who was not being paid for defending

Williams, had petitioned Judge Brown for funds to hire a psychiatrist. Brown offered to appoint a local one. "I don't want the local psychiatrist," Harry replied. "There's too damn much prejudice. I want somebody who is well known and well respected and frankly I don't believe any of the doctors you mentioned [from the Reno area] are really qualified anyway."

Judge Brown denied his request.

Claiborne then used $600 of his own money to hire Dr. Raymond Schmidt, who had acquired a reputation for his work at San Quentin Prison. Dr. Schmidt came to the Washoe County Jail, where the defendant was moved from the state prison as his trial date neared, and examined him for a day and a half. Schmidt came away convinced that Williams was legally insane and would become Claiborne's main defense witness at the trial.

Dr. Schmidt testified for nearly an entire day, repeatedly stating that, in his opinion, Williams was too insane to have understood what he was doing at the time of the murder. Schmidt said the defendant had not intended to kill anyone when he went to court that day, but became "absolutely powerless" to stop himself at the time of the shooting.

The prosecution then called Dr. Rudolph Toller and then Dr. Richard Brown to the stand. Bill had selected Brown as a prosecution expert because he was a "reasonable, centrist psychiatrist."

Claiborne hammered away at the doctor's testimony, seeking to define the point where Williams might have switched from legal sanity, to insanity. At one point, he got Dr. Brown to admit Williams might not have had control of himself after he fired the first shot. This, in some ways, paralleled Dr. Schmidt's earlier testimony. The key issue now was whether Williams knew right from wrong when he fired the first shot.

On redirect examination by DA Raggio, Dr. Brown testified that Williams did know right from wrong throughout the entire episode, though he may not have had total control over his actions. Brown said Williams had no recollection of the shooting incident. The psychiatrist went on to describe Williams as a methodical man until his marriage began failing a part three years before. Then, he found his methods no longer worked for him and he began blaming others for his failings.

Sharp exchanges between Raggio and Claiborne punctuated the trial, with Claiborne derisively referring to the district attorney as "Dr. Raggio."

When Judge Jon Collins was called to testify, he became the target of Claiborne's most ruthless personal attacks. Claiborne first pointed out that Judge Collins had brought his own court reporter with him from Ely to help work his cases in Reno the previous November. The defense attorney then described the account given by witnesses who said Collins had ducked behind the bench to avoid a shot and then crawled out of the room on his hands and knees, "leaving his staff in the courtroom." The implication was that the judge had acted in a cowardly manner during the shooting, though it had nothing to do with Williams' culpability for the crime.

Bill was familiar with Claiborne's often-vicious courtroom tactics and recalled the following:

> That was Harry Claiborne's style, especially if he didn't have the facts of the case working in his favor. He would "take off" on a witness. Harry believed in histrionics, a lot of courtroom drama. He recognized that many jurors liked his loud and demonstrative manner, particularly his antagonism of judges. Harry would purposely provoke a judge in front of a jury in order to have the judge rebuke him, thus garnering sympathy from some of the jurors. I liken it to a basketball coach intentionally drawing a technical foul in order to stir up the crowd.

Claiborne then decided to put the irrational, babbling Williams on the witness stand to demonstrate the level of his insanity to the jury. DA Raggio wisely chose not to pursue a withering cross-examination.

"Bill did not try to do much with him [Williams]," Claiborne later recalled. "He knew if he fooled around with him too long it was going to increase the damage to his case. Bill Raggio is not only the best prosecutor I ever worked against, but also one of the most clever. He was the ultimate. I beat him in some murder cases. But he was, God, the best ever. And I tried murder cases in I guess fifteen different states. Nobody can carry his briefcase."[2]

On the afternoon of July 11, 1961, Judge Brown instructed the jury on possible verdicts they could reach, ranging from first- and second- degree murder, to not guilty, or not guilty by reason of insanity. They then began deliberating the fate of Robert "Sandman" Williams.

Just prior to that, in his final argument, DA Raggio had asked the jury to send Williams to the gas chamber for "the most cold-blooded, brutal slaying in the state's history." Bill told them that Williams had "convenient amnesia" in forgetting the shooting and accused defense attorney, Harry Claiborne, of throwing up "a smokescreen to protect his client." Alluding to Claiborne's style, Bill told the jurors that Claiborne had "tried everyone in the courtroom except Robert Williams."

"Mr. Raggio wants to kill my client," Claiborne declared in his closing. He asked the jury to believe Dr. Schmidt, who said Williams had been insane for years and should have been committed. He urged them to believe that Dr. Schmidt was more credible because he "had no interest in the case" unlike Dr. Rudolph Toller, whom he labeled "a prosecution specialist."

"I selected psychiatric experts for the prosecution who I thought would sound the most reasonable to the jury," Bill would later remark. "Of course, we always ran up against the issue that the doctors were paid by the district attorney's office when they testified as expert witnesses for the prosecution. But since the defense side did exactly the same thing, I don't think that accusation had much of an impact on jurors."

Bill was correct. The following day the jury returned a verdict of first-degree murder. Three days later, Judge Brown sentenced Robert Williams to life imprisonment. In contrast to his disengaged demeanor throughout the trial, Williams now required help getting to his feet to hear the sentence and broke into uncontrollable sobbing as it was being read. When asked later how he felt about not getting the capital punishment he sought, Bill replied, "I was not surprised because I sensed a certain level of sympathy within the jury."

Harry Claiborne's take on the verdict was more in keeping with his flair for the dramatic:

> It must have been the best job I ever did in my life cause (*sic*) he got life in prison. If there was ever a sonofabitch ticketed for the electric chair, it was him [Williams]…I felt I saved his life, and of course, I did.[3]

His remark underscores the effectiveness of Bill Raggio as a prosecutor. It was rare when he did not get the sentence he sought, particularly in a capital case. Because of the foresight and attention to detail Bill put into preparation for every case, it was even more uncommon to have the verdict successfully appealed. Such a case involved the bizarre murder trial of five-time convicted felon, Joseph Walker.

# CHAPTER TWENTY-TWO

# Joseph Miles Walker

In December 1960, Joseph Miles Walker was serving a two-year burglary sentence under an assumed name in the Oklahoma State penitentiary at McAlester. In that month, Reno law enforcement authorities linked him to the murder, four months earlier, of Paul G. Allison, a fifty-nine-year-old camper-shell manufacturer from Santa Rosa, California. The connection had come about as the result of a Reno pawnshop employee identifying Walker as the person who pawned a ring belonging to Allison shortly after the murder.

District Attorney Raggio and Reno Police Chief Briscoe went to Oklahoma to question the prisoner. Initially denying the charge, Walker eventually confessed to the murder. He then described how he had been hitchhiking from Salt Lake City to Reno when Allison, who was been traveling back to California from a business trip to Montana, picked him up in his truck-camper near Elko. The two began drinking and soon Walker "just lost his head," stabbing Allison to death near Lovelock, Nevada. Walker then drove on to Reno before abandoning the truck in a downtown parking lot, with Allison's body inside.

After extradition to Nevada, Joseph Walker was indicted, and declared that, while he did kill Allison, the homicide was justifiable. In June 1961, Reno attorney John Squire Drendel was appointed by the court to represent him. The trial began on September 18, 1961 with Drendel immediately challenging the admissibility of the confession Raggio and Briscoe had obtained during their visit to the Oklahoma prison.

After a two-hour debate between attorney and prosecutor, with the jury absent, presiding District Court Judge Clel Georgetta ruled that an unsigned confession would be admissible as evidence; stating authority for allowing it was validated by the Nevada Supreme Court in the case of Thayne Archibald, who had just been executed the previous month. "I feel this is not the best rule involved," the judge declared. "I think the rule in other states is better."

Walker's oral confession was made in the presence of not only Raggio and Briscoe, but also a court reporter, Richard Williams, and Clint Gladden, Deputy Warden of the Oklahoma State Penitentiary. In admitting their testimony, Judge Georgetta was less reluctant: "I find no proof of any coercion, no promise of reward or threat and that the statements were made voluntarily." However, before the transcript could be read to the jury, the judge ordered references to five previous felony convictions expunged.

Deputy Warden Gladden came from Oklahoma to testify and told the jury that Bill made no promises or threats of force and that "the confession was voluntary on Walker's part." During the closing minutes of Gladdens's testimony, Bill asked him to comment on the incidence of homosexuality among prisoners in his facility.

Drendel vehemently objected to the question and asked that the jury again be removed for an argument on point. Drendel then prophetically stated, "Someday a higher court will review this case and such remarks as these will be shown as undue prejudicial error."

Joseph Walker took the stand in September 28, 1961, claiming that Paul Allison had made "unnatural advances" precipitating a fight that ended in his death. District Attorney Raggio attempted to counter Walker's claim by calling Allison's wife to the stand and asking her if "relations" between her and her husband were satisfactory until the time of his death. The widow's testimony seemed to refute Walker's allegation.

Defense attorney Drendel then asked Walker to describe the day of the killing. After finishing a bottle of gin, Walker said, Allison took off his clothes and said I should "be friendly." When Joseph Walker resisted,

Allison allegedly pushed him up against a sink, next to which was a large knife. Walker grabbed the knife and stabbed Paul Allison to death. His account paralleled information he gave during his confession in Oklahoma.

When asked by Drendel, Walker denied being a homosexual. When questioned further about how Allison's naked body got on to the bunk, his hands tied together with his own necktie, the defendant replied, "I don't know."

During cross-examination, Bill Raggio asked the defendant about the pawned ring: "Did you kill him with the intention of robbery?" Walker answered, "No." In the final moments of the cross examination, the district attorney addressed the most bizarre aspect of Allison's murder, a large soda pop bottle that had been inserted into the victim's rectum.

"You say you're not a homosexual?" inquired Raggio.

"Yes," Walker answered.

"Then how do you account for this bottle inserted in the body of Mr. Allison?"

"Mr. Raggio," Walker earnestly replied, "I don't account for that bottle."

After seven hours of deliberation, the jury returned a verdict of first-degree murder and recommended imposition of the death penalty. This was the first Washoe County District Court jury to recommend that penalty since the Robert Fox trial in 1952.

While the verdict was read, Walker remained calm, as he had during the entire trial. Following the proceedings, he asked to speak and thanked Judge Georgetta for appointing John Squire Drendel as defense attorney. "He did everything humanly possible," the newly condemned man said before being led away.

The judge then commended Bill and Assistant District Attorney Eric Richards for the "great care" with which they prepared the case and the "force and dignity" which they exercised during the trial.

Judge Georgetta, likewise, commended Drendel for his performance as court-appointed counsel. He said Drendel "never missed an opportunity to defend his client's rights."

On October 20, 1961, Joseph Walker was formerly sentenced to die in Nevada's gas chamber. The Nevada Supreme Court heard an appeal of the Walker case on November 12, 1961. Raggio and Drendel, good friends with enormous respect for one another, drove together to Carson City from Reno that day to argue opposing points to the jurists. Six days later the court affirmed the conviction.

Drendel doggedly pursued appeals on behalf of Joseph Walker, obtaining stays of execution, often days before the sentence was to be carried out. In May 1967, he convinced a majority of the justices on the Nevada Supreme Court that his client had not received a fair trial. Among the factors he cited, were errors made by Bill Raggio in asking about homosexuality in the Oklahoma penitentiary, which he did not connect to the defendant.

The high court ordered Joseph Walker to be retried. Bill quickly voiced concern that it would be difficult to obtain another conviction because of a recent U.S. Supreme Court decision, *Miranda v. Arizona*,* which would prohibit Walker's confession from being used at the retrial. Bill also saw problems in gathering all the material witnesses after six years.

Undaunted, Raggio presented an inspired case. The second trial ended on December 13, 1967 with Walker again being convicted of first-degree murder and sentenced to die. Yet, like others waiting on Nevada's "Death Row," he would be spared from the gas chamber by a U.S. Supreme Court decision outlawing capital punishment throughout the nation.

In October 2007, John Squire Drendel spoke about the prosecutorial "errors" citied by the Nevada Supreme Court in determining that Joseph Walker should be retried for murder:

---

*The 1966 *Miranda v. Arizona* decision by the United States Supreme Court held that both inculpatory and exculpatory statements made in response to interrogation by a defendant in police custody would be admissible at trial only if the prosecution can show that the defendant was informed of the right to consult with an attorney before and during questioning. The prosecution was also required to advise the defendant of his or her right against self-incrimination prior to questioning by police, and that the defendant not only understood these rights, but voluntarily waived them.

Bill Raggio was the smartest, most brilliant attorney I ever opposed in court. He had an incredibly sharp mind, was a deep thinker, well read and articulate—but absolutely ruthless in court. As an opponent, Bill was capable, focused to win, and because he was so well read he could recite poetry and quote French philosophers to the jury.

He had very few faults, one of them being that he would occasionally "overreach." By this I mean, when he felt very strongly about a case, it would occasionally trip him up. Mills Lane was the same. One time Bill made an opening statement in a [Joseph Walker] murder case that went beyond what the law allows. I was defending the accused, and because of this, the case was reversed on a technicality.

When asked later to comment on Drendel's observation, Bill said that his policy was to work hard on a trial, establish the chain of evidence, and have all his witnesses ready for everything they could possibly be asked.

"I was extremely thorough," he stated, "and would routinely go beyond what was required to make my point."

# CHAPTER TWENTY-THREE

# Lester Morford, III

Early on the morning of August 22, 1962, Jack and Patricia Foster, a honeymooning couple from Medford, Oregon, who had been married just three days before, were kidnapped at gunpoint from the parking lot of a downtown Reno motel. Their abductor was an eighteen-year-old itinerant farm worker from Santa Rosa, California, by the name of Lester Morford III. Morford had purchased a German-made .22 pistol and two boxes of cartridges for $16.95 from a pawnshop the day before and had spent the night getting high on toluene fumes from over a dozen tubes of glue.

Morford had, at first, intended merely to steal the Foster's car, but at the last minute ordered the couple into the vehicle and forced them to drive to Truckee, and then on to Lake Tahoe. About eight miles north of Crystal Bay, on the Mount Rose Highway, Morford ordered the driver, Jack Foster, to stop the car. He then shot Jack in the head, dragged the wounded man from the automobile and rolled him down a roadside embankment.

He then drove to an isolated area where he raped Mrs. Foster. He later repeated the offense at a second location before driving to Carson City, where the woman jumped from the car at a red light and escaped.

Morford sped off, but was arrested about an hour later by Nevada Highway Patrolman Larry Fister near the town of Silver Springs. According to the arresting officer, Morford surrendered meekly despite still having the pistol in his possession.

Later that day, a vacationer stopped his car on the Mount Rose highway to snap a photograph of scenic Lake Tahoe and discovered the wounded

Jack Foster. The man flagged down a passing motorist to go for help and soon authorities arrived. Bill Raggio later arrived with Lester Morford in tow.

Officer Fister had turned Morford over to Washoe County authorities and the killer was now guiding Bill over the same route he had forced his victims to drive earlier in the day. "He was cooperative," Bill would say. An officer accompanying them described Morford as "calm, cool and collected," showing no remorse.

Morford was later given a blood alcohol test at the same Reno hospital where Jack Foster lay in critical condition. The kidnapping occurred on Jack's 23rd birthday. He would die the following day. Mrs. Foster was also at the hospital, receiving treatment for abrasions and contusions, and was described by her attending physician as "extremely emotionally upset."

The incredibly efficient investigation, nearly completed on the same day as the crimes occurred, was, according to Patricia Foster, also handled with professionalism and sensitivity. After returning to Medford, she asked her brother to write a public letter on her behalf to the editor of the *Reno Evening Gazette*, expressing her gratitude—an extraordinary gesture considering all she had suffered. In closing, Foster said,

> If it were possible for the shock to be lessened by kindness and patience on the part of the investigating officers, your officers did everything possible. Now that you have a fine police force, give them your support and don't turn loose the criminals they have apprehended. Some people might have ill feelings for a town or area where this thing happened, but thanks to your officers, we have nothing but gratitude in our hearts for Reno and its people.[1]

Lester Morford confessed to murdering Jack Foster and raping Patricia. Eleven months later, on July 15, 1963, a three-judge panel heard arguments before deciding his degree of culpability and sentence. The tribunal, appointed by the Nevada Supreme Court, consisted of District Judge

John Barrett of Reno and Judges George Marshall of Las Vegas and Peter Breen of Tonopah.

In his opening statement, Bill said he would prove Morford was guilty of first-degree murder and called the crime "willful, premeditated and deliberate." Defense attorney Stan Brown hoped to convince the judges that Morford was incapable of premeditating murder and that he was acting under the influence of glue fumes.

Later in the morning, under questioning by Bill, a pale, but composed, Patricia Foster took the stand and recounted the events of the previous August 22. The legal proceeding ended on the following day. The panel of jurists handed down a decision of first-degree murder and sentenced Lester Morford to be executed.

In a letter to Nevada Governor Grant Sawyer, Morford's parents said they believed "the California Youth Authority was extremely negligent in their handling of our boy…The State of California has a moral responsibility in the actions of our son." Morford had been released from the custody of the Youth Authority just prior to his attack on the Fosters. "Our concern is for the life of our son…and to make the Nevada governor and Nevada Board of Pardons aware that this boy was improperly released and incapable of control." The letter ended with a plea to use their "influence to help us save our boy's life."

Governor Sawyer responded, "I have serious personal doubts as to the morality or the efficiency of capital punishment, generally. However, my personal views of the subject are of little significance. I must uphold the laws of the state, and as governor of the State of Nevada, I have no power of clemency or commutation. The matter is, therefore, entirely out of my hands."

Many, especially from California, used the Morford sentence as a platform to voice their opposition to the death penalty. Often the criticism became personal. One letter to the editor of the *Gazette* read: "District Attorney William Raggio is doing just the same thing as Morford did by getting him put to death—only slower."[2]

Stan Brown filed numerous appeals and federal court writs, hoping to spare his client from the gas chamber. Brown's arguments ranged from such trivial charges as that the DA had erred during the sentencing panel by using color photographs of the victim (instead of black-and-white), to claims that Morford had suffered from a "hostile environment" due to publicity surrounding the concurrent trial of another vicious murderer, Thomas Lee Bean.

Brown repeatedly argued that his client also was not advised of his rights before making a confession. Bill Raggio rebutted the claim by reminding the court that Morford received a fair hearing before a three-judge panel. He pled guilty to the shooting and under Nevada law, the panel sets the degree and punishment. The U. S. Supreme Court rejected hearing an appeal of the case.

Lester Morford was granted a stay of execution in April 1969. The last execution in the United States had taken place two years earlier, shortly before the high court ruled in *Witherspoon v. Illinois* that the death penalty could not be imposed without sufficient standards of directions to jurors. Morford's fate now hinged upon anticipated U. S. Supreme Court rulings related to other capital cases. Those were expected to set guidelines on the constitutionality of the death penalty on grounds that, in its current form, it constituted cruel and unusual punishment.

The lower federal courts were not anxious to deny appeals until the highest court had made its final ruling. Bill later observed that it was the "never-ending federal route of appeals" that also held up the imposition of sentences and "a person is not limited in the number of writs he or she can bring." "For all practical purposes," he later conceded, "those earlier high court decisions had ruled out the death penalty."

His prophetic 1969 observation that the high court had, for all practical purposes, already ruled out the death penalty, became a reality on June 29, 1972, when the U.S. Supreme Court ruled in the case of *Furman v. Georgia*. In that decision, the court split five to four in overturning the imposition of the death penalty. Although the majority agreed that the current application of the death penalty constituted cruel and unusual punishment in violation of the Eighth and Fourteenth Amendments to the U.S. Constitution, they could not agree as to a rationale, and did not produce a controlling opinion. Instead, each of the nine justices wrote separately, with none of the five justices in the majority joining in the opinion of any other.*

In September 1972, Lester Morford asked for a writ of *habeas corpus* claiming the death sentence violated his constitutional rights. In Reno, Federal District Court Judge Bruce Thompson, in keeping with the recent ruling in *Furman v. Georgia*, ordered Morford, along with several other Nevada death row inmates, to either be released from prison or resentenced by November 6.

He was subsequently resentenced by Washoe County District Court Judge John Barrett, one of the three judges who presided over his original hearing, to a term of life imprisonment without the possibility of parole. He would later commit suicide.

Bill Raggio's first term was grueling. He had faced the enormous challenges of reorganizing an antiquated and inefficient district attorney's office, fought rampant corruption in city government, endured slanderous insinuations about his character and relentlessly prosecuted vicious criminals. He felt he had given his best effort to the citizens of Washoe County and was now considering stepping down.

---

*In the following four years, thirty-seven states enacted new capital punishment penalty laws aimed at assuaging the High Court's concern about arbitrary imposition of the death penalty. Several statutes mandating bifurcated trials, with separate guilt-innocence and sentencing phases, and imposing standards to guide the discretion of juries and judges in imposing capital sentences, were upheld in a series of Supreme Court decisions in 1976.

# CHAPTER TWENTY-FOUR

# Reelection

As the 1962 election approached, Bill thought Deputy District Attorney Drake DeLanoy would make an excellent replacement, and encouraged him to run. DeLanoy declined, deciding instead to move to Las Vegas and enter private practice. As Bill considered the field of other contenders, he did not see one who he felt was ready for the office.

During his first term, Bill and his family had made enormous personal sacrifices. Throughout the Conforte extortion trial, and Bill's subsequent campaign against corruption in government, they had been subjected to insinuation and slights by not only strangers, but by acquaintances as well. The hours of preparation required to bring criminals to justice had left little time for the fishing and camping trips they once enjoyed. Always hanging over their heads was the threat of retaliation from unscrupulous people who were not used to being held accountable to the law.

Modernizing the DA's office into a more professional agency, one less dependent on corrupt law enforcement and city government officials, was not appreciated by all. By his own admission, Bill had "stepped on a lot of toes." Despite all this, he knew there was much work left to be done, and no one else yet ready to accomplish it. He announced his bid for reelection and braced for another round of smear and innuendo.

It was not long in coming. He would be challenged in the Republican primary election by city attorney Rick Breitwieser. Bill later recalled: "Rick was being financed by Joe Conforte and a number of other people who did not like having a tough district attorney, including some city council members with whom I was battling. Their campaign strategy was to label me as overzealous—a crusader."

In the unusually spiteful campaign leading up to the Republican primary election, Breitwieser accused Bill of having a "prosecution complex" and of only being interested in sensational cases "and not in protecting the people's interest." The DA, Breitwieser charged, "was more interested in obtaining a conviction, then first determining whether the suspect was guilty or innocent."

He was referring to the detention of Mrs. Belva Griffis on a murder charge. Mrs. Griffis had been held without bail for more than four months before she was cleared of the murder of her husband, neighborhood grocer Clarence E.L. (Jack) Griffis. Breitwieser claimed Mrs. Griffis had continually protested her innocence, yet the DA apparently was more determined to convict her than to lead an effort to uncover the facts of the crime.

Bill vehemently denied this charge, saying Breitwieser was "completely uninformed on criminal procedures and has no awareness of the facts or circumstances that surrounded the Griffis murder case." Mrs. Griffis, the DA went on to explain, was detained because she could not explain the presence of blood on her shoes. This, along with other circumstances, led to the charge. Though she proclaimed her innocence, Griffis was subsequently held without bail, not by the DA, but by order of a district court judge while hundreds of leads were being checked out.

Bill repeatedly offered Mrs. Griffis, through her California attorney, opportunities to take a polygraph test. The attorney had evidently neglected to pass that information along to her. Once he did, and the polygraph results were analyzed, Bill moved for dismissal of the charges.* Upon her release, Griffis authorized the DA to publicly state,

> She feels her case was properly handled…and had no desire to make this a political football by those persons who have sought her out for this purpose.

---

*Three teenagers were subsequently convicted of second-degree murder for the slaying, which occurred during an aborted robbery attempt. They are now serving time in state prison.

It would appear that my primary opponent from the city hall is so overzealous to be elected, for whatever purpose, he is more interested in innuendo and half truths then in ascertaining the true facts and circumstances, matters which I feel are a prime requisite for this office.[1]

Increasingly desperate, Breitwieser lashed out at Bill with a full page advertisement in the local newspapers accusing him of being responsible for Washoe County now having the nation's highest per capita crime rate. This had occurred despite the DA having increased the budget of the district attorney's office three-fold, from approximately $60,000 to $150,000 per year. The ad quoted Breitwieser: "My opponent is running on his record; I'm running because of his record."

Bill rebutted these charges, pointing out that while the population of United States has increased only 7% since 1957, the crime rate in the country has climbed by 34%. He said Washoe County, particularly the cities of Reno and Sparks, had a rate of increase even higher than the national average. He cited two factors for this. The first was that Nevada was "a twenty-four-hour state" making law enforcement "a full three-shift operation"; secondly, the national crime index figure was based on the number of crimes among members of the "permanent population." This did not account for the fact that the "actual" number of people in the state was multiplied many times by the tourists.

"Public apathy toward crime prevention and prosecution also seriously hampered the efforts of law enforcement officials throughout the country," Bill said. He pointed to the increasing juvenile crime rate, which was up 4%, as a steady contributor to the worsening general crime rate. He called upon parents to do everything in their power to initiate a better environment in the home.

Raggio blasted local politicians for interference in the administration of police duties and the relative lack of funding for more police officers. He ended by saying prison rehabilitation programs were not adequate and the current parole and probation system was too lax.

The intense primary campaign inflamed local fervor. Police reported a man breaking the back off a wooden bus stop at the intersection of Plumas and Mt. Rose Streets and throwing it into the trunk of his expensive, late-model car. The report further stated, "It was believed that part of the bench was stolen because it held a poster which read 'Vote for Raggio.'"

In September, Bill defeated Rick Breitwieser in the Republican primary election and began his campaign against the Democratic challenger, attorney and former Reno municipal court judge, Harry D. Anderson. The race would become even more rancorous than the primary had been.

Anderson had 10,000 political leaflets produced by a San Jose, California printing company. The leaflets contained an unflattering cartoon caricature of Bill jumping on a large phonograph record while ranting, "I stand on my record!" Looking on, was another crude illustration of a shapely young woman with a baby. In a dialogue bubble, the cartoon infant is asking, "What is wrong with papa?"—a reference to accusations made by Conforte minions that Bill had fathered Jackie Hitson's child.

Whatever clever advantage Anderson believed these handbills would provide, backfired on August 30 when he and his campaign manager, Reno attorney Sam Bull, arrived at the printing company to pick them up. San Jose police officers were waiting for them and confiscated the political handbills, because they violated California election law by not indicating the name of the sponsor. Anderson and Bull were questioned by the officers and released, pending an inquiry.

The following day, Harry Anderson told a *Gazette* reporter, "We did not know the existence of such a law...I just went along for the ride."[2] Later, Anderson would have second thoughts about the campaign literature because it was, he admitted, in bad taste and "did not reflect the type of campaign I wanted." He went on to say he had been given "some bad advice" about ordering the leaflets and instructed Sam Bull to destroy the remaining stock.

Bill Raggio countered with two issues that he believed made Anderson unqualified for the position of Washoe County District Attorney. The first was that his opponent had not even been astute enough to avoid violating California election law while producing his campaign literature. The deed showed he did not "display the dignity and surety" required of the office.

The second issue had to do with Anderson having previously resigned his position as a municipal court judge. The Nevada Bar Association, after investigating allegations of misconduct, had released a report stating that Judge Anderson did "improperly endeavor to use the influence of his judicial office to collect a legal fee." Anderson agreed that he had used poor judgment in the situation, but that his reason for resigning had to do only with the need to take care of some "family matters" in California. "It was right and proper that I was reprimanded, but that is as far as it went," Anderson replied.

Bill added that when Anderson returned to Reno from California in 1959, he applied for a position as assistant district attorney. "He didn't get the job," Bill said, without elaborating. Anderson immediately filed a $250,000 libel suit charging the DA with deliberately trying to defame him and ruin his reputation "by irrational and irresponsible statements."*

Bill bounced back, holding an afternoon press conference in his office at which he called the libel action was "ridiculous." "If he can't stand the heat," he said scornfully, "let him get out of the kitchen."

Like Breitwieser before him, Anderson claimed Bill was responsible for the high crime rate in Washoe County, because he prosecuted too many "sensational" cases. Bill called such accusations "electioneering, politicking and baloney."

In a 2008 interview, Bill would recall how discouraged he became by the way he had been portrayed in the local press, particularly by the *Reno Evening Gazette*. It reached a point where Bill had had enough, and invited the editor, John Sanford, to meet for lunch "to clear the air." Raggio said Sanford was "an old-style newspaper editor, a nice guy, but somewhat of a curmudgeon."

---

*November 3, 1962, Bill Raggio filed a motion for dismissal of Anderson's libel suit. The libel case was heard on December 11, but was subsequently dropped by Anderson before a verdict was rendered.

They met at the Riverside Hotel, along with his assistant Joe Jackson, who was a crony of some corrupt city council members and Chief Gregory. Bill told John of his concern that regardless of what the District Attorney's Office did, the newspaper criticized them.

"I explained that we were, like everyone else, human beings who occasionally made mistakes," Bill said. "But we worked hard to do our jobs and so did not understand his need to engage in such constant fault-finding."

Sanford replied that it was not his duty or his job "to report on anybody who wants to be a crusader."

Bill continued:

> I resented his barbed comment and replied (in much stronger language than I am using here), "So now I understand. If I make the least mistake, it will be reported by you; yet, if I make an extra effort in the office, you are going to ignore it. This can only mean that you are advocating mediocrity in public office." He disagreed with me at the time, but I had made my point. From that time on, I had excellent relations with both of the newspapers in town.

"Clearing the air" with John Sanford, paid off when, on October 27, 1962, just a week before the election, an editorial in the *Gazette* endorsed Bill Raggio and included a blistering challenge to his opponent's assertion that "somehow, or another, the district attorney is responsible for a crime wave in Washoe County":

> District Attorney Raggio has conducted his office efficiently and fairly, despite criticisms made by his opponents and some individuals around Reno who apparently want to return to its "wide open" base when the community was under the control of a greedy mob and had no respect for law, or the welfare of the residents of the city and the county. He deserves reelection. [3]

The bitter campaign ended on November 6, 1962. Notwithstanding all his hard work to rid the community of crime and corruption, and the dangers and indignities he and his family endured in the cause of a safer society, Bill won by barely 3,000 votes out of over 30,000 cast.

# CHAPTER TWENTY-FIVE

# Thomas Lee Bean

ill Raggio would personally try nine capital cases in his years as district attorney, many for crimes of unthinkable viciousness. However, none would match the case he prosecuted in the spring of 1963 for mind-boggling depravity and savageness.

"I've seen cases where I did not think it could get any worse. I'm now willing to believe almost anything." With those words, Bill Raggio informed the public of the barbarous, murder and mutilation of a twenty-four-year-old woman in Reno.

On the night of April 5, 1963, Reno Police Officer Mort Ammerman knocked on the door at 2640 Yori Street. He had received a report that the tenant, Sonja McCaskie, a former British Olympic skier, had failed to pick up her one-year-old son from the home of a babysitter.*

---

*Sonja McCaskie was born in Elgin, Morayshire, Scotland on February 19, 1939, the daughter of Dorothy and Henry McCaskie. Henry died several months later, leaving Dorothy to raise Sonja and her older brother and sister. In 1946, Dorothy moved the family to United States and eventually to Tahoe City, about fifty miles southwest of Reno, where Sonja was raised and graduated from Tahoe-Truckee High School. In the Sierra environment, Sonja learned to ski well and upon learning that the 1960 Winter Olympic Games were to be held in nearby Squaw Valley, she wrote the Ski Club of Great Britain asking to be included on their Olympic team. Sonja was given a tryout and qualified for a slot in the slalom competition. Though she would have preferred the downhill event, she competed in slalom, eventually falling during the final competition and finishing in last place.

The following winter Sonja competed with the team throughout Europe. After returning home, she continued to ski whenever possible and became a part-time instructor at the Slide Mountain Ski School. She hoped to polish her racing skills in order to qualify for the 1964 Winter Olympics; however, snow conditions in the Sierras during the winter of 1962-63 had been disappointing, and thus her practice time was unsatisfactory.

When no one answered, and finding the front door locked, Officer Ammerman checked the back door and found it half-open. Upon entering the two-bedroom duplex he beheld a sight so ghastly he could not at first comprehend it. "I kept thinking it was a mannequin," he would later recall. He quickly called for detectives.

During the subsequent investigation of the crime scene, authorities found the decapitated torso of a young woman, with three knives protruding from it, stuffed into a living room hope chest. Sonja's head, found beneath the torso, was wrapped in female undergarments and a white tablecloth. Her heart had been cut out and was lying on the floor. The woman's left foot, severed at the ankle, was lying nearby, wrapped in a blanket. Police Chief Elmer Briscoe said, "I worked on more than 150 murders, but never one like this…never one so vicious."

Four days later DA Raggio updated the press. Sonja was butchered in bed. Her killer then turned the mattress over and made the bed before leaving. In a kitchen cabinet, they discovered what appeared to be a thirty-inch-long bloody, homemade garrote constructed of hemp binder twine with clothespin handles.

Bill also disclosed the discovery of McCaskie's "little black book," a private diary containing the names of several lovers, along with the details of her intimate encounters with these men. Investigators had also turned up a book of poetry, primarily of a "morbid nature." Sonja evidently had contemplated suicide during periods of depression.

All this spurred a series of scandalous articles about Sonja's sex life, accompanied by provocative photographs. Chief Elmer Briscoe was appalled at the salaciousness of the media reports and in hoping to salvage Sonja's reputation, wrote an elegant clarification:

> The preliminary analysis of the writing habits of Sonja McCaskie indicates that she was a vivacious personality, serious about cultural development, artistically inclined and sentimentally sensitive. Her life has been punctuated with several emotional crises, which she survived with a normal amount of depression and in-

trospection under the circumstances. Her personal diaries and poetry indicate more than an average ability in that literary expression. Previous newspaper reports indicated an undue emphasis on sex activities. To the contrary, her writings indicate many friendships of a purely platonic nature and the normal amount of romantic affairs. She chose her friend's carefully. Her romances, known at the present time, have been conducted on a wholesome and discreet basis. Her writings indicated a desire for happy marriage and a full life.[1]

Nonetheless, every man whose name was mentioned in Sonja's diary was investigated and eventually cleared as a suspect in the crime. Twelve separate sets of fingerprints were found in her home. Investigators, realizing it must have taken hours to butcher the young woman, believed the killer might have had some special expertise or knowledge of anatomy. Though this theory later proved to be invalid, McCaskie was a secretary at the Blue Ribbon Meat Company in Sparks, and so police questioned and fingerprinted all the employees there. All were cleared as suspects.

In addition to her one-year-old son, McCaskie, who had been briefly married, was also the mother of two daughters. One was being raised by the father's parents and the other had been given up for adoption. As her mother, Dorothy McCaskie would later forlornly state, "Sonja just seemed to have a hard time trying to find her way."

As details of the murder were disclosed, the community became gripped in fear—bordering on panic—at the thought that such a monster resided in their midst. The Reno Police put every detective and available officer on the case. The district attorney's office, recognizing the public unease, worked around the clock. As the days passed, and newspapers were more frequently using terms like "baffled" to describe the investigation, the public held its breath, anticipating yet another grisly find.

A break in the case came from what at first appeared to be a minor clue. At the crime scene, investigators noticed a small instruction pamphlet for a 35mm camera—but no camera. After verifying that Sonja owned such a camera, police began to canvass every pawnshop in town. Their efforts paid off on April 13, when one shop dealer produced the camera, for which he had given $10 on the day after the murder. The receipt was signed "Thomas Lee Bean." Despite giving an incorrect address on the document, police quickly tracked him down.

Two officers arrived at the trailer home at 4135 Neil Road in Reno where Thomas, an eighteen-year-old Wooster High School student, lived with his father and brother. The officers asked Bean if he would accompany them to the station to answer questions regarding the camera he had pawned. He willingly agreed. Before leaving, they searched Bean's car and found a loaded rifle and pistol. After a more thorough search of his car later in the day, police found a radio missing from McCaskie's residence.

"He came down to the police station willingly," said Chief Briscoe, "and was quite cooperative at first." Bean remained calm, even when being fingerprinted. However, when police asked for his footprints, the young man became visibly nervous. Earlier news accounts of the crime had disclosed that a bloody footprint was found in the victim's house. Once Bean gave up his footprint, "He knew we had him," said Briscoe.

After obtaining the footprint, police led Thomas to be questioned by District Attorney Raggio. Suddenly, the yet-to-be manacled Bean bolted out the front door of the police station and raced up the street with twenty officers in pursuit. After chasing him for several blocks and firing five warning shots, Bean was finally tackled by Detective Ralph Andreini. Now handcuffed, the distraught Bean was heard to cry out, "Why didn't you kill me?"

Later that day, Thomas Bean was formally charged with the mutilation slaying of Sonja McCaskie. He immediately confessed to the crime, agreeing to lead Bill Raggio on a tour of the Yori Street home. As he provided grisly details of his actions that night, Bean was "methodical and remorseless" Bill recalled. The DA had taken the precaution of having the chilling reenactment not only tape recorded and photographed, but also captured on 8 mm movie film. Later, as Bean was being booked in to the Washoe County Jail, he turned to Bill and asked, "Is it pretty bad for me?" The DA paused a moment, then replied, "Always expect the worst in a case like this."

"Sonja was just a chance victim… Bean had no previous contact with her," Bill said at a news conference the next day. "The original motive was apparently rape. Bean had been prowling the neighborhood on other occasions obtaining women's undergarments from clothes lines."

The DA then described the makeshift garrote Bean made a few days before the murder. He carried that, along with a ten-inch-long knife, when he went prowling the night of April 4, parking his car a block from Miss McCaskie's residence at about midnight. Sonja had hung a white satin slip on her backyard clothesline shortly before going to bed and had left the rear door of the duplex unlocked. Bean took off his shoes (he wore no socks) and entered the home, crawling through the rooms making sure no one, except the sleeping woman, was home. He then went into her bedroom. When Sonja awoke, Bean strangled her. He then raped her.

He confessed to then having slashed the body open from the throat to the pelvis. Later, moving the corpse into the living room where he continued mutilating and dismembering it over the next five hours, all the while listening to Sonja's record albums on her stereo.

Bean was cautious not to leave fingerprints. "He used several pairs of gloves and a pair of nylon stockings to cover his hands while handling items in the apartment," Bill said. "He admitted the strangulation, dismembering the body, cutting out the heart and severing the foot."

Bean then took Sonja's 1962 Triumph TR-4 sports car for a joy ride at about 5:15 a.m., returning it back to her driveway with a damaged fender and wheel, about two hours later. He then walked to his own vehicle and drove home. When later asked why he returned the car to the murder scene, Bean replied, "Well, it was not my car."

"I'm completely surprised by his attitude," Bill said of the suspect at the time. "He was extremely nervous at first…but, after his escape attempt, his attitude became one of complete cooperation. He's one of the coolest suspects I've ever confronted. He talked to us about the murder without reluctance. He has not shown any apparent sign of remorse."

"I consider this to be a rare achievement of police work," Bill continued. "Hundreds of leads had to be followed up. In my eleven years as a prosecutor, this particular case has been the most difficult one, primarily because of the apparent absence of motive...I'm very much relieved that a person like this is still not at large." The district attorney then ordered Bean to be examined by a psychiatrist.

Thomas Lee Bean was born in Reno on October 16, 1945. His father, Elza "Roy" Bean, moved the family constantly because he had trouble keeping a job. In Thomas's short life, he had lived not only in Nevada, but in Oregon, Washington, Montana, Texas, California and Utah. He never remained in a school long enough to make friends—or to even learn to read.

On June 19, 1961, less than two years before the McCaskie murder, Thomas snuck onto the enclosed porch of a neighbor's house in Salt Lake City and attempted to strangle a fifteen-year-old girl sleeping there. She screamed and struggled. Bean fled, but was subsequently arrested.

Because his parents were soon moving to Nevada, Bean was turned over to the Nevada Youth Training Center at Elko without any prosecution in connection with the attempted murder. During his time in the institution, he was, according to later testimony by the facility's director, a model inmate displaying above average intelligence and progressing in his reading skills to a fourth-grade level.

In May 1962, though not psychiatrically ready for release, budgetary constraints required the state of Nevada to return him into his father's custody. By then Roy Bean had returned to Reno and divorced the boy's mother. Upon his release, Thomas Bean enrolled at Wooster High School. Principal Ed Dotson later described him to a reporter:

> [He was] one of those students you learn very little about. He was never disciplined by school administrators and did not participate in any extracurricular activities. He worked in the cafeteria

to pay for his lunch…but other than that, there's really nothing about school life that made him stand out.[2]

"Obviously insane" was the comment most commonly voiced by the public after Thomas Bean's arrest. His confession meant his fate would hinge solely upon the jury's interpretation of his mental state at the time he committed the crime. Despite the public outcry and widespread demand for punishment, many could not imagine that such an atrocity could be committed by a "legally sane" individual.

Bill Raggio had honed his skills in successfully prosecuting cases in which the "insanity defense" was employed, including those of Robert Fox and Robert "Sandman" Williams. Due to Bill's command of the complex nuances found in the McNaughton Rule, Thomas Bean's attorney would have a difficult task saving his client from the gas chamber.

Before the court could appoint a public defender, Harry D. Anderson volunteered to act as defense attorney. He asked the court for only $1 in compensation and $500 to hire his own psychiatrist to examine the defendant.

Anderson had been Bill's opponent in the contest for Washoe County district attorney the previous November. Because the race had been one of the bitterest political contests in local memory, Anderson would later spend a good deal of time refuting suggestions that he took the case as part of an ongoing grudge against the district attorney.

Judge Grant Bowen would preside over the trial, which began on July 1, 1963. Bill Raggio presented his case to the jury, saying that Thomas Lee Bean had planned and carried out this shocking crime fully understanding its nature and was able to distinguish between right and wrong.

Much of the prosecution's effort that day was in admitting into evidence Bean's sixty-six page admission of guilt. The veracity of this document was attested to by witnesses William Brodhead, Assistant Chief of the Reno Police Department, and court reporter Richard Williams. While Bill read the part of the interrogator aloud to the jury, the chief criminal deputy district attorney, Rick Ahlswede, read Bean's part.

"Don't do it now, I have a baby to support," read Ahlswede, quoting

Bean's description of Sonja's last words.

And later: "You ask the motive, I have none. It's been a childhood dream of mine to rape a girl, and I don't' know why. I've tried to kick it…I don't know why I cut her up. I just shoved the knife in and started to cut. That's all…I had no sensation while cutting her up."

The prosecution rested their case at 11:00 a.m. the following day. Defense attorney Anderson waived his right to an opening statement, saying that he intended to prove by psychiatric testimony that his client was insane when he attacked McCaskie. To support this claim, he called to the witness stand Dr. David Wilson, a lawyer, psychiatrist and professor at the University of California Medical Center in San Francisco. Dr. Wilson had spent a total of four hours examining Thomas Bean at the Washoe County Jail.

Wilson said Bean told him he had guilty feelings about a longstanding sexual aberration (to commit a rape), which manifested itself during his teenage years with his theft of women's undergarments. While prowling the Yori Avenue neighborhood, a freshly laundered white slip on Sonja's clothesline "led him to her." The psychiatrist further stated that "Roy Bean's association with a woman other than Thomas's mother," drove him from his home that night filled with rage.

All this, coupled with "other psychological problems and a combination of precipitous circumstances," resulted in the murder of the twenty-four-year-old McCaskie. "Somewhere in the evening he went over the bounds of control," the psychiatrist stated, "probably when he entered the house or sometime after…it was almost as if he was acting out a part."

Under cross-examination by DA Raggio, Dr. Wilson reluctantly agreed with Bill's assertion that at all times during his presence in Sonja's home, Bean was aware of what he was doing, could perceive what he was seeing and doing, and knew it was wrong, in the sense that it was against the law.

On July 3, the prosecution called two psychiatrists as rebuttal witnesses, Dr. Rudolph Toller, who Bill used frequently in such cases, and Dr. William Rapaport, a psychiatrist and superintendent of Agnew State Hospital in San Jose, California.

Dr. Rapaport testified that Thomas Bean had a plan to commit rape when he left home the evening of April 4 and was suitably armed with a garrote and a knife. "I cannot make a diagnosis of mental illness," Dr. Rapaport said, "but I can forecast that if he does become mentally ill it will be a form of schizophrenia…probably paranoid." Dr. Rapaport further told the jury that Bean was not psychotic at the time of the slaying and "nothing precluded him from knowing right from wrong." He said Bean had the capacity to plan the rape and slaying, and had already established a pattern of violence in his life.

In closing, Bill called to the witness stand seventeen-year-old Patsy Willis, who testified she had three dates with Bean between the time he killed McCaskie and the time of his arrest. During that period, he acted "respectfully" to her, did not appear agitated and discussed news reports of the McCaskie killing in a manner that did not suggest to her that he might be involved.

On July 8, defense attorney Anderson presented his final argument. Leaning on the judge's bench, he told the jury that his client "is facing the death penalty before he knows what life is…Every human being has the need to be wanted, and needed, and loved…We have to place him in an institution where he can be studied, otherwise how can we care for, or cure, his problem?" Andersen concluded by saying, "I ask you to return a verdict of not guilty and send this boy to his proper place."

District Attorney Raggio's final argument lasted two hours. He called the plea of insanity "a last ditch defense," and said it never fails that in cases of this type that "everyone but the defendant is on trial…society, his schoolmates, his father, the jury…Everyone is wrong but Thomas Lee Bean…Even Dr. Rapaport and Dr. Toller, witnesses for the state, are on trial." Calling Anderson's plea "a cowardly defense," Bill explained, "The act of hostility does not excuse him. It is a case where he did not use restraint, and this jury is not going to say if you are mad or angry, we will acquit you."

At one point in the summation, Bean commented aloud, causing Bill to wheel about and ask the defendant if he wanted to make a statement. "No sir, go right ahead," Bean replied.

"The mortal remains of Sonja McCaskie cling to this knife," said Bill, pointing to one of the knives removed from her body. "Rarely do I stand before a jury and say capital punishment is needed, but you know what the proper verdict is. You have choices…Only by one of them, can you look each other, and society, and the world, in the eye and say that this will never happen again."

The jury agreed, finding Thomas Lee Bean guilty of murder in the first degree. The verdict was rendered in just seventy-five minutes, believed to be the shortest length of a jury deliberation calling for the death penalty in the annals of Washoe County history.

As the jury foreperson delivered the verdict, Bean listened in the same detached manner he had manifested throughout the trial; a faint, sardonic smile creasing the corners of his mouth. When the jurors then filed from the jury box, Bean pushed his chair back slightly to face them. "Thanks," he muttered sarcastically.

On July 22, 1963, Judge Bowen sentenced Thomas Lee Bean to be executed. Prior to the sentencing, defense attorney Harry Anderson asked the court for a new trial, contending, among things, that the district attorney had used color photographs of the victim's dismembered body, instead of the more traditional black-and-white. Raggio responded with open distain: "Sonja McCaskie did not bleed in black-and-white." The motion was denied.

Anderson filed an appeal to the Nevada Supreme Court. Though he would die of a rare kidney disease the following January, other attorneys would carry Thomas Bean's case over a long series of appeals and federal writs, similar to, and simultaneous with, those of convicted murderer-rapist Lester Morford.

Bill Raggio would remain busy over the next eight years, personally handling most of the legal work in responding to these appeals, often at his own cost, in a frustrating and eventually futile effort to have Bean's sentence carried out.*

---

*Because of the Supreme Court ruling in *Furman v. Georgia*, Thomas Lee Bean was spared execution and continues to serve out a sentence of life imprisonment, without the possibility of parole.

CHAPTER TWENTY-SIX

# Raggio's Raiders

Under Bill's stewardship, the office of the district attorney expanded and became more efficient. He brought in the best and brightest assistants, who quickly learned from his example and became strong and accomplished members of the legal community. They soon labeled themselves "Raggio's Raiders."

All went on to successful careers. Several, such as Emile Gezelin, Jack Mathews, John Gabrielli and Larry Hicks became judges. Their experiences as young prosecutors would be remembered with fondness and gratitude throughout their lives, and were expressed by many at a "Raggio Raider's" reunion on July 12, 2008. Federal District Court Judge Larry Hicks recalled the early days:

> We all worked well together and had a great time in the DA's Office because of Bill Raggio. His great ethic flowed down from the top and created a model and an example for every one of us to take pride in. It shaped not only our professional careers, but our lives.

Larry Hicks first came to the Washoe County District Attorney's Office as a clerk in his second year of law school. Bill Raggio immediately assigned him to do the research and prepare the brief for a Nevada Supreme Court appeal of a death penalty conviction.

The offender, Pierce Spillers, while incarcerated in a prison north of Reno in 1966, escaped and broke into a nearby home, raping a woman who lived there. Spillers was subsequently tracked down by bloodhounds who trailed him from the house into the hills.

Raggio personally tried the case, even bringing a bloodhound and handler into court as demonstrative evidence. The victim identified Spillers as her assailant and he was found guilty. What created the controversy was that under Nevada law at the time, forcible rape was a capital crime. Bill's compelling argument convinced the jury that such punishment was warranted, and Spillers was given the maximum sentence. The verdict touched off an outcry of public disapproval by those, in and out of Nevada, who opposed the death penalty under any circumstances.*

Having prepared the brief, Hicks was asked by Bill to accompany him when he argued the appeal before the court. Bill asked him a few questions about the brief while they drove from Reno to Carson City.

"Then I watched him walk into the Supreme Court and argue a case that was so far above anything I had briefed him," Judge Hicks remembered. " I still, today, can only marvel at his insights into the law and his ability to argue and present the law. It was obvious that the Nevada Supreme Court justices all had this incredible respect for Bill Raggio."

Some in the legal community were skeptical of all the young assistant district attorneys Bill was hiring. Among them was Washoe County District Court Judge Grant Bowen. Judge Bowen, who heard the majority of cases presented by these eager assistants, jokingly called the DA's Office "Boy's Town." However, he came to respect their work ethic and knowledge. Bill remembered that transition, later saying:

> Soon, Judge Bowen would say things like 'You are not doing a bad job.' He thought we had a lot to learn. I grew to admire and respect him and even had a spittoon with his name on it placed in my office so he would stop spitting tobacco juice in to my plants when he came to visit.

---

*The outcry was amplified by those who felt the verdict was racially motivated; Spillers was black and his victim was not.

Larry Hicks added: "When you went into court with Bill Raggio's name on the pleading, you had a presumption of professionalism and of doing things correctly and effectively. If you fouled up, as some of us did, Bill would straighten us out—but with respect."

Judge Bowen's reference to the DA's Office as "Boy's Town" was not technically correct. In 1969, Bill hired young attorney Kathleen Wahl as the first female deputy district attorney not only in Washoe County, but in the State of Nevada.

"I believed that we should get the best people possible," he later said, "and we were a success because we did have the best people possible. I prided myself on the fact that I never asked anyone who I appointed to a position what his or her politics were."

Kathleen would agree, saying at the reunion: "Bill has always been a man of great integrity. Though I am a "yellow dog Democrat,* I would not only vote for Bill Raggio, I would campaign for him if he needed it."

Also at the Raiders reunion was Robert Barengo, former Speaker of the Nevada State Assembly, who related how, shortly after Bill hired him, he was given a traffic case to try before Judge Thomas O. Craven. While Barengo nervously sat in court waiting his turn, Raggio came in and sat down next to him.

"Do you know what you are doing?" Bill asked.

"Yes," Barengo replied, "I have a script."

Bill asked to see it, and after Barengo handed it to him, Bill got up and walked out of the courtroom with it—leaving the new deputy DA on his own. "Bill waited for me outside," Barengo said, "and told me 'No one who works in my office needs a script. You must be prepared.'"

Former Assistant DA Fred Pinkerton was in awe of his boss, telling of how Raggio once had to decide whether to go to trial against the son of a very prominent person in Reno.

"Bill came into my little cubbyhole of an office," Fred recalled, "and

---

*The expression arose from the notion that loyal Southern Democrats in the late-19th and early-20th centuries would vote for a "yellow dog before voting for a Republican." The term is now often used to describe any Democrat who will vote the party ticket under almost any circumstance.

said, 'I understand we have filed on Mr. [name withheld]. Do we have a case?' I replied that we had a solid case. Bill replied, 'Fine, go through with it.' I know Bill received a lot of heat from the community about that, but I will always remember his loyalty for backing me up and for his doing the right thing."* Rick Ahlswede, who in 1960 was Bill's deputy district attorney, had been nicknamed "The Noose" because of his energetic pursuit of death penalty verdicts. Far from being offended by the moniker, Ahlswede relished it, keeping a hangman's noose suspended from the ceiling in his office, as well as a working model of a guillotine on his desk.

The dark office joke was that he would seek the death penalty "on any case." However, as Larry Hicks later remarked, "Rick offered us trial skills and basic lessons on how to try a case and do it professionally. We all appreciated him very much."

Ahlswede recalled that after staff meetings, some of them would go out and hit a few bars, often in the seamier establishments along Commercial Row. "Bill had a strict rule about dress," Ahlswede said. "He wore a double-breasted trench coat the rest of us wore single-breasted trench coats, to show our subordinate rank."

The attire identified them as Raggio's Raiders and so most of the patrons would quickly vanish when they arrived. "The bartenders would typically pour us complimentary drinks," Rick added, "but while doing so say, 'These are on-the-house, but could you please drink up and leave—you're wrecking my business!'"

That double-breasted trench coat, bloodstained from visits to numerous crime scenes, became Bill Raggio's trademark. In April 1965, *Las Vegas Review Journal* columnist Jude Wanniski* followed Bill around for several days and wrote an article entitled, "Dick Tracy, Sam Spade Equals Reno's Mr. Raggio." In it, Wanniski stated that Bill Raggio was among the most colorful public figures in Nevada:

---

*The "heat" Bill received was because members of the prominent family felt the son should have been treated deferentially due to their social status in the community.

He may not be gubernatorial material, as many Republicans believe, but there's no doubt that he could adequately fill the bill if Hollywood ever wants to remake the Sam Spade movies. He wears a white, belted trench coat with traces of blood stains here and there which seemed a bit artificial until it became apparent that he's earned the trench coat.[1]

As the two men were driving through downtown Reno, a call came over the police radio in Bill's car reporting a shooting near the university. Raggio turned on the red lights and siren and raced to the scene. There about thirty young black men were angrily milling around the body of a friend who lay dead on the sidewalk in a pool of blood, a rifle by his side. A lone motorcycle police officer stood nearby, reluctant to approach the group until reinforcements arrived.

Wanniski then observed:

Raggio marched right into the crowd asking questions at random, rather than barking orders. He grabbed a rifle away from one screaming youth and when the boy tried to get it back, Raggio spun him away with such force that the boy, taller than Raggio, and about 200 pounds, skidded to the street. Soon three squad cars of police showed up and set about breaking up the crowd by force. Raggio quickly motioned them away and in the next seconds brought the shouting to a halt by walking into the middle of the group, quietly asking questions…He then asked the group if they'd mind driving down to the jail in their own cars to "help us get to the bottom of all this."

Every one of them not only agreed, but actually showed up at the police station within the next fifteen minutes. When he got

---

*Jude Wanniski later became associate editor of *The Wall Street Journal* from 1972 to 1978. As an advisor to President Ronald Reagan in 1976, Wanniski coined the term "supply-side economics" and was later called by Congressman Jack Kemp "the Thomas Paine of the Reagan Revolution."

back to his car his wife Dorothy looked up at him and said, "Oh Bill, you've got some more blood on your coat."

When asked years later about his signature blood-spattered trench coat, Bill spoke of how ironic his choice of profession turned out to be, saying that from an early age, his parents encouraged him to become a doctor.

> I probably would have, but I could not stand the sight of blood. I would almost faint if I saw someone with even a nosebleed. So I decided against it. Ironically, I ended up pursuing a profession which took me to countless accidents, suicides and homicides, with mangled bodies, dismemberments and decapitations—some of the most gruesome scenes imaginable. I occasionally wondered if I should have practiced medicine instead.

Before Wanniski returned to Las Vegas to submit his story about the "Sam Spade" of Nevada, Bill showed him around his office. Wanniski wrote:

> His offices in the new Reno courthouse are more spacious and polished than any other public offices in the state, including those in the Capitol. Asked if the voters resent this, he twinkles: "Heck no, the voters like to see me working in style."

Such an engaging personality and quick wit draws people in, and Bill Raggio was no exception. By the mid-1960s, he had already acquired a broad array of admirers, from the average working guy to the most famous and powerful people in the country.

# CHAPTER TWENTY-SEVEN

# "Everybody Seemed to Know Him"

B ill brought everyone into the fold," said his former protégé Judge Larry Hicks in 2008. Kathleen Thompson, *née* Wahl, elaborated:

> Everybody seemed to know him. I once went with Bill to San Francisco "to carry his briefcase" while he argued a case before the Ninth Circuit Court of Appeals. After the hearing, Bill took me down to the financial district to a famous restaurant called Jack's. As he walked along Montgomery Street, every other person we passed was saying, "Hey, Bill!"—and he knew everybody's name back!

Thompson would be even more astonished after the two were seated in the restaurant:

> I noticed one of the arriving diners was [world-renowned ballet performer] Rudolph Nureyev, who entered wearing a floor-length mink coat. Nureyev was seated elsewhere in the restaurant. A short time later, a waiter came to our table and said, "Mr. Raggio, Mr. Nureyev would like to meet you." Bill went over and spent some time with Rudolf Nureyev and his guests at their table.

Bill admitted to being well known. Largely through Hal Lipset, he met a great many people in San Francisco and became good friends with attorneys like Jake Ehrlich* and Melvin Belli.*

He was invited to participate in a regularly recurring luncheon with San Francisco's "movers and shakers." In addition to Lipset, Ehrlich and Belli, the attendees included attorneys Marvin Lewis, James Martin McGinness and Nathan Cohn, and retail giants John Livingston, who owned Livingston's department store, and Cyril Magnin owner of I. Magnin's. In addition to a variety of judges and politicians, the group included real estate developers like Lou Lurie and Ben Swig. "I was the only 'outsider' invited in," Bill later said.

The luncheon members became close and their humor sometimes outrageous. When Jake Ehrlich was invited to speak to a Nevada State Bar Association luncheon at the Dunes Hotel in Las Vegas, Bill picked him up at the airport and drove him to the venue. The auditorium in the hotel was filled to capacity.

Bill later recalled that because he was introducing him, Erlich gave Bill his speech and asked that he put it up on the podium for him.

"When I looked over the text of his speech, I saw that it was going to be a long, dry lecture about civil jurisprudence," Bill said, "so I took the speech out of the folder and replaced it with a copy of *Playboy* magazine. After my enormously laudatory introduction about what a great orator and defense attorney he was, Jake stepped up to the podium, opened the folder and saw only the magazine. Without batting an eye, he gave a brilliant extemporaneous speech about notable events in his career. Every-

---

*Jake Ehrlich had a forty-year career as a defense and divorce attorney. He authored a dozen books, including his memoir, which became the model for the television lawyer Perry Mason. Erlich's clients included celebrities, actors, writers, directors, musicians, sports figures, industrialists, madams, murderers, bigamists and petty crooks.

*Melvin Belli, who won over $600 million in judgments during his legal career, was known by admirers as "The King of Torts." His detractors, however, referred to him as "Melvin Bellicose," which he encouraged by raising a Jolly Roger flag over his Montgomery Street office building to proclaim a successful verdict, and then firing a cannon mounted on his office roof to announce the victory party that was about to commence. Belli represented numerous celebrities and high profile clients, including Jack Ruby for the murder of Lee Harvey Oswald. He was the author of several books on courtroom procedure.

one enjoyed it; but I think Jake remained half-angry at me for the rest of his life."

Long-time friend, Paul Lowden, attributes Bill's great success in life to the fact that "he doesn't take himself too seriously." Paul relishes Bill's "routines," and never tires of them.

"At a restaurant when the wine is being served," Lowden said, "Bill will often pretend to choke upon taking the first sip. After a few moments of Bill dramatically trying to regain his breath, he will then point to the glass, look up at the sommelier and gasp, 'This is very good!'" Lowden recalls that at other times, Bill would ask the server how much a dessert cost, and then order "fifty cents" worth.

Occasionally, Bill's sense of humor would create problems, as his good friend Las Vegas District Court Judge Charles Thompson vividly recalled in 2009. He and Bill had once visited the ruins of Machu Picchu in Peru. While waiting in the Lima airport for their flight back to the U.S., Bill informed Thompson that he was out of money and so Charles loaned him $75 in cash.

"About two months later," Judge Thompson recalled, "Bill walked into my chambers with his checkbook and commenced to sit down and write a check for $75. Because of his reputation, I was delighted to be reimbursed. However, in the lower left-hand corner of the check, Bill wrote the word 'bribe'. He thought I would not cash it because of that, but I needed the money and so I did."

Several years later, the Gaming Control Board was examining Bill for his position on the board of the Archon Corporation and found the check. Agents questioned Bill about it, to which he replied, "If that $75 were an actual bribe, then I paid off a mighty cheap judge."

Bill then asked the agents if they would, as part of the joke, go to Las Vegas, show the judge the check and read him his Miranda rights.

"They prudently declined," Thompson quipped.

One of Bill's favorite gags involves the kissing of a person's hand. Upon first seeing the intended "victim," he will theatrically approach so as to draw as much attention as possible. Then, in the case of a woman, gallantly raise the hand slowly to his lips and at the last moment, gently rotate his grasp and kiss the back of his own. With a man, Bill will initiate the traditional Old World gesture of respect and homage by kissing the person's ring, and, with the same rotating movement, peck his own.

The most famous "Raggioism" involves his asking an unsuspecting passerby if they have a $20 bill. Most would hear that as a request for money, rather than mere curiosity, which Bill insists it to be. The person questioned invariably hands over a twenty, which Bill accepts as a random act of generosity, slips into his pocket—and then walks away.

As this routine became better known, Raggio was forced to improvise. After becoming a state senator, he rarely missed an orientation meeting for new legislators, where those wearing purple badges, which identified one as newly elected lawmaker, were fair game.

Don Carano,* a long-time friend, found that, even after decades, the $20 bill mystique was too tempting to pass up. At a wedding in Santa Barbara in 2007, Don, Bill and Skip Avansino were at a restaurant, when Bill, always looking for a good deal, offered Don $20 for three bottles of his Siena wine (normally $25 per bottle). "We're Genovesi," Carano would say in a 2010 interview, "traditionally known to be tight with a buck. So I told Bill I would sell him the wine for his price if he would sign the $20 bill."

Don knew how rare an event it was when it was Bill parting with a $20 bill. "Bill signed it," said Carano, "and I now have it on a wall in the winery. Bill thought he got a good deal on the wine, but I think that twenty is going to worth a million dollars."[1]

Reporter Jude Wanniski not only marveled at Bill's wit, but his ability to remember the name of nearly every person he ever met:

---

*Don Carano specialized in business and gaming law before he established the Eldorado Hotel and Casino in 1973 on the site of the family's bakery in Reno. Today, the hotel has 817 guest rooms, ten restaurants, a casino, conference center and showroom. The Carano family is also partners with Circus Circus Enterprises in the Silver Legacy Resort Casino. Don and wife, Rhonda, own and operate the Ferrari-Carano Vineyards and Winery in Napa Valley.

In Reno, it's virtually impossible to sit and talk to him for ten minutes without interruption. In restaurants, the cook comes out of the kitchen to say hello to him. On the street, the truck drivers honk at him; cabbies slow down, yell and wave to him.

A hotel porter is sifting cigarette butts out of a wall sandbox, Raggio, walking by, hails him: "Freddie you find any gold yet?" and the porter turns around and grins.

Wanniski then described what happened when Bill walked into the Sands Hotel/Casino for a speech to the Las Vegas Kiwanis Club:

They almost shut down the casino for ten minutes while the bellhops, cocktail waitresses, pit bosses and owners jumped up to greet him. He knows everyone's name and razzes them all, asks the bellhops if they're "men enough to carry that blonde out of my room," rushes up to showroom Maitre d' Nick Kelly at five minutes before show time and asks if he can seat a party of twenty; introduces a casino owner as "too cheap to buy a drink"; asks a pit boss "which one is the honest dealer?" But all so obviously and lightheartedly tongue in cheek that he leaves behind him nothing but wide grins.[2]

# CHAPTER TWENTY-EIGHT

# Ol' Blue Eyes

During the late 1950s and early 1960s, before Las Vegas became the nation's entertainment capital, Reno hosted a large number of "big name" entertainers. Since its opening in late 1947, The Sky Top Room at the Mapes Hotel featured the likes of Frank Sinatra, Jimmy Durante and Milton Berle.

As the top law enforcement figure in the county, stylish and outgoing Bill Raggio soon found himself rubbing elbows with many of the nation's foremost celebrities.

"Whenever Sonny King and Jimmy Durante were performing in town," Bill recalls, "they would set aside one night to come over to our house on Robin Street for dinner. Vido Musso, a great saxophonist, would sometimes come with them. Vido would cook Italian food and end up using every pot and pan in the kitchen—making a complete mess— while Jimmy would play with my kids. Dottie had a wonderful time singing with Durante and Sonny King around her little piano."

In July 1960, the Cal-Neva Lodge at Crystal Bay, Nevada,* on the north shore of Lake Tahoe, became an even bigger celebrity attraction

---

*Since its opening in 1928, the Cal-Neva (so-named because the California-Nevada state line literally runs through the building) was managed by a succession of groups. By the 1940s, Elmer "Bones" Remmer, who was later mentioned as a mob associate of the San Francisco-based Lanza crime family during the Kefauver hearings, operated the casino. He was forced to sell in 1949, due to a large federal tax debt he had incurred. By March 1955, the Cal-Neva was being operated by a group of investors headed by Bert "Wingy" Grober. Grober had been in the hotel and restaurant business for many years, running the successful Park Avenue Steakhouse in Miami Beach. His liquor and meat supplier during that time was Joseph P. Kennedy and the two became lifelong friends.

than the Mapes. Frank Sinatra, Dean Martin[1] and two of Frank's business associates, Paul "Skinny" D'Amato and Hank Sincola, were approved for a gaming license and had purchased the lodge.

They then began a major remodeling, which included a larger entertainment venue called the Celebrity Showroom. The lodge's new eleven cottages and fifty-five hotel rooms were in high demand.

In the summer of 1961, it seemed like all of Hollywood had arrived. Mickey Rooney, the Andrews Sisters, the Modernaires, Dick Shawn, Vic Damone, Joe E. Lewis, Eddie Fisher, Juliet Prowse, Buddy Greco, Louis Prima and Keely Smith all performed in a single ten-week period.

Sinatra, Dean Martin and others, including Marilyn Monroe, would often go on stage to "sing for their supper." There was nothing quite like it in the country, perhaps in the world. As A.W. Moe stated in his book, *Nevada's Golden Age of Gambling*: "No one had more friends or power in the early 1960s than Ol' Blue Eyes. It seemed everyone wanted to visit the Cal-Neva Lodge."[2] Bill and Dorothy Raggio were no exception.

Bill recalled one evening in particular when he and Dottie went to the Cal-Neva Lodge for dinner and his good friend Sonny King introduced them to Frank Sinatra. Sonny, who performed around the country as the sidekick of the great Jimmy Durante, was also a popular lounge singer in Nevada and performed regularly at the Cal-Neva. Although, not technically a member of the famous Rat Pack,* Sonny was close to Frank and the others.

Bill continued:

> In addition to Frank being interested in meeting me because I was the district attorney of the county in which his business was operating, he had also heard about Joe Conforte and how I had helped put his Triangle Ranch brothel to the torch.

---

*The Rat Pack featured entertainers like Frank Sinatra, Dean Martin, Sammy Davis, Jr., Peter Lawford and Joey Bishop, who appeared together on stage in films in the early 1960s. They regularly performed in Las Vegas and their musical routines and zany comedy bits, many of which were ad-libbed, were instrumental in the rapid rise of Las Vegas as a popular entertainment destination.

Frank was clearly proud that, as a fellow Italian-American, I had, in his words, "Taken on a pompous, loudmouth like Conforte," and had successfully prosecuted him for his attempt to ruin my reputation through extortion. Frank apparently took a liking to me and whenever Dottie and I visited the Cal-Neva Lodge, he was a very gracious host.

During his contentious 1962 race for reelection against Conforte-supported opponent, Rick Breitwieser, Bill received a telephone call from Sinatra. "My secretary rushed into my office and excitedly said that Frank Sinatra is on the phone," Bill later said. "I picked up and he said, 'Hi Bill, this is Frank. I understand you're running for reelection and I would like to help you in your campaign.'"

Frank requested that Bill have some campaign scripts prepared and meet him in Los Angeles the following Friday. Bill asked his friend Harry Spencer to compose the requested material and join him on his trip. The two men arrived in Los Angeles about 5:00 pm and were met at the airport by three men in a limousine. One was noted film producer-director Howard W. Koch, who immediately passed along Sinatra's regrets that some medical testing had prevented him from personally picking them up.

Bill thought the limousine was there to take him to a small recording studio and so was amazed when they soon drove through the famous main portal of Paramount Studios.

"We arrived at Frank Sinatra's dressing room, which was actually a large, elegant bungalow," Bill said. "Several people were waiting. One took our scripts and began loading them onto a teleprompter, while I was taken to a makeup artist. I was now a bit embarrassed at all the attention."

Bill and Harry were then led outside and down the street to a large sound studio. The two men soon realized they were on the set of the film *Come Blow Your Horn*. To Bill's continuing amazement, the crew had designed an exact replica of the district attorney's office in Reno, down to the slightest detail.

"I was mortified that all these people were on hold waiting for me to show up to do these commercials," Bill would later say. "Howard Koch was producing *Come Blow Your Horn* and Harry and I were given chairs next to the director, Bud Yorkin. I was then called up to do several commercials. It was the first time I had ever seen a teleprompter. Later, when the tapes were delivered to local TV stations in Reno, they were astounded by the quality."

Several months later, Bill reciprocated Frank's generosity by inviting him to dinner at his home. Sinatra accepted, and one Sunday afternoon drove down to Reno from Lake Tahoe with his entourage of seven or eight people, including Skinny D'Amato and recording artist Buddy Greco, who was then appearing at the Cal-Neva Lodge. Bill barbecued and his mother Clara made pasta. Dottie took care of the rest.

Because her mom and dad entertained frequently, often having show business celebrities come to the house, young Leslie Raggio later remembered that it did not seem like "such a big deal" to her at the time. Yet Leslie admitted that something was more unusual about that particular Sunday evening, because so many of the neighbors were crowding in front of the house, or excitedly peering over the backyard fence at Mr. Sinatra.

Despite Frank's "bad boy" image in the press, he could be incredibly considerate to those he liked—Bill Raggio was one of those people. When Bill and Dottie were in Manhattan, they would always get by Jilly's on 52nd Street. This famous restaurant and bar was owned by Frank's best friend and bodyguard, Jilly Rizzo. "We were treated like one of the family," Bill recalled. When in midtown, they would go to Patsy's, a well-known Italian restaurant in the Theater District. There, owner and chef Pasquale "Patsy" Scognamillo "would always cook something special for us."

Jack Entratter, who then owned the Copacabana in New York City, always made sure the couple had a great table. Entratter had been responsible for helping start the careers of numerous entertainers such as

Dean Martin and Jerry Lewis, Johnny Ray and Frankie Laine. Later, as head of the Sands, he would help make Las Vegas the "Entertainment Capital of the World."

On one occasion, Sinatra arranged for Bill to attend a game at Yankee Stadium with then-retired baseball legend Joe DiMaggio. When the Raggios traveled to London, Frank arranged to have the Malm agency provide tickets to the best shows.

Bill would later say,

> Frank was a very thoughtful guy. He remembered my children's birthdays and brought them gifts. He was a very affable person and I had a good relationship with him. From time to time, he would call me, and it was usually to ask me to help somebody out, never anything having to do with my position as DA. I remember one time there was an orchestra leader performing at the Sparks Nugget, whose name I now can't recall. The man was ill, and when Frank heard about it, he asked if I could arrange to have this fellow driven to the airport, so Frank's private plane could get him to a hospital in LA. I saw Frank in good times and bad times, and he was like anybody else. Some days he felt good and some days he did not.

Anthony Summers and Robyn Swan, authors of the book *Sinatra: A Life*, fundamentally agree with Bill's assessment of Sinatra's enigmatic behavior:

> Aside from his natural abilities, Sinatra the man defied easy classification. Undeniably promiscuous, violent and self-serving, he could also be tremendously compassionate, loyal and generous.[3]

* * *

Frank Sinatra's association with organized crime figures had been well documented in the news since at least 1947, when he accompanied brothers Joseph and Rocco Fischetti, Chicago gangsters and cousins of Al Capone, to a meeting in Havana to pay their respects to Charles "Lucky" Luciano. Luciano, who could no longer enter the United States due to his deportation back to Italy the previous year, was undisputed leader of what was called "The Commission," thought to be a formal judicial body presiding over disputes among the nation's crime families.

Bill knew his friendship with Sinatra raised some eyebrows, but he believed much of what was said about Frank was not based on fact. "Most was gossip," Raggio said.

Some have pointed out that Sinatra must have known about these nefarious activities and thus was, to some degree, complicit in mob violence and crimes. It is difficult, however, for those who knew him well, or were helped by his generosity, to associate that proposition with the compassionate side of his nature.

While Frank's combative relationship with the press made him a highly visible target for such accusations, he was certainly not the only major entertainment figure with mob associations. By the 1950s, criminal elements controlled nightclubs, jukebox concessions and almost every facet of the music industry and, at various times, the film industry.

In 2003, Sonny King cut to the essence of the problem confronting entertainers: "If they [the mobsters] liked you, you worked all the time. They dictated what you were paid. If they didn't like you, you just didn't work."[4]

Sinatra later admitted that he knew members of organized crime:

> I spent a lot of time in saloons—and saloons are not run by the Christian Brothers. There were a lot of guys around and they came out of Prohibition, and they ran pretty good saloons. I was a kid. I worked in the places that were open. They paid you, and the checks didn't bounce. I didn't meet any Nobel Prize winners in saloons. But if Francis of Assisi was a singer and worked in saloons, he would've met the same guys.[5]

On more than one occasion, Sinatra publicly stated that he would not be disloyal to the people who gave him opportunities, especially early in his career. It would be largely out of this sense of "loyalty" that in the summer of 1963, Sinatra's world would be shaken because of his association with Chicago crime boss Sam Giancana.

Giancana, who was rumored to have been a driver at the 1929 St. Valentine's Day Massacre, spent much of his early life in prison. In all, he would be arrested over seventy times, three of those for murder. By the late 1950s, the ruthless Giancana had risen to the top of the Chicago mob and would, according to FBI records, eventually control an international crime empire which included interests in the Riviera, Sands and Desert Inn hotels in Las Vegas.

Giancana enjoyed the company of entertainers, and Frank Sinatra, the biggest name in the industry, soon became his favorite. The powerful and much-feared mobster often called upon Frank to give command performances. Though never proven, there were persistent rumors that Sinatra acted as a "front" for Giancana's ownership of the Cal-Neva Lodge. Such hidden ownership would have been necessary, because Giancana's name was included in Nevada's *Black Book*.

At the time of its inception in 1960, the *Black Book* (it actually had a silver-colored cover) was a list maintained by the Nevada State Gaming Control Board of eleven men who were not allowed into any Nevada gambling establishment because of "notorious and unsavory reputation which would adversely affect public confidence and trust in the gaming industry."

According to state law, Giancana could not even set foot in a casino— let alone own one. The Cal-Neva Lodge, with its unique location, half in California and half in Nevada, was perfect for his purposes. Here, he could visit the club regularly and, if questioned, say that he always stayed on the California side. This fine distinction worked for a while, and Giancana's presence on the property was never much of a secret, as columnist Herb Caen would write:

I saw Sinatra at the Cal-Neva when Sam Giancana was there. In
fact, I met Giancana through Frank. He was a typical hood, didn't
say much. He wore a hat at the Lake, and sat in his little bungalow,
receiving people.[6]

Things began to unravel one evening in July 1963, during a singing
engagement at the Cal-Neva by the McGuire Sisters. Victor LaCroix-
Collins, the road manager for the group, got into an argument with
Phyllis McGuire, who was Sam Giancana's mistress. Giancana, not
liking his tone, assaulted LaCroix-Collins. Frank Sinatra jumped in to
pull Giancana off and the brawl continued for several minutes. Undercover FBI agents who had Phyllis's bungalow under surveillance, witnessed the fight and informed the Nevada State Gaming Control Board.

An investigation was begun and subpoenas were issued. The Gaming
Control Board was careful not to announce it publicly. Sinatra's presence
in Nevada was very good for the tourist industry and, consequently, the
economy. Oddly, many tourists were drawn to Nevada, particularly Las
Vegas, by the aura of mobsters, who Frank publicly referred to as "The
Boys," and which evidently magnified these visitors' fantasies of the
town's illicitness. As such, the state was willing to handle this situation
in such a way that saved him, and the gaming industry, embarrassment.

Before the Gaming Control Board had completed their confidential
investigation of the incident, the *Chicago Sun Times* got wind of the
story through an anonymous source and published it. Wire services all
over the country immediately picked it up.

Believing the Gaming Control Board had fed the story to the press,
Sinatra was furious. At about 4:00 p.m. on August 30, 1963, he called
the chair of the Gaming Control Board, Ed Olsen, a forty-four-year-old
former wire service reporter. Sinatra insisted Ed come to the Cal-Neva
for dinner so they could discuss the problem.

Olsen replied that it would be unseemly for him to be on the premises
while the investigation was ongoing. He suggested Sinatra come to his
office in Carson City, after business hours, to avoid the press. The pro-

posal seemed to enrage Frank further, According to Olsen, Sinatra became more "menacing" and made a series of vague expletive-laced threats. Olsen described what occurred next in a memorandum:

> He [Sinatra] noted that he had other enterprises from which he makes his living, that the Cal-Neva is only incidental to his welfare but is important to the livelihoods of many "little people." I suggested it might be better for all concerned if he concentrated on his enterprises elsewhere and departed the Nevada gambling scene. He replied, "I might just do that…and when I do, I'm going tell the world what a bunch of f*****g idiots run things in the state.[7]

At 6:00 p.m. that day, two agents from the State Gaming Control Board, unaware of the Sinatra-Olsen telephone call two hours earlier, arrived at the Cal-Neva Lodge on a routine visit to watch the table count. When he saw the agents enter, Sinatra, still fuming from his conversation with Olsen, shouted across the casino to Skinny D'Amato, to "throw the dirty son-of-a-bitches out!"

D'Amato instead slipped two $100 bills into the crook of one of the agent's arms. When the agent asked if it were a bribe, D'Amato replied that it was merely a gift to thank them for coming to work over the Labor Day holiday weekend.

Bill Raggio later recalled that he was not directly involved in the problem. "I called Ed Olsen to inquire about the alleged incident at the Cal-Neva Lodge because it occurred in Washoe County," Bill later said. "It had nothing to do with my friendship with Frank. Mr. Olsen said, 'Bill, don't get involved in this, it is something we have to deal with,' meaning the Gaming Control Board had jurisdiction."

The bribe attempt, coupled with Sinatra's earlier intemperate remarks on the phone to Ed Olsen, forced the board to take strong and immediate action. Frank was subsequently ordered to explain himself and defend his actions before a meeting of the Gaming Control Board. Rather than dealing further with the board, Sinatra chose to surrender his gaming license and sell his shares in both the Cal-Nevada Lodge and the Sands Hotel/Casino in Las Vegas.

Nevada Governor Grant Sawyer stood behind the Gaming Control Board's decision and in his memoir, *Hang Tough!*, recalled a strange inquiry about the incident from no less than the President of the United States. On September 28, 1963, less than two months before his assassination in Dallas, President John F. Kennedy made a ninety-minute stopover in Las Vegas to give a speech at the convention center.

Riding in an open limousine with him from the airport were U.S. Senators Howard Cannon and Alan Bible, Congressman Walter Baring and Governor Sawyer. Kennedy turned to Sawyer and said, "What are you guys doing to my friend, Frank Sinatra?"

The Nevada Gaming Control Board investigation of Sinatra was still ongoing, and so Sawyer replied, "Well Mr. President, I'll try to care for things in Nevada, and I wish you luck on the national level." This polite way of telling the president to mind his own business, caused Kennedy to laugh aloud. Nothing more was mentioned.[8]

The governor later repeated to Ed Olsen what Kennedy had said. Olsen, was startled by the remark and replied, "That's about the highest degree of political pressure you could ever put into the thing."

Frank Sinatra, whose mother, Dolly, had been a Democratic Party ward boss in New Jersey for years, was an ardent supporter of John F. Kennedy's during his run for the presidency. Kennedy had been introduced to Frank in the late 1950s by actor Peter Lawford, a member of the Rat Pack, who was married to Kennedy's sister, Patricia.

After JFK won the presidential election in 1960, Frank was named director of entertainment for the inauguration festivities. Prior to this, Sinatra had introduced one of his girlfriend's, Judith Campbell, to Kennedy and the two began an affair that lasted for nearly three years. Sinatra also introduced Campbell to Sam Giancana, and soon the two men, president and mobster, were engaging in simultaneous affairs with the same woman.[9]

On February 27, 1962, FBI Director J. Edgar Hoover, who had learned of this connection, approached the president's brother, Attorney General Robert Kennedy, with the evidence. The president's relationship with Judith Campbell abruptly ended.

Robert Kennedy, who was in the midst of an intense campaign to prosecute mobsters, including Sam Giancana, cautioned the president to distance himself from Sinatra. At Robert's advice, President Kennedy changed plans he had already made to be a guest of Frank's at his home in Palm Springs, California in March 1962. Instead, the president chose to stay at Bing Crosby's home in the same town—though Crosby was a Republican. Frank was humiliated by the snub.

President Kennedy, though shunning Frank in public, remained cordial. It was during this time that the president visited Las Vegas and made the apparent attempt to pressure Governor Sawyer into dropping the case against him.

Public interest, however, continued to grow regarding the Cal-Neva Lodge incident, and it was, as Peter Lawford later said, "the end of old Frankie Boy as far as the [Kennedy] family was concerned."[10] On November 22, 1963, President John F. Kennedy was shot and killed while riding in a motorcade through Dallas.*

On Sunday December 8, 1963, just two weeks after the Kennedy assassination, Frank Sinatra, Jr., was kidnapped from Harrah's Lodge at South Lake Tahoe. The nineteen-year-old aspiring singer was abducted by two

---

*A lone gunman, Lee Harvey Oswald, was quickly apprehended, but was murdered two days later in the basement-parking garage of the Dallas Police Department. His killer, Jack Ruby, a Dallas strip club operator, had come to Dallas from Chicago where he had allegedly been involved in activities related to Sam Giancana's criminal enterprises in that city. Some, including G. Robert Blakey, a law professor and a foremost authority on the Racketeer Influenced and Corrupt Organization Act (RICO), speculated in his 1981 book, *The Plot to Kill the President,* that Giancana hoped, through his friendship with Sinatra, to influence President Kennedy into having the attorney general moderate his campaign against organized crime. However, once Frank became *persona non gratis* with the Kennedys, the mob's only recourse was assassination.

This theory was never proven, largely because Jack Ruby died without corroborating it. Sam Giancana was executed gangland style (seven shots to the head) in his Oak Park, Illinois home on June 19, 1975, the evening before he was to appear before a U.S. Senate committee investigating Mafia-CIA collusion in plots to assassinate Fidel Castro. Such plots, it was suggested, were in retaliation for Castro having nationalized numerous and lucrative mob-owned gaming establishments in Cuba.

men from a hotel room where he was eating dinner prior to his scheduled 10:00 p.m. performance that night with the Tommy Dorsey Orchestra.

In Reno, the Raggios were sitting down to a birthday dinner at the home of long-time family friend, Carl Giudici, when the phone rang.

Bill later recalled, "I received a call from Harry Claiborne who did legal work for Frank in Las Vegas. Harry said Frank's son, who had been performing at South Shore Lake Tahoe, had been kidnapped. He went on to say that Frank was coming up to Reno and asked that I meet him."

To avoid members of the news media waiting in the terminal building, Bill took Frank to a car waiting on the runaway apron. The two men then attempted to drive the sixty miles from Reno to Harrah's Lodge. Despite all the mountain passes being closed due a snowstorm, Bill attempted to make it over Spooner Summit on Highway 50. However, ice and deep snow prevented them from getting very far and, after Bill nearly spun off the winding, mountain road, he turned the car around and took Sinatra back to Reno.

There they set up headquarters in a three-room suite at the Mapes Hotel. "I suggested Frank set up his headquarters in Reno," Bill later said, "because he would need to deal with the FBI and other law enforcement people. I really had no jurisdiction over this, because the crime had occurred in Douglas County."

As the hours dragged on with no word from the kidnappers, Bill recalled how nervous Sinatra was. Frank's press agent, Jim Mahoney, expressed his concern that Sinatra was refusing to eat. As Bill later recalled, his mother Clara helped solve that problem: "My mother made some pasta and brought it to us. Frank had eaten her pasta before—liked it very much—and so he found this to be a nice surprise."

Offers of help, including airplanes, helicopters and mounted patrols came in from all over the world. Hundreds of messages of support arrived from political figures and entertainment celebrities. Sympathetic telephone calls were received, including one from Attorney General Robert Kennedy in Washington. Kennedy offered an all-out law enforcement effort. The multi-state manhunt eventually would employ twenty-six FBI agents, in addition to nearly 100 California and Nevada sheriff's deputies.

Bill sat with Frank over the next several days, waiting for the ransom demand, and would later say:

> Often it was just the two of us in the suite and so I really had the opportunity to get to know Frank and sound him out on many issues. Despite his lack of formal education, he was a very well informed man and could discuss almost any topic. One might think because he was a celebrity that he was only concerned in his own life, but he had a broad range of interests.
>
> We talked about his turbulent relationship with the press and the criticism he received for his often-acerbic treatment of reporters. I recall him once commenting to me, "You know, some days in my life I can't do anything without someone watching me every minute, from the moment I walk out the door. Some days I just don't feel good and so am naturally inclined not to be friendly."

On Monday, December 9, Sinatra received the first of seven phone calls with instructions from his son's abductors. To elude reporters, Frank used an unwatched basement exit in the Mapes and sped off to Ron's Gas Station in Carson City, thirty miles south of Reno. The awestruck attendant there told him, "Someone's been phoning you here. I thought it was a gag."

Another call sent Sinatra to a different gas station for more details regarding the ransom and release. That night Frank flew to Southern California to await at the home of his former wife, and Frank, Jr.'s, mother, Nancy, for further instructions.

Sinatra had offered the abductors $1 million if they would return his son safely. Inexplicably, the kidnappers said they only wanted $240,000. The ransom was dropped off at a specified location in West Los Angeles early on December 11, 1963. Two hours later, Frank, Jr., was released unharmed and arrived safely at his mother's home later that morning.

Less than a week later, the FBI announced the capture of three suspects.

The trio admitted to the crime and returned virtually all of the ransom money. They were subsequently sentenced to varying prison terms.

On December 28, 1963, a grateful Sinatra invited Bill Raggio and Harry Spencer to the Hollywood premiere of his latest film *Robin and the Seven Hoods*. Though they did not attend, Bill was not surprised by this gesture of Sinatra's gratitude. "During the subsequent years," he recalled, "Dottie and I would visit Las Vegas and often go to the Sands Hotel. We were always given a front table to watch the Rat Pack perform. Frank was very generous and always invited us to dinner after the show. It wasn't a close relationship, but it was a warm relationship."

Journalist Jude Wanniski later observed Bill's fondness for his friend Frank Sinatra in the décor of his office at the Washoe County Courthouse:

> He's probably the only law enforcement officer in the country who has on his office wall instead of a portrait of J. Edgar Hoover an autographed photo of Frank Sinatra, whom he has known for years. The Sinatra photo, the only one in his reception room, is there not to impress visitors; but to give them a chuckle and, more subtly, let them know all at once that he is what he is, no hypocrisy involved. Sinatra's a buddy even if the Gaming Control Board doesn't like him.[11]

Bill's portrait of Frank Sinatra hanging on the wall of the district attorney's office could be construed by some as an indication of his lack of professionalism, but nothing could have been further from the truth. In fact, Bill would spend his second term as DA raising the level of expertise and effectiveness of law enforcement in Washoe County to new heights and, in doing so, achieve extraordinary national recognition from his peers.

# CHAPTER TWENTY-NINE

# National District Attorneys Association

In January 1964, Bill Raggio celebrated his fifth anniversary as Washoe County District Attorney. He had weathered personal attacks on his character by the press and public and received challenges for his job from both outside and inside his own party. His detractors called him a "crusader" and suggested he was driven by aspirations to higher political office.

Bill disagreed, saying he did not have any political ambition or desire at that time other than being a good district attorney. "I had become very dedicated to making the district attorney's office more efficient," he later stated. "It was an era when professionalism in law enforcement was coming into its own."

To advance the goal of making the office more professional, Bill's predecessor, Jack Streeter, had helped found the National Association of County and Prosecuting Attorneys (NACPA).* Streeter would be the association's vice president from 1953-1955 and go on to become a Charter Member and Honorary Life Member of the NACPA.

As a deputy DA, Bill would attend association meetings with his boss, and immediately recognized the value of the organization in providing information on how to modernize.

---

*The organization's name was later changed to the National District Attorneys Association (NDAA).

Bill's genuine desire to make the office more successful in facing the legal challenges of his growing jurisdiction can be seen in his dedication to professional development. During this period, Bill was admitted to present cases before the U.S. District Court-Nevada, the Ninth Circuit Court of Appeals and the U.S. Supreme Court. He was also admitted as a Fellow of the American College of Trial Lawyers and served as secretary, and later president, of the Nevada State District Attorneys Association.

\* \* \*

Bill began serving as vice president of the 1,500-member National District Attorneys Association in 1961. The purpose of the organization was to acquaint prosecutors with new techniques in crime detection, keep them informed of current changes in law and evaluate proposed legislation. Its slogan was "Organized Law Enforcement vs. Organized Crime," and speakers in 1961 and 1962, respectively, included Virgil W. Peterson, head of the Chicago Crime Commission, and U.S. Attorney General Robert F. Kennedy.

Bill would proudly recall how well represented the association was, including all of the most prominent district attorneys from across the nation.\*

It was because of the talent and stature of such colleagues in the NDAA, that Bill Raggio was especially pleased when the organization named the thirty-nine-year-old Washoe County District Attorney "Outstanding Prosecutor of the United States for 1964."

Bill felt the award reflected the number of high profile court cases he had successfully prosecuted. All were widely publicized, with the Sonja McCaskie murder case receiving worldwide attention and inclusion in several detective magazines, which were popular reading at the time.

---

\*Among the more notable were Frank Hogan, DA of the Borough of Manhattan in New York City; Cook County State Attorney Jim Thompson, who later became governor of Illinois; Los Angeles County DA Bill McKesson; Garrett Byrne of Boston; Frank Newell, of Baltimore; John Corrigan, of Cleveland; and George Scott of Minneapolis. Due to Bill's west coast connection, he developed close personal and professional relationships with Alameda County DA Frank Coakley, Sacramento County DA John Price and, in particular, Tom Lynch, San Francisco County DA and later attorney general of California.

Bill also believed his colleagues took into consideration all that he did for the association, in particular the effort to establish a National College for District Attorneys. Bill, along with Washoe County District Court Judge Thomas Craven, had been successful in having a National Judicial College located in Reno and felt the nation would benefit from having a similar college for district attorneys.

Craven and Raggio both applied for grants from the Max C. Fleischmann Foundation, and both grant requests were approved, totaling $112,533.[1] Bill hoped the new National College for District Attorneys would also be located in Reno. Although the organization was grateful for his efforts in obtaining the funds, they decided to locate it in Houston Texas. As Bill later explained:

> This was because of the continuing stigma of the so-called "Nevada situation." In fact, during those years the National District Attorneys Association would not even agree to hold meetings here in Nevada, because we were considered a "sinful state" due to legalized gaming. I sometimes found this objection amusing, particularly when voiced by members from states like New Jersey, where *sub rosa* gambling had been flourishing in Atlantic City for years.

In speculating on reasons why the organization selected him as Outstanding Prosecutor of the United States, Bill Raggio modestly overlooked the fact that he was universally recognized as possessing a brilliant legal mind.

Throughout the 1960s he was regularly asked to speak at such prestigious events as Melvin Belli Seminars, state bar association conferences, university and law school commencement exercises and nationally televised programs dealing with sensitive legal issues. In 1964, Bill was invited by U.S. Attorney General Robert F. Kennedy to attend a National Conference on Bail and Criminal Justice in Washington, D.C., and he later returned to the Capitol to appear before the House Judiciary Subcommittee for his expert testimony regarding wiretapping legislation.

On the evening of July 18, 1965, a testimonial dinner was held in Reno honoring Bill Raggio for both his thirteen years of serving as Washoe County District Attorney and for being named Outstanding Prosecutor of the United States.

Organized by Harold Taber and John Squire Drendel, hundreds of guests attended. The honorary committee register, which consisted of family, friends, educators, politicians, media and business people, and colleagues in the legal community, was astonishingly comprehensive. Entertainers Jimmy Durante, Frank Sinatra and Frankie Fanelli, and sports figures Lefty O'Doul and Jackie Jensen were included. There were San Francisco society figures like Louis Lurie, John Livingston and Cyril Magnin. Among the luminaries from the legal profession were Jake Ehrlich, Melvin Belli, Marvin Lewis and Harry Wainwright. National District Attorney Association President George M. Scott, of Minneapolis, was on hand to make the presentation. Nevada Lieutenant Governor Paul Laxalt was master of ceremonies.

In March 1967, Bill succeeded Richard Gerstein, state attorney for Dade County, Florida, as president of the now-2,500 member NDAA. It was during a time when the nation was experiencing large-scale civil disobedience and deadly spasms of rioting.

In the opinion of the nation's prosecuting attorneys, this problem was due, in large part, to a shift away from the administration of justice. Recent court rulings, particularly those emanating from the U.S. Supreme Court, headed by Chief Justice Earl Warren, seemed to overprotect the accused, making convictions more difficult to obtain.

Moreover, an increasingly lenient attitude on the part of the courts toward those convicted of crimes, ranging from the unconstitutionality of the death penalty, to qualifications for parole, was enormously frustrating to those whose profession it was to seek justice for victims.

At his installation as president during a meeting in White Sulpher Springs, West Virginia, Bill spoke on a wide range of topics including recent U.S. Supreme Court rulings, riots and riot control, credit card fraud, changes in criminal procedures and limitations being imposed on prosecutors.

He noted there was a growing lack of respect for the law and called upon prosecutors "to lead the way in changing the philosophical guidelines which have inundated this nation in a tragic social experiment within the past several decades. The American public has paid a dear price in loss of lives, injured victims and theft of property. The average American's apathy has been replaced by fear for his very existence."

This fear, he concluded, had created widespread suspicion. However, as Bill was about to find out, such suspicion was not always found outside the NDAA.

\* \* \*

The elegant Monteleone Hotel in New Orleans was chosen as the site of the March 1968 national meeting of the NDAA. As the first anniversary of his two-year term as president approached, Bill wanted the event to be the most memorable in the organization's history. It would prove to be that, though due less to his organizational efforts, than the mercurial personality of the district attorney of Orleans Parish, Jim Garrison.

First elected DA in 1961, Garrison immediately established a reputation for being eccentric and flamboyant. The local media loved his regular raids on Bourbon Street bars and strip clubs. In January 1963, Garrison was convicted of misdemeanor criminal defamation during a widely publicized trial, after he publicly accused eight criminal court judges of racketeering and conspiring against him in a conflict over his office budget. Despite this, he was well liked not only by the public, but also by Bill Raggio and other members of the NDAA.

In a 2008 interview, Bill recalled that he was a close friend of Jim Garrison as a result holding offices in the district attorneys association. "I had taken him under my wing," Bill said, "and introduced him to other association members to try to get him involved. He was, to say the least, a unique individual."

In 1967 the NDAA conference was held in Los Angeles. Bill's hotel room was next to Garrison's and he soon began observing "some strange behavior."

"It appeared Jim had, for want of a better word, an 'obsession' with underage girls," Bill recalled, "some appearing to be as young as sixteen years-old. Surprisingly, when I mentioned my concerns about this to him, he did not deny his behavior. Because of this, I rather backed off from Mr. Jim Garrison."

Throughout 1967, Garrison constructed his famous conspiracy theory about the assassination of President Kennedy.* As the NDAA meeting in New Orleans approached, Bill and other board members were becoming increasingly alarmed by his erratic behavior.

As the host city NDAA member, Garrison would have certain ceremonial duties at the event. These concerns were somewhat assuaged when Garrison's assistant assured Bill that his boss would not use the convention to promote his own views concerning the assassination. With that pledge, they agreed to go forward with their plans to hold the meeting in that city.

Once the delegates had arrived, Bill recalled, problems arose. They had invited Vice President Hubert H. Humphrey to be the featured speaker. On the morning of the banquet, Humphrey's secretary called and advised Bill that the vice president was cancelling his speech that evening. Although the secretary did not say it, Bill sensed it had to do with Garrison's conduct. Bill quickly called a meeting of the executive officers, with Jim Garrison in attendance, and told them the vice president was not going to speak.

Garrison then told the group that he was going to act as the featured speaker in the vice president's place. Bill asked him what he intended to talk about.

---

*Though the alleged motive changed from time to time, the culprits Garrison focused on belonged to a "CIA-led, right-wing" conspiracy that included wealthy New Orleans businessman Clay Shaw, Lee Harvey Oswald and defrocked priest David Ferrie; who, like Oswald, was deceased by the time the grand jury indictments were announced. In March 1967, Garrison had Shaw arrested for the crime of conspiring to assassinate the president of the United States. Garrison later asserted that federal agencies, including the FBI and CIA, were working to stymie his investigation in order to protect President Lyndon Johnson and Vice President Hubert Humphrey, who Garrison believed were accomplices in covering up the conspiracy to kill the president.

"He replied that he was going to discuss the intrusion of federal courts into state affairs," Bill recalled, "and the activities of President Johnson in concealing vital evidence about the Kennedy assassination. 'I'm going to tell them,' Garrison fumed, 'about the f*****g president and the f*****g vice president.'"

Bill was shocked by Garrison's outburst and told him that, as the organization's president, he was not going to allow him to speak. "Garrison kept accusing me of censorship," he added, "but I finally made it clear to him that he not going to address the banquet."

Garrison then turned to an assistant and said, "Cancel the banquet, bolt the doors, guard them and don't let anybody in." He then stormed out of the room.

The NDAA board of directors unanimously backed Bill's decision not to let Jim Garrison speak. Bill then requested a refund from the hotel management for the cost of the banquet. "The manager said he could not do anything about that," Bill said, "because Garrison had been the one who made the arrangements. I suspect many people were not in accord with Jim Garrison, but because he was so powerful in Orleans Parish, they were fearful about standing up to him."

That night, 400 of the nation's top prosecutors and their spouses went without dinner.

Garrison's behavior toward the association turned into a major news story—one highly unflattering to the state of Louisiana. Governor John McKeithen came from Baton Rouge the next day and met with Bill. He apologized on behalf of the state, but was not willing to offer any criticism of Garrison's actions. Bill told a reporter shortly afterward, "Jim was a friend of mine ever since he was elected as DA… but his conduct [today] was completely irrational; he is an entirely changed man."

In 2008, Bill would say that Jim Garrison always needed to be in the limelight and thought he was smarter than everyone else was, adding,

I always found the mindset and the values in New Orleans to be curious. There was a certain flavor about the place. Most public officials ended up affording themselves the privilege of largess. They expected to go to restaurants, bars, any kind of services, and not have to pay for it. Jim Garrison had many friends there and, despite everything he did, I guess it should not surprise me that he later became a judge. It seemed that everyone in the state lived in fear of him.[2]

That would be Bill's last contact with Garrison. Harry Connick, Sr. defeated him in his bid for reelection as Orleans Parish district attorney and "proved to be an honest and highly respected public servant and a member of our organization," Bill later said.

Another member of the NDAA during this time was Dallas County District Attorney Henry Wade.[3] Wade, who could not have held a more contrary view of the Kennedy assassination than Garrison's, missed the opportunity to try Lee Harvey Oswald for the president's murder after Oswald was killed by Dallas nightclub operator Jack Ruby.

However, Wade would receive national attention for obtaining a conviction and death sentence for Ruby in March of 1964.[4] Coincidently, Bill's good friend, Melvin Belli, acted as Ruby's defense attorney at that trial, *pro bono*. When later asked about Melvin Belli's reasons for defending Oswald's killer, Bill would say, "Mel, nor I for that matter, ever felt there was enough real evidence of a conspiracy theory regarding President Kennedy's assassination."

Belli sought to convince the jury that Ruby was mentally ill when he shot Oswald, but said Bill, "Mel was the consummate attention-grabber, and so he defended Jack Ruby mostly for the publicity. If Oswald had lived, Mel would have wanted to defend him. That was the kind of guy he was. As far as publicity, that would have been the ultimate prize."

While he was president of the NDAA, Bill may have been involved in something many Nevadans might find difficult to forgive. "I probably played a significant role," he later confessed, "in New Jersey ultimately adopting casino gaming."

At the time, Brendan Byrne, the district attorney of Essex County, New Jersey, was the NDAA vice president. Byrne, said Bill, was particularly cautious and reluctant to even to visit Nevada for fear of being seen in the "Sin State."

Despite that attitude, in 1967 Byrne invited Bill Raggio to a meeting of the New Jersey Prosecutors Association, in Raggio's capacity as president of the NDAA, and introduced him to an aging state senator named Frank Farley[5] who was interested in the idea of using casino gaming to resurrect a blighted Atlantic City. Bill gave him his perspective on the pros and cons of legalized gaming and heard nothing more about it until Brendan Byrne became governor of New Jersey in 1974.

As governor, Byrne had come to see the advantages in a plan to revive Atlantic City by allowing legalized gaming there. He called for advice and Bill suggested that he come to Nevada and meet with gaming commissioners so he could better understand the process. "He evidently overcame his resistance to being seen in Nevada," Bill recalled. "The rest is pretty much history.[6]

# CHAPTER THIRTY

# The Political Waters (1964-1968)

eing honored by his peers as the "Outstanding Prosecutor in the United States" overshadowed Bill Raggio's debut on to the political stage. "I made my day in politics in late-March 1964," he recalled, "when I addressed the Clark County Republican Party Convention." Some Democrats felt Bill had already launched his political career months earlier when he began criticizing Nevada Governor Grant Sawyer and his administration for failing to take action to remedy inadequacies in the state's penal system.

As an assistant DA in the early 1950s, Bill had gotten to know Grant Sawyer, and they had once traveled together to attend a weeklong course for prosecutors at Northwestern University in Chicago. Bill also accompanied Sawyer on two occasions to Washington D.C., flying in a converted Nevada National Guard DC-3. On one of these trips, they both were sworn in to practice before the U.S. Supreme Court, under the sponsorship of U.S. Senator Alan Bible.

Bill had even campaigned for Sawyer during his 1958 race for governor. After his election, and despite their different party affiliations, Governor Sawyer invited Bill to attend some early discussions with respect to initially setting up his administration.

Bill would later remember First Lady Betty Sawyer as being "very diverse from Grant, a bit strident and probably the first governors' wife to assume a greater role in speaking out on issues in which she was interested."

Although an early supporter of Sawyer Administration's policies, the governor's increasingly liberal agenda, particularly when it came to public safety issues, put him on a collision course with Washoe County DA Raggio. As Jerome E. Edwards wrote in *The Maverick Spirit*:

> At times Sawyer's liberalism hurt him politically in conservative Nevada...It worried him that Nevada was incarcerating more people per capita than any other state and he was sensitive to the social conditions that put people into prisons. Sawyer wanted to get out of the cycle of putting more and more individuals into prison and then building more and more prisons.[1]

Bill's opposition to social forces that were considered by many to be a threat to public safety was not lost on the local Republican Party. Though Democrats held a three-to-one edge in voter registration in Nevada, Republicans were making inroads, particularly outside of Clark County.

In 1964, Bill and Paul Laxalt* were the two most recognized Republican officeholders in the entire state. Both men had won election to public office on the same day in November 1958; Bill to a second term as Washoe County DA, Paul to a first term as lieutenant governor. In that election, Laxalt had initially been running on a ticket with his predecessor, Lieutenant Governor Rex Bell, who was now running for governor. Bell, however, died suddenly of a heart attack on July 4, 1962, after attending a rally in the scorching summer heat of Las Vegas.

The ruggedly, handsome Bell had been a cowboy star in silent films and was married to the famed "It Girl," actress Clara Bow. After an unsuccessful attempt at running for the U.S. Congress in 1944, Bell became

---

*Paul Laxalt was born in Reno and raised in Carson City where his mother ran a small hotel and restaurant and his father, a Basque shepherd, spent much his time tending to flocks of sheep grazing in the high mountain meadows of the Sierras. Paul attended the University of Santa Clara and then served as a medic in the U.S. Army during World War II. In 1949, he received a law degree from the University of Denver. Laxalt returned to Carson City to practice law and served as the district attorney of Ormsby County between 1950 and 1954.

leader of the Nevada state GOP and in 1948 was an alternate to the Republican National Convention. He was elected lieutenant governor in 1954 on the same ticket with Governor Charles Russell.

In 1958, Democrat Grant Sawyer defeated Russell for the governorship, but the popular Rex Bell was reelected. So great was Rex Bell's statewide appeal that Bill was convinced Bell would have "easily been elected governor."*

Raggio and Laxalt had been acquainted since the mid1950s. Paul Laxalt would later recall that because there were so few lawyers in western Nevada that time, they all knew one another. When in Reno, Laxalt would make a point of dropping by the Mapes Hotel for a "briefing" on what was going on in the state (Reno was still the largest city in Nevada).

Invariably, Paul would find Bill Raggio there, usually in a group. Laxalt later remarked, "Bill always had people around him whom he trusted implicitly. I think that is one of the reasons he became as powerful as he did over the years."

Once elected as lieutenant governor, it became Laxalt's responsibility to lead the State's Republican Party. Early in the following election year, he decided Bill Raggio would be an excellent candidate to run against incumbent U.S. Senator Howard Cannon. Bill thought otherwise. During a 2007 interview, Laxalt recalled:

> I do not think Bill assigned a particular reason for declining to run for the U.S. Senate in 1964. I must say, it was one of the great surprises of my life that he did not. He called me in early summer and almost casually told me that he had thought it over and decided not to run.
>
> Here we were in an important presidential year with U.S. Senator Goldwater at the head of the ticket and the Republican Party

---

*Paul Laxalt decided not to take Bell's spot as candidate for governor and remained neutral in the primary as Las Vegas Mayor Oran Gragson defeated newspaper publisher Hank Greenspun. Gragson was later defeated by Democratic incumbent Grant Sawyer.

being on the rise in Nevada, and he [Raggio] calls and tells the captain that he is not going to play. I had no thought of running for the Senate, but did so because there was now no other candidate available.

In 2008, Bill spoke of his decision not to run that year:

Since neither Paul nor I had spent much time in Clark County, and were not well known there, I subsequently traveled to Las Vegas to "test the waters." I came back and told Paul Laxalt that it would be difficult because of the lopsided Democrat registration in Clark County. I suggested that he, being the state's lieutenant governor, at least had some name recognition and might stand a chance of winning if he spent more time down there.

Therefore, when he says that I declined to run in 1964, he is correct. However, I did not really take myself out of contention; I just decided that Paul was the better candidate.

Bill's evaluation of Paul as a strong candidate proved to be extraordinarily astute. In November, he nearly pulled off a stunning upset over incumbent Senator Cannon, losing in a recount by a razor thin margin of just forty-eight votes—out of 134,000 cast.

The election of 1964 was one of great importance to the nation. Social unrest stirred by civil rights issues, growing opposition to the Vietnam War and years of judicial activism, had reached the breaking point. The Nevada Republican Party was splintered by factionalism. Moderates, who felt the party should concentrate on policies that would stimulate economic growth in the state, were now being pushed aside by a right wing element with ideological ties to the John Birch Society and McCarthyism.

The Republican National Convention was held in July at the Cow Palace in San Francisco to nominate a candidate to challenge President Lyndon Johnson. Johnson had yet to win a presidential election, having assumed the office after the assassination of President Kennedy just eight months earlier.

The convention was a tension-filled affair. Conservative supporters of Arizona Senator Barry Goldwater openly clashed with liberal and moderate backers of New York Governor Nelson Rockefeller. When Rockefeller attempted to deliver a speech, he was booed by the convention's conservative delegates, who regarded him as a member of "the eastern liberal establishment." Despite the infighting, Goldwater was easily nominated. He chose William E. Miller, a congressman from New York, as his running mate.

In his acceptance speech, Goldwater declared that communism was the "principal disturber of the peace in the world today" and then delivered the phrase for which he would be most remembered: "I would remind you that extremism in the defense of liberty is no vice. And let me remind you also that moderation in the pursuit of justice is no virtue."

With those words, he lost the moderates and liberals within his party—effectively ending his chances of be elected. Lieutenant Governor Paul Laxalt loyally cast Nevada's six Republican Party delegate votes for Goldwater. In November 1964, President Johnson was returned to office in an electoral landslide.

Although politically conservative, Bill eschewed the radical right elements within his party whose message, he felt, had become increasingly paranoid. During the earlier Nevada Republican Party convention, in April 1964, he and Lieutenant Governor Laxalt worked successfully to pass a hotly contested resolution, the effect of which, as Robert Dickens would write in *The Maverick Spirit*, was to muscle out rightist splinter groups and mediate disputes between the far right and more centrist factions.[2]

Other mainstream Republicans, both locally and nationally, had also grown weary of the "far right," particularly the powerful John Birch Society, after its founder, Robert Welch, circulated a letter calling President Dwight D. Eisenhower "a possible conscious, dedicated agent of the Communist Conspiracy." Welch's charge against the highly respected Eisenhower eventually led many conservative Republicans, most prominently Barry Goldwater, and intellectuals like William F. Buckley, to renounce the group.

Though defeated in his race for the U.S. Senate, Paul Laxalt, as lieutenant governor, would remain titular head of the state Republican Party. Yet, as Bill later recalled, the party at that time "was dysfunctional, with low registration and in the grip of the ultraconservative John Birch Society."

Bill and Paul were among a handful of Republicans holding any kind of elective office. Together with party regulars, including Walt Casey, Bill Laub and George Von Tobel of Clark County; Archie Pozzi, of Carson City; Lucy Humphrey, of Washoe County; Roy Young, of Elko County; and Carl Dodge, of Churchill County, they would ultimately bring the party back together, though it would take nearly a decade to do so.

* * *

Bill used the 1964 campaign as a platform to attack the Sawyer Administration over what he considered its disregard for public safety. The DA publicly cited three major factors in the rising crime rate: early release of convicted felons from the penitentiary, parole without adequate supervision and lack of rehabilitation programs for prison inmates. Rehabilitation of inmates in the Nevada State Prison, the DA said, bordered on the ludicrous. The only job training the prison provided was work in the prison casino, "The Bullpen," this, despite a state law prohibiting ex-felons from working in Nevada's casinos once they were released.

When Governor Sawyer suggested that the Washoe County district attorney mind his own business, Raggio replied, "If the governor cannot mind the business he is charged with, than someone has to do it for him."

Raggio went on to say the major cause of the states increasing crime rate "certainly is not the way we prosecute the criminal." If the governor presented an adequate prison parole and rehabilitation program system, Bill would gladly support it."[3] Others in law enforcement agreed. Washoe County Sheriff Bob Galli remarked, "The parole board sees prisoners at their best; law enforcement officials see the results of them at their worst."

Reno Police Chief Elmer Briscoe concurred, saying it was a slap in the face of law enforcement that persons convicted of violent crimes are released without serving the minimum sentence.

Raggio was unrelenting, calling the parole system "a farce" and the parole board members professionally unqualified for the job. "We might start with the warden's qualifications to be the state's leading penologist," Bill remarked. "His appointment is another example of playing politics with public safety…If the governor's office would channel into the prison budget some of the funds it spends on public relations for the governor, much needed psychological services can be provided to the inmates."

Bill then brought a legal challenge against the parole board's decision to release the three young murderers of grocer Jack Griffis, after they had served only thirty months. In September 1964, the Nevada Supreme Court would agree with the DA and block the early release.

In response to that ruling, Governor Sawyer asked the 1965 Nevada State Legislature for a statute allowing prisoners convicted of certain crimes be made eligible for parole after serving just one-third of their minimum sentences. These crimes included nonviolent types, as well as armed robbery and second-degree murder.

A "Mother's March," orchestrated by District Attorney Raggio, descended upon the Capitol, but failed to stop Governor Sawyer from signing the legislation into law.

Bill immediately called upon his fellow district attorneys in the state to participate in "any effort which will allow a referendum on this most vital issue." To State Attorney General Harvey Dickerson's request for cooperation with the lawmakers, Bill replied, "I must respectfully state that I am unable to bend to the will of the legislature as you suggested."[4]

In August of that year, Bill expressed his concern that "court coddled criminals are going free here in Reno" and blamed "a liberal U.S. Supreme Court." He was referring to a series of Supreme Court rulings over the previous few years that appeared to weaken the ability of law enforcement to convict criminals.[4]

Most of those who were involved in the process of arresting and prosecuting criminals disagreed with the rulings, arguing that it was a new and reckless interpretation of the constitution by the high court.*

Because his no-nonsense approach to law and order appealed to so many Nevadans, Bill was urged by his fellow Republicans to run for lieutenant governor or state attorney general, but declined.

In June 1966, Bill announced that he would run for a third term as district attorney. Throughout his second term, he had continued to improve efficiency and expand service. The casework was now divided between three divisions, criminal, civil and investigations.

Raggio had pushed for consumer protection and was instrumental in overcoming opposition from the local retailers' association to help establish Reno's first Better Business Bureau.

The regular staff consisted of nine attorneys, four investigators and about a dozen secretaries and stenographers. Bill, whose annual salary was $15,000, was looking forward to a pay increase the following year to $18,000. He was now affiliated with over thirty-five professional, fraternal, veterans' and political organizations, as well as committees, boards, service clubs and other groups.

Because of his effectiveness and popularity as the county's top law enforcement officer, he ran unopposed.

Despite all the modernization and increased effectiveness of his office, one thing remained the same— he life of a district attorney was still a dangerous one, as Bill Raggio was about to be reminded.

---

*In 2008, Bill Raggio reflected on the concerns of law enforcement during that time and said, "During my latter years as DA, the Warren Court came down with many decisions, like Miranda, and we thought that it was a drastic change. As it turned out, we were probably over-alarmed. In retrospect, they did not have a major effect."

# CHAPTER THIRTY-ONE

# Jimmy Ing

District Attorney Raggio would again come into conflict with the Sawyer Administration, this time over security at the Nevada State Hospital. In early 1966, the *Reno Evening Gazette* published an investigative series revealing that a convicted felon, and others, had been granted passes from the institution and that there had been a number of escapes from the maximum-security ward.

In response, Bill sought a grand jury investigation into loose security at the hospital. When Governor Sawyer attempted to block the investigation, Bill took the case to the Nevada Supreme Court, which supported his argument to allow the probe.

The resultant grand jury report recommended sweeping changes at the hospital. Governor Sawyer called a special session of the state legislature and received a $100,000 appropriation for improvements.

In early November 1966, Bill was once again locking horns with the administration of the Nevada State Prison, after remarking, "We have one of the poorest examples of a prison in the United States."

Associate Warden Bill Frost responded that District Attorney Raggio was "acting as a puppet for a candidate for state office who lacks the courage to make these charges openly and directly." This was an obvious allusion to Paul Laxalt who was at the time running against the incumbent Sawyer for governor—an election Laxalt would win two days later.

Bill responded forcefully: "I have been criticizing the prison for years. Every time I hit a nerve, they bring up politics." [1]

The heated exchange between Frost and Raggio was initially triggered by a parole board decision to release a violent prisoner by the name of James Burton Ing.* Jimmy Ing had been arrested more than twenty times, the first in 1936. In 1938, he spent time for robbery in Illinois' Joliet State Prison. In 1959, he was arrested in Reno under the National Firearms Act for carrying a machine gun.

In 1963, Jimmy Ing was sentenced to the Nevada State Prison on charges of second degree burglary and assault with a deadly weapon after shooting and wounding a Washoe County Deputy Sheriff who was attempting to arrest him for the crime. Less than three years later, Ing was paroled for "good behavior" after having even served less than the minimum sentence.

The decision infuriated Bill, who had prosecuted Jimmy Ing and knew there was nothing "good" about his behavior. Ing was, in fact, one of the most ruthless criminals in northern Nevada history.

A few months after his release from prison, Jimmy was again arrested, this time for the murder of a bartender at a bar in Sparks. The victim was the father of a Reno police officer. A district court judge subsequently ruled that while it was clear Ing's car was used to transport the murderer, the crime could not be tied directly to him.

While still in custody for the crime, a handcuffed Jimmy Ing broke away from officers escorting him to his arraignment and attacked *Reno Evening Gazette* photographer Marilyn Newton. "He kicked me in the legs and stomach and then kicked my camera into my face, breaking my front teeth," Marilyn later recalled. "He then said to me, 'I'll see your camera on your grave.'"

The day Jimmy Ing was released from jail, both the Reno Police and the Washoe County Sheriff's Office each issued Newton a concealed weapons permit. She lived in fear.

Several months later, Marilyn Newton was with friends, including an off-duty Reno police officer and his wife, at the lounge in the Mapes Hotel, when local disc jockey Jack Joseph approached and asked Marilyn

---

*Ing, a surname often mistaken for Asian, was actually of Welsh origin.

if she would mind speaking to Jimmy Ing. Armed with her concealed weapon, and friends nearby to assist her if anything went wrong, Marilyn agreed.

"Ing said he wanted to buy me a drink and talk," Newton recalled. "I mentioned I was with friends but he assured me it wouldn't take long. So I sat down and he bought me a drink, and for the next forty-five minutes, or so, he apologized for having kicked me. His last words to me were, 'Next time I'll pose for you.' And he later did."

Jimmy Ing always had enough money to make bail and pay for good legal defense. He once claimed to a reporter that he had made millions in the wholesale liquor business in Alaska.[2] His attorneys were Harry Claiborne and Sam Francovich.

Ing became close to Sam and his family, and was a frequent houseguest. Sam's widow, Lillian Francovich, recalled in 2008 that Ing was "a gentle and friendly person who was good with our children." He was also a family man, with a wife and two small boys, living in a nice neighborhood on Mayberry Drive. This more charming side of Jimmy Ing's character, glimpsed by the Lillian Francovich and Marilyn Newton, was clearly at odds with his reputation as a violent criminal.

The headquarters for Ing's criminal activities was a bar he owned on East Commercial Row in downtown Reno. Police were often called there to investigate reports of tourists being mugged, or to look for stolen property from recent burglaries. At times, Ing was accused by victims of administering vicious late-night beatings around town.

Ing became the most active criminal in DA Raggio's jurisdiction. Bill later recalled:

> Some bodies were found buried out near Yerington, which we were reliably informed were probably his victims, but we did not have hard evidence. If anything crooked or criminal was going on in northern Nevada, he was probably involved. Ing was what I would call the King of the Demimonde; not connected to what some might call the Mafia, but a very bad individual none-the-less.

Jimmy was indeed a "bad individual." Upon his release from prison in 1966, he vowed not to return. On several occasions, he approached police officers and made taunting remarks about not being taken alive, saying, "The next time you stop me you are going to get what the other guy got [referring to the deputy sheriff Ing had wounded in 1963]."

On another occasion, he warned police, "If you are ever going to roust me you're going to need that [pointing at the officer's pistol]." Ing often remarked to officers that he knew they wanted to kill him and that he planned "to go out shooting."[3]

These threats extended beyond street cops. Jimmy Ing would spend hours sitting in his car near the Raggio home on Robin Street. When police would order him to leave, Ing would refuse; reminding them it was a public street and a free country. Sam Francovich tried unsuccessfully to convince his client to end that practice.

During this period, while Jimmy Ing was out on bail pending a trial, Bill Raggio's secretary received a threat and immediately passed it along to her boss. The male caller had said, "Tell Raggio if he goes ahead and prosecutes Jimmy Ing, he's going to end up in a mine shaft."

Bill was used to receiving such threats. However, when he subsequently learned, through informants, that threats were being made against his children, he had had enough. "I was used to threats and police protection of my home and family," Bill later said, "but that one really got to me. I knew Jimmy Ing was a tough customer and would probably stop at nothing."

Bill called Sam Francovich and told him to bring his client in to the DA's office immediately. When Francovich insisted upon knowing why, a livid Bill barked, "Never mind that, just bring him in!" When they arrived, Bill Raggio, Sheriff Bud Young and Reno Chief of Police Elmer Briscoe were waiting. In 2008, Bill recalled the conversation:

> I'm going to repeat this as close to word-for-word as I can, though I will clean up my language. I said, "Mr. Ing, I had you come here today so you could tell me to my face what's going to happen to me if we prosecute you."

Ing replied, "I don't know what you're talking about." I repeated the question. His attorney Sam Francovich then asked, "What do you mean?" I said, "We received a threat over the phone that if I prosecute him I am going to end up in a mine shaft. I wanted him to give him the opportunity to tell me to my face."

Ing repeated that he had not made such a threat, and Francovich argued that his client could not be responsible for the actions of other people. However, Raggio cut them both off saying this to Ing:

Let me make it perfectly clear, if I get more threats of any kind between now and this trial, I'm going to have them yank your ass off the street and you're going to rot in jail until this trial. And once you're convicted, you're going to rot in prison for as long as I have anything to say about it. If you're doing it, you better damn sure stop; and if you're not doing it, you better damn sure find out who is. That's the end of this conversation.

I never got another threat after that.

\* \* \*

On the morning of December 16, 1966, the lone caretaker of the main house on Wilbur D. May's Double Diamond Ranch, south of Reno, went out to breakfast, as was his routine. Shortly after he departed, burglars entered the dwelling through a bathroom window.

May was a wealthy businessman and philanthropist who, in addition to his sprawling 2,800 acre ranch near Reno, was the owner of a national chain of department stores. He also possessed one of the finest private art collections in the world. The burglars removed twenty-four paintings and numerous antique firearms. The artwork included pieces by Dubriffet, Ronault, Vlaminiek, Matisse and Picasso, among others. Although a priceless haul in today's market, authorities then valued the stolen art at about $500,000.

Bill suspected that Jimmy Ing was involved and called him into his office to persuade him to return the artwork undamaged. "He would not admit to the theft," Bill said. "I tried to prevail upon his conscience by saying, 'Why don't you do something decent in your life and see that we get these paintings back.' He proved he did not have a conscience by callously replying, 'It does not matter to me if those paintings are destroyed.'"

In February 1967, a less-direct approach was tried when an undercover police officer, acting as an intermediary for an insurance company, contacted Ing who then agreed to "arrange" ransom of all the stolen property. They decided on a price of $50,000.

The Stagecoach Inn Motel on West Fourth Street in Reno was selected by Ing as the place of transfer. At 10:45 p.m. on February 8, he arrived in his car and immediately removed a large, flat package encased in cardboard and carried it to the motel unit occupied by the agent. The package contained six paintings for which Ing was given $5,000 in cash. The intermediary asked for time to examine the paintings for authenticity before exchanging the remainder of the stolen art for ransom. Ing agreed and left.

An hour later, he returned to the motel and parked in the same place. He went to the rear of the car, pulled another flat cardboard box from the trunk and carried it back toward the driver's side door.

Over a dozen police officers and Sheriff's deputies were waiting in ambush nearby. One shouted for Ing to "Freeze!" Instead, he threw the box in the direction of the officer and then made a crouching, turning movement toward the car door. The police opened fire.*

Testimony at the subsequent coroner's inquest indicated that because of Ing's previous threats about "going out shooting," the officers assumed he was reaching for a gun, either on his person, or in the car. As it turned out, Ing was unarmed and there was no gun found in his car. All of the stolen art and most of the antique weapons were located and returned.

---

*Bill Raggio was in Carson City on the evening of the shooting.

The autopsy concluded Ing's death occurred "from numerous and multiple penetrating missile wounds." The coroner's jury deliberated just ten minutes before returning the verdict of "justifiable homicide." Marilyn Newton, who had been viciously attacked by him and, later, lived in near constant fear for her life, was relieved when informed of his death, saying, "I was told by officers that he was shot so many times, that when they rolled him over bullets literally fell out of him onto the pavement. And at his funeral, there was a wreath that said '22:1 and No Gun,' inferring that Ing was outnumbered by police twenty-two to one and was unarmed. I went to the funeral just to be sure he was dead."

As a career newswoman, Marilyn believed that an in-depth story about Jimmy Ing's criminal career would be interesting. However, she later received a tip that Ing's associates would put out a contract on her if she pried into details of his life. Marilyn reported this threat to the police. "They told me they would do what they could," she later said, "but they could not be with me twenty-four hours a day. I thought better of it and gave up the idea of this story about 'Nevada's Crime King.'"

Sam Francovich later stated that one of the Picasso paintings contained in the large package Ing threw at the police officers that night had been riddled by bullets or buckshot. Others claimed there was no damage to any of the artwork. Either way, Jimmy Ing's reflex reaction in throwing the painting at the police, eerily evoked Picasso's own wish for his work: "Art is not made to decorate rooms. It is an offensive weapon in the defense against the enemy."

# CHAPTER THIRTY-TWO

# Family

T hreats against Bill and his family, like those made by Jimmy Ing, were common and became a sad fact of everyday life.

By now, the Raggio family had grown to five, with the adoption of infants Tracy in 1961 and Mark in 1962. For their protection, the children were often reminded never to answer the front door or stand by the front windows. Tracy recalled that as a young girl she felt frightened, but "did not know what to be scared of."

Her dad regularly did not get home from work until nearly midnight. Because Tracy and Mark shared a bedroom near the front door of the house, she would often awaken at the sound of his key in the door lock and "be afraid that someone was going to attack him on the front porch. I would worry until he was inside the house."

Hunter Lake Elementary School was just a block from their home, but Dottie would stand each school day on the corner by their house and watch Tracy and Mark walk there until they entered the schoolyard. "Occasionally Dad would drive us to school in his big district attorney's car," Tracy would later recall. "After we got out and began walking into the school yard, he would turn on the car's loudspeaker and blaringly announce our arrival by saying something like, 'Have a good day and I'll see you at home tonight.' It was intended as a prank to embarrass us in front of our friends—and it worked."

Leslie, oldest of the three children by several years, knew her dad's work as district attorney involved associating with bad people. Once, when she was about nine years old, Leslie opened a bedroom door in the house and found her dad showing her mom projector slides on the wall. They were crime scene photos of the gruesome McCaskie murder scene, which Bill had recently presented to the jury in obtaining conviction of Thomas Lee Bean. Leslie just caught a glimpse before she was hurried out of the room by her mom; however, it was enough to make her frightened—for both herself and for her dad.

Leslie vividly recalls another evening, during the time her dad was prosecuting Joe Conforte for extortion, when neighbors ran to the house and pounded on the door to tell them that there was a cross burning on their lawn. For Leslie's protection, she was often walked to school by the police, and later, as a teenage girl, would be mortified at sometimes having police officers escort her while on dates with boys.

As daughter of the district attorney, the attractive, blond had to be careful of her associations and her behavior. "We really lived in a fishbowl," she said. In order to not disappoint her dad, she worked hard to be a model daughter, engaging in numerous extracurricular activities in high school and graduating with a near-perfect grade point average.

She loved her father and, during the elections, could not understand why some people would not vote for him. Once, one of her teachers put out a lawn sign endorsing Bill's opponent, Ed Fike. Young Leslie knocked on the door and demanded to know why.

She frequently found herself defending her dad's reputation against negative things being said about him by her classmates, who were just parroting political views they heard at home. Because most of her classmates' parents were not in the public eye, and so not subject to such slurs and criticism, Leslie was often upset that they did not recognize how hurtful it was.

During Bill's hectic years of administering and modernizing the district attorney's office, fighting for an effective system of justice in Nevada, dealing with the demands of his budding political persona and his duties as a national officer in the NDAA, it became increasingly more difficult for him to find time to spend with the family.

"My dad was so busy at work that in middle school I would sometimes wait up for him," Leslie recalled. "When I would hear his key in the door, I'd run out of my room to spend some time with him. Sometimes on the way home, he would pick up a pizza from Shakey's and we would sit in the breakfast nook at 11:00 p.m. eating pizza while working on my homework together."

Yet Bill still managed to find time to pick watercress and mushrooms with his family on a Sunday afternoon and even a few days for an occasional family vacation.

Daughter Tracy Woodring remembered a camping trip in the late-1960s:

> We would go to Silver Lake near Susanville, California for a week at a time. Dad would pull a trailer on his car. At night, we kids would sleep in the trailer while Mom and Dad slept outside in a tent. One night a bear came too close to us while on a foray of the campground's garbage cans and we awoke to the sound of shouting and witnessed our dad chasing a terrified bear around campgrounds with a gun in his hand.

It seemed the Raggio family vacations were seldom restful, but usually amusing. One such getaway was described in an August 4, 1964, article in the *Reno Evening Gazette*:

> Bill Raggio long looked forward to taking a few days off for a Lake Tahoe vacation. The first night he sprawled on the sofa. Just as he started to relax, his wife backed the car into a culvert and he had to get the sheriff and a tow truck, which meant getting off the sofa and an end to the relaxation. The next night his three-year-old daughter Tracy was bitten by a dog and, as he went to chase the dog away, he was bitten too. They both headed for Reno and the Washoe Medical Center for shots.[1]

Life on Robin Street was no less hectic. Tracy recalled the environment with fondness during a 2008 interview, saying, "My mom loved animals and we had many, turtles, fish, birds and dogs. The big dogs would stay outside and two smaller dogs would stay inside. Once, one of the big dogs got in the house and ate the standing rib roast Mom was cooking for dinner. There was always something going on."

While Leslie was a focused, mature, high-achieving middle and high school student, Tracy remembers that she and her little brother, Mark, were the "wild ones." Tracy, by then a pretty and confident veteran of pageants (which would later include her being crowned Nevada Little Miss), recalled that when her dad got home from work, he would often scold them if they had misbehaved. "Dad would often use a lot of lawyer terms that we didn't understand. I remember Mark once whispering to me during one of Dad's reprimands, 'What's an alibi?'"

Occasionally, the infraction would be so severe that it warranted a spanking. A "double spanking" would be administered if they lied about the misdeed. Such punishment was seldom necessary, however, for either Tracy or her younger brother, Mark—a handsome, flaxen haired boy with a disarmingly impish grin.

Dorothy "Dottie" Raggio was a very social person who enjoyed public affairs of all kinds. "She was very down-to-earth," Tracy said, "and the only people she did not care to be around were the pretentious ones."

Josephine Gezelin, wife of Judge Emile Gezelin, was very close to Dottie. "She was extremely outgoing and personable," Mrs. Gezelin said, "a hard person not to like. Dottie and Bill had wonderful parties and there was always such a wide variety of people at their house."

Trim, energetic and sincere, Dottie would go out of her way to help people and actively participated in her children's lives. When Mark had a paper route and needed to sell subscriptions to win a prize he wanted, Dottie was on the phone calling everyone she knew.

She loved to play the organ and small piano in the house, often aggravating the kids who were trying to hear their TV shows. Dottie insisted all her children learn to play the piano. Tracy and Mark, however, insisted upon learning other instruments and their mom eventually acquiesced, allowing Tracy to take guitar lessons and Mark to learn the accordion— an instrument Dottie abhorred.

Because Leslie was older than the other kids, she was expected to help raise them. Often this responsibility became overwhelming. At those times, she would turn to her "Grammy" Clara. Clara Raggio had been in a similar situation as a girl, tasked with helping raise her younger siblings on the Cardelli Ranch.

She maintained a small garden at her house, and showed Leslie how to can her own vegetables and make minestrone and other Italian dishes. The girl once saw her grandmother strewing shreds of paper around on the lawn and asked about it. Clara explained that it was to help the birds. "This material holds the nest together, Clara would say. Leslie recognized her Grammy's meaning: "I could see this was what she was doing for me...she was the rock of the family, a totally unselfish person."

The stress and peril of high profile lives can rupture a marriage and the Raggios were no exception. Dottie, like the wives of other visible and controversial public of figures of her day—Betty Ford, Pat Nixon and Joan Kennedy—had a problem with alcohol. Their relationship became strained and occasionally estranged.* "Perhaps if Dad had had a stronger person for a wife than Mom," Leslie conjectured years later, "He could have gone farther in politics."

For Bill Raggio and his family, living in the "fishbowl" of public scrutiny was just beginning to exact its toll.

---

*Nevertheless, Bill continued to be supportive, and they remained married until Dottie's death.

# CHAPTER THIRTY-THREE

# U.S. Senate Race (1968)

As the Nevada Republican Party prepared for its 1968 statewide nominating convention in Winnemucca, all eyes were on Bill Raggio to declare his intention to run for the U.S. Senate. Bill was now riding a wave of popularity in the northern part of the state, a status he had not always held.

Just a few years earlier, Bill's popularity had hit an all time low. Never one to duck a fight, he always seemed to be embroiled in controversy. He fought against early parole and for reducing sentences for marijuana possession. He made personal and political enemies in both parties when he tried to clean up corruption in the Reno City Council and police department. In addition, Bill suffered for years from defamatory rumors spread about him during his effort to put Nevada vice figure, Joe Conforte, behind bars.

Yet by 1968, Bill found himself increasing popular with a great many voters who had grown tired of civil unrest, President Johnson's idealistic social programs and the way the war in Vietnam was being conducted. Incumbent Democratic Senator Alan Bible seemed vulnerable because he was perceived to be a supporter of such policies.

The 1966 election had revitalized the Nevada Republican Party which made noteworthy inroads, despite the lopsided Democratic edge in voter registration. Ed Fike was elected lieutenant governor, Wilson McGowan as state controller and Paul Laxalt won a surprising victory over incumbent Governor Grant Sawyer.

Bill later attributed Laxalt's gubernatorial victory to several factors, including a lingering belief among many voters that Paul's forty-eight-vote defeat in the 1964 Senate race against Howard Cannon was the result of ballot tampering. In addition, Bill cited the support Laxalt had received from a large segment of Clark County's Mormon constituency and gaming community; Governor Sawyer's complacency; and an historical disinclination on the part of Nevadans to grant their governors more than two terms. "Paul," Bill said, "was affable, with great charisma, and able to put together a strong family team and as well as others with campaign expertise."

On April 26, 1968, in a speech before the state Republican convention, forty-one-year-old Bill Raggio announced his candidacy. The *Reno Evening Gazette* reported the news the following day on its front-page with the headline: "Raggio Runs, Says Nation Needs Change." It was located just below a slightly larger banner proclaiming: "H-Bomb Test Rocks Vegas."

Bill was entering the race several months behind his chief rival in the party, Lieutenant Governor Ed Fike. Fike, a soft spoken, some say lack-luster, Las Vegas businessman, was well known in southern Nevada. His four years as lieutenant governor had also given him important name recognition throughout the state. When Republican Governor Paul Laxalt announced he would remain neutral in the race, to avoid splitting the party, Bill knew his work was cut out for him.

He immediately challenged Fike to a debate, which the lieutenant governor refused, ostensibly to also keep from damaging the party, but more likely to avoid being mauled by Raggio's superior oratorical abilities. "I did not have any philosophical differences with Ed Fike," Bill would later say, "I just felt that I was the stronger candidate. The fact that he lacked substance on issues made him reluctant to debate me."

Without a debate to feature his more dynamic qualities, Bill headed to Washington D.C. on a "fact-finding mission," and associated photo opportunities. While speaking to a group in Maryland, Bill laid out his concerns for the nation, saying that there is something wrong in a country whose citizens are afraid to go outside in broad daylight. Of the Vietnam War, Bill called for a reassessment of the U.S. role and for other nations to step up support because "the free world all shares in the need to stop communism in Asia." Candidate Raggio also warned of "chronic deficits in our budget payments."

Upon his return to Nevada, Bill called for new procedures in the appointment for U.S. Supreme Court justices. This brought charges from southern Nevada that Raggio's opposition to the recent nomination of President Lyndon Johnson's friend, Abe Fortas, to the Supreme Court, was based upon anti-Semitism.

Bill called foul on the part of his opponent from the south, Ed Fike, and vigorously rebutted the allegation: "I'm opposed to Abe Fortas because I'm opposed to cronyism. Anyone who brands me as anti-Semitic is not interested in the issues, but in winning the election through downright dirty politics."

As the primary election approached, Raggio knew he was running behind and would need every vote he could muster. In such situations, family ties often transcend party affiliations. Bill's uncle, John Avansino, a staunch Democrat his entire life, would change his party membership so he could vote for his nephew in the Republican primary. The morning after that election, John appeared early at the Washoe County Courthouse to reregister as a Democrat—not wanting to remain a Republican any longer than familial loyalty and the county's business hours required him to.

On September 4, 1968, Ed Fike won the Republican primary election. An editorial in the *Gazette* applauded Bill's effort in making the race so close and speculated that, had he entered sooner, he may have had time to make a more significant impression on rural voters in the so-called "Cow Counties."[1]

Yet, Fike received twice as many votes as Bill in Clark County, and that is what likely settled the matter. The subsequent race between Alan Bible and Ed Fike was low key, reflecting the temperaments of the two candidates. In November, Bible easily retained his senate seat.

Throughout 1969, the district attorney's office continued to grow and function smoothly with a host of bright new talent. It was a relatively uneventful year for Bill Raggio, a calm before the political storm that was about to engulf him.

# CHAPTER THIRTY-FOUR

# U.S. Senate Race (1970)

On February 4, 1970, the Supreme Court of Nevada voted, in a three to two decision, to set aside the death sentence of Thomas Lee Bean. Their decision, influenced by the 1968 U.S. Supreme Court ruling in the case of *Witherspoon v. Illinois*, ruled that an error had occurred in the selection of jurors, because opponents of capital punishment had been excused.

District Attorney Raggio's response was scorching. He labeled the decision "the most outrageous and shocking in the history of the court" and accused the high court of "judicial legislation."[1] Chief Justice David Zenoff immediately ordered the Nevada Bar Association to investigate Raggio's remarks.

Bill was not intimidated. Rather than apologize, he continued venting his displeasure, telling the press that the court decision was "tortured out of recognition to bring with it an application of the U.S. Supreme Court decision in Witherspoon."[2] He called for the high court to rehear the case and, in lieu of that, provide guidelines for the new penalty phase.

On March 11, the court unanimously, and without comment, denied his request. Later that day, Chief Justice Zenoff called upon the Board of Governors of the State Bar of Nevada to initiate disciplinary proceedings against the Washoe County DA.

Bill fired back that there was no precedent for this decision in Nevada law and no provision for such a penalty hearing. "It's unexplainable and, in my opinion, totally uncalled for," he said. "Even the United States Supreme Court has not dictated such a holding."

Regarding the Chief Justice's demand for disciplinary action, Bill agreed as an officer of the court, he should be held to a higher standard than the public with regard to such criticism, though adding, "While my remarks may seem critical, they are in no way more critical than the opinions of the two dissenting Justices, Collins and Batjer."[3]

Feelings ran high throughout the state. Law enforcement officials, fellow prosecutors and much of the public, rallied to Bill's defense. Many were as exasperated by the court's attempt to curb Bill's right to free speech, as they were by the court's perceived determination to assist Thomas Bean in escaping the gallows. Chief Elmer Briscoe summed up the feelings of many, when he told a reporter, "The most shocking thing is not the decision by the high court itself with reference to this case, but that this court is in a position to threaten punishment, or disbarment, of a man who was named the Outstanding Prosecutor in the United States a few years ago and was honored as the President of the National District Attorneys Association. I'm sure no member of the Supreme Court can claim such distinction."[4]

A representative of the state bar immediately announced that their board of governors would not be stampeded into a hasty decision.

Thomas Bean reacted passively when notified in his death row cell of the Supreme Court ruling to block his impending execution. "Can I go to the yard?"—a request to be placed in the general prison population—was his only response.[5]

Because it was rumored that Bill was going to seek the Republican nomination for governor in that year, he was asked how the Supreme Court ruling might affect his future.

"I am making a very objective appraisal of the function that I serve as a prosecutor," he replied. "This decision will, I'm sure, have a very definite influence on what I do—whether or not I seek reelection to this office. It's a frustrating experience."[6]

Four months earlier, on September 30, 1969, Nevada Governor Paul Laxalt had announced he was retiring after just one term in office. He later cited among his reasons how nasty politics could be. "It was a tough, invasive experience...at times," Laxalt said. "It could be downright cruel, particularly when attacks were made against family and friends." In addition, he felt the need to spend more time with wife Jackie, from whom he was "growing dangerously apart."[7]

Earlier that month, Laxalt had been invited by President Richard Nixon to a meeting in the Oval Office. Nixon had learned of Laxalt's plans to retire and now urged the governor to run against Senator Howard Cannon in the approaching midterm election. Laxalt explained to the president his personal reasons for declining. "I'm not sure he related to any of them," Laxalt later wrote. "President Nixon was the consummate political animal."[8]

Despite Nixon's persuasiveness and the overwhelming attachment to history conveyed by the Oval Office, Laxalt chose to leave politics—at least temporarily.

In 2009, Bill Raggio would say,

> Laxalt's decision not to seek a second term was a real surprise. His term was not difficult from a financial or budgetary perspective, and Paul probably enjoyed the best relationship of any governor with the legislature. However, he did have to contend with issues involving Howard Hughes, reorganization of state government, reform of prisons and parole, as well as restoring Nevada's prestige with FBI Director J. Edgar Hoover and the advent of corporate gaming licenses.

Bill had previously met with the governor several months earlier after Laxalt's announcement that he was retiring. Reno attorney Frank Peterson, a close friend of Paul's since their days together as students at the University of Santa Clara, arranged the meeting to discuss Bill's wish to run for governor.

At the meeting, Bill listed the reasons he would be a good candidate. In addition, Bill told the governor that since his run for the senate in the

1968 primary election, he was now more interested in politics and a higher level of public service. Bill advised Laxalt that a recent poll showed him running twenty-points ahead of any potential Democratic candidate.

"I told him that Harry Spencer, who had assisted me in previous campaigns, was onboard for political advertising and advice," Bill said. "Frank Peterson thought that I should be the candidate for governor, and said so at the meeting. We were all set."

The governor seemed interested, but noncommittal.

They had no further discussion on the issue until the May 1970 Republican state convention convened at the Pioneer Theater in Reno. Governor Laxalt hoped to avoid what had happened at the convention two years earlier when Bill Raggio and Ed Fike split the party in their primary election bids. Both men had not yet made a formal announcement to run, and Laxalt wanted to try to work things out in advance.

Laxalt approached Bill about running for the U.S. Senate against Howard Cannon. Cannon appeared vulnerable because he had barely won the election in 1964. Bill advised Laxalt he wanted to run for governor and had a favorable rating in the state. "He repeated that the party would like me to run for the senate and added that they wanted Ed Fike to run for governor," Bill would later say. "I told Paul that Ed did not sell well because he was very thin on substance."

The next day, Governor Laxalt visited Bill at his office in the district attorneys' office, just across the street from where the convention was being held. The governor again asked Bill to run for the senate and let Fike run for governor. "We are going to have a good ticket, a Dream Team[1] for the Republicans," Laxalt said.

"Again, I stressed that it was asking a lot of me because I had a real shot at becoming governor," Raggio recalled. "I did not have any political baggage and I thought I could win. In addition, it was an election year for the district attorney position and if I lost, I was going to be out of office after eighteen years. What was I going to do?"

Before Laxalt left the office, he asked Bill to think more about running for the senate. Before Bill could do much thinking about it, the phone rang. It was Vice President Spiro T. Agnew.

Bill remembered the call:

> To get a call from the vice president urging me to run for the U.S. Senate was heady stuff for a small town district attorney. He said the president would have called personally, but was busy with the Cambodia operation. Agnew promised all the campaign funding I would need. In addition, the president would have his cabinet secretaries and staff out campaigning for me.

> He explained how it looked like a favorable race for us. Soon I received calls from several of the cabinet people, including Attorney General John Mitchell, urging me to run for the U.S. Senate.

After the barrage of calls from Washington, D.C., Bill spoke again with the Governor Laxalt and asked, "If I agree to take on this long shot-chance of beating an incumbent senator, and lose, what was I going to do?"

Laxalt replied that it was not an issue because "next year you will be sitting in the U.S. Senate." Raggio reiterated his point, stating that he would have to give up his job as district attorney in order to run. Bill told Laxalt that if he ran for governor, he would likely win; however, if he ran for U.S. Senate against a strong incumbent like Cannon, the probability would be high that he would have to start all over in private law practice at the age of forty-four.

"Laxalt then said to me," Bill recalled, "'if you should lose, we will open up a law practice together.' I still remained a bit reluctant and so he restated that it was a certainty we would do that."

Bill had seen how successful Grant Sawyer's law practice was since leaving the governor's office and felt that, should he lose the senate race, being in a private law practice with former Governor Laxalt would leave him with financial stability. Bill remembered the governor then sweetened the pot:

To further allay my concerns, Paul said that if I lost the race, and Ed Fike became governor, Ed would appoint me to any judicial position, either district court or Nevada Supreme Court, that opened up—if I decided I wanted that. He then provided me with a letter signed by Ed Fike agreeing to this. Those two incentives, Paul's promise of opening a law practice together if I lost, and a judicial appointment by Fike if he won, were what persuaded me to be a good Republican, give up my quest for governor and run for the U.S. Senate instead.

*Time* magazine later reported an account of the story:

In Nevada, Nixon wanted Governor Paul Laxalt to run against Cannon and told him so in a White House talk. "I need friends bad," the president said. When Laxalt insisted on retirement, and his decision threatened a party split in the state over his successor, Nixon had Agnew persuade Raggio, one of two Republicans who wanted the governorship, to run for the senate instead.[9]

On May 2, 1970, Bill accepted his party's nomination to run for the U.S. Senate. His speech to the convention began with an eloquent recitation of core Republican principles going back to the Party's first presidential candidate, Abraham Lincoln.

Bill then listed his personal qualifications and difficulty of his decision to run for the senate, one that "troubled" him more than any other decision in his life.

He described the three options with which he had grappled: remaining as district attorney, returning to private life—which, he said, would provide financial security for his family and had "great appeal in terms of Dottie and I regaining our lost privacy"—or seeking the U.S. Senate seat held by Senator Cannon, which would involve the rigors of opposing a well-entrenched incumbent with unlimited financing and recognition in populous Clark County.

"The governorship of this great state has much appeal to me," he said. "But one does not take lightly a request by his president and vice president. Again and again, I reviewed the alternatives in view of this development. Finally, last evening I came to my decision. I've decided to respond to the call of our president and hereby announce my candidacy for the United States Senate." [10]

It proved to be the most important decision of his life.

The next day Bill hit the campaign trail and came out swinging. "The Liberals have had their time and have failed and left chaos in their wake," he stated. "It is time that people of more conservative philosophy be given the chance to retrieve this nation from the wreckage that the Liberals have left to us."

By "wreckage," Bill was referring to a nation engulfed in a level of civil strife not seen since Appomattox. Many in the country, particularly younger Americans, had become disenchanted, not just with the more conservative norms of the time, but with mainstream liberalism as well. This created a counter-culture of social revolution in the United States, as well as in other industrialized nations around the world.

Once peaceful demonstrations to bring about social justice for minority groups and an end to U.S. military involvement in Vietnam, had turned into more strident, often violent, protests. Between 1960 and 1969, reported incidences of violent crime in the United States nearly doubled. Rioting in such cities as Newark, Los Angeles, Detroit and Chicago resulted in enormous losses of property and life. In the United States, political assassination had become a frequent occurrence.

In November 1969, a massive anti-war march on Washington, D.C., attracted over 500,000 demonstrators. Televised coverage of these legions of angry, young people massed in defiance of the elected government was distressing for many citizens who feared for the nation's very existence. By the end of the decade, politicians such as Richard Nixon and George Wallace, promising to restore "law and order," appealed to many Americans.

In early May, 1970, President Richard Nixon announced that he had ordered U.S. forces into Cambodia in an effort to destroy what had long been a sanctuary and supply conduit for communist forces fighting in South Vietnam. Many saw this action as an escalation of a war they were desperately trying to end. Campuses across the nation exploded in protest.

At Kent State University, over 1,000 Ohio National Guard troops were called in to restore order. Two days later, a company of guardsmen opened fire on a group of demonstrators, killing four and wounding nine others. Eight million students and teachers closed hundreds of universities, colleges and high schools across the country in protest.

Although the University of Nevada remained relatively calm by comparison, these events had a polarizing affect on the community. When a student at the Reno campus complained that her instructor had used obscenities in a classroom, Bill Raggio immediately admonished university administrators for not taking adequate disciplinary action against such behavior that "had occurred in a publicly funded institution."

Joe Crowley, who would later become one of the most respected presidents of that institution, was, at the time, a young professor there. He wrote a tongue-in-check letter, published in the *Gazette*, mocking Bill's stand on the issue.

In it, Crowley pointed out that such incidents were not widespread, and that, in this instance, the expletives in question had come from a history department teaching assistant. He objected to Bill's "harping" on the subject of obscenity in the classroom, and ended the letter on a theatrically sardonic note:

> No, friends, we must keep him here at home rather than in the senate where as a private citizen, par excellence, he can guard us from the forces of darkness, protect us from the prurience, stay us from temptation and serve unofficially as our grand expert— expunging expletives in the classroom, purging profanity on the job, blasting blasphemy in the home and waiting all the while for his inevitable canonization.[11]

The letter probably had little negative impact on Bill's race (the voting age at the time being twenty-one), and perhaps some positive effect from the more conservative segment of the population. Ironically, it helped catapult Professor Crowley toward the presidency of the university, as he explained in 2008:

> What is interesting about all this is that this letter, in a very real sense, made my career. It got a lot of attention in the newspapers. Within a few weeks, I was asked to fill a vacancy at the College of Arts and Sciences and ultimately became Chair of the Faculty Senate in 1971. When President Milam was fired in 1978, I let my name be brought up for that position, not believing that I had a chance to be elected. I went along rather reluctantly to run interference for another person who I wanted to win. But in the end, I got the job.

The Kent State killings would have a dramatic effect on the campaign from another, entirely unexpected direction. President Richard Nixon, seeking to soften public criticism about that event and the ongoing invasion of Cambodia, created a bipartisan, blue ribbon fact-finding committee to travel to Cambodia and report on the results of the operation. Incredibly, Nixon selected Bill's opponent, Senator Howard Cannon, as a committee member.

Bill would never forget that decision. "We were furious," he later said. "I was sure a deal had been made between the president and Cannon. However, we were in the midst of a campaign and I could not let it show. You just had to roll with the punches. That's what you did."[12]

Nixon, who early in his political career earned the moniker "Tricky Dick," had a Machiavellian knack for such political maneuvering. Though encouraging Raggio to depose the incumbent Democratic senator, Nixon also knew that Cannon, a retired Air Force reserve major general, was influential in military matters and a strong advocate of large defense appropriations. The president needed Cannon's public support of his Vietnam War policies and the senator did not appear to be unsympathetic.

Syndicated Washington columnist Clark R. Mollenhoff reported the difficulty Bill Raggio faced in the race, because of the president's hedging. On October 27, 1970, in a column entitled, "Blunder by White House in Backing Nevada Candidate," the Pulitzer-Prize winning Mollenhoff wrote:

> White House political bungling that has left Raggio in a deep hole. Raggio…is lagging several thousand votes behind Senator Cannon and he blames a good deal of it on inept political management at the White House. He called the White House immediately to complain that his action was undercutting from his campaign in a key area. White House strategists apologized to Raggio and said it was too late to take Cannon off the Vietnam panel and assured him that it would not happen again. For Raggio, the apologies were not satisfactory, for it turned out that one such political mistake was enough to wreck an important part of his campaign strategy…pointing to the past Cannon record of obstruction of Mr. Nixon's policies.

> Cannon went to Cambodia and came back in support of the Cambodian strike. This support thwarts the Administration from pointing Cannon out as in the "radical liberal" class.[13]

Reno journalist Dennis Myers observed that this was only part of the problem facing Raggio:

> It is difficult for a congressional candidate to run as a White-House-sponsored candidate. It locks him in on issues, it disciplines his reactions to events, it conditions public reaction to him. He is seen as something less than his own man.[14]

In an attempt to mitigate the damage they had done, the White House arranged an impressive and highly visible visit to Washington, D.C. for the candidate in June 1970. Bill and Governor Laxalt went together to meet with President Nixon and experienced a rather inauspicious entrance to the White House.

Upon arriving there the two men realized that neither carried any identification, not even a drivers license. The only thing Bill had with him was a campaign brochure with his picture on it. Despite that, the guards let them pass through the private entrance and into the Oval Office.

"Nixon was very charming and was clearly pleased that I had agreed to be candidate for the U.S. Senate," Bill recalled. "He echoed the promises made by Vice President Agnew that he would provide me all the help he could, including adequate funding for the campaign and public appearances in Nevada by cabinet officials on my behalf."

During the meeting, Nixon and Raggio discussed the Vietnam War and the need to take a hard stand against crime in the country.

Over the next few days, Bill would meet with top Nixon administration officials. He urged Attorney General John Mitchell to assist law enforcement officials in Nevada by increasing and continuing financial assistance for them. Mitchell was amenable, citing his concern that liberal Democrats in Congress were attempting to weaken the president's proposed legislation to fight crime in the country.

As president of the National District Attorneys Association, Bill Raggio had previously met Mitchell and later told the press he "was pleased that the attorney general is taking a strong position for legislation needed to fight crime."

Later, in a discussion with Secretary of the Navy John Chafee, Bill asked him to consider improving the Naval Ammunition Depot at Hawthorne and to approve additional housing for employees in nearby Babbitt. Bill then met with Secretary of State William Rogers, and was briefed on the recent developments in Cambodia, telling reporters, "I was reassured by the progress being made in the deAmericanization of the war in Vietnam and the role the Cambodian operation in helping this come about."

Before returning home, Bill also met with Vice President Agnew, Secretary of Interior Walter Hinckle, Secretary of Housing and Urban Development George Romney, Senator John Tower of the Republican Senatorial Committee, Harry Gant, Special Counsel to the President, and Jim Allison, Deputy Chairman of the Republican National Committee.

Once back in Nevada, Raggio hit the campaign trail. Governor Laxalt joined him on several occasions, or headed out on his own to campaign for the candidate. The governor also infused Bill's campaign staff with some of his own experienced political advisors such as Alan Abner and Hazel Gardella. Barbara Vucanovich would manage the Raggio for Senate campaign headquarters. Distinguished author Robert "Frenchy" Laxalt, the governor's brother, helped with speechwriting. Still there were problems with funding. "They did not entirely keep that part of the agreement," Bill said. "My campaign did not get all the funding that was promised by the Nixon Administration and was left with a deficit."

The campaign was, indeed, expensive and funding was vital for success, especially for a candidate with a wife and three children to support. Bill received campaign contributions funding from a variety of sources. One unusually large contribution came from an old friend. In 2008, Bill related the following:

> In the early summer of 1970, I received a phone call from Frank Sinatra's attorney, Mickey Rudin. He said Frank had heard about my run for the U.S. Senate and would like to help. I met with Frank in Oakland, California a few days later and he handed me a campaign contribution check in the amount of $25,000—a sizeable amount of money at the time [the equivalent of $132,000 in 2008].

Television political advertising was not as vital to a successful campaign as it is today, and candidates were expected to get out and "press the flesh." In 1970, the population of Nevada was a mere 489,000, the vast majority of whom lived in either Clark or Washoe counties. With such a relatively low number of registered voters, every vote counted,

Angelina (Avansino) Raggio and Ben Raggio with daughter, Florence, and son, William J. Raggio (c. 1899).

William Raggio, Sr., and Clara (Cardelli) Raggio with son Billy (c. 1929).

"Little Billy" Raggio, with his dog, "Mitzie" (c. 1932).

Bill Raggio earned the rank of Life
Scout in 1940.

Bill graduated from Reno High School in 1944.

Washoe County District Attorney, and later U.S. Senator, Ernest S. Brown was an early and influential mentor to Bill. (Photo courtesy of John Webster Brown)

# Vice Figure on the Town

JOE CAMPO, JACQUELINE HITSON, JOE CONFORTE, JOAN JOHNSON
Brothel owner and friend visited S. F. night club last November with trial witness and another date

# Prostitute's 'Kidnap' Plea Rejected

Continued from Page 1

and that "the man involved was Raggio."

The girl herself denied that she had been kidnaped or that Raggio was the father of her child.

## Protests Cancel Golden Speech

GREENVILLE, S. C., June 15 (AP)—Harry Golden, best-

to frame me so I had a witness with me at all times," said Raggio.

"Jacqueline is not being detained against her will and will be in court when the time comes."

house that was burned to the ground on court order three months ago.

(*Left to right*), Joe Campo, Jacquelyn Hitson, Joe Conforte and Joanne Johnson at a San Francisco night club in 1959. Note that newspaper caption mistakenly identifies Joanne Johnson as "Joan."

DA Bill Raggio watches as Joe Conforte's Triangle Ranch brothel burns to the ground on March 23, 1960.

Leaflet distributed during a 1962 political smear campaign against DA Bill Raggio. The young woman and baby talking (*at left*) are an allusion to persistent, though debunked, rumors that Bill had fathered Jacqueline Hitson's child.

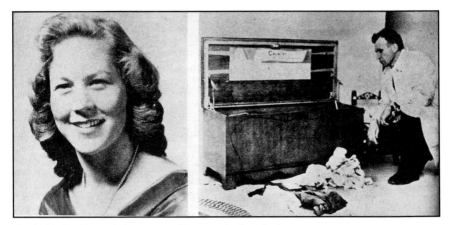

Sonja McCaskie and the scene of her murder/mutilation.

DA Raggio and Reno Chief of Police Elmer Briscoe consult during the McCaskie murder investigation.

Thomas Lee Bean (*left*), the man accused and convicted of murdering Sonya Mc-Caskie, is escorted to jail by Assistant Chief of Police Bill Brodhead.

Bill Raggio and Frank Sinatra at the Reno airport on December 9, 1963. Sinatra's son had been kidnapped at South Lake Tahoe. Bill would attempt to drive Frank there that night, but a heavy snowstorm in the mountains forced them to return to Reno.

Raggio's Raiders. Seated (*clockwise*): David Parraguirre, Gene Barbagelata, Rick Ahlswede, Bill Raggio, Clint Wooster, Bill Hadley, R. Gaynor Berry, Herb Santos. Standing (*left to right*): Larry Hicks, Paul Toland, John Peevers, Russ Schooley, Bob Canfield and Bill Cobb (c. 1965).

Bill and his friend, attorney Melvin Belli ("The King of Torts").

Grant Sawyer, Congressman Alan Bible and Bill Raggio in front of the U.S. Supreme Court Building in Washington, D.C.

Hal Lipset ("The Private Ear"), famed attorney Jake Ehrlich and Bill Raggio.

Former President Harry S. Truman meets with members of the National District Attorneys Association. Bill Raggio is second from the right.

Bill and publisher Hank Greenspun.

Bill and FBI Director J. Edgar Hoover.

The Raggio children (*left to right*): Tracy, Leslie and Mark.

DA Raggio meets California Governor Ronald Reagan in 1967 as Nevada Governor Paul Laxalt (*center*) and Charles Lanning, M.D., Chair of the Washoe County Republican Party, look on.

Bill showing off his catch in front of his home on Robin Street in Reno.

DA Raggio with Orleans Parish DA Jim Garrison in 1968. Garrison's bizarre behavior surrounding his well-publicized conspiracy theory regarding the 1963 assassination of JFK, disrupted the NDAA meeting in New Orleans that year.

ANNUAL BANQUET of the National District Attorneys Association convention was cancelled Saturday afternoon by Jim Garrison, right, after William Raggio, left, asked him not to speak at the affair. Photo above was taken earlier in the week, as the convention started. Raggio, of Reno, is president of the association.

# Garrison Cancels Talk, Claims Censorship Try

NEW ORLEANS (UPI)—Dist. Atty. Jim Garrison abruptly cancelled a scheduled speaking engagement before the National District Attorneys Association Saturday claiming the association tried to censor his speech.

The controversial district attorney said the leadership of the association, asked him Saturday afternoon to omit such strong criticism.

But Garrison said he refused and, instead, cancelled both his speech and a banquet which his office was to have sponsored.

Raggio, a Republican, later said he had an advance agreement, worked out some time ago with Garrison's office, assuring the association the district attorney would not discuss the assassination.

Raggio, of Reno, Nev., said Garrison broke the agreement

(See Garrison, Page 4, Col. 1)

Bill files to run for the U.S. Senate on July 13, 1970. (*Left to right*): Bill, Governor Paul Laxalt, Dorothy, Tracy, Leslie, Mark and Bill's mother, Clara.

Bill discussing strategy with President Richard Nixon in the Oval Office early in his 1970 campaign for the U.S. Senate.

Bill with U.S. Attorney General John Mitchell campaigning in 1970. Dorothy Raggio is on the elephant's trunk. The banner on the side of the GOP mascot reads, "Win Big with Bill Raggio."

and candidates for statewide office were expected to travel to nearly every inhabited site in the state to ask for support. Because Nevada covers over 110,000 square miles, geographically the 7th largest state in the country, this presented a challenge for the Raggios.

"Dorothy and I would pack up the car with my son and daughters and travel to almost every town in the Nevada," Bill later recalled, "chatting over fence lines with ranchers in between." Under Dorothy's direction Leslie, Tracy and some of their girlfriends, formed "Bill's Belles." This ensemble would dress in old-fashioned dresses and entertain crowds with songs and dancing wherever they stopped.

Dottie and the children canned hundreds of jars of pickles; labeling them with campaign messages to be handed out along the campaign trail. The pickles were so delicious that, in some parts of state, Dottie became more famous than Bill.

For years thereafter, people, especially in the rural counties, still talked about her pickles, hoping Bill would run for statewide office again so they could enjoy his wife's famous delicacy. Speculation about the ingredients was piqued when a photo appeared in newspapers showing the kids sitting around the Raggio kitchen table, slicing onions for the pickle jar; each melodramatically protecting themselves from the effects of the onion by wearing sunglasses, a slice of bread hanging from their mouths.

Bill was required to attend nearly every public event in the state. Although he had not ridden many horses, it was necessary in Nevada to ride one in parades. Bill's friend, Sharon Green, a barrel racer on the rodeo circuit, had a horse she sardonically named "Flash." Sharon would lend him Flash for parades.

"I always felt sorry for the horse because he was used to good riders," Bill said. "I rode Flash in Fallon, Lovelock and Elko, as well as in the Reno Rodeo Parade. When I rode Flash in a parade in Battle Mountain, we went up and down the street three times because the town was so small."

In 2008, Paul Laxalt recalled that during a campaign stop they made together for a parade in Winnemucca, Bill had forgotten to bring his cowboy boots. "That probably is an indication of why he did not do well in the Cow Counties," Laxalt said. "It would have cost him votes if he joined that parade in street shoes. I happened to be wearing a beautiful pair of custom-made boots that had been presented to me as governor by a famous boot maker in Texas. Since Bill and I were about the same size, we swapped footwear."

Laxalt then added amusingly, "To this day Bill has never returned them. I loved those boots dearly for the short time that I had them."

In Eureka and Austin, Bill rode a llama, and in Las Vegas, he rode a tame Brahma bull in the Helldorado Parade.

While in Las Vegas, Bill was asked to speak to an organization called the West Side Caucus. This group was comprised of black businesspeople and community activists, who regularly interviewed candidates for office. Bill knew the members of the West Side Caucus were overwhelmingly in favor of Democrat candidates and were unlikely to support him. Nevertheless, he decided to try it. The interviewers were polite, though, at times, "condescending."

> Toward the end of our meeting, one man asked me, "Mr. Raggio, if you are elected U.S. senator, how many blacks will you appoint to your office?" The question caught me a bit off guard because I had not really thought about that. Therefore, I took a gamble and replied, "If I appoint just one, it will be one more than Senator Cannon has on his staff." As it turned out, the senator did not have even one African-American in his office. After that, some of the West Side Caucus members seemed to treat me with more respect. Maybe I even picked up a vote, or two.

In August 1970, Bill met a second time with President Nixon while both were attending a national conference of the Law Enforcement Assistance Administration in Denver. On September 13, Vice President Spiro T. Agnew came to Las Vegas and appeared at two functions in support of the candidate: a $1,000 per person cocktail party attended by 200 Republican supporters and a $100 per couple dinner, which drew 1,600 guests.

Some of the nine "bright young candidates" Nixon had chosen to win back a majority in the U.S. Senate, like Minnesota's Clark MacGregor, were not enthusiastic about receiving public support from Agnew. However, the vice president's strident campaign rhetoric was popular among most Republicans. Bill's campaign manager, Alan Abner, was one of them, saying that Agnew was "tremendously popular here [in Nevada]. Not just with Republicans but with Democrats too—'Hard Hats.'* A guy like Agnew really speaks their language."

While the funds raised would be useful to Bill's campaign, Agnew's words fell short of the mark in stirring the Nevada electorate. Dennis Myers would write, "Agnew's speech in Las Vegas was not at all tailored to Raggio's Nevada needs; rather it pursued Agnew's national agenda with its denunciation of a 'drug culture' in things like rock and roll lyrics."[15]

Journalist Clark Mollenhoff agreed:

> Even as Raggio's spot television commercials have tried to emphasize Cannon's wobbly position on Vietnam, Cambodia and military preparedness, a host of administration speakers, including Vice President Spiro Agnew, have given Senator Cannon such light criticism that it has almost amounted to an endorsement.... Agnew raised about $300,000 for Raggio's campaign, but he also set the pattern for failing to criticize Cannon...Raggio has been left to carry his own attacks on Cannon.[16]

Senator Cannon highlighted this failure of the Nixon Administration to criticize him, when he later boasted with sardonic pleasure that he had not even made Vice President Agnew's 1970 list of "radical liberals."[17]

---

*Term used at the time to describe politically conservative blue-collar workers, often from the construction trades.

Not all the political blunders affecting Bill's campaign for the U.S. Senate were emanating from the White House. Perhaps the oddest twist occurred on the evening of October 21, 1970, when non-candidate Governor Paul Laxalt found himself debating Jack Anderson on television. Anderson was America's premier investigative journalist and produced a nationally syndicated newspaper column and radio program from his hometown of Salt Lake City.

The debate occurred one week after Anderson, "on a slow news day,"[18] wrote a column accusing Lieutenant Governor Ed Fike of corruption. Anderson claimed that in addition to serving as lieutenant governor, Fike was also the vice president of a corporation negotiating a land purchase from the state of Nevada. Further, Fike purchased property along the Colorado River from the state "at a suspiciously cheap price, and his company stood to make more than $2 million by developing the land."

"State politics," Anderson continued, "simply does not hold enough interest for a national audience, but there was something special about the frontier flavor of Nevada politics, mingled in those days with mob influence in casinos....To give it a national flavor we added some tidbits about a campaign stop in Las Vegas by Vice President Spiro T. Agnew to stump for Senator Bill Raggio. In blatant violation of state rules with regard to corporate meddling in campaigns, signs announcing Agnew's visit and a rally for Raggio had been plastered on casino marquees."

When Governor Laxalt publicly questioned Anderson's credibility, the journalist challenged him to debate the issue. Laxalt accepted. Anderson immediately received a call from Bill Raggio's opponent, Howard Cannon. "Senator Howard Cannon begged me to cancel the debate," said Anderson, "fearing I would make a poor showing against the polished Laxalt thus sealing the election for Fike and dragging other Democrat candidates down to defeat."[19]

Cannon need not have worried. Laxalt, a gifted debater, was off his game that night and Anderson quickly knew he had the advantage. "Just a few moments in to his [Laxalt's] opening remarks," Anderson wrote, "I realized with satisfaction that he had not done his homework."[20]

Bill Raggio watched the debate on TV in Las Vegas along with Ed Fike and some of Governor Laxalt's close advisors.

Bill later said that "Jack Anderson started off by throwing a couple of curve balls at Paul. Instead of being a debate about the issues, it became a debate about Paul Laxalt. Paul tried to defend himself and fell flat on his face. It was the only time I had ever seen Paul at a loss. Everyone in the room was amazed at how Paul was whipped in this debate."

During the thirty-minute event, Laxalt repeatedly expressed his indignation on behalf of the citizens of Nevada. "Here in Nevada, we're a little bit sensitive about this. We feel we've taken enough of this type of irresponsible criticism from eastern columnists and it's time to fight back." Unfortunately, he never got on track addressing the issues at hand. Anderson was briefly on the defensive about charges that his interest in the election was because both he and Howard Cannon were Mormons, then switched topics to the Raggio campaign.

Jack Anderson charged that federal laws were violated when corporations, in the form of Las Vegas hotels, advertised Vice President Spiro T. Agnew's September 13 visit. The columnist went on to accuse Gaming Control Board Chief, Frank Johnson, of violating the Corrupt Practices Act when he called Las Vegas hotels asking them to advertise Agnew's visit. "The Corrupt Practices Act ought to be obeyed; particularly by those who preach law and order," Anderson said.

Governor Laxalt replied that the allegations against Frank Johnson contained "half truths" and "innuendos." He pointed out that "in 1964, when [Democratic] President Lyndon Johnson came to Las Vegas, you couldn't see anything but his name." Anderson then referenced his column, saying that not only were the hotel marquees illegal, but some booths in Las Vegas hotel lobbies, set up in Raggio's behalf, violated Federal law.

Bill's angry response appeared the next day in the news:

> Anderson talks like he writes his column, without specific facts and, I am now convinced, without real knowledge. Some volun-

teers from my campaign committees arranged to be in the hotels. The signs they made mentioned nothing of my name. They were there to push the rally at the airport for the vice president. That's it. They were volunteers and not hotel people in any sense… This is an example of the smear tactics Anderson uses. It's hard to believe his credibility is not shot.[21]

Interest in the debate was high, but when it was over, the bulk of the viewing audience believed the governor—intentioned, or not—was skirting the issues.

Shortly after the Laxalt-Anderson debacle, the Nevada State Bar Association decided to withhold its recommendation on possible disciplinary action against Bill until after the penalty hearing for convicted slayer Thomas Lee Bean. That hearing was scheduled for November 16—two weeks after the election. Bill requested an immediate decision, so that he would not have the continuing uncertainty hanging over his race for the senate, but was denied. These were all distractions he did not need.

The political bungling surrounding his campaign was only part of the problem. Howard Cannon steadfastly refused to debate Bill and did not otherwise offer much of a target. As an aide to the fifty-eight-year-old senator boasted, "He's the most arch middle-of-the-roader I know."[22]

Raggio and Cannon were close on issues like Vietnam, crime and campus disruption. Bill's strongest issue was the economy, blaming the nation's woes on "the free spending liberal Democrats in Congress, like Senator Cannon."

By the end of October, Las Vegas oddsmakers had made Cannon a seven-to-five favorite. The White House, still believing they could capture a sizable number of the state's conservative Democrats, hurriedly sent a series of dignitaries to Nevada to campaign for Bill, including First Lady Pat Nixon. Mrs. Nixon was a native of Nevada, her father a miner in Ely, and so was a crowd favorite, particularly in the north.

Bill appreciated such appearances, but was still concerned that he had not received the full amount of campaign funding promised him by Nixon when he agreed to run for the senate. Cannon, on the other hand, seemed to have limitless financial support.

The campaign rhetoric heated up during a late October exchange in the press. Cannon stated that Vice President Agnew's visit trip to Las Vegas, and an imminent visit by President Nixon, polarized voters.

"It irritated a lot of people who might not have been irritated otherwise," Cannon stated. "The day after Agnew spoke at Raggio's dinner, which was televised throughout the state, the Cannon campaign headquarters was deluged with requests for yard signs and there was a substantial increase in the core of volunteer workers."[23]

Bill ignored Cannon's remarks about the Agnew visit, instead pointing out a recent gaffe committed by the senator with regard to a critical piece of gaming legislation in Congress.

"Pathetic performance and dangerous neglect by Cannon has endangered Nevada's legal gaming industry," Bill said. "Cannon let the recent anti-crime bill slip through the Senate without taking precautions to protect Nevada's legal gambling. If, after a dozen years in the Senate, he cannot still spot such obvious dangers to one of Nevada's major sources of income, than his seniority counts for absolutely nothing."[24]

A week before the election, the *Reno Evening Gazette* endorsed Bill Raggio. However, the two major southern Nevada newspapers were hostile. "I'm not whining," Bill told reporters. "I guess I just assumed that on the news pages you could get at least fair and equal treatment."

Bill spoke of how the *Las Vegas Sun* blasted the vice president's visit to that city. Bill said that the editor, Republican Hank Greenspun, "told me with his own lips that he had to support Cannon because Cannon had helped get a presidential pardon a few years ago when Greenspun was convicted of a felony."[25]

In late October, Zane Miles, the editor of Carson City's *Nevada Appeal*, resigned in protest after newspaper chain owner Don Reynolds forced an editorial endorsement of Howard Cannon on that newspaper. With that, Bill decided to confront the publisher.

Donald W. Reynolds was a hardnosed businessman. *Forbes* magazine called him remarkably "consistent in ruthlessness," with "a single-minded devotion to business" and "not much use for compassion."[26] Reynolds had once bragged about breaking the legs of a union picketer at his photoengraving plant by running over him with his car during a labor dispute.

Bill knew of Reynolds's reputation, but still needed to vent his dissatisfaction.

"I felt I was not getting a fair share of news coverage for my campaign and met with Don at his office," Bill said in 2008. "I told him that while he certainly had every right to endorse a candidate in an editorial, the day-to-day news reporting should be more fair and equitable."

Reynolds replied coldly, "You're not going to tell me how to run my newspaper." Annoyed by what he perceived as a gross injustice, Bill responded forcefully. "Let me tell you something. If I'm elected, you are not going to be telling me how to be a U.S. senator."

Reynolds just glared at the brash young man, but the newspaper's assistant editor, Don Digilio, who was also attending the meeting, now wore a stunned look of incredulity that someone would speak to his boss in that manner. Bill felt emboldened.

"Mr. Reynolds," he said, "you are finally going to have to give me some ink because President Nixon will be coming to Las Vegas and you are going to have to cover that story." With that, Bill left the office.

On October 31, 1970, President Nixon came to Las Vegas to make a speech to a big rally at the convention center. On the way to the venue that day, Bill had found himself alone with Nixon in the passenger compartment of the presidential limousine.

Bill later described that unforgettable ride:

> Nixon and I got in the big limo and drove down the Las Vegas Strip. The casino marquees contained messages welcoming the president. Not everyone was happy that he was in town. Some along the way were waiting with anti-Nixon placards. A few even made hand gestures of disrespect. To that, Nixon said to me, "I just smile and return them the favor"—although he was careful to keep his middle finger below the window so people couldn't see.

Later at the convention center, Nixon delivered his speech. While the Republican gubernatorial candidate, Ed Fike, was along side, the president's words were primarily about Bill Raggio and the U.S. Senate race.[27]

The next day, Bill fully expected to find a photograph of himself and President Nixon in the *Las Vegas Review Journal*. It did not materialize. He later recalled with amusement:

> There was a photo in the paper that had originally been taken of me, Fike and Nixon standing together. However, Don Reynolds had my image cropped out so that only Fike and Nixon appeared. Don got the last word and I learned a valuable lesson about trying to buck newspapers. Don Reynolds and I grew to respect one another over the years and became pretty good friends.

Two days before the election, Ed Fike sealed his defeat by publicly stating he would do away with sales taxes in the state if elected. Donal "Mike" O'Callaghan,* Fike's Democratic opponent, who had started the race twenty points behind in the polls, knew at that moment he would win the election. That night, O'Callaghan was on the radio pointing out that Fike failed to understand the Nevada Constitution which did not allow removal of the tax without it first being on the ballot for voter approval. O'Callaghan won by 6,000 votes.

It is difficult to gauge just how much Ed Fike's problems with the Colorado River property scandal and his sales tax remarks contributed to the defeat. Of the "Dream Team" Governor Laxalt had envisioned at his September 1969 meetings with Bill, only two of the six were elected, Robert List as attorney general and Wilson McGowan as state controller.

Bill Raggio lost in his bid for the U.S. Senate. The final vote tally was 73,357 to 50,451. He carried eleven of the seventeen counties in the

---

*O'Callaghan was born September 10, 1929 in La Crosse, Wisconsin. After becoming a highly decorated combat veteran in the Korean war, where he lost part of his left leg, O'Callaghan became a high school teacher and boxing coach in Henderson , Nevada. (He was Sen. Harry Reid's history teacher and later promoted Reid's political career). O'Callaghan's political career began in 1963, when Governor Grant Sawyer appointed him as director of the newly established Department of Human Resources.

state, including Washoe. Yet, he lost in populous Clark County, where Democrats had a three-to-one edge in voter registration due to a powerful union base and a sizable Mormon population, who, in 1970, still voted predominantly Democratic.

Bill was gracious in conceding defeat, and years later said, "The voters were smarter than I was and they reelected Howard Cannon as they should have. He had seniority, and some incumbency, and a lot going for the state. Even after such a tough race, Howard and I remained good friends until his death."

The day following the election, Bill received a telegram from President Nixon:

> *Dear Bill,*
>
> *I want to express my respect and appreciation to you for waging such a gallant battle in your campaign. From personal experience, I know the disappointment that you and your family must feel at this time. I am sure however that you will not allow this defeat to discourage you and your efforts to continue to provide leadership for our party and the nation. Mrs. Nixon joins me in extending our very best regards to you for the years ahead.*
> *— Richard Nixon.*[28]

Bill later said that although he liked a career in public service, he never liked politics very much, especially the campaigns.

> I did not like a lot of the people that you have to deal with in the campaign. I particularly disliked having to go out to raise money or spend time each day calling people for contributions. When you first file for political office, you think you have many friends out there who are going to go all out to help in the campaign. It is surprising to learn that about half of them go to the weeds and you never hear from them.

What makes up for that, Bill said, was the many new people whom he had never met, but who believed in him, who came out to help. "That was a wonderful experience for me," he said. "I have always appreciated the great friendships we made around the state during that campaign."

Bill would recall the sense of disillusionment that followed the election:

> After I lost the Senate race, I became somewhat despondent. The disappointment came because, obviously, I hate to lose, but also because I was faced with the prospect that I had to leave the district attorney's office within a month or so, because my term was up. So I had to decide what I was going to do.

Bill said he was relying on Governor Laxalt's pledge to him that they would start a law firm together. When he did not hear anything from Laxalt about this for some time, Bill finally contacted the now former governor, and asked him about it. In 2008, he related what transpired:

> Laxalt said that he had talked with his brothers and "they just don't think it will work out." I was astounded by his reply, and so he tried to put me down easy. Yet the fact remains that Paul did not keep his word to me. His promise was one of the big reasons I had agreed to run for U.S. Senate in 1970, instead of for governor. I firmly believed I would have been elected governor, so Paul's later decision not to start a law partnership left me with a bad feeling. I was let down.

# CHAPTER THIRTY-FIVE

# Private Life (1971-1972)

For several months, Bill felt adrift. He had years of legal training and courtroom experience but could not now use it. He considered going into personal injury law because he liked pleading a case before a jury. "I really enjoyed trial work," he said, "I guess I was part ham, but I purely enjoyed it."

In February 1971, Bill Raggio decided to accept an offer to become a partner in the well-established Las Vegas law firm, Wiener, Goldwater, Galatz. Lou Wiener and David Goldwater were trial lawyers and Neil Galatz specialized in personal injury cases. Bill thought it would be wise moving to Las Vegas. It was the largest city in Nevada and, by then, he had become well known there.

"I believed I would be a good adjunct for their law firm, and also felt it was time to begin making some better money and provide my family with more financial security," he said.

Also in the firm was a young lawyer, J. Charles Thompson. Bill became a mentor to Thompson, who, in his unabashed admiration of Bill, directly credits that fortuitous circumstance with his success in life. In 2008 interview, Thompson would tell of how he once joined Bill on a trip to Winnemucca to gain some experience in obtaining depositions.

Near the end of the meeting, the young attorney decided, on his own, to ask one final question: "Do you have anything more you want to add?" The person being deposed then went for several more minutes adding information that eventually "killed the case."

At the first opportunity, Bill took Thompson aside and firmly pointed out a lesson he would always remember: "Never," said Bill, "ask a question unless you already know the answer."

Raggio is unreserved in his praise for his former protégé, who went on to become a district court judge:

> Chuck Thompson is a consummate judge and the best trial judge the state has ever seen. Often judges would recuse themselves from cases, not because of a conflict of interest, but because the cases were difficult, high-publicity, "lose-lose" situations—frequently referred to as "career killers." Chuck has such integrity that he never refused any of those cases and did not care about the political fallout from them.

In early 1971, Bill was dealing with some "political fallout" of his own. The Board of Governors of the Nevada State Bar had been ordered by Nevada Supreme Court Chief Justice David Zenoff to take disciplinary action against Bill for public remarks he had made the previous year, critical of a ruling by the high court regarding the legitimacy of Thomas Bean's death sentence. Because of that ruling, Thomas Bean was allowed a second penalty hearing, held on November 17, 1970.

At that hearing, Bill Raggio, who had been defeated just two weeks earlier in his race for the U.S. Senate, presented such a compelling case that the death sentence was once again imposed.

The bar association had decided against a public hearing, which Bill had requested, and chose to wait until after his senate race to complete their investigation. In answering their writ, Bill said he had not intended being disrespectful to the court and that there had been a great deal of inaccurate emphasis placed on his remarks. He said his statements were in no way directed at the court itself, or to individual members, and claimed it was not his intent to interfere with a fair trial for Bean. Bill said he did not believe he violated any ethical standards in commenting on the case.

On July 13, 1971, the Supreme Court approved the recommendation of the bar and Bill Raggio was officially reprimanded. The reprimand did not prevent him from practicing law, but acted "simply as a public statement." The court, they stated, became the center of controversy and public confidence in the system of administering justice may have been eroded.

The document concluded:

> The inner motivation which caused Mr. Raggio to speak out in such an intemperate fashion, is unknown to us and we shall not indulge in presumptions or inferences adverse to him. We are never surprised when persons, not intimately involved with the administration of justice, speak out in anger or frustration about our work and the manner in which we perform it, and we should protect their right to express themselves. A member of the bar, however, stands in a different position by reason of his oath of office and the standards of conduct which he is sworn to uphold. Conformity with those standards has proven essential to the administration of justice in our courts. Mr. Raggio offended them, and, as recommended by the board of governors, we reprimand him therefore.[1]

Newspaper editorials immediately took up the cause again. Both those defending Bill's actions, as well as those who felt the disciplinary action was not harsh enough, accused the court of lacking "guts." Raggio, however, would remain silent—and the issue soon went away.

Bill's recent move to Las Vegas spurred speculation in the press about his future. *Gazette* political pundit Bob Stewart wrote:

> It should be remembered that he was asked by the vice president of the United States to seek a seat in the Senate...Raggio has never hinted that he was promised anything if he would give the senate contest a try...President Nixon made it clear during the

campaign that he liked Raggio. The question now is how much did Nixon like Raggio? [1]

That question would be answered in late 1971, when Bill received a telephone call from Harlington Wood, Jr., then-Director of the Executive Office for United States Attorneys and later Deputy Attorney General of the United States. Mr. Wood was calling to extend President Nixon's offer of the position of United States Attorney for the District of Nevada. In 2009, Bill described the conversation:

> I told him to let me think about it, but I didn't know if I was interested. I had just left a prosecuting attorney office after eighteen and a half years and gotten into private practice. The salary Mr. Wood offered, $30,000 a year, was no longer as attractive as it might have been when I was making only $19,500 as a county district attorney. I also had reservations about the job. The U.S. Attorney in Nevada had never been his own man because the federal strike force ran the show. They made all the decisions and the U.S. Attorney was just a figurehead.

The strike force Bill was referring to was created in 1961 by Attorney General Robert F. Kennedy to rid Nevada of corruption.

After the Kefauver Committee expired, the senate established the Permanent Subcommittee on Investigations, the "Rackets Committee," which held hearings from 1957 to 1963, and was chaired by Arkansas Senator John McClellan. These investigations culminated with the testimony of mob informer Joe Valachi. A number of people, including Dave Beck and Jimmy Hoffa of the Teamsters' Union, were sent to prison. Robert Kennedy, who acted as a special counsel to the committee in the late 1950s, brought with him his fixation with the mob when he ascended to the nation's highest law enforcement position in January 1961.

In his memoir, Governor Grant Sawyer recalled learning from Nevada Attorney General Roger Foley in the summer of 1961 that the U.S.

Justice Department wanted him to deputize sixty-five federal agents to carry out statewide raids on every major casino in Las Vegas and Reno.

Sawyer, who was a political ally of the Kennedys, and who considered himself a personal friend of the president, immediately flew to Washington, D.C. and met with Robert Kennedy. Sawyer later wrote, "He [Robert Kennedy] looked at Nevada, as many people did then, as a den of iniquity. Everybody who lived in, or came to, Nevada was corrupt, including me, and to clean up the state he was ready to assign a substantial force of agents to raid it."

The attorney general was in no mood that day to compromise, so Governor Sawyer went directly over to the White House and asked the president to call off the raid. "I got the impression," Sawyer wrote, "that he knew nothing about his brother's plan...He made no commitments, but the raids never occurred."[3]

Despite the raids being cancelled, the federal strike force "invaded" Nevada in less-overt ways, wire-tapping the phones of top casino executives and joining with the IRS to investigate their tax returns. Ironically, because many of the FBI methods were later ruled to be illegal, several solid IRS tax evasion cases were dismissed.

Federal strike force activities continued, at varying levels of intensity, over the next twenty-five years. As Grant Sawyer pointed out, even before the strike force arrived, Nevada already was home to more federal agents per capita than any other state in the nation.[4]

In a 2009 interview, Las Vegas Mayor Oscar Goodman, for many years a defense attorney for some who were accused of crimes by the strike force, described the environment by saying, "It was a war down here during those days. It was not a game. Every day, day-after-day, there was a major search, a major arrest, a major subpoena issued. It was really the United States of America versus Nevada. I like to think that most of the time we [Nevada] prevailed."

Bill Raggio had been offered the position of U.S. Attorney because of a scandal involving the current occupant of the office, Bart Schouweiler. Schouweiler had allegedly attended a party with some friends at a brothel owned by Joe Conforte. Attorney General John Mitchell, according to what Harlington Wood later told Bill, was "livid because he [Schouweiler] had brought disrepute to the office." Mitchell privately demanded Bart

Schouweiler's resignation, which he provided, but not before publicly blasting the methods of the strike force.

On February 13, 1972, in reporting his resignation, the *Nevada State Journal* wrote: "The difference between a Nevadan U.S. Attorney General, and some of the day helpers assigned here by the Justice Department, is that Schouweiler doesn't believe everyone who lives in the state is a crook or a hoodlum." An accompanying news story speculated that Bill Raggio would likely be appointed as Schouweiler's successor.

Bill did not believe Schouweiler was corrupt, and the brothel where he allegedly attended the party operated legally. "However," Bill later remarked, "it did show some bad judgment on his part by taking favors. I think he was a little too cozy with the likes of Joe Conforte."

Bill's coolness to Nixon's job offer prompted a personal visit by Harlington Wood to Bill's law office in Las Vegas.

Wood told Raggio that the president would very much like him to accept the position of U.S. Attorney, adding they would increase the salary and give Bill full authority in the state of Nevada, even over the federal strike force. The offer of "full authority" was based, Wood continued, on the confidence they had in Raggio's ability to do the job. He added that the only reason they did not give such authority to previous U.S. Attorneys, was that they did not have the level of experience that Bill did.

Bill said he was pleased they had that much confidence in him:

> I told Mr. Wood that the offer was tempting, but I still had concerns about my future. He then said that if I accepted the job, they would eventually consider me for the next federal judgeship, including a seat on the Court of Appeals. Despite all this, I refused.[5] As it turned out, [Attorney General] John Mitchell went to prison and both Vice President Agnew and President Nixon later resigned. I probably made a wise decision.*

---

*In October 1973, during his fifth year as vice president, Spiro T. Agnew was charged with having accepted bribes in excess of $100,000. On the condition that he resign the office of vice president, Agnew was allowed to plead *nolo contendere* to a single charge of failing to report $29,500 of income received in 1967.

On August 9, 1974, President Richard Nixon, with virtually no political support and facing the certainty of impeachment, resigned the office of the presidency.

On February 21, 1975, John Mitchell was found guilty of conspiracy, obstruction of justice, and perjury for his role in the Watergate break-in and cover-up and would serve nineteen months in prison.

Many were surprised when Bill refused the position of U.S. Attorney. Some saw this as evidence that his move to Las Vegas was being politically motivated—to position himself for another run for statewide office. Asked about this later, Bill admitted giving the political element some thought when he was considering the move.

However, Las Vegas had changed considerably since Bill's first statewide campaign in 1968. This was largely due to the arrival of Howard Hughes, who in November 1966, quietly slipped into town with his entourage on a night train and moved into the top floor of the Desert Inn.[6]

A few weeks later, Desert Inn co-owners Moe Dalitz and Ruby Kolod asked Hughes to vacate his rooms so they could make it available to high rollers coming to town for the New Year's holiday. Howard refused, and instead purchased the place for $13.25 million.

Hughes, who already owned a considerable amount of undeveloped real estate in the Las Vegas area, then went on a hotel-casino buying binge between 1966 and 1968, eventually acquiring the Castaways, New Frontier, Landmark, Sands and Silver Slipper, all with large parcels of adjoining property.

In 1957, Hughes, then already in near-total isolation, hired former FBI special agent, Bob Maheu. Maheu was to become his personal emissary. Strangely, in the thirteen years Bob Maheu worked for Howard Hughes, they never met face-to-face. Communication was always by phone or memo.

As K.J. Evans wrote in the *Las Vegas Review Journal* series, "100 People Who Shaped Nevada," many believed Hughes was on a "mission to demob" Las Vegas and open it up to legitimate business. Between his buying out so many old-timers in the casino business, and escalated federal law enforcement by the strike force, mob activity declined dramatically.

"He cleaned up the image of Las Vegas," said Maheu. "I have had the heads of large corporate entities tell me they would never have thought of coming here before Hughes came."[7]

To help this process along, Governor Paul Laxalt arranged for Hughes to be licensed to operate casinos without having to meet the requirement of appearing in person before the Nevada State Gaming Commission, something the reclusive Hughes had no intention of doing. Maheu appeared before the Commission as Hughes' surrogate and later remarked, "Laxalt saw Hughes as a better option than the mob."[8]

Bill Raggio came to know Bob Maheu well and, when running for the U.S. Senate, received a political contribution from him on behalf of the Hughes Corporation.

On November 5, 1970, Howard Hughes was secretly carried from the Desert Inn on a stretcher and flown to the Bahamas. Six years later, in continued seclusion, he would die from dehydration, malnutrition and, Maheu believed, willful neglect by his attendants.

Yet, Hughes' adventure in Nevada opened up the gaming industry to corporate investors. In 1969, the state legislature passed the Corporate Gaming Act and, in time, most of the major casinos, including those owned by northern Nevada gaming pioneer, Bill Harrah, had "gone public."

However, the federal strike force stayed busy. In the 1980's scandals involving skimming by organized crime operatives at the Stardust, as depicted in the Martin Scorsese film, *Casino,* brought national attention to the problem. However, by 1999, the National Gambling Impact Study Commission concluded: "All evidence presented to the Commission indicates that effective state regulation, coupled with the takeover of much of the industry by public corporations, has eliminated organized crime from direct ownership and operation of casinos."

Governor Laxalt, who presided over the events that set this implausible change in motion, did not always find the results entirely to his liking. In a 2008 interview he stated:

> I would far rather meet with the so-called old-timers than the corporate types that I dealt with later, because if one of the old-timers, like Moe Dalitz, ever gave you his word, that was it. It was solid. Corporate types always seem to find a gray area so they can get out of an obligation.

Bill Raggio's new law partners, David Goldwater and Louie Weiner, represented several clients with ties to organized crime, including Moe Dalitz, who writer Alan Balboni described as "the foremost of those men with shady pasts who created modern Las Vegas."[9]

Bill had a passing acquaintance with Dalitz, and later remarked how the stigma of early mob affiliations endured:

> The one thing most of them wanted was respectability and acceptance, and, for the most part, it was not forthcoming among a population where their intentions were carefully scrutinized. Dalitz, Fitzgerald and the Wertheimer brothers were recognized as important figures, contributing to their respective communities and very generous toward local causes. Yet, because of their past, they never received the respect they had hoped for.

When Bill first moved to Las Vegas, he took an apartment with the intention of buying a home and staying. Dottie came down on weekends, and they would go house hunting. Bill kept finding something wrong with the houses they viewed.

Finally, Dottie recognized the problem and said, "Bill, you really do not want to live in Las Vegas do you?" Bill had to agree. "I had nothing against Las Vegas," he later explained, "but I had my roots in northern Nevada and missed the hunting and fishing and spending time at Lake Tahoe."

Ultimately, Bill convinced his law partners that they should open an office in Reno, to establish a statewide presence. He opened a small office there, and was soon joined by his cousin, Ray "Skip" Avansino, who had been with Lionel, Sawyer and Collins in Las Vegas, and, like Bill, wanted to return to northern Nevada.

Within a year, Wiener, Goldwater, Galitz & Raggio decided to close their Reno branch. Bill chose to stay in Reno and amicably ended his association with that firm. Soon, larger law firms in the state would recognize the value of having statewide offices. "I was the first lawyer to see the value in having law offices at both ends of the state," Bill later quipped, "my idea might have been a just bit ahead of its time."

In 1973, Skip Avansino would leave the firm to establish Avansino, Melarkey, Knobel and Mulligan. Bill would briefly set up a law firm with Lee Walker, Clint Wooster, John Pilkington and Jeff Clontz.

Eventually, Bill and Clint Wooster, who had also served as an assistant district attorney in Washoe County while Bill was DA, would join with a bright young attorney, Michael Lindell, in establishing Raggio, Wooster and Lindell. The firm handled an occasional criminal trial, but focused primarily on civil law.

It was, at first, strange for Bill coming back to Washoe County and practicing law after so many years there as a prosecutor. Though most of his deputy DAs had been replaced, and his new practice rarely pitted him in a criminal proceeding against the DAs office, there were always reminders of his strong stance on lawbreakers as the county's top law enforcement official.

An amusing example of this came in November 1971, when as a private attorney, Bill sent a letter to the State Board of Pardons requesting clemency for a kidnapper he had sent to prison.

As DA, Raggio had convinced the man to provide testimony against his accomplices during the trial. Consequently, he was now in danger for his life and living in isolation from the general prison population. Nevada Supreme Court Justice John Mowbray, a Pardons Board member, used the opportunity to take a good-natured jab at the tough former DA by asking that Bill's letter be made a matter of public record "in view of the former district attorney's many appearances before this Board in opposition to such action as requested today." The Board honored his request, and voted unanimously to place the man on probation for the remainder of his sentence.[10]

Throughout 1972, Bill Raggio worked to put together his law practice. He enjoyed the new challenge and, largely because of name recognition from his district attorney days and two statewide political campaigns for U.S. Senate, the firm attracted numerous clients.

Nonetheless, Bill found that he missed public service and despite his aversion to certain aspects of politics, decided to run for the Nevada State Senate.

# CHAPTER THIRTY-SIX

# State Senate (1973)

Nevada's biennial, "citizen legislature" would allow Bill to continue to build his law firm while achieving his desire to serve the public. On May 25, 1972, he announced his intent to run for one of the two open seats representing Washoe-Storey Senate District 1.

An editorial in the *Reno Evening Gazette*, which had in the past routinely endorsed Bill Raggio for public office, was now endorsing another candidate, C. Clifton "Cliff" Young,* and was not kindly toward the former district attorney's candidacy. Referring to Bill as a "once popular politician," who had "gone sour," the editorial went on to say that Raggio "bit the hands of the taxpayers" upon leaving the DA's office by seeking $3,288.60 in accumulated sick leave.

He then "demanded that the people of Washoe County pay a $554.64 bill for moving his personal property from the plush district attorneys quarters the taxpayers have provided him."[1]

Bill knew what had prompted this change of attitude on the part of *Gazette* editor Warren Lerude. During the Thomas Bean trial, Bill had joined in a motion made by the defense counsel to prevent the newspaper from printing the names of jurors.

---

*Clarence Clifton (Cliff) Young was born in Lovelock, Nevada. He graduated from the University of Nevada in 1943 and saw combat as an Army officer in Europe during the war. He later graduated from Harvard Law School and was admitted to the Nevada bar in 1949. Young was elected to the U.S. House of Representatives from Nevada in 1953 and served until 1956. After an unsuccessful bid for the U.S. Senate, he was elected to the Nevada State Senate and served until 1980. He would go on to become President of the National Wildlife Federation and was elected to the Nevada Supreme Court in 1984, later serving as chief justice.

"Lerude was a strong advocate of 'freedom of the press' and did not approve of anything that appeared to be 'prior restraint,'" Bill later said. "I simply felt otherwise. That this was a high profile case with strong public feelings and I felt steps should be taken to insulate the jurors from outside pressure. The court agreed."

Despite these niggling accusations by the newspaper, Bill ran well ahead of the other five contenders for that district, garnering 7,324 votes in the state Republican primary election the following September. Four of the others had either been, or were currently, state senators, including the incumbent Cliff Young. Young polled the second highest number of votes, ensuring his name would also be placed on the general election ballot.

The unusually large number of senators, and former senators, on the general election ballot was due to recent reapportionment by the state legislature, which left many without districts. Washoe-Storey Senate District 1, had become a multi-member district with four seats in the state senate. Incumbent senator and former Reno Mayor Len Harris was eliminated in the primary election, leaving Bill in a four-way race for two senate seats against Young, former Storey County Senator James Slattery and former Assemblyman James C. Bailey.

Bill campaigned for better drug education for youngsters, measures to strengthen law enforcement and restoration of capital punishment for some crimes. He urged the reappraisal of priorities in expenditures of tax revenues in order to provide additional help to the neediest on welfare.

On Election Day, November 5, 1972, while President Richard M. Nixon trounced South Dakota Senator George McGovern in one of the most lopsided presidential elections in American history, Cliff Young (22,870 votes) and Bill Raggio (22,374 votes) claimed the two state senate seats by a wide margin over their opponents.

Bill would be arriving in Carson City during a period of enormous social and political change throughout the country. The Nevada Legislature, to which he had just been elected, had recently undergone a transformation like none other in its 109-year history.

While the Nevada Constitution, Articles 1 and 15, required that legislative apportionment be based on population, the legislature had been using a variety of other plans to determine how representation would be accomplished—none of them commensurate with population.

The state senate was comprised of one senator from each county, no matter how thinly populated the county was. In addition, each county was apportioned at least one member in the state assembly. This method had the effect of over-representing the rural counties at the expense of urban areas.

The 1960 census showed Nevada's population as being 285,278, ranging from as many as 127,016 in Clark County to as few as 568 in Storey County. With seventeen members in the state senate, apportioned one per county, the ratio of representation between those two counties was an astonishingly imbalanced 224 to 1.

In order to assure a fair distribution of seats in the U.S. House of Representatives, the U.S. Constitution requires a decennial census. Beginning in 1962, a series of U.S. Supreme Court decisions required states to ensure these districts were equal in population and that both houses of state legislatures be apportioned on the basis of population, then referred to as the "one-man-one vote" rule. [2]

Most Nevada legislators balked at such interference by the federal government and adjourned their 1965 regular legislative session without addressing the matter of apportionment. In order to rectify Clark County's underrepresentation in the state legislature, Democratic Assemblywoman Flora Dungan filed suit against Governor Grant Sawyer to force the issue.

Once *Dungan v. Sawyer* was heard in federal district court, Nevada's apportionment formula was determined to be unconstitutional. Governor Sawyer called a special legislative session to settle the matter, reminding the legislators that if they failed to redistrict the state properly, they would almost certainly be facing judicial reapportionment. The special session was convened on October 25, 1965 and adjourned twenty days later. [3] Traditional legislative power of the rural counties had now shifted dramatically and permanently to the urban areas of Nevada.

By 1971, the assembly established single-member districts, though in order to achieve incumbent protection and make the constituencies more manageable, created odd district boundaries reminiscent of traditional partisan gerrymandering.

The Senate resisted this change and retained multi-member districts, largely to protect incumbents in both Las Vegas and Reno who lived in close proximity to one another other.[4] The redistricting plan retained the same composition of the two houses—twenty members in the senate and forty in the assembly.

During Bill Raggio's first session in 1973, the Nevada State Senate would retain a sizeable Democratic majority. Of the twenty seats, only six would be held by Republicans. Of those six, only one, Chic Hecht, would represent a district in southern Nevada.

The senate majority leadership consisted of Mahlon Brown, an attorney from Las Vegas, whose engaging personality had made him an effective leader since 1965, and Floyd Lamb, chair of the powerful Senate Committee on Finance. Yet, the most respected and influential member of the state senate was James I. Gibson.[5] Gibson was the premier legislator in terms of historical perspective, intellectual ability and thoughtfulness. An engineer by training, he was the master of the budget, working his slide rule to compute dollar amounts while people testified.

Richard Bryan,[6] who would go on to become state attorney general, governor and U.S. senator, came to the state senate in the same year as Bill. In 2008, Bryan recalled the nonpartisan atmosphere of the body, saying Bill Raggio, though a Republican soon forged a very close relationship with majority members, particularly with Jim Gibson.

"Whereas Raggio had charm and pizzazz," Bryan noted, "Gibson was the Rock of Gibraltar and, although a Democrat in the majority, quite nonpartisan. Back in the late '70s, there were very few philosophical differences between Republicans and Democrats in the legislature."

Bryan went on to say that many in the legislature were concerned about Raggio's reputation as "a fire-breathing prosecutor," worried that he would be a single-issue person, arguing all the time about longer prison sentences and the like.

"However," Bryan added, "I was pleased to see how seamlessly his transition was from prosecutor to legislator. Bill, even then, was a man of considerable intellect and immense personal charm, and he fit into the state senate like a glove."

Bill Raggio would later comment about the "seamless transition" of which Bryan spoke:

> My oath as a prosecutor was to enforce the goals of the state and represent the state in criminal matters as well as civil matters. As a senator, I had to look at the whole picture, not only the criminal cases, but everything else we do.

Dan Miles, long-time Senate Fiscal Analyst with the Legislative Counsel Bureau (LCB), said in 2009 that despite the tough, conservative, law-and-order attitude Bill Raggio brought with him to the senate in the 1970s, Jim Gibson, the Democrat, "was even more conservative." Senator Raggio would later agree with that assessment.

That is not to say either man was close-minded. Partisanship was nearly nonexistent then, certainly worlds away from the current political climate. "I deplore partisan politics, "Bill said. "We did not have that when I was a young senator. Once the election was over, we worked together."

As a new legislator, Raggio would cut his legislative teeth on two emotionally charged issues of national interest: implementation of *Roe v. Wade*, the U.S. Supreme Court decision legalizing abortion,[7] and ratification of the Equal Rights Amendment.[8]

Feelings ran high on both sides of the abortion issue. State Senator Mel Close, a member of the Senate Committee on Judiciary, and a Mormon, whose church doctrine opposed abortion, articulated the dilemma faced by many legislators when he said he was "incensed" by the decision of the Supreme Court which "usurped the authority" of the state.

Though conceding the state must abide by the high court ruling, which had made Nevada's existing state law prohibiting abortion obsolete, Senator Close encouraged the body to create "the strictest abortion bill Nevada could constitutionally enact."

Freshman state Senator Raggio would quickly learn the difficulty of having to set aside one's personal feelings in order to uphold his recently administered oath of office. On February 16, 1973, Assembly Bill 319 was introduced. The bill was drafted to comply with the High Court ruling, permitting licensed physicians in Nevada to perform abortions, except where limited by certain conditions.

After much heated debate, the bill was approved by both houses and entered in the Nevada Revised Statutes on May 3, 1973. Bill had some familiarity with the subject from his days as district attorney, when he tried a doctor who was performing abortions and had gone on record supporting the law.[9]

During a 2008 interview, Bill recalled his soul-searching decision to vote for the legislation. He sought advice from Bishop Green of the Reno Catholic diocese, who told him that despite the church's doctrine with regard to abortion, he had an obligation to follow the nation's laws and in doing that, the church could not fault me.

> I appreciated his counsel. I am not sure many bishops today would give the same. Many legislators were reluctant to do that and allowed their personal religious beliefs to influence their vote. I could have argued that because I was a Catholic, I was going to refuse to change the law. But, I saw that as a violation of my oath as a senator, because the Supreme Court decision is the law of the land, as much as is an act of Congress. As such, I did vote to change our state law to conform to *Roe v. Wade.*

The other tough decision Senator Raggio faced in his first session was whether to vote for ratification of the Equal Rights Amendment (ERA). The Nevada Assembly took up the ratification issue in January 1973. However, the resolution failed in the senate, with Bill Raggio voting no.

Bill's primary concern was that the amendment would require women to be subject to the military draft and serve in combat (the draft would not be abolished until later that same year). It also seemed to broaden the circumstances under which abortion was legally permissible.

The senate held lengthy hearings on the subject and many people came to testify for and against the amendment, including Phyllis Schlafly, spokesperson for the Eagle Forum, who was known throughout the country for her opposition to the amendment.[10]

"It was a difficult vote because there was much to be said on both sides of the argument," Bill recalled. "I realized later that the ERA was not going to have as radical an effect on society as I first thought; but I also recognized it was not going to create all the changes its supporters promised."

It was a busy term for the new senator from Washoe County. Bill was appointed to six committees, including the powerful Senate Committee on Finance—the first freshman ever to be seated there. He proved to be independent from the beginning, voting his conscience and what he felt was in the best interest of the state. Bill would often be the single dissenting vote on a variety of issues, both in committee and on the senate floor.

Senator Raggio was particularly protective of any changes to the criminal justice system that he felt might hobble law enforcement or the courts, and remained a conservative voice against what he felt was the declining moral standards in the country.

As an example, when fellow Republican Senator Cliff Young sponsored a bill to lower the age at which girls could legally obtain birth control pills, from sixteen to fourteen, Bill was the only member on the Senate Health and Welfare Committee to vote against it. Despite such emotionally charged issues like abortion and the ERA, there were few philosophical differences between the two political parties.

However, that was about to change. For in the same year Bill was elected to the Senate, a thirty-seven-year-old electrical company personnel administrator from North Las Vegas also arrived. His name was Joe Neal.[11]

Neal would be the first African American senator in the state's history. He later recalled in his 2008 oral history that the ideological difference between Democrats and Republicans in the senate was so slight that, "I was the only true Democrat that was there."[12]

Senator Neal was intent upon shaking things up. The controversial and generally unpopular causes Neal took up in his first session are found in bills he sponsored to abolish the death penalty, provide equal pay and benefits for female employees, employer-provided childcare, cash assistance to needy children and the establishment of a consumer affairs unit. Neal knew these bills did not have a chance of passing. Most died in committee. However, he also knew that the press would carry stories about them and that would spur public discourse on the issues.

Senator Raggio would later recall Neal's first session:

> When Joe Neal arrived, he was very liberal and stood out. Therefore, it took him a long time to fit in. Even his fellow Democrats were not very receptive. This was not because of his race, but because of his positions, which, as I mentioned, were very liberal.

Bill told of how Senator Neal got off to a bad start by voting against a resolution to memorialize Senator Jim Gibson's father who had recently died. "I guess it was designed to prove he was going to be against everything," Bill said. "Some of his fellow-Democrats took him aside, however, and convinced him to change his vote, in a later re-vote, on the same resolution."

During this first session, Senator Neal was the primary sponsor of a bill that must have appeared to be aimed at infuriating his fellow freshman Bill Raggio. Senate Bill 422 allowed the restoration of civil rights to some ex-felons under certain conditions. Neal felt this was important in providing them opportunities for these ex-offenders in finding employment. The bill initially had some opposition.

As Neal later recalled, "Then one day a guy by the name of Jim Slattery shows up. I didn't know Jim Slattery from Adam, but I did know that he had been a senator. He came to me and asked if I needed any help with that bill. I said 'yes,' and he took that bill, and he ran it through the legislature."[13]

Slattery had lost his district due to reapportionment and later ran unsuccessfully against Bill Raggio and three other candidates in the 1972 race for the state senate. The lanky and loud Slattery was extremely conservative, especially with regard to progressive social legislation. It was an open secret that he was largely financed by Joe Conforte, who had political influence in the former state senator's home base of Storey County.

It was not until after the bill passed into law, that Neal learned Slattery had it amended just enough to allow his patron, Joe Conforte, to have his civil rights restored. Conforte had forfeited those rights as the result of a felony conviction for attempting to extort then-District Attorney Raggio in 1959.

Senator Raggio had been the only senate member to vote against the measure.

Senator Neal later stated he was irate at being tricked by Slattery to help a "whoremonger."[14] It was the only piece of legislation Neal would be able to pass during his first session.

In April 1973, as the legislative session wound down, Senator Neal shook things up again, by publicly charging that his fellow senators were not allowing more of his legislation to pass because of racial discrimination.

The outcry was immediate. An ill-tempered Senator Warren "Snowy" Monroe of Elko, blasted his fellow Democrat: "Neal's legislation is not getting passed because it is not acceptable."

Senator Raggio offered a more concise rebuttal at the time:

> He [Neal] has contributed a great deal of input, but the issues are decided on merits, not on who introduces them. In some ways, Senator Neal has rendered himself ineffective by taking stands that are inappropriate. I commend him for sticking to his principles, but you have to see the other point of view.

During his first session, Senator Raggio cosponsored dozens of bills and resolutions and was primary sponsor of eight bills, most dealing with law enforcement and public health issues. Of these, three passed into law.

Coe Swobe, who served nearly twelve years in the legislature, remembered in 2010 how impressed he was:

Bill Raggio knows how to frame issues correctly to build public support. He is exceptional at educating his audiences. As it would turn out, no one ever had a more positive influence on the state than Bill Raggio. He could have been many things, but I always felt that he did not seek the position; the position sought him.

By the time the 57th Session of the Nevada State Legislature adjourned, Bill had been named Outstanding Freshman Senator and, despite his being in the minority party, was considered a rising star in that legislative body.

Yet, before that prophecy would come to pass, Bill decided to take one more shot at statewide office.

# CHAPTER THIRTY-SEVEN

# Race for Lieutenant Governor (1974)

"It is an open secret," Bill Raggio told a reporters in January 1974, "that I would seek the governorship should Governor Michael O'Callaghan decides to vacate the office and seek election to the United States Senate."[1]

Bill had no illusions about the popularity of the Democratic governor, nor his ability to be reelected to that office if he chose.[2] Other factors entering his decision to run, would include the political climate in the state and the effect of the national situation on local races. "I am not referring to Watergate,"* Bill said, "which I see as a diminishing political issue, but rather such things as the energy crisis and the state of the economy."

By March 9, speculation in the media was high, fueled by the results of a public opinion from the previous fall. The poll, conducted by the Las Vegas company of Dr. Wayne Pearson, touted by one paper as "the most scientific and reliable pollsters in the state,"[3] showed Bill Raggio ahead of all Nevada Republicans in a potential primary election for the Nevada governorship.

Yet, Bill's hope of someday living in the Governor's Mansion was once again dashed when Governor O'Callaghan phoned him on April 5,

---

*"Watergate" refers the Watergate office complex in Washington, D.C. where, in June 1972, five men were arrested for breaking into the Democratic National Committee headquarters, which was located there, to, among other things, place "bugging" devices on the telephones. Evidence led investigators to an office in the White House. The resulting attempt by President Nixon and his staff to cover-up the crime led to the discovery of other illegal activity. The scandal ultimately led to the resignation of President Richard Nixon and the indictment and criminal conviction of several top administration officials.

1974, to say he was going to announce his run for reelection the following day. Raggio later said the governor had made his decision not to run for U.S. Senate primarily because he preferred living in Nevada.

Immediately following O'Callaghan's announcement, Bill was non-committal about his plans. Yet, many were surprised when on July 17, nine weeks before the state primary elections, Bill announced his bid for the office of the lieutenant governor.

Challenging the forty-seven-year-old state senator in the Nevada Republican primary election was Rex Bell Jr., a thirty-nine-year-old former Clark County justice of the peace, and son of the wildly popular lieutenant governor who had died while campaigning for governor in 1962.

Their campaign was spirited, but civil, and on September 4, 1974, Bill Raggio defeated Bell by a margin of 10%, to become the Republican Party nominee for lieutenant governor.

His Democratic opponent in the race would be Bob Rose,* who, in 1971, became Bill's successor as Washoe County district attorney. In that 1970 race, Rose had defeated Bill's long-time deputy district attorney, Rick Ahlswede. Bill contacted Bob just after the election to congratulate him and offer assistance in making an easy transfer to the office.

In 2010, Justice Robert Rose would say of that transition: "I was handed a very good office by Bill Raggio. He was a great prosecutor and a good administrator." Bill would later recall his relationship with Rose as one in which they were always "respectful of each other." Indeed, the campaign would be one of the more civil in state political history.

The candidates agreed on many issues, including having any change to state's "right to work" laws be put to a vote of the people. Both agreed that strong action was required to help the mining industry, particularly small mining concerns. Even on the issue of the ERA ratification, the two were close.

---

*Robert E. Rose graduated from New York University School of Law School in 1964 and gained his early legal experience as law clerk at the Nevada Supreme Court. He would eventually entering civil law practice with the firm of Goldwater, Taber & Hill in Reno. He would go on to be appointed as a district court judge, and serve three terms on the Nevada Supreme Court.

The one issue they came down on opposite sides was that of abortion. Rose was pro-choice and said the Supreme Court decision on abortion was the law of the land. Although Bill had remained true to his oath of office as a state senator, and voted to change the abortion ban in Nevada to comply with *Roe v. Wade*, he remained philosophically opposed to the practice.

He told a news conference at the Las Vegas Press Club just three weeks before the election that he favored a strong "right to life" amendment "recognizing the existence of life at inception and protection of that basic life of an unborn child." When asked if he was basing his convictions on religious reasons, Bill replied, "That happens to be my belief as a Roman Catholic. We are all products of our environment and religious background is part of that environment; but I do not legislate on the basis of my religion."

Though his truthfulness was honorable, the Nevada electorate was overwhelmingly pro-choice and Bill knew voicing such views was far from being politically expedient.

The Watergate scandal loomed above the 1974 election, putting all Republican candidates in a defensive posture, though none was actually involved in the intrigues of Nixon's inner circle. During the race neither the press, nor the Democratic candidate, tried to tarnish Bill's by bringing up his earlier association with some of the conspirators.

The most recent attempt to do so had been a year earlier, in July 1973 when the *Washington Star-News* published a report that Watergate investigators had discovered a fake organization operating out of a White House basement back room and run by Nixon attorney Herbert Kalmbach. Through it, Kalmbach had funneled $1.5 million in cashier's checks to Republican campaigns in 1970, including Bill Raggio's run for the U.S. Senate.[4]

Bill was quoted as saying President Nixon and Vice-President Agnew both encouraged him to run in the race and had "enlisted the support of a large number of individuals who contributed to my campaign," which spent about $200,000 in the race. Further, he had never heard of the organization named in the investigation. Bill pointed out that 1970 election laws did not require the various committees who aided him to report where their contributions came from.

This issue did not arise during the race for lieutenant governor, as likely from the civility of the contest, as the reputation Bill Raggio had earned for his honesty and integrity. In fact, on campaign funding reform, which was a major issue in the 1974 election due to such abuses, both candidates were outspoken in their support for changes in the law limiting the amount of individual contributions and for publicly identifying contributors.

President Nixon resigned under threat of impeachment in the midst of the 1974 election. If that was not enough unnecessary, political baggage for Republican candidate Raggio to carry, the new president, Gerald R. Ford, immediately pardoned the former president before he had even been charged with a crime.

On September 12, the *Las Vegas Sun* reported Bill's reaction to the presidential pardon:

> The president's action seems untimely especially since no charges have been formally established. Speaking as a former prosecutor, it does disturb my concept of equal justice. However, I do believe the president acted in good conscience in what he thought was in the nation's best interest.[5]

It seemed that President Nixon had once again managed to interfere with Bill's chances for being elected to a statewide office. Despite all this, Raggio campaigned across the state, as he had four years before, and Dottie's famous pickles were soon being distributed door-to-door by campaign workers.

Though both candidates had recent ties to Las Vegas, it was not enough to create sectional allegiances. As such, Bill received strong endorsements from newspapers, including those in Las Vegas, such as the *Valley Times* and the *Las Vegas Review Journal*, as well as his hometown *Reno Evening Gazette*. The editor, Warren Lerude, had not always agreed with Bill, yet his almost reluctant-sounding endorsement seemed to frame the candidate's qualifications better than a glowing tribute:

> This newspaper has endorsed opponents over Raggio in the past and the editors and publisher have fought freedom of the press fights and pitched disagreements with the strong-willed District Attorney. Raggio outweighs Rose in experience and that most important ingredient of leadership, forcefulness…The endorsement the *Gazette* offers is born out of the conviction that the better man should be elected, whether that man and this newspaper have seen eye-to-eye all the time in the past or not.[6]

Bill also received strong endorsements from the National State Education Association, the State of Nevada Employees Association and the Nevada Homebuilders Association of Southern Nevada. As a state senator for just one session, he had the respect of many colleagues, including Democrats, such as Senator Helen Herr, who worked in her southern Nevada district for his election. Even the stars seemed to be in a most propitious alignment for a Raggio victory, as Bill learned in an October 1974 letter from Professor James Monroe Harvey, a Las Vegas astrologer and expert in "the science of universal law and vibration," who predicted Bill would win.

However, Rose was an attractive thirty-four–year-old, former state Democratic Party chair, with a large following of young and enthusiastic volunteers. Throughout the campaign, Rose and his workers knocked on thousands of doors in Clark County. On Election Day, he prevailed, receiving 85,935 votes to Raggio's 68,362.

Bill's daughter Leslie, a student at the University of Santa Clara, had come from California to be with her dad on Election Day. The next morning, as she was preparing for her return flight, Bill offered to drive her back to school. Leslie was delighted to have the opportunity to spend time with her dad, a rare occurrence given his hectic life. "I was crying all the way back," she recalled. "I was so sad for him." Bill understood.

"When you lose an election," he would later say, "it is always much more disappointing for your family than it is for you."

Bill told Leslie that he had been through tough times before and "the only thing you can do is pick yourself up in defeat and go on." He reminded her that it unlikely he would be leaving his children a large inheritance. "The only thing of value I can give you," Bill said, "is my good name."

The 1974 midterm election produced a virtual sweep for Democrats across the country. A nation unsettled by scandals in the Republican Party, soaring inflation, and a deepening recession, saw an increase in Democratic strength in both houses of Congress and state governorships. Nevada Governor Mike O'Callaghan catapulted into a second term with over 67% of the vote.

Two bright spots for Nevada Republicans was the election of popular former-Governor Paul Laxalt, who bucked the tide to win a seat in the U.S. Senate over Democrat Harry Reid. Attorney General Robert List squeaked by Democratic challenger Richard Bryan. Each race was decided by less than 750 votes. In keeping with his respect for the electoral process, Bill congratulated his opponent stating, "He'll be a very capable lieutenant governor and I pledge my cooperation in the senate during the forthcoming legislature."

When pressed for further insight as to why the election went badly for him, Bill said he believed a loss of some Republican votes to the Independent American Party[7] was a factor in the defeat. Indeed, the IAP candidate for lieutenant governor, Jack Long, received over 12,000 votes that would have likely gone to Bill due to the party's strong anti-abortion platform. Not enough votes to have carried him to victory, but certainly enough put him within striking distance.

However, Bill felt the biggest factor against his not being elected was the strong tendency among voters to have the governor and the lieutenant governor be of the same party.

However, Republican Senator Bob Dole, of Kansas, who barely won reelection that year, saw the national drubbing of Republican candidates as being the result of one thing: "The wreckage of Watergate," he stated, "is spread over the landscape."[8]

In 2010, Robert Rose would concur with Dole's assessment, saying:

> When I look back on it, I see that even the greatest campaigner could not have won that race if they were Republican, because it was the Watergate year. Between [Governor] O'Callaghan being a Democrat and Watergate, Bill had an awfully tough race. I would say that he probably would have beaten me had it not been the Watergate year.

Bill Raggio would never again run for statewide office.

United States Senator Harry Reid, reflecting on Bill's three races for statewide office, in August 2010 said,

> I believe the Republican Party never used him properly in the statewide races—and that was Nevada's loss. Yet, Bill picked himself up after those defeats and did what was best for the state. He became a very successful lawmaker and did great things for Nevada.

# CHAPTER THIRTY-EIGHT

# Learning to Make Law
# (1975-1977)

As the result of the Democrat's success in 1974, when Bill returned to the state legislature for the 1975 session, he would be one of only three Republican members of the Senate. The three legislators took their meager numbers with good humor. Cliff Young later commented that they were able to "hold caucus meetings in a phone booth." The junior member of the caucus, Bill Raggio would sardonically tell his colleagues that he was making great strides toward higher office, as evidenced by the fact that after just one session, he was "already the Assistant Minority Whip."

Governor O'Callaghan presented a budget emphasizing social programs, but called for more restricted spending in the wake of lower than anticipated revenues from sales and gasoline taxes. Most of his agenda was approved, except for the ERA.

Indeed, the legislative and executive branches were in such harmony that the governor did not veto a single bill in 1975 (and vetoed only one bill the previous session).

The 58th Session of the Nevada State Legislature ended on May 22, 1975. It had been the longest in the state's history—122 days. Although some were disappointed with the length and results, Senate Majority Leader Mahlon Brown saw much that was positive. "There were new members with new ideas," he said, "and more citizen input on proposed legislation than ever before."

However, Bill Raggio and the rest of Washoe County's legislative delegation came away frustrated with the mechanics of the process. The session started slowly due to insufficient staff, particularly in the number of bill drafters, and was poorly managed. Though a great deal of work was accomplished, many felt it should not have taken 122 days to complete.

There was a consensus for reorganizing the process. Senator Raggio suggested reforms to make the legislature more productive, including the use of a consent calendar that would allow for the posting of non-controversial bills and their passage without a formal floor vote.

Moreover, both Raggio and Young were feeling disillusionment about their futures in the Senate, questioning whether they would run again. Both felt the length of the session had adversely affected their respective law practices, and each did not hide the fact that they were disappointed by the paucity of Republican representation.

\* \* \*

By 1976, Bill Raggio and Cliff Young began to see glimmers of hope for the Republican Party in Nevada. The Watergate albatross was beginning to lift, in large part because of the entry of a Washington outsider into the GOP presidential race, California Governor Ronald Reagan.

Reagan's appearance on the national scene renewed public interest in the party's message at all levels of government. At that time, Nevada hosted a presidential primary, and while Republican President Gerald Ford made only one brief, primary election-eve visit to the state, his opponent, Ronald Reagan, toured Nevada several times, touting his close ties to U.S. Senator Paul Laxalt. Consequently, on May 4, Reagan won a significant victory over Ford in Nevada, receiving 66% of the vote, to the president's 29%.\*

In the 1976 general election, incumbents Raggio and Young were challenged for their two Washoe Senate District 1 seats by Democrats Marshall Bouvier, Dennis Myers and Libertarian Party candidate Bob Hemenway.

---

\*Jimmy Carter would go on to defeat Gerald Ford in the November presidential election.

Of the three, Myers, a twenty-seven-year old journalist and student at the University of Nevada, was the most effusive, proposing ideas on a myriad of subjects, though remaining largely non-confrontational. "I'm not running against Raggio or Young, in fact, I think a lot of both men," Myers said. "I'm running for the senate because I think it has regressed through the leadership over the years."[1]

Myers was particularly anxious to keep Senator Floyd Lamb from resuming his seat as Chair of the Senate Committee on Finance.[2] It was widely rumored that Lamb was personally profiting from his position.

In June 1976, Senator Lamb stood trial on four counts of income tax evasion. Testimony disclosed that he had received "special legislative consulting fees" from Harrah's Hotel Casino in 1971. According to a *Nevada State Journal* report of June 4, 1976, Lamb's legislative colleagues, from both parties, were surprised by that news, wondering what a "special legislative consulting fee" was and why Lamb had not disclosed it publicly.[3]

Federal District Court Judge Roger Foley dismissed three of the four counts, and ruled for acquittal on the last. Despite continued widespread belief in Lamb's corruption, he was later reelected and remained popular with his constituents. [4]

On Election Day, November 3, 1976, Raggio and Young easily defeated their three challengers. Contrary to their hopes of gaining additional Republican seats in the Senate, they would remain outnumbered by Democrats, seventeen to three, with Senator Carl Dodge also retaining his seat. Bill Raggio was named Senate Minority Floor Leader, and would serve on the government affairs; legislative functions; and health, education and welfare committees.

Because the majority party had decided to increase their numbers from five to six members on the seven-person Senate Committee on Finance, the Republicans were left with only one seat, which was filled by Senator Young. Bill told reporters he was not happy about being bounced from his seat on the Senate Committee on Finance, "but that's a policy we Republicans can't determine." Senate Democrats selected James Gibson as majority leader and assembly Democrats chose Joe Dini of Yerington as Speaker.

The 59th Session of the Nevada State Legislature opened on January 17, 1977. Before tackling new issues, the legislature had to deal with an old one—whether to ratify the Equal Rights Amendment.

The measure had come before them during the 1975 legislative session, failing in the assembly and losing in the senate by a vote of twelve to eight, despite Senator Raggio having voted for it.

The surge of states ratifying this amendment had slowed to a trickle. By 1977, the amendment was still far short of the required 38 states necessary to approve ratification, with some states having rescinded their initial ratification.

This turnabout was largely due to the efforts of groups opposing the amendment, most visibly, the conservative Eagle Forum and socially conservative religious groups. In Nevada, where the Mormon Church was well represented and politically powerful, the ERA was not acceptable. In 1976, Church leaders described it as "a moral issue with many disturbing ramifications for women." Spencer Kimball, President of the LDS church, declared it "would strike at the family, humankind's basic institution."[5]

To many, the church's influence in the senate was evident.[6] "I had nothing but high praise for Jim Gibson," Bill would later say, "but there is no question that he was greatly influenced by his Mormon background on the Equal Rights Amendment and abortion. I'm not saying that in a pejorative way, because he was truly dedicated."

Despite this concerted effort to oppose passage of the ERA, it would pass in the state senate in a most unpredictable manner, set in motion by Senator Joe Neal.

During his first two sessions, Neal came to realize he was at an educational disadvantage over many of his colleagues, but was able to overcome this, with the assistance of the Secretary of the Senate, Leola Armstrong[7] by learning the rules of parliamentary procedure as thoroughly as possible. He virtually memorized *Mason's Manual of Legislative Procedure.*

In it, he found a little used rule dating back to 1864, which required every member within the bar of the senate to vote yea or nay—no abstentions—when a measure was invoked by three members. Senator Neal led off with one of his signature, long-winded addresses calling for passage of the ERA and lulling those opposed to ratification into concentrating on other matters.

As his speech ended, Neal invoked the rule. By prearrangement, two Clark County Democratic senators quickly joined him. Senator Neal later recalled, "I saw Raggio pull his rulebook out and started looking at it, and he looked back at me, and he started laughing. I guess he knew he was going to vote for the passage of the ERA, but he didn't know how it was going to get passed."

The debate on the resolution went on for about two hours and then a vote was entertained. The roll was opened and the senators voted ten yea, eight nay and two abstentions. Democratic Lieutenant Governor Bob Rose ordered the two abstentions placed in the nay column, so the vote was now tied ten to ten. Rose then voted to break the tie. His yea vote allowed the ERA to be adopted by the state senate. In his 2009 legislative oral history, Neal recalled that moment:

> I saw Gibson had his head in his hands...Gibson took it pretty hard. I didn't know why he took it so hard until after his death, and I was at his funeral. Some of the people from Salt Lake City came to his funeral and made the statement that he had told them that the ERA would never pass. Then I understood why he took it so hard.[8]

The assembly, however, did not pass the resolution that session and, though it would be reintroduced by each succeeding legislature through 1981, Nevada would remain one of fifteen states that have yet to ratify the ERA.

"Women have gone ahead and gotten most of the rights that they wanted," Bill Raggio said in 2008. "I don't think the ERA substantively made that much difference. It was more a matter of status that people wanted to prove. I voted against it for these reasons the first time, and then after analyzing that, I voted for it the next time. Looking back, I think I was wrong, both times."

As amusing as that might sound, it points up an important fact-of-life for a legislator, one that Bill understood early in his senate career, noting that, "Most issues are complex, rather than simple. Testifiers, especially skilled lobbyists, can make compelling arguments for both sides of an issue. Often, there is a fine line between voting one way or another."

The 1977 session addressed many such weighty issues, but none was more important to the economic growth of northern Nevada than Senate Bill 198, which sought to establish the Washoe County Airport Authority. The bill was championed by Senator Bill Raggio, who felt the current control of the airport, by the city of Reno, was "too provincial a base for the airport to develop the way it should." The bill would face tough opposition, but eventually passed.

On May 7, 2003, the Airport Authority of Washoe County celebrated its 25th anniversary by honoring the "Father" of the Authority, Senator William J. Raggio. At the ceremony, a bronze bust[6] of the senator was unveiled in the terminal to remind travelers of his vision for the future—and his determination. In his speech that evening, Raggio recalled the difficulties he faced in making others see what he envisioned. As in his DA days, had stood up to the Reno City Council and their mismanagement of the airport.

"At the time of the legislation, I was being pilloried because I was doing this," he recalled. "It took a lot of years for people to realize it was the best thing. It is bittersweet now to be honored…They were saying I was trying to steal the airport from the city and I had to take a lot of blows and darts and comments, but I shrugged them off because I knew we were doing the right thing."[10]

Efficient operation of the airport meant low landing fees, which encouraged increased air service—vital to a tourist-based economy. In the first twenty-five years since enactment of the Washoe County Airport Authority Act, passenger traffic at the Reno-Tahoe International Airport nearly tripled, to over two million arrivals a year.

Also, during the 1977 legislative session, Senator Raggio found himself accused of "a direct conflict of interest" and being "completely unethical" because a member of his law firm represented the Washoe County Teachers Association. Somewhat surprisingly, this charge came from Senator Carl Dodge, one of Raggio's two Republican colleagues in the senate.

Bill quickly responded that he had already made it clear that he did not intend to vote on the legislation in question. He then joined several fellow senators in vigorously defending the right of any legislator to speak out on any issue.

"I will be the judge of my qualifications and my concerns," Raggio said. "I know what my duties and responsibilities are and I suggest that others mind their own house."

The Nevada legislature is not a full-time body he added, but composed of citizens from all walks-of-life who have concerns, biases and prejudices. A legislator could have direct involvement in legislation and abstain from voting, and by abstaining, in effect, cast a no vote, which would have just as much impact as active participation.

"The people who elect us know our backgrounds and interests," Bill said. "And each of us, as the occasion arose, either through disclosure or non-voting, have been our own judge of our ethics or conflicts."

\* \* \*

By the end of the session, Bill was displaying mastery of the legislative process. Despite being in an almost laughable minority of three, and only in his third session, he was the prime sponsor of forty bills, nineteen of which passed into law that year.

When the legislature adjourned on May 13, leaders of both houses expressed pleasure with the way things had gone during the 113-day session.

Much had been completed during the session. Gaming laws were rewritten, a four-year medical school was approved for the University of

Nevada, Reno and the Tahoe Regional Planning agency was reorganized. In order to streamline government, sixty-three boards and commissions were eliminated. In addition, a full-time parole board was established, long a wish of former district attorney Raggio.

After the session, Bill returned to building his law practice. By now, he had gained expertise in a new field of the law, which would draw him into the, sometimes-shady, world of Las Vegas casino financing and international intrigue.

# CHAPTER THIRTY-NINE

# Gaming Lawyer

In 1976, the course of Bill's legal career would take a new turn, one that would eventually earn him a reputation as one of the country's preeminent attorneys in the field of gaming law. Until that time, he had not represented many clients before the Gaming Control Board or State Gaming Commission.

However, in that year he received a call from Lou Karras, whom Bill had known when he was with Hal Lipset's detective agency in San Francisco. Karras, who now lived in Las Vegas where he was head of security at the Hacienda Hotel/Casino, suggested Raggio call Paul Lowden, part owner of the Hacienda, regarding a legal matter.

Bill was not previously acquainted with Lowden, though their paths may have crossed as early as 1961. That year, a teenage Lowden had arrived in Nevada with little but his musical talent and a dream of making it big in the entertainment business.

His first job was as a piano player at the Riverside Hotel, just next door to DA Raggio's office in the Washoe County courthouse. He would soon move to Las Vegas and work as a keyboardist accompanying numerous headline acts. In 1979, Paul would be named musical director at the Flamingo.

Despite having no formal business training, Lowden possessed an aptitude for investing. By 1972, he and a group of partners raised $250,000 and bought a 15% interest in the Hacienda. Soon, one of Lowden's partners brought in Allen Glick, a decorated Vietnam War veteran and land developer from San Diego. Glick purchased majority control of the hotel casino.

Lowden, who acted as the Hacienda's entertainment director, expanded his casino holdings in 1975, by purchasing a share of the Tropicana for $500,000. Soon thereafter, amid reports that organized crime was skimming large amounts of cash from the Tropicana's counting room, federal and state law enforcement agents began investigating.

In 1976, Lowden asked the Tropicana's majority owners to buy out his investment. When they refused to do so, he simply walked away rather than jeopardize his casino owner's license by continuing a business connection with the Tropicana's mob associates.

Paul would eventually regain his investment in 1979, after Joseph Agosto, who controlled the casino operation, pled guilty to skimming charges. Agosto, and several of the Tropicana's owners, were forced out by the State Gaming Commission.

Meanwhile, a similar scandal was brewing at the Hacienda. The twenty-nine-year-old Glick, who also controlled the Stardust and the Fremont hotel-casinos, was being investigated. Glick, who would later admit to acting as a "front" for hidden mob interests in the casinos, was now facing legal and financial problems. He agreed to sell the Hacienda to Lowden for $21 million. The Gaming Control Board, questioned the propriety of Lowden's proposed sources of capital and recommended against allowing him a license as majority owner of the Hacienda.

In 2008, Lowden spoke about the situation. "It was not my association with Glick that caused the problem," he explained, "rather, that I was borrowing money from two gentlemen who the Gaming Control Board felt would have a hidden interest in the casino. These two men were highly reputable individuals. One was Howard Harmer, a bishop in the Mormon Church, and the other Glendon Johnson, President of the American National Life Insurance Company of Dallas, Texas. Consequently, they [the Gaming Control Board] wanted to deny my application for a gaming license."

Lowden was introduced to Bill Raggio, who agreed to represent him.

"When Phil Hannifin, a member of Gaming Control Board, learned that Bill was handling my appeal," Lowden later recalled, "he advised him to collect his fees in advance. In other words, I did not have a chance of winning."

While other applicants had been approved, Lowden had been turned down. His only recourse was to go before the State Gaming Commission, which would require a unanimous vote to overturn an adverse ruling by the board.

Bill was able to get the Gaming Commission to delay the hearing. He then spent an enormous amount of time in Las Vegas over the next several months putting together the case, preparing documents and exhibits, obtaining affidavits and responding to every allegation. When he was finished, Bill felt it was "an airtight presentation."

"That was the toughest application I ever handled," Bill said in 2009. "After that, I would represent numerous clients before the Gaming Control Board and the Gaming Commission. Gaming law is of great interest to me and a challenging field of law."

Gaming law is "challenging" because state law defines a gaming license as a revocable privilege, rather than a right. An applicant can be turned down for any reason, without recourse to an appeal. If the board or commission finds anything they do not like, or believed an applicant was concealing something, that person could be turned down.

Later, the Nevada Supreme Court ruled that, while a new applicant for a gaming license could be turned down for almost any reason, an existing licensee could not have a license removed without grounds and due process.

Bill later observed that Nevada statutes determining how members of the Gaming Control Board and Gaming Commission were selected helped maintain a good balance of experience and perspectives. "Some have been critical of this process," he said, "however, in my experience, I have not seen a decision of the Gaming Control Board or Gaming Commission influenced by politics. We have been fortunate to have good, qualified people in those positions."

In early 1977, Governor Michael O'Callaghan appointed Harry Reid to succeed Peter Echeverria as chair of the Nevada Gaming Commission. Because of the skimming scandals in Las Vegas, it was a busy and sometimes dangerous time for commission members.[1]

On July 21, 1977, Bill presented his case on behalf of Paul Lowden before the State Gaming Commission in Carson City. He argued that the board came to "the totally unwarranted conclusion" that Lowden's plan to finance the purchase was "fraught with hidden interests."

It was particularly shameful, Bill continued, that the Gaming Control Board had relied on the testimony of convicted felon Ramon D'Onofrio, who told board investigators that hidden interests were involved in Lowden's bid to take over the Hacienda.

During his efforts to raise money for the deal, Lowden became involved with D'Onofrio, who told him that overseas money was available. The deal turned out to be a scam, Bill said, "that made the plot of *The Sting* read like a nursery rhyme."

Bill pointed out that D'Onofrio feared another term in prison, and felt his best defense was to take offensive action against Paul Lowden, which he did by outlining the alleged hidden interest scheme. "It is patently unfair to accept the word of a felon, an accused perjurer and a self-confessed con artist," Bill added.

The commission ruled to approve Paul Lowden's application to take over the Hacienda. Bill's scrupulous rebuttal of each allegation against his client was most compelling and commission chair Harry Reid complimented Bill for preparing such a strong case, despite being burdened with other duties, "such as being in the legislature." He then quipped that he hoped Raggio "had not been too good of an advocate in that he swayed my mind wrongly."

Reid then took the unusual step of rebuking the Gaming Control Board for having done a sloppy job. The Board's evidence in the Lowden case, he said, "would not hold water in anything; in an eighth grade government class."[2]

\* \* \*

Ramon D'Onofrio was not the only "con artist" Lowden was dealing with at the time. Earlier, he had been put in touch with a man in Brussels by the name of Joseph Dorey, who, ostensibly, directed an investment company called Sceptre. As Bill later recalled, "Paul paid him an 'upfront fee,' which is usually a bad indicator. If you are paying an upfront fee, it may figure that it's going to be a scam. At that time, however, funding was hard to find and Dorey evidently came highly recommended."

After receiving the fee, Dorey kept making excuses about when the loan would be available. Lowden and Bill decided to fly to Brussels and confront him. Dorey, however, was not available, though the two men found a very legitimate-looking two-room office, with a secretary, when they arrived. As they would later learn, it was just a facade. In a 2008 interview, Paul Lowden would recall that he and Bill finally located Dorey, a British citizen, in a London hospital and paid him a visit.

Joseph Dorey was an extremely overweight man with health problems. However, Raggio and Lowden knew they could rely on Dorey's greediness and so were eventually able to overcome his suspicion and lure the man to Las Vegas on the pretense of receiving another large upfront fee. Bill's private detective friend, Hal Lipset, bugged the ceiling light in Lowden's office. Hal then set up in an adjacent room to record the meeting.\* Dorey self-incriminated himself on tape. "We then called the Metro police and had him arrested," Lowden recalled. "I'll never forget the way Dorey was biting his lip when the officers arrived."

Joseph Dorey pled guilty to fraud charges and was extradited back to England. However, before Lowden could recoup his initial investment, Dorey liquidated his assets. Recognizing that a lengthy court battle would cost more than he would receive in a judgment, Lowden decided not to pursue legal action.

Bill would remain Paul Lowden's personal attorney, close friend and, in 1982, business associate, when he began serving as a director, vice president, secretary and corporate counsel for Sahara Resorts. Bill retained

---

\*This practice is legal under Nevada law as long as one party to a conversation knows that it is being recorded.

those corporate positions when Paul Lowden reestablished his holdings under the Archon Corporation.[3]

* * *

So quickly had his reputation grown as one of Nevada's foremost experts on gaming law, that just four months after the ruling in the Lowden case, Bill was contacted by Beverly Hills' attorney Mickey Rudin.

In 1976, Rudin collaborated with Frank Sinatra and Hank Greenspun to purchase 400,000 shares of stock in the Del Webb Corporation, which operated four casinos in Nevada. After the purchase, which constituted 8% of the corporation's common stock, the three men asked the company to pay for the investigation necessary to license them.

However, the Del Webb Cooperation, anticipating Frank Sinatra would face considerable opposition in obtaining a license, sold their stock to Ramada for $10 million, and the three partners did not pursue the license.

Bill Raggio's most celebrated appearances before the Gaming Control Board and State Gaming Commission occurred just two years later when, in February 1981, he would act as counsel for Frank Sinatra, who was seeking a license as a consultant of entertainment and public relations at Caesars Palace.

In 2009, Bill recalled having received a call from Frank Sinatra's attorney, Mickey Rudin. Frank, said Rudin, wanted Bill to represent him before the Gaming Board and Commission. Raggio agreed. "Frank had always been there for me, and so I said yes," Bill later remarked.

What made the hearings unusual was that they were unnecessary. Under what was commonly referred to then as "Sinatra's Law," Nevada did not require entertainers to hold a key employee license in order to enter and perform in a gaming establishment. Moreover, Frank had no immediate plans of acquiring ownership of a casino. Rather, he had decided nearly twenty years after having surrendered his gaming license over the Giancana affair, to "clear his name."

Frank asked Caesars Palace, where he was performing, to submit his name to the State Gaming Commission for a key employee license. Caesars did so, but refused to pay the hefty cost of the background investigation. Sinatra, eager for his day before the commission, bore the entire cost himself—nearly $500,000.

Attorney Raggio did extensive research, spending a great deal of time obtaining information under the Freedom of Information (FOIA) Act from the FBI, DEA and IRS.

Bill later said,

> We needed this because several allegations were obviously going to have to be refuted, particularly Frank's association with Giancana, which resulted in his having to surrender his license in the first place. In looking over that material, it was apparent much of it was not based on fact, and a lot of it described situations where, as an entertainer, Frank played in places where the demimonde, i.e., the underworld, had interests. There was no denying that he knew these people, but there was no proof of any kind, that he was involved in any of their activities.

Although Bill obtained a vast amount of information about his client from the FBI, it was incomplete. It would not be until after Frank's death in 1998 that a, more-or-less complete file, containing both headquarters and various field office documents, was available for release under the FOIA. That file contains nearly five decades of investigative work and is 2,403 pages long.

Director J. Edgar Hoover first had Frank Sinatra investigated in the early 1940s as a suspected communist because of his active support of equal rights for African Americans. The record indicates a later obsession with his life, including Sinatra's association with gangsters and the, often-lurid, details of personal relationships, seemingly unrelated to any criminal activity or the nation's internal security.

In addition to reports from extensive spying by FBI agents, the file contains an enormous amount of unsubstantiated information fed to the FBI by scandal-mongering journalists. In exchange for this information, the FBI occasionally doled out unflattering data about Sinatra back to the press. As journalist Pete Hamill wrote in his book, *Why Sinatra Matters*, Frank was "the most investigated American performer since John Wilkes Booth."[4]

At 9:18 a.m. on February 11, 1981, Chair Richard Bunker gaveled to order a meeting of the Gaming Control Board in the Las Vegas City Hall to hear testimony on Frank Sinatra's fitness for a key employee license. Among those testifying to Frank's good character and generosity were Los Angeles County Sheriff Peter Pitchess; Catholic priest Father Herbert Ward, who directed St. Jude's Ranch for Children; publisher Hank Greenspun; and film actors Kirk Douglas and Gregory Peck. In addition, Bob Hope submitted a sworn affidavit. Ronald Reagan, who had been inaugurated as president just twenty-two days before, sent a letter attesting to Frank's good character.

Bill Raggio then addressed the board, saying that under the FOIA, Frank had petitioned the government for all his records and had received "fourteen pounds of FBI files and another thirteen, or so, pounds of IRS files," all of which were made available to the board's investigative staff.

Bill told the board members that most of the information in those files was unsubstantiated or irrelevant. He further asserted that, though the FBI was "out to get Mr. Sinatra," it had failed to do so. The IRS had reported that "while the taxpayer (Sinatra) had openly consorted with Mr. Giancana...the evidence supporting a joint financial or nominee interest between the taxpayer and Giancana is lacking."[5]

Sinatra was the last person to testify that day. He was questioned by board members for nearly an hour regarding numerous allegations about his personal and business associations with members of organized crime over the years.

Of the most serious and relevant charge, that he had a close relationship with Chicago mob boss Sam Giancana, Frank adamantly denied anything but a passing acquaintance. The basis for much of the board's questioning came from allegations made in recently released memoir called *The Last*

*Mafioso*, by former Los Angeles crime boss Jimmy "The Weasel" Fratianno, who was now in hiding under the FBI's witness protection program.

Former Gaming Commissioner Clair Haycock, former Clark County District Attorney George Franklin, and others, had previously expressed in the press their objections to Sinatra receiving a Nevada gaming license. However, there was no testimony given during the Gaming Commission hearing to refute Frank's answers.

This may have been because the Gaming Control Board was not a law enforcement agency and so did not have power to subpoena witnesses; nor could it obtain information directly from the FBI, or other police agencies. It was widely believed that because Sinatra's approval for a license was going to be, in the words of Las Vegas journalist Ned Day, "a lead pipe cinch," few wanted to invoke his ire needlessly, by testifying against approval of a license.

Paul Lowden, who attended the hearing, vividly recalled the contrast in body language between Bill Raggio and Frank Sinatra as they sat beside one another: Bill, exceptionally poised and eloquent; Frank, exasperated, scowling, answering questions with clipped, often defensive, replies.

Terry Care, who would later serve in the state senate with Bill Raggio, was also in the audience that day as a journalist and remembered Frank's bearing. "A one point our eyes met and locked for a few moments," Care later recalled. "It was obvious to me that Frank knew I was a reporter and glared at me with great disdain. Everyone, of course, knew about his unconcealed contempt for the press. I finally looked down to jot some notes and, after about two minutes, when I looked up again, Frank was still glaring at me exactly as he had been before. I must admit, it was a bit unnerving."

At the completion of the testimony, Chair Bunker ended the nearly six-hour meeting by making a motion to recommend to the Nevada Gaming Commission that Sinatra be approved for a six-month license. The board approved the recommendation unanimously. As Frank exited, spectators gave him a thunderous ovation.

A week later, the Nevada State Gaming Commission took up the matter of Sinatra's gaming license application. On hand was Frank's usual entourage, wife Barbara, Mickey Rudin and Frank's bodyguard, Jilly Rizzo. Since Caesars Palace was technically the applicant, retired Brigadier General Harry Wald, president of Caesars, attended, along with the company's legal counsel, Peter Echeverria, a former chair of the Gaming Commission.

Bill Raggio opened the proceeding with a review of what he called the "very thorough, precise and extensive investigation which was conducted by the Gaming Control Board and its staff over the last thirteen months." It had been an investigation, he reminded the commissioners, that was far more thorough than any previously done for an equity interest license, let alone for a key employee. Bill pointed out Sinatra's cooperation with control board agents, by providing them with three separate interviews over the last year.

He warned that much of what had been said about his client was "inference and innuendo, and gossip and rumor," and that such unsubstantiated information often blurred the facts, and told the commissioners:

> As to the more serious allegations, I would say this to you: Mr. Sinatra has not denied that he, like many other public figures, over a good many years, has met or known persons reputed to be members of some type of organized crime society, but he has denied that he was ever involved with them, or been in business with them; ever dealt with them, or allowed them to interfere in any way with his business or personal life. There is no evidence in all these investigative files, in the efforts of all those who have access to these files, there is no evidence to refute that.[6]

Several testifiers followed, including entertainment attorney Vincent Chieffo, Jilly Rizzo and Mickey Rudin. All refuted claims that Frank was closely related to organized crime figures. This testimony covered allegations going back to the 1940s, but concentrated primarily on activity at the Cal-Neva Lodge in July 1963.

It was their recollection, they said, that Sinatra had likely been in Los Angeles at the time of the altercation between Giancana and Victor LaCroix-Collins in Phyllis McGuire's bungalow; a fight in which, LaCroix-Collins claimed, Frank personally intervened.[7]

Sinatra followed these witnesses and testified for about fifteen minutes. He spoke of his September 1963 abusiveness toward Gaming Control Board Chair Ed Olsen and the two Gaming Control Board agents who later appeared at the Cal-Neva for a routine table count over the Labor Day weekend. Frank attributed his ill temper to business concerns arising from an overflow crowd during that busy holiday weekend.

A hint of defensiveness appeared to creep into his testimony as Sinatra pointed out that he had heard talk of "undesirables and nefarious people" frequenting other casinos. "By the same token, strangely enough, you also later heard that he [Giancana] was at the Christmas Tree [a casino between Reno and Lake Tahoe] but nothing was ever made about that."[8]

Commissioner Carl Dodge vigorously questioned each testifier. Dodge, a lawyer by training, also served with Bill Raggio in the state senate. When asked about his long-term intentions, Sinatra replied that, while he was only seeking a license as a key employee and not an equity owner, he "would not rule the latter out in the future."

Though careful not to appear disrespectful of Sinatra's stature in the community and good deeds, Dodge suggested that it might be prudent for the commission to approve a license for only a six-month period, as had been recommended by the Gaming Control Board a week before. This, he argued, would allow for the outcome of a trial going on in Westchester County, New York, and certain grand jury proceedings in New York City, both of which were focusing on underworld figures alleged to have close relationships with Frank.

Chair Reid, however, in a lengthy summation of the commission's findings, laced with numerous flattering examples of Mr. Sinatra's warmth and munificence, called for a vote granting an unlimited gaming license. The motion carried four to one, with Commissioner Dodge dissenting.

Bill was, of course, satisfied with the outcome. He had especially enjoyed the experience of reuniting with Frank, later saying, "I frequently stayed at Frank's home in Palm Springs during the preparation and around the time of the hearings. This gave me a chance to get to know him again and meet his new wife, Barbara. It was an interesting time. I would not see him again after that, other than when he performed."

# CHAPTER FORTY

# Lobbyists

The presence of lobbyists in the legislative process has always raised the specter of impropriety. In his book, *The Sagebrush State: Nevada's History, Government and Politics,* Michael W. Bowers describes how the dominance of interest groups in Nevada politics has changed over time. Nearly 100 years of railroad and "Bank Crowd" influence was dealt a "staggering blow" in 1958 when Grant Sawyer was elected governor, bringing "the end of machine politics in Nevada." [1]

Not surprisingly, gaming interests filled the void and became extremely powerful in the state. As Nevada's chief industry, "gaming has been extraordinarily successful in getting preferred candidates elected to office in large numbers." [2]

Though without the financial resources of the casino industry, teachers' organizations also have been successful in obtaining their goals in Nevada, due largely to their ability to put thousands of volunteers into action for, or against, a candidate. In addition, what Bowers refers to as media power brokers, such as Don Reynolds, Michael O'Callaghan and Hank Greenspun, have traditionally exerted great influence upon the Nevada political scene.

The importance to organized interests in decisions made by the legislature can be seen in the growing number of lobbyists. In 1975, there were about 350 registered lobbyists. By the 2009 session, there were more than 1,100, creating a lobbyist-to-legislator ratio of eighteen to one.

Regulation of lobbyists in Nevada began in 1973. Prior to that time, lobbyists were not required to register, nor did they have to identify the group or groups for whom they lobbied. In some instances, they were even permitted to sit in chambers with legislators as they voted.

When revelations of questionable campaign contributions arose as part of the Watergate investigation, voters in Nevada prepared to put an initiative on the ballot to regulate lobbying. This stirred the legislature to action, quickly passing a bill requiring lobbyists to register with the Secretary of State. During the 1975 session, additional legislation was passed requiring lobbyists to prepare monthly reports on their expenditures, including entertainment, gifts and loans to legislators.

By 1979, lobbyists were required to wear identification badges while in the halls of the legislature, and the registration site was moved from the Office of the Secretary of State to the Legislative Counsel Bureau. Increasingly stringent reporting measures were passed in subsequent sessions so that by the 1995 session, lobbyists were required to specify which legislator received the benefit of an expenditure, as well as the amount. As Bowers observed:

> Not wanting to find themselves on a list of those frequently wined and dined by lobbyists, a distinction that election opponents would surely use against them, many legislators avoided gifts and free meals they were so willing to accept in past sessions. To no one's surprise, spending by lobbyists on legislators dropped by more than 90% between the 1993 and 1995 sessions after this new law took effect.[3]

Such measures would make one believe that lobbying was a bad thing. However, legislators, and those knowledgeable about the workings of the legislative process, hold quite the opposite opinion.

Senator Raggio believes that many who have not served in a legislative body "can have a warped impression of a lobbyist, and what he or she does."

A lobbyist, he explained, is a legislative advocate who openly represents a cause and who makes him- or herself, available to respond to questions that legislators may have about the cause. "We have good ones and we have not so good ones," Bill noted.

"A good lobbyist," he continued, "is one who advocates a cause in a forthright manner, in a highly competitive spirit, if necessary. The good lobbyist tells both the good and the bad, never misleads, is not abusive and respects the process regardless of whether the cause is won or lost...We could not function without them, anymore than without staff at the legislature."

Of all the lobbyists Bill Raggio had known, Jim Joyce, "was probably the best and most effective that I ever dealt with in my legislative career." Ironically, the two first became acquainted while Joyce was working on U.S. Senator Howard Cannon's reelection campaign against Bill Raggio in 1970. Joyce would begin his career as a lobbyist at the state legislature in 1973, the same year Bill entered the senate.

"Jim Joyce was a political consultant for my opponent, then-Senator Howard Cannon. Largely through Jim's efforts, I lost," Bill recalls, adding dryly that "many people today still feel that my losing that race was Jim's major political accomplishment." However, in losing that election, Bill gained great respect for Joyce's abilities, and would engage his assistance in the 1974 race for lieutenant governor.

Jim Joyce went on to handle many political campaigns after that, including Bill's state senate campaigns. According to Bill, Joyce "had an uncanny ability to evaluate a candidate for the strengths and weaknesses of the race. There are many who have held office in the state...who may never have held those positions except for Jim."

To those who found his avocation suspect, Jim Joyce was almost incredulous: "The perception is that no one can be as successful as I have been lobbying and politically without being corrupt, shady, dishonest, immoral and amoral," he once declared. "Nothing is further from the truth."[4]

Jim Joyce died in 1993 at the age of fifty-four.

Lobbyist John Pappageorge, who was once described in a survey of legislators and fellow lobbyist as the "best in the game" and a person of "unparalleled integrity and skill," explained his low-key technique in a March 2009 interview. According to Pappageorge, it was important that a lobbyist understand how much work a legislator has to fit into their 120-day session. The number of bills they must hear makes their time extremely important.

> To help them and me, I get to the Legislative Building early and sit at a table closest to the elevator. When a legislator passes by I ask them a quick question or provide them with what I believe is new information. I think the legislator appreciates a quick update because their time is so limited. They too may have questions they need answered. I may ask how they feel about a certain issue and if they need more information. Often this encounter will take only a few seconds.

Despite his day at the legislature starting before 7:00 a.m. and generally ending late in the evening, Pappageorge jokingly says that because of his early morning elevator watch, his day "is over by 8:00 a.m., because that is when the committee hearings begin and talking to a legislator becomes difficult."

Developing trust and respect is a two-way street between lobbyist and legislator. John Pappageorge has the utmost of both for Senator Raggio. "Once Senator Raggio gives his word, it is unshakeable, as long as the information you have given him remains factual," Pappageorge said. "He will think through every possible issue. Occasionally, Senator Raggio will let me know when he can no longer support my position on a bill because new information has surfaced, or, in some cases, he has changed from not supporting it, to support. I am always sure of one thing: He's done his homework."

The relationship between lobbyist and legislator, when conducted with mutual respect for one another and the process, is enormously important to the efficient functioning of the state. This is not to say legislators rely entirely on information from lobbyists and legislative staffers. Some, like Bill Raggio, also sought to learn things on their own, through the sharing of ideas and travel.

# CHAPTER FORTY-ONE

# Tax Reform and Sagebrush Rebels (1979)

In August 1978, Bill Raggio was part of an eighteen-member delegation chosen by the National Conference of State Legislators to visit the People's Republic of China. Also selected from Nevada were state senators Mel Close and Richard Bryan, and Assemblyman Robert Robinson. The group had been invited by the Chinese government, though not as official guests, to meet with their officials to discuss housing, health care and education in China and the United States. The tour would include visits to several major cities including Canton, Beijing and Shanghai. While in Beijing, the legislators would tour the Ming Tombs, the Forbidden City and the Great Wall.

Though President Nixon had opened up relations with this "closed society" by making an official visit six years earlier, the U.S. and the People's Republic would not achieve formal diplomatic recognition until 1979. Senator Bryan jokingly suggested that sending Bill Raggio to China nearly compromised that important international accord.

At that time, Bryan was starting his run for the Office of State Attorney General and later said he felt that his opponents "appeared to be a very weak field, and so I felt confident that I could take some time out from campaigning."

Unbeknownst to Bryan, Raggio intended to do a bit of campaigning for him. Bill had smuggled in a 4'x4' campaign poster that proclaimed "Bryan for Attorney General" and plastered it up on the Great Wall of China.

Moments after a surprised Richard Bryan came across his campaign poster 6,000 miles from home, nearby guards, ever vigilant for signs of anti-government activity under this still tightly controlled communist regime, quickly tore it down, but did not detain Bill or the others.

Upon arriving in Shanghai a few days later, Bryan received a call placed by what sounded, authentically, like an international operator who barely spoke English. In 2008, Senator Bryan described what happened next:

> Then an American voice came on, kind of distant and muffled, saying he was calling from the Secretary of State's office in Nevada and informing me I had not filed properly to run for attorney general. There was something wrong with my application, though the details were vague, and I needed to sign something within the next twenty-four hours. Of course, I became immediately agitated and dismayed because I was so far away. What I found out later was that I had been suckered into another Raggio prank.

* * *

That same year of 1978, Governor Mike O'Callaghan announced he would not be running for a third term.*

Of O'Callaghan's time in office, Bill Raggio would later say,

> He turned out to be one of our most popular governors. Mike was totally engaged in the office and was extremely interactive with the legislature. In fact, he was the first to defy a tradition by which governors in the past only came to the Legislative Building to deliver the State of the State message and to present the Executive Budget. Governor O'Callaghan, however, was in the legislature's hallways almost daily, on the phone, often at ungodly morning hours.

---

*O'Callaghan would become executive editor of the *Las Vegas Sun,* a job he held until his death in 2004.

Though Raggio and O'Callaghan had their differences over the years, the two shared a bond of mutual respect. Years later, Bill would receive a letter from Mary Colleen O'Callaghan-Miele, daughter of the governor saying, in part, "My father always spoke highly of you—sometimes a little louder than at other times."

O'Callaghan's decision not to run for reelection prompted a race between Republican Attorney General Robert List and Democratic Lieutenant Governor Bob Rose. List's rise through the political ranks had been meteoric. At age thirty-one, he was elected Ormsby County district attorney and just four years later, in 1974, became state attorney general.

List had developed a favorable working relationship with outgoing Governor O'Callaghan and, with no primary election opposition and substantial campaign funding, he defeated Rose, receiving 56% of the vote.

Despite heavy Democratic voter registration in Nevada, Rose suffered from a bitter primary election campaign against former state senator John Foley—who then refused to endorse Rose in the general election. In addition, List was able, with the support of a friendly press, to give Rose a liberal image, a potent label in conservative Nevada.[1]

Except for Rose's defeat, the Democratic Party did well in the election. Myron Leavitt was elected as lieutenant governor and most other statewide offices went to Democrats. Despite (or because of) having his campaign poster hung on the Great Wall of China by Bill Raggio, Richard Bryan was elected as state attorney general, garnering an impressive 74% of the vote. Republicans did make some gains in the legislature, however, winning nine more seats in the assembly and two in the senate.

The 1978 election included two important ballot initiatives. Question 5 was a nonbinding referendum on the ERA, which showed an overwhelming number of Nevada voters, 123,952 to 61,768, opposed ratification. The other measure, which would limit real property tax to 1% of market value, passed, but to become law would require a second vote of approval during the next election.

In an effort to forestall voter approval of this Proposition 13-like property tax cap question in the coming election, Governor List, during his State of the State address in January 1979, called for a 30% reduction in property taxes, a repeal of the sales tax on food and a tax deferment for the elderly. In order to accommodate these cuts, he suggested a budget calling for economizing in some areas, such as the system of higher education, and a no-growth policy for most other agencies.

In addition, the 1979 legislature passed a budget cap statute limiting General Fund spending and allowing increases only in correlation to population growth and inflation.

Despite facing an overwhelming Democratic majority in both houses, the new governor was able to pass most of his proposals, largely because of the legislature's tradition of working with the executive branch for the good of the state, and its equally long tradition of fiscal conservatism.

The most important piece of legislation that session was a $244 million tax reform bill calling for a 27% reduction in property tax. A special election was necessary to amend the state's Sales and Use Tax of 1955, to exempt the sale of food. That election was held on June 5, 1979 and the issue was approved by majorities in sixteen of the seventeen counties.

Adding to the economic woes in southern Nevada, the federal strike force made a sufficient case to have the Tropicana casino closed for skimming and having hidden ownership interests related to organized crime. In addition, the Aladdin was slapped with a fine of $12 million for also having hidden ownership interests.

In the state legislature, Senate Bill No. 185 was introduced to allow Nevada gaming authorities to use wiretaps to help discover more hidden casino interests. The bill died in the Committee on Government Affairs in a five to two vote. Dissenter Carl Dodge had argued that the Gaming Control Board "looked bad" because, despite knowing about the hidden interests, it could not make a case without information obtained by wiretaps.

Senator Raggio, who joined the majority vote in killing the legislation, and who had more practical experience investigating crimes than any others member of the legislature noted: "There is a place for wiretapping in investigating serious crimes committed under circumstances that otherwise would be difficult to solve. Those circumstances are covered by present (wiretap) law. I have some reluctance to extend it because... there is a very grave danger of abuse."

Bill's continuing expertise in the legal profession was borne out by his selection that year to the prestigious American Board of Criminal Lawyers, an exclusive national society for outstanding criminal trial lawyers. The standards for acceptance included successful "major felony trial experience and exceptional recommendations from distinguished jurists and current Fellows attesting to the candidate's high ethics as well as their litigation skills in the area of criminal defense"—in essence, the nation's best criminal trial lawyers.

The 1979 legislature also passed a measure to gain control over 49 million acres of federally controlled public land in Nevada. This was proposed by a public movement, labeled the "Sagebrush Rebellion," which reflected a belief that federal land policies in western states were the result of the government's ignorance of geographic conditions.[2] Some blamed large mining interests for denying them the right to use the land. As these Sagebrush Rebels bridled under the lack of attention being paid to their concerns, the dialogue grew more rancorous, with sporadic incidents of violence against government offices and employees.

While Senator Raggio objected to any acts of violence and the stridency of the debate, he did support certain issues espoused by members of the movement. Among the measures he sponsored during the 1979 session was Senate Committee Resolution 25, which admonished the Bureau of Land Management to cease its consideration of certain Nevada lands for designation as wilderness areas.

The difficult 60th Nevada Legislature adjourned after setting a new record for duration—133 days. The coming session would be noted for its progress in achieving long needed tax reform, but would also be remembered for the rekindling of an old feud in which Bill Raggio and Joe Conforte would once again lock horns.

# CHAPTER FORTY-TWO

# An Old Foe (1981)

In June 1980, Bill Raggio announced he would seek reelection for a third term. The fifty-three-year-old minority floor leader said he would base his reelection campaign on a "sound record of past achievement and new programs to meet the challenges of the 1980s."

Listing priorities for the upcoming session, Raggio called for sound economic and fiscal policies, improved transportation systems and highways, continued strict gaming control and a better definition of nuclear waste disposal policies.

Cliff Young, his usual running mate for the other at-large, Washoe District 1 seat, had decided not to seek reelection. Of his time working in the senate with Raggio, Young would recall in 2009: "Bill was one of the most able persons I have ever served with, and that includes the U.S. Congress—and there were certainly a number of very able people there."

In departing, Young endorsed Republican Assemblywoman Sue Wagner for his vacated senate seat. Wagner had come to Nevada in 1969 from Arizona, and five years later, as a homemaker raising two small children, ran successfully for the state assembly. After three terms in the assembly, she decided to run for the senate in 1980.

In her 2005 memoir, *Through the Glass Ceiling*, Wagner would recall that Cliff Young endorsed her because they shared much of the same ideology, while she and Bill disagreed on key issues. When confronted by the choice of running in tandem with Bill (in what was then termed a "single shot"), as he and Cliff Young had done so often in the past,

Wagner heeded the recommendation of her campaign staff that she distance herself from Bill and run separately.[1]

With no Democratic Party candidate opposing them on Election Day, Raggio and Wagner easily won the two at-large Washoe County senate seats. Wagner, campaigning countywide for the first time, was the top vote getter. Of the approximately 74,000 votes cast in Washoe County, Raggio received about 29,000 and Wagner received about 32,500. Clearly proud of having garnered more votes than the veteran Bill Raggio, she later wrote that this had resulted from her having gone door-to-door throughout the county, and the fact that many women voters were probably energized by her candidacy.

When asked at the time about having received fewer votes than her, Bill replied, "Frankly, Sue Wagner and I had a fairly easy race. I was more concerned about legislative races statewide resulting in more balance in the 1981 legislature."

The results of the 1980 election in Nevada demonstrated the growing conservatism of the electorate. In the presidential race, Ronald Reagan won, receiving 62% of the vote to incumbent President Jimmy Carter's 27%.

Senator Paul Laxalt also had an easy race for reelection. Already popular throughout the state, his well-publicized friendship with Reagan made Laxalt a prohibitive favorite and carried him to victory in every county, garnering nearly 60% of the overall vote.

Yet, other races proved the state was still Democratic in its voting habits.[2] Congressman Jim Santini was reelected with nearly 70% of the vote. In the legislature, Democrats held the same party majorities as in 1979, a fifteen-to-five margin in the senate and a twenty-six-to-fourteen margin in the assembly.

Property tax cap Question 6, which had passed overwhelmingly in 1978, was defeated. In an advisory referendum question, voters rejected the placement of the MX missile system in Nevada by a margin of two to one.[3]

On January 19, 1981, in his second State of the State address, Governor List called for austerity because of the adverse effect the national economic recession was having on Nevada's gaming industry.

\* \* \*

The main achievement of the 1981 Legislative session was tax reform. In order to stave off a proposal similar to California's Proposition 13, the legislature, along with Governor List, approved a measure that would reduce property taxes (paid almost entirely by Nevada residents) and raise sales taxes (part of which would be paid by tourists). Due to this plan, voters would reject passing the 1% property tax cap into law during its second attempt in the 1982 election.

Toward the end of the session, Senator Raggio sponsored legislation that would outlaw houses of prostitution within twenty-five miles of a city with a population of more than 60,000, and within twelve miles of a federal interstate highway in the area of such cities. Coincidently, the only brothel in the state that would be adversely affected by the measure was Joe Conforte's Mustang Ranch.

The media saw this as a rekindling of the twenty-two-year feud between Raggio and Conforte. Bill disagreed, citing law enforcement problems and depicting the brothel as "a breeding ground for serious crime."[4]

There was much evidence to support Raggio's contention. Since leaving the District Attorney's Office in January 1971, he had watched a resurgence of Conforte's corrupt influence in both Washoe and Storey Counties.

In that year, Storey County legalized brothels. A long-time Conforte nemesis, Reno Chief of Police Elmer Briscoe, was forced to resign. In 1973, the Reno-Sparks Convention Authority, after a controversial vote, purchased property from Conforte that would become the Wild Creek Golf Course. Conforte kept adjacent land, which immediately increased in value by $1 million.

In January 1976, a Washoe County grand jury investigation found close ties between Reno and Sparks public officials and Joe Conforte. The jury cited examples of Conforte's influence, but no indictments were handed down.[5]

Two months later, revelations by investigative journalists told of a 1974 meeting in Palm Springs, California between Conforte and organized crime figures from Philadelphia and Los Angeles to discuss building a hotel-casino on Conforte's property adjacent to the newly constructed Wild Creek Golf Course.

A year later, the Mustang Ranch suspiciously burned to the ground in what was claimed to be an arson fire. With the $350,000 insurance settlement, Conforte rebuilt a larger and more lavish brothel. The following year, in May 1976, Argentine heavy weight boxer Oscar Bonavena was shot to death outside the brothel.[6]

In April 1977, Joe and Sally Conforte had been arrested on ten counts of federal income-tax evasion. Sally was ultimately fined $10,000 and given a suspended sentence. Joe faced a minimum five years in prison. The couple appealed the ruling, and when the U.S. Supreme Court refused to hear the case, Joe fled the country. His previous stay in the federal correctional facility at McNeil Island, Washington, on an earlier tax evasion conviction, had not been a pleasant one and Joe had sworn not to return to prison. Sally remained behind and continued to run the Mustang Ranch.

In support of Bill's contention that the brothel was "a breeding ground for serious crime," Washoe County Sheriff Bob Galli testified before the senate's judiciary committee. Galli said the proposed legislation would "eradicate a long-standing cancer in the side of the Reno community." The sheriff told lawmakers about Conforte's ties to organized crime figures and how shutting down Mustang Ranch would help to clean up Reno's image.[7]

Before fleeing the country, Conforte had tried to sell the Mustang Ranch for $20 million. Yet, as a local news story pointed out, "If Raggio's law passes, the Mustang Ranch would probably be worth closer to $20,000."[8]

Some speculated that creating an enormous monetary loss to his old antagonist might have been part of the timing of the measure; however, Bill had actually proposed it first in 1975.

The earlier version of the bill would have outlawed brothels within fifty miles of any major city. Senator Raggio discussed it with Senator

Floyd Lamb while the two car-pooled from Reno to Carson City one day. According to Raggio, Lamb then drafted the bill but said he wanted to wait and see if he could get a majority of the twenty members behind the measure, before he introduced it. Lamb then let the bill sit on his desk until session ended.

When asked about it later, Senator Jim Gibson recalled that Lamb had drafted the legislation and then insisted it stay on his desk. Gibson, who years before had sponsored the measure outlawing prostitution in Clark County, said Raggio wanted the bill introduced and voted on the floor. "But it was Floyd's bill," Gibson explained. "It was his idea to hold it until we got enough votes to ensure passage. Therefore, I went along and agreed. Floyd did the counting, and my memory is that he got within one or two votes of the eleven we needed."

Gibson further stated that he had heard rumors over the years of Lamb's possible business involvement with a Lincoln County brothel. "I accosted him about it," Gibson said, and Lamb "produced a lot of papers" and convinced Gibson that he sold the land in 1970, though at one point admitting that he might still be "the technical owner" of the property.[9]

In 1976, Bill Raggio told reporters that the fifty-mile proposal had nothing to do with any Lincoln County brothel. "No one would give a damn in Clark County," he said, "because brothels adjacent to Clark are more than fifty miles outside the Las Vegas City limits." Raggio said he favored putting the bill on the floor in 1975 to force all of the state senators to take a stand on the issue, but Lamb refused to do it that way. "I wanted to let them face muster on it," Bill said.[10]

Of Lamb's reason for not introducing the measure, Bill would provide an amusingly loaded reply in 2009: "Trust me. Floyd was the last person in this state who would ever want to close down a brothel."

On May 30, 1981, Senator Raggio finally got his chance to see how fellow solons would "face muster." Before the vote, Bill made a powerful argument that his bill was not his attempt to satisfy a vendetta against brothel owner Joe Conforte, or to moralize against prostitution. He cited law enforcement reports detailing incidences of crime at the Mustang Ranch ranging from murder to assault to drug possession.

Opponents of the bill, led by Senator Virgil Getto of Fallon, called it "a very serious encroachment on another county's business" and a threat to local autonomy. Getto, who represented four rural counties that licensed bordellos, including the Mustang Ranch in Storey County, spoke of creating "a serious precedent" that could result in prostitution "being barred in other areas during the sessions ahead."

Senator Spike Wilson, a Democrat from Washoe County, said that "This is a social question and not a business question. There's no justification for keeping the joint open."

In his 2008 oral history, Senator Neal recalled that Assembly Speaker Joe Dini, who represented Lyon County where brothels were legal, asked him to help stop the bill from passing. Neal, along with Dini, felt that it was the individual county's prerogative to decide on brothels.

Senator Neal noted that during debate about the measure on the senate floor he decided "that the best thing that I possibly could do was to just laugh this thing right out of the senate, so I started telling jokes...When the vote came, Raggio lost the thing by one vote. He couldn't get angry with me because he saw what I had done to him—had made it funny and just laughed it right out."

In 2008, Senator Raggio would say, "Joe Neal took the issue on for some unexplained reason. I believe he was contacted on behalf of those interests and he succeeded in getting the votes to kill the bill in the senate. I'm not going say much more than that."

On June 4, 1981, the legislature adjourned after another record-breaking session—137 days. It had been a redistricting session and membership of the legislature was increased from sixty to sixty-three, in order to cushion the reapportionment blow to rural counties. The assembly now consisted of forty-two members and the senate had twenty-one. The newly created Northern Congressional District was also formed and would be filled in the subsequent election.

As the 1983 legislative session approached, Bill began to see glimmers of hope that he and his fellow Republicans would not remain the minority party forever.

# CHAPTER FORTY-THREE

# Plight of the
# Citizen Legislator (1983)

Due in large measure to the country's deep and continuing economic recession, Governor Robert List would serve only one term in office. His tax package, which reduced property taxes by an average of 50% and increased the sales tax rate from 3.5% to 5.75%, had met little opposition from legislators who, like the governor, were also aware that property tax relief was necessary to keep voter initiative Question 6 from becoming law.

More than 75% of Nevada's revenue was based on gaming and sales tax. However, these taxes are the most unstable and the most difficult to project in estimating future revenue over a two-year period.

It was in times of economic recession, when revenues from sales tax and gaming were in decline, that Nevadans most needed state services, such as food stamps, welfare payments and unemployment compensation. The Nevada electorate directly contributed to this situation in their overwhelming desire to shift the revenue burden away from property tax and income tax. When hard times arrived, the electorate would hold Governor List accountable.[1]

When List sought reelection in 1982, he barely survived the Republican primary and lost to Democratic challenger, Richard Bryan, in the general election, receiving only 42% of the votes.

Governor List's term was, according to Bill Raggio, "beset with financial woes," a contrast to his eight years as an "efficient and highly competent attorney general."

"Bob List never really appeared comfortable in his role as governor," Bill later remarked. "He became somewhat aloof and seemed to talk down to his constituency. In addition, there were constant rumors concerning his personal life and the First Couple's marriage. To their credit, however, the marriage was held together during his term and Kathy served as an elegant and dedicated First Lady."

Bill said that he appreciated working with Governor List, though as a junior member of the senate he was not called upon that often to provide advice or input.

Despite Lists reelection defeat, there was good news for Bill Raggio and his fellow Republicans in the 1982 election. The party took more statewide offices than they had since 1930. Former State Senator Chic Hecht ousted U.S. Senator Howard Cannon and former Assemblywoman Patty Caffereta was elected state treasurer. Darrell Daines and Brian MacKay were elected as state controller and attorney general, respectively. Barbara Vucanovich won the Congressional race for District 2.

\* \* \*

Nevada had experienced unique revenue problems since its inception, as Mark Twain humorously observed in *Roughing It*:

> [Nevada] could not well carry such a load as a state government, since it had nothing to tax that could stand a tax, for undeveloped mines could not, and there were not fifty developed ones in the land. There was but little realty to tax, and it did seem as if nobody was ever going to think of the simple salvation of inflicting a money penalty on murder.[2]

There was, however, nothing humorous about the most difficult problem facing the 1983 legislature— taxes. While there was general agreement that additional revenue was required due to the decline in sales tax caused by the recession, there was no agreement on how that should be done.

The governor, assembly and senate each proposed a different tax plan.

Some have argued that the assembly proposal, which called for a 35% increase in property taxes, was superior to that of the senate plan that would increase property taxes by 30% and include a 5% tax on wholesale soft drinks. However, the senate plan passed into law due to the senate's "stronger, more mature leadership."[3]

Although he was successful in pushing other parts of his agenda through the legislature, Governor Bryan did not remain in full control of his party and was often challenged by Democratic senate leaders who had not supported him in the primary election.

Another influential Democrat, Lieutenant Governor Robert Cashell, would leave the party soon after the session ended. Cashell, like several others in the assembly and senate, would find that their moderate values and pro-business philosophy made them feel less welcome in an increasingly liberal Democratic Party.

President Reagan and Nevada Senator Paul Laxalt were eager to capitalize on such sentiment, with programs like "Operation Crossover." Laxalt and Cashell had long been friends in the previously less-partisan atmosphere of Nevada politics. The lieutenant governor was soon invited by the president to visit him at White House. In a 2009 interview, Cashell described the event:

> President Reagan said to me, "I need you to be on our team," and so I replied that I would do my best for the country. Reagan then repeated, "I know that, but I need you to be on our team." When the president asks as he did, well, you just pack your bags and move across the street right away. In fact, President Reagan was so charming and engaging, that by the time you were done shaking hands with him you are already feeling guilty for not having switched parties sooner.

After he switched to the Republican Party, Bob Cashell heard from former Governor O'Callaghan. "He really chewed me out," Cashell said. "However, at the same time, he said he understood that I was a conservative businessman and how persuasive President Reagan could be."

Cashell then pointed out, "O'Callaghan also knew that without moderate Republicans, he would not have been elected governor, and Laxalt would not have been elected without the votes of moderate Democrats. This is an important element of Nevada politics, which fringe factions often ignore."

Governor Bryan understood this too, but also recognized Bob Cashell had nicely positioned himself to make a run for the Governor's Office. Much to his chagrin, Cashell was quickly appointed as chair of two new commissions on economic development and tourism that Bryan had fought so hard to create.

Within just two years, due to the intercession of Laxalt and Raggio, new-party-member Bob Cashell was named Chair of the Nevada Republican Party.

Of Senator Raggio, now-Reno Mayor Cashell said, "When I was president of the senate, Bill was the minority leader. He was so damn smart I had to be on my toes all the time. I could never let down. It is not that he was going to screw anybody, but he was just so smooth that you might not see something coming if you weren't paying attention all the time."

\* \* \*

In addition to dealing with revenue plans, the 1983 legislative session showed there was "no doubt that gambling interests were in control of legislature."[4]

The powerful lobby was successful, among other measures, in killing a lottery bill; preventing significant increases in gambling taxes; severely limiting benefits to tip earners; and making the collection of gambling debts legally enforceable.

Senator Raggio was again accused of having of conflict of interest because the previous year he had begun serving as a corporate officer for Sahara Resorts, which owned several large Las Vegas hotel/casinos. His firm also handled legal business for other gaming properties.

In August 1983, Raggio sent a strongly worded letter to the editor of the *Reno Evening Gazette* refuting the accusation, declaring no legislative body in the country—from Congress to city councils—should be comprised of individuals who are without any preconceived ideas.

Each member, he said, has diverse viewpoints, depending on background, education, social contacts, business, profession or constituency and such diversity contributes in a positive manner to the give-and-take process of enacting legislation.

He pointed out that in the future Nevada might consider going to a full time "professional" legislature, though it would require adequate compensation and additional costs.

Yet, that would likely not solve such problems, "since much of the same criticism is leveled at legislators in such states by those who were on the losing side of any issue, or disagree with decisions which are made in the process."

Bill referred to the 1977 Ethics Law, which he supported, as providing realistic guidelines for both legislators and public officials and stated that he had "meticulously followed these guidelines." In conclusion, he added a caveat: "The guidelines should not be so restrictive that only an isolated and non-representative segment of the citizenry would be willing to serve in such positions."[5]

The 1983 Legislative session adjourned on May 22. During this session, Senator Raggio had regained a seat on the Senate Committee on Finance and consequently the Interim Finance Committee during the off-session.

He would remain busy for the remainder of 1983 and into 1984 with those legislative duties as well as dedicating his time and energy to numerous service and civic groups and nonprofit organizations. Bill would resume his duties as a board of director of the National Conference of Christians and Jews (he had previously been a board member from 1966-1970) and become an advisory board member of the E.L. Wiegand Foundation, focusing on grants for education and health.

His law practice would also make demands on his time. Within months, Bill would find himself in one of the most dramatic federal trials of the decade, defending an old friend against slanderous testimony from Bill's old nemesis, Joe Conforte.

# CHAPTER FORTY-FOUR

# Judge Harry
# Claiborne Trial (1984)

O n October 7, 1983, sixty-eight-year-old Floyd Lamb, Chair of the powerful Senate Committee on Finance, was indicted by a federal grand jury on the charge of interference with commerce by extortion.

Lamb had received $23,000 in cash from FBI undercover agent Steven Rybar, the first of three agreed-upon installments toward a "finder's fee" of $150,000. In return, Lamb promised to use his influence in securing Rybar a $15 million loan from the State Public Employees Retirement System. Lamb would be found guilty and serve seventeen months in federal prison. Two weeks after his conviction, he resigned from the Nevada State Senate where he had served for twenty-six years.

Floyd Lamb's arrest came at the conclusion of a three-year-long FBI sting, code named "Operation Yobo."[1] The operation, designed to uncover suspected high-level political corruption in Nevada, was conducted simultaneously with a broader and much publicized FBI sting known as Abscam.[2]

Rybar, posing as Steve Reilly, a financial adviser for the Doctors Fiduciary Trust, a fictitious company set up to provide tax sheltered investments to a group of out-of-state physicians, who sought favors, such as zoning changes and loans, in exchange for bribe money.

Rybar was initially introduced to Lamb by fellow Democratic State Senator Gene Echols. Echols, who like Bill Raggio was first elected to the senate in 1972, was also indicted and later convicted of accepting a bribe. He also resigned his senate seat. Others caught during the Yobo sting were Clark County Commissioners Jack Petitti and Woodrow Wilson, and Reno City Councilman Joe McClelland. All were convicted.

Rybar, it turns out, had also tried to ensnare Senator Raggio.

"I had my law practice downtown (Reno) on the eighth floor of the First Interstate Bank building," Raggio recalled. "I was a state senator, then, but also in private practice. One day, a man came in saying he was a physician and wanted my help in getting his investment group to be able to build a hotel casino in Reno. I told him that there was a moratorium on casino building in the city at the time and that I could not help them, although I could assist his investors if they wanted to build in another part of the county."

Rybar was adamant that they wanted to build in Reno itself and asked the senator if the physician's investment group were to give him some money, would he intercede with influential people and "get it done."

"As an attorney," Raggio points out, "I could have taken the retainer they offered, and that would not have been a crime; however, taking the retainer knowing at the time that I was not going to produce the results they wanted would have been unethical."

Rybar was persistent and continued asking Bill if additional money might help him with the decision. "I finally told him that I was not interested and that I would not waste his time or his money by promising something I could not do. At the time, I did not think of the offer as anything other than a retainer, nor did I suspect that it was part of a sting."

Only months later did Bill learn that this was part of an FBI operation to ensnare public officials for corruption. "One thing has always bothered me, though," Senator Raggio later said. "While some public officials were disgraced because of the sting, the strike force should have published a list of those who did not take the money—for the sake of fairness."[3]

Though Bill Raggio had been on the sidelines most of the time watching this drama unfold, he would soon find himself in the midst of the fray when in December of 1983 the federal strike force announced the indictment of Raggio's former courtroom adversary, and old friend, Harry E. Claiborne.

In 1978, on the recommendation of Nevada's Senator Howard Cannon,

President Jimmy Carter had appointed Claiborne federal judge for the United States District Court for the District of Nevada. Claiborne's unorthodox and antagonistic courtroom style, upon which his legend was built, also proved to be his "Achilles Heel."

His ostentatious life manner; public associations with reputed organized crime associates, like Benny Binion, with whom he frequently lunched; and subsequent rulings, often in favor of those being prosecuted by the strike force, raised the ire of federal law enforcement. A concerted effort was made to remove him from the bench.

The strike force first tried to make a case against the judge for having illegally bugged the home of a former girlfriend, but the grand jury failed to indict. This only made Judge Claiborne more outspoken in his undisguised contempt for the intrusiveness of the federal strike force in Las Vegas; a unit he publicly referred to as "a bunch of crooks out to destroy Nevada."

Spearheading the effort to indict Judge Claiborne was Joe Yablonsky, the FBI Special Agent for Southern Nevada and inspiration for the code name Yobo, given to the sting operation.

The belligerent Yablonsky had not made himself welcome in the state from the time of his transfer from Cincinnati to Las Vegas in 1980. Upon his arrival, he publicly proclaimed that, for far too long, Nevada had operated "like a foreign protectorate…We've had to plant the American flag in the desert."[4] *Time* magazine claimed that Yablonsky had told acquaintances he, above all, wanted Judge Claiborne's picture hanging on his office wall—as a trophy.[5]

In a 2009 interview, Las Vegas Mayor Oscar Goodman, who was part of Judge Claiborne's legal defense team against the federal charges, made clear his feeling about the FBI Special Agent, declaring, "as far as I'm concerned, Yablonsky was a bum, and acted like a bum, and as a result, directed his energy toward Harry Claiborne."

In late 1983, while the federal grand jury was still considering charges against the judge, Bill Raggio received a telephone call from Claiborne, who told him the strike force was "out to get him" and that he wanted Bill to represent him after any future indictment.

"He said a grand jury was going on and asked me to fly down to Las Vegas to meet with him," Raggio recalled. "I flew down there, met with him and agreed to represent him. The strike force was after him because, unlike other federal judges, Claiborne was willing to rule against their cases. I made some inquiries on his behalf."

On December 8, 1983, a federal grand jury announced an indictment charging Judge Claiborne with taking bribes, obstructing justice and filing false income tax returns.

Government prosecutors quickly won a change of venue from Las Vegas to Reno, believing Claiborne's popularity in southern Nevada, and the general antipathy toward the federal strike force there, would make their case more difficult to try.

The mind-set of northern Nevadans differed dramatically from those in the south. As Michael Vernetti points out in his biography of Harry Claiborne, "Las Vegas' much tarnished image as a mob playground caused Reno citizens to adopt an attitude of moral superiority." Consequently, a Reno jury would be less suspicious of the government's case and more inclined to convict a flamboyant Las Vegan like Claiborne.[6]

When later asked about this curious change of venue, Bill Raggio said, "The fact that the change of venue was allowed before any examination of the jurors was, to my mind, a highly unusual situation."

The media ran the story of Claiborne's indictment hours before the grand jury announced it. Many were infuriated about this "leak," from what was, by law, a secret deliberation.

Two days later, during a meeting of an interim study committee, Senator Raggio suggested the state consider passing a law making it a felony for government officials to leak information. In addition, Raggio raised the question of whether the state should amend its "shield law" to require reporters to divulge the sources of leaked information. "Some strong punishment has to be considered," he said. "It's reprehensible that people in high places are leaking information. It is trial by ordeal and innuendo, not trial by justice."

The six-member committee was tasked with providing recommendations to the upcoming 1985 legislature on how to revamp the county grand jury system. Coincidentally, Judge Claiborne had been scheduled to appear before them that day to testify on his views. He cancelled his appearance, however, after word of his indictment leaked out.

Bill confirmed to the committee that he had accepted a request by Claiborne to act as counsel in the judge's upcoming trial. He said that involvement in the Claiborne case would not influence his thinking on the committee.

Another jurist invited to testify that day was Clark County District Court Judge Stephen Huffaker, who said leaks to the press could destroy the reputations of innocent people who may never be indicted. Huffaker found it "appalling" that a reporter called him for his reaction an hour *before* Claiborne's indictment was officially announced. He urged the committee to recommend making it a misdemeanor for government officials to leak information, and called upon the press to exercise more restraint.

Senator Raggio agreed, noting that freedom of the press is a fundamental right and guarantee. "I don't know if we can expect them [the press] to shut up on leaks when they come on silver platters," he said. "However, it might be impractical to rely on governmental officials to admit their guilt. That's why an exemption to the state's shield law requiring reporters to divulge the sources of leaks may be necessary."

The committee, he pointed out, had jurisdiction over county grand juries, but not the federal grand juries. "I favor county grand juries," Bill said. "But federal grand juries are Star Chambers. You don't need a witness and you can rely on hearsay evidence to indict someone. It's ridiculous."

Bill's characterization of the federal system could not have been more appropriate than in the case against Judge Harry E. Claiborne, especially when it was soon learned that the bulk of the state's evidence hinged upon the testimony of convicted felon, incorrigible liar and Bill Raggio's old adversary, Joe Conforte.

Federal authorities had been negotiating with Conforte for his return to the United States from Brazil where the brothel owner fled in 1981 after finding himself in the worst legal jam of his life. In addition to a recent conviction on federal income tax evasion, a Washoe County grand jury had indicted Conforte for attempting to bribe Lyon County DA John Giomi in order to gain his influence in obtaining a brothel license. Washoe County District Attorney Mills Lane was awaiting the result of that trial. If convicted, Lane planned to have Conforte declared a habitual criminal, which would send him to prison for life.

In exchange for Conforte's testimony that he had bribed Judge Claiborne on two different occasions, federal prosecutors agreed to reduce his prison sentence from twenty years to just fifteen months on the income tax charge. They persuaded Mills Lane to agree to only an eighteen-month sentence on the state bribery charge, to be served concurrently, and not pursue his effort to have Conforte declared a habitual criminal.

For good measure, the federal government agreed to erase the brothel owner's tax liability debt of nearly $20 million. It was, as John Smith wrote in his biography of Oscar Goodman, *Of Rats and Men*, "...one of the sweetest, and most outrageous, deals in the history of the Justice Department."[7] Such was Joe Yablonsky's fervor to hang Claiborne's picture on his wall.

Many were angered by the government's generosity to Joe Conforte. According to a *Las Vegas Sun* story at the time, Nevada IRS Director Gerald Swanson accused the IRS, the FBI and the Justice Department of setting him up on false charges because of his resistance to the deal. Swanson was subsequently transferred to the Dallas IRS office.[8] *Sun* editor Hank Greenspun called the arrangement clear evidence of a "federal vendetta" against Judge Claiborne.[9]

Upon hearing of the deal, Bill Raggio went to see Mills Lane, who was now held the DA position Bill had for sixteen years. "We discussed his proposal to work with the FBI during the Claiborne trial," Bill said, "and their request to have him dismiss some state charges against Conforte. I let him know that I thought it was wrong. He went ahead and made the deal with the federal people."

The trial began on March 15, 1984 at the federal courthouse in Reno. Presiding would be seventy-seven-year-old Judge Walter E. Hoffman, a semi-retired federal jurist from Virginia. Normally, the Chief Judge of the Court of Appeals for the Ninth Circuit would have jurisdiction selecting the judge. However, he invoked his right to pass that decision on to the Chief Justice of the U.S. Supreme Court.

As such, Chief Justice Warren Burger, reputedly no admirer of Judge Claiborne's public persona, selected Judge Hoffman for the job. Hoffman, who shared Justice Burger's political philosophy and rigid sense of respectability, had presided over the October 1973 trial of Vice President Spiro T. Agnew, on similar charges.

Hoffman would have the highly unusual opportunity of ruling in both cases to deny motions arguing that certain Constitutional officers could not be tried in federal court prior to being impeached by the U.S. House of Representatives.

Judge Hoffman's reputation as a hard-nosed authoritarian, who offered little latitude during trials, helped compel Agnew's attorneys to work out a deal with federal prosecutors to plead no-contest to one count of income tax evasion, a fine, no prison time and his resignation as Vice President, all of which Hoffman accepted.

No two personalities could have been less alike than those of attorney Oscar Goodman and Judge Walter Hoffman. Goodman had earned his reputation with a fiery courtroom style. He was unapologetic in his representation of notorious figures from the world of organized crime, which had earned him the moniker "Mouthpiece for the Mob." It could not have helped his relationship with Judge Hoffman that Goodman had, less than a year before, gotten Las Vegas crime figure Jimmy Chagra acquitted on charges that he assassinated U.S. District Court Judge John Wood, Jr., of Texas.

Goodman's method was to file a flurry of pre-trial motions and argue every aspect of the process to ensure his client was fully protected. Hoffman, on the other hand, was not used to being challenged.

When it became clear the judge was going to deny all thirty-defense motions, Goodman became infuriated. He later recalled, "it got to a point where he [Judge Hoffman] and I were shouting at each other so loud that Claiborne actually reached over and pulled me down and said, 'He's going to send you to jail if you don't shut up.'"

Co-counsel Raggio knew what they were up against from the beginning, believing that Judge Hoffman was convinced of Claiborne's guilt and would do whatever it took to prove it. "He was bound-and-determined that Claiborne would be removed from the bench," Raggio said. "He tried to act impartial, but it was a tough act. For example, we were holding a special session of the legislature [March 29, 1984], a one-day session, and so we asked for a one-day recess so I could attend. He denied it, saying I could go, but Oscar would have to stay and try the case."

Bill had been selected for the team in large part because his smooth, deliberate style would balance Oscar Goodman's more animated delivery. "Oscar," Bill would later say, "is a colorful, flamboyant individual, but is also a very polished defense attorney, very good in court, very good before juries. He could also be bombastic, and I think that was an irritant to Judge Hoffman, who was used to running the court precisely the way he wanted it run."

The bribery charges against Claiborne hinged upon the word of Joe Conforte that on December 12, 1978 he had given the judge $30,000 cash in return for "taking care of" subpoenas against two of his Mustang Ranch prostitutes.

Conforte would further claim that in March 1979, he visited the judge in Portland, Oregon, where Claiborne was presiding over a circuit court, and paid him $55,000 to intercede with the Ninth Circuit Court of Appeals in overturning his income tax conviction. A Multnomah County grand jury subsequently heard evidence on that charge and found it insufficient to bring an indictment.

Judge Claiborne was acquainted with Conforte as the result of legal work he had done for him over the years. Before being elevated to the federal bench, attorney Claiborne had harnessed his considerable legal talent to keep Conforte out of prison on a federal Mann Act violation. However, Claiborne refused Conforte's subsequent request to represent him at his trial for income tax evasion, citing his lack of expertise in federal tax law.

In 2009, Oscar Goodman recalled how anxious he was to be the one to cross-examine Conforte and "tear him apart" on the witness stand:

> Bill Raggio was tireless in his preparation of the case; both as far as motions were concerned, as well as the trial of the case. He had an instinctive dislike for Joe Conforte, not only professionally when he was with the District Attorney's office; but he really disliked him personally.

> While I wanted to cross-examine Conforte in the worst way, Bill's will prevailed and once Conforte took the stand Bill ripped him a new rear end. The "the ripping of the new rear end" was basically what caused the government to drop all of the a venal counts against Claiborne for which Conforte was the primary and sole witness.

Raggio did, indeed, "rip" Conforte on the stand, beginning with his opening remarks in which referred to him as a "pimp" and "whoremonger" so often that an uncomfortable female juror entreated the judge in a note to have him stop.

"Mr. Raggio," said Judge Hoffman, "just call him 'Conforte.'" The judge then addressed Conforte's lapses into vulgarity by saying that he "may get his mouth washed out" before his testimony went much further.

The old feud was apparent in Conforte's testimony, as he tried to personalize the dialogue in an effort to throw Bill off track. He often laced his answers with gratuitous comments, such as how he had contributed to Bill's political campaigns, or that he leased the property for the Mustang Ranch from a Raggio cousin. When Bill later asked him if he had operated other brothels in Storey County, Conforte heatedly replied, "Yeah, you burned one of them down!"

Bill ignored such taunts and spent the day methodically debunking the testimony. At one point, Conforte, evidently still smarting from the craftiness of the extortion case Bill had put together against him in 1960, blurted out, "You are not going to trip me up this time!"

Conforte, however, was incorrect. In the course of his meticulous trial preparation, Bill had discovered numerous inconsistencies in the government's case. One, in particular, would provide the most dramatic moment in the trial.

Over his many years of preparing for trial, Bill developed the habit of going through the evidence in chronological order and writing down relevant dates. One of the pieces of evidence in this trial was Conforte's passport.

"The prosecution had put it in evidence for some purpose, I never really understood," Raggio later commented. "While looking at it, I noticed the date that it was issued in New York City was the same date as alleged in the criminal indictment of bribery."

During subsequent cross-examination, Bill was able to get Conforte to admit that he personally picked up his passport on the date it was issued. Bill, therefore, had him boxed in as being in New York City at the time he was supposed to be bribing Judge Claiborne in Reno.

Judge Hoffman had reluctantly agreed to issue a subpoena to have John Rolf come from the passport office in Washington D.C., to testify and supply documents establishing that Conforte had appeared personally in New York City on the date the passport was issued.

What amazed Raggio and Goodman the most was, with all the expertise the prosecution had—including the FBI and IRS—they never noticed this blatant discrepancy.

"Even more astonishing," Bill added, "they did not even see what was coming as the result of our getting the subpoena for the passport agent. We took them completely by surprise."

What happened next would astound Bill and everyone else in the courtroom. Even decades later, when describing it, his head shook in disbelief:

> At the conclusion of the passport agent's testimony, Judge Hoffman called us up to the bench, including the four federal prosecutors. Having just been confronted with evidence that it was impossible for Conforte to have been there on the day the bribe

was said to have taken place, he turned to the prosecutors and said in exasperation, and I quote, "What do we do now?" And I stress here the word *we*. I looked over at Oscar, incredulous at what we had just heard. It was now apparent to everyone in the courtroom just how biased Judge Hoffman was.

After some discussion with the prosecutors, Judge Hoffman ruled to allow the date of the bribe to be "on, or about" the day the prosecutors had originally stated in the indictment.

Later in the trial, Judge Hoffman would object to splashy headlines on the front page of the *Las Vegas Sun* in support of Claiborne. Early one morning, he spent eleven of his own quarters to empty a news rack in the lobby of the courthouse of its contents before arriving jurors might see them. He then ordered all the *Sun's* newspaper racks removed from the building until the end of the trial. When Sun editor Hank Greenspun arrived to attend the trial, Judge Hoffman ordered him to sit by himself in a far corner of the courtroom.

The day after the shocking passport testimony, Bill called to the witness stand the manager of the apartment complex where Judge Claiborne had lived when Conforte allegedly passed him the $30,000 bribe. Once again, the federal prosecutors were about to be embarrassed by their overeagerness to convict at any cost.

Oscar Goodman described the event in a 2009 interview, saying that before the trial began, federal prosecutors had given Conforte a tour through the apartment complex where Judge Claiborne lived, which happened to be adjacent to the federal courthouse in Reno.

Though the government did not take him into the actual apartment where Claiborne had resided, they did take him into an apartment they believed was the exact image of Claiborne's. However, it was a "mirror image," with everything in that apartment being on the opposite side. That is, if Claiborne's bedroom was on the left as you walked into his apartment, it was on the right, in the apartment Conforte saw. In his testimony, Goodman said, Conforte described an apartment that was, "basically, upside down."[10]

Goodman then added, "There is a Jewish word that Senator Raggio likes, *shanda*. I'm not a great expert on Yiddish, but I think it means 'shame' or 'shameful.' That is exactly the way Bill and I characterized the conduct of the government in this case, '*shanda*.'"

Raggio showed the jury video of the apartment interiors. This, and the conflicting descriptions between the testimony of Conforte and the apartment manager, made it clear that Joe Conforte had never been in Harry Claiborne's apartment. Once again, the federal prosecutors were mortified—and Judge Hoffman's frustration was palpable.

The next day, Conforte's attorney, Stan Brown, took the witness stand. Brown, who was dependent on Conforte for the bulk of his income, corroborated his earlier testimony. In addition, Brown admitted to having secretly recorded conversations with his friend and long-time legal colleague, John Squire Drendel, who had been an early member of the Claiborne defense team.

Conforte, it was believed, had a vendetta against Drendel going back to 1961. At that time, just days before Conforte's appeal before Nevada Supreme Court on his extortion conviction, young Jackie Pearson (*née* Hitson) publicly announced that her testimony during the Conforte extortion trial the year before was untrue, and that she had been coerced by DA Raggio to save his reputation.

The Washoe County grand jury quickly convened and after determining her to be lying, indicted Mrs. Pearson for perjury. Drendel agreed to represent her at a meeting in Bill's office the following day. Both Bill and Drendel believed she was being used by Conforte in his desperate attempt to stay out of prison. Drendel advised his client that it would be in her best interest to plead guilty to the perjury charge and accept probation, instead of going to trial and risking prison time. She accepted. Conforte was furious with Drendel, believing he had conspired with Bill against him. It was an affront Joe Conforte never forgot.

So when it later became known that Drendel had spoken about the Claiborne case briefly with Stan Brown, who was, by that time, a material witness for the prosecution, Drendel was forced to remove himself from the defense team and suffered damage to his otherwise sterling reputation.[11] It would seem Conforte had exacted his revenge.

Yet, under skillful examination by Oscar Goodman, Drendel may have gotten the last laugh, taking the stand angrily, though convincingly, and thoroughly destroying the credibility of his former friend, Stan Brown.

"I knew Stan Brown ever since I started to practice law in Reno," Bill Raggio later said. "His downfall was that he resorted to the easy way to make a living and decided to represent the pimp Joe Conforte for the money. Until then, Stan Brown had been a pretty legitimate lawyer."

Yet, Bill felt that Judge Claiborne may have been responsible for much of his own predicament because "he was very outspoken about the strike force and the federal prosecutors, and he invited them, I guess, to go after him. Unfortunately, for the FBI, they bought into this story that Conforte used to get his charges dismissed."

When later asked why the federal prosecutors would risk so much on the word of an acknowledged liar, Bill was philosophical: "Their attitude as a prosecutor, and my attitude as a prosecutor, is that you don't always get choirboys as witnesses. You get the guys who are around the individual you are trying to convict."

After twenty-two days, testimony from ninety-six witnesses, and the introduction of nearly 200 pieces of evidence, the jury began its deliberation. Eventually, they were unable to agree on a verdict on all six counts and hung ten to two for acquittal. The judge declared a mistrial.

Before the case went for retrial, and despite being convinced in the innocence of their client on all counts, Raggio and Goodman offered Judge Claiborne another option.

"We suggested to him that, if he were willing, we would make an offer that he would resign as judge and pay his tax penalties, because they were mostly inadvertent as a result of his drinking," Bill said.

Claiborne would hear nothing of it.

"I think the fact that he did have a drinking problem was one of the reasons he did not give it consideration," Bill continued. "At that point, the federal prosecutors might have been willing to accept something like that because their main goal was to get him off the bench."

Oscar Goodman had much the same take on it, adding, "…and Judge Claiborne never backed away from anything. When you have a client who says, 'I'm right,' you go to bat for him and you do the very, very best you can for him. That's how it works."

The second trial began four months later in July 1984. Bill Raggio would not be part of the ongoing defense team. The federal prosecutor had dropped all but two counts of income tax evasion.[12] Judge Claiborne was convicted on both. Bill later said the only thing Judge Claiborne was guilty of was having "incompetent accountants and not keeping accurate records."

Judge Harry Claiborne would serve seventeen months in prison, during which time he was impeached by the U.S. House of Representatives, tried by a twelve-member committee of the senate and removed from the federal bench.* Oscar Goodman would continue to represent him throughout the Congressional proceedings. Upon his release from prison, Claiborne was once again allowed to practice law in the state of Nevada, though not in federal court. He died in January 2004.

Joe Conforte again fled to Brazil to avoid prison on subsequent tax evasion charges and remained bitter about what he considered Bill Raggio's "personal beef" with him. In a November 1986 telephone interview from Rio de Janeiro, Conforte told a *Gazette-Journal* reporter, "If I knew then about the federal laws what I know now, I would have had him [Raggio] indicted on a criminal civil rights charge."[13]

* * *

The April 1984 mistrial had resulted largely from the careful preparation and expert courtroom technique of Bill Raggio, which exposed Conforte's fabrications and misrepresentation of fact. This was particularly impressive because over his entire legal career, Bill had acted as a defense counsel in criminal cases just a handful of times.

---

*The only impeachment ever handled this way. The full senate was later given three dense volumes of testimony and evidence to read in two weeks. The full session of the senate convicted the judge after just five hours of deliberation (during which Claiborne was not allowed to call witnesses).

Jan Nielson Little, a member of the federal prosecuting team, when interviewed by Michael Vernetti nearly twenty-four years after the trial, vividly recalled Bill Raggio's "magnificent performance." Little was particularly impressed by Bill's scrupulous questioning of the passport agent for what seemed to her like hours. An examination so thorough, she remembered, it left no doubt in the jurors' minds that Joe Conforte was in New York City on the day he claimed to be bribing Judge Claiborne in Reno.[14]

"I have a great affection for Bill and respect him and admire him," Goodman would later say, "not only as a great public servant and a great lawyer, but as someone whose word is his bond. Bill Raggio did not get a fee for the Claiborne case; he did not spare a moment of his time other than in representing the judge. He put himself into it fully and completely. I am sure he did it solely out of admiration for the judge."

In 2008, John Squire Drendel said, "Judge Harry Claiborne was a friend of my wife's, and I knew and liked him. I did not know much about Bill's political life then, but when he took the case to help Claiborne during his trial, we were so grateful, my wife and I [both Democrats] walked precincts for him."

Bill Raggio would soon need all the political supporters he could find, as he was about to enter into one of the nastiest campaigns of his career.

State Senator Jim Gibson, U.S. Senator Howard Cannon and Bill
Raggio in Washington, D.C. (c. 1976).

Nevada Governor Mike O'Callaghan and Senator Bill Raggio had
their differences over the years, but shared a bond of mutual respect.

Newly elected State Senator Raggio hands a very large bill to Secretary of the Senate Leola Armstrong during the 1973 legislative session.

Senator Raggio giving a speech from the floor of the old senate chambers.

Senator Raggio questions a testifier in committee as Senator Mike Sloan (*left*) looks on (c. 1979).

Bill Raggio (*right*) plasters a "Bryan for Attorney General" banner on the Great Wall of China in 1978, much to the chagrin of Richard Bryan (*next to Bill*). State Senator Mel Close is to the left of the banner.

Bill and Cliff Young plan their state senate reelection strategy in 1976.

Bill talks with President Jimmy Carter, as daughter Leslie looks on.

*In. Bill – Who got the whole thing done! with admiration and respect Love, Francis Albert 1981*

Bill represented Frank Sinatra in his effort to obtain a gaming license before the Nevada Gaming Control Board on February 11, 1981. The inscription reads: "*To Bill—Who got the whole thing done! With admiration and respect. Love, Francis Albert.*" Sinatra used his first and middle name as a term of endearment when corresponding with those closest to him.

After the Gaming Control Board hearing, actors Gregory Peck and Kirk Douglas, who had appeared as character witnesses, congratulate Bill on his effective presentation.

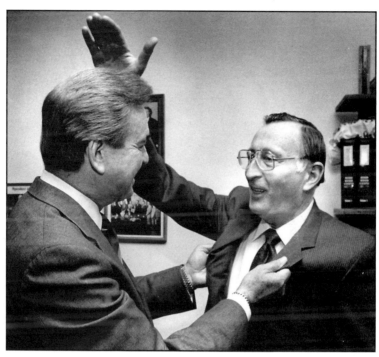

Senator Raggio jokingly implores Assembly Speaker Joe Dini for his blessing.

Governor Richard Bryan (*center*) signs legislation. Looking on are, *left to right*, John Sande III, Senator Bill Raggio, Senator Sue Wagner, Assemblyman Bob Sader, Secretary of State Frankie Sue Del Papa and Lieutenant Governor Bob Miller.

Attorney Oscar Goodman (*left*) and Harry E. Claiborne in 1987. (Photo courtesy of the *Las Vegas Review-Journal*)

Bill greets President Ronald Reagan upon his arrival in Reno (c.1984).

Governor Bob Miller (*center*) signs legislation as Assemblyman Lynn Hettrick (*left*) and Senators Dina Titus and Bill Raggio look on.

Congressman Jack Kemp and Bill Raggio greatly admired one another.

Once Bill began accumulating power, he frequently found his steps dogged by reporters. In this case it's *Reno Gazette Journal's* Bill O'Driscoll (*left*), Cy Ryan of United Press International, and later the *Las Vegas Sun* (*right*), and Patrick Graham of Associated Press bringing up the rear. (Photo courtesy of Dennis Myers)

Nevada state senators on a fact-finding visit to the Yucca Mountain Nuclear Waste Repository in southern Nevada (c. 1995). Seated (*left to right*): Senators Lawrence Jacobsen, Dean Rhoads, Sue Lowden, Bill Raggio, Randolph Townsend and Mike McGinness.

Chair of the powerful Senate Committee on Finance. (Photo courtesy of Bob Cook)

Governor Kenny Guinn and Senator Raggio not only shared an excellent working relationship, but were also close personal friends.

The 2003 Senate Committee on Government Affairs. Standing (*left to right*): Senators Warren Hardy, Dina Titus, Randolph Townsend and Terry Care. Seated (*left to right*): Senators Sandra Tiffany, Ann O'Connell and Bill Raggio. (Photo courtesy of Bob Cook)

Bill and Paul Lowden in Italy, 1997.

Former President George H.W. Bush chatting with Bill. The two have known each other for years and share a mutual respect. (Photo courtesy of Bob Cook)

Senators Joe Neal and Bill Raggio just before Neal's retirement from the Senate in 2004.

Senator Raggio and campaign advisor Greg Ferraro get news of victory in the 2008 Republican primary election over Sharron Angle. (Photo courtesy of the *Reno Gazette Journal*)

Senate Majority Leader Raggio discussing an issue with Assembly Speaker Barbara Buckley, late in the 2007 session. (Photo courtesy of Brad Horn)

Raymond "Skip" Avansino, Bill Raggio and Don Carano in 2002. Taken in northern Italy at Skip Avansino's daughter's wedding, this snapshot was later dubbed "The Godfather" photo.

Negotiating on the floor of the senate during the contentious 2009 session (*left to right*): Senator Terry Care, Majority Leader Steven Horsford and Senators Bill Raggio, Michael Schneider (*back to camera*) and Randolph Townsend. (Photo courtesy of Brad Horn)

Bill and Dale Checket were married on April 27, 2003. (Photo courtesy of Bob Cook)

Bill and Dale Raggio walking across the Nevada State Capital Mall in 2007.

# CHAPTER FORTY-FIVE

# Not One to Hold
# a Grudge (1985)

On May 24, 1984, Bill Raggio announced his bid for a fourth term. He stressed his experience and a near perfect attendance rating (exceeding 98%) over the previous three sessions. Bill pointed to the crucial issues of education and taxation awaiting the 1985 legislature, and how his seats on key committees such as Finance, Judiciary and Taxation, would provide the voice his constituents would need.

His Democratic opponent was forty-two-year-old Dave Bianchi, an agent for the Northwestern Mutual Life Insurance Company. The candidates remained so civil toward one another during the initial few weeks of the campaign, that the local media was referring to the race in terms of "nice" and "gentlemenly."

The two sparred mildly over gun control and capital punishment. On the issue of education, Bianchi, whose wife was a teacher in Washoe County, said he believed the state had "come to the point where teachers are treated as second class citizens" and he would favor salary hikes that will keep quality teachers in the state and keep them from jumping to higher paying administrative jobs.

Bill denied that Nevada teachers are treated as second-class citizens, saying Nevada teachers were tenth in the nation in average salaries. However, he added, "we need to ensure that what we're doing is guaranteeing a high quality of education." He also suggested tests to determine the competency of teachers.

Both men agreed tax hikes would probably be necessary, but that it was a complex issue requiring a great deal of scrutiny. "We need to place limitations on tax increases," Raggio said, "to lessen the burden on taxpayers and especially real property owners. Raising taxes must be a last resort." Both candidates disapproved of ballot Question 12, a proposed constitutional amendment that would require a two-thirds vote of the legislature, and a majority vote of the electorate, before sales, gaming, excise taxes and fees could be raised.

By mid October, the race had turned spiteful. A Bianchi newspaper ad blasted Raggio with its "Get Rid of Someone Who Represents Las Vegas" banner, and began running ads saying that Raggio's twelve years in the state senate had been tainted by "conflicts of interest," raising the obvious ethical implications that accompany such charges.

This was solely based on Bianchi's belief that as vice president and legal counsel for Sahara Resorts, Bill must have used his considerable influence in persuading other legislators to vote in favor of the gaming industry. To this, Bill quickly responded that as a member of the finance and taxation committees, he had purposely abstained from voting on such matters, or engaging any other activity that might give the appearance of a conflict of interest. "I've been there six sessions," he cracked sarcastically. "You'd think he [Bianchi] would have a longer laundry list."

"Who has more of a conflict?" Bill asked in return. "My opponent is a registered lobbyist for insurance agents. His wife is a schoolteacher. If you talk about conflicts, you'd better not live in a glass house." In fact, the Democratic candidate did have the endorsement of teachers' groups.

Bill had always been supportive of the teachers' union and they had supported him. Yet now, the union had decided to endorse Bianchi. Bill went to see Rita Hambleton, local president of the Teachers Union in Washoe County.

I asked her why, after I had long supported their organization and supported teachers' pay, they chose to endorse my opponent. She replied, "That was the way it came down [from the National

Education Association]." I was very disappointed and said to her, "Let me get this right. What you are telling me is, unless you are a Democrat, or you are a Republican running in an uncontested race, the teachers' union is not going to support a Republican?" She replied that I was, essentially, correct.

Even greater frustration came from a lack of complete support within his own party. Republican Senator Sue Wagner was running for reelection as well, and she and Bill had agreed to support one another. While Bill's contest turned out to be, in his words, "one of the closest races I ever had," Wagner had little opposition. When Bill turned to her for her public support, she declined stating that her supporters did not think that she should "get involved" in Senator Raggio's race.

"It did not make a lot of sense that she would not endorse me," Raggio said many years later. "I believe she made this decision because she was positioning herself to run for higher office and did not want to jeopardize the bipartisan support she had from Democrats. She did not want to alienate anybody on my behalf."

Her refusal of support troubled him and, according to Raggio, "impaired, to some extent, whatever relationship we had later on. I worked very closely with Sue. I appointed her as the chair of the Judiciary Committee and supported her when she ran for lieutenant governor. Yet, when the chips were down, she did not keep her promise to support me in that race. I am a firm believer that if you give your word on something—you keep it."

On November 6, 1984, Bill Raggio won reelection more handily than anticipated.

Back in Carson City, he was once again chosen as senate minority leader. The Republican caucus would now consist of eight members. In addition to returning Senators Bob Ryan, Sue Wagner and Lawrence Jacobsen, four new Republican members replaced Democrats in the senate. These included Dean Rhoads from the Northern Nevada Senatorial District; Kenneth Redelsperger from the Central Nevada Senatorial District; and

Ray Rawson and Anne O'Connell from Las Vegas. O'Connell won the seat vacated by Floyd Lamb, who resigned in disgrace on September 29, 1983. Senators Raggio and Jacobsen would fill the two seats on the Senate Committee on Finance, allocated to them by the Democratic majority.

\* \* \*

The 1984 election had been another good one for the Republican Party. The state had voted overwhelmingly for the reelection of President Reagan. Though still outnumbered by Democrats in voter registration, Nevada Republicans gained major victories in important areas.

The Nevada Republican Party also enjoyed increased prestige from the close personal relationship between President Reagan and U.S. Senator Paul Laxalt. Several high-level government appointments went to Nevadans and Frank Fahrenkopf was appointed chair of the Republican Party National Committee.

The immediate impact on the state was the new Republican majority in the assembly, the first since 1971. New assembly leadership and chairs of important committees were receptive to gaming interests. As the session progressed, gaming lobbyists were able to influence major legislation that would have adversely affected them, like an attempt by Democratic Senator Don Mello to increase gaming taxes and Governor Bryan's proposal to assess casinos for the cost of hiring new Gaming Control Board agents. In addition, the industry was able to gain some exemptions from existing taxes.

The 1985 session was one of the most bitterly fought and politicized in the state's history up to that time. No better example of this acrimony was when, in the closing days of the session, the Republicans in the assembly voted retroactive bonuses to state employees and university personnel—but refused it to public school teachers. The press labeled this action as a punishment of the teachers for not endorsing Republican candidates in the 1984 election. The decision to refuse bonus payments to teachers appeared even more "mean-spirited" after the assembly followed up by voting elected officials a 19% increase in salary.

Bill led the senate Republicans in repudiating the action of the assembly and restored the retroactive bonus for teachers. Certainly, he was annoyed with the teachers association for deciding not to endorse him in such a close race because of his party affiliation. Nevertheless, he opted to avoid the kind of vindictiveness being displayed by his Republican colleagues in the assembly.

Putting his personal feelings in check, he sponsored Senate Bill 522 to restore bonus pay to teachers. The measure passed, but not before Raggio insisted that it contain language affirming that the legislature would never again consider retroactive pay for public employees. "You don't get it in the private sector," he said.

The 1985 Legislative session mercifully ended on June 4. It would be the last session for Democratic Senator Thomas "Spike" Wilson, who decided not to run again after a distinguished sixteen-year career. His departure would end years of compelling debates between him and Senator Raggio, which many felt were the most urbane and articulate ever heard on the senate floor.

Senator Randolph Townsend would later comment that if a person wanted a feel for what the Lincoln-Douglas debates must have been like, they should find the exchanges of ideas between Spike Wilson and Bill Raggio in the *Senate Journal.*

"Wilson was a lawyer and a gifted courtroom orator," Townsend said. "I was fascinated by both of their debate and legal skills—though half the time I did not understand what the hell they were talking about."

In 2010, Wilson would comment on his legislative experience, with unsurprising eloquence. "One's conscience and intellect were the guide, not partisanship or party politics," he recalled. "That tradition seems to have weakened over the years, to Nevada's loss. Bill Raggio always listened to committee hearings and the debate on the floor, and reached his conclusions independently, and voted on the merits of the subject. Legislation affects and defines the future and Bill was always mindful of its public purpose and consequences."

In September 1985, Bill was invited to speak at a gathering of the

Washoe County Teachers' Association—the same organization that refused to endorse him the previous November.

In his introduction, association executive director Don Purcell told the audience that while they did not support Raggio in his last election, he was now "a true friend of education." Purcell promised that the teachers' association would "appreciate and remember" the senator's efforts on their behalf during the waning days of the legislature to reason with fellow his Republicans over the issue of incentive pay for schoolteachers.

In his address, Senator Raggio said he hoped the association would not take either political party for granted, saying teachers "are not taken for granted" and that "all legislators recognize the complexities of being a schoolteacher." However, he ended on a somber note, warning that as a member of the Committee on Finance, he would not be part of a "conduit to funnel money to groups" without knowing what he was voting on.

Bill's development as a legislator was noted in the *Reno Gazette Journal*, which pointed out that despite his being in the minority, with no committee chair duties, he had the "highest batting average" (.916) of any senator, managing to pass eleven of the twelve measures of which he was the primary sponsor.[1]

Over the last seven legislative sessions, Bill had become exceptionally well versed on all major issues, particularly the state budget, which he studied meticulously. No senator worked harder at learning his job than he did, and Republican colleague Senator Carl Dodge observed, "Bill devoted considerable thought to what it would be like to be majority leader."

\* \* \*

Amid the numerous private and community-service board meetings, running his law firm and his work on behalf of fellow Republican candidates, Bill and Dottie managed to squeeze in several trips during 1985. Along with other legislators and their wives, they visited Taiwan to promote Nevada tourism and attended the annual meeting of the National Council of State Legislatures in New Orleans.

During 1985, Senator Raggio was also recognized for his skill and integrity outside the political arena. In November, he was named a fellow of the American College of Trial Lawyers. Membership was a high honor and gained only by invitation of the Board of Regents. The college, an association of (then) about 4,000 Fellows in the United States and Canada, has as its mission to improve the standards of trial practice. Bill's induction into the ranks of this prestigious society took place at a meeting of the Fellows of the American College of Trial Lawyers in London, England.

The year ended for Bill with a touching tribute. On December 11, 1985, the Anti-Defamation League of the B'nai B'rith, one of the nation's oldest organizations to stand for the security of minority groups, presented Bill Raggio its Torch of Liberty Award during a black tie affair at Reno's MGM Grand Hotel.

The award was presented by the league in recognition of distinguished service and strong leadership in preserving liberty, counteracting bigotry and advancing the course of human rights, dignity and equal opportunity.

In presenting the award, master of ceremonies, the Reverend Monsignor Leo M. McFadden, said that achievement in a free society is more than just the attainment of personal success. "In his lifelong pursuit of human ideals," the Monsignor said, "Senator Raggio has been active in numerous other community services as well, serving on the advisory board of the Salvation Army for many years and as a member of the board of directors of the National Conference of Christians and Jews. Compassion, creativity, industriousness and humor find no finer expression than in the life of Senator Bill Raggio."

Bill would soon bring those qualities to his first leadership position. In 1986, Raggio's untiring work to rebuild his party and elect Republican legislators reached fulfillment with a majority in the senate. The Old West culture of swagger and bombast in state government had been slowly changing and was now about to be replaced by one more respectful of decorum and reasoning.

# CHAPTER FORTY-SIX

# Majority Floor Leader (1987)

Early in 1986, Legislative Counsel Frank Daykin retired. A gifted attorney, he had been with the Legislative Counsel Bureau since 1963, and had personally drafted thousands of measures, including the law that allowed corporate ownership of casinos. Daykin had also written the "one-man, one-vote" legislation, which led to state reapportionment resulting in a dramatic shift of representation to urban areas. Frank was known for his impartially and commitment to making the Nevada Revised Statutes consistent and grammatically correct. This gave rise to the pet term "Daykinism" for his precise use of the language.

Bill Raggio was master of ceremonies at Daykin's retirement dinner at the Ormsby House in Carson City. He told the audience, "Many of us [legislators] would not have accomplished one iota but for his genius, ability and extra effort."

Bill then wryly speculated that Frank might have included Daykinisms in love letters to his wife: "Will you, or would you, or shall you, or should you, marry me?" Of Frank's almost painful faithfulness to the "letter of the law," Raggio quipped, "There's one thing you can say about our Frank; he is not a textual deviate."

Although not running for reelection in 1986, it would be a busy election year for Bill. He had already established himself as the dominant party leader in the state[1]—recruiting candidates, raising campaign funds and driving toward his goal of Republican legislative majorities.

Bill anticipated the major issues in the upcoming session—education, liability insurance reform and affordable health care reform—and wanted to get the Republican message out early and often.

He had some background in the field of health care since joining the board of directors of Sierra Health Care Services in 1984. It was an offer he initially declined because he was already busy as a board member of Sahara Resorts.

Later Bill explained that after the legislature passed laws providing for health maintenance organizations, which he thought were a real advancement in providing meaningful access to health care and helping to lower the costs of health care, they asked him again and he agreed to serve. Bill would remain on the board for the next twenty-two years.

In October 1986, Bill's sixtieth birthday party was held at the venerable Coney Island Bar and Grill. The tiny establishment had seen better times, and the neighborhood had declined, but "The Coney" retained a faithful following generation upon generation.

Several months later, at the invitation of President Reagan and his wife, Bill and Dottie would attend a June 26, 1987 concert and reception at the White House. While no one would mistake the Coney Island Bar for the White House, those acquainted with the down-to-earth Raggios knew they had just as memorable a time at each.

Over the years, Bill and Dorothy attended several of the Reagans' White House social gatherings. "I do not want to pass myself off as having been close to the Reagans," Bill later said. "I did meet them on several occasions."

\* \* \*

Bill had long recognized that because the time between the September primary election and November general election was so short, damage Republican candidates did to each other in the primary, could often not be repaired in time for the election. By 1986, the ferocity of the primaries seemed to be increasing as party unity disintegrated into heated debates over social issues. Traditional financial support groups were abandoning the Republican Party in lieu of giving money directly to candidates who sponsored particular issues.

"After fourteen years in the minority," Bill later said of the situation, "it became obvious to me that the machinery of the Republican Party could not be relied upon to help recruit candidates or to fund campaigns if we were ever to gain a majority in either house of the legislature. There was increasingly antagonistic partisanship and too much effort being expended on one-upsmanship, turf battles and who was going to hold power—all of which obviates against working together and solving problems."

To help remedy this, Bill instituted the Republican Senate Caucus, also called the Senate Republican Leadership Conference (SRLC).

"So we came up with a plan to go out and seek the best candidate possible to win seats," Bill recalled. "We then would back that candidate from day one, regardless of the primary. In 1986, we took control of the senate. That was a direct result of our effort."

State Senator Randolph Townsend of Washoe County became part of that process. In 2010 he said, "It allowed us to run campaigns intelligently and no longer be dependent upon a party that was increasingly independent from us."

In this way they were able to utilize like-minded relationships to develop campaign funding that would support their candidates. The SRLC, Townsend continued, did not care what a person's social philosophies were, because "it was a waste of our time dealing with social issues."

If the candidate were pro-life and running in a district where the electorate was heavily pro-choice, they would talk to him or her about the problems they would face in getting elected.

"We never tried to change a person's position on such issues. A person should be able to believe what they want to believe," Townsend said. "The only thing Senator Raggio insisted on was that our candidates adhere to the basic Republican principles of limited taxation, limited government, free market enterprise and a belief in individual's own capabilities."

Republicans were able to maintain the majority in the state senate for all but one of the next ten biennial sessions. This would require something besides a successful mechanism for funding and vetting candidates, and that ingredient was a wise leader.

Senator Townsend explained how in addition to being a strong leader, Bill selected winning candidates who he knew would go on to make capable committee chairs.

"He was able to train, mentor and encourage us to be the best chairpersons possible," Townsend recalled. "That is crucial, because that is where your policy comes from, and that is what campaign donors are looking for."

According to Townsend, when groups look at Senator Raggio, they may not always agree with him, but they always have respect for his knowledge of the budget and his ability to be fair and balanced.

"Many who get power are only interested in maintaining it and jealously guarding their advantages," Townsend said. "Raggio understands that by developing a better team, it makes him a better leader."

Legislative Counsel Bureau Director Lorne Malkiewich, who is responsible for training new legislators at the beginning of each session, said Senator Raggio regularly attended these training sessions because he was interested in developing the skills of all legislators—regardless of party.

Because Senator Raggio has such institutional memory, Malkiewich says, he is familiar with what things have failed before and why they failed. He is also unselfish about sharing his knowledge of the process with others. "As an example," Malkiewich said, "he would discuss with them the importance of not losing the trust of others by going back on your word."

If a legislator gave his or her word too easily, Bill would tell them, they would find themselves left with two equally bad options: to continue following through with a bad bill; or, having to go back on their word — irreparably damaging their reputation for dependability.

Malkiewich added that there were some things that "you just cannot teach."

"Few possess the innate ability that Raggio does of knowing when to vote," Malkiewich said. "Sometimes he will ask questions that direct others to the knowledge that he wants them to have. Sometimes, he will call for a vote in the middle of a hearing when his intuition tells him that the members of the committee are prepared to vote the way he wants."

During the 1986 election season, Bill's public message and tireless effort on behalf of SRLC candidates paid off in November when voters gave the Nevada State Senate its first Republican majority in twenty-two years. The twelve-to-nine majority was achieved with the election to the upper house of three state Assemblymen: Erik Beyer, Charles Jeorg and Mike Malone. All three had replaced Democrats.

Two-term Democratic Senator Randolph Townsend, finding his party to have turned "too far to the left," ran for reelection as a Republican candidate. Though Townsend won handily, it was a politically dangerous decision. Two other party switchers, who had gone from Democrat to Republican in the assembly, were defeated.[2]

The new majority party caucus selected Senator Raggio as floor leader and chair of the Senate Committee on Finance. As Robert Dickens described in *The Maverick Spirit*, Bill was about to change the culture of the institution:

> Raggio immediately set the tenor for the senate. Throughout his senate career, he had been recognized for his gentlemanly demeanor, his ability to remain unruffled in times of great stress, even for his impeccable dress, complete with stylish suits and French cuffs. No cowboy boots, no public bluster, no frontier bawdiness…His legal background and his moderate conservatism, coupled with his reserved personality, led him to emphasize the importance of decorum, of respecting the integrity of state officials, of following established procedure and process.[3]

Bill sought to create a more professional milieu and knew the importance of finding a common ground for compromise, rather than seeking confrontation. "He discovered," Dickens wrote, "that most men and women in the legislature responded better to calm reasoning and humor than to bombast and bluster. His was a leadership that exercised power with finesse."[4]

Said former Lieutenant Governor Bob Cashell, "Bill is a diplomat. He will include his worst enemy in the conversation, and before it's over with, they're buddies."

As much as Bill Raggio would have liked it, the 1986 election did not maintain a Republican majority in the assembly. The Democrats selected Joe Dini of Yerington as Speaker. Dini, who owned and operated a small casino in rural Yerington, and had held the leadership position in 1977, proclaimed of the upcoming session: "We'll get done fast because there will not be a lot of politicking going on. Bill Raggio and I get along fine. He's a class act. We can sit down and work out our problems, get past the issues, play it straight up."

Dini was considered a moderate and, like Raggio, a mediator. His style would be a definite change from retiring Republican Assembly Speaker Bill Bilyeu of Elko, who had been a polarizing force, politicizing the position of Speaker more than his predecessors, and using it as a bully pulpit from which to pontificate his personal views.

On the evening of January 21, 1987, Senate Majority Floor Leader Raggio appeared on television to give his party's response to Governor Richard Bryan's State of the State message. "This legislative session will not be easy," he said, describing the state's growing needs in education, public safety, welfare, infrastructure, health care and tort reform. "The population of the state has grown almost 8% since the end of the 1985 legislative session. While this growth was expected, as lawmakers, we never anticipated the level of growth in many vital programs."

Revenue projections had dropped appreciably, he warned, and whatever method was approved to remedy that, tax increases must be equitably applied.

When Bill became majority leader in January 1987, Democratic Governor Bryan and Bill Bible, Director of the Department of Administration, went to see him in his new office and asked him about the things he needed to do about his priorities.

"The legislative issues were very nonpartisan then, as opposed to the national politics," Bryan recalled in 2008. "A big factor was that Bill was a very likable guy. I had great respect for him and I have always liked him. Despite the fact that Bill was a Republican, he was not an ideologue, he was a pragmatist."

Raggio took over the majority leader position long held by Senator Jim Gibson, who would now become minority leader. Because Gibson was considered a conservative, change in control in the senate produced few philosophical changes.

Senator Raggio warned, however, that there might be some conflicts between houses because "there are going to be a lot of new faces who are going to have to feel their way along, which might bring on some conflict."

However, Donald Driggs, a political science professor at the University of Nevada and a longtime observer of the legislature, said in the *Reno Gazette Journal* that Raggio "mingles well with Republicans and Democrats" and should be "a soothing influence" in the legislature.[5]

Most of the new Democratic majority in the assembly came from the southern part of the state and demanded Clark County leadership on the Assembly Committee on Ways and Means. The caucus selected Assemblyman Marvin Sedway of Las Vegas. Sedway had been groomed as a replacement for State Senator Jim Bilbray, who had been elected as a member of the U.S. House of Representatives. Yet, he opted to remain in the assembly so he could chair that powerful money committee.

Sedway, a doctor of optometry, was born in New York City in 1928 and moved to Nevada at age thirteen. His Uncle Moe was a partner of mobster Bugsy Siegel and his father ran the race book in the Flamingo Hotel.

"I'm not an apologist for my uncle and the other people he associated with," the irascible assemblyman would later say. "We put up statues in

Las Vegas to all the great Mormon pioneers who made Las Vegas what it is today. If they are going to put up statues, they should put up statues to people like Bugsy Siegel. That may sound ridiculous, but before the advent of Mr. Siegel, Las Vegas was just a wide spot in the road."

Marvin was first elected to the legislature 1982. His style was as publicly confrontational as Bill Raggio's was not. "It's going to be interesting," Bill commented at the time, drolly understating the blistering disagreements that would characterize their professional relationship.

\* \* \*

The 1987 Nevada citizen legislature consisted of engineers, insurance agents, ranchers, miners, laborers, company presidents, homemakers, teachers, casino owners, lawyers, writers and a doctor. By the time the session ended, in May 1987, they had managed to avoid major tax increases for the average citizen. No new property taxes were levied for state purposes, other than for bond redemption, and there was no increase in sales tax. Revenues came primarily from an increase in the gaming tax, which provided 44% of the state's revenue.

In addition, mining taxes were increased and a three-cent-per-gallon increase on gasoline went into effect to provide for repair and construction of roads, much of which was anticipated to be paid by tourists. A five-cent-per-pack tax on cigarettes was also enacted and the legislature called for an independent study of Nevada's overall tax structure, the first study of its kind since 1960.

Moreover, the legislature passed sweeping reforms in the way insurance companies operated and legislation to help the medically indigent, including a bill designed to provide greater assistance to senior citizens in need of medical treatment. A measure was passed to create an attractive environment for new corporations to organize in Nevada, limiting the liability of corporate boards and stockholders, making Nevada the first western state to pass such a law.

During the session, other issues arose, such as testimony before the Senate Committee on Finance by Phyllis Schlafly. Her hope was to convince legislators to oppose a constitutional convention for passage of a balanced budget amendment. Nevada was one of thirty states (thirty-four states must ratify to convene) which had requested such a convention. A measure to repeal that request had passed the state assembly.

Both Senators Raggio and Gibson were in favor of the constitutional convention. Schlafly, who originally founded the ultra conservative Eagle Forum in order to resist passage of the Equal Rights Amendment, believed such a convention would only create "chaos and controversy" by allowing special interest groups to alter the U.S. Constitution in other ways.

Raggio noted that supporters of a constitutional convention included Senator Paul Laxalt and President Reagan. If amendments to the constitution were recommended, three-fourths of the states would still have to ratify them before passage. Bill rejected Schlafly's argument because it "doesn't show enough faith in the American public to reject any nonsensical ideas."

During the 1987 session, the new majority leader was challenged by the state's judicial branch over their share of the budget. The autocratic Supreme Court Chief Justice, E.M. "Al" Gunderson, unhappy with the level of proposed funding for the judiciary, claimed the right, under the state constitution, to court order their funds, thus circumventing the legislative appropriations process.

Senator Raggio would later remember the confrontation.

"It was not a bluff," Bill recalled. He [Justice Gunderson] really did think he could appropriate funds that way. Therefore, I paid the Chief Justice a visit soon after his pronouncement and suggested he continue reading the state constitution until he arrived at the provisions under which the legislature could remove judges." Gunderson would later accept the legislatively approved funding level.

Justice Robert Rose served on the Supreme Court from 1989 to 2007. During a 2010 interview, he recalled when, as Chief Justice, he would often testify before the Senate Committee on Finance, chaired by Senator Raggio. "Bill took almost a paternalistic view of the Nevada judiciary and the Nevada courts," Rose said. "It was a very important thing to him. If you had a good program, or a problem, he could be very receptive. Not to say it was a giveaway. He would listen, but he made you show everything."

Justice Rose added that because Bill was such "a great lawyer," and had so much practical experience with courts at every level, "you didn't have to draw him a lot of pictures."

"Bill's purpose," he continued, "was to make sure that the Nevada judiciary functioned, and functioned the best it could with the money it had. If you asked every chief justice in the last twenty years, they would say the same thing about how Bill took care of the courts. We all really appreciate what he has done for the judiciary."

The 1987 session also included the formation of Nevada's eighteenth county, ingloriously named "Bullfrog." The county was established in a misguided attempt by the state legislature to obtain additional federal funding from the placement of the unpopular Yucca Mountain Nuclear Waste Repository in Nye County.

The legislature, over the objections of many, including Senator Raggio, voted to create tiny Bullfrog County in the unpopulated area around the proposed dumpsite. Because this new county had no population, and consequently no county administrative apparatus, Carson City was designated as the county seat and any federal payments for establishing the nuclear waste site in the new county would go directly into the state treasury.

Nye County, which stood to lose that federal funding, challenged the legality of the new county. A Nevada district court later found Bullfrog County to be in violation of the state constitution, because it had no residents. The state legislature abolished it during the next session, returning the 144 square miles back to Nye County.

Senator Raggio predicted this outcome in 1987, saying from the senate floor, "Historians will look back on this, because it will be reversed at a later date, whether by the court or by the legislature, and laugh at us for being part of such a shenanigan."

If Bullfrog County was the ridiculous, Assembly Bill No. 116 was the sublime. Few pieces of legislation created as much introspection among Nevada legislators as did the vote to make the birthday of Dr. Martin Luther King, Jr. a state holiday.

Two years earlier, after the 1985 Nevada State Legislature failed to pass a bill that would have created the holiday, Governor Bryan issued an executive order establishing the Martin Luther King, Jr. Holiday Commission to investigate feasibility and costs.

In January of that year, Bryan had used one of the executive branch's two yearly discretionary holidays to commemorate Dr. King's birthday. This practical application helped legislators in the 1987 session better evaluate the financial impact.

New Senate Majority Leader Raggio believed that Dr. King had been "a great American and one who led a great and worthwhile cause" and so had, on the very first day of the 1987 session, arranged a special tribute to the fallen civil rights leader.

Such praise, however, did not prevent Bill from treating the matter before the Senate Committee on Finance with the same objectivity and mindfulness of the public trust that he would any other issue. He questioned the bill's sponsors, Assemblymen Morse Arberry and Wendell Williams, at length concerning the economic impact on public and private employers who would need to pay time-and-a-half wages to employees working on the holiday.

The assemblymen responded that funding set aside for one of the governor's discretionary holidays, coupled with added tax revenue from tourists to the state over the three-day weekend, would more than compensate for any additional payroll costs. Indeed, because Nevada remained one of the few states that did not recognize the holiday, numerous organizations and associations had refused to consider it as a destination for their gatherings.

Others testified for passage of the legislation, some against. One opponent testified that he was opposed to the holiday because of FBI reports indicating Dr. King had been a member of "over thirty communist-front organizations." To this, Senator Raggio rhetorically asked, "Do you think President Reagan would have approved the national holiday if Martin Luther King were a communist?"

The bill was approved in committee and sent to the full senate for a vote. Years later, Bill would recall that as long as the senate was controlled by Democrats, notably Majority Leader Jim Gibson, Mahlon Brown and Floyd Lamb, they would never have agreed to it. "I would assume some of that was because they had strong Mormon beliefs," Bill said, "and, at that time, an African-American was not eligible to participate in any meaningful role in their church. I think it went beyond that though, and included some personal objections to Dr. King."

Senator Raggio added that, whatever the reason, the Democrat-controlled senate would never agree to that holiday. It was only after the Republicans took majority control of the senate that the measure was approved. He pointed out that it had been Republicans who historically championed civil rights, where Democrats, particularly Dixiecrats like George Wallace and Lester Maddox, had always opposed such legislation. "This comes as a surprise to many people," Bill remarked. "I think too much history has been forgotten."

When the measure came to the senate for a vote after passing unanimously in the assembly, Bill Raggio rose in support. He pointed out that because he had not served on the committees that processed this measure in previous sessions, he did not have to face the decision until now.

He had misgivings about the concept of a holiday honoring Dr. Martin Luther King, or any other individual, largely because of the economic impact upon the state. However, he felt that "anything that this legislature can do to erase any remnants of bigotry or racial prejudice which exist in this country ought to be done."

Senator Raggio then told of his experiences during his time in the military when he was stationed in the Deep South; of how shocked he was by the oppressive extent of racial segregation. "I could not conceive that this could be America," he said. "I made a pledge to myself at that time that I would not be party to any system or procedure that would perpetuate that kind of conduct on the part of citizens of this country."

Bill ended his speech by saying that while other people made great contributions to the country and were not honored with a holiday, he supported this measure not just for what Dr. King had done for African-Americans, but what he had done "for the conscience of all Americans."

The bill passed by a vote of sixteen to five, a constitutional majority.

\* \* \*

Although the arduous 1987 session required him to be in Carson City for the first six months of the year, Bill's professional expertise was on demand throughout the country. In that year alone, he was welcomed in to several legal organizations whose missions were to foster excellence in ethics, civility and legal skills.

Among these honored positions was an appointment to the Criminal Law and Administration of Justice Committee of the Council of State Governments; the Law and Justice Committee of the National Council of State Legislators; Advocate of the American Board of Trial Advocates and Master of the Bench of the American Inns of Court. Closer to home, he was named to the Old College of Reno Board of Trustees, the Nevada American Revolution Bicentennial Commission and named Citizen of the Year by the Nevada Judges Association.

The coming session would reflect a passing of the old guard, not only in its loss of experience, but also through a continuing decline of civility and a level of discord and public hostility not seen before in legislative history.

# CHAPTER FORTY-SEVEN

# Pension Fiasco (1989)

Senator Jim Gibson, though now minority leader, and physically weakened by his long battle with cancer, remained a quiet power in the legislature. Humorously referred to as "The Godfather of the Mormon Mafia," a small, but effective, collection of Mormon lawmakers, Gibson still commanded enormous respect from legislators in both parties. As one lobbyist put it at the time, "Gibson's the ballgame in Carson City."[1]

When he died in August 1988, at the age of sixty-three, his passing was greeted with genuine grief and a staggering sense of loss that such an extraordinary leader, who so many had relied upon for so long to guide the state through its increasingly complex problems, was no more.

Hundreds attended his funeral in the sweltering Las Vegas heat, including the Nevada Congressional delegation, dozens of his colleagues from state government and prominent figures in the Mormon hierarchy. His old friend and former senate Majority Leader, H. Mahlon Brown, spoke, as did Governor Richard Bryan and others. Governor Bryan described Gibson as a well-educated engineer who was considered an expert on state budget issues and a champion of progress in education.

Bill Raggio, who served beside Gibson in the legislature for sixteen years, gave the most powerful eulogy of the day, words that would never be forgotten by the Gibson family and others in attendance. Calling James Isaac Gibson "Nevada's most powerful and effective lawmaker… and one of Nevada's greatest public servants," Raggio brought the mourners to tears in closing, when he forlornly declared, "The task has been completed. The session is over. With our love, Jim Gibson, *sine die*."*

Because of Gibson's extraordinary diplomatic skills and political acumen, many doubted whether he could be replaced, or whether the legislature would now have the ability to do its business as efficiently.

Yet, even under Gibson's influence, the biennial sessions had grown longer. Although the 1987 session ran over 150 days, few demanded reform. Complaints about inefficiency were now being voiced, most prominently concerning the legislature's inclination to ignore major bills until the frenzied final days of the session.

Assemblyman Bob Sader, a Democrat from Washoe County, summed up the concern of most: "There is no Democratic leader in the senate with that kind of force of moral character. He was a clear leader, and now there is no leader." However, one name was mentioned most often by legislators to assume that mantle—William J. Raggio.

The *Reno Evening Gazette* reported,

> A Republican, Raggio is one of the longest serving senators, covering sixteen years, eight regular and two special sessions. He has risen to majority leader and acquired a broad reputation for competence and expert political craftsmanship, especially in building bipartisan partnerships and non-sectional coalitions on key issues such as prison expansion and education funding.[2]

Bill had been grooming himself over the previous sixteen years for such a role, and described his bond with the late Senator Gibson: "We were very much alike. We worked closely for four sessions and I can't tell you any area where we fundamentally disagreed."

Dan Miles, Senate Fiscal Analyst, who worked closely with both men during those years, was more specific during a 2009 interview:

---

*\*Sine die*, literally "no more days," is the term used by legislative bodies to announce the final adjournment of a session.

Senators Gibson and Raggio were alike and I can tell you why they
were so successful. It's very simple. They both worked harder than
anybody else. Both were gracious and fair-minded. Both understood
that the legislative process is generally a compromise process, and
not everyone gets everything they want—no matter how powerful
they are.

Bob Cashell, Nevada's Lieutenant Governor from 1983 to 1987, concurred with Miles's assessment of Raggio's ability: "Bill understood he
was not always going to get the whole pie, but he always made sure he
got a slice. He knew he'd get the rest later."

When Dan Miles retired in 2000, he sent Senator Raggio a note of
thanks in which he wrote, "I feel fortunate to have worked with many
fine legislators over the years, but none have done a better job or made
more of a difference than you."

* * *

Bill Raggio sought reelection in 1988. Unlike the tough and rancorous
campaign mounted against him by Democratic challenger Dave Bianchi
four years earlier, this time Bill would have no serious opposition. It
was as if the Democratic Party, so determined in 1984 to dislodge him
from his senate seat, now tacitly recognized his importance to the effectiveness of the coming session. They did not put forward a candidate.[3]

Despite a dearth of challengers, Bill still campaigned. In September,
he was endorsed by the eight thousand members of the Nevada State
Education Association (NSEA). The Washoe County Teachers Association had publicly praised him the year before for helping teachers during
the closing days of the 1987 session, and promised to "appreciate and
remember" his efforts on their behalf.

Despite that promise, it is unclear if such an endorsement from them
would have been forthcoming had the Democratic Party run a strong
candidate. Bill, and Senator Sue Wagner, who was also running unopposed, were among only a handful of state Republican candidates to receive the NSEA endorsement that year.

In October, Senator Raggio and Washoe County District Attorney Mills Lane appeared before the Reno Rotary Club to debate ballot Question 4, a proposition calling for district and Supreme Court justices to be appointed rather than elected. This ballot measure, proposed by Raggio, was a modified version of the so-called "Missouri Plan," used at that time to appoint judges in twenty-seven states.

Under Bill's proposal, those interested in judgeships would apply to a seven-member commission comprised of the Chief Justice of the Nevada Supreme Court (or his or her designate), three members of the state bar association and three lay people. The committee would interview candidates and recommend three to the governor. The governor would then select a judge. Judges would then have to submit to retention elections if they chose to run for additional terms of office.

This system, Senator Raggio argued, would free judges from the "degrading" need to solicit campaign contributions, adding that passage is necessary to "take Nevada out of the dark ages" and ensure the selection of independent judges who are not beholden to contributors. "How would you feel walking into a courtroom knowing that the attorney on the other side made a substantial contribution to the judge?" Raggio would ask.

District Attorney Lane contended that passage of the question would place selection of judges in the hands of "an elite group that would reward friends and punish enemies. The person with the most merit would not be appointed; it would be that person in most political favor with the governor." Raggio admitted the plan was far from perfect, but that it is much better than the present system.[4]

Prior to the election, the media reported a huge disparity in campaign contributions between candidates in the race, saying Raggio "was suffering from an embarrassment of riches."

According to his financial disclosure forms, after spending $24,000 of the $84,000 he had collected, Bill was sitting on a campaign contribution nest egg of nearly $60,000. He defended himself against accusations that he had spent far too much to defeat such weak opposition by saying that a candidate had a responsibility to get his or her message out to the people they represent. Bill would channel these funds to other Republican candidates who needed help in future campaigns.

Under Nevada's campaign finance laws, considered the least restrictive in the nation, no candidate was required to provide a detailed accounting of how excess campaign funds were spent, and there were no laws prohibiting politicians from converting campaign funds to their own personal use.

Throughout his career, Bill Raggio's regular use of his own excess campaign contributions to assist other Republican candidates was just part of his continuing effort to keep his party strong in the legislature. Despite his demanding schedule, there were few requests for public appearances, or for his participation in fundraising events, that Raggio would not honor on behalf Republican colleagues and candidates. Political observers believe it was such loyalty, which he expected in return, when combined with his prodigious intellectual gifts, industriousness and keen judgment that produced in Bill Raggio the powerful leadership qualities comparable to those of the venerated Jim Gibson.

When not campaigning in 1988, Bill was busy with a variety of other activities. In April, he was recognized by the Ann Martin Women's Political Caucus for his support of 1987 Sex Education\AIDS Legislation. The mission of the organization, part of the National Women's Political Caucus, was to organize at a local level to ensure that women were fairly represented in elective and appointive political offices, to affectively raise women's issues in every election and to see that women held policy-making positions in the political parties.

In August, Reno hosted the National Council of State Legislatures (NCSL) annual meeting. Bill had been an active member in the organization for years and was instrumental in making the event a success. In appreciation of his excellent work as a leader in the Nevada legislature over the previous decade, Bill Raggio received the NCSL's Distinguished Leadership Award for 1988.

Also in August, Bill and Dorothy Raggio celebrated their fortieth wedding anniversary at a party arranged by their children at the El Dorado Hotel. Four generations of Raggio's were present, as well as scores of other family members and friends.

A home movie of their 1948 wedding and reception was shown. Bill quipped humorously throughout, at one point explaining, "The people in the reception line were the ones who brought gifts." At the end of the event, the two renewed their wedding vows in a ceremony officiated by retired Reno Justice of the Peace William Beemer.

In the opinion of many guests, and the media, it was the delightful Clara Raggio, who surpassed her son, Bill, as the life of the party. Indefatigable and independent, Clara would again be mentioned in the press three months later.

The story described how ninety-year-old Clara, with other women of the American Legion Auxiliary No. 1, sold little paper poppies each November 11, to provide money for the personal needs of hospitalized veterans. This happened to be the 50th anniversary of the end of World War I, and Clara had been out each November since that day.

Wrapping herself against the Reno cold, the sprightly Mrs. Raggio and others, happily received whatever people wished to give. The largest single gift that Clara accepted came from a fellow she calls "that boy of mine." Bill Raggio, attorney, state senator and good guy, handed over $50 for his poppy. [5]

On Election Day, November 8, 1988, George Herbert Walker Bush was elected as the forty-first President of the United States, defeating Massachusetts Democratic Governor Michael Dukakis. In Nevada, Governor Richard Bryan, having served just two years of his second term, defeated incumbent Chic Hecht to become U.S. Senator. The state constitution allowed Bob Miller to maintain his lieutenant governor's post as well as become "acting" chief executive. Consequently, he would remain both governor and president of the state senate for another two years. Miller, however, did not request a budget for the Office of Lieutenant Governor and returned that salary.

In 2010, Senator Raggio would speak of his close relationship with Dick Bryan during his six years as governor, and continuing throughout their lives:

I had the pleasure of serving with him in the state senate, and knew him to be competent, caring and willing to listen. He was the ultimate politician and I doubt anyone has enjoyed political life more than he. His quick wit and dry sense of humor endears him to people, and certainly has contributed to his ultimate political success as governor and United States senator. Bonnie and Dick Bryan were a delightful First Couple.

Bill Raggio easily won his reelection bid, and Republicans added an additional seat in the state senate. When the January 1989 legislature opened, senate Republicans would have a thirteen to eight edge. The number of Democrats being now being so few, they would lose a seat on three committees.

Bill's money committee counterpart in the other house, Assemblyman Marvin Sedway, defeated a strong challenge from a former GOP state chairman to win by only 814 votes.

Among the new faces in the senate were Democrat Dina Titus, a UNLV political science professor, and Republican Hal Smith, who won the seat left vacant by the death of Senator Jim Gibson.

One political observer pointed out that the entire nation seemed to be in a period where the electorate desired stability, returning more than 84% of incumbents to state legislatures. The power of incumbency, and the resulting amount of campaign contributions going to incumbents, seemed to have slowed political turnover to a crawl.

Upon the death of Jim Gibson, Senator Joe Neal was selected as minority leader. Neal's style and philosophy differed dramatically from Gibson's. Lacking the broad bipartisan senate support Gibson had, Neal would need to form coalitions necessary to develop major legislation and see it passed.

On March 23, about midway through the session, *Las Vegas Sun* columnist Jeff German wrote of how the recent Jim Gibson Day at the legislature reminded him how badly the late senator was missed: "Without Gibson, Clark County has no one to match wits with his longtime friend and political adversary Senate Majority Leader Bill Raggio of Reno."[6]

Mr. German pointed out that during the previous session, Minority Leader Gibson met daily with Raggio "fine tuning the senate's engine… the two men had a magical working relationship." He added, "Raggio, who without question is in a class by himself these days, has no such relationship with Gibson's successor, Senator Joe Neal of North Las Vegas."

Senator Randolph Townsend recalled the situation as resulting from "a culture clash" between the two that had gone back to their earliest days together in the senate.

"Bill came from what Tom Brokaw called 'The Greatest Generation,'" Randolph recalled. "Joe was ten years younger and a product of the 1960s, with its philosophy of "power to the people." Part of this philosophy was the belief that the 'White Establishment' was the enemy."

Townsend remembered how Neal let his 1960s enthusiasm get the better of him in his oratory from the floor, rhetoric that was not culturally acceptable to Bill Raggio. "Conversely, Neal, in his fervor to help minorities and those politically underrepresented, believed Bill stood for everything he did not," Townsend noted. "That is not to say they did not respect each other. They put that aside to be colleagues and I think that shows the quality of the people they are. You don't have to be best friends with people to be effective."

Senator Neal had become minority leader after a bitter internal struggle within the Democratic caucus, but was unable to gain respect from many of his Democratic colleagues. Consequently, he could not hold the caucus together to provide a strong single voice of moderation.

Senator Neal defended himself against comparison with Raggio, saying that while Bill was "very slick," he was also too cunning. "I would say he [Raggio] is average as a leader. He may not pressure others, but they are afraid to oppose him."

In replying, Bill would later say, "Joe Neal and I have been friends for years. We came into the senate together. I would've liked to work more closely with Joe, but I'm not sure he had the full support of his party."

Jeff German suspected that regional, rather than partisan, issues might present problems for the northern majority leader during the session, and described talk of a coup within the ranks by southern Republicans:

> The uprising, quietly being spearheaded by Republican Majority Whip Bill O'Donnell of Las Vegas, is designed to make sure Raggio remembers to be kind to southern Nevada. Raggio says he knows nothing about a pending revolt, but at the same time, insiders say he recently reminded O' Donnell about the merits of "loyalty."[7]

Marvin Sedway, chair of the Assembly Committee on Ways and Means, fired the first shot in the contentious working relationship he and Senator Raggio would have throughout the next few months, announcing that taxes would be raised.

Bill indignantly replied, "I'm not going to be pinned to the wall on the second day of the session." Sedway then warned him, via the press, saying, "I had my training wheels on before, now I have a whip." Then, to emphasize his point, he pulled an actual rawhide whip from a nearby bookshelf.

Journalist Jane Ann Morrison wrote at that time: "Some of them wield their power like a jackhammer, busting up the opposition with intimidation. Others use their clout with a feather touch of the conductor's baton…with subtle arguments and offers of beguiling compromise."[8]

While the "conductor's baton" had been wielded by Gibson and, later, his successor Bill Raggio, there was no question who was the master of "jackhammer" power.

Sedway and Raggio clashed over funding on almost every major budget item: universities and public schools, prison construction and law enforcement, social programs and medical care. Despite reduced revenues and enormous pressure from agencies and lobbyists, the two men managed to fashion a budget acceptable to both houses.

In May, Sedway, a two-pack-a-day cigarette smoker (when smoking was still permissible in government buildings), became so engrossed in a debate on the floor of the assembly that he inadvertently set his beard on fire while attempting to light a cigarette.

He later joked with the press about the incident: "If I'm going to die of smoking, I want it to be from the inside, not the outside." Sadly, by the time of this quip, Sedway had already been diagnosed with inoperable lung cancer.

During the legislative interim following the 1989 session, Bill Raggio, Marvin Sedway and their wives would find themselves on the same two-week tour of the former Soviet Union. Though cool to one another at first, as the trip progressed, the two men were drawn together by their common experience. By their return home, both learned that, at heart, they were driven by what was in the best interest of the state.

Lorne Malkiewich, legislative counsel during the 1989 session, later recalled that while the two men shared the same goal of doing what was best for the state, their methods differed.

> Marvin Sedway could be very angry at times and say things he probably regretted. I believe it was Senator Raggio's legal training that served him well here. When a person becomes a lawyer, and they take a case, they don't let that case define them as a person. It is just their job to provide effective defense or representation for that person.
>
> This can sometimes take the form of personal attacks between attorneys, or between judges and attorneys. Yet, once the trial is over, these individuals will often have more respect for one another because of the acknowledgment of each other's ability in doing the job well.

Marvin Sedway died in July 1990 at the age of sixty-one. Shortly before his death, he told a reporter, "I'm not really the S.O.B. people think I am."[9]

His wife, Kim, a nurse, had been able to care for him at home until his passing. After his funeral, she wrote a note to Bill Raggio:

*Dearest Bill,*

*There are no adequate words to express my gratitude to you for your kindness, concern and generosity and above all for the friendship you have shown especially during these last most difficult weeks. I cannot thank you enough. Marvin and I have always treasured your and Dorothy's friendship, and now I still do.* *—With love, Kim.*[10]

As Bob Dickens later wrote: "It was Nevada's misfortune not to witness Sedway and Raggio collaborate in helping to bring Nevada into the 21st century."[11]

* * *

Ed Vogel, writing for the *Nevada Appeal* near the end of the 1989 session, described Senator Raggio as a "one-man state senate":

In the mornings, Raggio presides over the Senate Finance Committee. Then he becomes the floor leader during the voting sessions. Later in the afternoons, he huddles with other key legislators to hammer out the deals that may finally close a legislative session. No job is tougher or more important. [12]

"A lot of this job is hand-holding," Raggio told Vogel. "A lot of these legislators have personal problems. They don't all like each other. You play the mediator's role. Sometimes you play the chaplain."

"You have to get some things done," Bill continued, "Somebody has to take control. I have always been a guy who has to have a full day. I would vegetate if I wasn't doing something all the time."

In order to produce needed revenue, the 1989 legislature raised the mining tax, cigarette tax and insurance premium tax, and allowed an increase in a number of county levies. However, all the important work completed by the Nevada's 65th Legislature was overshadowed by the furor over a large increase in pension amounts for legislators.

While the legislature would typically increase the calculation by a small amount every four years, Senator Don Mello of Sparks now proposed a measure that would immediately increase pension benefits by a whopping 300%.

In 2009, Raggio recalled that Senator Mello was looking forward to retirement and decided that the existing pension amount was not enough. He saw immediately that, despite the good economic times, "it was not only inappropriate to push this heavy increase; but political suicide." He convinced Senators O'Donnell and O'Connell to change their minds and join him in voting no.

"If they had not," Bill later remarked, "I believe they would have been defeated for reelection. With the exception of our few dissenting votes, it passed both houses and became law."*

Senator Townsend voted for the measure, later saying that by the time Raggio had advised him against it, he had already pledged his support to Senator Mello and would not go back on his commitment, adding:

"Mello was a tyrant, who would yell and threaten people in his committee. He began collecting the pension as soon as the session ended. There was no doubt in anyone's mind that the whole thing had been about his retirement. I'm the only one still serving, who voted for the 300% pension increase."

Governor Bob Miller, who had warned that he would veto the measure, quickly did so and returned it to the legislature, where his veto was promptly overridden. The public outcry was overwhelming, causing many legislators to regret their vote immediately. Governor Miller threatened to call a special session to have the Legislators' Retirement Law provision changed.

Majority Leader Raggio opposed such a special session, saying it would be "a bad mistake" for the governor. "A Special Session ought to be called for issues of the greatest importance," said Raggio, "not to avoid political damage to a party."

---

*Only Republican Senators Raggio, O'Donnell, O'Connell and Democratic Senator Bob Coffin voted against the pension. Republican Senator Hal Smith abstained.

It was estimated that a single-day special session would cost the state $70,000. Bill assured the governor that the problem would be corrected during the 1991 session without the state wasting the money. "Besides," Bill said, "there would be 'unrelenting pressure' on the governor to include in the special session agenda such issues as abortion and the shortfall of $14 million in the welfare budget."

Raggio pointed out that both Democrats and Republicans voted for the pension increase and that "everyone should stand muster at election time." The majority leader said that convening a special session would mean that replacements would have to be named for Senator Mello and Assemblyman James Banner of Las Vegas.*

While waiting for various legal opinions to sort themselves out, the controversy continued to burn. Democratic Assemblyman Matthew Callister of Las Vegas said, "A number of legislators, including myself, were very much concerned with the retirement of Senator Mello. I don't know if we were suckered. His retirement is evidence that perhaps some legislators were only interested in lining their own pockets."

Governor Miller ordered a special session. Senator Raggio immediately issued a statement accusing the governor of misusing his office for blatant political purposes. Though both Republican and Democrats had voted for the pension increase, the bill had come out of the Democrat-dominated assembly and so they would likely bear the brunt of voter wrath at election time.

Republican Senator Charlie Jeorg decided to boycott the special session. Bill counseled him against it, saying it was irresponsible and would cost him votes during his 1990 reelection bid.

The Sixteenth Special Session of Nevada legislature opened on the morning of November 21, 1989. Replacements for Senator Mello and Assemblyman James Banner were seated. It took just two and half hours to repeal the pension increase.

---

*Assemblyman Banner had resigned on September 1, 1989, and Mello, who had pushed through the pension increase, immediately retired and was receiving the new maximum amount of $36,000 a year.

Lost amid the resentment over such a large increase is the fact that, given the amount of time and effort they contribute to keep the state running, Nevada's part-time legislators were (and are) woefully underpaid.

In 1989, they received a salary of $130 per day, and $66 in *per diem*, for the first sixty days of the session, and then only *per diem* from the sixty-first day until the end of the session. Most had businesses from which they are taken for much of the year, not to mention the expenses of meeting their off-session responsibilities on various committees and tending to constituent needs.

Testifying before the state's eleven-member Blue Ribbon Commission on the Legislative Process in 1988, Senator Raggio said he would prefer that legislators receive a fixed salary based on the length of legislative session. When asked if the current pay for legislators was too low, he replied, "I don't know of any legislator who serves or runs because of pay," adding that, legislators who served in rural counties, often covering thousands of square miles, should be given a larger travel subsidy.

Legislators and political observers of the process frequently point out that this is not just an issue of fair compensation for service. More importantly, it has the effect of restricting the economic, social and cultural diversity of the legislature by limiting such public service to only those with the financial means to support themselves during their terms of office.

It is a difficult job, one which is often unappreciated by those who are being served. In a letter to Senator Raggio at the close of the 1989 session, State Attorney General Brian MacKay articulated the dilemma:

> I want to take this opportunity to thank you for all your efforts to make Nevada a better, more effective, more efficient place to live. I recognize and appreciate your task is a thankless one, so I think it is especially important for you to know that those of us who must deal with the state government on a daily basis realize that you try to do your very best in spite of the media's often fictional portrayal of your action…I congratulate you on your dedication, your perseverance and your hard work.[13]

\* \* \*

On October 24, 1989, Bill Raggio was honored as National Distinguished Eagle Scout. Given Bill's numerous awards and accolades over the years, one would think this would be just another. Yet, it touched him deeply and during the ceremony, he told the audience, "I have received a lot of recognition of my life, but I think the Eagle Scout badge was the one I cherish the most. It took a lot of effort and time to earn it."

During his years in scouting, Bill earned an excessive number of merit badges, and though he had achieved Eagle Scout status before his troop was disbanded due to the onset of World War II, he did not receive the badge until years later. In a 2008 interview, Bill spoke of the positive impact scouting had on his life:

> I suppose that today many kids look down on scouting as being too regimented. Yet, I think it is one of the best programs in which I was ever involved and one that had a lasting influence on my life. Scouting taught me the importance of principles, morals, achievement. Scouting also taught me the importance of getting along with others in order to accomplish a common goal. I considered it one of the greatest honors I have ever received when I was named a National Distinguished Eagle Scout in 1989.

Perhaps the most important lesson Bill took from his years in scouting is contained in the Boy Scout Motto: "Be Prepared." Throughout his life, associates in both the legal profession and the legislature would cite his exhaustive preparation as the single most influential factor in his success.

However, not even Senator Raggio was prepared for what was about to happen in Carson City. Voter dissatisfaction with the pension vote and the intensification of regionalism between north and south was about to change the political landscape, resulting in what would become one of the most difficult legislative sessions in recent memory.

# CHAPTER FORTY-EIGHT

# The Session from Hell (1991)

Bill Raggio's warning about the consequences of having voted for the 300% pension increase during the 1989 session came to fruition the following year.

Public backlash first hit home in the summer of 1990, when six incumbent legislators failed in the primaries. While Bill did what he could to help Republican candidates in both houses, he focused most of his effort on the reelection of Senators Mike Malone of Las Vegas, Erik Beyer of Reno and Charlie Jeorg of Carson City, all of whom were in close races.

In addition, Bill worked to help old friend and former Assemblyman Bill Farr in his effort to defeat Democrat Len Nevin in the race to fill the seat from Sparks vacated by the retirement of Senator Mello.

In early October, Democrats were infuriated by a series of Republican television advertisements. One showed Bill Raggio working at his desk while a narrator warned the audience that a Democratic-controlled state senate would mean higher taxes for Washoe County. "Northern Nevada needs to keep the Republican senate majority to protect your interest," it proclaimed while flashing the images of five Republican senate candidates.

Another ad cautioned that if Las Vegas Democrats gained control of the body, $16 million more in state tax dollars would go from Washoe County to Las Vegas, a reference to money Clark County legislators claimed was owed their constituents as the result of a recently discovered accounting error made by the Washoe County Assessor's Office.

Bill defended the ads against accusations that they were inflammatory and designed to scare northern voters, saying they only mirrored promises being made during Democratic campaigns in Clark County. He added that Democratic senators from the south were also pushing the idea of a "fair share" sales tax plan, allowing counties with larger populations, like Clark, to keep a higher share of the sales tax they generated.

Such legislation would require them to change the current formula for the distribution of sales tax revenue statewide established in 1981. That formula had long favored Washoe County, and, in the decade since it was created, led to Washoe taking in $99.7 million in sales taxes generated elsewhere; this, while Clark County gave up $107 million, Elko County gave up $27 million and Carson City, $15 million.

Senator Raggio warned that northern Democratic senate candidates would be powerless pawns of those from the south. "If they are elected," he said, "they will become freshman members of the very group that is advocating these changes. They will have little or no voice in assuring that northern Nevada also receives its fair share."

A letter from a Democratic Party member soon appeared in the *Reno Gazette Journal* questioning Bill Raggio's actual allegiance to northern Nevada, because, as a corporate officer of Sahara Resorts, which operated southern Nevada casinos such as the Sahara, Hacienda and Pioneer Hotel and Gambling Hall, he "has a vital interest in the growth of Southern Nevada."[1]

Far more strident was the response of the Democratic State Party Chair calling for Raggio's resignation. "As the second most powerful politician in Nevada," Segerblom said, "he should use his position to promote all regions of Nevada, not just his personal power base. It is unconscionable for him to use his leadership position to deny any part of the state its fair share of state tax revenues."[2]

Raggio responded that he had no intention of resigning. "Their reaction speaks for itself. We must be hitting a nerve." He stated that southern Nevada legislators had already proposed legislation that would change the formula by which tax dollars were distributed to the counties, and referred to the "fair share" uproar in the south as a "bogus issue" and a "political charade."

Ironically, much of the funding for those campaign ads came from southern Nevada. Las Vegas political journalist Jon Ralston warned readers not to be misled in the belief that the majority of southern Nevadans wanted Bill Raggio removed from office. "Nothing could be further from the truth," Ralston wrote. "Most politically savvy gaming industry executives, and the business community, remain in Republican hands as a conservative foil to any more liberal measures they view as detrimental to their bottom lines."[3]

These people knew that a business tax would top the agenda of the 1991 session and so contributed to Republican candidates in hope of receiving a fairer hearing on the issue. Ralston quoted one southern Nevada business leader as saying, "The cost of my gaining stability may be more money going to Washoe County and UNR in northern Nevada."

Despite a coffer full of campaign funds from the south, Bill was unable to save the majority in the senate. On November 7, 1990, voters turned out in large numbers across Nevada and Democrats not only retained their majority in the assembly, but also captured the senate by an eleven-to-ten margin.

During the race, Democrats had successfully labeled Senator Mike Malone of Las Vegas as a "Raggio tool," because he had refused, at the end of the 1989 legislative session, to sign on as a cosponsor of a "fair share" tax bill being circulated by Clark County legislators.

Before the election, Senator Joe Neal publicly scolded Malone and other southern Nevada Republican legislators. "Are they going to be the party of the north as their leader Bill Raggio dictates?" said Neal. "Or are they going to stand up for the people of southern Nevada?"

In the northern part of the state, Senator Erik Beyer and Charlie Jeorg lost their seats to Democrats. All three of the defeated senate incumbents had voted for the 300% tax increase, despite Senator Raggio's strenuous counsel against doing so. Several Democrats who voted for the pension measure were also defeated.

Senator Sue Wagner was not up for reelection in 1990, but decided to run for lieutenant governor. She had also voted for the pension increase the previous year and, in her memoir, recalled being advised by her campaign strategist to take out a full-page ad in Las Vegas newspapers apologizing for her vote. Feeling that it would have the effect of bringing more attention to the issue, she decided to explain to voters that she had made a "rare bad decision." It worked. Wagner was elected as Nevada's first woman lieutenant governor.[4]

Also in 1990, Sue Wagner would make a bold political move of another kind. Sensing conservative legislators would attempt to change the state's eighteen-year-old law permitting abortion, Wagner led a drive for a referendum to have the public enact a statute bringing the state into compliance with *Roe v. Wade*. Question 7 won handily and prohibited the legislature from changing Nevada's abortion law without a new referendum.

Outside observers might find such overwhelming support for this measure at odds with the conservative bent of Nevadans, especially considering their recent rejection of the ERA. However, as political scientists Driggs and Goodall pointed out, Nevada's individualistic political culture "focuses on the centrality of private concerns."

This culture, they suggested, placed a premium on limiting both governmental and non-governmental community intervention into private activities to keep the marketplace. Viewed from outside Nevada, this attitude was most apparent in the legalization of prostitution in much of Nevada.

"The 'right of privacy,'" they added, "was also important to the typical Nevadan, as evidenced by 63% of the electorate voting in 1990 to restrict the legislature from making changes in the 1973 abortion law."[5]

\* \* \*

Senator Raggio was disappointed by the results of an election that now put him back in the minority—no longer chair of the powerful Committee on Finance. He could see the obstacles ahead, and it was not just the issue of a fair share.

With twelve of the twenty-one state senators now from Clark County (four of them in the Republican caucus), his continuing leadership role was not a certainty. In addition, redistricting during this session would undoubtedly move even more legislative seats to the south, and, given the lopsided voter registration favoring Democrats in Clark County, made a return to majority status by Republicans seem improbable.

This appeared to be especially true in light of the election of Democratic Governor Bob Miller, who had been serving as acting governor for the last two years. Raggio was stoical, saying, "I was in the minority for fourteen years, so I know how to function in both majority and minority positions."

The Republican caucus again chose Bill as its leader. Senator O'Donnell made the usual rumblings about the need for southern Nevada leadership; but most understood it would take all of Raggio's experience, intellect and political skills to navigate through the increasingly hostile political landscape of the coming session.

Yet, not even the veteran Raggio could then envision what pundit Jon Ralston later called, "One hundred sixty-one days of agony...some of the most mean spirited, ugly and unseemly behavior in legislative annals."[6]

Officially, it would be known as the 66th Nevada Legislature, but to those involved in the process, it would ever after be referred to as "The Session from Hell."

A hint of the approaching discord occurred a month before the 1990 election, when senate Democrats removed Senator Joe Neal from his position as minority floor leader. Randolph Townsend later recalled the circumstances, saying that Senator Jack Vergiels initiated a successful coup against Neal.

Vergiels, Townsend remarked, was an expert at manipulating the legislative process for political purposes. Democratic legislators claimed that the reason for this action was that Senator Neal was alienating potential campaign contributors.

"It was a total dethroning," Randolph said. "Not only did Joe lose his leadership position, but he was passed over as chair of the Committee on

Finance in favor of Senator Nick Horn. Horn's assignment to that position was part of the deal Vergeils made to get enough votes to oust Neal. Being deprived of two positions that he'd spent the last eighteen years earning, Joe was left with a certain degree of bitterness that he kept forever."

The new majority leader, Jack Vergeils, was a fifty-four-year-old Las Vegas university professor. Though not as gifted an orator as his predecessor, Senator Raggio, and weaker on policy issues, Vergeils was a shrewd political operative whose single goal was to get Democrats elected—and reelected.

Not to be pushed aside without a fight, Senator Neal responded by insisting that, because the decision to remove him had been made between, not during, a session, senate rules allowed him to remain as majority floor leader. Vergeils nastily disagreed: "He [Neal] is a genius in his own mind."

After receiving an opinion by the legislative counsel that his ouster from the party's leadership had not violated senate rules, Neal shook things up further by declaring he might consider nominating Raggio as majority leader.

"If I nominate Raggio," Neal said, "then he becomes majority leader by a vote of the senate, not by a vote of a party." Although an accepted practice in the U.S. Congress for a legislator to organize in another political party, a subsequent legal opinion later held that it was not permissible to do so under rules governing the Nevada senate. Bill declined to comment on Neal's ploy, or on the Democratic Party infighting.

The session moved slowly. By April 30, the 100th day, and just a month before the targeted adjournment date of May 31, only 120 bills had been sent to the governor for signature—about 700 fewer than average for that period.

Now facing a $300 million budget deficit, the passage of a controversial business activity tax, the bitter "fair share" issue and thorny redistricting decisions, the level of partisanship in both houses became so intense that it seemed to preclude any chance at compromise.

The process slowly ground to a halt.

No one seemed able or capable of taking charge. Even the experienced assembly speaker, Joe Dini, was unable to inject life back into his house. A disheartened Senator Raggio later said, "It's ten times worse than any other session."

As the legislators slogged on, June 30, the end of the fiscal year, loomed ahead. After that date, the state would be out of funds to operate. In desperation, lobbyists took over and began brokering deals among legislators who were no longer speaking to one another.

In an example of the old adage that, "politics makes strange bedfellows," Jim Joyce, Richard Bunker and Harvey Whittemore, representing gaming interests, joined with John Cummings and Billy Vassiliadis, of the powerful teachers' association lobby, to craft necessary legislation and compromises on the business tax and teachers salaries. The two groups were traditional competitors over issues revenue and appropriations during past biennial battles.

Minority Leader Raggio used the leadership vacuum to his advantage, halting progress on the tax package by focusing attention on the provocative fair share issue. On June 27, Senator Raggio introduced an amendment to the proposed fair share bill that would greatly reduce the loss to Washoe County.

Democratic Senator Dina Titus angrily derided the proposal during a floor debate, calling Washoe County a "sponge" that has been soaking up taxes raised by Clark and other counties. Referring obliquely to Raggio, Titus said, "I never cease to be amazed by the audacity of Washoe County."

Senator Raggio responded, "Too many inflammatory remarks have been uttered," and warned of greater divisiveness in the state as a result. Not surprisingly, his amendment was roundly defeated.

Under the new sales tax distribution formula, Washoe County would lose $6.6 million in sales taxes in the current year and $13.2 million in 1992 and 1993. Washoe was also required to reimburse Clark County $2.2 million a year, over the next three years, for mistakes made by the county assessor. Yet, Washoe County would not be obligated to repay the rest of the $93 million it received from other counties under the 1981 distribution formula.

Washoe County citizens were more angered by having to reimburse Clark County than by anything the legislature had done in memory. Their argument was that the act was purely punitive, deliberately designed by Clark County lawmakers to penalize Washoe taxpayers for an error that was not their fault.

Despite their victory, some southern Nevada legislators remained disgruntled when they later realized that Raggio had anticipated this legislative battle two years earlier, and had cleverly managed during the previous session to cut the amount of sales taxes Clark County Democrats sought to recover from Washoe County from $13 million to $6.6 million.

An editorial in the *Reno Evening Gazette* praised Raggio for what he was able to accomplish against the irate and suspicious majority from the south. "Raggio," it said, "has become the closest thing to a folk hero that Washoe has had in a long time."[7]

Arguably, Bill's most brilliant political move during the 1991 session was in seeing the defection of Assemblywoman Patricia Little from the Democratic caucus as an opportunity to rally lethargic assembly Republicans into derailing the Democrats' districting legislation. The assemblywoman had objected to her party's reapportionment plan and Bill, with the assistance of Senator O'Connell, used her alienation to design a strategy which led to an eventual agreement on redistricting that was more favorable to the Republicans.

Bill's keen political instincts were also apparent in the final hours of the session when, upon realizing he had not achieved certain goals on class size and accountability in education, positioned himself to make political gains for his party in the following election year.

Rising to the floor of the senate, Senator Raggio made an eloquent plea for increasing the amount of teacher's salaries—a measure he knew was going to pass anyway.

Senator Townsend would later comment, "Bill is like a three-dimen-

sional chess grandmaster, seeing twenty moves ahead and fully understanding the policy and political implications of each of those moves.
He is also a formidable gin rummy player."

\* \* \*

On June 30, 1991, just hours before the end of the fiscal year, the legislature approved a $2.2 billion budget. New revenue would come from
a business activity tax based on average number of employees. To assuage
concerns of the gaming industry, a cap of $100,000 per tax quarter was
included. In addition to this, a variety of fee and county sales tax increases,
levies and transfer taxes were imposed or allowed. Senator Raggio voted
against the legislation and later explained that the difficult economic
times required a more fiscally prudent approach. An economic downturn
was occurring throughout the country, he said, and there was every
reason to expect that we would eventually feel its impact in this state,
which we did.

Senator Raggio then added:

> Nevertheless, many legislators refused to recognize this potential
> and opted, instead, to rely on overly optimistic revenue projections
> in an effort to fund many growing social needs. Unfortunately,
> this was done without regard to whether the increases in revenue
> were real or illusory. We cannot address fully every need ex-
> pressed by someone representing a special cause or special in-
> terest. Far too many legislators, although well intentioned, simply
> refuse to recognize this.

Although the 1991 redistricting process was aided by improved data
collection methods and state-of-the-art computer mapping techniques,
partisan and regional bickering turned it into the most difficult and controversial reapportionment task in the state's history. The legislature
chose to retain the same number of seats, twenty-one in the senate and
forty-two in the assembly. Washoe County lost one senate and two assembly seats to Clark.

Bill Raggio became particularly creative in order to save the senate seat of his old friend, conservative Republican Lawrence "Jake" Jacobsen, by helping create a new district for him stretching from Douglas County north for nearly seventy miles in a narrow corridor along the eastern Sierra Nevada Mountains and into part of Bill's own district in west Reno.

\* \* \*

With control of both houses and the governorship, Democrats were under pressure to accommodate their reliable constituency of state employees, and so seriously considered changes to the restrictive collective bargaining elements in Chapter 288 of the Nevada Revised Statutes.

In 2010, Senator Raggio talked about the reason the legislature never adopted collective bargaining for state employees. His main concern was that the governor and the public sector unions would get together before the legislative session began and engage in binding arbitration. "This," said Raggio, "would decide nearly 90% of the state budget, with the legislature having almost no say in how the majority of the money is spent in the state budget."

Technically the legislature would still have the opportunity to vote against such a proposal, Bill continued, but the pressure against changing it would be enormous, once something had been determined through binding arbitration.

"It was very political for the Democrats," Bill said. "Whether being led by Speaker Dini, or later Perkins, both of those individuals came to me and said, 'You have got to kill this bill. We have to pass it, but you have to kill it.' They felt compelled to support it, but hoped it would not pass, because they knew that it would have this negative effect. Even when the Democrats had a majority in both houses in 1991, and passed out a collective bargaining bill, Democratic Governor Miller vetoed it."

In June 1991, while the legislature was still in session, an advertisement in the *Gazette* announced the impending merger of the law firm of Raggio, Wooster and Lindell with the firm of Vargas & Bartlett.

Because John Sande III, of Vargas & Bartlett, was a lobbyist for several interest groups, including the Nevada Bankers Association, the Nature Conservancy, the Western States Petroleum Association and the Washoe County Airport Authority, some questioned whether this change constituted a conflict of interest.

Senator Raggio had always gone to greater lengths than the ethical standards required. He voluntarily did not sit on the Human Resources Committee because of his association with Sierra Health Services; nor was he a member of the Judiciary Committee, which dealt with gaming matters, because of his professional association with Sahara Resorts.

State ethics laws required that a legislator announce potential conflicts before voting on matters. Lawmakers may still vote on the issue, unless they have a financial interest that "a reasonable person" would believe constitutes a conflict of interest. Bill made a habit of not voting on matters that even remotely hinted of conflict.

He explained the merger, saying that he and his law partners had been looking for the resources that a larger firm could provide, including a presence in Las Vegas, and had been discussing the matter with several law firms. The actual merger with Vargas & Bartlett would not occur until July 1, after the session ended.[8]

The biennial tradition of attempting to impugn by association the integrity of Senator Raggio, once again quickly played itself out.

In April, about midway through the session, Bill lost his old and trusted friend, former Reno Police Chief Elmer Briscoe. Just before his death, Briscoe asked that his "closest friend," Bill Raggio, deliver his eulogy. In it, a grieving Raggio said Elmer's "most precious legacy was real friendship, unflagging loyalty and his devotion to profession, society and family."

Bill was also called upon during that time to speak in Chico, California at a memorial service for Muriel Corbett, the wife of Roger Corbett, his first investigator with the district attorney's office.

Muriel and Roger had taken the risk of hiding Jackie Hitson, the star witness in the 1960 extortion trial of Joe Conforte, for which Bill was ever grateful. In a note to Bill after the service, Roger thanked him for granting Muriel's "final request" by speaking at her memorial service. "That was a difficult assignment," Roger wrote, "but you met it with characteristic dignity and sympathy. I shall always be grateful."

* * *

Amid the ill feelings that marked interaction between legislators during "The Session from Hell," Bill strove to maintain decorum and respect for the institution.

In May, he paid tribute on the senate floor to the memory of Sol Dartch, who Bill had known for many years. Sol operated a one-chair shoeshine concession at Harrah's in Reno. Due to financial hardship early in life, Dartch, an African American, was unable to attend school and was illiterate.

Senator Raggio told of how Dartch comported himself with pride in his personal appearance and of his ability to discuss events of the day, despite the fact that he could not read a newspaper. "Sol knew nearly everyone," Bill said. "He mingled with the high and mighty. Yet he greeted all who walked by with genuine warmth."

By the time Raggio had convinced him that he was not too old to enroll in an adult literacy program, Dartch was dying. When he passed away, his obituary stated there were no known relatives and no funeral. "It was probably the only time he ever had his name mentioned in the newspaper," Bill said, in closing. "Yet, people like Sol Dartch *do* make a difference."

Raggio's words deeply moved those in attendance and seemed to calm the stridency of the body— at least momentarily. Long time local columnist Rollie Melton wrote Bill a letter the next day, calling his words about Sol Dartch one of his "greatest speeches" and thanking him for "being a man who speaks the eloquent language of a loving heart."[9]

Throughout his senate years, Raggio refused to give up these charming traditions of the legislature. While legislators would often eulogize former colleagues or the passing of a prominent person in the state, Senator Raggio would often rise to say a few flattering words about an ordinary citizen. He particularly enjoyed recognizing high school classes, boy and girl scouts, athletic teams and other youth groups, who were visiting the legislature. As Melton observed: "Media members and lobbyists moan about the delays, but Raggio is not about to leave a compliment unsaid to guests of the day."

Also during the hectic 1991 session, the legislature enshrined Senators James Gibson and B. Mahlon Brown into its Hall of Fame. Bill Raggio did not pass on the opportunity to remind the body, now virtually at a standstill, of how productive and efficient were the days before political partisanship had rendered the art of compromise nearly obsolete.

After 161 days, the 66th Legislative session was finally over. It had taken a harsh personal and economic toll on many of the legislators; nearly six months deprived of family activities and their sources of livelihood.

There was a physical toll as well. Some suffered from health issues related to stress and exhaustion. In the senate, Committee on Finance Chair Nick Horn, battling cancer, was often forced to miss chemotherapy to attend to his duties.* Democratic Senator Tom Hickey, a heart patient, removed himself from a hospital bed to be taken to the floor of the senate in a wheel chair so he could vote on the reapportionment bill.

In an August 12, 1991, letter to Bill Raggio, the late Guy Shipler, *Time's* correspondent in Carson City and the legendary "Dean of the Capitol Press Corps," humorously quipped that he had worried Bill might sue him for defamation of character from an article he had written three weeks before. "I knew when I was writing the column," Shipler said, "that naming you as the session's most effective leader sure as hell wasn't the greatest compliment in the world. Actually, you'll never get the real credit you deserve for sticking your neck out, knowing there would be harsh critics to contend with."

---

*Senator Horn died the following April.

Shipler went on to say that Bill's critics claimed he was using his "exceptional political skills" exclusively for his, and his party's, own purposes, "but none of them showed the same expertise—or guts—to do anything about it themselves."

In closing, Guy Shipler wrote:

> What gripes them more than anything else is that you *were* effective when they weren't, in the most difficult and challenging political situation of the decade. You saved what little there was to be saved, when nobody else did.[10]

# CHAPTER FORTY-NINE

# The American Legislative Exchange Council

Among the scores of organizations to which Bill Raggio belongs, none provided him with as much far-reaching influence and prestige as the American Legislative Exchange Council (ALEC).

The first ALEC meeting was held in Chicago in 1973, chaired by Congressman Henry Hyde of Illinois. Though its featured speaker was Nobel laureate economist Milton Freidman, only fourteen state legislators and eight members of Congress were present. Their mission was to form a nonpartisan, public-private partnership of America's state legislators, promoting economic growth and traditional values, what the organization termed the Jeffersonian principles of free markets, limited government, federalism and individual liberty.[1]

During the Reagan years, ALEC grew in profile, stature and credibility. President Reagan was a champion of the council's philosophy, saying, "For state legislators who appreciate the critical value of free enterprise, ALEC offers the strong support, legislative research and networking... ALEC and I are soldiers in a common cause."

Membership in ALEC was not limited to just state legislators. Members of the public, private-sector business people and federal office holders were included in the ranks.

By the early 1980s, ALEC member and Republican Congressman Jack Kemp of New York had built a coalition in Congress that pushed through radical cuts in capital gains and income taxes.

Many believed that Kemp's tax cuts ushered in America's most productive decade and the greatest peacetime economic expansion in world history—six million new businesses, twenty million new jobs and a 32% surge in real national income.

Many ALEC members saw similarities between Kemp's and Raggio's philosophy and work ethic. They admired the way both came to the table prepared, were trustworthy and the fairness with which they treated others.

Like Kemp, Bill Raggio would prove to be an influential force in the organization. As an early member of ALEC, he had served on the board of directors since 1983 and was selected the organization's National Chairman for 1993.

At the time, ALEC was veering toward becoming more a vehicle of social, rather than fiscal, conservatism—a change that threatened its very existence. Ron Scheberle, Chairman Emeritus of the ALEC Private Enterprise Board, was unequivocal in his praise for Bill's leadership during the crisis:

> I would say without hesitation that ALEC would not be in existence today had it not been for Bill Raggio. ALEC went through some tough times over the years, just as all organizations do, and his leadership skills were startling. Bill spent a great deal of time developing a strong set of bylaws, so we had guidance and direction. That piece—the free market, free enterprise, pro-business focus—is where the organization provides its guidance, that is to say, the fiscal conservative aspects of legislation, rather than the social conservative issues, such as abortion, prayer in school, etc.

During that time, Bill would meet President Reagan on several occasions, but more frequently, Vice President Bush. Senator Raggio minimizes his role as being just one of the ALEC Board members in attendance at these meetings. However, others report he was more than just a face in the room, and that both the president and vice president not only knew of Bill's reputation, but valued his opinion.

Jerry Watson, a long time ALEC member, said in 2009, "Bill Raggio is the most respected member of ALEC. Bill has his fingerprints on every piece of legislation in the country. His advice reverberates far beyond the state of Nevada."

That year, ALEC chose Colorado Springs, Colorado as the venue for its annual meeting. It would prove to be the most successful meeting in the organization's history. In addition to the keynote address by President George H. W. Bush, six members of the president's cabinet would also deliver speeches. One, Secretary of the Department of Housing and Urban Development Jack Kemp, would be receiving ALEC's highest honor, the Thomas Jefferson Award.

On August 6, 1992, President Bush addressed the nearly 2,000 ALEC members in attendance at the Broadmoor Hotel in Colorado Springs. After thanking outgoing National Chair Fred Noye for the introduction, the president said, "You have done a great chairman's job and I know that your shoes will be ably filled by Bill Raggio, over here, from the state of Nevada. Bill flew in with us last night from Reno on Air Force One, and all the White House stationery and matchboxes from the plane are missing. But he swears there's no correlation whatsoever."

In 2008, Bill Raggio described the flight:

> It was an interesting flight. After getting a personal tour of the airplane's interior, the president invited me to sit with him in his private compartment. A pair of bedroom slippers with the Presidential Seal on them caught my eye. I thought, at the time, how unique it would be to own them. Later, when President Bush accused me in his speech of petty larceny for taking everything I could find bearing a Presidential Seal, I was almost sorry I hadn't taken those slippers, too.

Bill would, after completing his term as national chair in 1993, also receive the Thomas Jefferson Award, joining such distinguished past recipients as Presidents Reagan and Bush and Wisconsin Governor Tommy Thompson, among others.

Having put the ALEC house in order, Bill Raggio would soon set about doing what he could to accomplish the seemingly impossible task of regaining the majority in the Nevada senate.

# CHAPTER FIFTY

# "A Fiscally Prudent Approach" (1993)

ill Raggio turned sixty-five in October 1991. The previous year, the "dapper and ruggedly handsome" state senator appeared on the Nevada Newswomen Association's list of list of "Top 10 List of Most Watchable Men." While others might look at their sixty-fifth birthday as a time to slow down—Bill Raggio was just hitting his stride.

He ran unopposed for reelection in 1992, and so dedicated his time and energy to working for the election of Republican Party candidates.

In February, several weeks before the SRLC held their annual fundraising breakfast in Las Vegas, Bill Raggio invited a select group of influential lobbyists and political operatives to a more intimate gathering, or, as Jon Ralston would write, "to twist the arms of the arm twisters." The columnist criticized this closed gathering as an example of how Nevada politics was run, and power was maintained, by a select few. Quoting a political insider, Ralston described Nevada politics as being "like a Frank Capra movie without Jimmy Stewart."[1]

Senator Raggio disagreed with the sinister implication, saying that the process was organizationally better suited to achieve success on issues that would benefit citizens of Nevada.

The SRLC subsequently decided that Sue Lowden would challenge Senate Majority Leader Jack Vergeils, and that Las Vegas attorney Mark James would run against Democratic Assemblywoman Saundra Krenzer, for one of the two seats in the new Clark County Senate District No. 8.

Lowden was well known to Las Vegans as a television news reporter and anchor. She gave up her TV career after marrying Sahara Resorts owner Paul Lowden, and becoming vice president of the company.

Mark James had been "bitten by the political bug" while interning in the office of U.S. Senator Paul Laxalt. He originally considered running for an assembly seat, but Raggio, seeing great political potential in this bright, young attorney, convinced him to run for the senate.

"Bill told me the Republican Party would do everything they can to help me," James would later recall. "He said I was going to have to work hard and walk a lot of precincts and that it would be a tough race. Bill followed through with what he promised and it helped my race enormously. He started out as a great mentor right from the very beginning."

The two political newcomers were both running in strongly Democratic districts. Success would require them to capture not only all the Republican and independent voters in the district, but a good percentage of registered Democrats as well. By Election Day, each would have spent nearly $200,000, much of which was provided through the diligent pursuit of campaign donors by Senator Raggio.

Though the candidates benefited from Bill's political skill and advice, they also endured criticism from their association with the man who many southern Nevadans believed had deprived them of their fair share of state sales tax revenue. Sue Lowden's long personal and professional association with Bill, combined with her challenging an incumbent Democrat who held the majority leadership position in the senate, made her task especially daunting.

One campaign brochure distributed by the Vergeils camp, failed even to mention Lowden's name—but not Raggio's. Bill complained to the press, "Everyone down there [Clark County] is running against me," rather than against the Republican challengers. [2]

Vergeils ran a television ad portraying Sue Lowden as being "in the pocket" of "northern Republican Senate Minority Leader Bill Raggio," and this, by association, made her complicit in helping divert millions of dollars owed to the taxpayers of Clark County.

In response, Lowden said, "I will fight for every penny that deserves to be down here in southern Nevada, but to think I would be a puppet for any man is sexist." Lowden accused Vergeils of "resorting to desperation tactics because of a lackluster legislative record in which all he did was to raise our taxes and vote himself a pension increase."

In mid October 1992, Sue Lowden and her opponent debated the issues. Despite Vergeils being the senate floor leader and a university professor, Lowden appeared more poised and knowledgeable on the issues.

As Senator Raggio had predicted at the close of the 1991 session, the slumping national economy finally made its way to Nevada and revenue levels, anticipated by the legislature when approving spending in the biennial budget, did not materialize.

Consequently, Democratic Governor Bob Miller had been required to make deep cuts in state agency budgets in early 1992, which affected services to Nevadans and compensation to state employees. In addition, a business tax passed in the previous session capping the burden on large companies, primarily in the gaming industry, was now viewed as unfair to small businesses.

During the campaign, Senator Raggio came out against repealing the tax entirely, but promised to seek refinement to alleviate the burden on smaller businesses. "We need to take out the disincentive to create jobs," he said. "Disgruntled small business owners claim that they have cut staff and hours or withheld pay raises to stay afloat since the tax was initiated."

On Election Day, voter dissatisfaction directed toward incumbents was felt across the nation. President George H.W. Bush was defeated by Arkansas Governor Bill Clinton. In Nevada, Sue Lowden defeated Senate Majority Leader Jack Vergeils by a margin of nearly 15%. Bill Raggio was not surprised by Sue Lowden's victory, saying, "She was a television anchorwoman, photogenic and had a lot of charisma. She worked hard and campaigned hard. I think Vergeils may have taken it for granted because he had such a voter registration edge."

It was Mark James's race, however, that would provide some of the greatest drama in Nevada electoral history, and upon its outcome would hinge Bill Raggio's return to senate majority leadership.

At the end of ballot counting on election night, James was ahead by only twenty-four votes out of over 41,000 cast. Nevada's secretary of state, Cheryl Lau, ruled that because overseas absentee ballots were mailed out late, she would allow an additional seventeen days for those ballots to be returned.

When the additional 160 ballots were counted, James's lead increased by eight votes, to thirty-two. His opponent went to court and a recount was held that validated James's victory.

"A second court action was considered," Mark James later said, "to test the legality of the extension granted by the secretary of state, a Republican. However, my opponent, Assemblywoman Sandi Krenzer, graciously declined to contest the election further, and conceded. Whenever I want to inject humor into a conversation, I tell people that I was elected by 'acclamation.'"

James's victory gave the Republicans the majority they had been hoping to regain. The profound affect Bill Raggio would have as majority leader on the lives of Nevadans over the next fourteen years, all came about by the slimmest of margins—just thirty-two votes.

However, Bill needed to survive one more critical test when Clark County Senator Ray Rawson challenged him on the leadership position and his chair of the Senate Committee on Finance.

Rawson, a Las Vegas dentist, sought to win the influential posts from Raggio as a way to lessen tensions between Washoe and Clark Counties. He announced that he had the support of the five other southern Nevada Republican senators—a majority of the caucus— and so would be replacing Bill Raggio. When asked by a reporter how Senator Raggio had taken the news of this attempted coup, Rawson responded truthfully, "He didn't take it well. He felt it was a backstabbing; a betrayal."[3]

Senator Raggio was unavailable for immediate comment, but quickly flew to Las Vegas to meet with the group. He later emerged from a two-

hour closed-door session as both majority leader and chair of the Committee on Finance. "I'm going to work as hard as I can to defuse sectionalism as a basis for how we treat issues," Raggio said. "We're going to
unite together. 'Fair share' has been decided and it's behind us."

When Senator Rawson was later asked what had transpired during the
meeting, he would only comment that Bill "won the vote"—inferring
that he had been able to persuade at least one southern Nevada senator
to change. That person, according to Bill, was Sue Lowden.

As a concession, Bill selected Senator Rawson as vice chair of the
Committee on Finance, a position previously held by Senator Jacobsen
the last time the GOP had been in the majority. Some in the press wondered how Rawson's attempted coup would affect this working relationship with Senator Raggio.

"There was never any retaliation by Senator Raggio," Randolph
Townsend later recalled. "Bill was never that way. When the fight was
over, it was over."

With Mark James now "officially" elected, the Republicans held a
one-seat majority in the senate. Yet, given the degree of voter dissatisfaction, the seats they had hoped to gain in the assembly did not materialize. In fact, Republicans suffered a net loss of seven of their twenty
seats in that body.

With Raggio now chairing the Committee on Finance, the budget
would be scrutinized like never before. Ever the diplomat, Senator Raggio
would only say, "I'm optimistic good compromises will be reached."

* * *

On January 18, 1993, the 67th Nevada Legislature convened. High on
Senator Raggio's list of priorities was to implement "a fiscally prudent
approach" in forecasting revenue projections. No longer, he said, could
legislators rely on overly optimistic projections in order to justify the
funding of growing social needs or pet projects.

To this end, Bill was successful in passing legislation to create the
Nevada Economic Forum. Consisting of five members, the Forum would

meet just prior to the beginning of each legislative session to provide a revenue forecast which both the legislative and executive branches would be required to use in approving state government budgets.

The Forum would then meet again approximately thirty days prior to the adjournment of the session to make any necessary revisions to the biennial forecast. The group could also meet at any time to make preliminary projections of future state revenue. The five members would be required to have backgrounds in finance, two appointed by the legislative leadership and three by the governor.

Other key issues during the session would contain cost saving measures, including the reorganization of government agencies, sweeping reform of the state's business tax, education funding and, most importantly, saving the state's workers' compensation program, called the State Industrial Insurance System (SIIS), from a projected $2.2 billion long-term debt.

Senator Townsend, who regained the Chair of the Committee on Commerce and Labor, had been working on the issue since 1987. Governor Miller proposed a bill that would abolish the SIIS board and put control and responsibility directly under the Office of Governor. Townsend, driven to see necessary reforms enacted before the end of the current session, set out to work with all parties involved. The situation was extraordinarily complex.

Lobbying was intense and complicated as gaming interests (referred to as "gamers"), were pitted against small business, small business against labor, labor against gamers, gamers against doctors—and so on. It would be called by legislative insiders, "the fiercest political fight in years."

High-powered lobbyist Harvey Whittemore energetically worked the halls of the Legislative Building, meeting with lawmakers on both sides. Townsend's friend and former political foe, Jack Vergeils, now a lobbyist, used his experience from years with the SIIS, as well as his celebrated political skills, to help sort through the complexity of the system and accomplish needed reform.

By implementing the seldom-used Committee of the Whole, where all twenty-one senators simultaneously hear testimony and question testifiers, Senator Townsend was eventually able to assuage all concerns enough to hammer out a deal and avoid the pending economic catastrophe. Then-assemblyman Pete Ernaut said of the compromise, "When everyone walks away from a deal equally unhappy, you have a pretty good deal."

In mid-June, the assembly approved the workers' compensation measure and sent it to the senate for approval. Just after the voluminous, 155-page bill was passed out to the senators, Majority Leader Raggio ordered that the rules of the senate be suspended and called for the bill's approval the following day. Democratic Senator Bob Coffin of Las Vegas protested, asking that they be given a few days to read the newly amended legislation.

Bill used this opportunity to remind veteran senators, and educate the newer ones, that the Democratic leadership in 1991 suspended the rules on bill processing "a whole month and ten days" before the end of session. Now, with only thirteen days left in the current session, it was necessary for him to suspend them as well.

Senator Raggio further informed them that the assembly had imposed new conditions, among them, barring lobbyists from the floor during recesses. This "off-limits rule" for lobbyists, Bill said, would now also apply to the senate. When Senator Coffin again protested what he considered Raggio's heavy-handedness, the majority leader replied, "We like to keep the voting in floor committee meetings to committee members only."

The SIIS reform measure was passed by the senate and signed by the governor.

Senator Townsend later recalled that particular piece of legislation as being the most memorable of his senate career, and not just because of the enormity of the effort required to pass it.

"Bill never once meddled," Townsend noted. "He never once came to me and said that lobbyists were complaining about my methods, which I'm sure many did; or to suggest I do something different. I don't think he ever trusted anyone else with his back like he did me on that huge workers' compensation mess."

By April, four months into the session, activity in the legislature had come to a virtual standstill. Senator Raggio was at loggerheads with Governor Bob Miller and the Democrat-controlled assembly on a number of issues, including a massive bill to reorganize government agencies. Among Miller's proposals to help state government run more efficiently, was to expand the authority to the Governor's Office in transferring funds among departments. Bill saw this as relinquishing legislative power over the state's purse strings, and would have no part of it.

The most vocal and heated exchanges between Governor Miller and Senator Raggio had to do with the governor's proposal to save $22 million by closing several of the prison system's "honor camps" throughout the state, releasing 1,000 inmates convicted of nonviolent crimes back into the community. This was an element of larger pending legislation being promoted by the Miller Administration, called the Facility Capacity Act. Senator Raggio argued that public safety should not be a tradeoff to balance the budget.

Though Governor Miller argued that closing the honor camps was not a budget issue, but rather criminal justice reform supported by law enforcement to allow space for violent criminals, to Bill, the move was reminiscent of the 1960s, when Democratic Governor Grant Sawyer sought to cut costs by initiating an early release program for offenders throughout the prison system. As Washoe County District Attorney, Bill had protested such a move in the press and as a testifier before legislative committees. He had even orchestrated a Mother's March on the Capitol to denounce the release of prisoners into their communities.

On a more personal level, Bill knew the capacity for crime of these "non violent" offenders, as in the case of honor camp escapee Pierce Spillers, who committed rape after an escape from such an "honor camp."

In addition, Jimmy Ing, released under the Sawyer Administration plan after serving just one third of his sentence, immediately threatened the lives of then-DA Raggio and his family, before dying in a hail of police bullets.

Instead of closing these minimum security camps to increase the available funding, Raggio proposed reopening a low-level nuclear waste dump near Beatty in exchange for a $25 million payment to the state from the dump's prospective operator, U.S. Ecology.[5]

This proposal was soon clouded by controversy when it was learned that Bill's law firm, Vargas & Bartlett, one of the state's most influential lobbying enterprises, represented U.S. Ecology, thus creating a potential conflict of interest.

When asked about this, Bill initially denied that U.S. Ecology was a client of Vargas & Bartlett. However, after fact checking with the law firm, he soon reported that Vargas & Bartlett did represent the company, and he had been unaware of the association until he checked.

As a fellow member of the law firm pointed out, there had been no conflict of interest or impropriety. Senator Raggio, he said, initially did not know that another attorney at Vargas & Bartlett had U.S. Ecology as a client. The law firm employed fifty attorneys and had over 2,500 accounts. At the time, Raggio had only been with the firm since mid-1991, so it was unlikely he knew more than a fraction of the firm's clients.

Despite this being an understandable mistake for the average person, it was a rare gaffe for Bill Raggio, one he considered the Miller Administration responsible for creating in order to undermine his alternative revenue plan by reopening the dump. Five days later, U.S. Ecology withdrew its offer.

When the governor's Facility Capacity Act measure came before the Committee on Finance, Bill was prepared to even the score. He patiently allowed each of the seven members on the committee to speak on the measure, beginning with the Democrats.

Senator Matt Callister strongly defended the bill. Although just a freshman, Callister, rather than Senate Minority Leader Dina Titus, seemed to collide more often with Senator Raggio on hot button issues during the session.

Chair Raggio then had the Republican members speak. When they were finished, he took his turn, assailing the Miller Administration as "irresponsible." Their use of "gimmicks" to balance the budget, he said, "is completely intolerable and inappropriate." He then raised the specter of Willie Horton[6] by describing the danger of 1,000 newly freed inmates roaming the streets. Callister responded, saying that Raggio was engaging in demagoguery and that he and other opponents of the governor's budget were only concerned with protecting their careers.

Senator Raggio had the last word. "If this bill was to address prison reform, it could conceivably have merit," he said. "But as proposed by the governor as a means of balancing the budget, it has no place in a legislative session."

With that, he called for a vote. The measure was defeated in committee along party lines, by a vote of four to three, setting the stage for a political battle over whether to raise taxes, cut programs—or both.

Just before midnight on June 30, as the fiscal year ticked down, Senator Callister rose to the senate floor to request an amendment to eliminate rural honor camps and certain rural services for the elderly, and use the savings to fund urban needs. When Senator Raggio responded, "Let's quit delaying and put this budget process to bed," an angry Callister muttered the word "coward" loud enough to be heard by many in the gallery.

A quick recess was called as senate Democrats met. Veteran Senator Ray Shaffer of Clark County told them they did not have the votes for such last minute changes, "Find the eleventh Democrat," Shaffer said, "or Raggio is going to stop us. We have to realize we're living in Raggio's house."

When the recess ended, a calmer Callister publicly apologized to Senator Raggio, but then immediately sought an amendment cutting additional rural programs. He ended by criticizing the status quo funding of class-size reduction, welfare benefits and the "screaming needs" of the mentally handicapped.

Majority Leader Raggio reminded the body that the budget before them had the support of the assembly and the governor. "This is a responsible budget. Barring a disaster worldwide, you need not worry about revenue projections," Raggio said. "I suggest we get on with the job and bite the bullet." The senate then voted in favor of the appropriations bill. Governor Bob Miller signed a $6.2 billion state budget into law—one minute before the midnight deadline.

Additional revenue needed to balance the budget came from increases in the sales tax and certain fees. Difficult decisions had to be made, including Senator Raggio's decision to kill in committee a measure to restore $18 million in schools cuts that the governor had implemented earlier in the year due to revenue shortfalls. Many school districts were forced to scramble for alternative funds to cover expenses before the approaching school year commenced.

The legislature also approved sweeping reforms in the state business tax, making it more equitable for all businesses, regardless of size. In addition, they completed adjustment on the bitterly contested "fair share" legislation from the previous session and approved a massive reorganization plan for state government agencies.

Though they had met the deadline for passing a budget before July 1, the senate session ran on into the next day. A weary Bill Raggio blamed the delay in adjournment on senseless bickering and a backlog of unprocessed amendments arriving from the assembly just before midnight.

A week earlier, Senator Raggio had charged the governor with offering the legislature a misguided budget proposal. However, he knew all the proposals that had been offered were just devices to avoid facing the inevitable: the state had no stable revenue and no one was willing to propose a new source.

He addressed his colleagues at that time, telling them that they "would not be able to skirt the tax issue any longer because it will make the current crunch look like a walk in the park." One lobbyist concurred, saying, "Come 1995, when they walk into this building $100 million upside down, they will know what a real crisis is like." [7]

# CHAPTER FIFTY-ONE

# The Purse Strings (1995)

On April 22, 1994, former President Richard M. Nixon died. In reporting the event, Nevada newspapers included a local slant, recalling how Bill Raggio's political future had been so dramatically altered by Nixon's national political agenda in 1970.

Later that year, Jon Ralston would articulate what many were thinking while reading those newspaper accounts: "He [Raggio] rules the upper house with an iron hand, but it is always encased in a velvet glove. It seems almost a shame that he never got to ply his trade in the U.S. Senate."[1]

The phenomenon of the 1994 mid-term Republican sweep, which gave that party its first majority in the House of Representatives since 1954, played out in Nevada as well. On Election Day, the state assembly found itself with a twenty-one to twenty-one split, a curious situation that required two speakers and two chairs for each committee. In the senate, the Republicans picked up two more seats giving them a thirteen-to-eight majority.

Bills excitement over his party's November 8 gains in the legislature was immediately tempered by a family crisis. On that same day, Dorothy Raggio underwent surgery to remove a tumor from her lung. In her weakened condition, she contracted pneumonia and fell into a coma. The prognosis was not good.

However, just before Christmas, she miraculously regained full consciousness and eventually grew strong enough to leave the hospital. Bill happily told his friend Rollie Melton, "We have a beautiful Christmas present! Dottie is off the respirator and will likely be home soon."

Bill was again named Majority Leader by his caucus and passed out committee chair assignments. In order to help develop skills as an effective chairperson, as he had done so well with Randolph Townsend, Bill assigned the important chair of the Taxation Committee to Sue Lowden and the equally significant chair of the Judiciary Committee to Mark James.

Bill told the press that he did not anticipate early partisan fighting and, indeed, bitter sectional issues, which had erupted during the previous session, were largely absent in 1995.

Senator Raggio worked well with his money committee counterpart, Assemblyman Morse Arberry, chair of the Assembly Committee on Ways and Means. A newspaper article speculated that after twenty-two years, this might be Bill's last session, one in which he would be "a kinder, gentler leader," exhibiting one "last burst of statesmanship."

Minority Leader Dina Titus did not agree, either about Raggio's intent to retire or about a "gentler" approach to the south. "I think we have to play defense with the leadership held by the north," she said, "or Raggio will get back at us for 'fair share' a nickel here and a nickel there." [2]

The issue that would receive the most attention during this session was not the budget, but the growing influence of the gaming industry on the legislative and executive branches of state government. In 1995, gaming profits hit an all time high and with it came increased pressure from gaming interests for favorable legislation.

Casino owners did not always leave political activity to lobbyists. Steve Wynn, the eloquent and charismatic head of Mirage Resorts, became a political force in the early 1990s and "strongly encouraged voter registration among his thousands of employees, openly communicated his political concerns to them and contributed heavily to pro-gaming candidates." [3]

"Steve Wynn was one of the best supporters of Republican candidates we had," Bill said. "I had good relations with him, as I did with most of the gaming operators. I do not think they thought I was going to do their bidding, but they felt that I understood their problems. Though I did not curry their favor, I felt they were an important sector of our economy and that their issues deserved to be heard."

During a 2010 interview, Wynn was asked about allegations by some Raggio adversaries that he was overly influenced by large, southern Nevada gamers:

> Do you know why that one allegation always went away? Because it wasn't *true*. He would never do most of what we asked him to. He had a nice of way of turning people down. Nobody could hold a position like Bill and be in the so-called "pocket" of anybody. He never would've had the credibility that he developed. Ultimately what Raggio did was to stop a few ideas that would've broken the industry in half and put everybody out of work.

Yet during the 1995 session, gaming made its presence known. Reno attorney Harvey Whittemore, Las Vegas advertising executive Billy Vassiliadis and Richard Bunker, former head of the Gaming Control Board, became informal advisers to Governor Miller, assisting him in working with legislators.

By June 18, as the legislature raced toward adjournment, the Republican-controlled senate became the object of condemnation. Critics charged that the gaming industry had increased the number of lobbyists and the number of bills in an ambitious agenda to save casinos millions of dollars.

Legislative Counsel Bureau records showed that in 1995, twenty-seven lobbyists were representing the Nevada Resort Association and other casino interests at the legislature. Billy Vassiliadis was defensive, saying the industry had long been accused of conducting business with legislators behind closed doors. "We are out of the back rooms," he said. "We are in committees. We're testifying publicly and talking to the press."

Because an even split between Democrats and Republicans in the assembly made it generally more moderate on budget and labor issues, the senate was called upon to introduce the bulk of the gaming bills.

These measures included numerous reforms the industry wanted in the SIIS, as well as a bill to increase information sharing about employees between casinos, a measure some labor advocates claimed could lead to blacklisting.

A tort reform measure, Senate Bill 474, was introduced making it more difficult for casinos and businesses to be held liable for the wrongful acts of their employees. Language had been inserted to make it retroactive, so that it would cover most current claims against the casinos, including a large judgment against the Las Vegas Hilton by ex-Navy pilot Paula Coughlin. The retroactivity called for in the bill, would ignite controversy and leave Nevada—once again—with a tarnished reputation.

During a 1991 convention of the Tailhook Association* at the Las Vegas Hilton, Coughlin, and other women, was forced to walk through a "gauntlet" of drunken naval and marine officers in the hotel hallways while the men groped and fondled them. This behavior occurred in the presence of Hilton security personnel who were nearby observing, but who evidently failed to act.

The resulting scandal rocked the nation and infuriated President George H.W. Bush (a former naval aviator), eventually leading to career-ending reprimands for numerous admirals and other high-ranking Navy and Marine Corps officers.

Paula Coughlin sued the Hilton and proved to a jury that the hotel management and security were aware such "gauntlets" had existed during past conventions there, and should have done more to protect female guests. In 1994, a Las Vegas district court decision awarded Coughlin $5.2 million.

During the 1995 legislative session, the case was still pending a decision before the Court of Appeals for the Ninth Circuit.* When rumors spread around the Legislative Building that Barron Hilton was making personal telephone calls to legislators in support of Senate Bill 474, critics accused the industry of trying to circumvent the judicial process.

A bitter floor debate ensued between Senators James and Coffin with regard to an amendment introduced by Coffin to remove all retroactivity

---

*A U.S.-based, fraternal, non-profit organization, supporting the interests of sea-based aviation, with emphasis on aircraft carriers. The word *tailhook* refers to the hook underneath the tail of some aircraft that catches the arresting wire suspended across the flight deck in order to quickly stop the landing plane.

*The appeals court would decide in her favor and she received the amount awarded.

in the bill. In a subsequent vote, the amendment was defeated. Senator Neal rose to say that the world was watching Nevada and seeing the state government as corrupt. Governor Bob Miller recalled in February 2011, that he had informed the legislature and those lobbying for the bill "in no uncertain terms that I would not only veto it, but call a press conference to condemn its passage."

A subsequent torrent of negative national publicity ensued when Paula Coughlin arrived in Carson City to lobby personally against the bill. A week later, the clause allowing retroactive application of the law was removed by the Assembly Judiciary Committee. The bill's most vocal supporter, Senator James, did not object, and the amended bill passed both houses.

In the senate, only two legislators voted against Senate Bill 474—Neal and Coffin. Senator Raggio was absent that day for the vote.

Before voting "yea" on the bill, Minority Leader Titus said, "I recognize the need to protect the gaming industry...which provides 65% of the jobs and 60% of the tax dollars. At the same time, we cannot let them dictate state policy and ride roughshod over those who worked so hard to help make the gaming industry the success it is today."

She then angrily directed her criticism at Senators Raggio and Lowden, who were executives of the Sahara Gaming Corporation, as well as Senators Randolph Townsend and Mark James, who represented gaming clients in a professional capacity.

"The frustrating thing is that people with connections to the gaming industry seem to abstain only on certain issues and not on others," Titus said. "When it's convenient, or in their best interests, they abstain, otherwise they vote. I think it clearly contributes to the perception that the senate is in the hip pocket of gaming."

Senator Raggio recognized that Titus was referring to an earlier vote on Assembly Bill 58, which directed the State Gaming Control Board to investigate union leaders organizing in casinos. Lowden and Raggio voted on the measure, despite one of the Sahara Resorts Corporation's properties, the Santa Fe Hotel and Casino in Las Vegas, being locked in a protracted dispute with the culinary union.

Bill later rebutted Senator Titus's insinuation, saying he and Senator Lowden were not obligated to abstain. "There is no need for me to abstain on a bill that has something to do with procedures in gaming. That's not a conflict of interest. There has to be a pecuniary interest of some kind."

Raggio denied the casino industry held sway over the senate, describing the current legislature as a rivalry between free enterprise on one hand and liberals and labor unions on the other.

"This is a more Republican legislature and so is more business oriented, and that's gotten some of the liberals angry," he said. "It is a legal industry in Nevada and now it's a legal industry in just about every state. You can't say it's a legal industry and then say it shouldn't participate."

That was the kind of thinking that gamers like Steve Wynn appreciated. "Bill," Wynn would later say, "is one of the few people who has deep insight and keen understanding of how the state works and how to balance the interests in the state."

He went on to describe Raggio as a person who was able to sort through an incredible amount of information and identify what was important. That was a rare enough a skill, Wynn said, but to be able to function within a group "with that kind of clarity and still be collegial," was even more uncommon.

"It is a much more complex and deeper challenge," he added. "I see that kind of dynamic personality and common sense in a lot of executive types, but in the legislature, it's much rarer… I have known Bill Raggio for over forty-two years and while he doesn't always agree with you, if he gives you his word, it is his bond. He's the best. He just is the best. He's just the consummate professional."

\* \* \*

In April, the Economic Forum reported to the legislature that tax revenue from unusually high profits in gaming portended a windfall to the state of up to $60 million over the coming biennium. A scramble ensued on how to spend it.

Democrats, lead by Governor Miller, wanted to use it to enhance kindergarten through grade twelve (K-12) education, particularly smaller class sizes for third grade. Senator Raggio was cautious, saying he foresaw deficits in the second year of the 1995-1997 budget, which would result in less from the windfall than expected. A compromise was finally reached.

On July 4, 1995, the last day of Nevada's 68th Legislature, Senator Raggio and Assembly Speaker Dini worked together feverishly to complete business. The two men combined for fifty-two years of legislative experience and knew how to get the job done—though the 1995 session was testing that.

"This is the most hectic session I have ever been involved in," Senator Raggio told Geoff Dornan of the *Nevada Appeal*.[3] Raggio and Dini blamed the last minute confusion on the size of the "freshman class."

Nearly half the assembly members were new and did not know the process, rushing at the last minute to push through bills on issues important to them. "Everybody's got an issue," said Bill, racing down the hall to Dini's office. The two lawmakers had enormous respect for the other's abilities.

"Raggio is very bright and never quits," said Dini. Bill responded that he had learned from Dini not to put his name on too many bills. "I put my name on thirty bills one year and he [Dini] held every one of them." Looking down at a stack of bills in his hand, Raggio told Dornan, "I have nothing in here with my fingerprints on it."

To be sure, Senator Raggio had become master of finding components of legislation being proposed by others, often those in the other house or party, and use them to forward initiatives he desired. He would then let that bill "carry his water."

In this way, Bill would skillfully piece together, from a number of other measures, the sum of the resulting legislation he desired. This denied his political foes the opportunity to "hold hostage," as a bargaining chip, legislation he might otherwise have had to introduce and thus be identifiable as his.

Bill told Dornan that inexperienced legislators had to learn to overcome the frustration of finding that some of their legislation was just not going to pass. "They must," Bill said, "be able to step back once in a while and say, 'This ain't the real world.'"

The hardest thing a new lawmaker must learn, he continued, was to say "no" to a constituent or fellow legislator. Bill noted that Senator Rawson was renowned for having a difficult time denying such requests. "If he were a woman," Raggio said in good humor, "he'd have been pregnant all the time."

By the end of 1995, there was no doubt Bill Raggio was the most influential person in the legislature. No piece of legislation was approved without his imprimatur, and virtually every penny spent by the state required his blessing.

As Jon Ralston observed:

> Rarely has Nevada had a lawmaker who could accomplish so much without saying anything. Raggio's very presence determines how legislation is written or not written, a barometer of what the governor and his comrades think they can pass through the Senate gatekeeper.[4]

As the session wound down, rumors surfaced that it might by Bill's last. At age seventy, with his wife recovering from a life threatening illness, and facing the unpleasant prospect of running for reelection the following year, many believed he was considering retirement.

Republicans took time during a final floor session to pay tribute to their leader. As one observer later put it, it appeared as if he were guest of honor at a surprise retirement party. Senator Rawson, Bill's heir apparent in such an event, gave a moving testimonial and Bill was presented with a set of golf clubs—a traditional retirement gift.

Senator Raggio was clearly touched by the gesture, and spoke eloquently of how much he appreciated their kindness. Yet, when Senator

Townsend was asked if this was, in fact, a retirement party for Senator Raggio, he chuckled and replied, "Don't bet on it. He'll be back."

# CHAPTER FIFTY-TWO

# Master of the Endgame (1997)

Clara Cardelli Raggio died on January 13, 1996, at age ninety-seven. She had lived independently all but the last five years. "She was a very compassionate, caring person," said her son Bill, "and a wonderful role model for my children and their children. She was the most important influence in my life."

The daughter of one of Nevada's pioneer families, Clara turned early adversity into becoming a strong, self-sufficient woman who understood the dignity of hard work, the honor of civic duty and the importance of instilling in her only son values that would serve him well in later life. Her love and guidance prepared Bill Raggio to be the man he became and, in turn, touched the lives of untold Nevadans and would resonate for generations.

Bill inherited his mother's empathy and consideration for those in society who needed help the most. As such, Clara would have been proud to witness a small ceremony later that year, just a few blocks south of where Bill had grown up.

The gathering was to honor the opening of the William J. Raggio Plaza in Reno, an apartment building designed to meet the needs of residents with severe physical handicaps. The plaza was named in Bill's honor because of his vision and leadership in pioneering legislation to better the lives of Nevada's neediest.

During his speech, Bill thanked his wife Dorothy, who, despite her poor health, attended that day, for her support in helping raise awareness for the project.

The Truckee Meadows Human Services Association in 2011 awarded him with their "Politician of the Year" award. In nominating him, the association noted that as far back as 1979, Bill had sponsored legislation to assist low-income people obtain affordable and safe housing for their families. Over his career, he had championed personal assistance services for the low-income disabled and the cause of Nevada's family of survivors of traumatic brain injury.

In 1995, when a critical legislative measure recognizing American Sign Language as the official language of deaf Nevadans appeared to be lost, Bill stepped in to save it. The deaf community had worked for six years on that bill and without Senator Raggio's intervention, "the dignity and culture of the deaf people would yet be recognized."[1]

In addition, Senator Raggio spearheaded the enactment of a small surcharge on telephone bills to provide access service to the deaf. "I kind of championed their issues from session to session," Bill would later say, "because they were a relatively small group and not heavily supported."

The following year, Bill would receive the Golden Hand Award from the National Association of the Deaf. The nomination concluded by describing Senator Raggio as "That rare politician who has used his power to help the powerless, his 'insider' knowledge to promote inclusion and his preferential status to level the playing field for all Nevadans regardless of color, economic circumstance or disability."

Bill's interests and support covered a broad segment of society. In addition to being honored for helping the disabled, the year 1996 also brought such distinctions as the Nevada Wildlife Federation's Legislative Conservationist of the Year Award; Life Membership in Friends of the UNR College of Education; Guardian of Small Business Award from the National Federation of Independent Business; and the Augustus Society's Italian American of the Year.

On April 15, 1996, ending months of speculation, Bill Raggio filed to run for his seventh term of office. Those closest to him hinted that while he did not want to run again, his sense of duty compelled him to reconsider—duty not only to his constituents, party and his caucus, but also to the state.

He knew the legislature was poised on the brink of political, sectional and philosophical divisions that would create chaotic, partisan infighting, the likes of which had never been seen in that body. He also knew that only strong leadership could avoid that and there was no one yet ready to take the helm.

Bill had the knowledge, and that knowledge equated to power. As Jon Ralston would write that day, "When he files today, the man who runs Carson City will be sending a message that, after nearly twenty-five years, still nobody does it better."[2]

The Democratic Party did not put forward a challenger.[3] When Bill pointed out to Dottie that this was the third consecutive election in which he would not have significant opposition, she replied, "My God Bill, has it ever occurred to you that no one else would want the damn job!"

By 1996, the culture of the legislature had changed dramatically. Gone were the years when the art of consensus building was a respected tool of power. As Lorne Malkiewich would say in 2008, an even more chaotic process would have likely evolved had not "members of the caucuses of both houses understood Senator Raggio's ability to see through the complexity of numerous issues at one time. You just don't walk in the door and do that."

\* \* \*

Before Senator Raggio created the Economic Forum, which began its work during the 1995 session, senate fiscal analysts came under great pressure toward the end of budget negotiations, as legislators tried to make the revenue forecasts fit their spending initiatives.

In 2009, former Senate Fiscal Analyst Gary Ghiggeri would talk of just how much the staff appreciated Senator Raggio's trust in them.

"We spent a great deal of time on preparing reports each day," Ghiggeri said, "to make sure we did not embarrass the senators if some of the information was inaccurate. Senator Raggio was one of few senators who actually took the time to read them and he understood how much work was involved in their preparation."

Most LCB staff members appreciated Senator Raggio's presence, but not all.

Jan Needham, for many years a bill draft advisor for the legislative legal division, observed that some of the women in the legislature found Senator Raggio's courtly manners, and pre-feminist terminology, offensive. "Although, it never bothered me in the least," said Needham in a 2010 interview.

When she first arrived at the legislature in the 1980s, several senators told Jan that because she was a woman she would never make it in that type of work. "Senator Raggio was never that way," she recalled. "In fact, once he learned I liked boxing, he would always make it a point of talking with me about the latest fights. He once went to a Mike Tyson bout in Las Vegas and brought me back a Tyson hat as a good-natured practical joke—because he knew I did not like Tyson."

Bill Raggio was not only making an impression on the LCB staff, but also those in his law firm of Jones Vargas.* Michael Alonso, a newly hired attorney fresh out of law school at the University of Southern California, recalled how awed he was by Bill Raggio's poise, wisdom and consideration, and how grateful he was for his guidance.

When Jones Vargas was involved in an $80 million-dollar sale of property on the Las Vegas Strip, Bill, fellow attorney John Sande III and Alonso flew to Las Vegas to meet with attorneys for the buyers. Bill told the twenty-eight-year-old Alonso he would be going in alone. Alonso was nervous and so asked what he should do once he got in the room.

"Don't give them anything. Not one thing," Raggio instructed.

Alonso then went into the meeting with the group of high-powered corporate lawyers. The lead attorney immediately asked, "Where's Raggio? Where are the big guns?"

Alonso told them that he was the only one they would be meeting with. The lead attorney became visibly irate and angrily asked, "Why

---

*In 1997, Vargas & Bartlett merged with the equally prestigious firm of Jones, Jones, Close & Brown, to form Jones Vargas.

does Raggio disrespect me by sending a boy to do a man's job?" He then stormed out. "The others began the meeting," Alonso later recalled, "and as we started going down the list of demands, I followed Bill's instruction not to give them anything. By page three, one lawyer says, 'Are you going to concede anything?' I replied, 'No.'"

With that, they abruptly ended the meeting and sent Alonso on his way.

Bill Raggio had called it correctly, because the buyers did come back and sign the deal without the benefit of the changes they were requesting. However, because it was a transaction regarding gaming, it took months for the buyer to obtain approval of a gaming license to close the deal.

The night before the scheduled closing, Alonso was on the phone and got into an argument with the other side about closing adjustments, a relatively small amount of $150,000 in an $80 million deal.

Bill entered the room during that late evening conference call, listened to the quibbling for a few minutes, then walked over and hung up the phone.

"I was clearly not happy that my deal was blowing up in front of me," Alonso later recalled.

> "What do we do now?" I asked Bill. He replied, "Mike, let's go eat some spumoni." So the two of us went out and had some spumoni ice cream and then Bill went to bed and, unlike me, slept like a baby. The next day, they accepted our terms, just as Raggio knew they would. I never learned so much as I did from Bill on that deal. Rather than his hanging up on them ruining my reputation—it made it.

Alonso clearly holds Bill Raggio in the highest esteem, pointing out that Bill "knows what the right thing is, and always does it." Alonso bridles when others say that because Bill is on the board of a large gaming corporation there must be a conflict of interest.

"There are many more legislators who are government employees and who benefit directly from increased budgets to their agencies," he said, "yet, rarely do they recuse themselves from votes like Senator Raggio does. With Bill Raggio, the state of Nevada comes first—and I don't even know where Jones Vargas is on that scale."

\* \* \*

On November 8, 1996, Bill won a seventh term in the Nevada legislature. Because he did not face a serious challenge during the campaign, he used his time and resources to help fellow Republican candidates across the state.

One of the most bitterly fought races was in Clark County between incumbent Senator Sue Lowden and Democratic challenger Valerie Wiener. Wiener, the daughter of Bill's former Las Vegas law partner, Lou Wiener, had aggressive support of the Culinary Workers Union.

Lowden and her husband, Paul, were large shareholders in the Santa Fe Hotel Casino, which had been involved in a yearlong strike with that union. Bill knew that Lowden was vulnerable and worked hard for her reelection. In the end, she was defeated. "The Culinary Workers Union targeted Lowden and worked hard to unseat her," Bill said. "She was a strong legislator and I hated to see her leave."

As the final election returns came in, it was clear that senate Republicans would retain a net majority of three seats. Democrats remained in control of the assembly, though their majority edge had now dropped to just eight seats. As Bill Raggio drove home from a victory party that night, a skunk ran in front of his car. "I suppose it was an omen of some sort," he later joked.

The Assembly Democratic Caucus met and named Joe Dini as speaker and Richard Perkins as majority leader. In the Republican caucus, Raggio was returned as majority leader and Chair of the Committee on Finance.

Before that occurred, Senate Minority Leader Dina Titus, the only southern Nevadan holding a leadership post, tried to shame the six southern members of the Republican caucus into dumping Bill by saying they lacked the courage. "Raggio has controlled the money for so long that the Republicans are afraid to buck him. He has a whip over them," she said.

Though southern Nevada now held thirty-nine of the sixty-three seats in the state legislature, unlike Senator Titus, few grumbled that their leaders were from the north end of the state. Seven of the ten legislators with the greatest longevity came from areas other than southern Nevada. Most southern lawmakers were satisfied that Bill Raggio and Joe Dini paid proper attention to the south.

On Election Day, Nevada voters also approved a constitutional amendment to enact term limits for a number of elected officials in Nevada, including members of the legislature. These provisions specified a lifetime twelve-year limit on an assembly members and senators.

The period would begin with the general election in 1998. Therefore, 2008 would be the last eligible election year for a member of the assembly who had been elected in 1998 and each election thereafter.

Senators who had been elected in 1998 could run for office in two additional elections—2002 and 2006—for a total of three terms or twelve years in office. However, because Senator Raggio was next scheduled to run again in 2000, rather than 1998, his final term was not set to expire until November 7, 2012. Few at the time, anticipated the seventy-year-old senator would even come close to approaching that limit and many expected him to announce his retirement from the legislature before the 2000 election campaign.

Before the session began, lawmakers and staff moved into their newly remodeled Legislative Building which afforded them additional office space and security. The first few months of the session contained little sense of urgency. Good economic times, coupled with Senator Raggio's pressure over the previous session for a conservative fiscal policy, had left the state with a budget surplus.

By April, the session schedule had become so lax that Senate President Pro Tempore Jacobsen lamented, "Everybody seems to be taking Thursdays and Fridays off. We've got to start forcing attendance in some manner."

Yet by July, these three-day a week floor sessions had been propelled into a frenzy of last minute activity and all night sessions. Tempers flared. In May, Senators Raggio and Titus engaged in a nasty squabble while debating Senate Bill 215, regarding campaign reform. Minority Leader Titus had introduced companion legislation and new amendments, holding up a final vote on the bill for several days.

On May 15, after she rose to propose yet another amendment, Majority Leader Raggio, in an unusual show of force, cut her off, threatened her with sanctions and maneuvered the Republican majority into not allowing her to speak again on the issue.

Senator Neal lashed out at Raggio, accusing him of an abuse of power "in stifling the voice of the minority." Later, Senator Titus attacked Raggio's motives, saying he only complained about violations of the rules of decorum when it suited his purposes.

Before adjourning for the day, Raggio defended his action, saying it was in keeping with the Mason's Manual, the rules of procedure used in the Nevada legislature. "This subject has been debated to the point of *ad nauseam.* Her amendment was just a rehash of everything we just argued."

The following day, both Senators apologized for their "intemperate remarks." Senator Raggio said, "We can have as much debate as we want on any issue, but we must observe the rules. Personalities and motives will not be discussed on the senate floor."

Ed Vogel, covering the tiff for the *Las Vegas Review Journal,* wrote that Raggio and Titus had been sniping at each other for the last few months over partisan issues. "Ironically," Vogel wrote, "Titus began the session in January vowing to tone down the amount of criticism of Raggio she dished out on the majority leader in the 1995 session."[4]

In 2009, Bill was asked about his long and contentious working relationship with Senator Titus. He replied, "I always had great respect for Senator Titus, but I felt there was too much partisanship, and maybe we [Republicans] were also to blame."

Because he had always worked so closely with Senator Gibson, Bill said, he anticipated that he and Senator Titus would have the same rapport.

"I would have discussions with Senator Titus about working together when the sessions would start," Bill noted, "and she agreed. However, within a few days, she would get on the senate floor and start throwing verbal brick bats at me over some issue. It just kept getting a little more difficult over time and that is kind of what started this process of division and partisanship [in the state senate]."

Senator Randolph Townsend later said that despite her best efforts, Senator Titus was just never comfortable in direct negotiation with Senator Raggio.

"Senator Titus did a marvelous job as minority leader," Randolph later said. "I do not know why she could not sit down and talk to Bill. It may have had to do with her feminist values being offended by his chivalrous style. I think Bill truly wanted to be able to deal with her directly, but it just never happened."

Thus, Townsend became the go-between for the two senators and continued in that capacity until Dina Titus left the senate. "I was the one who communicated nearly everything that went on between them outside of their direct contact in committee rooms or in the senate chambers. I'd be lying if I didn't say it was time consuming and, often, exhausting for me."

In 2010, now-Congresswoman Titus reflected upon her years in the Nevada senate. She said partisanship had evolved from regional differences, the south against the north, urban Las Vegas against the "cow counties," in which she included Washoe. However, as Reno grew and began to experience the same urban problems as Las Vegas, their differences lessened. Political parties in Nevada, she added, also reflected the mood of national partisanship.

More women were elected, she noted, and redistricting altered the equation, as the south got more seats in the legislature. "This changed the way we did a lot of our business," Titus said. "The old ways of drinking and fighting and negotiating in Jack's bar across the street no longer worked anymore."

> I think in the early years, the differences Bill and I experienced were generational. He is kind of Old School, Italian and Northern, where I was Southern, New Generation, and a woman. Yet, over

the years, our differences became less as we kind of grew old together in the senate.

I think from the outside, Bill Raggio and I looked like we were greater adversaries than we really were. We worked together, especially in the last ten years, more so than the first ten years. There was great mutual respect between the two of us. I do not know anyone who is wilier or smarter than Bill is at working the system, controlling that budget and finessing the end game.

* * *

Among the major issues that engaged the 69th Nevada Legislature was education reform. Governor Bob Miller, who was in his final and unprecedented tenth year in the Governor's Mansion, had established this as his legacy package. Consequently, he and Senator Raggio would engage in their most heated battle yet.

In February, Miller, along with Senator Titus, excoriated the Republican majority leader for questioning the governor's approach to reform. This compelled Senator Raggio to take the highly unusual step—for him—of calling a news conference to rebut their charges and accuse the governor of "using threats to coerce Republican senators into approving his programs."

However, Raggio was more comfortable with the situation than he let on, knowing that his bi-partisan style unusually drew regular Democratic support, often from Senator Bernice Mathews or Senator Jack Regan.

Raggio was gravely concerned about the state of education in Nevada, which had the highest high school dropout rate in the nation. He and Governor Miller also saw education reform as a major component in a strategy for curbing the rising rate of juvenile crime by reaching children early enough to give them the hope and the tools for a productive future. The two, however, disagreed on the method.

In addition to his belief that class-size reduction did not provide enough "bang-for-the-buck," Senator Raggio wanted greater accountability and standards, particularly in literacy, as a precursor to supporting Miller's "a computer-in-every-classroom" plan.

The accountability Bill Raggio demanded was included as a key component of the Nevada Education Reform Act (NERA), which Bill put together with the help of LCB staffers Pepper Sturm and Jeanne Botts. Bill would later credit the two, and their long hours of research and time spent testifying on behalf of the measure, with convincing the legislature and the governor to pass it into law.

"I even had support of the teachers' union," Bill noted with mild surprise.

Nevertheless, a number of legislators felt NERA was too much, too soon. Senator Joe Neal, just prior to the final vote, gave a lengthy address saying he was "skeptical" of the plan because it had not made a thorough enough study of all school districts and all curriculums. He was concerned that students in poor and politically disenfranchised districts would be further disadvantaged by certain aspects of the reform legislation.

Senator Raggio rose and offered an impassioned and eloquent rebuttal, saying the senate had for too long made excuses and "thrown money at a problem." The problems were still there, he agreed, and while the current measure was not a perfect one, it was a good one.

"I know the good senator was not content when I read the statistics," Raggio acknowledged. "A lot of them refer to people, like his own constituents, whom we have discarded—whom we have left to flounder."

His voice rising with emotion Senator Raggio concluded:

> If there is nothing else I have ever been party to in this session, or the sessions in which the good senator and I had both served, it will be that at least we tried to do our best to make a difference in what is the most important priority that we address here—education and the future of our children.

> So, I invite you to come along and help. We can all be critics, but we have done that, Senator, for twenty-five years, both you and I. Now it is time to march ahead, shoulder to shoulder, with our colleagues and with the education community. So let's cut out the alibis. Let's make a commitment to our kids and to their

future so that they can have the same advantages that all of us have enjoyed.

A roll call vote was then taken. Senate Bill 482 passed unanimously. "The Nevada Education Reform Act," Bill Raggio would later say, "was my greatest accomplishment as a legislator."

*  *  *

Before the session ended, legislation allowing for the establishment of charter schools was also approved, in the hope that it would encourage creative methods of education. The measure included safeguards to prevent the schools from becoming bastions of the economic elite.

In the end, Miller's third grade student-to-teacher ratio of ten to one was reduced to sixteen to one. The $27.5 million agreed upon for computers did not provide all the updated technology the governor hoped for, but created a sound base for future legislatures to expand upon. A *Reno Gazette Journal* editorial noted, "Governor Bob Miller and Senate Majority Leader Bill Raggio showed a good deal of statesmanship in their compromise on K –12 education funding."[5]

There were some complaints about the session, as well. The gaming industry once again appeared to be the big winner, gaining almost everything they requested and resisting once again the call for a tax on gross profits for casinos.

In addition, two questionable pieces of legislation were dramatically changed at the last minute, circumventing any deliberation on the issues. This included a 500-page amendment to the Electric Restructuring measure, making radical changes to the Public Service Commission. The other measure was a thirty-seven-page amendment presented by the Prime Cable Television lobby that, essentially, gutted a previously debated bill regarding telecommunications regulation.

Early lollygagging by some legislators drove the session to 169 days. This would help make a stronger case for Senator Raggio's proposal to limit the length of the sessions to 120 days. As one observer put it, "There is a great need to speed up the process and make it more efficient and economical. We need to end the game playing, hostage taking and childish tantrums that prevent good government from happening."

Columnist Jon Ralston observed that, despite the continuing transition to an increasingly younger group of legislators, and the emergence of many lawmakers of "substance," such as Assembly Majority Leader Richard Perkins, Assistant Majority Leader Barbara Buckley and Assemblymen Mark Amodei and David Parks, it was still Senator Raggio's legislature.

"He owned it," Ralston said. "He wielded power within his house and caucus without appearing to do so; he directed money where he wanted it to go, usually to northern Nevada; he dominated the horse-trading that characterizes the sessions, and the seventy-year-old was never better."[6]

In a post-session poll taken of legislators and lobbyists, Bill was selected as "The Most Effective Legislator of the 1997 Session," receiving three times more first-place votes than anyone else. On being selected for the honor, Bill would say only, "I can't please everyone, but I try to call them fairly. I'm mindful of the dignity of the process."[8]

Participants in the poll were encouraged to make comments, which would be kept anonymous when later published in the *Las Vegas Review Journal.* One contributor recalled how energetic and impeccably dressed and groomed Senator Raggio appeared in the closing hours of the session "in a building otherwise dominated by bleary-eyed zombies." Another simply declared, "No one knows the game better."

However, there was certainly nothing simple about this game.

Senator Raggio won the endgame in 1997, as he now seemed to do almost every session. Yet his endgame victory actually came a month before the session adjourned, when he and Assemblyman Morse Arberry, Chair of the Committee on Ways and Means, held a private meeting to discuss budget items. During the discussion, Arberry agreed that the assembly would process three bills regarding sexual predators, including one, Senate Bill 101, a chemical castration measure.

Later, when it became obvious that the Democratic caucus would not support two of the measures, including Senate Bill 101 (something Senator Raggio likely anticipated when the deal was struck), Arberry was forced to renege. Even though the Republican caucus also found the measures too repulsive to approve, to Raggio, Arberry had given his word.

Shortly before the end of session, Senator Raggio found the perfect hostage in Assembly Bill 339. The measure would have required the state to make an appropriation of nearly $3 million to help pay health insurance benefits for retired teachers, and was vital to the teachers associations' reputation for delivering on their lobbying efforts.

Ralston wrote of the maneuver: "Raggio is like Israel when it comes to paying ransoms; he won't. The hostage was DOA when it arrived in the senate, a victim of a master's power play."[8]

By the end of the last night of the session, Senator Raggio had demanded a heavy, some say punitive, penalty from the assembly for having not kept the deal, by winning funding for three major pet projects of senate Republican caucus members.

Probably as important, Bill had provided his side with important political weapons to use against the Democrats in the 1998 election. Though retired teachers would be angry with him for killing their health insurance assistance, they would be equally incensed at Democrats, who traded it away for a chemical castration bill.

Randolph Townsend, who knows Senator Raggio's methods better than anyone, would later say of his friend and colleague:

> If someone disagrees with Bill's policies it is never an issue. However, if they tell him something and do not honor it, he will not tolerate that. His ways of letting that person know can take several forms, and they almost never see it coming. Whether it is through the legislative process, a policy issue, or an issue at the end of the session, Bill knows how to exact his pound of flesh.

# CHAPTER FIFTY-THREE

# Pain and Partisanship
# (1998-1999)

Despite making a near-miraculous revival from a coma in late 1994, Dorothy Raggio remained gravely ill with cancer. Following the 1997 session, Bill sought to spend as much time as possible attending to her. They took a cruise to Hawaii and in the fall of that year joined Paul and Sue Lowden at a European conference of gaming attorneys.

Afterward, the Raggios celebrated their fiftieth wedding anniversary "early"; both couples renting a villa on Lake Como, along the Italian-Swiss border. "They must have just had a feeling about it," Paul Lowden would later say, referring to the chance that Dottie might not make it until the following August. "And it turned out to be a pretty good time."

On April 4, 1998, the American Cancer Society, with Honorary Chairpersons Governor and Mrs. Bob Miller, held the Silver Baron's Ball at the Reno Hilton in honor of Dorothy and Bill, "for providing inspiration through their strength and courage in facing this devastating disease." Five hundred people attended, though Dottie was unable to do so. Bill and their three children were there, as well as their grandchildren, four of whom performed musically.

Dorothy died three days later.

On April 13, over 900 people attended her funeral mass at Reno's Little Flower Catholic Church, all entering through an honor guard from law enforcement agencies. Bishop Philip Straling presided, accompanied by Monsignor Robert Bowling and family friends Monsignor Leo Mc-Fadden and Father Frank Murphy.

Daughter Leslie Righetti gave a touching eulogy, referring to Dottie as a kind woman who always sent early Christmas cards to her grandchildren, each card containing an affectionate personal note and a silver dollar taped to the inside. "I am confident," said Leslie in closing, "my mother will be remembered as the thoughtful person she was."

Though Dorothy never tried to influence Bill's decisions in the legislature, her concern for public policy and how it affected the average person, led her to become active in a number of organizations.

She was a member of the PTA and sat on the boards of the Make-a-Wish Foundation and the Nevada Girls Training Center in Caliente. In 1977, Governor O'Callaghan appointed her as the first public representative on the state Board of Dental Examiners, a position in which she served for many years. The Dorothy Raggio Memorial Scholarship endowment was established at UNR by family and friends to carry on her tradition of caring.

In a moving tribute, columnist and long-time family friend Rollie Melton wrote,

> Through the couple's half century together, whether he was the young district attorney or the foremost legislative hitter, she was his omnipresent sounding board. She knew Bill Raggio better than any other person, and was patient with his torrid agenda and even with most of his critics…No man had a more graceful, loyal cheerleader.[1]

* * *

The 1998 political campaign began a few weeks after Dorothy's funeral. Although Bill would not be running in this election, he was not out of range of political fire. In May, a *Las Vegas Review Journal* article sought to remind voters that neither house of the legislature had been led by a southerner for fifteen years. A number of lawmakers were speculating that a change might occur in 1999.[2]

Senator Dina Titus was most critical of Bill, accusing him of showing a lack of sensitivity to Southern Nevada interests. "Raggio is the old guard," she said. "He is hanging on for Reno until the end." Titus said this was particularly true of the legislative "pork," those projects decided upon with funds left over after the budget appropriation process had been completed. She felt the south did not get a proportionate share.

Former Governor Kenny Guinn would later comment on such charges:

> Bill Raggio always looks at what is best for the people of Nevada. He never thinks of himself, or of the state, as being north and south. Although once it got down to there being only so much money left, he always considered those who elected him at the end, but this is only after he had considered all the other areas and needs of all the people.

An example of this had occurred at the end of the 1995 session when Bill engineered a $3.2 million grant to bail out the National Automobile Museum in Reno, which was on the verge of defaulting on bank loans. Although no other pork barrel project was as large, he did see to it that $2.5 million was set aside for the Railroad Museum in southern Nevada's Boulder City.

Most did not see a problem with the northern leadership. Republican Jon Porter, of Boulder City said, "He supports our needs whether we live in Las Vegas or Reno."

Assembly Majority Leader Richard Perkins, a Democrat from Henderson, said,

> There's a perception that southern Nevada loses under northern leadership, but I've never been able to find a single solitary issue where the south has suffered. We in the south are our own worst enemies. The people in the north serve longer and become leaders. Here, we have greater turnover and a lot of new folks.[3]

Many political watchers observed that the 1998 campaign had been "cleaner" than previous ones. This change was probably due to legislation championed by Senator Raggio in the previous session to prevent negative campaigning, by empowering the Ethics Commission to act as, what some later labeled, "the truth squad" for election campaigns.

Ethics Commission members could now hold public meetings to consider whether campaign advertisements and statements were appropriate and question candidates about their purpose in, what Bill Raggio termed "airing dirty laundry about each other."

Candidates, who lied about opponents, could be fined up to $30,000. Bill was confident these changes, if later upheld in court, would lead to less negative campaigning. "It should have a chilling effect on people," he said. "I think they will be a little more careful about what they say about an opponent."

Recent judicial races in Nevada, at all levels, had become notorious for running more malicious campaigns than those for non-judicial offices. Bill's former "one-shot" running mate in the state senate, Cliff Young, now the Chief Justice of the State Supreme Court, took Bill's lead and established the Committee on Judicial Ethics and Election Practices.

However, Justice Young was not optimistic about the prospects for change, saying, "In judicial races you can't campaign on a platform, so you get all the negative things you can get on your opponent. Ultimately it becomes a contest between the spin doctors."

The chief justice questioned whether legislative or judicial panels constitutionally could stop negative speech. Courts routinely held that campaign statements are protected under the first amendment. "I'm a little cynical," he said. "But we have to give it a try."

In 2010, Senator Raggio would reflect on the issue. The remedy when somebody slanders you or libels you, is to go sue them, he explained, however, that takes two or three years in court and so in the course of a short campaign, it is ineffective.

Bill continued, "Therefore, we were trying to figure out some way that we could get an immediate action. I proposed that we provide the Ethics Commission with authority to allow somebody to file a complaint when something malicious or untrue was said about them in a campaign." The commission would then have five or ten days to review it and respond.

The law would be challenged in 2002 by the American Civil Liberties Union of Nevada and the Nevada Press Association.

An effort to abolish the "truth squad" during the 2003 session failed when Senator Raggio insisted that the provisions remain in the law. However, the law was subsequently declared unconstitutional in a U.S. district court ruling, which held that it violated the due process clause of the 14th amendment. In 2005, the state legislature would eliminate the Ethics Commission review of campaign statements.

Bill would later say, "I never thought it was a bad process, but that is what happens when you go up against the media, who think that any time you restrict someone in any way from expressing himself, it is to be a violation of freedom of speech."

Throughout the 1998 campaign, Bill worked hard to reach voters about the importance of passing a ballot measure to control the length of legislative sessions. Passage would ensure a constitutional amendment to limit legislative sessions to just 120 calendar days. Passage would also require the governor to submit the Executive Budget to the legislature at least fourteen days before the start of each session. The overall change would, according to proponents, promote greater efficiency, result in millions of dollars in operating cost savings and allow the citizen-legislators less time away from their families and sources of livelihood. The most recent legislative session, in 1997, which had lasted a record 169 days, and cost $15 million, provided impetus for the measure.

Senator Raggio had been calling for such a measure for twenty years, and was now about to see it come to fruition. Dina Titus, who had originally disagreed with Bill on the need for a 120-day session, joined him in endorsing the measure. However, she warned that other states with limited regular sessions seemed to require numerous special sessions to finish business. The ballot question passed overwhelmingly on Election Day, and would take effect with the 1999 legislative session.

Two days after the election, Bill was again selected as majority leader. With the defeat of Democratic Senator Ernie Adler by Republican Mark Amodei, the senate now held a twelve-to-nine majority. Senator Bernice Mathews was reelected to her second term and now held the distinction of being the only Democrat in the senate from outside Clark County.

Gaming interests once again were the largest contributors of campaign funds to candidates. Gamers had become increasingly interested in the politics of neighboring California, where voters were considering the expansion of casino gambling on Indian reservations.

Nevada gaming interests funneled large amounts of campaign contributions to defeat the proposition and also defeat candidates like Governor Gray Davis, who favored expansion of "Las Vegas style" gaming on reservations throughout the state. Despite their efforts, the measure passed. Tribes in other states would soon follow California's lead.

The potential impact on tourism, due to casino gaming in California, did not bode well for Nevada. The blow would likely be strongest in northern Nevada, where casinos in Lake Tahoe and Reno already had to contend with unpredictable seasonal problems, such as snow in the high Sierra Nevada Mountains, which curtailed the ability of travel from California.

Yet, in 1998, Nevada's gaming industry was booming and few seemed to be paying attention to the dark economic clouds forming on that western horizon.

* * *

The 1997 election brought change to the executive branch. Republican Kenny Guinn defeated Las Vegas Mayor Jan Laverty Jones in the race for governor and former Clark County Commissioner Lorraine Hunt was elected lieutenant governor. Thus, in addition to majority control of the senate, there would also be a Republican presiding over it and a Republican governor.

Kenny Guinn came to the statehouse with a broad range of experience as an educator, administrator and businessperson.* Of outgoing Governor Bob Miller, Bill would later say, "We had many disagreements on issues, but I felt that kindled mutual respect for one another. We were both strong willed, both having been prosecutors, and interestingly, two Nevadans who had served as president of the National District Attorney's Association."

Bill admired the way Miller had wisely surrounded himself with very capable staff:

> Among them were Scott Craigie, who served as Chief of Staff, and later Director of the Department of Health and Human Services. Judy Matteucci was an extremely capable director of the Budget Division; Larry Struve headed Labor and Commerce; Roland Westergard was Director of Conservation and Natural Resources; Stan Jones remained head of Employment Security; Gerry Griepentrog was director of Human Resources, who was assisted by very capable administrators such as Del Frost in Rehabilitation and Linda Ryan in Welfare. Garth Dull headed Transportation and former budget director Bill Bible became head of the Gaming Control Board.

* * *

The 1999 legislative session began on February 1. Secretary of the Senate Jan Thomas began by reading a poignant letter from Leslie Righetti to her father, offering moral support as he began his fourteenth legislative session, now without his wife Dorothy.

---

*Born in Exeter, California, the son of migrant farm workers, Guinn began his professional career as a teacher in Las Vegas, Guinn eventually became Clark County superintendent of schools from 1969 to 1978, earning a Ph.D. in education along the way. During this time, he would become involved in the legislative process, participating on numerous panels to study education policy in Nevada and testifying before committees. Guinn would later become vice president of Nevada Savings and Loan, then president and head of the Board of Director's of PriMerit Bank. From 1988 to 1993, he was CEO of Southwest Gas Corporation, later becoming Chair of that company's Board of Directors. He served on the boards of various other organizations and had, most recently, been interim president of the University of Nevada, Las Vegas.

Leslie's letter ended with a touch of humor, observing that with 120 day limit, and the session ending on May 31, her dad would be able to attend his first grandchild's high school graduation on June 6.

Bill used that remark to cue his colleagues for action: "Be prepared to work and you'll be able to enjoy June with your families instead of sitting around here griping with each other."

Newly elected Governor Guinn immediately sent a hand-delivered note to Senator Raggio asking for a meeting so they could get things off to "a smooth start" between the two branches of government. Guinn first came to know Senator Raggio, on more than an informal basis, in 1973 when he began participating on issues related to education and testifying before legislative committees.

In a 2009 interview, Governor Guinn recalled those days: "As young person, in my thirties, I wanted to hook up with what I saw as a rising star in the legislature. That decision paid off for education." Guinn said he thought of Bill Raggio as his legislative mentor "because he had a way of guiding a person in the right direction."

As a governor, Kenny Guinn would often go to the legislature to testify personally on bills he cared about, rather than send a surrogate:

> I would go comment on it in committee and tell them that I was prepared to sign the bill. I learned that technique from Bill Raggio and it was very effective. Bill did not give me inside information, but would give me suggestions on how the system worked and on techniques to accomplish more goals. If a person with my experience needed to go to Bill to get down to the depths of issues, it just gives you an idea of the scope of his knowledge.

This close bond between Governor Guinn and Senator Raggio would last a lifetime.

Both men believed in quality education for Nevadans, and the 1999 session would hear much debate on these issues. By early March, the impact of newly implemented high school standards became evident when the state Department of Education announced that nearly 2,000 seniors failed to pass the new proficiency examination and were in danger of not graduating.*

As an incentive, Governor Guinn proposed using a recent tobacco settlement windfall to establish what he termed the "Millennium Scholarship."[4] This would allow every qualified high school graduate in Nevada an opportunity to receive a college education.[7]

In an effort to improve the quality of education in the state, the legislature also changed the 1967 Nevada Plan for education funding, by combining the Class-Size Reduction (CSR) Program with the Distributive School Account (DSA).[5]

The Nevada Plan, had to be tweaked each session to accommodate changes brought on by growth in the state.

"Most people do not understand the Nevada Plan," Governor Guinn said in 2009, "but it is a fair plan that has stood up to challenges in the court system. The Plan withstood those legal tests because it has an equalizing factor that follows for the complex diversity of the state."

Bill Raggio later recalled meeting Guinn for the first time in early 1973. Bill was a freshman legislator and Guinn was running the state's largest school district. Guinn pulled him aside in Carson City and said he wanted to talk about the Nevada Plan.

Bill asked what the Nevada Plan was, and Guinn explained it was the blueprint used by the state to calculate basic support to the public schools. He then went on to give Bill a basic course in the intricacies of the state's budget and education funding formula.

"At the time Kenny must have thought," Bill said self-deprecatingly, "Where do they get these people they send to the legislature?"

Guinn proved to be an invaluable resource when it came to understanding facts and figures, Raggio said, and he had a clear vision of what Nevada needed.

---

*The senate passed a bill late in the 1999 session to spend $300,000 on summer school classes for students who had not been able to pass the mathematics proficiency test. Senator Raggio introduced that bill in the face of demands by some educators to lower the score or exempt students from the test.

Because Guinn understood the intricacies of such systems, he was an opponent of term limits for legislators, saying there was nothing as effective in dealing with complex issues as longevity.

"You just cannot fund projects one year and not the next. It takes a long time to grasp some systems." Guinn said. "It takes a long time to replace someone with Bill Raggio's expertise."

Dan Klaich, Chancellor of the Nevada System of Higher Education, is astonished by Raggio's ability to synthesize a discussion down to its essence. "You don't see many people who can do it," Klaich said in 2010. "There are several reasons he can. You have to have an encyclopedic memory, which he definitely does. You have to have the ability to listen carefully to what people are saying and figure out what the core of their belief is, and what is fluff. Then you have to be able to put it all together. Bill is a master of that."

Chancellor Klaich added that Bill knows just how long the discussion should go and can cut off a discussion without offending the participants."Bill is firm but not offensive," Klaich concluded, "and is a marvelous role model for anyone who wants to be a leader."

As a follow up to mandating higher standards for K-12 students during the previous session, the 1999 legislature approved $7 million to create four regional teacher-training programs across the state called Regional Professional Development Programs.

Longtime educator Bill Hanlon would zealously promote the concept, later commented, "Legislators almost always mistake activity with achievement." Bill Raggio, Hanlon said, was the exception.

At 11:44 p.m., with just sixteen minutes left on the final day of session, the 70th Nevada Legislature adjourned sine die, to which Senator Raggio teasingly lamented, "We have time to spare."

The legislature's first experience with the 120-day limit, received mixed reviews. Some, like Senator Ray Rawson, felt issues were given greater scrutiny under a session with unlimited days, though he did not think annual sessions were the answer, either.

Assembly Speaker Joe Dini had no problem with the new limit, saying,

"It was a good session. We did not raise any taxes, and the governor made sure we did not raise the fees. I think we took care of everybody."

Jim Richardson, a longtime lobbyist for the Nevada Faculty Alliance would say of Dini and Raggio, "It would've been extremely problematic to make the 120 day session work without them."

\* \* \*

While most knew Bill was adjusting to Dorothy's recent death, many did not know of an extremely serious health issue that was preying upon his mind throughout the grueling session.

On December 30, 1998, just weeks before the legislative session was to begin, Bill was diagnosed with melanoma. For years, a mole on the left side of his face had been routinely misdiagnosed. Upon seeking a second opinion, a biopsy was performed. The mole was determined to be cancerous and surgically removed.

Bill thought that would be the end of the problem, but in December 1999, he learned the cancer had returned and metastasized down his neck in the form of stage-three melanoma. After removing a lump in his neck, doctors referred Bill for a treatment called Interferon, which like chemotherapy would have debilitated him for a year.

Looking for alternatives to that, Bill was referred by Dr. John Dooley to the M.D. Anderson Cancer Center in Houston, where Dr. Kie-kian Ang, a noted radiological oncologist, found him a suitable candidate for treatment. In the spring of 2000, Bill underwent successful radiation therapy on his face and neck over a period of six weeks.

After the 1999 session ended, family and friends worried that Bill would have trouble adjusting to life alone. Governor Guinn recalled that Bill would often decline evening engagements saying that, "He had to go home and feed the dog." John Sande, III spoke of how he worried about Bill "wandering around that big house all alone."

Yet Bill did his best to fill the days with interim legislative duties and extensive travel. In that year alone, he journeyed to such diverse destinations as Indianapolis, Ireland, Barcelona, Singapore and Quebec. The year before, he had traveled to Taiwan and Japan along with Governor

Miller and some southern Nevada business people to promote tourism to Nevada. Bill had paid his own way on that trip because he was interested in the issue.

In April, Bill was the recipient of the Lifetime Achievement Award at a gala held by the National Italian American Foundation at the Rio Hotel pavilion, with 800 people in attendance.

In July, Bill was honored for his contribution to UNR Wolf Pack athletics over the years and, amusingly, received his letterman jacket for being on the university's basketball team fifty-five years earlier.

He accepted the honor with his usual grace and humor, acknowledging that there were few men on campus then, since most were off fighting in World War II, and so it was not very difficult to make the team. "I wasn't much of a basketball player. I think I scored just one point the entire season."[6]

In that year, Bill also received the UNR Alumnus of the Year Award, presented to him by President Joe Crowley during halftime of the school's homecoming football game.

Kenny Guinn later provided his own tribute Bill Raggio's contribution to the people of Nevada: "He became the finest legislator I have been associated with in my forty-plus years, because he had the ability to think ahead. It turned out we all had a friend in Bill Raggio."

However, some would disagree with Guinn. The political climate of Nevada was changing in step with the national trend toward partisanship and non-cooperation between the parties. A growing ideological rift within the Republican Party would magnify the problem. All this converged as the coming legislative session faced the thorny and traditionally heated task of reapportionment and redistricting, and was about to test Bill Raggio's ability like no other session before.

# CHAPTER FIFTY-FOUR

# Redistricting: An Opportunity Missed (2001)

Senator Raggio would keep to his usual busy schedule throughout 2000, willing to appear almost anywhere to help raise funds, not only for his party, but for worthy causes throughout the state.

In April, he was guest of honor at a dinner hosted by the American Cancer Society. The theme was a 1960s "Shindig," and, in a departure from the usual cocktail attire required at such events, 400 prominent Reno area residents dressed as hippies and "flower children."

Bill, however, arrived in a business suit, and later deadpanned while at the podium, "I don't know what everyone is laughing about. I was told to wear what I did in the 1960s, so that's what I did." Then, without missing a beat, added, "I was prosecuting your kind of people back then."

Later in the year, Bill would be honored at a dinner hosted by the American Lung Association of Nevada. Over 700 people attended and the event raised over $200,000 for lung disease prevention education programs. He would later receive the Nevada State Medical Association's Nicholas J. Horn Award in recognition of his distinguished contribution to health care and medicine in Nevada.

On June 24, 2000, South African Anglican Archbishop Desmond Tutu spoke in Reno at the invitation of the Millennium Speaker program. Bill Raggio, a board member of the E.L. Weigand Foundation, which supported the program, presented a Nevada tribute to the 1984 Nobel Peace laureate.

He recalled having spent ten days in South Africa in July 1993, when, as national chair of ALEC, he led a contingent of state legislators and business people invited by the then-apartheid government to exchange ideas. While there, they also met with rights activist Archbishop Tutu in Soweto, the impoverished and overcrowded slum near Johannesburg where blacks were then forced to live.

In welcoming the archbishop to Nevada, Senator Raggio said he would never forget the lively 1983 discussion he had with Tutu, after which he told his traveling colleagues, "That guy is going somewhere." Bill then confessed to the audience: "How little did I realize just how far!"

\* \* \*

The election season began in April with a rift at the Washoe County Republican Convention. Several social conservative delegates walked out because pro-choice activists were allowed to participate. Raggio lamented this fissure, saying, "I've been through a lot of these wars, and the other party doesn't beat us. We beat ourselves."

Between July 31 and August 3, Bill, along with Governor Guinn and other prominent Republican state leaders, attended the party's national convention in Philadelphia. Delegate Raggio helped draft platform language opposing a nuclear waste dump in Nevada. At the conclusion of the convention, Nevada delegates joined the majority in selecting George W. Bush as the party's candidate for president.

Back in Reno, Bill would begin his reelection campaign. His would be the only senatorial seat being decided that year in northern Nevada, and he would have no opposition from the Democrats.

During that year, two initiative petitions were launched to increase taxes. Senator Joe Neal championed one of the ballot measures, which sought to raise the maximum tax rate of casino gross gaming revenues from 6.25% to 11.25%. Neal admitted that the ceiling was excessive, but explained that casinos had an opportunity in 1999 to negotiate a hike to 8.25% that he had proposed, but were way "too arrogant" to talk about the issue, despite being "prodded by Senator Raggio to do so."

The Nevada State Education Association also circulated an initiative to establish a net profits tax on businesses. Governor Guinn, whose staff was in the midst of a study on state income and spending, asked Neal and the union to defer their initiatives and let the upcoming legislature work out the issue. Both refused. In the end, Neal would fail to get his initiative on the ballot, and the NEA measure was halted by a state Supreme Court ruling.

Two other initiatives were also on the ballot that year, one approving a new section of the Nevada constitution recognizing marriage as only existing between a male and a female, and the other legalizing the use of medical marijuana. Both passed by resounding margins.

Two days after being reelected to his eighth term, Bill Raggio was again selected as majority leader and chair of the Senate Committee on Finance. Initially, Republicans would have the same twelve to nine majority as they did in 1999; however, Democratic Senator Ray Shaffer would soon switch parties, giving them a thirteen-to-eight edge. For the first time in Nevada political history, an election had resulted in no new faces in the senate. The session would begin on February 5.

Republican George W. Bush was elected president and won the state of Nevada, receiving about 5% more of the total popular vote than his opponent Vice President Al Gore. As such, Bush would receive all four of Nevada's electoral votes. Nationally, he had won 271 electoral votes to Gore's 266 (The U.S. Constitution requires a minimum of 270 votes to win). Though Gore had won the popular vote by over 500,000 votes, Bush had succeeded in obtaining one electoral vote more than the minimum required for victory.

Bill Raggio had been selected at the Nevada Republican Convention earlier that year to act as one of the state's four electors. On December 19, at a ceremony in the state capitol building, they cast their votes, one of which happened to be the 271st.*

---

*Just twelve days earlier, a U.S. Supreme Court ruling had stopped a recount of votes in four Florida counties, thus awarding all that state's electoral votes to Bush.

Arguments were immediately put forth that the Electoral College was archaic and that the presidential election should be decided by winner of the popular vote. Bill disagreed:

> If the election were based upon popular votes, the candidates would spend all of their time on the west coast, the industrial areas surrounding Chicago and the Atlantic seaboard. If you study the history surrounding the creation of the college, it is for exactly that reason. The small states would not have joined the union without some assurance that they wouldn't be overshadowed by the states with larger populations.

In late November, Bill became ill and went to the doctor for a checkup. The physician immediately sent him to Saint Mary's Regional Medical Center where a six-way heart bypass surgical procedure was performed. Before going under the knife, Bill joked, "I hope my doctors are Republicans because I don't want a recount."

The medical procedure was successful, though it would take Bill months to regain his strength.

Before the 2001 session began, Governor Guinn met privately with GOP and Democratic lawmakers to discuss upcoming legislation and renew his pledge of no new taxes. However, the governor warned that if changes were not made, the state would be facing a $1 billion deficit by the end of the decade.

As the session got under way, many legislators voiced concern that the relatively new 120 day limit would make it impossible to complete both their usual biennial business and the thorny task of redistricting required of them that year. Senate Majority Leader Raggio felt otherwise, encouraging his fellow lawmakers to focus on the business at hand in order to complete their work as scheduled.

In May, the Economic Forum determined that the governor's proposed budget would need to be trimmed by $121.5 million due to a decline in tax revenues. The two main sources of income, gaming and sales taxes, which accounted for about 75% of the revenues, had dropped dramatically. Analysts said the decline in gaming taxes was largely due to the slowdown of new mega resorts in Las Vegas and fewer California gamblers crossing the border due to the increase in casino gaming on Indian reservations. California residents also faced skyrocketing energy costs and a drop in disposable income.

In response, Senator Raggio proposed that the state take a larger share of property taxes from growing counties, including Washoe, rather than raise taxes.

Twenty years earlier, to prevent passage of a California Proposition 13-type ballot initiative to cap property taxes, lawmakers agreed to increase sales taxes as a primary source of revenue and give most of the existing property tax dollars to the counties. Now, said Senator Raggio, the state deserves a larger portion of that revenue.

"The problem is the taxes we are collecting are not being allocated in proportion to the responsibilities," he explained. "I'm not saying that we should take anything away. I'm talking about future growth." Bill said the plan would not alter current revenue distribution but would increase the state's share in future valuation growth. He believed it would be clear to everyone that looking forward to a state share of any new property taxes would be fair. A hearing was held, and, as Bill recalled in 2009,

> They came out in droves, all of the lobbyists for the local school governments, all of those who obviously shared, or received property tax, and testified that this would be the undoing of the whole financial structure. My idea did not go very far, but evidently, I was on the right track because in later special sessions we have had to take property tax revenue from local governments. I guess I was a little ahead of my time.

As the session wound down, the debate over reapportionment became rancorous. Senator Raggio led Republicans and rural lawmakers in an effort to increase the number of seats in the legislature in order to ensure areas outside Clark County were adequately represented.

In addition to this redistricting, the state's rapid population growth over the past decade now allowed it to form a third congressional district. Republicans and Democrats vied for an advantage in the new district, pressured daily by national party leaders who were intent on capturing the seat for a House of Representatives that held just a five-seat (Republican) majority.

By the morning of the 120th day, Democrats had agreed to add six state legislators, which would protect northern seats, but insisted the deal include a majority of registered Democratic voters in the new congressional district. Since Democrats typically have lower voter turnout, Democratic leaders were pushing for a 52% to 48% ratio. Republicans wanted the new district split fifty-fifty.

Bill later recalled the problems that occurred. He had entered into an agreement with Speaker Richard Perkins that they would expand the senate by two seats, and four in the assembly.

"Perkins gave me his word on that," Bill said, "but when we got into the actual negotiations on reapportionment and redistricting, he informed me that we had a problem with the redistricting on the Congressional seat we were adding in Clark County."

Bill felt the Democrats reneged on the promise to expand the state legislature because they did not get everything they wanted in the creation of this new congressional district. It certainly would have been better for the area outside Clark County to have a larger number of legislators, Bill added, and, obviously, it would not have impacted Clark County because they would have also gotten more.

"I am chagrined to this day," Senator Raggio admitted, "because I thought he had given me his word on that."

Bill recalled another problem that adversely affected his party in the legislature during that session. Thanks to what he called a "breakdown of leadership in the assembly," things did not work out as well for the Republicans as they had hoped:

Assemblymen Lynn Hettrick and Peter Ernaut were working on redistricting with the Democrat leadership, and we were trying to work together to be sure that the assembly Republicans were treated fairly. On the last evening that this was being finalized, Hettrick was supposed to be coming in to work on this, but did not show. I called him at his home in Gardnerville and he told me he wouldn't be able to come in. He said he'd had a couple of martinis and was not coming back that night. As a result, the assembly Republicans did not get all they wanted to work out in the redistricting. It was startling.

Bill concluded that, because of this, the Republicans "lost the seat that Jake [Senator Jacobsen] would have ended up with if we had expanded the legislature like we wanted to, and like we were promised. We would not have lost that night."

No compromise was reached before the end of the regular session. To complete the redistricting process, Governor Guinn called a special session to be convened on June 14, including twenty-three additional measures for reconsideration.[1]

The special session lasted two days and, despite some foot-dragging by assembly Republicans, a redistricting agreement was reached. The agreement would keep the legislature at sixty-three members and provide a new congressional district evenly split between Republicans and Democratic voters.*

Under the plan, Washoe County would retain all four of its senate seats. All senate incumbents would be protected with one exception. The senate seat held by Douglas County's Republican senator, Lawrence Jacobsen would be absorbed into the district of Republican Senator Mike McGinness of Fallon.

The state's two rural senate districts grew in size. Senator Dean Rhoads would now represent a district encompassing over 75,000 square miles.

With regard to other matters before the legislature, there was the usual horse-trading. During the negotiations, several bills were held hostage

---

*The new Third Congressional District seat was won by Republican Jon Porter.

by each side. The assembly voted down a measure for funding a school financial accountability program that had been supported by Senator Raggio.

In response, Raggio delayed votes on a measure switching child welfare services from the state to the counties, which was a pet project of Assemblywoman Barbara Buckley. "I have a hunch that bill will be resurrected," Raggio said of his school financial accountability measure. Once the assembly reconvened, the first action was to pass his school finance measure, and within thirty minutes Buckley's stalled child welfare services bill was approved by the senate.

"This is a disgusting display of control," said Democratic Assemblywoman Chris Guinchigliani. Others that session saw it differently.

Republican Senator Mark James viewed it more as Bill's unique ability to work with members of both parties and reach across the aisle. "Senator Raggio provided leadership not just for the Republican side, but for the Democratic side as well," James said. "He is a truly unique leader, and I don't want this to sound like hyperbole, but I cannot imagine that there is a leader like him in another state legislature that has so much respect across party lines."

In 2010, Assembly Speaker Barbara Buckley would recall that as the new Assembly speaker, she experienced "a bit of a learning curve" in dealing with Senator Raggio. "He always intimidated me a little bit, before I got to know him," Buckley recalled. "One thing I learned early on is that he has an ability to put someone at ease very quickly because he can be very charming and very funny. In time, I also learned his negotiating style, which simply put is: He will not be moved before he is ready to move."

Speaker Buckley explained that no matter how many times she might approach him with what she considered a fair proposal, he would decline discussion. "This is because he had already figured out the day he was going to move," she said. "Over the years, Senator Raggio has learned that he can get a lot more if he holds out."

Lorne Malkiewich also recognized a pattern in Senator Raggio's negotiating strategy, though he thought it might be better termed an "intuition.":

> What makes a leader great is in his or her ability to know the precise moment to push in one direction or another. Raggio will typically answer the very first time with "No." After more research, and more pressure on him, he will sometimes begin to give in and say, "Maybe a little." Finally, after much time and discussion, he may go along with it—but at the point when he does, he wants it clear that you owe him.

\* \* \*

Shortly after the 2001 special session concluded, Republican State Senator Bill O'Donnell blasted Senator Raggio in a story carried on the front page of the *Las Vegas Sun*. O'Donnell said he was leaving the legislature when his term ended in 2002. He criticized members of the GOP caucus who failed to support him in his recent move to wrest the majority leader job from Raggio and "bring control of the leadership position to the south."

"Legislators are more afraid of Raggio and more concerned with their own reelection than doing what is morally correct," said O'Donnell. He likened Bill to dictators such as Joseph Stalin and Idi Amin, and said the majority leader ruled by fear and punished lawmakers like O'Donnell who did not support him. O'Donnell said he was discouraged and felt he was blocked from doing what he wanted to do because of people like Raggio, Assembly Speaker Richard Perkins and lobbyist Harvey Whittemore.

During the last days of the 2001 regular session, O'Donnell had surprised Raggio and other Republicans when he voted to block a Republican redistricting bill from passing out of committee. Ironically, that redistricting plan would have likely helped O'Donnell win reelection.

Senator O'Donnell had once so infuriated the late Assemblyman Marvin Sedway for "grandstanding" over a piece of legislation with which he had little to do, that it prompted the pugnacious Sedway to exclaim,

"I'd like to tear his liver out with my fingernails!"[3]

In 2009, Bill Raggio was less dramatic in his reaction to O'Donnell's behavior, noting that he was "a very emotional guy."

"He would often come to my office in tears," Bill said, "and I would have to console him. He had a habit of telling lobbyists he would support them and then changing his mind and vote otherwise. As majority leader, they would come to me and I would have to help straighten things out between him and the lobbyists several times."

Bill added that in two elections, he had to go with O'Donnell to meetings of supporters and convince them to support the senator, "otherwise, he would not have been reelected." In newspaper polls as the end of the session, O'Donnell was often voted as the state's worst senator. "I have never really known when, or why, he turned on me," Raggio said, "but I think he resented me at the end."

Mark James did not recall Senator Raggio as being threatening or heavy handed, saying it just "was not in his nature." For James, Raggio's philosophy could best be described in the advice he often gave that it was "more important to be respected than feared."

Mark James stated that Senator Raggio elicited the compliancy needed from his caucus, and the compromise he needed from people, because they respected his wisdom and the reason he was making his decision.

"You never got that undertone that he had a personal agenda," James noted, "and when he was being tough about an issue, he was doing it for the right reasons. And that's how he got us to follow."

Joe Brezny, who later acted as manager of the Senate Republican Caucus, would say in 2009, "It is about compromise. If they are smart enough to be tactical, the legislators will take something back to the electorate. If they show up as ideologues; going to change the world; not tactical; starry-eyed; it is Senator Raggio's job to remind them they have a constituency to care for."

At the end of the 2001 special session, Jon Ralston wrote of the senate majority leader:

Bill Raggio is still the best there is—maybe the best there ever was—in the building. This was the first session, after all the recent whispers, where his age showed, and he lost on one thing he really wanted—legislative expansion. It was what he wanted, right? [2]

# CHAPTER FIFTY-FIVE

# Caucus Revolt (2003)

On March 9, 2002, Bill received one of the great honors of his life when the University of Nevada, Reno unveiled the new William J. Raggio College of Education building. In previous years, he had been the guest of honor at several other such dedications, among them the Raggio Parkway at the Desert Research Center in Reno; the William J. Raggio Math and Science Center at UNR; and the William and Dorothy Raggio High Tech Center, Western High School, Las Vegas.

This most recent honor had a personal facet, because Bill had grown up just a few blocks from the site of the new building, and, as a boy, the campus had been his playground. Throughout his life, Bill would retain a warm attachment to the place. Not only was he an alumnus, but his late wife, Dorothy, and his three children, had all had attended the university.

The ceremony was attended by over 200 well-wishers, including legislative colleagues, members of the university system's board of regents, state officeholders, fellow alumni and longtime friends. University President John Lilley addressed Bill in his speech, saying, "It is an honor to recognize your career and your good name."[1]

Bill was humbled by the dedication, saying, "Coming here as a freshman in 1944, I never imagined I'd ever have a building named for me." He then jokingly added, "Thank you for not checking my transcripts."

"I like to be involved in finding ways to help students, staff and professors excel in our state's universities," Senator Raggio said of his legislative obligation. "That's what we're entrusted to do."

Fellow Senator Bernice Matthews attended, and remarked, "Sitting on the Finance Committee next to him, sometimes we don't agree on some of the things that fell through the cracks, but I can tell you he's always looking out for education."

Senator Randolph Townsend agreed. "He is probably the most misunderstood champion of education there is," he said. "He's always believed the money that goes for education needs must be well spent."

University system Chancellor Dan Klaich would later say that when it came to supporting education, Bill Raggio didn't just talk about it—he did something about it. "He has pushed more actual dollars into the classrooms than anyone else," Klaich noted.

Chancellor Klaich added that it sincerely bothers Senator Raggio when others say he champions only UNR. "He takes just as much pride in what he has done over time for UNLV and the state and community colleges," Klaich said, "as he does in what he has done for his alma mater in Reno."

During a 2009 interview, Joe Crowley, who served for over twenty years as one of university system's top lobbyists, said Raggio always had a keen interest in education and always listened.

Crowley said the university system moved into some high-cost domains, such as the School of Medicine, which began to grant degrees in 1980,* and there was concern that a north-south rivalry would stand in the way of university funding. Many, who were affiliated with UNLV, believed they had been deprived of the better projects and felt that the new medical school should be located there.

Wanting to keep the medical school in the north, Senator Raggio was sensitive to the south's complaints, especially in recognizing that the preponderance of the state's medical needs were in that region, where the population was greatest.

Bill used his knowledge of the budget, and his position on the Senate Committee on Finance, to defuse the situation by helping to build a strong medical presence in the south.*

---

*From 1969 to 1980, UNR provided pre-med training, but students would then have to leave Nevada to earn their M.D.

*Joe Crowley: "The cost of operating a major medical center drives the discussion, and so to offset those costs we offered inexpensive options, with residencies for doctors and surgery programs that were entirely based in the south [despite the school being located in the north] rather than anywhere else in the state, because that was where the medical caregiving needs were the greatest."

One of the reasons UNLV lagged behind UNR in obtaining funding, Crowley explained, was simply that the UNR lobbyists knew how to "do politics."

Joe Crowley, Robert Dickens and Jim Richardson of UNR, were the primary lobbyists for the state system of higher education. While they were technically lobbying in the interest of the entire university system, they were also interested in their own university in the north.

Joe Crowley recognized this and would often suggest to the president of UNLV that he provide lobbyists from there to the state legislature.

As an example of knowing how to "do politics," Joe Crowley cited the process by which UNR was able to improve the percentage of indirect costs they were able to recover.

Indirect costs, or "overhead" are actual costs that incurred when research, education or outreach projects are performed at the university. They cannot always be specifically identified with a particular sponsored project and so are accounted for on a pooled basis, using a rate determined the U.S. Department of Health of Human Services.

Under President Crowley's guidance, UNR focused on investing in research cores, renovation of research space, faculty start-up packages and research administrative staff. This would allow them to recover a greater allowable amount of facilities and administrative costs from all grants and contracts.

Ramping up investment in research projects would require legislative approval. Crowley later explained that because he and his fellow lobbyists understood how the chair of the Committee on Finance, Senator Raggio, approached such issues, "they were very patient."

"At the time I became university president," Crowley recalled, "UNR was only recovering 25% of its indirect costs. We decided to go to Senator Raggio with incremental 25% increases. Once he was able to get the first 25% increase to build research institutes, he would tell us, 'Don't come back.' We would then patiently wait for one entire session to elapse before we would bring up the proposal for the next 25% increment."

During the interim between requests, the lobbyists would constantly keep this information in front of Senator Raggio. "In this way," Crowley explained, "over the course of six sessions, we were able to increase direct costs in a way that allowed the UNR to receive 100%. This would not have happened without Bill Raggio. He understood how it would benefit the university system and made it a priority."

For such reasons, there was no doubt in Joe Crowley's mind that the new $21 million college of education building at UNR should be named in Bill Raggio's honor. "It is the perfect choice," Crowley said during the dedication ceremony. "He doesn't get enough credit for what he's done for higher education in this state."[2, 3]

Also in the spring 2002, Bill received high acclaim from halfway around the world. Pope John Paul II conferred upon him the Papal honor *Pro Ecclesia et Pontifice*. The award, also called "The Cross of Honor," is the highest medal bestowed upon a lay person by the Papacy and is given "for distinguished service to the church."

When nominating him for the Papal honor in September 2001, Reno's Bishop Philip Straling called Bill "a devoted member of the local church and a respected public servant." Among the contributions that were cited on behalf of the Catholic faith community, were Bill's efforts through the E.L. Wiegand Foundation to help make substantial contributions to the new Bishop Manogue High School and to a Carmelite monastery in Reno, as well as a parish church building in Battle Mountain.

In addition, he was hailed for his work with the Foundation, through the Millennium Speaker Series, to bring to Nevada lecturers such as Nobel Peace Laureates Archbishop Desmond Tutu and Ireland's John Hume, which, according to Straling, "has contributed to bringing our community closer together in reconciliation and healing."

About his religion, Bill would say in 2008, "I think it's important to have faith and God in your life, although I don't wear it on my sleeve."

* * *

In December 2001, the St. Paul Companies, one of the nation's leading malpractice insurers, withdrew from the market. The company insured about half of Nevada's doctors, and, by mid-2002, no other insurer had expanded its business to cover them. In Nevada, many physicians, particularly obstetricians, stopped taking patients. The busy trauma center in Las Vegas was forced to close its doors in July, because doctors refused to work without insurance. On July 31, Governor Guinn convened a special session of the legislature to remedy the emergency.

The session lasted three days. The main sticking point for a compromise arose not from the suggestion to cap non-economic damage awards (so-called "pain and suffering") at $350,000, but rather from the number of exceptions to that cap. The assembly wanted eight exceptions including cases involving death, brain damage, paralysis, total blindness, amputation and sterility.

The senate wanted only two, cases involving gross malpractice and those in which there was "clear and convincing" evidence that the award should exceed the cap.

Senate Majority Leader Bill Raggio said that while a $350,000 cap permitting no exceptions would probably be ruled unconstitutional, a cap with as many exceptions as the assembly wanted would likely provide little benefit.

"I feel somewhat used in this process," Raggio said. "Our purpose here is not to help lawyers. It isn't to help doctors financially. We're here to help the public, who needs to have adequate and affordable health care."

The final agreement passed, setting a cap of $350,000 and giving plaintiffs three years after an injury to file a lawsuit against a health care provider. This compromise also allowed judges the authority to grant awards that exceed the cap if they found clear and convincing evidence for a higher award.

In November 2002, Governor Kenny Guinn's popularity across party lines was evident in his overwhelming reelection victory over Democratic challenger, Senator Joe Neal.

In his State of the State address, Guinn called for nearly $1 billion in new taxes. He said it was time to stop putting off the tough decision and recognize that gaming and sales taxes alone, which comprised the bulk of the state's revenue, were not a stable enough base to continue to meet the needs of a growing state. "It is the only choice," he told the legislators. Inaction in the face of such a financial crisis would be "political cowardice."

The governor went on to present a plan for cutting the budget deficit by increasing taxes on businesses, live amusement, cigarettes and alcohol. Guinn also proposed a property tax of fifteen cents per hundred of assessed value, which, when implemented in fiscal year 2005, would generate $100 million. Such a move, he said, would stabilize Nevada's revenue structure.

The governor told his audience that the time for relying on cuts to fill the budget gaps was over. "I refuse to balance the budget on the backs of our children, senior citizens and the poor," Guinn said. "This," he added, "was the time for courage and leadership.

With the retirement of Joe Dini after thirty-six years in the assembly, the emerging leadership, Speaker Richard Perkins and Majority Leader Barbara Buckley, would be sorely tested. Even Senate Majority Leader Raggio, with all his experience and savvy, would be hard pressed to keep his caucus in line during the bitter tax battle that was about to take place.

Yet, Governor Guinn was confident that his friend and political ally could create a consensus that would bring such crucial tax reform. "Bill Raggio," the governor said, "is, by far, a better closer than anyone."

The 2003 session, however, would present challenges (and perhaps some angst) for Senator Raggio as a "closer," because it would be the first time he would be faced by a legislative bloc, in this case, within his own party, that refused to negotiate.

This bloc of "No Tax" individuals, according to Republican former Senator Mark James, "refused to think that far ahead about how the state will function. If you see these people in debate or interviews, they really do not have solutions or understanding."

Mark James noted that Senator Raggio was the most fiscally conservative person he had ever met. However, given that "the state government of Nevada is woefully underfunded," he said that Raggio recognized that even fiscal conservatives could not allow the state to go bankrupt and added that as legislators, we "did not have any choice":

Are we going to let people out of prison? Are we going close schools? If we do not fund these services, the judiciary will step in and dictate how we spend these funds. Senator Raggio will always ask the "No Tax" people what they are willing to do. Their reply is always that they will cut expenses. Raggio would then ask, "Where would you cut?" To that they usually reply in generalities about government waste, but the fact is, they can never put their finger on anything specifically.

Governor Guinn agreed, saying that people who vote "'No" on everything, or "Yes" on everything, are not good legislators. "The problem in 2003 occurred," Guinn said, "when people like Assemblyman Hettrick and Assemblywoman Angle did not provide alternative plans. They would vote 'No' on tax plans other people submitted, but wouldn't offer a plan themselves."

The adamant stand taken by Hettrick, Angle and others against taxes was not without some support in the state. Michael Bowers points out in his book, *The Sagebrush State*, that, as of 2003, Nevadans were "virtually obsessed" with the taxes they pay, despite "one of the lowest state and local tax burdens and the eleventh highest per capita income among the fifty states."

The majority of Nevada voters, he wrote, were so fearful of having their taxes raised that they amended the Nevada constitution, "to prevent the state collecting inheritance taxes from the estates of deceased individuals, despite the fact that this provision also precluded the state from picking up its share of the federal estate tax. Nevada was the only state not to do so and lost millions of dollars in taxes that reverted to the federal treasury."[4]

Moreover, in 1994 and 1996, Nevadans passed the so-called Gibbons Tax Restraint Initiative, requiring a two-thirds super-majority vote of the legislature to raise taxes. This change would become enormously important to the outcome of the 2003 legislative session.

While many important issues were considered by the legislature during that session, including implementation of the Bush Administration's No Child Left Behind education reform act, the tax issue would overshadow them all.

Eventually, the governor's budget, which included some tax increases, passed in the senate by the required two-thirds majority, but did not pass in the assembly.

In a 2009 interview, Senator Raggio recalled that at the beginning of session the entire legislature, including the senate Republican caucus, agreed that everything would be on the table. Because of findings by a Blue Ribbon Commission that he had put together during the interim, the governor suggested a gross receipts tax. Several members of the caucus were against such a tax, and so continued to discuss it during the regular session, in the so-called "core" group.* As the session went on they came to no conclusions as to the amount of taxes that were necessary, or what taxes would be part of the revenue package.

Senator Raggio worked closely with Senator Townsend, a member of the Committee on Taxation, to come up with a scenario that would not include a gross receipts tax.

"However, the governor, lobbyists and the assembly majority were pushing hard for inclusion of such a tax," Bill later said. "So there came a point where I had to announce publicly that the gross receipts tax was dead, so we could move on."

Senator Ann O'Connell had, from the beginning of session in February, believed the governor's tax plan and budget was intended to protect the gaming industry, and so voted against it and similar plans. In her 2008 legislative oral history, O'Connell would say that it was the most divisive issue in her twenty years at the legislature. She recalled how at 10:00 p.m. one night, Senator Raggio told the Committee on Taxation to bring him back a tax bill that night, or they would have to go into a special session.

Senator O'Connell and others on the committee again reviewed the various scenarios. "When the gross-receipts tax came up, I made the

---

*The "core group" was a select group of legislators from both houses, and both parties, who regularly met behind closed doors to work out differences on the issue.

motion to kill it," she said. "After we killed [it]—I got the votes to kill it—then the Tax Committee came up with a proposal of $511 million of new taxes, which would really take care of the 'rollover,' which were the expenses that were already stated that had to be paid for."

They then returned to caucus with other Republicans in the majority leader's office. Senator Raggio, she continued, did not like the $511 million, and so that bill never got to the floor. The next morning, Bill called for a Committee of the Whole.

"He usurped the power of the Tax Committee," declared Senator O'Connell. "They were going to get that gross-receipts tax if they possibly could. I always felt very badly for Mike McGinness who chaired the Tax Committee. It was a big insult to him to take the chairmanship away from him and do what they did. Of course, that really started a division in the caucus."[5]

Senator Raggio, however, viewed it differently: "The Taxation Committee was no longer functional. Mike McGinness did feel that he had been usurped, but it was a matter of necessity and not one of having confidence in him. I just reached a point where we were into a special session and had to get something done."

Senator O'Connell also felt she had been frozen out of the deliberative process. "From that point on," she said, "Guinn did not call me into any more meetings, to say the very least." The division on the tax issue, she explained, permeated all of the other issues. "It became a very personal thing to where those of us who objected to going any higher than the $500 million became ostracized from even the caucus meetings. We were not informed of the caucus meetings, and it was ugly."[6]

During a 2010 interview, Senator Raggio disagreed with Senator O'Connell's recollection of events, saying,

That is just the opposite of what happened. They refused to come to our caucus meetings. Maurice Washington, Ann O'Connell, Bob Beers, Barbara Cegavske and Sandra Tiffany were having little meetings up in one of their own offices. I would send for them to come down and discuss the revenue issues and they would not come down. In fact, for a leader who always had good relations and control of his caucus, I was mystified that these people were hiding from me.

Senator Randolph Townsend later gave an account of a deal he made with Senate Minority Leader Dina Titus about a month before the end of the regular session. Upon learning that Senators O'Connell, Tiffany and Cegavske were planning a coup to wrest the leadership position from Raggio, Townsend realized the senate rules had to be changed to protect the majority leader.

"I went to Senator Titus," Townsend would say in 2010, "and said to her, 'Here is what's going on, let's make a deal. Bill does not know about this. I am making this arrangement without his authority or knowledge.'"

Townsend then advised Senator Titus that after such a rule change, some Democrats would be required to vote for Raggio as majority leader. Because they were essentially forming a coalition, they then negotiated committee chair assignments, with Senator Townsend agreeing to "one or two" Democratic chairs. When the deal was completed, Randolph went to tell Senator Raggio that he had worked out a solution—and, whether Bill liked it, or not, it was necessary. "All I told him was that it was ugly," Townsend recalled. "He did not ask me what the deal was."

Senator Townsend then met with "O'Connell, Tiffany and the others who were part of the plot" and confronted them about their plan to remove Senator Raggio from the leadership of the caucus.

"It was the most uncomfortable I have ever been in the legislature," Townsend said. "I couldn't tell Bill I was meeting with them, because I could not have him try to save himself. That was not a good idea because he would be too personally involved. I just told them I knew about their plans and that we were prepared for a fight."

The three senators dropped their plans to try and remove Senator Raggio from the majority leadership position, and so the senate rule changes were unnecessary.

"Senator O'Connell was a very principled woman who voted the way she believed and there is nothing wrong with that," Senator Townsend later said. "However, when you are part of the team, it's not about you, it's about the team. And when you plan a coup, or an internal fight, it isn't about being right; it's about being able to count. The first rule of politics is to learn how to count."

When the regular session adjourned on June 2, there was still no agreement on a tax plan to fund either education or the general budget. Governor Guinn immediately called a special session to have lawmakers develop a tax plan sufficient to meet all the appropriations and other spending measures that were passed during the regular session.

Two tax bills were killed in the senate during the first special session with four of the senate's thirteen Republicans—Warren Hardy, Ann O'Connell, Sandra Tiffany and Barbara Cegavske—voting against the bills both times. Three other senate republicans—Mark Amodei, Maurice Washington and Mike McGinness—joined them in voting against one of the tax bills.

Assembly Minority Leader Lynn Hettrick said at the time that although Senator Raggio was probably "the most powerful politician in this building," he still was not able to get all the Republicans in his caucus to vote his way. "But, like anything else," Hettrick remarked, "you can't control everything all the time."[7]

On June 12, 2003, Assembly Speaker Richard Perkins sent a letter to Governor Guinn, formally notifying him that "there is disagreement between the assembly and the senate relative to adjournment." Perkins suggested that the governor consider saving Nevada taxpayers the $50,000 per day it cost to hold the session, by allowing legislators to "adjourn for a period of time so that we can continue to seek compromise and obtain counsel of those experts who can help prevent unintended consequences of our revenue plan that will be passed into law."

Senator Raggio did not agree with Perkins's suggestion to adjourn, but Governor Guinn chose to dissolve the special session—the first time this had been done in the state's history.

Senate Fiscal Analyst Gary Ghiggeri later recalled that during the 2003 special sessions he would spend hours on the senate floor tediously repeating the same figures. "It was like the movie *Groundhog Day*. The alarm would go off and we would go over the same issues, every day, at the same time."

The governor ordered another special session, the twentieth in the state's history, to convene on June 25, 2003, as an extension of the earlier special session that he had dissolved on June 12.

As the session began, Bill blasted assembly Republicans, accusing them of working to fracture the party by blocking tax proposals that had a majority of support.

"We are destroying each other in the Republican Party," he said, "and some of this rhetoric that is going on is going to have some serious political consequences. I don't know how you can serve here in the legislature and say, 'I'm not going to vote for any new taxes.' I don't think that meets the responsibility we have."

Raggio had just led the Senate Committee of the Whole to approve an $870 million tax plan, which included a payroll tax and increased levies on cigarettes and alcohol. Assembly Republicans had promised to ensure that a two-thirds majority could not be obtained, unless the plan did not involve more than $800 million in taxes.

Bill suggested that any lawmakers who want cuts in social and health spending should visit clinics for the mentally retarded or physically disabled. "Go out and look at those clinics, look at the kids on the waiting list and your heart will burst," he said.

The tax measure, Senate Bill 8, passed out of the senate Committee of the Whole with the necessary majority. The bill was similar to the second bill that was killed in the first special session. Senators Cegavske, Tiffany, Washington and Carlton voted "No." Senator O'Connell abstained.

The assembly could not muster the two-thirds majority and so the measure remained in impasse.

State Attorney General Brian Sandoval, a former assembly member, testified before the assembly that lawmakers would be in violation of the state constitution if they failed to pass a balanced tax-and-spend plan by July 1,—the beginning of the fiscal year. When asked, Sandoval admitted he had no idea what the punishment would be for lawmakers if they violated that tenet of the Nevada constitution.

When July 1 arrived, the state was without a budget. Governor Guinn then took the extraordinary step of suing the legislature for violating the Nevada constitution by failing to fulfill its constitutional duty to approve a balanced budget and appropriate funds for public education by the beginning of the new fiscal year.

The Nevada Supreme Court heard the case of *Guinn v. The Legislature of Nevada*, and on July 10, 2003, Chief Justice Deborah Agosti handed down the court's decision in a vote of six to one:

> Nevada's public educational institutions are in crisis because they are unable to proceed with the preparations and functions necessary for the 2003-2004 school year...Due to the impasse that has resulted from the procedural and general constitutional requirement of passing revenue measures by a two-thirds majority, we conclude that this procedural requirement must give way to the substantive and specific constitutional mandate to fund public education.

> Therefore, we grant the petition in part, and order the clerk of this court to issue a writ of mandamus directing the legislature of the state of Nevada to proceed expeditiously with the 20th Special Session under simple majority rule.

A flurry of legal motions was filed in state and federal courts on behalf of twenty-four Republicans from the assembly and senate, petitioning the Nevada Supreme Court to rehear its July 10 decision.

Notwithstanding this decision, Senator Raggio publicly declared that the senate would not pass out, and he would personally not support, any state budget that did not receive a two-thirds majority. "I do not agree with the court's analysis," he stated at the time.

On July 22, an $836 million compromise tax package for funding the public schools and state government received a two-thirds vote in both houses of the legislature.

After a seventeen-to-two vote in the senate, with only Senators Cegavske and Tiffany dissenting, the assembly quickly followed with a twenty-eight-to-fourteen vote on Senate Bill 8.

Assembly Democrats vowed earlier in the day to pass a less appealing alternative tax measure, if the compromise developed by the senate did not receive their two-thirds vote.

Despite the supreme court ruling that only a simple majority would be required for passage, most lawmakers wanted to meet the supermajority threshold to comply with the higher standard for taxes required by voters in 1996, and avoid further judicial appeals.

Final approval was assured when Republican Assemblyman John Marvel of Battle Mountain voiced his support for what he admitted was an imperfect tax plan. Marvel would give the tax plan the two-thirds supermajority in the assembly.

He pointed out that the state was facing a constitutional crisis with the threat of taxes being raised by a simple majority. "We must uphold the constitution," he said. "I think it raises too much tax, and I think the appropriation is too high, but, if we're going to do the business of the state of Nevada, I reluctantly say I will vote for this bill."

In his 2008 Legislative Oral History, Marvel would recall:

> I get charged now with being a tax-and-spender, but my motive for that was to get our schools open. My vote was for the kids, not for raising taxes…It was the right decision. As far as I'm concerned, if you're going to be a statesman, be a good one. It turned around and got me in the end,* but at the same time, it was for the right reason."[8]

---

*Marvel was defeated in the 2008 election.

Senator Raggio was livid with the process:

> It was a farce. The four legislative leaders would meet, and we
> would get an agreement. Assembly Minority Leader Hettrick
> would agree and sign off on it, but would then come back and
> say he could not get his caucus to support it. What must be em-
> phasized is we weren't talking about whether or not to raise
> taxes; we were only talking about the difference, over the two-
> year period, between $715 million and $836 million. This is all
> lost in the discussion and their historical recall, because they are
> all out there today saying they would not raise taxes. That is
> simply untrue.

In 2010, Assembly Speaker Barbara Buckley agreed with Raggio's
assessment, saying, "They are not, as they claim to be, 'No Tax' people;
they just disagreed with Senator Raggio on how much."

Lobbyist Pete Ernaut, who had served as Governor Guinn's chief of
staff during his first term would later add, "There is an old saying that
'Any jackass can tear a barn down.' Kenny [Guinn] made some tough
decisions. The kids today deserve teachers and books and decent classrooms just as the kids that came before them."[9]

In 2009, Guinn would say, "Everybody can argue about it now, but
what kind of shape would the state be in today if we had not done that?
It would be devastating."

The 20th special session ended on July 22, 2003. At twenty-seven
days, it was the longest special session in the state's history and capped
a total of 169 days of legislative work.

Bill Raggio saw a positive side to the nearly six months of deliberation.
"I wouldn't call it the worst session, but it was the longest and most difficult
session I have been in," he said. "We were able to develop a tax plan
without a business income tax. That's was important. That is a win."

\* \* \*

This would be Senator Joe Neal's last session. Bill Raggio's conservative political philosophy often left the two men little common ground. Yet, as Bill would later say of their thirty-four years together in the Nevada State Senate, "We developed a mutual respect for one another over the years, even though we were miles apart on issues, especially when Joe first came to the senate. However, as I told him recently, 'Here we are at the ends of our careers; you're beginning to sound a lot like me and I'm beginning to sound a lot like you.'"

\* \* \*

In the midst of the bitter 2003 regular session, Bill was married at the Governor's Mansion. His bride, Dale Checket, formerly of Hillsboro Beach, Florida, had been a long time friend of the family.

Dale was born and raised in Sydney, Australia. At an early age, her parents divorced and her mother, Kathleen, took Dale to the Philippines. There, Kathleen met, and later married, Everett Checket.

Everett had been stationed in the Philippines with the U.S. military during World War II. After arriving there as a sergeant, his intellect and willingness to take on the most difficult assignments earned him a field commission. He would rapidly rise through the ranks to become a lieutenant colonel. After the war, Everett was appointed by General Douglas MacArthur to direct the war crimes trials of Japanese military figures. He would later be an official witness at the executions of Generals Homma and Yamashita.

Dale attended Sacred Heart School in Tokyo and, when her father returned to the United States to work on his M.B.A. at Harvard, she was enrolled in a private girl's school in Washington, D.C. Everett later returned to Asia as director and executive vice president of Mobil Oil Worldwide Marketing and Refining Division.

Dale went back to Sydney, where she attended college and, in 1962, married a chemical engineer. Two years later their son, David, was born.[8]

The marriage proved to be unworkable and when her parents moved back to the United States in 1966, Dale and David obtained a six-week visa to visit them in New York City. Upon learning of her marital difficulties, Everett suggested she go to Reno, establish residency and get a divorce.

Her dad recommended an attorney to Dale and she left for Reno. The attorney turned out to be unacceptable. "Fortunately," Dale would recall, "I was staying at the Whitney Ranch, in the Damonte area of Reno, and the kindly Mrs. Whitney said, 'I'll get you a fine attorney.'"

Mrs. Whitney recommended Bill Raggio to handle her case. Over the years, Dale never forgot Mrs. Whitney's term "fine attorney" and was especially pleased after meeting with him and finding him to be so considerate and helpful in handling her case.

Since Dale only had a visitor's visa, she could not legally obtain a Nevada divorce. Bill called a friend at the immigration office in San Francisco and her visa was extended. He then handled the divorce.

While Dale was waiting out her residency requirement, Dorothy Raggio and her son, Mark, would often visit her. Mark and David, who were about the same age, would play together. Dale remained in Reno from September 1966 through May 1967 and then returned to New York City.

There, she began a career with Puritan Sportswear, eventually remarried and moved to Florida in 1974. Her husband died suddenly of a previously undetected heart problem in 1980.

About that time, she applied for U.S. citizenship. Because Florida was experiencing waves of immigration from Haiti at the time, the Immigration and Naturalization Service was inundated. Dale's paperwork was not processed for years.

She had stayed in touch with the Raggios over the years and when Bill and Dottie visited Florida occasionally, they would get together for dinner. As such, she decided to ask Bill if he would help with her citizenship application. He made some inquiries and the problem was corrected. Dale was naturalized as a citizen of the United States in 1983.

In the years after Dorothy Raggio's death, Dale and Bill remained in touch. In 2000, while on business in Miami, Bill called Dale. "He asked me to dinner that night," she recalled, "but I had previous plans. He then asked if I had plans the following night. I told him I had a hair appointment." Dale agreed to meet him for a late dinner after her hair appointment, at which they "felt an immediate attraction." Over time, they decided to end their "long-distance" relationship—and get married.

On Christmas 2002, Dale came to Reno to meet Bill's family and friends. Among the latter were Kenny and Dema Guinn. Dale and Dema instantly became friends. "We are often mistaken for one another," said Dale, "especially at times when we inadvertently dress alike or wear our hair the same."

Dale and Bill had planned to be married at a local Carmelite monastery chapel in a private ceremony, but Dema had other plans. "If there was ever anyone who should be married in the Governor's Mansion," said the First Lady, "it's Bill Raggio."

On April 27, 2003, just prior to the formal wedding at the Governor's Mansion, Bill and Dale were married at St. Teresa of Avila Catholic Church in Carson City in a ceremony attended by family and a few close friends. Skip Avansino and Bill's daughter, Leslie, were the official witnesses.

Father Robert Buchanan repeated the ceremony later at the Governor's Mansion, with Governor Kenny Guinn and First Lady Dema, standing up for the couple. A poignant moment occurred just as the couple were about to exchange vows, when Bill's good friend, Father Frank Murphy, was brought forward in a wheel chair.

Bill and Dale had originally asked Father Murphy to perform the ceremony, but he was now hospitalized with terminal cancer. He was thought not to have the strength even to leave his bed, and had already been administered his last rites.

As the wheelchair neared the bride and groom, Father Murphy, with great effort, pushed himself up out of the chair. Steadying himself for a moment, he looked at Bill and said, "I promised you I would stand at your wedding." It was a heartrending moment for all present. "Father Frank" would die before the year was out.

In 2010, Senator Raggio recalled that he had first met Murphy when he was with the bishop's office and that he would occasionally say mass at the Raggio's parish church, Our Lady of the Snows.

"When Dottie was quite ill with her lung and liver cancer," Bill explained, "Father Murphy intervened and had me meet with Sister Pat at the Carmel monastery. She turned out to be a saint assisting with Dottie."

Father Murphy would visit also and he and Bill struck up a friendship:

> It was more than just a priest-parishioner relationship. I would even call him my confidant. It actually worked both ways, as he would often talk to me about personal matters of his own. Therefore, after Dottie died, we spent time together, going out to dinner and so forth. He loved to talk about politics, but no matter what I said, I could never convince him to become a Republican. He did tell me he voted for me, but did not want to reveal openly that he had supported a Republican.

Bill added that he always called him "Father Frank," even though Murphy insisted he use just "Frank." "I told it him it made me feel younger, even though I was older than him," Raggio joked. Then on a more serious note: "Father Frank made each of us who knew him feel like we were the most important person in his life. I don't think I ever heard him speak ill of anyone."

\* \* \*

The day after the wedding, Senator Raggio was back to work at the legislature. The honeymoon would be postponed though, not only through the end of the regular session on June 2—but by the two special sessions as well.

In the summer, the couple traveled to the east coast so Bill could introduce Dale to his many friends. Among those they visited was U.S. Senator Harry Reid. Reid had, years before, been Nevada's lieutenant governor. Bill recalled him to have been an effective president of the senate. "Harry was very low-key and non-confrontational. He was quiet and I recall seeing him often jogging around Carson City by himself to keep in shape."

On August 4, 2003, Harry Reid sent a note to Bill, reaffirming their mutual respect; but also, in the current atmosphere of highly partisan politics at both the national and state level, providing a reminder of a time, not too long before, when both sides worked together for the common good. In it he wrote, "You are a legend and I'm grateful for our decades of friendship." [10]

In August 2010, Senator Reid would recall his first meeting with Bill Raggio in the early 1960s. Harry was at the time a law partner in Las Vegas with Drake Delanoy, who had worked for Bill as a deputy DA in the Washoe County. Drake, said Senator Reid, "remained a huge fan of Bill Raggio."

Whenever Bill was in Las Vegas, he would visit their law office, and that is how the two met. "I remember Bill came into my office one day and was looking at the several plaques and awards that I had displayed on the walls," Reid recalled. "'Harry,' he said, 'all those things put together, and two-bits, will buy you a cup of coffee anywhere in town.' I recognized the truth in what Bill was saying and that day has come to my mind often over the years."

After the end of the 2003 session, many people were predicting the fall of Senator Raggio as a force in the senate, and it remained to be seen if he could hold things together. But first he would have to withstand a painful personal tragedy.

# CHAPTER FIFTY-SIX

# Good Compromises (2005)

On February 19, 2004, Bill and Dale traveled to San Juan Puerto Rico where Bill was to attend a meeting of the Senate Presidents Forum, a non-partisan, non-profit, educational organization, serving the information and networking needs of the presiding officers of the fifty state senates in the United States. As they were unpacking, the phone rang. It was Bill's daughter, Leslie. "The first thing she said was, 'Is Dad sitting down?'" Dale later recalled. "I knew then the news was going to be very bad." It was. Bill's son, Mark, had died suddenly of a heart attack at the age of forty-one.

Bill was staggered with grief at the news. Stunned, the couple immediately returned to the airport and were able to find seats onboard a flight returning to the continental United States.

Mark William Raggio had attended Reno High School and the University of Nevada, Reno, where he earned a degree in business management. During college, he worked at the *Reno Gazette Journal* and upon graduation continued there. He was soon promoted to circulation manager. He would go on to help with the national launch of *USA Today*.

Mark changed careers in 1987, entering an accelerated management program with Nevada Bell in Reno. He eventually joined the management staff of Pacific Bell in San Francisco and, later, U.S. West Communications in Phoenix.

By 2001, Mark was executive director of Digital Subscriber Line (DSL) products in the Consumer Division of AT&T. He was on assignment in Morristown, New Jersey when he died.

Mark's sister, Tracy, later recalled that while their dad's schedule often precluded him from attending the children's organized activities, such as little league games and cheerleading events, he did find time to take Mark hunting and fishing. They particularly liked rafting, and when Mark was in his early teens, they took a voyage on a wild river in the Andes Mountains of Chile. They were joined by Paul Lowden and his son, Will, Bill Raggio's namesake.*

A memorial service was held for Mark Raggio at the Carmel Monastery chapel in Reno on February 19. Despite still carrying enormous grief at the loss of his own son, Paul Lowden would attend. In addition to the traditional Catholic hymns and prayers, Mark's long time companion, Shannon Smith, read a poem in his memory. Mark's family and friends would later establish the Mark William Raggio Scholarship Endowment for the School of Business at UNR.

Given his already rapid rise through the executive ranks of AT&T, and his command of innovative communications technology, one can only imagine how successful Mark Raggio might have become in the world of business. Yet, a fellow employee would later remark that what he would most remember about Mark was his "infectious laugh and good-natured kidding."

\* \* \*

In April 2004, Bill announced he would seek reelection to the state senate.

The political fallout from the 2003 legislative session had created bitter divisions within the Nevada Republican Party. Bill acknowledged that some in his caucus were angry with him because of the tax issues the previous session. "Certainly there were bad feelings in the end," he said, "but two-thirds of the legislature did what it had to do."

Evidence of the deep divisions could be seen in the strain it put on the relationship between Bill Raggio and Ann O'Connell.

In 2008, O'Connell spoke of this. "Bill Raggio is a dear, dear man,"

---

*In a crushing blow to both the families, seventeen-year-old Will Lowden would die tragically just a few weeks before Mark.

she said. "He's probably one of the most thoughtful men that I can ever remember having worked with...Very gracious. But don't cross him.

When a person has a different opinion than Bill, O'Connell explained, he can be adversarial. "He's two personalities to work with, just very, very thoughtful, very, very concerned about his group—but 'father knows best' is his style of operating. I kept reminding him that every one of us was voted in the same way to get to the legislature, and so I felt that my opinion is as important as his opinion. He never quite bought that [laughter]. I don't know why. But as a friend, I don't think you can have a better friend. As far as politics goes, we don't have the same philosophy."[1]

In 2010, Bill Raggio commented on Senator O'Connell's remarks:

> In the 2003 session, when we had to raise taxes, Ann O'Connell, Sandra Tiffany and Barbara Cegavske fought me tooth and nail and refused to discuss it. On the final day, when we were going to vote on this, the three of them came into my office with tears in their eyes and said if I need them, they would vote with me. I have never disclosed this before, but I must give them credit. Though Ann abstained in her vote, and the two others voted against it, they did come to the table, after weeks and months.
>
> We should've done this together, instead of this political posturing all the time. Many people are more concerned about how they are viewed on personal issues, than how well they govern. We knew something was necessary, we knew we had to fund the budget...we had to bite the bullet.

He and Senator O'Connell were very close until her reelection campaign in 2004. Over the years, Bill said, he was her confidant and she came to him often for personal advice and advice on legislative matters. Bill made her committee chair and said that he had nothing but very deep respect for her. "I was mainly responsible for her being in the Senate Hall of Fame afterward," he said.

"She described me in her legislative oral history as someone who was hard to get along with." Senator Raggio continued, "That was absolutely not true. This is an unfortunate residue of her service."

After Senator O'Connell was defeated in the 2004 Republican primary election, Senator Sandra Tiffany blasted the campaign of Joe Heck as being deceptive about O'Connell's stance on taxes during the 2003 session.

Taking her lead, the press reported that anti-O'Connell funding came from a political action committee called "Citizens for Fair Taxation," which reported receiving $199,000 in gaming industry contributions by early September. The group's agent was Michael Alonso, an attorney with Jones Vargas.

Bill Raggio denied even knowing about the PAC's existence:

> To this day, it is apparent that Senator O'Connell and her minions felt that Senator Townsend and I were not supportive of her and her campaign against Joe Heck. I told her numerous times that was not the case; I did not ever know, or talk to, Joe Heck during that campaign.

> She got a burr under her saddle that somehow we were not supportive, but the facts were we gave her full financial support, attended her functions and spoke on her behalf. But sometimes you get ideas in your head and you cannot dislodge them.

Raggio added that after Joe Heck defeated Ann O'Connell, and Assemblyman Bob Beers beat Senator Ray Rawson in the Republican primary, it caused a division within the party.

In 2009, Senator Randolph Townsend defended the position Raggio had taken:

> Bill is not asking you to agree with his policies, he is not asking you to always vote with him. He's just asking you to give the same kind of commitment that he does, study your issues so you

can defend your positions and if you tell somebody something—you'd better honor it.

Townsend said that nothing aggravates Senator Raggio more than when everyone leaves a caucus meeting agreeing on an issue and then when it comes time to vote, "two of them get out of the corral, but then later say, 'I'd of been there if you needed me.'"

"I know Bill still wonders," added Senator Townsend, "how, during the 2003 session, O'Connell, Tiffany and Cegavske could look him in the eye and tell him they would do one thing, and then go do something else."

Townsend then described a 2004 fundraiser for Senator O'Connell held at the home of a supporter in Las Vegas. Randolph and Bill flew down to present O'Connell with a $5,000 campaign contribution from SRLC, as well as their own personal contributions. Upon arriving they knocked on the door. The hostess, on seeing who they were, immediately shut the door in their faces. Raggio pushed the door open and while he was giving the door-slammer an earful about civility, Townsend went in and gave O'Connell the checks.

"The people in that room were the core of the party's right wing in Las Vegas," Senator Townsend later said. "If they had asked us for our help, they would've won that race. They hated Bill and they hated me. It was just unnecessary that it cost her [O'Connell] a seat in the senate, and Rawson lost to Beers. It was totally unnecessary. We lost two twenty-year senators in one day."

\* \* \*

In November 2004, Bill won reelection to an unprecedented ninth term in the Nevada State Senate, taking nearly 68% of the vote.[2]

During the campaign, Senator Raggio had stressed that no new taxes would be approved in the coming session:

The state will have limited revenues to meet its needs as result of high growth, but it will have to manage. We must address the needs of the mentally ill, the physically impaired, children with disabilities and those who are dependent or without means. At the same time, we need to support the court system and correctional facilities to ensure that criminal justice is swift and certain. This will require fiscal restraint and experience in a very difficult budget process.

Both Joe Heck and Bob Beers won senate seats in the general election. Democrats gained a seat when John Lee of Las Vegas defeated Senator Ray Shaffer. This would leave the Republicans with a twelve- to-nine majority in the senate. Democrats would continue to hold a majority in the assembly by a margin of twenty-six to sixteen.

In setting the tone for the coming session, Assembly Speaker Richard Perkins said, "My number one issue will be just to bring some respect and civility to the legislative process." Senator Raggio acknowledged that the process would probably run more smoothly in the assembly now that the Republican minority was smaller.

Bill was referring to the so-called "Mean 15," whose equivocation about the amount of tax increase they would support in the 2003 session resulted in two special sessions, costing taxpayers over $500,000 in administrative costs. Republican Minority Leader Lynn Hettrick lost five members between sessions—two being replaced by Democrats, two deciding not to run and the fifth, Bob Beers, winning a seat in the senate. [3]

Early support for an effort by some southern Nevada Republican senators to oust Raggio from his leadership position did not materialize. He would also remain as chair of the Committee on Finance. Las Vegas Senator Dennis Nolan was selected as assistant majority leader and Senator Mark Amodei as president pro tempore. Senator Sandra Tiffany, who remained vocal about her displeasure with Senator Raggio, would find herself without either a caucus assignment or a committee chair, despite her being in the majority party. "My life is suspended," she said.

However, this is not to imply Raggio was dishing out punishment for being attacked by a group of fellow Republicans during the previous session. Senator Barbara Cegavske would remain as both a committee chair and a member of the Committee on Finance. Newly elected Senator Bob Beers, one of the more vocal members of the intractable assembly Republican caucus in 2003, was selected by Raggio to be vice chair of the Committee on Finance.

\* \* \*

Before the 73rd Session of the Nevada Legislature began, the 21st Special Session would be called by Governor Guinn to consider matters relating to the possible impeachment of State Controller Kathy Augustine, the first time the Nevada legislature had ever considered an impeachment proceeding. Augustine was a former colleague of many of the legislators who would decide her fate, having served in both the assembly and the state senate.

On November 11, 2004, the assembly unanimously adopted three Articles of Impeachment for "Misdemeanor or Malfeasance in Office." Controller Augustine pled not guilty to all. On November 29, 2004, the senate began its trial of the second-term Republican controller, who had been removed from the office pending the outcome of the proceeding. Her attorneys argued that, while Augustine had already been fined $15,000 for three willful ethics violations, those violations were not serious enough to warrant a removal from office.

Five days later, the senate voted to dismiss the first Article of Impeachment and "not sustain" the second. The senate "sustained" the third article and approved Senate Resolution No. 5, censuring Augustine, but allowing her to resume office.[4]

Bill Raggio felt there was something more behind the censure than appeared on the surface. "I think the Kathy Augustine situation was, in reflection, overblown," he said. "She wasn't the best-liked person, particularly by the opposite party. Her detractors were looking for anything and everything to criticize her about. Before the charges went before the ethics commission, I think she should have been given the opportunity to resign, had she been willing to do so. That would've been a far better result than what occurred. The procedure was very distasteful."

\* \* \*

The major issues facing the 2005 legislature would be education and property tax relief, especially in southern Nevada where property values were skyrocketing due to rapid growth. In addition, lawmakers would have to decide what to do with an anticipated budget surplus of nearly $600 million, the result of an upturn in Nevada's economy and the broadened state tax base achieved during the 2003 session. Governor Guinn suggested using $300 million to provide motor vehicle registration rebates, but only after his proposed $5.7 billion budget for the coming biennium had been approved.

Because Guinn was serving out his final term, some legislators were positioning themselves for the coming governor's race. Among them were two Democrats, Senator Titus and Speaker Perkins. A *Las Vegas Sun* article later pointed out that while the Democrats were staying quite vocal about their legislative agenda, even holding weekly press conferences, "Raggio, on the other hand, has kept quiet on his own priorities."

Speaker Perkins termed the Democratic strategy a double-edged sword. He knew that Republicans would not be as aggressive in promoting an agenda, "because of their leader's political savvy."

Senator Raggio later said that experience had taught him to maintain a good poker face in politics. "If I had any priorities, I wouldn't tell you, because then they would hold me hostage. I'm going to take it a day at a time, an hour at a time and get the job done. If you let frustration enter into it, you'll never make a good decision."

By April, one meaningful issue had already been settled. A compromise on property tax relief resulted in completed legislation and the governor's signature. Both houses had worked in a bipartisan manner, their leadership building consensus and, eventually, agreement.

The new law capped property tax increases at 3% annually for owner-occupied homes and owners of low-income apartment complexes. For all other property owners, the cap would be 8% a year. As part of the compromise agreement, Senate Majority Leader Raggio found a way to have a payroll tax reduction measure, championed by freshman Senator Bob Beers, passed into law.

On April 28, 2005, the legislature approved a law barring the death sentence for those who commit murder before age eighteen. This measure brought Nevada into compliance with a recent U.S. Supreme Court ruling that held those under the age of eighteen are more likely to lose control because their brains are not yet fully developed. Although passage of the measure was a foregone conclusion, Senator Raggio, in keeping with his long established principle that criminal justice be "swift and certain," protested for the record.

Bill recited the details of the brutal Sonja McCaskie murder and dismemberment. Thomas Bean, he reminded the senate membership, was seventeen at the time and, as district attorney, Bill had won death sentences at both of Bean's trials. He rejected the high court argument saying, "It's disturbing to me that we have to adopt this now as a law. The same court has held in cases of abortion that juveniles are mature enough to make those decisions, and juries have always had the ability to take the age of the defendant into consideration."

\* \* \*

As the session neared its end, the usual question arose about whether Senator Raggio would return. Bill replied that he would. The senate suited him, he said, and he saw his primary job there as guarding the state's finances.

Sig Rogich, former White House assistant to the president for President George H.W. Bush in 1989, and later U.S. ambassador to Iceland, had known Bill for more than forty years. "I've always viewed Bill as kind of an anchor in state government," Rogich said at the time. "He has an amazing ability to make things happen. He's a consensus builder, and yet never loses sight of what is the dearest thing to him: the purse strings."[5]

As the session approached the 120 day limit, negotiations became predictably contentious. The main sticking point was conditions under which the Millennium Scholarship would be continued. The primary bargaining chip in that discussion was how full-day kindergarten would be implemented. Senate Republicans offered to consider funding for full-day kindergarten, if individual schools were given the option to decide whether to employ it.

Assembly Majority Leader Barbara Buckley said Democrats might be willing to back off their position on full-day kindergarten. "Bill Raggio is a master negotiator," she said. "We [southern and rural lawmakers] always want to go home sooner than he does because we don't sleep in our beds at night. He is a master that way. However, in the end, he is fair; and we are fair. I'm sure we'll be able to work it out."

Governor Guinn proposed, and the senate approved, a $100 million fund that schools on the No Child Left Behind watch list could use to improve; or, if they wished, add full-day kindergarten. Speaker Perkins, however, wanted to use $50 million of that fund to pay for full-day kindergarten at all schools.

For days, the assembly and senate leadership met behind closed doors to address these and other issues. Having been a district attorney, Bill Raggio likened these meetings to jury deliberations, which are also not open to the public. "These are core meetings to negotiate the end game, he said. Raggio would later say that experience had taught him that without some closed meetings, legislators could not "talk as freely and so didn't make as good decisions."

In the final push, after working for thirty straight hours, lawmakers were unable to reach agreement on key issues before the mandated deadline of 1:00 a.m. on June 8, 2005. Dozens of bills were still in the pipeline.

Governor Guinn immediately called a special session to be held from 3:00 a.m. to 6:00 a.m. and rushed over to the Legislative Building to broker deals between exasperated lawmakers.

Guinn had crafted the special session proclamation so that lawmakers could vote on only the most crucial issues. After securing agreements on how to fund full-day kindergarten and the Millennium Scholarship, the governor then specified another ten bills that could be addressed. These included the senate's $53 million "pork bill," Barbara Buckley's measure to allow lower-cost prescription drug purchases from Canada and an omnibus tax cleanup bill, estimated to save Nevada businesses $5.8 million a year.

Due to the sheer mechanics of drafting and then printing the bills, coupled with repeated rounds of redrafting due to tired staff members overlooking errors, Governor Guinn was required to extend the special session proclamation three times, by hourly increments. Political maneuvering also contributed to the delays. Despite deals having been made, lawmakers, in their suspicion of the other house, continued to roll the most important measures to the bottom of the agenda — just in case.

In the end, they agreed on a $22 million appropriation to provide full-day kindergarten for at-risk schools and a compromise bill on restructuring the Millennium Scholarship program to keep it viable for another decade.

Despite its quarrelsome ending, the session was considered by most to be a success. Scores of other bills were passed addressing K-12 and higher education, health care, consumer protection, child welfare, water, energy conservation and public safety. In addition, most Nevadans would be receiving a tax rebate from the budget surplus. Majority leader Buckley would say, "What I'm most proud of is the very large number of bills that represent good public policy."

Senator Bill Raggio demonstrated that he still wielded considerable power in the legislature. The senator won approval of $32 million for a math and science building at UNR, one of his top priorities. In addition, $10 million was allocated for UNR's Nevada Cancer Institute. For the Reno-Sparks area, Senator Raggio was able to get $5 million for a homeless services center and another $1.5 million for cultural and recreational projects.

The *Las Vegas Sun* noted, "Given the shift of legislative power to southern Nevada, this has to be considered a victory for the north." Senator Dina Titus, recalling remarks made earlier in the session by some assembly members that Raggio's age was getting the best of him, said admiringly, "The mistake people made was to underestimate him. I think he came out great."[6]

Many political observers marveled at how Bill, who emerged from the session two years before "battered and bloody," with his caucus in disarray and his party fracturing along philosophical lines, had so quickly "turned it around."

"Basically it looked to me," said veteran lobbyist Sam McMullen, "that at the end of the last session they were not even functioning as a caucus. This time, every day they have been having caucus meetings and communicating and airing their differences. That probably is the strongest hallmark of why they did better."[7]

Senator Bob Beers agreed: "From what I understand, last session there was some people who felt there was consensus on various issues that he [Raggio] just ignored and went with his own concept. This time he went out of his way to find out what we all thought. And I know he did some things that the caucus wanted done that he himself did not want done."

However, Democratic Assemblywoman Sheila Leslie from Washoe County observed what she saw as cracks in "the master's armor." "I still think his caucus frustrates him," she said. "The old style of leadership isn't working the same way anymore."

Yet, Leslie conceded that Raggio worked things to the benefit of northern Nevada. "He is clearly the master of the legislative process when you look at the pork bill and what he was able to deliver for Washoe County. It was very clear he was still in charge."[8]

In its traditional end-of-session poll, the *Las Vegas Review Journal* asked legislators, lobbyists and press members to rate the performance of lawmakers. Barbara Buckley and Bill Raggio were voted as the best legislators. Buckley was lauded for her talent "working the caucus and the rules." Of Raggio, remarks ran from, "He still knows and does what is best for the most," to, simply, "Look at the final score."

Sandra Tiffany was selected as the worst senator. Several respondents commented on her ethics.[9] Sharron Angle was named worst assembly member.[10]

After the session, *Las Vegas Review Journal* journalist Ed Vogel interviewed Governor Kenny Guinn who responded to criticism by Angle for his having increased the size of state government. He noted, with irony, that those legislators, still in office, who had resisted his tax plan in 2003, all voted for the 2005-2007 budget—a budget that was 23% larger than the previous one.

"Even Assemblywoman Sharron Angle voted for the record budget," the governor observed.[11]

\* \* \*

In 2005, Chief Justice of the Nevada Supreme Court Nancy Becker, a Democrat, wrote in a note of appreciation, "Senator, your support and mentoring have made me a better person and member of the judiciary. Thank you for always being there for me." The following year, Federal District Court Judge Brian Sandoval would call Bill "the greatest statesmen and lawyer that I've ever known."[12]

Bill Raggio's lifetime of working to improve the legal profession and the field of criminal justice would be recognized by others during 2004 and 2005. He would be named Honorary Chief Deputy, Washoe County Sheriff's Association; receive the Legislative Advocate Award from the Nevada Disability Advocacy and Law Center, 2005; and be given an Outstanding Award from the National Council of Juvenile Family Court Judges.

In conjunction with this, Bill was honored for his commitment to the Children's Cabinet and Nevada Partnership for Homeless Youth for compassionate and effective leadership to Nevada's Division of Mental Health and Developmental Services.

James E. Rogers, Chairman and CEO of Sun Belt Communications and interim chancellor of the Nevada System of Higher Education, sent a letter to Bill in 2005 advising him that the largest classroom at UNLV's Boyd School of Law would be perpetually named the William J. Raggio classroom. "This way, we will thank and recognize you for your service," Rogers wrote. "And thanks for being a great role model for our profession."[13]

One of the many attorneys for whom Bill had been a role model was Michael Lindell. In September 2005, Lindell retired after having spent twenty-seven years—nearly his entire career in private practice—in partnership with Bill Raggio.

Their relationship had an unlikely beginning. Lindell had graduated from UNR and the University of Alabama law school. As his service in the U.S. Army Judge Advocate General Corps was about to end, he returned to Reno for a few days to look for employment.

Having concluded his scheduled interviews with other firms, Lindell decided to visit each law firm in the major office buildings in Reno to hand out his resume and ask if anyone in the firm was available and interested in speaking with him about a position.

About noon, he reached the offices of Raggio, Walker and Wooster. Bill Raggio and Clint Wooster were just leaving for lunch and asked the young man if he wanted to join him. During their meal, they saw promise in Lindell and subsequently hired him as an associate in the firm. "It was the ultimate cold call," Lindell recalled.

The young lawyer was soon dazzled by Bill's talent in the courtroom. "He's a great trial lawyer," Lindell said, "far better than I ever could hope to be." Lindell would spend most of his career working behind the scenes and out of the limelight.

He was in awe of Bill's gift for remembering almost everything he ever heard. He would later recall how he would often spend an enormous amount of time preparing for a complicated case that Bill was going to take to court. A day or two before trial, Bill would ask him to go over the pleadings, discovery, evidentiary and other legal issues, interim court proceedings and rulings, and the positions and anticipated positions and strategies of both the firm's client and the opposition, including any settlement discussions on either side, and his view of the likely outcome of the issues during and at the conclusion of the trial. Bill would listen and occasionally ask questions. When the court date arrived, Bill would go in and present a flawless case—from memory.

After nearly three decades together, it took Michael Lindell only five words to sum up his feelings for his law partner: "Bill Raggio is my hero."

# CHAPTER FIFTY-SEVEN

# An Air of Incivility (2007)

In May 2006, Bill Raggio met with the newly hired president of UNR, Milton Glick, who was moving from Arizona State University. Glick sent a note thanking Bill for meeting with him and observed, "It is clear politics in Nevada is very personal and I look forward to your tutelage and help."

As Glick surmised, a feature of Nevada's individualistic political culture had traditionally been personal relationships between the state's legislature, governor and interest groups.[1]

However, with the loss to retirement of people like Joe Dini and an increasingly partisan and dogmatic approach to lawmaking, Bill Raggio might well remain the last vestige of what was once referred to as "a political life based on a system of mutual obligations rooted in personal relationships"—where a person's word was his or her bond.[2]

As if to emphasize this changing culture, two former legislators from that era, Lawrence "Jake" Jacobsen and Carl Dodge, died in July 2006, just three days apart.

With forty years in the assembly and senate combined, Jacobsen had been the longest serving legislator in Nevada history. In 1941, he had been a survivor of the Japanese attack on Pearl Harbor aboard the cruiser USS *Astoria*, and later distinguished himself in several major naval engagements, including the invasion of Guadalcanal, where the *Astoria* was sunk by enemy gunfire.

In eulogizing Jacobsen, former governor and U.S. Senator Richard Bryan said, "He was a product of the old school, before the corrosive influence of partisanship infected the political process at the state and national level. He was always a gentleman. He believed in civility and courtesy and that they were not signs of weakness, but of respect for the other person."[3]

Carl Dodge was born in Reno, but lived most of his life in Fallon. Following graduation from the University of Nevada, Dodge earned a law degree from Stanford and then served in the Navy during World War II.

Returning to Fallon after the war, he was elected to the state senate in 1958 and would serve six consecutive terms, many of them as part of a three-member Republican minority caucus, along with Bill Raggio and Cliff Young. Dodge was remembered for his intellect, eloquence and ethical standards, as well as for being the primary author of the state's Distributive School Account. His distinguished service in the legislature ended in 1980 when he resigned to take a seat on the Nevada Gaming Commission.

Both Senators were inducted into the legislature's Senate Hall of Fame.

\* \* \*

Limited by the state constitution to two terms, the 2006 election would be the last for Governor Guinn.

Bill had immense respect for Governor Guinn and spent a great deal of time with him during the legislative sessions. "Of all the governors with whom I served during my legislative years, I probably had the closest relationship with Governor Kenny Guinn," Bill Raggio said in 2009. "Much like Governor O'Callaghan, Guinn enjoyed coming to the Legislative Building during our sessions and I probably conversed with him, or had him in my office, two or three times daily."

Bill noted that Guinn was "readily accepted by the Democrat leadership in both houses, as well."

"While some partisanship occurred of necessity on some issues," Bill added, "there was an air of civility between leadership, and between the legislators and the Executive Branch, which has seriously deteriorated since that time. In my early years, we would have spirited elections, not mean, not nasty, not filled with partisan venom. When it was over, we worked together to find acceptable and responsible solutions to our state and national problems."[4]

Senator Raggio later wrote the Introduction to an Executive Summary of the Guinn Administration, Moving Nevada into the 21st Century, 1999 to 2006, in which he said of the governor:

> Whenever I think of Kenny Guinn, I think of another great American optimist—President Ronald Reagan. To Ronald Reagan, America always had the potential to be "prouder, stronger, better," because, in the famous political tagline that he used, it was always "morning again in America." So it has been with Governor Guinn and our great state. Under his leadership, it has always been "morning again in Nevada." We are a prouder, stronger, better state, because of this humble, friendly man's principled leadership.[5]

In addition to a close working relationship with Kenny Guinn, Bill enjoyed a social one as well. He was often invited to stay at the Governor's Mansion during hectic legislative sessions, when he did not have time to make the forty-mile drive to his home in Reno. Bill would frequently joke that he was the only legislator in the country to whom the governor "brought coffee in the morning."

The admiration Bill and his wife had for the governor also extended to First Lady Dema Guinn. "She worked more assiduously at her job than any other first lady I have known," Bill said. "She spruced up the Governor's Mansion and the grounds, largely at her own expense, to the point where it was a showcase. She took on many substantial issues and personally created and hosted many important events."

An ardent student of Nevada history, Dema was struck by the lack of historical artifacts and paintings at the mansion, which had been newly renovated during the Miller Administration. She contacted the staff at the Keck Mining Museum at UNR and the Nevada State Museum, but soon discovered that both museums' budgets were so minimal, they could not offer additional displays of historical artifacts.

She took it upon herself to raise funds to augment their budgets and improve their ability to serve the citizens of Nevada. From this, came the annual Tin Cup Tea and the Chuck Wagon BBQ, which were highly successful in raising funds for both museums.[6]

"She took her role as First Lady seriously," Bill said, "and was indefatigable in her support for her husband. All had better be ready for an onslaught from her for what she perceived as unwarranted criticism of the governor."

* * *

The race for governor in 2006 pitted Senate Minority Leader Dina Titus against five-term U.S. Congressman Jim Gibbons.[7] In addition to becoming the most expensive race in the state's history, it would also be one of the most negative.

Gibbons faced allegations of impropriety on a variety of issues, from knowingly employing an undocumented alien as a domestic employee, to sexually assaulting a woman in a Las Vegas parking garage after an evening of drinking with his campaign staff, though the Clark County District Attorney's Office decided against filing criminal charges on the latter.

On Election Day, Gibbons received 278,984 votes to Titus's 255,675. The Democratic candidate carried Clark County, Nevada's most populous, but lost the other sixteen.

"As someone who has high respect for Titus's capabilities," Raggio recalled, "I think there is no question that she lost for several reasons: her failure to get much of the rural vote; the split with the heavily Mormon (Jim) Gibson faction in Clark County; and the fact that she came across in her personal appearances a little bit acerbic, for example, her use of salty language at times. In addition, some statements she made in previous legislative sessions, such as calling the northern part of the state a "sponge" that has been soaking up taxes raised by Clark County, were, unfortunately for her, remembered."

On January 3, 2007, Jim Gibbons was sworn in as Nevada's twenty-ninth governor. In his inaugural address, he said he would seek to put the contentious election behind him and set a bipartisan tone for his administration. Retiring Governor Kenny Guinn, whose relationship with Gibbons was strained, was not in attendance, explaining that attention should be focused on the new governor.

Senator Raggio, later commenting on the incoming governor's speech said, "I hope everyone picked up on the unity theme. We've had too much divisive politics."

Democratic Assemblywoman Sheila Leslie was listening to Governor Gibbons, and observed: "The dynamics have shifted. You have a very experienced legislature and a governor who has been in Washington for ten years. The political climate is very different here. While Washington is filled with partisan sniping, in Nevada we have to work together to find solutions."[8]

The "dynamics" of the legislature were indeed changing. In the assembly, the election had resulted in an increased number of Democrats, who now held a twenty-seven to fifteen seat edge—one short of being "veto proof."

Despite all this, a demonstration of unconcealed partisanship occurred in the first moments of the new legislative session when freshman Republican Assemblyman Ty Cobb defied legislative custom by loudly voting "No" during a roll call vote to seat Barbara Buckley as speaker of the Nevada assembly.

Traditionally, leadership members are first chosen by their parties and then ratified by votes on the floor of the assembly and the senate. In the interests of civility, previous ratifications had always been unanimous. Cobb, who occupied the seat formerly held by Republican Assemblywoman Sharron Angle, known for her unwillingness to compromise, later said that as a Republican, he "didn't feel right voting for a Democrat for the position."

Later, Buckley, the first woman Speaker in the 142 year history of the assembly, commented that she would not take it personally, but that Cobb's gesture did not bode well for the freshman. "People who lack a sense of judgment sometimes run into trouble with legislation because they don't reach out to people," Buckley said. "You can't do anything unless you get a majority. It doesn't matter if you have the best ideas." [9]

In the state senate, Democrats picked up another seat when long time Las Vegas educator Joyce Woodhouse upset Senator Sandra Tiffany.

Tiffany had remained openly critical of Senator Raggio since the 2003 session, when she and fellow Republican Senator Barbara Cegavske were the only two members of the Republican caucus to vote against the final budget appropriation measure.

Despite this, Bill adhered to the policy of the SRLC to support every Republican candidate selected in the primary election, and so had worked for her reelection. In a January 2007 note to Senator Raggio, Tiffany thanked him for his "generous and ongoing support."[10]

The senate was now more closely divided, eleven Republicans to ten Democrats. Bill was again voted as majority leader by his caucus. As result of the razor thin party split in the senate, he was required to juggle committee-meeting times for the upcoming legislative session. This was necessary to maintain seven total members on each of the panels, while still keeping a Republican majority. As he began his eighteenth regular session of the legislature, Bill announced that, given the continuing Democrat control of the assembly, compromise would be the order of the day.

In 1979, the Nevada legislature had passed a budget cap statute that limited general fund spending based on a formula using population growth and the rate of inflation. However, the economic health of the state had not made those provisions necessary to consider until 2007-2009 budget cycle.

The formula in the statute now required Governor Gibbons to submit a budget that did not exceed $7.1 billion, which he did with a proposed budget amount of $6.8 billion. However, this figure was over $1 billion short of combined agency requests for funding. Drastic cuts in the cost of state government would have to be made.

Complicating the overall budget process was a newly enacted "Education First" provision, a voter initiative pushed by then-Congressman Jim Gibbons, which forced lawmakers to approve public education funding before they could appropriate funds for other services.

Senator Raggio, never a big fan of the initiative, stated, "It has served no useful purpose and, in reality, poses a roadblock to the finalization of a legislatively approved budget, which must deal fairly and adequately with all aspects of required state funding."

Because the education portion had to be decided before the rest of the budget, the negotiating process would require a strong "closer," and in Bill Raggio, the Republicans held an advantage.

As an example, just a few days prior to the end of the regular session, and following weeks in a negotiation cycle of "close and impasse" (close to an agreement, then impasse), legislative leaders were only a few million dollars apart on the nearly $7 billion budget. Suddenly Senator Raggio declared that he had had enough, and told assembly Democrats to deal, or he was turning the negotiations over to the hard-line conservatives in his barely manageable caucus, led by Senator Bob Beers.

This would have been the Democrats' "worst nightmare," because Beers and his anti tax cohorts, relished saying "no" to government funding on nearly everything. Though Senator Beers was as surprised as the Democrats were by Bill's pronouncement, the tactic did get the process moving again.

*Las Vegas Sun* reporters J. Patrick Coolican and Joe Schoemann, quoted an anonymous source close to the negotiations as saying, "Raggio was exhausted from having to deal with the Beers faction...They had little interest in settling with Democrats if it meant giving too much to all-day kindergarten or not extending a cherished, although small, tax cut on business set to expire this year."[11]

The reporters explained that the faction had to be kept in the negotiation process because the budget would include small fee increases, which required a two-thirds majority in both houses.

The final budget deal included Republicans receiving a large business tax cut advocated by Senator Beers, and Democrats getting full-day kindergarten for sixty-three schools. Most other state agencies were required to make cuts in their operating budgets of 4.5%.

Ralston pointed out that Bill Raggio "was not so much ideologically driven, as process driven."

No better example of this was seen than when Senator Beers tried to advance his Tax and Spending Control (TASC) amendment through the legislature. The amendment would have limited the growth of state spending to no more than the state's population, plus the general inflation rate—with any excess revenue being returned to the taxpayers. However, because that formula was overly simplistic, it also contained a long list of exceptions and restrictions.

Bill opposed the plan saying it would "have serious unintended consequences." One example, he said, would be the ban on unfunded mandates for state or local government. As an example, Raggio said, adding more judges in Clark or Washoe counties to deal with growing caseloads would be an unfunded mandate. Yet, the duty to provide Nevadans adequate public safety would require this.

Bill said the measure was not needed because the state already had a statutory cap on spending growth since 1979, and "we have not had a legislature violate that cap."

Raggio rejected Beers's claim that the state was overtaxing people. He pointed out that Nevada was ranked the fourth best state in the nation for its business climate, thirteenth lowest in property taxes, had the forty-eighth lowest in spending per capita by state governments and the fortieth lowest in public debt per capita. Because state government has been prudent, Bill added, the amendment is unnecessary.

Rather than challenge Bill's data, Senator Beers replied that the TASC was "a matter of personal belief about what is the role of government." This remark seemed to contrast their differing styles of governance: the pragmatic, information-based process used by Raggio, as opposed to a more ideological approach. The measure died in the Senate Committee on Finance, with only Senators Beers and Cegavske voting for it.

Although an advocate of funding for education, Senator Raggio demanded accountability and quality. Earlier in the session, he had become frustrated with the State Board of Education for having resisted reform measures passed by previous legislatures, and proposed stripping the board of its power over public education,

Previous governors and legislatures had been unable to get the board to act on needed reforms. In 1997, after Raggio's initial attempt to abolish the Board of Education was killed, he developed and saw passed the Nevada Education Reform Act, which included legislative oversight committees to pursue reform and create standards for school districts.

Now, a decade later, in 2007, Bill claimed the Department of Education was making almost no progress in developing standards for education and there was clearly, "a vacuum in leadership."

Raggio pointed out that while public schools consumed 35% of the state's general fund budget, the governor and legislature had no control over the department.

"The state board wants to move back to the past by eliminating or reducing the structure we put in place," he said. "We [the legislature] have primary responsibility for the state system of public education."

Bill proposed Senate Bill 540, which would change the Board of Education from a governing board into an advisory panel reporting to the superintendent. The governor would be responsible for appointing a superintendent.

Minority Leader Dina Titus liked much of the bill, but objected to having the governor select the superintendent. The State Board replied that it was a "complicated situation" and they needed to study it more. A frustrated Raggio responded, "If you don't want to deal with something, you study, study and study."

Bill continued to battle for accountability in education, bristling when Superintendent of Education, Keith Rheault, told the Committee on Finance that budget cuts would likely require eliminating the norm-referenced student proficiency test, in lieu of a standardized required under the federal No Child Left Behind Act.

Senator Raggio had long been a proponent of the test because it measured how Nevada students compared with other students across the nation.

"I'm tired of hearing that there's too much testing," he declared. "We're providing the bulk of our financial resources to K-12 education and we need to have an assessment. We need to know where the money is being spent and if it is cost effective."

Despite Bill's efforts, norm-referenced testing was stopped in Nevada after the 2007 session due to budgetary considerations.

\* \* \*

While at times during the 2007 session Senator Raggio was unable to keep his caucus together, he did manage to defend higher education, a priority for him. He was also able to move forward his measure to end the direct election of judges.

Due to a last-minute rush of legislation seeking passage before the constitutionally mandated deadline of 1:00 a.m. on June 7, Governor Gibbons was required to call a special session for later that day. The senate finished work at 8:49 p.m. "We voted, we won, we lost, but in the end I think we served the people of this state well," said Senator Raggio afterwards.

Appropriations made outside of agency budgets, commonly referred to as "pork projects," included a number of grants designed to help the disabled, medical programs for the indigent, a program to help inmates return successfully to society, aid to rape victims and child assault prevention.

In a subsequent newspaper editorial, Rosetta Johnson, president and CEO of Human Potential Development, thanked Senator Townsend and Senate Committee Finance Chair Raggio for their commitment to helping people with co-occurring disorders.

"As a nonprofessional lobbyist," Ms. Johnson wrote, "I was treated with respect and helped to navigate the bewildering legislative process. Our legislative process in Nevada does provide its citizens a voice to express their needs and concerns. I am grateful."[12]

The largest single appropriation on the list went to the Nevada Cancer

Institute at UNR. At $10 million, the funds were provided to build additional laboratory and clinical space for research and to purchase equipment, conduct outreach and education, and implement preventative health strategies.

Three million dollars was allocated for the Lou Ruvo Brain Institute to help in the treatment and curing of a variety of brain diseases. Although considerably less than the $10 million he had sought, successful Las Vegas business executive, Larry Ruvo, was satisfied.

About Bill Raggio, Ruvo would later say,

> He has great insight and he knows when he can win, and when he can't. He cuts to the essence and is able to convince people it is the right way, because it is the only way to accomplish something. He does business the old-fashioned way, on a handshake. He will never give promises he cannot keep.

> It is hard to think of a state legislator who has done more for the State of Nevada then Senator Bill Raggio. While you may not always have agreed with him, you always knew that he gave you his honest assessment. I think Mark Twain summarized my feelings about Bill Raggio best when he said, "Always do right. This will gratify some people and astonish the rest."

In July 2007, Bill Raggio traveled to Philadelphia to attend a national meeting of ALEC, where 2,000 state legislators and business leaders from across country gathered. The featured speakers were President George W. Bush, former U.S. Senator Fred Thompson, former Arkansas Governor Mike Huckabee and former Speaker of the House of Representatives Newt Gingrich.

A highlight of the meeting was the announcement that the ALEC board of directors, in a highly unusual display of appreciation, had established the annual William J. Raggio Excellence in Leadership and Outstanding Service Award. During the Philadelphia meeting, Bill would be the first recipient of this honor for his "extraordinary contributions to ALEC through his dedication and involvement with this organization over the last thirty years."

In October 2007, Bill lost two women of great significance in his life. On October 7, Carmelite Sister Patricia Ann Kelly died. Sister Kelly had come into the Raggio family's life when Dottie was in the final stages of terminal cancer. Her frequent visits to their home, and the spiritual guidance she provided, were a great comfort to them during that dismal period.

Eleven days later, on October 18, Bill's long time executive assistant, Dorothy Souza, also died of cancer. Dorothy had been with Bill at both Jones Vargas and the legislature, for nine years. Her warm and engaging personality was a perfect complement to Senator Raggio's style. Dorothy's loss was felt by all who knew her.

Throughout Dorothy Souza's long illness, Senator Raggio kept her job open and his wife, Dale, stepped in, despite having no previous experience in the law, politics or the legislative process.

The coming two years would be the most difficult of Bill Raggio's political career. A strong effort mounted by ultra conservatives within his own party would nearly unseat him in the senate, and the increasing self-isolation of Republican Governor Gibbons would require every bit of Bill's leadership skills in an effort to save the state from financial ruin.

# CHAPTER FIFTY-EIGHT

# Challenge from the Right (2008-2009)

In March 2008, Bill and Dale joined a Nevada delegation on a visit to Taiwan. Over the years, Bill had cultivated a good relationship with his counterparts in that country, not only to share his experiences in governance, but also to promote Nevada tourism and other commercial opportunities beneficial to the state. As a result, he was highly respected by lawmakers and business people in Taiwan, who, on this visit, asked Bill for his advice on liberalizing their local gambling laws.

Consequently, Bill presented a "white paper" on Taiwan's gaming and tourism development opportunities. He prefaced his address to the forum by saying, "I'm not here to tell you whether or not to legalize gambling in any form, or to what extent, but if you were considering that, we would certainly help you with our expertise."

He noted that while the United States, in general, had been affected by the global economic slowdown, Nevada was the only state where citizens and corporations alike do not pay income taxes. He pointed out that Macao had used Las Vegas expertise to build their casinos, and positive results came quickly. In 2006, the twenty-four casinos in Macau overtook the Las Vegas strip as the world's top gambling center, taking in nearly $7 billion dollars in gambling revenue. Many in Taiwan were interested in duplicating that success.

Dina Titus, also traveled there as part of the delegation. She and Bill Raggio had served together in the state senate for twenty years, most of it as leaders of the opposing parties. Upon returning from Taiwan, she sent her former political adversary a note expressing how much she enjoyed the trip. "It was fun to step out of our worlds and be friends," Dina wrote.[1]

While Raggio and Titus's relationship warmed over time, Bill's connection with Governor Jim Gibbons seemed headed in the opposite direction.

As early as 2007, Jon Ralston wondered how effective Jim Gibbons might be as governor without people around him with legislative experience.

Bill would later say that he was able to work fairly well with Governor Gibbons during his first legislative session in 2007, as did the entire Republican senate caucus.

Although relations between the governor and Democrat leadership were hardly cordial, Bill was able to negotiate, on behalf of the governor, to save at least four of Gibbons's most important issues, including a reduction in the business payroll tax rate, the empowerment program for schools, the National Guard Academy program and transferring some room tax to road assessment.

By 2008, a host of personal problems confronted the governor. He was being sued by a woman he allegedly attacked in a Las Vegas parking garage. Gibbons had also come under investigation by federal prosecutors for improperly accepting gifts, and possible payments, from Warren Trepp, majority owner of a Reno software company that was awarded military contracts when Congressman Gibbons served on both the House Intelligence and Armed Services Committees.

More damaging allegations followed. Gibbons admitted he had pressured FBI agents to pursue criminal action against a former business partner of Trepp's, and the Elko County Assessor charged that the governor had attempted to influence him into lowering tax liability on property Gibbons had recently purchased there.

The governor's long rumored extramarital affairs became public in early 2008 when he sued his wife for divorce based on "incompatibility"—and Dawn Gibbons subsequently accused him of cheating and listed the names of several women.

Throughout all this, Senator Raggio remained loyal to both the governor and the First Lady, refusing to comment publicly on the series of embarrassments, and continuing to suggest to others that they respect the office, if not the man.

Yet, as the governor's behavior became more unpredictable, and his decision-making more illogical, Bill would find himself in an increasingly difficult position; one that would sorely test his statesmanship and sense of decorum.

During the interim between the 2007 and the 2009 sessions, the governor's popularity with voters fell dramatically. Polling conducted in June 2008 indicated an all-time low 10% approval rating, with 59% disapproving.

In 2010, Bill Raggio would talk of how all these matters appeared to have distracted the governor, creating disharmony not only in his personal life but also among his staff. "For whatever reason," Bill said, "the governor was facing constant changes in his staff, either through departures, terminations or defections."

Mike Dayton, his first chief of staff was removed; Steve Robinson, his legislative liaison, and Josh Hicks, his second chief of staff, both resigned. "And as a result of the continuing rift with Diane Cornwall," Bill said, Mendy Elliott, deputy chief of staff, was relegated to a secretarial position in the Department of Business and Industry. Ben Kieckhefer, the only information officer on the governor's staff who earned high respect from the media, was transferred to obscurity in the Department of Health and Human Services.

"It seemed as if the governor could not get along with almost anyone who worked with him," Bill added, "and it is telling that none of these persons are supporting him in his campaign for reelection in 2010."

\* \* \*

In the summer of 2008 the Nevada Supreme Court heard arguments about the legality of the term limits passed into law by voter initiative in 1996.

Proponents of term limits believed that incumbents held an overwhelming advantage during elections, especially in attracting campaign donations, and that the longer politicians held office, the friendlier they became with special interests, while losing touch with their constituents.

Opponents argued that term limits took away the freedom of the people to elect the candidate of their choice and that those voters had been effective in using the ballot box to remove elected officials who no longer deserved the position.

In a state with a citizen legislature, like Nevada, lobbyists were already serving as subject-matter experts. With lawmakers now limited to twelve years, while lobbyists and bureaucrats were not, the legislature would become easier, rather than more difficult, for special interests to manipulate.

Senator Raggio worried about the future of the Nevada State Legislature with term limits in place. "You lose historical reference in large measure, for example, the reasons why bills were passed years ago," he explained. "It takes a long time to understand the state budget process, never mind policies and the reasons behind those policies. It takes time to get to a goal. Even twelve years can be a short time in that process."

Bill was also concerned that the first session to be impacted by a large influx of new faces in the legislature due to term limits would be 2011, a session that would require reapportionment and redistricting. Because Nevada had experienced such rapid growth over the last decade, it was probable that a fourth seat in the House of Representatives would be added. The legislature would also have to decide whether to expand in size beyond its current sixty-three members.

In July, the issue became moot when the Nevada Supreme Court unanimously upheld term limits and clarified what constituted a "twelve-year term."

Senator Raggio could serve until November 7, 2012. Bill stated that he felt an "obligation" to run for a final term, arguing the state needed his leadership as it heads into what is expected to be bloody battles over shrinking revenues and reapportionment.

April 13, 2008 was the deadline for filing to run for elective office in Nevada. As that day arrived, Bill had no serious challengers in his run for reelection. Yet, just moments before the 5:00 p.m. closing time at the office of the Secretary of State, Sharron Angle arrived and filed to run against him for his Senate District 3 seat.

Angle, a former assemblywoman and one of the, so-called "Mean 15," had served from 1998 through 2005. During her time in the assembly, she prided herself on her unwillingness to compromise on almost every issue.

At the end of the 2003 session, Jon Ralston reported the results of the *Las Vegas Review Journal* poll of legislators, lobbyists and the press. In the category of "Worst Assembly Member," or what Jon Ralston termed "Just Wasting Space," Angle won "hands down." "No one was even close," he wrote.[2]

Working to cultivate an image as a conservative maverick, Angle's dogmatic approach caused her to have a difficult time drawing other legislators to her issues.

"We used to have a joke called '41 to Angle,'"* Democratic Assemblywoman Sheila Leslie would later say. "She took great pride in voting 'no' for everything. We have some very conservative people in the assembly, but she was the only one voting 'no' on a technical cleanup bill. The lobbyists didn't talk to her and the legislators wouldn't talk to her. When you vote 'no' on everything, no one wants to deal with you."

Bill Raggio was disappointed when he learned Angle had filed at the last minute to be his challenger in the primary election. "I thought her credentials were minimal," he said. "She served four terms in the assembly and during all those years was of absolutely no consequence. She prided herself on voting 'no.'" Frankly, I did not believe that she would command a lot of support."

"Over the years," Bill added, "she has always been more interested in her personal success than in helping to solve issues."

Before Senator Raggio could fully concentrate on the campaign, he was faced with having to help resolve a gigantic shortfall in the state's budget.

---

*The Nevada Assembly consists of forty-two members. Sharron Angle often was the only "no" vote.

After emptying the state's Rainy Day Fund of $914 million, Governor Gibbons suggested a special session of the legislature to remedy the remainder of the problem. Others disagreed.

Senator Raggio, who had originally sided with Democratic leaders in saying that the special session was unnecessary, later acceded to the governor's wishes.

The governor finally called for a special session to be held in June 2008, and then, as Dennis Myers wrote, "Nothing happened...Days passed with no guidance on what he wanted them to do when they arrived in Carson City."[3]

Democrats were confounded by the governor's lack of leadership. Speaker Barbara Buckley said, "The governor is saying he believes we have a budget crisis, but is proposing no solutions to deal with it. I find that ludicrous. To now just abdicate his responsibility to come up with suggestions to ensure a balanced budget just defies logic."

Buckley was grateful, however, for Senator Raggio's presence in the decision-making process, calling him "an honest and dedicated public servant," and commended him for working with her toward a bipartisan solution.

Bill also worked with the governor's staff throughout the budget negotiations to make certain many of the legislatively agreed-upon budget cuts were in the final legislation.

The governor eventually submitted a budget. Curiously, given his well publicized "no tax" stance, his program called for reinstatement of sales tax on complimentary meals served by casinos. That recommended tax increase passed in the Democrat-dominated assembly, but died in the senate.

By the time the special session convened on June 27, most of the details on closing the $1.2 billion shortfall had already been worked out in closed-door meetings between assembly and senate leadership.

In the twelve hours the special session lasted, the legislature enacted painful cuts to education, public health programs and the operation of state government. The remainder of the shortfall would come from a 3.3% cut in agency operating budgets, tapping a school textbook fund and canceling some transportation projects.

As a safeguard against further erratic behavior on the part of the governor, legislators used a concurrent resolution, rather than a bill, to describe the cuts they had approved—because a concurrent resolution is not subject to veto.

Governor Gibbons was soon on television blaming the lawmakers for the budget crisis because of the budget "they" had approved in 2007.

Almost before the Democrats could, an irate Senator Raggio responded, "The governor pointed toward the legislature saying they over promised and overspent. I would take issue with that. It's my recollection that the governor proposes the spending level in the budget. The governor did not recommend in his 2007 budget any spending reductions."

\* \* \*

With the end of the special session, Bill Raggio turned his attention to the political challenge presented by Sharron Angle. He knew that the Democrats were going to make a powerful run both statewide and nationally in 2008 and was not pleased the Republican Party was being weakened by divisiveness.

This was the first time since 1984 that Bill had a serious challenge to his senate seat. Angle had built her power base outside the Republican establishment and narrowly lost to Dean Heller in the 2006 Republican primary for Nevada's Second Congressional District seat.

She had been successful by going door-to-door and engaging each voter on a personal level. It was thought by many in her camp that the eighty-one-year-old Raggio would not be up to competing with her at that level, especially during the heat of summer. They would soon be proven wrong.

Bill and Dale began spending their mornings canvassing the district. On any given day, they would be assisted by numerous volunteers including State Republican Party Chair Sue Lowden and her husband Paul, and numerous other supporters such as former Governor Guinn and his wife Dema, Reno Mayor Bob Cashell, former councilman Dave Howard, At&T President Hal Lenox, Carol and George Del Carlo, and Bill's daughter, Leslie Righetti.

Later, Senator Raggio would jokingly speak of how Guinn's popularity made him ineffective as a precinct walker. When surprised residents saw who it was, they would invite him in and offer him a beer. "So he didn't cover much ground," Bill quipped.

"We had major funding and a major outpouring of supporters from all walks of life," Bill would later say. "This included endorsements from the Chamber of Commerce, people like U.S. Senator John Ensign, former Congresswoman Barbara Vucanovich, District Attorney Dick Gammick and Mayor Bob Cashell. I would say we were endorsed by almost all of the leaders of our state and communities."

Bill received support from groups that would not normally endorse Republican candidates, such as the teachers' union and the National Education Association. This was fodder for Angle's campaign, which used it against Bill as "proof" that he was not a true conservative. Raggio replied, "I'm not going to tell people not to endorse me. Her lack of endorsement speaks for itself. Her only endorsement was from what I call the Ron Paul group, which, in effect, makes her a Libertarian who has chosen to wear the Republican label. In many ways, this is a fight for the soul of the Republican Party in Nevada."

Bill particularly enjoyed knocking on doors that already had Angle signs on the lawn. If no one answered, he would leave a leaflet, first writing on the back "Sorry I missed you. I would appreciate your vote on August 12." To those who answered the door, he would say, "I'm Bill Raggio and I'm your state senator." He would then inquire about any concerns the person might have, and ask for their vote.

Once back at home, Bill would spend his afternoons and evenings writing personal notes to voters or making phone calls.

He told *Las Vegas Sun journalist* David McGrath-Schwartz that the campaign had "energized" him and he was delighted by the level of support he was receiving.[4]

Even the nuns at the Carmel monastery in his district, realizing Bill was in a close race, all volunteered to change party affiliation from Democrat to Republican so they could vote for him in the primary election. When Bill heard about it, he humorously reassured them that, "It's only a venial sin (as opposed to a *mortal* sin) to be a Republican."

Part of Sharron Angle's campaign strategy was to convince Republican primary voters that, for all Raggio's influence, the northern part of the state had not fared well during his tenure. "I don't know that we benefited in northern Nevada from his power and influence," she said, blaming Bill for allowing northern Nevada seats in the legislature to move to southern Nevada during the past reapportionment sessions. "While population dictates redistricting," she conceded, "he should have gotten the number of districts increased."

Bill found the claim amusing. During the last reapportionment session in 2001, he had been the chief proponent for expanding the legislature, but could not persuade the assembly to go along with the plan.

Raggio called her claim "disingenuous" and reminded voters that he had a commitment in 2001 from Assembly Speaker Perkins to enlarge the legislature so that the north would not lose any seats, while the south would gain what they proportionately deserved.

However, in a subsequent battle over the makeup of a new congressional district in Clark County, "Perkins withdrew the commitment he had made me to enlarge the membership," Bill said. "If my opponent had all the power she claims to have had, where was her voice in the assembly at that time?"

The Angle campaign was strongly supported by a conservative PAC that had long been pressuring candidates and incumbents to sign what they called the "Taxpayer Protection Pledge" promising "no-new-taxes."* The group dogmatically held that Nevada had a spending problem and not a revenue problem. [5]

Ultra-conservative Republicans and Libertarians railed against Senator Raggio for not taking the pledge and because he advised his political colleagues to stop making broad pledges not to raise taxes:

---

*Toward the end of the Reagan presidency, taxes would be a fundamental issue with ultra conservative Republicans. Grover Norquist, head of Americans for Tax Reform, created a no-new-taxes pledge and began encouraging candidates at all levels of government to sign it. The pledge version for state legislators simply states that the signer will "oppose and vote against any and all efforts to raise taxes."

It's time to quit the bluster. I'm not championing higher taxes or new taxes. I'm just pointing out the problems we face and what the options are. Contrary to what a lot of these political candidates throw out there, including Angle, Nevada is not the fifth or sixth highest taxed state in the country. According to the Tax Foundation, we are the second, only to Alaska, in having the lowest tax burden per capita in the nation. We don't have a state income tax, we don't have a corporate income tax, yet I got chewed up for saying we're not over-taxed.

Raggio refused to be put in a situation where his flexibility in bargaining with the Democrats would be taken away. He called Angle's anti-tax message "dishonest." While Angle had voted against all the major spending bills in 2003, as part of her opposition to the tax increase, Bill reminded voters that she did vote "yes" in 2005 on each of the budget bills, approving spending measures in excess of the 2003 budget. "I don't call that conservative," he said, "I call it hypocritical."

Angle supporters regularly accused Senator Raggio of not being a "true Reagan Republican," calling him a "RINO," Republican in Name Only. Bill found this ludicrous, since he had known Ronald Reagan far better than any of his detractors had. As a member of ALEC, Bill attended policy meetings with the president at the White House, and was invited by the Reagans to social gatherings.

"The party needs to get back to the principles of Ronald Reagan and that is to stick to their basic principles of free enterprise and limited government," Bill said. "Don't speak ill of other Republicans—and don't make pledges not to raise taxes any time. Ronald Reagan raised some taxes."* They need to take a page out of his book."

He also chastised the right wing of his party for creating lack of unity among its members. "Until the party unites itself and focuses on defeating Democrats and liberals," he complained, "it won't succeed. Like the

---

*President Reagan's policy regarding taxes was that they were undesirable, yet sometimes necessary. During his eight years in office, Reagan approved thirteen tax increases, including one in 1982 that was the largest in the nation's history. He also cut taxes on a number of occasions.

Birchers in the 1960s, these right wing elements will argue that they need to rid their party of everybody who doesn't agree with them. Time will tell how distorted that concept is."

On August 13, 2008, Bill Raggio won the Republican primary election by 550 votes out of 9,200 cast, equating to a 53% to 47% margin over his challenger.

In addition to funds, endorsements and a legion of volunteers and campaign workers, Bill utilized the services of a Nevada firm, Advanced MicroTargeting, that specialized in a high-tech campaign strategies.

Joe Brezny, who directed the day-to-day operations of the campaign and was later manager of the senate Republican caucus, had used the company when he successfully managed Mitt Romney's presidential primary campaign in Nevada earlier that year.

Brezny explained that most elected officials don't know much about running campaigns. "They are wired differently," he said, "and think in a certain way. However, a few, like Bill Raggio and Barbara Buckley, can think like a political operatives. Bill was acutely present in the 2008 primary campaign. He questioned us a lot and asked many very tough questions."

"One reason Senator Raggio won, Brezny said, "is because he was smart enough to surround himself with the best." But, as Brezny was quick to point out, it was not the only reason. "A lot of people love Senator Raggio and what has done for the state of Nevada," he said. "They realize the power that they have in northern Nevada is because of him. So, we had people who came out of the woodwork."

One of the "best" Bill surrounded himself with in that campaign was his friend and trusted advisor, Greg Ferraro. Ferraro had known Bill since he began lobbying at the legislature in 1989. During the time of Dorothy Raggio's illness, and in the aftermath of her death, the two grew closer. When Ferraro was later diagnosed with early stage melanoma, similar to what Bill had survived in 2000, Bill helped him through the stressful process, seeing that he obtained attention from the best specialists in that field.

As the 2008 election cycle neared, Bill turned to Ferraro to oversee the general operation of the primary election campaign, primarily focusing his talents primarily on the message, polling and spending.

In a 2011 interview, Ferraro would say of that campaign: "His opponent's attacks were mostly personal, the subtext being that because of Bill's age he would not have the vigor to mount a successful campaign. We did not respond on that level, nor did we panic even when the poll numbers closed a bit, as they do in every election. Instead, we decided to prove that Bill was strong and energetic."

Ferraro recalled that Senator Raggio worked harder than anyone did, out every single day, regardless of the summer heat, walking precincts in his district and working well into each night making calls and writing letters. "Republican voters want to see a candidate not only with energy and desire, but also someone with the ability to get things done," Ferraro said. "He won because he is Bill Raggio."

Reflecting on Bill's political career, Ferraro added:

> In November 1970, Bill lost a tough race for the U.S. Senate. One of the great ironies is that voters made a choice that in fact turned out to be a very good one. Had it not been for that, Nevadans would be bereft of the Carson City master who, empowered by the giant spirit of his small state, set the course for the Nevada we know today.

Three days after his primary election victory over Sharron Angle, Bill spoke about the race. Months before the election, he recalled, long before any challengers appeared, he and Dale discussed whether he should retire from the state senate or seek a final term.

"Dale was extremely supportive of whatever decision I wanted to make," Bill said, "although I think she privately hoped that I would retire, or to use her expression, 'go out on top.'"

Bill said he had been privileged to represent Washoe County and the interests of Northern Nevada in the state senate since 1972. He recognized that the dynamics of the state has changed dramatically since that time. The structure of the legislature and the issues had changed as well.

"I believed we needed to have some strong voices in the legislative process," he said, "especially with the impending loss of leadership due to term limits. This was not an ego trip for me. I felt I had an obligation and a responsibility to run."

Bill added that while he had experienced competitive elections over his career, he never faced an opponent as deceptive as Sharron Angle, or where his record was so distorted and his reputation so besmirched. "It is very apparent to me," he said, "that she will stop at nothing to further her own personal ambition."

Bill gave as an example of Angle's deceptiveness, how she drew the ire of National Rifle Association Executive Vice President and CEO Wayne La Pierre for falsely claiming she had the organization's endorsement of her candidacy.

In another example, Angle claimed that Senator Raggio was against property tax relief, because he would not support her initiative. "However," said Bill, "in 2005, when we voted a property tax cap to limit individual homeowner's property taxes to 3%, she was the only one in the legislature to vote against it. This is because she wanted to further her own ambitions with her name on a property tax initiative. When she later tried to accuse me of being against property tax limitations because I didn't support that tax initiative, my reply was, 'We passed the law; we do not need to change the Constitution.'"

Regarding the 2003 tax increase, Angle tried to paint Bill as a "tax-and-spender." Yet, over the years, he had gained respect from both parties as a conscientious fiscal conservative.

Her campaign ads repeated the message that a person with principles would never compromise. Bill was incredulous: "If that were true, you would never end a legislative session. Yet, people listen to her and believe that diatribe."

In 2008, Reno journalist Dennis Myers would ask Senator Raggio to comment on the suggestion that some in his party treat programmatic matters, like spending and taxes, as moral issues rather than public policy issues. These Republicans, Myers observed, consider compromise not as a necessary legislative tool, but as ethically wrong.

Senator Raggio replied, "I've had to deal consistently with a house of the other party and we would have gotten nowhere if we were not willing to compromise. If we were going to put good and evil labels on things, we might as well not have shown up." [6]

Bill told his staff that he did not want to run a "nasty campaign," saying that if he had to rely on the kind of support Angle was receiving, he would just as soon not win.

"I did not want to be beholden to that type of support or committed to doing nothing," he noted, "which was essentially the message she was sending out. Legislation is the art of compromise, but there is no compromise in their minds. It is either all their way or the highway."

Political scientist Eric Herzik noted that intolerance on both social and tax issues was damaging the Republican Party's ability to attract a wide spectrum of voters needed to win elections. "Instead of bringing people into the tent, they are throwing people out of the tent."[12]

Customarily the candidate who loses in a primary election calls the victor to offer congratulations and support. Sharron Angle never called. "What does that tell you?" Raggio quipped dryly.

* * *

The general election was held on November 4, 2008. Senator Raggio retained his senate seat, garnering nearly 64% of the vote over his Democratic challenger.[7] Nationally, Democrats swept into power gaining majorities in both houses of Congress and elected Illinois Senator Barack Obama as President, over Arizona Republican Senator John McCain.

In Nevada, Obama won by a margin of 12%. Regarding the national election, Bill would later say, "Who would have guessed his victory in Nevada would give such large numbers to a Democrat, and an African American? I am not proud to say that Nevada was once called the "Mississippi of the West. Obama is charismatic and a good campaigner."

However, Bill could see the national Democrat trend coming. In a 2009 interview, he explained:

Whenever you have a recession, the party in power usually loses. It was a perfect storm. You had an unpopular president. People were tired of war. There's no question that many people who supported the war against terrorism agree that the war has been mishandled. You had the impact of Hurricane Katrina. In fairness to George Bush, if you begin with terrorist attacks on September 11, no president has ever been faced with anything that severe, unless it was Abraham Lincoln or maybe Roosevelt during World War II.

Former Senate Minority Leader Dina Titus rode the Democratic wave in defeating Republican Jon Porter in his bid for reelection to the U.S. House of Representatives. It was an expensive and bitterly fought campaign.

With Titus's departure from the state senate, thirty-five-year-old Democratic State Senator Steven Horsford, of Clark County, a relative newcomer to the body and, like Obama, an African American, was elevated to senate majority leader.[8]

Horsford's meteoric rise to the top leadership position was largely the result of his intellect, drive and skill as a political operative. The latter resulted in his receiving credit for having helped engineer the election of two relatively unknown Democratic senate candidates in upset victories over conservative Republican incumbents Bob Beers and Joe Heck. Their defeats resulted in the Republicans losing their majority in the state senate for the first time in sixteen years.

Many observers, including Senators Raggio and Townsend, insisted that resources, which could have gone to help boost candidates in the November election, had been needlessly depleted in order for Raggio to fight off the challenge by Sharron Angle in the primary. Nevertheless, Bill had to concede that it might have still been an impossible task:

The Democrats had all the money they needed nationally and, through the efforts of Senator Reid, they had more money than they needed in Nevada. Money poured into the state, particularly to unseat southern Nevada candidates Heck and Beers. We raised a great deal of money and I, personally, raised a great deal of money through the Senate Republican Caucus and by the Majority Leader's Fund. Yet the Democrats were able to meet the funding requirements to match independent efforts that were put forth for those counties. There is nothing we could have done to win those races.

Senator Raggio was not pleased with what the election results boded for the future. "We have this Republican Party that seems to be intent on 'eating its own,'" he said.

Bill felt that because of the far right's influence, there had been a large defection from the party, especially from Independents and Libertarians who insisted on running candidates that drew votes from the Republicans, like John McCain.

In November 2008, Bill said:

It is obvious that this anger the radicals exhibit is fanned and fumed by talk shows. Talk shows are a form of entertainment that these people take as gospel. These commentators and talk show hosts are entertainers. That is how they make their living. Look at Rush Limbaugh, Hannity and the like. They spent six months, day-by-day, hour by hour, skewering John McCain because he was not conservative enough, and that he wasn't a "real" Republican. Yet at the end of the presidential campaign, they expected their listeners to vote for McCain. A lot of them did not vote for him, or support the party, because they had been traumatized for six months. These people have simply forgotten Reagan's "11th Commandment" of not speaking ill of other Republicans.

* * *

The 2009 legislature convened on Monday, February 2. Senator Raggio received a call from the new majority leader, Senator Horsford. "We had a discussion the first day. He was very gracious and said we would work together."

Following the previous session, relations between Governor Gibbons and Democrats had deteriorated rapidly. Revenues were falling and forecasts were dire. The governor had called two special sessions to deal with the revenue shortfalls, and lawmakers had been able to agree on reductions without raising taxes.

Bill's relationship with some members of his own party had turned as well.

When Republican Assemblyman Ed Goedhart, of Amargosa Valley in southern Nevada, published a "Fiscal Blueprint" recommending all cuts and no flexibility on taxes to solve the budget deficit, Senator Raggio responded in an open email, accusing Goedhart of using a document written for him by Las Vegas anti-tax activist Chuck Muth "for his own publicity proposes." Bill's email read, in part:

> *Since you indicate that you had no intention of voting for any tax increases of any kind you really have removed yourself from any part of the potential solution to solving our serious budget crisis. If we are to balance a budget and ensure delivery of essential services, taxes may be an option, albeit a last option. I have some long-term experience in this legislative process and I really don't think I benefit from the advice you are offering.*[9]

After submitting his *Executive Budget*, which included a 36% cut in higher education and a 6% cut in salary and benefits for teachers and state workers, and then threatening to veto any legislation that contained new or increased taxes, Governor Gibbons went into isolation.

While his predecessor, Governor Guinn, had been in the Legislative Building almost daily, often testifying before legislative committees on behalf of measures he supported, Governor Gibbons rarely was seen, provided no leadership and little relevant input. Instead, he sent his staff to testify.

While many of them were qualified individuals, high turnover in their ranks, through defections and terminations, prevented them from having much influence on the lawmaker's decisions.

Senator Raggio immediately criticized the budget cuts as being too draconian. By now the majority of legislators, including much of the senate's Republican caucus, which normally would be working to implement a Republican governor's budget, had become indifferent to Gibbons.

They, like everyone in the Legislative Building, knew that Senator Raggio held the real clout in the party, and it would be up to him to help resolve the $2.3 billion budget crisis.

Bill began work with the new majority leader, Senator Horsford, and their counterparts in the assembly, to reach a compromise on measures to rescue the state.

Senator Raggio warned that Nevada was facing the "most serious financial crisis" he had seen in his thirty-seven years of political service. "We have to concern ourselves with how we get through this next biennium," he said, "and how to provide essential services, but at the same time not impose unrealistic, unfair financial burdens on the people that have to pay the cost of it."

While assembly Democrats held a veto-proof majority, senate Democrats would require at least two Republicans to vote with them to reach the two-thirds majority necessary to override a veto. The final decision would be in Senator Raggio's hands, though he downplayed the notion early on. "I'm going to do precisely what is necessary in the best interest of the state," he said. "That's what I was elected to do, and not to represent my party or any special interest group."

Bill insisted any tax increase would have to have an automatic expiration date, called a "sunset provision," and be revisited in the following session. "If the economy improves and we don't need them, then they'll be gone," he explained.

Another of his conditions for voting for a temporary tax plan was that there be, what he termed, "a credible, objective tax study" conducted by an independent consultant such as Price Waterhouse, the Urban Institute or "someone of that caliber."

In that way, Bill said, if the study was completed by the following session, "there will be something that the public can understand, whether or not new taxes are needed, tax increases are needed, and whether we are spending the money wisely on essential services."

If those conditions were met, Raggio said, then he, and at least one other member of his caucus, would vote for the plan, thus giving the senate enough votes to override the governor's veto.

The Nevada Constitution granted the governor five working days to act on a measure coming from the legislature. Should that period elapse without any action, the measure would automatically pass into law. With the legislative session mandated to end June 1, lawmakers would have to have the appropriation measures to him no later than 5:00 pm on Friday, May 22.

Majority Leader Horsford was confronted with a difficult task, requiring him to learn his job quickly while at the same time using a fine diplomatic touch to keep the Republican caucus happy for their two needed votes.

As would be expected of someone learning his job, he occasionally tripped up. In the early morning hours of May 21, after the details of the $780 million budget package had been already worked out, the two party's differed on how much to change public employee pensions, health benefits for retirees and collective bargaining between the local governments and employee unions. Republicans insisted their votes on the tax package were conditioned upon significant reform. Talks between the two parties on these issues had broken down.

At 2:30 a.m., Senator Horsford attempted to keep business going by invoking a little used procedural rule—"Call of the House"—to force three wayward Republican senators back to the floor. This required the senate sergeant at arms to find and return these individuals to the senate chamber, even if it was necessary for them to be taken into custody. During this time, Horsford even refused a request for a restroom break, though the requesting senator ignored him and left chambers.

The majority leader soon lifted the order after two of the three senators returned (the other lived well out of town and had gone home). Senate members then spent the next hour hearing bills, arguing the propriety of Senator Horsford's tactic and debating the issues holding up the tax package.

Horsford defended his move, saying the tax package had to be on the governor's desk the following day, "otherwise we have the governor's budget, with all its cuts." He said Democrats had already agreed to sig-nificant reforms on public employees benefit and health plans, as well as the collective bargaining issue, and felt it was time to get it resolved.

When the meeting adjourned at 4:00 a.m., Senator Raggio said of the Senator Horsford's ploy, "It was not a wise tactic. I think what the dis-tinguished majority leader has done tonight, works to his disadvantage. I told him earlier our folks are tired. We haven't reached an agreement. I think we can."

Despite these occasional meltdowns, the tight deadline generated a generally bipartisan spirit throughout the session. However, later that day, all the hard work nearly came undone with a level of high drama rarely seen in the senate chambers.

Desperate anti-tax forces, represented by Republican consultant Robert Uithoven, used rumors of potential conflicts of interest as a way to peel off "yes" votes. The targets were Senators Hardy and Raggio.

Senator Hardy was first on the "hit list." After hearing about the threat of an ethics complaint against him for a conflict of interest, Hardy had earlier stepped away from his role as lead Republican negotiator on changes to pay and benefits for public employees.

The potential conflict arose because Hardy was president of the Asso-ciated Builders and Contractors, on whose board sat the president of the Greater Las Vegas Chamber of Commerce, Steve Hill. The Chamber was lobbying assiduously to curtail public employee pay, benefits and collective bargaining. Because Hill technically acted in a supervisory position over Hardy, the senator said he would, on the advice of legislative counsel and with "an abundance of caution," abstain from voting on the public employee measure.

About six hours later, the Nevada Supreme Court voted unanimously that the Ethics Commission be barred from taking any action against Hardy based of the constitutional doctrine of separation of powers. The court ruled that only the legislature could determine whether its members can vote on an issue, or if they must disclose potential conflicts of interest before voting. Of the ruling, Hardy said he was gratified that lawmakers were now "assured that there won't be an unfair, politically motivated attack on their ability to vote."[10]

A few hours after Senator Hardy stepped down as negotiator, Senator Raggio announced that he would be abstaining from the crucial vote on the tax package. Unbeknownst to him, an attorney from Jones Vargas had testified earlier in the session on the tax bill, and Raggio had just learned that he might be threatened with an ethics complaint as a result. He made his decision on the legal opinion of Legislative Counsel Brenda Erdoes.

Senator Raggio then gave an impassioned speech, decrying such attacks on legislators' integrity, saying, "I will follow the opinion. I will abstain. I will do so reluctantly because my first obligation here, under the oath I took, was to do what's right for the state."

Bill added that outside activists were seeking to thwart the tax package. Political operative Robert Uithoven, head of the Western Alliance Fund, a conservative PAC that had been airing radio ads opposing the tax increases, brought the issue to light, but later denied Senator Raggio's charges that he threatened to file an ethics complaint.[11]

Bill ended his speech by defending the ideal of citizen legislators, while pointing out how increasingly untenable that concept was becoming:

> Maybe we ought to decide whether or not we want ordinary people who have some interest in being in the legislature...who were trying to do their duty and doing it sincerely, and let's make sure they don't feel threatened every time. I'm getting a little irritated with this kind of activity.

These two stunning events, coming just one day before the legislature's self-imposed deadline, seemed to derail the plan to override the governor's veto. A recess was called and when the senate session resumed, Majority Leader Horsford took the floor and announced he was introducing a resolution that would provide an exemption to Senate Rule 23, which provided ethical guidelines, including those governing conflicts of interest. The resolution, now necessary due to the recent Supreme Court ruling in the Hardy case, would allow both Raggio and Hardy to vote on the measures in question.

In his announcement, Horsford said that Nevada's system of citizen legislators was founded on the principles of transparency and disclosure of personal conflict of interest. He congratulated Senator Raggio for his commitment to these ethical principles.

Because the issues at hand were of such great importance to the state, Horsford explained, "All legislators should have the ability to execute their sworn constitutional duty to balance the budget of the state and represent the interests of Nevada citizens."

The senate then voted on—and passed—the resolution.

The following day, Friday, May 22, was even more nerve-wracking. Before 3:00 p.m., the senate settled the public employees' benefits and collective bargaining reform issues. The only two items remaining to close the budget agreement were Senator Raggio's earlier conditions of "sunset provisions" on taxes and an objective study of the tax state's structure.

As expected, Bill then put forward his amendment to provide a firm two-year "sunset" on most of the tax package. It failed to pass in a voice vote. Democratic Senator John Lee then offered an amendment that proposed a sunset provision based on a trigger mechanism. This passed on a party line vote.

Raggio insisted on an unconditional sunset. Senator Hardy agreed, saying, "I cannot support a tax package without a true sunset." In the hallway outside the chambers, lobbyist Mike Hillerby, former chief of staff for Governor Kenny Guinn, told a *Review Journal* reporter, "I'm not sure there are the votes in the senate until someone blinks."[12]

After meeting with LCB legal staff members, Senator Horsford took the senate floor with an amendment containing the unconditional two-year sunset provision Senator Raggio had proposed earlier, explaining, "I care more about this state and my children's education than scoring an internal policy victory." However, his amendment also included language for an interim commission to review the state's tax structure.

Senator Raggio replied that, while he was grateful for the sunset provision, the interim commission was unacceptable, as it seemed to include language about specific taxes. He asked for a recess so he could study it in caucus.

It was now within an hour of the deadline to have a bill to the governor's office and tension on the floor, and in the gallery, was palpable. So much so, that when Senator Bob Coffin heard Bill's insistence on a recess to review the amendment, he shouted, "No! No!"—compelling Senate President Brian Krolicki to bang the gavel for order.

After about ten minutes, the Republican caucus returned. Senator Raggio announced he would not support Senator Horsford's amendment unless the interim commission language was removed and a "credible" tax study was approved.

Realizing Raggio would not allow him even a small victory, and with precious minutes ticking away, Horsford relented and agreed to delete the objectionable provisions in the amendment. The bill passed the senate seventeen to four, with five Republicans voting for it.

Just six minutes earlier, in another part of the Legislative Building, Assembly Speaker Buckley interrupted comments on the tax measure and called for a vote. It passed twenty nine to thirteen.

When comments about the bill resumed, Assemblyman John Carpenter of Elko County asked to speak. He had been one of the so-called "Mean 15" who defied increasing tax increases in 2003, but was now the only assembly Republican to back the 2009 tax measure.

Because of term limits, it would be Carpenter's last session. He told his colleagues that the vote had been the toughest decision in his twenty-two years as a legislator, reminding them that throughout those years he had worked to improve schools and colleges and reduce class sizes. "My own children and grandchildren have received fine educations," he added, saying that all children in the state should have an opportunity for quality education. "I asked the Lord," Carpenter said, "and the Lord said this is the thing you should do. Tonight you're going to sleep. And sleep well I did."

Escorted by several police officers, a staffer carried the budget bill across the plaza from the Legislative Building to the state Capitol, arriving at the governor's office just before closing time of 5:00 p.m.

The final legislation contained a yearly increase in taxes and fees of $390 million to finance the state's $6.7 billion biennial general fund budget. These included a higher sales tax and an increase in vehicle registration fees. Large businesses would pay higher payroll taxes, a move not seriously opposed by most business groups. Smaller businesses would receive a tax break.

Senator Barbara Cegavske, who joined fellow Republican Senators Washington, McGinness and Amodei in voting against the bill, called the tax on business "a job killing tax and a business killing tax" that would result in more layoffs.

Lawmakers also cut many critical services affecting children, families and the aged. Raggio referred to the measure as "bare bones."

Jon Ralston said, "It is far from a badge any of them should wear with honor." He went on to say that the "real travesty" had been in the way many Republican legislators, "using simple minded, fatuous rhetoric," had voted against a tax increase, but only after voting hundreds of millions of dollars in spending for K-12 education and the overall spending package.

This, said Ralston, would allow them during their reelection campaigns to say that they "supported education, but hypocritically opposed the revenue package to fund it…This is the worst kind of craven and disingenuous behavior."[13]

The 75th Nevada legislature adjourned just before the 120-day deadline, overriding twenty-five of Governor Gibbons's record forty-one vetoes, and working to finalize a handful of last minute bills.

The governor's method for deciding which bills to veto was often a mystery, even to his staff. In one case, he vetoed an increase to a gas tax in Washoe County, even though it had already been approved by voters there. He also vetoed a bill that would have created a rainy day fund for education, a concept he had gone on record earlier as supporting.

Later in 2009, Bill Raggio recalled the session as the most difficult of his career. "There were a lot of egos that had to be assuaged in order to come together," he said, pointing to the many differences of opinion between, and within, each party and each house. "It was an unusual set of vibrations, if you want to call it that."

In addition to those impediments, Raggio said, "We had a governor who made himself irrelevant to this process and was not communicative at all. I only spoke to him four or five times and those were usually calls that I placed to him."

However, Senator Raggio worked very closely with at least three people from the governor's office: Josh Hicks, his chief of staff; Mendy Elliott, deputy chief of staff; and Andrew Clinger, budget director. "They were very efficient, high quality people and great to work with," Raggio would say, adding that despite the governor's disengagement from the process, these three staffers kept communications open so he could keep them informed about the process.

Raggio said he had advised the governor, before the session began, that the economy was most likely going to slip further than anyone had anticipated and that Gibbons could make the case for some tax increases. "He could have cited his stand on taxes, recognizing that some cuts were too deep and these were extraordinary circumstances," Bill recalled. "He could have said, 'I think for the good of the state we're going to have to accept some tax increases.' That's where I came from. But the governor stuck to his principles."

"In fairness to the governor," Bill continued, "the Democrats did not make him feel welcome when the legislature began. The Democrat leaders in both houses were very vituperative in their comments. I did not agree with him altogether, but I always respected the office of the governor. And whenever it came up, I tried to be defensive. I tried to be a supporter, not of his positions necessarily, but of his right to express them."

Assembly Speaker Buckley recalled during a 2010 interview that, very early in the governor's term, a number of Democrat's were extremely frustrated with him. He was disengaged, Buckley explained, and appeared to be expending a significant amount of time on personal issues. She said there were numerous distractions and they would not hear from him for years. "Therefore, we were always very quick to be disdainful of the governor," she admitted. "So we would talk about him and sometimes it would leak out into the public domain. Senator Raggio would always say, 'You must respect the office of the governor even if you don't respect the occupant.' He was right; I needed to be more statesmanlike. It was good advice and I took it."

\* \* \*

Senator Horsford received praise from many quarters for the job he had done as a fledgling majority leader. Jon Ralston applauded him for deciding to "lose the battle to win a war" in order to benefit the state. He was referring to Horsford having allowed "the master of the legislative endgame, Bill Raggio, to do what he does best—run out the clock — but to sacrifice for the short term to preserve the long term." [14]

In late 2009, Bill Raggio discussed the job done by the majority leader, saying Senator Horsford learned a great deal, but also made some errors through inexperience. "Everything you do should be done to try to accommodate the minority," Bill said, "because you do need them sometimes."

About the last minutes of debate on the budget, when Senator Horsford included new changes to the tax measure, Senator Raggio said, "I guess he thought that I would not read that amendment, or that he would be able to push it through and I would be required to vote for it."

Bill said that every time they met in core meetings, he told the Democrats his conditions for voting with them on the tax measure.

"They kept saying that they did not support our conditions. It was as if they did not listen. It was as if they did not think we were serious. I told them that they did not have the votes for the tax plan unless they agreed."

"If he [Horsford] had not blinked," Raggio added, "we would have stuck to our guns. I don't look at it as 'coming out on top.' I was holding to a bargain; to an agreement."

Throughout the 2009 session, Bill made every effort to keep his caucus informed and "on board." They had all agreed that some taxes would have to be raised and that the amount would be $780 million over the biennium. "Everyone understood that," Bill said, "and everyone agreed that was the number."

The caucus, he said, agreed to restore essential services and that any tax plan would have to entail a sunset provision. They debated issues regarding the taxes and agreed on no gross receipts tax and no taxes on net profits and net proceeds, which the senate Democrats were pushing. The caucus decided to use all sales tax to fund any shortfalls.

That plan was on the table, Bill noted, until the last moment, "when Senator Hardy figured it would hit Clark County, which already had an 8% sales tax, too hard." As such, the caucus decided on a payroll tax, which would be "sunseted."

They talked about mining tax, because the mining industry was being viewed as getting the best tax rate in the state's economy. However, both Senators McGinness and Rhoads said they would not support the measure if mining taxes were increased, because it is too important to their local economies.

Bill then spoke of how the final bill played out:

> Senator Washington committed in caucus saying, "Don't worry, Bill, I'm there. I will vote for it." But on the floor, he did not. When I asked him what happened, he said he "just could not vote for it at the last minute." Senator Amodei never indicated that he was not going to vote for it, but on the floor he made a statement and gave as his reason that we did not treat state employees fairly enough and therefore he could not vote for it. While I have great admiration for Mark, and think he is a brilliant guy, I thought it was a lame excuse. Senator McGinness never indicated in caucus that he would vote against the tax plan, but, for whatever reason, he did. Still, a five-to-four majority of Republican senators voted in favor of the measure.

Senator Raggio never voted for a tax increase unless it had the support of a majority of the Republican caucus. Beyond negotiating the tax plan in the 2009 session, he was, as always, thinking on multiple levels. He knew that 2011 would be a reapportionment year and the Republican minority would have limited influence on redistricting.

A "sunset" on the revenue would force Democrats to deal with him again to solve the fiscal crisis anticipated when the legislation expired. Likely needing Republican votes to override a possible veto in 2011, Democrats might be willing to make concessions on drawing the new political map of Nevada.

While two of Bill's colleagues, Senators Randolph Townsend and Warren Hardy, agreed that gaining leverage for future redistricting had been a consideration, both said later that Bill's primary focus was on reforming the state's tax code.

By allowing this "quick fix" in 2009, and with more information on the state's tax structure from his proposed study during the interim, Bill hoped the sunset provision would compel lawmakers to develop fundamental changes to the tax codes in 2011.

The success of both strategies would be predicated on Democrats not picking up two or more seats in the senate during the 2010 election—and not electing a Democratic governor.

Assembly Speaker Barbara Buckley spoke of the tremendous respect she has for Senator Raggio:

> If you watch the struggle of factions within the Republican Party, Senator Raggio is clearly of the old school, an old school Republican, who believes he can be conservative without being so conservative that you forget why you have government in the first place. He is very pragmatic. He is not going to be swayed by people who govern by sound bite; that is not true governing.

With the coming of 2010, Barbara Buckley's words would become extraordinarily prophetic. Some of those who preferred government "by sound bite" would initiate a vengeful campaign to drive the senator from office, not fully appreciating that after a lifetime of law enforcement and law making, Bill Raggio was too tough a guy to be bullied into something his conscience would not allow.

CHAPTER FIFTY-NINE

# The Price of Conscience (2010)

In the waning months of 2009, a handful of local Tea Party[1] activists in Reno proclaimed the formation of the "Committee to Recall Raggio." Angry at the recent tax increases approved by the legislature, over the veto of their anti-tax champion, Governor Jim Gibbons, the group accused Senator Raggio of lying about his stand on tax increases during his 2008 reelection campaign. Granting a recall election would require petition signatures from 25% of those Washoe Senate District 3 voters who had cast ballots in the 2008 election. Few seemed interested, and the much-ballyhooed crusade to remove Bill Raggio from office soon vanished.

Those who knew of his contributions to the people of Nevada were troubled by the malicious nature of these attacks.

In a letter to the editor of the *Reno Gazette Journal* on December 8, 2009, Dr. Robert McQueen, emeritus professor of Psychology at UNR and former member of the Washoe County School District Board of Trustees, wrote that he took strong issue with "a small group of Washoe County residents" who were seeking the recall:

> From the day Raggio first took a seat in the Nevada State Senate, he has won steady praise from his colleagues on both sides of the political aisle. It would be difficult, indeed, to identify a local political figure who has displayed more sterling qualities than has Sen. Raggio. I know I speak for many of my Washoe County friends when I salute the work and character of Sen. Bill Raggio.[2]

Although Bill was never concerned about the success of the effort to recall him, he was dismayed by the tone of the rhetoric and insulted at being called a liar.

In 2009, Bill said,

> I'm a conservative, a Reagan conservative; I've never been an extremist. I disagree with these folks out there who call themselves Republicans, but are, in fact, Libertarians, and who don't want to hear facts and turn a blind eye to what is necessary. You have to do what is right for the state and not play party politics, or in this case, divisive politics. I said early on when the Economic Forum numbers came in last year we realized that the revenues were far short of what anybody imagined.

> During my campaign, I said I would not want to raise any taxes and that is true. But that was before we got those numbers at the end of last year. We saw that it would decimate education and health and human services and public safety if we did not raise some revenues. So I committed early that through the budget we would determine what essential services were needed. We made deep cuts.

Senator Raggio stated that Nevada was at a point where it could not cut any more "unless we want to start firing state workers, taking wheelchairs away from the disabled, closing rural clinics and making people wait five years for mental health treatment." Further cuts to the prison budget could not be made, he added, without endangering society.

Even if legislators were willing to take responsibility for dismantling state programs, Senator Raggio said, they would be prevented from doing so by federal law. In that regard, he said, the state cannot be run like a private business.

"The courts don't step in when a private business doesn't provide some service," Bill explained. "But, the courts step in when the state doesn't provide some essential services, i.e. prisons, mental health, education and compliance with the Americans with Disabilities Act. The private sector doesn't face that consequence."

In 2009, former Governor Guinn would agree: "When people say they want smaller government, they just don't understand what they mean by government. That's what you don't have with Senator Raggio. He sees the total picture. He understands."

As an example, Guinn explained, people in Clark County voted bond issues to build more schools, but then would not fund teachers for them. "People want very tough crime laws, but they do not want to pay for policemen, or for prisons," he said. "Some say, 'I don't want government,' but they do not really think what government is. It's important that at the very least they understand what their voting about.This problem cannot be solved with all cuts or all taxes."

\* \* \*

Due to the severity of the continuing downturn in Nevada's economy, revenue projected in the 2009 legislative session did not materialize. By February 2010, the state was dealing with a deficit of over $800 million. Governor Jim Gibbons called for a special session of the state legislature to convene on February 23, 2010 and fix the budget problem.

Before the opening of the session, town hall meetings were held to allow public input on remedies for the deficit. Although hundreds of citizens testified, fearing cuts to vital state services upon which they depended, few people offered suggestions.

Senator Raggio attended and was not optimistic. "This is ugly," he said. "I don't sleep at night knowing what we are going to be doing in the coming special session. If you think this is bad, in the next regular session we will be looking at problems three or four times bigger."

At one point, Bill interrupted the testimony to explain that the legislature in a special session is bound by law to adhere to the governor's agenda. He did not remind them that Nevada voters had the opportunity to give the legislature power to call its own special session and set the agenda, but had voted that measure down in 2006.

"I have to tell you, I wish there were other options," Raggio said.

"We've been working 24/7 to try and minimize the impact of these cuts...very frankly, I'm your elected representative, and I don't have a clue where to look [for more cuts]."

Governor Gibbons set the tone for session on the first day, by blasting legislative leaders of both parties during a television interview with reporter Sam Shad, for having failed to cooperate with him:

> I want to work with all of them, and over the course of the past several months, we have given them every chance—including Senator Raggio, including Senator Horsford and all of the members of the legislature—to meet with me and see what is going on with the budget....We have briefed them time and time again in my office here in Carson and in Las Vegas. We have gone over to listen to their ideas. We have worked together through this process so it has surprised me that Bill Raggio has never showed up at most of these meetings.

While the governor had often publicly criticized Senator Horsford, the Democratic majority floor leader, no one could recall a governor making such a personal attack on his own party's leader in the senate.

Visibly angry at hearing of the governor's comments, Senator Raggio initially remained silent, but the capital was abuzz waiting for his response. Bill had always reminded others that they should respect the office of governor, if not the office holder, and had refrained from publicly criticizing Governor Gibbons, despite his disappointment in the chief executive's lack of leadership and ethical behavior over his preceding three years in office.

As a concession to his dissatisfaction with the governor, Bill had recently endorsed Brian Sandoval, Gibbons' strongest opponent in the upcoming Republican primary. It was an act that Senator Raggio, out of party loyalty, had never before taken with an incumbent Republican governor.

Former Democratic Governor Richard Bryan was at the legislature that day, and remarked that Bill Raggio had always been extraordinarily deferential to governors from both parties. "I think he has been very restrained in terms of comments about Governor Gibbons," Bryan added, "[whom] I know he has disagreed with in the previous session. So I was frankly shocked to see the attack."

Assembly Speaker Barbara Buckley later said, "After the governor's attack, it was interesting to watch Senator Raggio when he had had enough. The governor failed to follow the conventional protocol and statesmanlike behavior that governed the executive and legislative branches for decades. Senator Raggio found that kind of behavior horrid. Someone needed to speak up and Senator Raggio didn't hesitate to call him out."

The next morning, Bill decided to answer Gibbons from the floor of the senate. In addition to the governor's inexcusable breach of protocol, he felt that the remarks were an attack on all legislators and threatened the delicate working relationship he was trying to maintain between Republicans and Democrats. When Bill rose to speak, the chamber fell unusually silent:

> I am both puzzled and amazed at the governor's statement, which was reported in the RGJ.com, indicating that I did not "show up" at most of the meetings the Governor's Office held concerning the budget process prior to the start of the special session.

> Either the governor's memory is failing or he has been misinformed, or he is intentionally distorting the facts. Prior to the session we have had at least eight meetings between the governor's staff and legislators and our fiscal staff. I personally attended two at the governor's office when the governor was also present. I attended another one at the governor's office when he was not present. As to the other five held in the Legislative Building with the governor's staff and the fiscal and budget personnel, I was present for all of them and the governor did not personally attend any.

I do not understand why he wants to pick a fight with me—
unless it is for political reasons because I am supporting his primary opponent—but my commitment has been at all times to
have the legislature work together with the Executive Branch to
reach a consensus, if at all possible, on how to deal with the excessive shortfall of $890 million.

Later in 2010, Senator Raggio spoke of how the special session started
out on the wrong foot. Just before it began, he said, the governor brought
Lynn Hettrick, the former assembly minority leader, onboard as his deputy
chief of staff. "Lynn had the respect of the legislative leadership," Raggio
said. The governor also hired Robin Reedy, formerly with the Treasurer's
Office, "who was a tough negotiator on his behalf, but rather acerbic in
her demeanor and tended to be confrontational at times."

Prior to the session, Raggio explained, the governor invited legislators
to meet with him and his staff to discuss revised budget proposals, all
the time reiterating his stance of no new or increased taxes or fees. A
series of meetings ensued, perhaps eight in all, attended by the governor's
aides, the legislative leadership, money committee members and fiscal
staff from both the budget office and the legislature.

The governor then outlined his proposals in a televised State of the
State address on February 8, which was followed by the Democratic response, provided by Senator Horsford.

Senator Raggio was asked to join with him in delivering this response,
but declined because it would appear that they were pitting themselves
against the governor. "I really wanted to defuse that dynamic," Raggio
said, "so we might be able to work together to reach a solution."

In light of his efforts to keep divisive rhetoric to a minimum, Bill was
chagrined when, on the first day of the special session, he was handed a
report of the governor's comments. "I was shocked to read this statement,
particularly targeting me, the senate majority leader from his own party,"
Raggio said. "I was tempted to issue a rebuttal immediately but I thought
about it and decided I should make a formal statement during a regular
senate session to correct this blatant and uncalled for misrepresentation."[3]

More ill feelings between the governor and the legislature arose when Gibbon's attempted in his proclamation agenda to put severe limitations on what measures the legislature could consider and how long the session would last.

It also didn't help matters, Bill remarked, that before the special session began, the Governor's Office issued a press release stating that he had spent $15 for "a new veto stamp."*

Yet, after Senator Raggio's strong response from the senate floor on the second day of the session, things quickly changed. Republican Senator Mark Amodei soon asked Senator Raggio if he would meet with Lynn Hettrick. Raggio agreed to do so, and later recalled that he "was pleasantly surprised when told that the governor wanted to come over and meet with me. We had a congenial discussion in my office and I told him I had put any differences aside. The governor and Hettrick said they would like to participate in the process."

As a result, Bill said, the governor's budget director, Andrew Klinger, along with Hettrick and Reedy, joined with the legislative core group to work out a final budget plan for the remainder of the biennium.

During these meetings, which were conducted over a period of three days, "a lot of give and take occurred," Bill said. "To his credit, the governor was willing to compromise."

As an example, the assembly Democrats wanted no more than a 5% cut in K-12. Assembly Republicans had proposed a 7.5% cut. The senate Republican's position was that since any cuts primarily involved personnel costs, teachers, academicians and the like had to be treated the same as state workers, since this was the traditional formula used in developing all previous state budgets.

The governor was finally willing to agree to a 7% cut. Bill insisted that higher education be treated the same as K-12, and as a final compromise, he proposed a 6.9% cut, which was agreed upon.

The 26th Special Session of the Nevada Legislature adjourned at 2:16 a.m. on March 1, 2010. In addition to the 6.9 % cut to higher education,

---

*There is no "veto stamp." A veto is made official by the governor's signature.

resulting in a general fund savings of about $44 million, K-12 education funding was also cut 6.9%. The legislature also reduced operating expenditures throughout state government, including education, recovering about $304 million. Transfers from various reserve accounts added another $197 million. Money from Clark County capital projects funding, the Millennium Scholarship fund and uncollected taxes, amounted to $129 million. Fee increases to mining, banking and various services provided by the secretary of state would raise another $53 million.

The governor did not veto the agreement, and so had to defend his "no tax" promise. Interviewed by Jon Ralston soon after, the governor said he had to accept increasing fees because it was part of the compromise, later admitting when pressed by the interviewer that a "fee is a tax" and acknowledging breaking his no-tax pledge."[4]

For having accepted the revenue increases in the compromise, the governor was excoriated by the no-tax zealots, effectively losing a large segment of what was left of his dwindling political base. The spokesman for a Nevada anti-tax group called Citizens Outreach, declared that the governor's "non-stop parsing and telling of falsehoods about breaking the Pledge are worse than breaking the Pledge itself." [5]

Later, Senator Raggio would say,

> In the end, the revised budget was passed. The assembly voted for it too, including all Democrats and some Republicans. Eight Republicans [Christensen, Cobb, Goicoechea, Goedhart, Gustavson, McArthur, Settlemeyer and Woodbury] voted no; however, my perception is that most of them, as in 2003, secretly hoped it would pass and they could claim they didn't vote for it. It is another example of voting to get reelected, rather than doing what is necessary in the best interest of the state.

\* \* \*

Jim Gibbons, pursued reelection for governor despite having the lowest popularly in the history of the office. On June 8, he made more history by being the first incumbent governor to be defeated in his own party's primary since statehood, losing to former assemblyman, state attorney general and federal court judge Brian Sandoval. It was no surprise.

What was surprising, however, was the result of the bitterly fought Republican primary campaign for U.S. Senate, where Sharron Angle was selected to challenge incumbent Democratic Senator Harry Reid.

Former state senator Sue Lowden, an early favorite to be the candidate facing Reid, and who consistently led in statewide polls as the favorite to defeat the incumbent senator, lost ground during the primary campaign due to some highly publicized gaffes and later had additional votes siphoned off by a third competitor, Danny Tarkanian.

"Sue Lowden," Bill said, "was the initial front runner, who was well qualified and supported by the national Republican establishment. She lost the primary to Angle, largely through efforts of both the Reid campaign strategists and the likes of the National Tea Party Express, the Club for Growth and similar ultra-conservative operations who chose to endorse and fund Angle—a strange combination to say the least!"

Upon learning that Angle had won, Bill Raggio, who in 2008 had been challenged by her in an acrimonious race for his state senate, stated,

> I would say there are a lot of Republicans who will find it difficult to support Sharron Angle. Abolishing the Department of Education, phasing out Social Security—those are pretty extreme positions. I think any incumbent is vulnerable, but you have to have somebody that is also acceptable if you're going to win.

On May 10, a month before the primary election, Senator Raggio commented on how he saw things shaping up—and he was concerned. The hard-right conservatives—"whether they come under the label of Libertarians or the Tea Party"—had penetrated the Republican Party, he stated. To what extent, he did not yet know. Most people are not that interested in politics until general election time, Bill explained, "so these ultra conservatives go and make themselves delegates to a county convention or a state convention and take control of the party machinery."

They want to rid the party of anybody that does not agree with them. There can be no disagreement, even on social issues. On a national level, they are even going after Republican senators who voted for bailout money—when Bush was president! They are changing the whole make up of the Republican Party and in the long run it will be disastrous. Unfortunately, it brings out the worst in a lot of people. I think both parties have extremists and I find it difficult to believe that the majority of Americans really want that kind of polarization in our political process.

God forbid if Sharron Angle becomes a Republican nominee for the U.S. senate. I would never support her. I know her, and I know she is treacherous and deceitful, and will do anything to win.

\* \* \*

On July 22, 2010, former Governor Kenny Guinn died. The robust and energetic seventy-three year old was fatally injured after a fall from the roof of his Las Vegas home while he was removing leaves. Personable and forthright, Guinn was one of the most popular governors in Nevada history and had a reputation as a pragmatic leader and skilled political mediator who could get things done.

Upon learning the news, Bill Raggio said, "I'm personally devastated. I thought so much of him and worked with him very closely, probably closer than with any other governor. My heart aches for his family."

At his funeral mass, more than 1,200 people filled the pews at St. Joseph, Husband of Mary Catholic Church in Las Vegas. Bill was asked to give a eulogy and it proved to be one of his most eloquent and heartfelt.

Offering perhaps the highest praise that can be bestowed on a person, Raggio said there was virtually no difference between Guinn the public figure and the man he knew in private life. "He pursued that vision without sacrificing his strong personal faith," Raggio said. "He fought for the common good of the people he was elected to serve."

Bill defended the former governor for his most controversial decision: a call for a gross-receipts tax on business in 2003. "This subjected him to heavy criticism, some of which lingers to this day, from thoughtless people," he said. "The passage of time has, of course, proved him right."*

Nonetheless, Bill pointed out, Kenny Guinn remained one of the state's most beloved public figures and because of his service, "We are a prouder, stronger, better state," Bill said.

Pete Ernaut, Guinn's former chief of staff, said the governor was the first one in the office in the morning and the last one to leave at night— "Not most days, but every day," poring over the state budget, always looking for ways to improve public services. "He cared more about others than about himself," Ernaut added. "He had a great will to succeed because he knew it mattered that he succeed. People were counting on him."

After the funeral, mourners were invited to a hot dog and beer reception. "It was the way Kenny would have wanted it," his wife Dema said. "It was the way he lived and it was what he would have enjoyed."

\* \* \*

By October, the Reid and Angle campaigns had reached an extraordinary level of venom. Few could recall a race where both candidates were so vehemently disliked by so much of the electorate.

Attempts by Angle's advisers to soften her extremist image proved futile because of her inability to refrain from making outlandish remarks. She called for a "phase out" of Social Security and Medicare and elimination of the Energy and Education Departments and the EPA. A deeply religious woman, Angle referred to the separation of church and state as an "unconstitutional doctrine" and warned of "Second Amendment remedies" if her ideology was not advanced through the electoral process. She agreed with a radio talk show host that there were "domestic enemies" sitting in Congress.

Many voters in Nevada were also disenchanted with Senator Reid, who had become a lightning rod for anger about the worsening recession. By mid-to-late 2010, the severe decline in the state's construction and tourism

---

*The gross-receipts tax idea did not pass, but the legislature ended up raising taxes in 2003, after a controversial vote in a second special session.

industries had left nearly 200,000 out of work and looking for a job. Including those who had given up looking for work, the actual jobless rate in Nevada was in excess of 20% of the workforce, nearly rivaling figures from the Great Depression. In addition, the state had the highest home foreclosure rate in the nation, and that figure was still rising.

Reid had been beaten up by Republicans on almost every issue for two years and was facing an election year when a broad spectrum of Nevadans were blaming the national Democratic leadership for the deepening recession. He was given only a slight chance of winning reelection against a viable Republican opponent. The selection of Angle, however, gave Reid the opening he needed.

Frustrated by the absence of a "viable" GOP challenger, and fully conscious of Angle's lack of qualifications for the position, the 200-strong "Republicans for Reid" list was established. In addition to some of the state's most influential lobbyists and businesspeople, Senator Reid also received endorsements from such high visibility Republicans as Wayne Newton, Reno Mayor Bob Cashell, former First Ladies Dawn Gibbons and Dema Guinn—and Bill Raggio.

Sharron Angle was endorsed by several top Republicans, including former Congresswoman Barbara Vucanovich, Congressman Dean Heller, former Governor Bob List and state GOP Chair Mark Amodei. Absent from that official list was U.S. Senator John Ensign, former U.S. Senator Paul Laxalt and Angle's primary opponent, Sue Lowden.

Bob List dismissed Reid's Republican supporters as just a few people with economic or personal ties to Reid and his agenda. "We've closed ranks quite well behind Sharron Angle. That's why she's running so well," List declared.

Bill Raggio explained his endorsement of Reid, one far from enthusiastic, in a statement released on October 7, 2010. Bill said he had been a strong supporter of Sue Lowden in the Republican primary, but after her defeat, largely though the efforts of the National Tea Party Express, he indicated publicly that he would evaluate the two candidates, Senator Reid and Sharron Angle, as the campaign unfolded.

Only one candidate, Senator Harry Reid, had sought his endorsement.

He had not heard from Sharron Angle or talked with her since long before she decided to run against him for the state senate two years earlier. "After losing to me in a primary," Bill said, "during which she ran a very negative campaign and distorted my record—referred to me as a liar and a RINO— I never heard one word from her, or a concession, or an offer of support. Instead, she lent aid and comfort to an effort to recall me as state senator."

However, these were personal issues, Bill added, which he was willing to put aside.

"What is difficult to overlook is her record of being totally ineffective as a four-term assemblywoman," Bill said, "and inability or unwillingness to work with others, even within her own party, and her extreme positions on issues such as Medicare, social security, education, veterans affairs and many others."

Raggio said some of her supporters told him that the party needed her vote in the U.S. Senate, and that she could not do much harm as a junior backbencher. "Since when should this be the criteria on how we select and vote for a U.S. Senator to represent our state?" Bill responded.

Senator Raggio noted that he was a lifelong Republican—unlike Sharron Angle, who changed parties when it suited her. He espoused the words of President Reagan, whom he knew personally, to never speak ill of other Republicans. "In other words, quit calling dedicated people like former Governor Guinn, and many other good Republicans, RINO's and other derogatory terms," Raggio said.

Bill's inability to accept her extreme and often even radical ideas and positions did not in themselves preclude an endorsement. However, coupled with remarks she had made in a secretly taped conversation, disavowing the Republican Party saying it had "lost its standards and principles," did.

"For all these reasons," Bill said, "I am unable to support Sharron Angle. We need someone in the U.S. Senate who can be effective, work with others and best represent the interests of our state."

Senator Raggio qualified his decision by saying that he was not pleased with, or supportive of, many of the issues that Senator Reid has supported, and had told him so.

"I believe he understands that he must vote more strongly to represent the views of his Nevada constituency in the future," Raggio said, "rather than a liberal agenda which many feel drifts toward Socialism in America. With that caveat, I will reluctantly vote for Senator Reid's reelection."

Bill added that he opposed almost all of President Obama's agenda. "Barak Obama is not president because of the way I, and others like me, voted. I voted for Senator McCain, who lost in large part because ultra conservative voices bashed both him and President George W. Bush for over a year and then in the last few weeks asked us to vote for McCain!"

Bill concluded: "I truly believe most Nevadans, and for that matter, most Americans, are disgusted with negative campaigning and would like to see civility restored to the political process, with both parties working together and seeking responsible compromises in difficult and complex issues."

Bill asked Greg Ferraro to review the statement prior to release. Upon considering the political consequences of this message, Ferraro suggested Bill make a few minor modifications. He will never forget Senator Raggio's unequivocal reply: "Don't change a word!"

Ferraro later pointed out that, ironically, Bill never joined the "Republicans for Reid" group, despite it containing numerous luminaries within the state Republican Party. When asked why, then, did Raggio choose to make an independent endorsement of Reid, rather than simply not endorsing Angle, Ferraro speculated: "I think he felt he needed to send a powerful message."

Sharron Angle's campaign responded to Raggio's endorsement by lashing out at him, calling him a "good ol' boy career politician who does not believe in Republican principles."

Of all the Republicans who endorsed Harry Reid's reelection, Bill became the lightening rod for the far right backlash. The Clark County Republican Party immediately issued a statement calling his decision outrageous and demanded that Republican senators refuse to reelect him to a leadership position.

Others, like Jim Uster, former chair of the Clark County Republican Party, came to Senator Raggio's defense. "Sharron Angle's unmitigated attack on his character and track record was a clear indication that she is too far outside mainstream," said Uster, "so much so that she would be unable to represent Nevada effectively in the U.S. Congress."[6]

He also warned that it would be smart for Angle's allies to leave the Raggio issue alone. Despite what loud voices from the far right were proclaiming, Raggio's political credibility is hard to match in Nevada.

However, this did not happen, and for the remainder of the impassioned campaign, Bill Raggio would, on an almost daily basis, be either applauded or vilified in the media for his stance.

Near the end of the campaign, polls showed Sharron Angle was running evenly, or slightly ahead of her opponent, though Senator Raggio was not convinced. "Early on, while attending an ALEC event, I told my friend Lew Uhler, one of the National Tea Party Express organizers, that they had supported the wrong candidate and as a result Reid would win."

On November 2, Senator Harry Reid defeated Sharron Angle by 40,000 votes, a margin of nearly 6%.

Five days later, Senator Raggio discussed the Nevada and national mid-term elections, describing both as the most angry and uncivil that he had ever witnessed in all the years since he first voted in 1948.

Bill believed that it was not surprising that the National Tea Party Express was attracting so many individuals facing economic problems resulting from the recession. "In tough times," he explained, "the majority of voters lash out and vote *against* rather than *for* almost anything, whether it's candidates or issues."

Nationally, the GOP recaptured the House of Representatives and gained six seats in the senate. Democrat Congressional incumbents who were defeated, lost not so much on their own records, Bill believed, but because of a vitriolic campaign against then-Speaker Nancy Pelosi, who had championed the Obama administration objectives, including health care, bailouts of banks and other sectors, stimulus funding, tax increases and other contentious issues.

"Political venom spewed forth from both ultra-conservative and ultra-liberal talk shows and think-tanks throughout the campaign," Bill said. "In Nevada, over my objections in the 2009 legislature, the primary election date had been moved back from mid-August to early June, resulting in the most protracted and costly general election campaign in the state's history." Indeed, both Reid and Angle had each spent over $20 million on their campaigns.

Other Election Day victories for Republicans included Brian Sandoval, who Senator Raggio had encouraged to resign from the federal bench to run for governor.

Lieutenant Governor Brian Krolicki was easily reelected, overcoming the effects of criminal charges, which were filed against him, citing violations of internal operations in his office as state treasurer.

"They were charges brought by the Democrat attorney general," Raggio later explained, "and in my opinion, since I was very familiar with the circumstances, were completely unwarranted. As a result, Brian Krolicki should have a bright political future, as well as Governor-elect Sandoval, if he puts the interests of the state, as a whole, as his first priority, rather than any political agenda."

Congressman Dean Heller won easily and former State Senator Joe Heck defeated Dina Titus in her bid for reelection to Congress. "Another victim of the anti-Pelosi campaign," Bill said.

As senate minority floor leader, Senator Raggio had spent the campaign trying to focus his efforts on adding Republican seats in the state senate in order to regain the majority, as well as supporting Republican candidates for other state and local offices.

The SRLC voted to support incumbents Barbara Cegavske and Dennis Nolan, as well as candidates for open seats in the state senate—Ben Keickhefer, Assemblymen James Settlemeyer and Joe Hardy, Bob Larkin, Phil Salerno and Clark County attorney Michael Roberson. The caucus had traditionally discouraged primaries because they are divisive and costly and aid the other party.

"Unfortunately, this came at a time when the leadership of Nevada Republican Party had been taken over by the ultra conservatives," Bill said, "led by activist Chuck Muth and the likes of the Nevada Policy Research Institute. They wanted candidates who would sign no-tax pledges and would vote against any increased spending of any kind, insisting that further cuts in the state budget should be made."

As such, they promoted candidates to file against the caucus-endorsed candidates in the primary election, including Ty Cobb, Jr. against Ben Kiefhefer; Elizabeth Halseth against Dennis Nolan; and Patrick McNaught against Joe Hardy.

This resulted in Senator Nolan's defeat. "Dennis had been a dedicated assemblyman and senator," Bill later said, "and one who voted his convictions even if his vote was not popular."

Raggio worked to raise considerable amounts for both the caucus and for his own campaign and leader's funds, in order to fund all of the state senate campaigns as fully as possible. He also spent considerable time contacting contributors encouraging them to make contributions to SRLC endorsed candidates.

"All of our general election candidates won," he said, "with the exception of Phil Salerno, a good man who was up against the odds in registration and a highly regarded opponent in Assemblywoman Sheila Leslie."

\* \* \*

In mid-November, the senate Republican caucus unanimously elected State Senator Mike McGinness of Fallon as the new minority leader and State Senator Barbara Cegavske of Las Vegas, as assistant minority leader.

During an interview with journalist Ray Hagar on November 16, McGinness acknowledged that Raggio probably lost his longtime role as state senate Republican caucus leader because of his support for Harry Reid in his recent U.S. Senate campaign against Republican Sharron Angle.

Senator McGinness added that this was not Raggio's only move that upset Republicans, noting that the former minority leader's support for increasing taxes in the 2003 and 2009 sessions had angered many in his party.[7]

Senator Raggio would later say that following the election, Republican Party leaders began a campaign to have him replaced as leader of the caucus. According to Raggio, this included phone banks for robotic calls "and resolutions from some Republican Party groups, threatening our Republican state senators with retaliation if they did not vote to replace me with Senator Mike McGinness."

"Senator McGinness had, months earlier, informed me that despite the fact Senator Cegavske and one or two others wanted a change, he would never challenge me," Bill added.

In the end, Raggio decided he did not want to have discord in the caucus, "or subject these individuals, even those like Hardy, Rhoads and Kiekhefer, who were supporting me, to further political pressure. I thus agreed to withdraw and make it unanimous for Senator McGinness."

As Bill explained in an interview on November 18:

> I also felt it would help to unify the party, which I have been a part of for over half a century. Further, I requested that I not be reappointed to the Senate Finance Committee since the state budget would be the main issue in the very difficult 2011 session, and I wanted our caucus to have a free hand to work with the governor, and since most had made their own campaign commitments to deal with the extreme budget gap. I recognized that these commitments would probably be at variance with my own concepts.

Bill added that he found it a bit ironic that his efforts in helping to elect, or reelect, all of these individuals, resulted in such a lack of support.

In October, according to the contribution and expense report from Senator Raggio's Leader's Fund, $5,000 was contributed to Senator McGinness and $10,000 to Senator Cegavske, who had been targeted by Democrats because she was deemed vulnerable.

The fund also recorded $10,000 in contributions to Assemblyman Don Gustavson (R-Sparks), a newly elected state senator and a critic of Raggio's Reid endorsement and James Settelmeyer, a conservative assemblyman who won the state senate seat vacated by Senator Mark Amodei.

"But even more ironic," said Bill, "is the fact that if anyone speaks his or her mind and supports a candidate of the opposite party, it will result in some sanction, particularly from those ultra conservatives who constantly cite the U.S. Constitution and the Bill of Rights. I guess their view is that if you are a Republican, and an elected official, you forego the right of free speech!"

Senator Raggio added that he had always been mindful that he was elected not just by Republicans, but as well by Democrats and Independents. "I did not take an oath to follow any party's platform," he stated, "and I would suggest that if legislative candidates did so they would probably never get elected, or would put themselves in a position where they simply could not function."

Asked if he now regretted his decision to endorse Senator Reid, Bill replied,

> All I can say is that I did what I thought was right and apparently more people agreed with me than disagreed, because Reid won by 40,000 votes. So, I guess I am with the majority of the people. The Republican Party simply put up a candidate who could not win.

The decision to end Senator Raggio's tenure as senate leader was met with a strong reaction on both sides. Public opinion ran high and Bill received dozens of emails, of which only about ten were critical of him. He personally answered each.

One critic summed up the far right conservative feeling about Senator Raggio in a public letter, saying, "If the Nevada Republican Party is going to succeed in drawing more popular support, it must be united, behind simple, clear, well-articulated and non-negotiable principles…none of that was likely to happen under Senator Raggio…Raggio was beyond reform."[8]

An old friend and former political adversary, retired Supreme Court Justice Bob Rose, interviewed shortly after the decision, commented about how unfortunate it was:

> There always are consequences if you go against another party member. Bill has the courage of his convictions and expressed his opinion, an educated opinion. If something is really in the best interest of the state, he will do it regardless of the political consequences. He has always been that way.

In late November, Senator Raggio reflected on the events of earlier that month, pointing out that the *Las Vegas Review Journal*, the state's largest newspaper, and the only major newspaper to endorse Sharron Angle, had recently announced the sacking of its publisher, Sherman Frederick, and its editor, Tom Mitchell.

"There is an old saying that 'what goes around comes around,'" Raggio said. "These two had made the newspaper into what appeared to be an organized anti-Reid organ on a constant and daily basis, not just in editorial content, but in news articles and the publishing of continual 'poll' results, which proved to be totally inaccurate in that race. Obviously, the image and perception of the paper as an organ of fair reporting had been severely tarnished and its credibility went out the window."

He said that he has always respected Sherman Frederick, who he was first introduced to in the late 1980s by columnist Jon Ralston. Bill added that he "was disappointed to see him move to the extreme right in his beliefs."

"[Tom] Mitchell, on the other hand, should never have been an editor of a major newspaper," Raggio continued, "since he held such firm Libertarian, biased and almost anarchist views. Both Governor Guinn and I, and others with like opinions, who had voted for any tax increase, even though necessary at the time, were excoriated by him in his editorials and other rantings."

As one example, Raggio cited Question 1 on the 2010 ballot. This measure would have authorized the merit selection of judges, similar to, but an improved version of, the system already used to fill vacancies in the judicial system.

Senator Raggio had sponsored the measure and, with the support of Assembly Speaker Barbara Buckley, it passed two successive sessions. "[It] was endorsed by both the *Reno Gazette Journal* and the *Las Vegas Sun*—special thanks to Brian Greenspun, its publisher—and supported by diverse groups, including business and labor, attorneys and lay people," Raggio stated.

Justice Sandra Day O'Connor agreed to be the honorary chairperson, along with individuals such as Irwin Molasky and former Supreme Court Justice Bill Maupin. Greg Ferraro and R&R Partners put an effective media campaign together.

"Nevertheless, the measure lost on the ballot largely through efforts of the likes of [Chuck] Muth and [Thomas] Mitchell," Bill said. "Justice O'-Connor met with editorial boards throughout the state and was well received, except for Mitchell at the *Review Journal*, who treated her with disrespect, and went on to crusade against the measure in his editorial comments."

Bill Raggio was used to accepting political setbacks; however, he could not accept such displays of disrespect. This lack of civility, often accompanied by a condescending air of self-righteousness, bothered him because he had always been courteous to others, considerate of their reasoned opinions and expected the same in return.

Six years earlier, in April 2005, Bill gave a speech to the Catholic Committee on Scouting in Reno. In it, he credited his boyhood years in scouting as having "made me what I am today." He quoted the words of the 19th century British educator and theologian, John Henry Cardinal Newman, from the treatise "The Idea of the University."

"The true gentleman," Newman said, "never speaks of himself except when impelled, has no ears for gossip or slander, interprets everything for the best. He is never mean in his disputes, never takes an unfair advantage, never mistakes personalities or sharp sayings for arguments... He observes the maxim of the ancient age that we should ever conduct ourselves towards our enemy as if he were one day to be our friend."

In November 2010, higher education system Chancellor Dan Klaich would speak of how Bill Raggio was indeed a "true gentleman." He had known Senator Raggio for over thirty years and recognized that, while everyone has a sense of self, the best leaders take it out of the process:

> You have to know when to check your ego, and that's what Bill is able to do. It is truly amazing because he is such a significant person, yet able to treat everyone as a peer.

> I love Bill for who he is and what he's done for the state over the last five decades. He has given his entire adult life to the service of the state, selflessly and remarkably. What's not to like about Bill Raggio?

# EPILOGUE

*For what is a man, what has he got?*
*If not himself, then he has naught;*
*To say the things he truly feels,*
*And not the words of one who kneels;*
*The record shows, I took the blows...*
*And did it my way.*

— Lyrics from "My Way" *

On January 5, 2011, Senator Bill Raggio announced the end of his career in public service. His statement read:

I had hoped to complete the remainder of my tenth elected term, but my physical mobility simply does not allow me to function fully, and therefore it is time for me to step aside for someone who can give the position a 100% effort.

I am hopeful the [Washoe County] commissioners will take the opportunity to appoint someone well-qualified, who shares my political values and who will commit to working with others and across party lines to do what is in the best interests of our communities and our state.

Dale and I look forward to retirement from elected public service; however, I intend to stay active in our law firm and certainly look forward to remaining involved in the decisions affecting the future of Nevada and in a position to offer assistance, if asked.

---

*Bill Raggio's favorite song, written by Paul Anka and made famous by Bill's friend, Frank Sinatra.

I am extremely honored and privileged to have been allowed to serve in public office for more than fifty-six years. To the citizens of Washoe County, I extend my sincere gratitude for your support for so many years.

Bill had undergone recent back surgery, yet, more pertinent to his decision, was a painful torn Achilles tendon, which greatly impeded his mobility. He had hoped a procedure could be found to repair the tendon, but after consulting in 2010 with one of the nation's foremost surgeons in that field, Bill learned the probability of success was too low to risk the surgery.

News of his retirement spread like wildfire and produced an outpouring of emotion, most despairing of the fact that he would be not be there to lead the 2011 legislature through what would likely be its most difficult session.

When asked if he felt badly about leaving at such a precarious time in state's history, Bill admitted he did. "But they've got new people," he said. "They are competent and hopefully they will realize the importance of putting sectionalism and partisanship aside. And, look, nobody is irreplaceable."

He offered some words of advice:

Stick to your values. Keep your ears and eyes open to all sides, and if you think you are wrong, don't be afraid to change, yet have some principles you believe in. That's why I'm a Republican.

On January 18, 2011, former assemblyman Greg Brower was appointed as Bill's replacement by the Washoe County Board of Commissioners.

On April 19, 2011, Bill Raggio was inducted into the Nevada Senate Hall of Fame.

## ACKNOWLEDGMENTS

It would have been impossible for me to tell a story of this magnitude without the assistance and support of so many. I am grateful to have had that.

First and foremost, I must thank Senator Bill Raggio, who, despite believing he had not lived an interesting enough life to merit such a biography, graciously (and patiently) bore my prodding and poking into his life. He not only allowed me access to volumes of his personal papers, but also sat for nearly fifty hours of interviews over three years. Whatever praise this book might receive will largely be due to his candor, self-effacing humor and photographic memory.

There are also two women in my life to whom I must give special thanks. The first is Senator Raggio's wife, Dale, without whom this book would never have been written. Because Senator Raggio comes from a generation where it is considered bad form to talk too much about oneself, it required Dale's subtle, though persistent, "nudging" of him to make it happen. Dale's love and dedication to her husband is without equal and I am deeply indebted to her for everything she has done to see that this amazing story was told.

The other woman I must thank is Marion Sandoval. I have known Marion for over thirty years and her intercession in my life not only resulted in my meeting Senator Raggio (and all that subsequently resulted from that), but also meeting my wife, Becky. Marion's encouragement and support over the years is something for which I will always be grateful.

Many others have been of great help, including Robert "Tom" King and Allison Tracy of the University of Nevada Oral history Project; oral historians Dana R. Bennett and Dale Erquiaga; the staff of the Nevada State Library and Archives; and the Nevada Historical Society. I am also indebted to the Legislative Counsel Bureau Research Division staff, particularly Director Don Williams, Michael Stewart, Ricka Benum, Teresa Wilt and Nan Bowers.

I am also appreciative of those who took the time to provide me with interviews, including: Michael Alonso, Joe Brezny, Billie Brinkman, John W. "Web" Brown, U.S. Senator Richard Bryan, Speaker Barbara Buckley, Don Carano, Senator Terry Care, Claire Jesse Clift, Mayor Bob Cashell, Tracy (Raggio) Chew, Joe Crowley, Fred Davis, Drake Delanoy, Robert Dickens, Perry DiLoreto, John Squire Drendel, Bill Farr, Lillian Francovich, Sam Francovich, Joesphine Gezelin, Gary Ghiggeri, Mayor Oscar Goodman, Governor Kenny Guinn, Bill Hanlon, Senator Mark James, Chancellor Dan Klaich, U.S. Senator Paul Laxalt, Michael Lindell, Paul Lowden, Lorne Malkiewich, Senator Bernice Mathews, Betty Melarkey, Dan Miles, Governor Bob Miller, Lila Mill, Jan Nedham, Marilyn Newton, John Pappageorge, U.S. Senator Harry Reid, Senator Dean Rhoads, Leslie Righetti, Justice Bob Rose, Larry Ruvo, John Sande III, Ron Scheberle, Jack Streeter, Senator Coe Swobe, Judge Charles Thompson, Congresswoman Dina Titus, Senator Randolph Townsend, Congresswoman Barbara Vucanovich, Jerry Watson, Senator Thomas "Spike" Wilson, Steve Wynn and Justice Cliff Young.

Journalists, past and present, whose work has been instrumental in telling this story include Herb Caen, Guy Clifton, Anjeannette Damon, Ned Day, Guy Farmer, Jeff German, Brian Greenspun, David McGrath-Schwartz, Ray Hagar, Clark R. Mollenhoff, Ed Montgomery, Jane Ann Morrison, Jon Ralston, Brendan Riley, Cy Ryan, Steve Sibelius, Guy Shipler, John L. Smith, Bob Stewart, Ed Vogel, Jude Wanniski, Caleb Cage of the *Nevada Review* and photojournalists Cathleen Allison and Brad Horn.

Special thanks to Geoff Dornan, of the *Nevada Appeal*, who patiently answered all my questions each time I buttonholed him in the halls of the Legislative Building, and to Dennis Myers, of the *Reno News & Review*, who helped me wrap my mind around some of the more complex elements of Nevada history and politics—and of whose analytical skills I remain in awe.

I am also indebted to the talent and professionalism of the staff at Hellgate Press, especially Harley Patrick, an excellent publisher and editor, who has, once again, made me look smarter than I am.

Kudos to Bob Cook, of Cook's Photography in Reno, for his outstanding work preparing the photos for this book.

I would like to remember the late Dr. Robert "Doc" Topmiller, a gifted scholar, author and tireless humanitarian, for broadening my world view and helping me understand that the only "impossible" things in life are those you don't try.

Thanks also to my wife Becky and my children Casey, Hilary and Colin for your patience and support while I was "away" at my desk so much; and, to my best friend, Steve Orr: Thanks for your unwavering faith in me over the last forty-three years.

# APPENDICES

# Legislative Biography and Achievements

## WILLIAM J. RAGGIO

Republican

Washoe County Senatorial, District No. 3

Attorney at Law

*Born*: 1926—Reno, Nevada

*Educated*: Louisiana Tech; University of Oklahoma; University of Nevada, Reno, B.A.; Hastings College of Law, University of California, J.D.; Boalt Hall School of Law, University of California, Berkeley

*Married*: Dale Raggio

*Children*: Leslie Ann Righetti, Tracy Lynn Woodring, Mark William Raggio (deceased 2004)

*Military*: USNR; USMCR, Second Lieutenant, 1944-1946

*Hobbies/Special Interests*: Hunting, fishing, golf

### LEGISLATIVE BIOGRAPHY—2011 SESSION

*LEGISLATIVE SERVICE*: Nevada Senate, 1973-2011 (first elected November 1972)— thirteen special and twenty regular sessions (longest Senate service in Nevada history). Senate Minority Floor Leader, 1977-1979, 1983-1986, 1991, 2009; Senate Majority Floor Leader, 1987-1989, 1993-2007. Senate Committee on Education, 2011; Senate Committee on Government Affairs, 2007-2011; Senate Committee on Health and Human Services, 2011; Chair, Senate Committee on Finance, 1987-1989, 1993-2007, Member, 2009; Vice Chair, Senate Committee on Legislative Operations and Elections, 2007, Member, 2009. Legislative Commission: Alternate, 1975-1977, 1981-1988, 1991-1993; Member, 1973-1975, 1977-1979, 1981. Interim Finance Committee (IFC): Member, 1973-1976, 1983-1986, 1991-1992; 2009-2010; Vice Chair, 1987-1988, 1995-1996, 1999-2000, 2003-2004, 2007-2008; Chair, 1989-1990, 1993-

1994, 1997-1998, 2001-2002, 2005-2006. Member: IFC Subcommittee to Review Allocations for Homeless, 2007-2008; IFC's Subcommittee to Review Public Works Board Matters, 2007-2008, 2009-2010. Chair, Interim Retirement and Benefits Committee, 2007-2008; Member, 2009-2010; Member, Committee to Consult with the Director, 2007-2008, 2009-2010; Chair, Legislative Committee on Education, 1997-1999, 2001-2003, 2005-2006; Vice Chair, 2007-2008; Member, 2009-2010. IFC's Subcommittee to Conduct a Review of Nevada's Revenue Structure, 2009-2010; IFC's Subcommittee for Federal Stimulus Oversight, 2009-2010; IFC's Subcommittee to Conduct a Review of Nevada's Revenue Structure Working Group to Review Responses to the Request for Proposal, 2009-2010; Legislative Commission's Subcommittee to Study the Requirements for Reapportionment and Redistricting, 2009-2010.

*AFFILIATIONS*: State Bar of Nevada; Washoe County Bar Association; American Judicature Society; American Trial Lawyers Association; Alpha Tau Omega; Phi Alpha Delta; Elks; Republican State Central Committee; Washoe County Republican Central Committee; Reno (Host) Lions Club; American Legion; Prospectors; American Board of Criminal Lawyers, 1979-1982; Director, Sierra Health Services, 1984-2006; Senior Partner, Jones Vargas, Reno/Las Vegas; Executive Advisory Board, E.L. Wiegand Foundation; Board of Trustees, E.L. Wiegand Foundation; American Legislative Exchange Council, Board of Directors 1983-2011, National Chairman, 1993; Director, Archon Corp.; Board of Directors, Senate President's Forum, 1993-2009.

*PERSONAL AND PROFESSIONAL ACHIEVEMENTS*: U.S.: District Court–Nevada; Court of Appeals–Ninth Circuit; U.S. Supreme Court. Assistant DA, Washoe County, 1952-1958; DA, Washoe County, 1958-1970; House of Delegates, American Bar Association, 1967-1970; State Chairman, Junior Bar Conference, 1957-1960. Nevada State DA Association: President, 1960-1963; Secretary, 1959-1960. Former National President National DA's Association: Board of Directors, 1961-1970; V.P., 1961-1966; President, 1967-1968; Honorary Life Member, 1970. Fellow, American College of Trial Lawyers; Board of Trustees, Washoe County Community Action Program, 1964-1967; Reno Board of Directors, National Conference of Christians and Jews, 1966-1970, 1983-1987; Republican nominee, U.S. Senate, 1970; Republican nominee, Lt. Governor, 1974; Young Man of the Year, Reno-Sparks Jr. Chamber of Commerce, 1959; Brotherhood Award, NCCJ, 1965; Distinguished Service Award, Nevada Council on Crime and Delinquency, 1970; Columbus Day Committee, 1967; Truth in Action Award, World Association of Detectives, 1967; Fellows Award, National Salvation Army; Honoree, Better Business Bureau of Northern Nevada, 1971; Torch of Liberty Award, ADL of B'nai B'rith, 1985; Honorary Membership, International Association of Firefighters, Local 731. Criminal Law and Admin. of Justice Committee, CSG; Nevada American Revolution Bicentennial Commission; Old College of Reno Board of Trustees; Law and Justice Committee, NCSL; Advocate, American Board of Trial Advocates; Master, American Inns of Court. Citizen of the Year, Nevada Judges Association, 1987; Boy Scouts of America National Distinguished Eagle Award, 1989; Eagle of the Year Award, 1988. NCSL Leaders Award, 1988; Honoree, Nevada Lung Association, 1990; Hall of Fame, Washoe County Regional Transportation Commission, 1990; Excellence in Public Service, NTLA, 1990; Outstanding Graduate Award, Washoe County Teachers Association; Outstanding Prosecutor in the United States, 1965; SIR Award, Associated General Contractors of Northern Nevada, 1994; Most Effective State Legislator, The Ralston Report—1993, 1995, 1997, and 2001; Senate Majority Leader of the Year, National Republican Legislators Association, 1995; Nevada Society of Respiratory Care, 1995; the Third Most Influential Person in Nevada, the Las Vegas Sun, 1995, and the Second Most Influential Person in Nevada, the Las Vegas Sun, 1997; Honorary Membership, Legislative Conservationist of the Year, Nevada Wildlife Federation, 1996; Life Member, Friends of College of Education, UNR, 1996; Guardian of Small Business Award, NFIB, 1996; Landsman Association Award, S.F., 1996; Golden Hand Award, National Association of the Deaf, 1997; Italian American of the Year Award, Augustus Society, Las Vegas, 1997; No. 1 Nevada Legislator of the Year, NAIB, 1997; Nevada VAD Presidential Award, 1997; Silver Baron Honoree, American Cancer Society, 1998; Hispanics in Politics Award, Las Vegas, 1998; Grand Pioneer Award, Northern Nevada Black Cultural Awareness Society, 1998; Nevada Prosecution Advisory Council Award, 1998; Who's Who in America, 1998-2001; Outstanding Alumnus, University of Nevada, Reno, 1999; Junior Achievement Hall of Fame Award, 1999; Lifetime Achievement Award, National Italian American Foundation, 1999; 22nd Annual Honor Award, American Lung Association, 2000; Nicholas J. Horn Award, Nevada Medical Association in Recognition of Distinguished Contributions to Health Care and Medicine in Nevada, 2000; President, Education Foundation, Inc. (Washoe County School District); Bible/Elston Educational Leadership Award, TMCC, 1999; UNR Athletic Foundation, Jake Lawlor Award, 1999; Distinguished Service Award, UNR Alumni, 1997; President's Medal, UNLV, 2000; Nevada Law Foundation; Civic Leader of the Year Award, Greater Reno Chamber of Commerce, 1999; Headline Maker of the Year Award, Reno Media Press Club, 2001; Outstanding Service Award, Airport Authority of Washoe County, 2001;

Appreciation Award, Nevada Highway Patrol Association, 2001; Certificate of Appreciation, National Rifle Association, 2002; Papal Honor Pro Ecclesia et Pontifice, 2002; Honoree, Knight of Camelot, Opportunity Village, Las Vegas, 2002; Chapel of Four Chaplains inductee and name inscribed on the Legion of Honor Wall in the Chapel at Valley Forge, PA, 2002. Dedications: College of Education Building and William J. Raggio Math and Science Center, UNR; Raggio Parkway and William J. Raggio Plaza, Reno; High Tech Center, Western High School, Las Vegas. The Nevada Public Education Foundation Hall of Fame inductee, 2003; honored as Father of the Airport Authority, Airport Authority of Washoe County, 2003; Dean's Award, UNR School of Medicine, 2003; President's Medal, Truckee Meadows Community College, 2003; Good Efforts Matter Award, Nevada Diabetes Association for Children and Adults, 2003; Honorary Chief Deputy, Washoe County Sheriff's Association, 2004; Honoree, American Lung Association, 2005; Legislative Advocate Award, Nevada Disability Advocacy and Law Center, 2005; Academic Achievement Award, The College of Collaborative of Washoe County, 2005; Outstanding Award, National Council of Juvenile Family Court Judges, 2005; honored for commitment to the Children's Cabinet and Nevada Partnership for Homeless Youth, Nevada Legislature's Nevada Homeless Youth Awareness Day, 2005; honored for compassionate and effective leadership to Nevada's Division of Mental Health and Developmental Services, 2005; Distinguished President's Medal, Desert Research Institute, 2006; Champion of Education Award, Washoe County Education Foundation, 2006; Lifetime Achievement Award, Nevada Republican Party, 2006; Heart of Gold Award, American Heart Association, 2006-2007; William J. Raggio Excellence in Leadership and Outstanding Service Award, American Legislative Exchange Council, 2007; Special Friend Award, Nevada Association of School Boards, 2008; Recognition, Nevada Peace Officers' Standards and Training Commission, 2008. Best Senator, Las Vegas Review-Journal Poll, 2009; Herbert Harley Award, American Judicature Society, 2010; Transparent Courthouse Award, Institute for Advancement of the American Legal System, Denver, 2010; Nevada Governor's Points of Light Award, Nevada Energy, 2009; The Father of Regional Planning Award, Truckee Meadows Regional Planning Governing Board, 2011; "Hero of Higher Education," Nevada Faculty Alliance and UNR Faculty Senate, 2011; Honorary Cochair, "Rat Pack" Reno Symphony Orchestra Program, 2011; Lifetime Achievement Award, Nevada Arts Council, 2011; Distinguished Service Award, Washoe County Board of Commissioners, 2011; Nominee for Honorary Doctorate of Humane Letters, University of Nevada, Reno, 2011; Inducted into the Nevada State Senate Hall of Fame, 2011.

DEDICATIONS: College of Education Building and William J. Raggio Math and Science Center, UNR; Raggio Parkway and William J. Raggio Plaza, Reno; High Tech Center, Western High School, Las Vegas. The Nevada Public Education Foundation Hall of Fame inductee, 2003; honored as Father of the Airport Authority, Airport Authority of Washoe County, 2003; Dean's Award, UNR School of Medicine, 2003; President's Medal, Truckee Meadows Community College, 2003; Good Efforts Matter Award, Nevada Diabetes Association for Children and Adults, 2003; Honorary Chief Deputy, Washoe County Sheriff's Association, 2004; Honoree, American Lung Association, 2005; Legislative Advocate Award, Nevada Disability Advocacy and Law Center, 2005; Academic Achievement Award, The College of Collaborative of Washoe County, 2005; Outstanding Award, National Council of Juvenile Family Court Judges, 2005; honored for commitment to the Children's Cabinet and Nevada Partnership for Homeless Youth, Nevada Legislature's Nevada Homeless Youth Awareness Day, 2005; honored for compassionate and effective leadership to Nevada's Division of Mental Health and Developmental Services, 2005; Distinguished President's Medal, Desert Research Institute, 2006; Champion of Education Award, Washoe County Education Foundation, 2006; Lifetime Achievement Award, Nevada Republican Party, 2006; Heart of Gold Award, American Heart Association, 2006-2007; William J. Raggio Excellence in Leadership and Outstanding Service Award, American Legislative Exchange Council, 2007; Special Friend Award, Nevada Association of School Boards, 2008; Recognition, Nevada Peace Officers' Standards and Training Commission, 2008.

# The legislature may be able to replace Bill Raggio, but his absence will surely be felt

by STEVE SEBELIUS

One of the last things that Bill Raggio said before retiring from public life was simply untrue.

"Nobody is irreplaceable," said the longest-serving state senator in Nevada history. "You will find that out."

It's more likely we'll find people are irreplaceable, and that while the state of Nevada will surely march on, it won't march as true as it would have had Raggio not ended his unbelievable 56 years of public service before the 2011 Legislature.

Yes, Raggio's role was diminished considerably. Democrats won control of the state Senate in 2008, thrusting him from the majority into the minority. In 2010, he endorsed U.S. Sen. Harry Reid over Republican nominee Sharron Angle (a woman who once ran against him). The price for speaking his mind? He was deposed as Republican leader. He voluntarily stepped down from the Finance Committee after that, and accepted committee posts more common to a freshman than the dean of the Nevada Legislature.

In his 38 years in Carson City, Raggio showed he was the master of the game, brokering budget compromises, outmaneuvering political opponents, doling out favors and collecting them in return. Almost every observer of the process knew Raggio would be a player no matter where his office was located. In fact, many relished the revenge Raggio doubtless had waiting for the coup-plotters who'd churlishly knocked him from his decades in leadership.

If anyone feared Raggio's wrath, he's now provided something even greater to fear: His absence. The simple-minded on the right look at Raggio with contempt because he supported taxes in 2003 and again in 2009.

But Raggio is old enough to remember a time when Republican didn't mean "somebody who wants to shrink government to the size it can be drowned in a bathtub." He remembers a party that stood for something, for small but competent government, and that didn't consider a tax an erosion of liberty. He remembers Oliver Wendell Holmes, who said taxes are what we pay for living in civilized society.

To Raggio, the radicals on the right were savages, nihilists, "John Birchers," as he famously put it on the steps of the Legislature in 2003. He had more in common with Democrats than with those strange people who claimed his party affiliation but had none of his affection for the System as It's Supposed to Work.

And he would have again: Raggio was considered the key in the upper house to reaching a two-thirds supermajority required to raise taxes, without which almost nobody believes the 2011-2013 budget can be balanced. No, that's not quite right: The budget can surely be balanced without new taxes. But not responsibly so. And if nothing else, Raggio was a responsible lawmaker. The visions of a decimated university system, of K-12 education, of already parsimonious social services reduced even further—which so delight those who hate government—were Raggio's nightmares.

He gave as his reason for leaving before his final term expired in 2012 the reduced mobility that came from foot and back problems and breathing difficulties. Surely, Raggio had shown some of the ravages of age in recent years. But there were many observers who thought he'd never leave. For them, a legislative building without Bill Raggio is akin to a baseball game without a pitcher—everybody is standing around wondering how the thing is going to work.

We will find out, and soon. But it's not going to be the same. Because no matter what Raggio said on his way out, there are irreplaceable people.

The Washoe County Commission will appoint someone to fill Raggio's term, but no matter whom the commissioners pick, it will be a successor, not a replacement.

(c) Stephens Media LLC, 2011. Reprinted with permission. All rights reserved.

# *SUN* EDITORIAL: A Distinguished Legacy

*Longtime senate leader retires after a career filled with accomplishment*

Sen. Bill Raggio, who for years led the Republicans in the Nevada Senate, announced his resignation Wednesday, and he will leave a huge void in Carson City this year.

A skillful lawmaker and shrewd negotiator, Raggio has been the linchpin in the Legislature for years. He has a knowledge of the budget and the legislative process that is unequaled. Raggio worked across the aisle without compromising his principles, and he won the respect of both Republicans and Democrats.

His retirement was a shock to many politicians and legislative observers, who figured he would finish his final session this year. Raggio was deposed as caucus leader late last year because he endorsed Democratic Sen. Harry Reid's re-election bid over a Republican who had smeared him in a previous campaign, but Raggio said that was not a reason for his resignation. The 84-year-old Raggio cited poor mobility—he has undergone back surgery and has a severed Achilles tendon.

Republican Gov. Brian Sandoval said the Legislature "will never be the same," saying "if Nevada had a Mount Rushmore for public servants, Bill Raggio's image would be etched on its face."

Indeed.

Raggio's career in the Senate began in 1972 and he became not only the longest-serving senator in state history but also one of the most influential. Nothing moved through the Legislature without Raggio's knowledge, and his list of accomplishments is long. Republicans and Democrats appreciated his steady leadership and willingness to listen and negotiate.

Senate Majority Leader Steven Horsford, a Democrat, called Raggio "a Nevada hero." Incoming Assembly Speaker John Oceguera, a Democrat, said Raggio "was sometimes a fierce opponent, but his service was distinguished by a true love of Nevada and a commitment which rose above party politics to do the right thing for our state."

Whether people agreed with Raggio, a native Nevadan, they couldn't question that he was doing what he thought was best for the state he loved.

However, in recent years, Raggio didn't neatly fit into his party, which morphed into the Party of No. Raggio, however, was able to forge common ground—he said compromises could be made without giving up principles—to push the state forward.

Raggio called himself a "traditional Republican." He championed low taxes, a friendly business environment, limited government and higher education, which he said helped business and the economy. Raggio didn't despise government, as some conservatives do. He saw a role for it, as the country's founders did. Despite those in his party who demanded litmus tests, like no-new-taxes pledges, he voted for tax increases when he saw a compelling need.

For that, and his support of Reid, he was called a RINO—Republican in name only—by Tea Party supporters, who ridiculously tried to recall him. Anyone who observed his career knows he was certainly a true conservative.

Over the years, there were occasions when we disagreed with him on issues, but we certainly admired his integrity, his principled views and his skill. Raggio is an all-too-rare elected official, and his absence in Carson City will be felt.

From the *Las Vegas Sun*, Friday, Jan. 7, 2011. Reprinted with permission.

# Raggio's exit leaves a big vacuum

By JON RALSTON

Bill Raggio is the only elected official who almost made me cry.

It was June of 1997. I had written a column accusing Raggio and others of lying in an attempt to smear a Democratic state senator who had settled a court case with the majority leader and others. For a couple of weeks, Raggio, with whom I frequently interacted, froze me out. And then he sent word he wanted to see me.

Like many lawmakers and lobbyists who met with him over the years, I was not prepared for what was coming. He expressed his disappointment in me, compared me to people he knew I despised, pushed all my buttons. He had carefully thought it through, I later realized, but it was devastating.

I held back tears, but my eyes were moist as I walked out of his office. Like many a legislator, lobbyist and, yes, Southern Nevada, I had been taken to the woodshed by the master of subtle incisions—you didn't know you were bleeding until you left the room.

As he departs the scene, unimaginably, after 56 years in public life, Raggio leaves behind an unmatched legislative legacy, much of it palpable in the form of laws, buildings and programs but much of it invisible to the naked eye. The man who left his mark on more bills than anyone in state history probably should be immortalized in a biography titled, "Never Leave Fingerprints."

Thus, there is a palpable sense of mourning, especially in Northern Nevada, that no other elected official could achieve upon retirement. Bill Raggio is not dead, but an era is. And I come not to bury him but to praise him.

Raggio was the Master of the Game, in every facet. He worked harder than anyone. He knew the budget better than anyone. He had better relationships with lobbyists and the media than anyone. And he was smoother, funnier and classier than anyone.

The cliche is as appropriate here as anywhere I can think of: Sixty-two members of the Legislature every two years were playing checkers; Raggio played chess, and he was a grandmaster to boot.

Put another way: Raggio walked into the legislative labyrinth every two years as the only one who knew the way to the exit. And before he led the rest of the denizens there, he had almost always accomplished what he wanted—anything from education accountability measures to an ornament on the end-of-session Christmas tree to some business-friendly measure.

I often referred to him as Sir Bill through the years. He truly was the courtly lord of the manor, albeit now an octogenarian who may have lost a few steps—yet still miles ahead of his peers and still possessed of a freakish endurance that allowed him to outlast everyone.

There will be those who say he symbolized everything wrong with Nevada—the consummate good old boy who thrived in the state's incestuous politics, helping his law partners and cronies, serving on company boards. But while there may be a patina of truth to that characterization, it is so overwhelmed by his good works as to render it all but irrelevant.

Too, the notion that he was not a conservative is just silly, more evidence that the word has lost all meaning. Raggio may not have been invited to the Tea Party, but he did more for conservative causes than any of the nouveau right. He staunchly opposed many labor initiatives and was adamant that state employees should not have collective bargaining rights. Business interests had no better friend than Raggio, and he single-handedly squelched thousands of Democratic initiatives.

But Raggio was flexible enough, not in the pejorative sense attributed by litmus-testing, tea-swilling folks, to realize that circumstances change and that sometimes programs needed funding and taxes need to be raised. He funneled millions to the North, but he was also a statesman in the truest sense of the word.

The past few cycles took their toll. He was furious that Sharron Angle challenged him in a primary in 2006. And despite putting the best face on it, he was shattered when Mike McGinness ousted him as minority leader, ostensibly because he snubbed Angle for Harry Reid in the Nevada Senate race (as many, many Republicans did privately).

Yes, Raggio has an inoperable, severed Achilles tendon that limits his mobility. But while he is a proud man and would not want to hobble around the building, I think he would have put up with the pain if he were still leader.

I have always considered it a political tragedy for Nevada that Raggio never got to do what he did in Carson City in Washington, D.C. He tried and failed to become a U.S. senator. He was easily that good and would have been a leader there, too.

A day after that unforgettable meeting 14 years ago, Raggio called and asked me to dinner, as if nothing had happened. But now, something has happened that has changed everything. When we walk into the Legislative Building on Feb. 7, Bill Raggio will not be there.

It makes me want to cry.

From the *Las Vegas Sun*. Reprinted with permission.

# Raggio leaves some loose ends but, overall, a very sound legacy

By JANE ANN MORRISON

State Sen. Bill Raggio, the master of the art of the deal, is irreplaceable, despite his protestations to the contrary.

No matter who is chosen to fill his seat, no one knows the state's budget as well as he does after 38 years in the Senate. Frankly, no one is as good at getting what he wants without leaving any fingerprints as Sir William.

His surprise announcement Wednesday that he is retiring because "my physical mobility simply does not allow me to function fully" brought back a flood of memories of the man I first met in 1987, the first time I covered the Legislature.

He was the Senate majority leader and key to all things happening in the Legislature. This was in the days when there was no 120-day limit and the session dragged on for six months or so. It would be 4 in the morning toward the end and the reporters would look haggard but Raggio looked fresh and alert, as if he could go on forever. His stamina and style were part of his success.

Nothing passed if he didn't want it to pass because he was a master at trading votes and using the budget to provide funding for someone's pet projects, much like U.S. Senate Majority Leader Harry Reid.

Raggio's endorsement of Democrat Reid over Republican Sharron Angle, viewed in context, might have been a mistake. It certainly seems to have sparked this pivotal turning point in his career.

That was why he was ousted in the fall from his GOP leadership position by Fallon state Sen. Mike McGinness. After that, Raggio, 84, said he didn't even want to be on Senate Finance, where he had ruled whether he was in the majority or minority.

Would he have resigned if he still were leader of the Republicans? I can only wonder.

Over the 23 years I knew him, I came to admire him but also let him have it in the chops more than once.

We agreed on some issues, most recently on the need to appoint judges based on merit selection rather than elections. We agreed Nevada needs a more stable tax base than it has.

(c) Stephens Media LLC, 2011. Reprinted with permission. All rights reserved.

# The Opinion of the *Reno Gazette Journal* Editorial Board

*Raggio's resignation will leave Washoe County, state poorer...*

Bill Raggio, who served Washoe County and this state from a seat in the state senate for 38 years, has been a Nevada politician in the best sense of the phrase.

For all these years, what's best for the state has been his number one priority. For Raggio—and numerous other lawmakers of his generation—service in Carson City rose above party labels and above strict ideology. He wasn't interested in "making a statements"; his priority was to get the job done. And that's exactly what he did.

In an age when politics has come to resemble a football game—what matters first is the color of the player's jersey and the guy in the other jersey is to be defeated at all costs—we can ill afford to lose the Bill Raggio's of the world.

Like the late Sen. Lawrence Jacobson, a Minden Republican, Bill Raggio, who announced his resignation from the state senate effective January 15, is tough to pigeonhole. Just when you think you've got him pegged as an unswerving conservative, he surprises you.

Hardly anyone who served in the Nevada Legislature in the past 40 years could squeeze a penny harder than Raggio. Yet, no one could claim to be the bigger advocate for public education, for K-12 and for higher education, either.

But he didn't go easy on educators. When he was dissatisfied with the State Board of Education's work on school standards, he pushed the sweeping reforms that led to the development of some of the toughest standards in the nation.

Nothing showed Raggio's philosophy and leadership skills, however, better than his role in finally winning approval of a tax increase in 2003 that ended a stalemate in the Legislature that was threatening to damage the state's education system. It was painful, but it was necessary. While some legislators were willing to simply say "no" and turn their backs, Raggio understood the damage that the lack of an agreement could do to the state, and he worked with Gov. Kenny Guinn—as he would later with Gov. Jim Gibbons—to get the budget passed.

Some Nevadans saw Raggio's willingness to cooperate with those he fundamentally disagreed with as a sign of weakness, as a betrayal of core values. And they saw that again in 2010 when Raggio bucked his party's voters and announced his support for longtime U.S. Senator Harry Reid, a Democrat, over former Assemblywoman Sharron Angle, a Republican. As loyal as anyone in the state to the Republican Party, Raggio believe that Reid in the U.S. Senate would be better for the state, and he had the courage to say so publicly, while many in the party who shared his conviction simply kept their mouths shut.

There is no irreplaceable man or woman, of course. The Washoe County Commission now has the unenviable task of replacing Bill Raggio, at least until the 2012 election.

Regardless of the commission's pick, however, we'll all be a bit poorer when Raggio is no longer at his Senate seat. The Legislature will be poorer. Nevada will be poorer.

This editorial appeared in the January 7, 2011 edition of the Reno Gazette Journal, reprinted by permission.

# Evolution

Republican Bill Raggio went from militancy to moderation. The GOP went the other way.

By DENNIS MYERS

The announcement was made just before 11 o'clock the morning of Jan. 5. In politics across the state, a mixed metaphor described the reaction: The news spread like wildfire and landed like a sledgehammer.

At lunch in Reno's Gold 'n' Silver Restaurant, a favorite café for long-time Nevadans, including local government officials, the news could literally be seen spreading from booth to table to booth.

That evening at Casale's Halfway Club, a favorite Italo-American hangout since 1937, a few people still hadn't heard. A bartender turned from a chattering crowd to "Mama" Inez Casale and said, "Bill Raggio quit."

There it was, the news that, in an instant, changed Nevada politics. Plagued by a severed tendon that followed back surgery, Washoe County Sen. William Raggio announced his resignation, effective Jan. 15, after the longest senate tenure in state history. This is one of the few instances when a public figure's retirement for health reasons was taken more or less at face value. "I don't think anything else would have made him do this," said one legislator.

There were reminders of the way the state's turnover leaves fixtures like Raggio behind. On KRNV, an anchor and a reporter mispronounced Raggio's name (Rawggio, akin to Nevawda).

But the real meaning of Raggio's legislative career, beyond his specific accomplishments, was the evolution in his political style from militant to moderate and the deterioration in dialogue and civility over four decades while he became a leader of resistance to those trends.

## The Hardliner

Raggio himself began his public career in a mode that would have fit neatly into today's politics. As a hard-right district attorney with a law-and-order orientation, he was like chalk squeaking on a blackboard to liberals. He had a take-no-prisoners style in both law enforcement and politics. His law-and-order orientation was so pronounced that President Nixon and Vice President Agnew—running a 1970 midterm election law and order campaign against what they called "radiclibs" (radical liberals)—recruited a reluctant Raggio, who was already running for governor, into an unsuccessful U.S. Senate race. Among the state's major political figures, he was probably the most polarizing. After taking that style into two unsuccessful statewide campaigns, an opinion survey showed he had a very high "antipathy quotient" among the public.

But when Raggio entered the legislature, he learned quickly that he needed Democrats and interest groups he had previously demonized. At his first legislature, there were only six Republicans in the Senate—and that number went down in the next election. If he wanted to get anything done, he would have to learn to work with the other party—and he did. His evolution into the legislative process was probably eased by the fact that the majority floor leaders in his first sessions were Democratic conservatives. And once he started dealing with Democrats as actual people instead of as vague others—something he rarely had to do as a prosecutor—politics for him became easier and more congenial.

That didn't mean Raggio wasn't still capable of getting rough. He once sponsored legislation to damage an old adversary from his district attorney days, brothel lord Joe Conforte. The Senate did him the favor of killing the bill.

Many of the comments that followed his resignation announcement focused on him as a defender of Washoe County, which obscured the fact that it was Raggio himself who provoked the biggest financial setback the county suffered during his terms. In 1990, he stirred up north versus South feelings by telling voters in Washoe County that a Democratic majority in the Senate would hurt the north. It was no longer an age when something said in one region was not heard elsewhere, and his comments exploded in Southern Nevada, where he had effectively cast his Southern Republican candidates as defenders of the north. He ended up losing Senate races at both ends of the state and the Southerners headed north determined to punish him. They enacted "Fair Share," which forced Washoe to repay subsidies it had been receiving from the rest of the state.

But Raggio also learned from these episodes. Thereafter he defended the North without demonizing the South. It was another step in his learning to value amity and respect for an adversary's point of view. (And Conforte did himself in.)

### Devolution

But as Raggio was tempering his style, his party was headed back to where he started. Politics was changing, though national trends took a while to bleed down into state legislatures. In 1980, Ronald Reagan was elected president, which moved the political frame of reference to the right and set in motion more meanspirited politics. This was in defiance of Reagan's own example. He reached out to Democratic leaders like Edward Kennedy and cultivated Democrats in both houses of Congress. His first budget was opposed by Republican "new right" senators but supported by "blue dog" House Democrats.

Reagan is the Republican president with whom Raggio most closely identifies, but many of Reagan's followers, such as the National Conservative Political Action Committee and evangelical leaders like Jerry Falwell favored a more confrontational, adversarial politics than the president. Leading figures like Robert Dole, Barry Goldwater and Jack Kemp increasingly became targets of rightists.

Raggio probably did not realize initially that this new harsh tone of the party was anything but temporary, a burst of venting after years in the wilderness. But over time it became apparent that it was here to stay. Raggio had once used his share of vituperative rhetoric—after he condemned in acidic language the reversal of a death sentence, the Nevada

Supreme Court opened an investigation of his use of free speech—but as a legislator he had learned how to make his case without questioning the motives or good will of his opponents.

Year by year, the temperature level of politics rose, and the rhetoric became harsher. As these trends moved into state GOPs, Raggio himself became a target. In 2000, a conservative activist circulated a CD of a song called "Won't You Come Home, Bill Raggio?" along with some printed matter calling him a RINO—a "Republican in name only." The claim was preposterous—Raggio had been the party's candidate for U.S. Senate in 1970 and for lieutenant governor in 1974 and had taken the Senate Republican caucus from 3 out of 20 senators in 1975 to regular majorities in the 1990s.

But the newcomers to the party—Reno Mayor Bob Cashell calls them the RINOs—were increasingly intolerant of bipartisanship, and Raggio was an exemplar of it. (During the same period, Nevada's current lieutenant governor and new governor both were branded with the RINO label.)

It took time for these trends to catch up to Raggio. His consistent success at both legislative accomplishment and building up the party kept him unassailable. Rarely has an elected official who did not hold statewide office so dominate the state's politics. One deft move that fueled Raggio's rise to statewide power came after 1982, when Republican governor Robert List was defeated for reelection, leaving a vacuum in the in-state leadership of the party. Raggio made it clear he had no interest in filling that vacuum and foreswore any further statewide races. It meant he was no threat to other rising Republicans and freed him to concentrate on building the GOP's fortunes in the Senate, which he did with enormous success.

### The New Hardliners

In 2003, the Assembly Republican caucus held the legislature hostage for weeks, using a minority control provision in the state constitution to halt all business and keep the legislature meeting through the regular session and two special sessions in order to get its way on a tax hike package. Raggio was appalled, less by the tactics than by the attitude of disrespect for majority opinion. It reminded him of the polarization of the Republican Party during the mid-1960s, particularly the 1964 presidential campaign when the John Birch Society and the GOP were linked.

"If the Republican Party continues to be the party of the far right, rather that what I term 'Reagan-type conservatism,' the party will never elect people," this one-time far rightist said. "We cannot be the party of the far right. That doesn't sell. And if that means moderate or RINO in some people's eyes, so be it. ... I believe in free enterprise, I believe in limited government, and I believe in fiscal responsibility. But in Reagan's eyes, that meant a lean government, not a mean government. And it also, if I recall, meant everybody was welcome under the Republican tent, even if you didn't agree on everyone's social issues. And I want to emphasize that. I helped resurrect this party with a fellow named Paul Laxalt in the early '70s when the John Birchers had taken over this party. Took us 10 years to dig out. I'm not going to let all that effort fall by the wayside and let radicals take over the Republican Party. Not while I'm in it."

That was outside the frame of reference of his critics, many of whom were children or unborn in the 1960s.

Raggio argues that his views have not changed over the years. Though there are some demonstrable exceptions, there is merit to his assertion. He has been a solid conservative throughout his legislative years, though he never had much in common with those lawmakers who—as the late former governor Kenny Guinn described them—"do not believe in government" and latched onto the GOP as their vehicle. Raggio never confused their stances with real conservatism.

Raggio is not well known for specific bills he got passed because he tended to work on issues and policies through the budget process. (He was a member and usually chair of the Senate Finance Committee.) But he occasionally did sponsor significant bills, one establishing the regional planning process in Washoe County, another creating the Washoe County Airport Authority.

One of his bills, an education accountability and standards measure for kindergarten though high school enacted in 1997, is noteworthy for the way it demonstrates how he worked. Democrats and the powerful teachers union were suspicious of it, and Raggio did not get everything he wanted in it. But because he had a history of cooperation on other issues with both groups, and they had come to trust him—and because he was able to bring the Democratic governor on board—he was able to get most of what he wanted. He had advanced a conservative initiative with support from the teachers and Democrats.

"I obviously had, over the years, to work with the teachers union," he said. "They were generally supportive, but they were very resistant to any kind of reform, and so I had to get them involved, and I had to get Gov. [Robert] Miller involved. And so we were able to do that, come together. You know, there was some give and take there. We had to agree to some class size reductions. But overall, I think it was a giant step in the state for K-12 because it paved the way for a lot of reforms, and they're still ongoing."

### Legislative Devolution

But it was just that kind of cooperative relationship with Democrats that drove Raggio's right wing critics crazy. They didn't want Republicans to "come together" with the enemy. And they were having impact. The parties started using huge swaths of legislative time to hold regular caucuses behind closed doors to enforce party policy. This was a sharp break from the past when partisanship at the legislature was understated and party discipline unknown.

Reno attorney Thomas "Spike" Wilson, who served in the Senate for 16 years, some of it with Raggio, has said, "I don't think we ever had a party caucus when I was there."

"It seems like they caucus on every vote," Raggio said. "You know, we didn't do that in the past. ... Once the election was over, everyone was willing to sit down and compromise and now that's a four-letter word to some of these extremists."

Those who obstruct, he said, "don't belong in the process, whether they're Republicans or Democrats. Legislation is still the art of compromise, and over the years that's been my mantra. You know? I've had to deal consistently with a house of the other party. And we would have gotten nowhere if we weren't willing to compromise, and if we were going to put good and evil labels on things, we might as well not have shown up. Now, there's some that still feel that way. I think they're an impediment to accomplishment."

If some Republicans did not like their leader's style, Democrats watched it with envy. In 2009, shortly after Raggio forced Democrats to reduce planned tax hikes, former Democratic senator Terry Care told the Las Vegas Business Press, "Bill Raggio is a pleasure to watch. I could tell you all kinds of Bill Raggio stories. You know, he's been in the majority, I think, since the 1991 session, maybe the 1993 session. He's 82 years old. You wouldn't believe it to watch him because he has a lot of energy that people that age, if they ever get that far, don't come close to having. He's very bright. He's shrewd. He is about five steps ahead of you on everything, and even as we know from this last session, when he's in the minority, he still has a way of being very effective and, in many cases, getting what he wants. … We've had our shouting matches and our debates, but man, I hold deep, deep respect for him."

As the years passed and the benchmarks of age appeared and passed— heart surgery, the death of his wife—Raggio still seemed indefatigable. There was a point when his weight fell alarmingly because of his heart problems, but he continued to hold the twin posts that were as much re-flection as source of his power—Republican floor leader and member of the Senate Finance Committee (which he chaired when the GOP held the majority), where he developed an encyclopedic knowledge of the state budget. And he still practiced law full time when the legislature was out of session.

The notion that Washoe County will be at the mercy of Clark County, which has received so much attention since Raggio's announcement, is overstated. The alliance between Washoe and the small counties against Clark is outmoded. In recent years, legislators from the two urban counties have formed close alliances because of the common problems of both their areas. There will always be competitions for funds among the dif-ferent parts of the state, but that is as much urban-versus-rural as it is North-versus-South.

Raggio's departure from the legislature is a substantial setback to the state's new Republican governor. The Washoe senator has always been a legislative leader who is very oriented to governors' programs, even when—as in the case of Jim Gibbons—the governor did his best to alienate him. He has done his best to get their programs enacted. Some legislators felt he was too willing to serve as a cat's paw for GOP governors. Raggio even supported Gov. Robert List's now-infamous "tax shift" from property to sales tax reliance that has led the state into chronic budget crises.

After a lifetime of service to the Republican Party, Raggio does not expect to play much of a role in it now. In November, time finally ran out for him with the far right of his party, when he was forced out by his Republican colleagues as floor leader after he grudgingly endorsed Democrat Harry Reid's reelection as U.S. senator against putative Republican Sharron Angle.

After he announced he would resign, Raggio said, "I'm not in favor very much with the party leadership at this moment. … They've been passing resolutions around the state in the last year that are very critical of me, so I'm not sure that I would have a role in the organized party."

But that doesn't mean he won't speak out if he sees something that particularly interests—or bothers—him.

"And on occasion I might even pop off, which I have done in the past occasionally."

Raggio is at relative peace with his legacy. After he announced his retirement he found himself giving some thought to things he might have done differently as a legislator. He thought open meetings had been extended too far, and that the Nevada Ethics Commission—which he helped create—has gotten out of control "to the point where good people just don't want to subject themselves to some of these requirements."

But he said, "Otherwise, I think there's very little I would have done differently, in reflection."

# CHAPTER NOTES

## PROLOGUE

1. Robert E. Dickens, "William Raggio: Personality, Power, and Politics," in *The Maverick Spirit: Building the New Nevada*, edited by Richard O. Davies (Reno: University of Nevada Press, 1999), 226-227.

## 2. THE WASHOE

1. Mark Twain, *Roughing It* (New York: New American Library, 1962), 297.
2. Angelina Raggio *née* Avansino, Avansino Family History (unpublished, circa 1940), 5.
3. *Ibid.*, 4.

## 3. BEN RAGGIO

1. *Reno Evening Gazette*, 20 October 1930
2. *Nevada State Journal*, (Month and date unreadable) 1894
3. *Reno Evening Gazette*, 18 June 1901
4. *Reno Evening Gazette*, 6 June 1909

## 4. RENO

1. *Reno Evening Gazette*, 19 November 1923
2. *Reno Evening Gazette*, 20 November 1923
3. *Reno Evening Gazette*, 22 December 1923
4. *Nevada State Journal*, 10 September 1896

## 5. WINGFIELD

1. *Time*, 13 September 1937
2. *Nevada State Journal*, 11 July 1917

## 6. CARDELLI

1. *Reno Evening Gazette*, 26 January 1924

## 7. "LITTLE BILLY RAGGIO"

1. *Reno Evening Gazette*, 1 November 1928
2. *Reno Evening Gazette*, 17 October 1989

## 8. FORMATIVE YEARS

1. *Reno Evening Gazette*, 10 January 1941

## 10. LEARNING THE LAW

1. Eleanor was the wife of crooner and stage and screen star, Rudy Vallee. They were

married in a small, private ceremony in Berkeley, California in 1946; she was 19 and he 45. Bill and Dororthy were the official witnesses. The Raggios and Vallees socialized frequently over the ensuing years. Rudy and Eleanor would remain together until his death in 1986. Eleanor wrote of their marriage in her book, *My Vagabond Lover.*

2. *San Francisco Daily Journal*, 26 February 2003

3. The Phi Alpha Delta Law Fraternity now claims six U.S. presidents among its membership, with the addition of Jimmy Carter and Bill Clinton.

### 11. ERNEST BROWN

1. *Reno Evening Gazette*, 10 October 1938

2. *Reno Evening Gazette*, 2 September 1936

### 12. PRACTICING THE LAW

1. *Nevada State Journal*, 13 September 1917

### 13. DEPUTY DISTRICT ATTORNEY

1. The O'Brien arson case is described in Melvin Belli's 1982 opus Modern Trials (a five-volume set). A photo of Deputy DA Raggio Bill appears in the section covering demonstrative evidence.

### 14. MCCARRAN

1. Robert Laxalt, *Nevada, A History* (Reno: University of Nevada Press, 1977), 72.

2. A simplified version of the complex (McNaughton) rule would be:

(1) A person is punishable for a crime if he knew he was committing the act and that it was contrary to law—even if it was done under the influence of an insane delusion.

(2) To establish the defense of insanity, it must be proved that at the time of the crime the defendant had such a defect of reasoning as to (A), not know the nature and quality of the act or (B), did know it, but did not know it was wrong.

(3) A person is legally responsible for his act even if they committed the crime because of an insane delusion as to the existing facts and as a consequence of these false circumstances (providing they would not constitute a legal defense if they were true.)

3. The Fox sentence was later commuted and he was eventually pardoned.

### 15. PROSTITUTION IN NEVADA

1. Guy Louis Rocha, *Presentation by Nevada State Archivist on the History of Prostitution in Nevada* (August 4, 1999).

2. William D. Rowley, Reno: *Hub of Washoe County* (Woodland Hills: Windsor Publications, 1984), 51.

3. After the executive order was lifted following the end of the war, Madam Mae Cunningham reopened a brothel at 900 East Commercial Row, employing 11 prostitutes and a staff of 8 other employees. A complaint was filed and the defendant was enjoined from using the premises because it was a public nuisance. Cunningham appealed, and the Nevada Supreme Court rendered a landmark decision that confirmed the legal basis for abating a brothel as a public nuisance. The court also negated the appellant's argument that enacting

statutes outlawing houses of prostitution within 400 yards of a school or church or on a main street of a town, does, by implication, legalize such houses in other areas.

In a reaction to the Supreme Court ruling, the 1949 Nevada State Legislature passed Senate Bill 218, which defined as the public policy of the state "to allow houses of prostitution in compliance with county or city ordinance." Governor Vail Pittman vetoed the bill, however, saying, "Such legalization would result in sensational and sordid publicity throughout the Nation and the world, to the inestimable damage of the good name of our state and its citizens."

### 17. CONFORTE

1. *Nevada State Journal*, 21 November 1959.

2. *Nevada State Journal*, 2 July 1960.

3. *San Francisco Chronicle*, 9 March 1960.

4. *San Francisco Chronicle*, 3 April 1960.

5. *San Francisco Examiner*, 29 June 1960

6. *Sacramento Bee*, 1 July 1960

7. *San Francisco Examiner*, 2 July 1960 (article reprinted with permission)

8. "One-on-One With Mustang Ranch Owner," I-Team with George Knapp. Las Vegas, NV: CBS-KLAS. May 1, 2008

9. *Nevada State Journal*, 3 July 1960

10. *Nevada State Journal*, 5 July 1960

11. *San Francisco Chronicle*, 13 July 1960

12. *San Francisco Chronicle*, 21 September 1960

13. *Las Vegas Review Journal*, 11 December 1986

14. Lyon County followed suit in March 1972. Later in the decade, Churchill, Mineral and Nye Counties legalized brothel prostitution in restricted areas.

15. *Reno Evening Gazette*, 14 November 1986

### 18. ORGANIZED CRIME

1. *Los Angeles Examiner*, 13 June 1953

2. *Nevada State Journal*, May 21 1976

3. *Ibid.*

4. *Fortune*, April 1934

5. Virgil W. Peterson, Operating Director, Chicago Crime Commission, testimony before the Special Committee to Investigate Organized Crime in Interstate Commerce, the United States Senate Eighty-First Congress, second session, June 22-23, 28; July 6, 7; and August 16, 1950.United States Government Printing Office, Washington, D.C., December 18,1950.

6. *Reno Evening Gazette*, 18 November 1949

7. Demaris, Ovid, *The Last Mafioso: The Treacherous World of Jimmy Fratianno*, (New York: Bantam Books, 1981) 66-68. Six years later, 50-year-old Louis Strauss disappeared. Jimmy Fratianno, who had once shared control of the Los Angeles crime family, confessed to the FBI that he had personally strangled Strauss to death in the Ontario, California.

According to Fratianno, "Russian Louie" Strauss, who moved to Las Vegas after his acquittal for murdering Sherwood, subsequently attempted to blackmail Las Vegas casino owner Benny Binion. In revenge, Binion promised the Los Angeles crime syndicate a percentage of his next casino if they "took care" of Strauss. In lieu of the percentage promised, Fratianno claimed he was later paid $60,000 for carrying out the hit. Binion emphatically denied these accusations.

Though Strauss's body was never found, knowledge of his execution became wide spread. For many years afterward, in establishments frequented by underworld figures in Las Vegas, it was common to hear someone describing an event that was extremely unlikely to occur, by using the morbidly-humorous expression: "When Russian Louie hits town."

8. Michael S. Green, "Hank Greenspun: Where he Stood," in *The Maverick Spirit: Building the New Nevada*, edited by Richard O. Davies (Reno: University of Nevada Press, 1999), 85.

9. Under the previous system, casino employees were hired based on whom they knew, rather than what they knew. If they did not have this kind of "juice," they likely would not work. Employees did not question decisions made from above. The safest attitude was summed up in the phrase "dummy up and deal." The less one knew about what was going on, the better.

10. John L. Smith, *Of Rats and Men: Oscar Goodman's Life from Mob Mouthpiece to Mayor of Las Vegas* (Las Vegas: Huntington Press, 2003) 74.

11. Bill Raggio, and others, later credited banker Eddie Questa for helping prevent underworld investors from making inroads into the Reno area, as they had in Las Vegas during the 1940s and 50s. The premise being that Questa's First National Bank lent northern gaming operators money at 6% per cent, while his competitors in the south were demanding 12%.

### 19. CORRUPTION

1. *Reno Evening Gazette*, 11 May 1960

2. Bill would remain forever grateful to the members of the grand jury whose dedication and courage contributed toward ending corruption in Reno city government and law enforcement. They were Lee Frankovich, foreman, Harvey Sewell, assistant foreman, and Stanley Jones, secretary. Other members included, C.W. Lingenfelter, Jesse Acrea, Adam Alger, Dwight Anderson, Robert Bond, Zetta Capriotti, Sam Hammond, Robert Harker, Brian La Veaga, Bill Ligon, Al Nagel, Ed Peckham, Ed Redman and Margaret Shaw.

3. *Reno Evening Gazette*, 31 January 1961

### 20. THAYNE ARCHIBALD

1. *Reno Evening Gazette*, 1 April 1960
2. *Reno Evening Gazette*, 6 April 1960
3. *Reno Evening Gazette*, 9 April 1960
4. *Reno Evening Gazette*, 8 April 1960
5. *Reno Evening Gazette*, 23 August 1961

### 21. ROBERT "SANDMAN" WILLIAMS

1. Claiborne, Harry Eugene. Interviews by Bruce Alverson (2002-2003). *Nevada Legal*

*Oral History Project: A Co-Operative Project of the Ninth Judicial Circuit Historical Society, Nevada Judicial Historical Society and University of Nevada Oral History Program* (Unpublished), 201.

2. Claiborne, oral history, 206
3. Claiborne, oral history, 205-206

## 23. LESTER MORFORD, III

1. *Reno Evening Gazette*, 22 September 1963
2. *Reno Evening Gazette*, 13 September 1963

## 24. REELECTION

1. *Reno Evening Gazette*, 20 August 1962
2. *Reno Evening Gazette*, 1 November 1962
3. *Reno Evening Gazette*, 27 October 1962

## 25. THOMAS LEE BEAN

1. *Nevada Daily Register*, 15 April 1963
2. *Reno Evening Gazette*, 13 April 1963

## 26. RAGGIO'S RAIDERS

1. Jude Wanniski, "Dick Tracy, Sam Spade Equals Reno's Mr. Raggio," *Las Vegas Review Journal*, 29 April 1965. (Reprinted with permission from the then-editor of the *Las Vegas Review Journal*.)

## 27. "EVERYBODY SEEMED TO KNOW HIM"

1. So famous is Bill for this gag, that among the scores of interviews the author conducted for this book, nearly everyone began with the same anxious question: "Did he get your $20?"(Yes, he did.)
2. Wanniski, op. cit.

## 28. OL' BLUE EYES

1. Though being licensed by the Nevada Gaming Commission, Dean Martin later decided not to seek joint ownership in the Cal-Neva.
2. Al W. Moe, *Nevada's Golden Age of Gambling* (Tacoma: Puget Sound Books, 2001) 90.
3. Anthony Summers and Robbyn Swan, "Sinatra: The Life—Interview with Anthony Summers and Robbyn Swan." Interviewed by Rick Porrello, *AmericanMafia.com*, June 2005
4. Anthony Summers and Robbyn Swan, *Sinatra: The Life* (New York: Alfred A. Knopf 2005) 44.
5. Pete Hamill, *Why Sinatra Matters*, (New York: Little, Brown & Company 1998)146.
6. John W. Tuohy, "The Cal-Neva Lounge." Rick Porrello's *AmericanMafia.com*, January 2001.
7. Grant Sawyer. Interviews conducted by Gary E. Elliott, narrative composed by R.T. King. *Hang Tough! Grant Sawyer: An Activist in the Governor's Mansion* (Reno: University of Nevada Oral History Program, 1993), 235

8. Sawyer, *Hang Tough!* 90-91

9. Sam Giancana and Chuck Giancana, *Double Cross: The Explosive Inside Story of the Mobster Who Controlled America* (New York; Warner Books 1992) 282.

10. Touhy, "Cal-Neva Lounge."

11. Wanniski, op. cit.

## 29. NATIONAL DISTRICT ATTORNEYS ASSOCIATION

1. Max C. Fleischman, heir to the Fleischman Yeast (later General Foods) fortune, was a philanthropist who had lived in Glenbrook, Nevada. The Max C. Fleischmann Foundation was established upon his death in 1951. The Foundation's trustee at the time Bill applied for the grant was Lester Summerfield, who had been district attorney in Washoe County from 1919 until 1931. In 2009 dollars, the 1964 $112,533 grant amount would be equivalent to $762,000.

2. Jim Garrison's highly publicized, though ill fated, investigation into a conspiracy surrounding the assassination of President Kennedy largely faded into obscurity. Garrison, embarrassed after the 1969 acquittal of Clay Shaw as a conspirator in the Kennedy assassination, was defeated in his reelection bid. He would soon recover and, in 1978, was elected as a judge of the Louisiana State Circuit Court of Appeals where he served until his death in 1992.

In 1991, Oliver Stone's film *JFK* was released—depicting Jim Garrison as a hero. However, Bill Raggio's March 1968 observation of Garrison as "an entirely changed man," would be echoed by Rosemary James in the December 23, 1991 issue of *Newsweek* when she compared the "real" Jim Garrison to the film version in *JFK*. James concluded, "He [Jim Garrison] went from a highly intelligent eccentric to a lunatic in the period of one year."

3. Henry Wade would make another far more enduring contribution to the national debate as the respondent in *Roe v. Wade*, the famous Supreme Court decision on the right to an abortion.

4. Ruby's conviction was subsequently overturned by the Texas Court of Criminal Appeals based on a ruling that he could not have received a fair trial in Dallas due to the level of pre-trial publicity. In January 1967, just prior to his retrial, Jack Ruby died of cancer.

5. Senator Frank "Hap" Farley was the most powerful legislator in New Jersey state history. He served 34 years in the New Jersey State Legislature and was head of the state's Republican Party. Farley would later withdraw support for casino gambling in Atlantic City, an act many attributed to his having second thoughts about the increased scrutiny it would bring to his political machine. He was defeated for reelection in 1971.

6. After casino gambling was approved in Atlantic City, the Nevada Gaming Control Board would not sanction a Nevada license for any company who wanted to set up outside Nevada. The policy was finally changed on condition that the regulatory process in the other state was the equivalent of that in Nevada.

## 30. THE POLITICAL WATERS (1964- 1968)

1. Jerome E. Edwards, "Grant Sawyer: A Liberal Governor for a Conservative State," in *The Maverick Spirit: Building the New Nevada*, edited by Richard O. Davies (Reno: University of Nevada Press, 1999), 146.

2. Dickens, "Personality, Power, and Politics," 225

3. *Reno Evening Gazette*, 2 October 1964

4. Among the most important of these High Court cases were: *Fay v. Noia*, in which the court extended the availability of federal habeas corpus to persons convicted of crimes in state courts, thus opening the door to an often-protracted appellate process; *Escobedo v. Illinois*, a precursor to the more famous 1966 *Miranda v. Arizona* decision, which determined the right to an attorney before questioning; and, *Mapp v. Ohio*, incorporating 4th Amendment rights into the Due Process clause of the 14th Amendment to create the "exclusionary rule," which prevents the use of evidence gained by so-called "illegal searches."

## 31. JIMMY ING

1. *Reno Evening Gazette*, 7 November 1966
2. *Reno Evening Gazette*, 7 February 1967
3. *Ibid.*

## 32. FAMILY

1. *Reno Evening Gazette*, 4 August 1964

## 33. U.S. SENATE RACE (1968)

1. *Reno Evening Gazette*, 4 September 1968

## 34. U.S. SENATE RACE (1970)

1. *Reno Evening Gazette*, 6 February 1970
2. *Nevada State Journal*, 6 October 1970
3. *Ibid.*
4. *Reno Evening Gazette*, 5 February 1970
5. *Reno Evening Gazette*, 6 February 1970
6. *Reno Evening Gazette*, 5 February 1970

7. Paul and Jackie Laxalt would divorce in 1972. In 2008, Bill Raggio would recall: "With the later exception of Dema Guinn, I was probably much closer to Jackie Laxalt than to the other First Ladies. Jackie was certainly her own person and she brought a lot of class to her position. She was responsible for restoration of the Governor's Mansion, which had fallen into a state of semi-neglect, and both she and Paul brought a new style and charm to the executive branch, much like the Kennedys arrival at 'Camelot.' Even though Jackie was beset by some personal challenges, the couple kept any element of marital discord from becoming a public issue until well after he left the governor's office."

8. Paul Laxalt, *Nevada's Paul Laxalt, A Memoir* (Reno: Jack Bacon & Company, 2000), 181.

9. "Politics: The President's Candidates," *Time*, 27 July 1970

10. Text of Raggio speech May 3, 1970 (Raggio Collection)

11. *Nevada State Journal*, 29 August 1970

12. Dickens, "Personality, Power, and Politics," 227

13. Clark R. Mollenhoff, "Blunder by White House in Backing Nevada Candidate," *Des Moines Register*, 17 October 1970

14. Dennis Myers, "Raggio Redux," *Reno News & Review*, 12 June 1996 (Reprinted with permission.)

15. Myers, "Raggio Redux"

16. Mollenhoff, "Blunder by White House"

17. *Reno Evening Gazette*, 24 October 1970

18. Jack Anderson and Daryl Gibson, *Peace, War, and Politics: An Eyewitness Account* (New York: Tom Doherty Associates 1999), 145.

19. Anderson, 147.

20. Anderson, 147.

21. *Reno Evening Gazette*, 22 October 1970

22. *Reno Evening Gazette*, 24 October 1970

23. *Reno Evening Gazette*, 29 October 1970

24. Representative Walter Baring of Nevada caught the oversight and inserted language in the bill that continued to decriminalize gambling in Nevada.

25. *Reno Evening Gazette*, 22 October 1970. In 1950, Hank Greenspun pled guilty to violating the Neutrality Act by having provided arms to Israel. He was fined $10,000.

26. *Forbes*, April 1934

27. John Woolley and Gerhard Peters, *Richard Nixon, XXXVII President of the United States, No. 421, Remarks in Las Vegas, Nevada 31 October 1970*, University of California, Santa Barbara, *http://www.presidency.ucsb.edu/index.php*

28. President Richard M. Nixon letter to William J. Raggio, November 1970 (Raggio Collection).

## 35. PRIVATE LIFE (1971-1972)

1. Opinion on the recommendation of the Board of Governors of the State Bar of Nevada in the matter of William J. Raggio by the Nevada Supreme Court of Nevada, No. 6142. 13 July 1971.

2. *Reno Evening Gazette*, November 1970

3. Sawyer, *Hang Tough!*, 90.

4. Sawyer, *Hang Tough!*, 90-91.

5. Though disappointed, Harlington Wood conferred with Bill later about who should be appointed to that position. Bill nixed several candidates. Wood eventually relied on Bill's suggestion to appoint Devoe Heaton as the U.S. Attorney for Nevada.

6. The 61-year-old Hughes, a Texas billionaire, had made his reputation as a dashing playboy and innovative businessman. Inheriting the Hughes Tool Company at age 19, Hughes went on to become a Hollywood movie producer, aircraft inventor, dare devil aviator, and mining mogul. By the time of his arrival in Las Vegas, he had descended into mental illness; a paranoid recluse, addicted to pain killers since being severely injured in a plane crash twenty years earlier. The reason for his visit to Las Vegas was a mystery, although seven months before that, Hughes had sold his stock in TransWorld Airlines for more than $546 million and was looking to invest in a tax-friendly industry and state.

7. A. D. Hopkins and K. J. Evans, *The First 100: Portraits of the Men and Women Who Shaped Las Vegas* (Las Vegas: Huntington Press, 2000) 278.

8. *Ibid.*

9. Alan Balboni, "Moe Dalitz: Controversial Founding Father of Modern Las Vegas,"

*The Maverick Spirit, Building the New Nevada,* edited by Richard O. Davies (Reno: University of Nevada Press, 1999) 25.

   10. *Nevada State Journal,* 14 October 1971

## 36. STATE SENATE (1973)

   1. *Reno Evening Gazette,* 26 May 1972

   2. In 1962, the U.S. Supreme Court ruled in *Baker vs. Carr* that federal courts could act in cases in which action, or inaction, by state legislatures led to malapportionment. This was followed in 1964, by *Reynolds v. Sims,* in which the high court interpreted the federal constitution to require that both houses of state legislatures be apportioned on the basis of population, referred to then as the "one-man-one-vote rule."

   3. Don W. Driggs and Leonard E. Goodall, *Nevada Politics and Government: Conservatism in an Open Society* (University of Nebraska Pres., 1996) 76.

   4. *Political History of Nevada* (Eleventh Edition), issued by Dean Heller, Secretary of State, edited by Rene Parker and Steve George (Carson City: State Printing Office, 2006), 312."The session was characterized by angry attacks on the U.S. Supreme Court, hostility, and dismay. At least 20 plans were introduced to reapportion the state, and a final plan was adopted to increase each chamber by three seats—to 20 members elected from 13 districts in the senate and 40 members elected from 16 districts in the assembly. In the senate, Clark County had 8 members; Washoe-Storey counties, 6 members; and the rural counties, 6 members. The assembly had 16 members from Clark County, 12 from Washoe-Storey counties, and 12 from the rural counties...On March 21, 1966, the three-judge panel of the federal district court reluctantly ruled that the adopted plan was constitutional and approved....The court noted, however, that the adopted reapportionment plan "...is not the fairest and best plan that the Nevada Legislature could possibly enact."

   5. *Political History of Nevada,* 314. James I. Gibson was born in 1925. He attended the U.S. Naval Academy and served as a naval officer in both World War II and the Korean Conflict. Gibson, a Democrat, represented Clark County in the state assembly and moved to the senate in 1967, where he would become an important addition to the influential Senate Committee on Finance. He was respected for his integrity and willingness to work and cooperate with others, making him a powerful force over his 30 years in the legislature.

   6. Richard Hudson Bryan was born in 1937. He graduated from the University of Nevada 1959 and earned his law degree from the University of California, Hastings College of Law. In 1963, he was admitted to the Nevada Bar. A Democrat, Bryan served as a member of the Nevada Senate from 1972 to 1978, and as the state's attorney general from 1979 until 1983. He was elected governor in 1982 and U.S. senator in 1988. In 2001, Richard Bryan left the senate and reentered the practice of law as a shareholder in the firm of Lionel, Sawyer & Collins.

   7. *Roe v. Wade* held that a mother may abort her pregnancy, for any reason, during the first six months. The Court based its ruling on the mother's constitutional right to privacy provided in the Due Process Clause of the Fourteenth Amendment. At the time of this decision, abortion was legal in only four states, Alaska, Hawaii, Washington and New York. In Nevada, abortion was illegal, except to save the life of the mother or another child.

8. The ERA, which supporters hoped would become the 27th Amendment to the Constitution, was intended to guarantee under federal, state, and local law that a person could not be denied equal rights because of gender. The proposal was sent by Congress to the states for ratification on March 22, 1972. Initially, its swift passage looked promising, with 22 of the necessary 38 state ratifications obtained in the first year.

9. On February 17, 1961, Dr. Thomas Wyatt of Crystal Bay, Nevada was convicted of attempting to perform an abortion on a woman sent to his office by the Washoe County district attorney to solicit such an illegal service. Testimony at the trial indicated the doctor had performed numerous such procedures in the past. Before his sentencing date, Wyatt and his wife fled to Mexico. Shortly thereafter, he engaged in a shootout with a man attempting to burglarize the trailer home in which he lived. Dr. Wyatt killed the intruder, but only after he and his wife were wounded in the gun battle. Wyatt was eventually extradited back to Nevada and given a two-year prison sentence.

10. Schlafly argued that the amendment would deny a woman's right to be supported by her husband; woman would be drafted and required to serve in combat; privacy rights would be overturned; and abortion rights and homosexual marriages would be institutionalized. Her primary underlying concern was that the ERA would grant excessive power to the Congress and to the federal courts.

11. Joseph M. Neal, Jr., was born in Mounds, Louisiana, on July 28, 1935. After four years in the United States Air Force, Neal attended Southern University where he graduated in 1963 with a degree in political science and history. He later attended and graduated from the Institute of Applied Science in Chicago, Illinois, where he studied civil identification and criminal investigation. Joe Neal would serve in the Nevada Senate from 1973 until 2003.

12. Joseph M. Neal, Jr., interviewed by Dana R. Bennett, *Nevada Legislature Oral History Project*, 12, May 2008. 13.

13. *Ibid.*

14. Neal, oral history, 16.

## 37. RACE FOR LIEUTENANT GOVERNOR (1974)

1. *Reno Evening Gazette*, 14 January 1974

2. Of Governor Michael O'Callaghan's popularly, Senator Richard Bryan would say in 2008: "He was so popular that people in his home town of Henderson mortgaged their homes to support him. He just had a way about him in dealing with people, that if you talked to him you would never forget him. He related well with everyone. He was overweight, had a chipped tooth and a wooden leg; yet, once you met him you never forgot him. It was also important to remember that O'Callaghan had lived in Northern Nevada as a member of the Sawyer Administration, so he was not just a southerner. It is hard for northerners to understand, but, at least in those days, southerners did not care if a northerner ran the state; however, northerners really did care whether a southerner ran the state."

3. *Reno Evening Gazette*, 9 March 1974

4. Herbert Kalmbach was convicted of illegally raising $3.9 million. He served 6 months in prison and was fined $10,000.

5. *Las Vegas Sun,* 12 September 1974

6. *Reno Evening Gazette,* 18 October 1974

7. The Independent American Party of Nevada is an offshoot of the American Independent Party movement of the 1960s, which espoused limited constitutional government, fiscal restraint, maximum personal freedom and the reassertion of states' rights. The party enjoyed its greatest popularity during the 1968 presidential election, when Alabama Governor George Wallace received nearly 10 million votes. During the 1972 presidential campaign, Wallace was the target of an assassination attempt that left him paralyzed for life, and the party never recovered its momentum.

8. *Reno Evening Gazette,* 6 November 1974

## 38. LEARNING TO MAKE LAW (1975–1977)

1. *Reno Evening Gazette,* 27 October 1976

2. Floyd Lamb, a southern Nevada rancher, represented the wild and wooly image of mid 20th century western politics. With flowing white mane, and rugged suntanned face, scarred from a lifetime of brawling, Lamb was originally elected as state senator from sparsely populated Lincoln County. When redistricting in 1971 eliminated his seat, Lamb promptly moved to adjacent Clark County, where his brother Ralph was the no-nonsense sheriff, ran for election and won—all without interrupting his term of office.

Floyd's temper was legendary. He was known to have engaged in fistfights with fellow solons after contentious senate meetings, and of dragging lobbyists across his desk by their neckties. Once, during the annual Helldorado Parade through downtown Las Vegas, Lamb's horse was acting insubordinate. He dismounted, and before a large crowd of onlookers, punched the horse in the nose so hard the stallion dropped to ground. It wobbled back to its feet and was docile for the rest of the parade.

3. *Nevada State Journal,* 4 June 1976

4. Elazar, Daniel J., *American Federalism: A View from the States, 2d Ed.* (New York: Crowell, 1972), p. 88-89. In Nevada's individualistic political culture, Elazar wrote, "most politicians are interested in office as a means of controlling the distribution of favors or rewards of government rather than as a means of exercising governmental power for programmatic ends...Since political corruption is not unexpected, there is relatively little popular excitement when any is found unless it is of an extraordinary character."

5. Kathryn L. MacKay, *Utah History Encyclopedia,* "The Equal Rights Amendment," *http://historytogo.utah.gov/utah_chapters/utah_today/equalrightsamendment.html*

6. Sue Wagner and Victoria Ford, *Through the Glass Ceiling* (Reno: University of Nevada Oral History Program 2005), 139.

7. Leola Armstrong would retire in 1981 from the position of Secretary of the Senate after 24 years and become executive director of the public watchdog group Common Cause/Nevada. She died in 2004.

8. Neal, oral history, 30.

## 39. GAMING LAWYER

1. Frank "Lefty" Rosenthal, a convicted felon who specialized in "fixing" sporting events,

and who posed as Glick's assistant, was required, in 1976, to apply for a state gaming license. It was denied because of his criminal background. Rosenthal hired attorney, who eventually took the case to the Nevada Supreme Court. The court affirmed the state's broad rights in granting privilege licenses. The U.S. Supreme Court refused to hear the case.

In December 1978, Rosenthal came before the Gaming Commission represented by Oscar Goodman. The Commission unanimously voted to deny his application. Rosenthal blamed the chair, Harry Reid. In the ensuing months, Reid received threatening phone calls, was offered bribes and had a bomb put on his car (though they failed to detonate). Despite all this, the FBI conducted a secret five-month investigation of Reid, to determine if he was now "connected" to the mob. The investigation had been prompted by innuendo overheard during a wiretap between two reputed mobsters. Reid was subsequently vindicated.

2. Nevada State Gaming Commission, *Transfer of Interest Among Licensees, Casino Operations, Inc., dba Las Vegas Hacienda*. Transcript of Proceedings. 21 July 1977. 92-94.

3. Bill Raggio resigned his position on the Board of Directors of the company, and certain of its subsidiaries, in May 1999 due to a potential conflict caused by his position on the board of another gaming company, a position that he no longer holds. Bill was reappointed to the Board of Directors of Archon in December 2000.

5. Hamill, *Why Sinatra Matters*, 146.

6. Kitty Kelley, *His Way: The Unauthorized Biography of Frank Sinatra* (New York: Bantam Books 1986), 468.

7. Nevada State Gaming Commission, *In the matter of: Desert Palace, Inc., dba Caesars Palace, Frank Sinatra, Applicant. Transcript of public hearing* (Non restricted item No 80-51), 19 February 1981. 11.

8. Some of the documents that publicly appeared in the complete FBI file on Sinatra released after his death in 1998 were not available to Bill Raggio in preparing for Frank's 1981 hearings before the Gaming Control Board and Gaming Commission. Among those documents were statements by Victor LeCroix-Collins and Phyllis McGuire about Frank's participation in the Cal-Neva incident, as well as reports by FBI undercover agents who witnessed the altercation; all of which refuted testimony given at the hearings by Sinatra and his associates.

When asked about this in a 2009 interview, Bill said he could only build a factual case based on the information the government had been willing to provide. If the FBI had included those statements and reports in his 1981 FOIA request, they would have been considered at the hearing.

9. Gaming Commission hearing, Sinatra. 50.

## 40. LOBBYISTS

1. Michael W. Bowers, *The Sagebrush State, Nevada's History, Government and Politics* (Reno: University of Nevada Press, 2002), 58.

2. *Ibid.*

3. Bowers, *Sagebrush State*, 61.

4. A. D. Hopkins and K. J. Evans, *The First 100: Portraits of the Men and Women Who*

*Shaped Las Vegas* (Las Vegas: Huntington Press, 2000), 317.

### 41. TAX REFORM AND SAGEBRUSH REBELS (1979)

1. Russell R. Elliott, *History of Nevada, 2nd ed.* (Lincoln: University of Nebraska Press, 1987), 361.

2. Due to the extremely dry climactic conditions in Nevada, traditional homesteading proved more difficult than in most other states. The 160 acres granted under the federal Homestead Act was not of a practical size in this harsh environment.

By the late 19th century, most of the arable land with direct access to existing water supplies had been claimed by the railroads and a few wealthy landowners. Consequently, settlers were forced to homestead land surrounding a lesser water source, such as a well, and graze livestock on adjacent public land. That practice continued into present times.

In 1970, the Federal Land Law Review Commission recommended to President Nixon and Congress that they retain land in federal ownership "whose values must be preserved so that they may be used and enjoyed by all Americans." By 1977, the Nevada Legislature established the Select Committee on Public Lands to effect changes in public lands policies and to encourage other western states to join Nevada in that effort.

In 1980, a bill was introduced in Congress by Republican Senator Orin Hatch of Utah to allow states, such as Nevada, to take transfer of some federal public land. It failed to move forward. With 16 cosponsors, Hatch reintroduced the bill in 1981. This provided a huge morale boost to long-aggrieved public lands users, other than conservationists, and started a two-year newspaper, radio and television fight for the legislation.

Though the bill did not pass, it received enormous press attention. The election of President Ronald Reagan, who had once referred to himself as a "Sagebrush Rebel," diminished the intensity of the political battle, largely because Reagan appointees slowed the pace of wilderness designation legislation.

### 42. AN OLD FOE (1981)

1. Wagner, Sue and Victoria Ford. *Glass Ceiling*, 243. In March 1980, Sue Wagner's husband, Peter, along with three other employees of the Desert Research Institute, was killed in a plane crash in the Sierra Nevada Mountains. Despite this personal tragedy, Sue was able to resume campaigning later in the year.

2. Elliott, *History of Nevada*, 363

3. In 1979, the U.S. military planned to hide an arsenal of mobile nuclear missiles in the Nevada desert to deter what was believed to be technological advances in the Soviet Union's first strike missile capability.

4. Bill's effort to sway public opinion against legalized prostitution was not just directed against Conforte's business. One of his more interesting appearances, with regard to this issue, came a few years earlier when he attended the Nevada Public Health Association's annual educational conference, in Hawthorne, Nevada. There, he debated the pros and cons of legalized prostitution with Margo Saint-James, a former prostitute, representing the COYOTE (Call Off Your Old Tired Ethics) organization of San Francisco, which advocated the decriminalization of prostitution. Saint-James would go on to seek the Republican nomination for president in 1980.

In 2009, Bill recalled:

"Hawthorne was not what I would call a 'contemporary town.' I was someone who had shut down brothels and prosecuted a pimp, and so obviously was on the 'other side.'

"My argument was that the least offensive thing about prostitution was the prostitute. It was everything that goes along with it—the pimps, the demimonde, drugs, and the fact that it attracts bad elements. It is hardly an industry that is going to add a lot of diverse elements in your economy. The debate was civil and, given the sentiment of the audience, I was in the minority—but being in the minority never bothered me."

5. In 1982, a Storey County grand jury would conclude a 2-1/2 year probe, stating that Conforte had unusual influence and power in the county. The jury implicated district attorney Virgil Bucchianeri and Sheriff Bob Del Carlo, but no indictments resulted.

6. In the late 1960s and early 1970s, Bonavena had been a serious contender for the world heavyweight boxing title. After being knocked out in the 15th round of a fight with Mohammed Ali in 1970, he began a slide into obscurity. Joe Conforte brought him to the Mustang Ranch in 1975 to train for a comeback. The fighter began an affair with Joe's wife, Sally, and soon believed he would be replacing Conforte as the proprietor of the Ranch. When Conforte learned of this, he banished both Oscar and Sally from the brothel grounds. When Bonavena later returned to confront Conforte, he was shot and killed by one of Joe's bodyguards. The shooter, Ross Brymer, was found guilty of manslaughter and served 15 months in prison.

7. *Reno Gazette Journal*, 14 November 1986

8. *Nevada State Journal* , 20 May 1981

9. *Reno Evening Gazette*, 9 July 1976

10. *Reno Evening Gazette*, 31 May 1981

## 43. PLIGHT OF THE CITIZEN LEGISLATOR (1983)

1. In February 5, 2009, Dennis Myers wrote in the *Reno News & Review* that state legislators and county governments had gone to the "sales tax well" so often that Nevada now had one of the highest sales taxes in the nation. "Politicians learned that it was a low-political-cost levy: The rate of collection is so gradual that people, particularly the working poor, have no idea how heavily they are being taxed. The influential, book-length 1960 study *Financing State and Local Government in Nevada* called the sales tax a 'sucker tax.'"

2. Twain, *Roughing It*, 297

3. Bowers, *Sagebrush State*, 111

4. Elliott, *History of Nevada*, 366

5. *Reno Evening Gazette*, 11 August 1982

## 44. JUDGE HARRY CLAIBORNE TRIAL (1984)

1. Floyd Lamb had long been suspected of corruption. Two years before his arrest, he reportedly sent then-Legislative Counsel Frank Daykin to Las Vegas to attend a meeting with several casino operators, including Frank "Lefty" Rosenthal and Allen Glick. Brendan Riley, Associated Press correspondent in Carson City, heard one result was a bill that would benefit Rosenthal, whose mob ties were hindering his ultimately unsuccessful efforts to win a gaming license, and others by softening gaming laws. Riley learned the senator tried to hide

his role by having the bill introduced in the Assembly. Lamb denied his involvement, but several sources confirmed otherwise and Riley wrote about the measure's origin. The morning the story ran, Lamb, newspaper article in hand, entered a packed Senate-Assembly Judiciary Committee meeting, spied Riley in an aisle seat and kicked him hard in the shin with the toe of his cowboy boot (Brendan would later say he could feel the bone bruise for a year thereafter).

After Lamb stalked out of the hearing room, Riley left to write about the assault. He saw Lamb at the door of the Senate chamber and confronted him. Lamb called Riley a liar and slapped him hard across the face. When the now-furious Riley stepped toward the senator, Leola Armstrong, Secretary of the Senate, kept matters from escalating by stepping between the two men and pushing Riley away. Years later, Riley said Armstrong likely saved his AP job in Carson City, one he held for 37 years, because AP probably would have transferred him—or worse—had he thrown a punch. The news story resulted in Lamb's bill dying in the Assembly.

2. Operation Abscam was named for a fictitious Arab sheikh, Kambir Abdul Rahman, who tried to bribe U.S. government officials to, variously, purchase asylum in the U.S., involve them in an investment scheme, or help him get money out of a Middle Eastern country. That investigation ultimately led to the conviction of a United States senator, five members of the House of Representatives, one member of the New Jersey state senate, members of the Philadelphia city council, and an inspector for the Immigration and Naturalization Service.

3. The "fairness" issue aside, political exposes, such as Watergate, Abscam and Yobo, fed a growing public mistrust about the integrity and motives of their elected officials. This helped fuel the demand for term limits and the growing use of ballot initiatives and referendums to circumvent the legislative process.

In time, term limits would drain necessary experience and institutional memory from the process, making it less efficient and more reliant on staff and lobbyists for information and guidance.

The initiative process would have an equally negative effect. Complex issues, normally decided upon after committee hearings into all facets of the matter, were put to the voters in the form of slogan or synopsis.

Ironically, in the immediate aftermath of Operation Yobo, some honest officials received damaging backlash. U.S. Attorney Mahlon Brown III, son of the long-time state senate majority leader, deserved praise for his part in the operation. He personally knew most of those indicted and their families. Instead of trying to derail the probe, he urged the FBI to move forward. While his sense of integrity should have been admired by his fellow Nevadans, many resented Brown's participation. He subsequently lost his race for the Office of State Attorney General, one that he had earlier been favored to win.

4. Richard Woodbury and Anastasia Toufexis, "Law: The Trouble with Harry," *Time*, 2 April 1984.

5. *Ibid.*

6. Michael Vernetti, *Lies Within Lies: The Betrayal of Nevada Judge Harry Claiborne* (Las Vegas: Stephens Press, 2011) 122.

7. Smith, *Of Rats, 166*

8. *Las Vegas Sun,* 3 December 1982

9. Smith, *Of Rats,* 166-167

10. FBI agent Bruce Wick was called to testify by the defense to refute Conforte's testimony. Under questioning by Raggio, Wick admitted that he was assigned by the prosecutors to photograph the interior of Claiborne's apartment, particularly an "eating bar" where Conforte swore he had worked out a bribe amount with Judge Claiborne. When Wick found that such an "eating bar" did not exist in the one-bedroom units, like that rented by Judge Claiborne, he was directed by the apartment manager to a studio apartment, because, as Agent Wick testified, "the studio apartments were the only ones that had a bar such as that in them."

11. Drendel was replaced by Oakland, California attorney J. Richard Johnson who specialized in federal tax law.

12. During a 2008 interview, journalist Dennis Myers, who covered both of Judge Claiborne's trials, spoke about a major flaw he observed in the federal justice system with regard to the Claiborne case: "I always thought the second trial revealed one of the failings of the grand jury system. They [federal prosecutors] shopped the case around for months trying to get and indictment and grand jurors would not go along. Therefore, they lure Conforte into the deal and they finally get the indictment. Then they drop Conforte from the case for the second trial. If he wasn't part of that second case, the indictment should not have stood, because only his testimony made it happen in the first place."

In addition, Myers was amazed that the prosecutors chose to retry the judge at all, since his first trial had ended with the majority of jurors (10-2) voting for acquittal. Myers later contacted a justice department official to find out who authorized the retrial, and was told the decision had been left to the prosecutors on the scene.

13. *Reno Gazette Journal,* 14 November 1986

14. Vernetti, *Lies Within Lies,* 135.

## 45. NOT ONE TO HOLD A GRUDGE (1985)

1. *Reno Gazette Journal,* 11 July 1985

## 46. MAJORITY FLOOR LEADER (1987)

1. In "Raggio Redux," Myers points out that in 1982, when Republican Robert List was defeated, and numerous other GOP candidates around the state fell, Bill Raggio was widely expected to try to turn his new image and his dominance in the party into another statewide run. "Faced with this tantalizing prospect, Raggio backed away, publicly declining any further statewide races," Myers wrote. "It was a deft maneuver, taking him out of the role as a competitor to other Republicans and increasing his influence within Party and Legislative circles."

2. Senator Townsend attributes part of his success in being reelected after switching parties, to the Democrat decision to run an opponent against him who had also switched parties—though from Republican to Democrat. This removed "switching" as a campaign issue. Townsend, like Bob Cashell, was also asked personally by President Reagan (in Townsend's,

case by telephone call) to consider switching parties.

　　3. Dickens, "Personality, Power, and Politics," 229.

　　4. *Ibid.*

　　5. *Reno Gazette Journal*, 20 January 1989

## 47. PENSION FIASCO (1989)

　　1. *Reno Gazette Journal*, 20 January 1989

　　2. *Reno Gazette Journal*, 17 January 1989

　　3. William Hamma, a registered Democrat and political science teaching assistant at UNR, filed just to keep Bill from running unopposed. Bill's only other challenger was Libertarian Party candidate David Palmquist.

　　4. Question 4 would be defeated in November 1988. This was not the first time Senator Raggio had proposed this plan for selecting Nevada judges and he would continue to push for its passage for the remainder of his legislative career.

　　5. *Reno Gazette Journal*, 13 November, 1988

　　6. *Las Vegas Sun*, 23 March 1989

　　7. *Las Vegas Sun*, 11 August 2001

　　8. *Reno Gazette Journal*, 18 January 1989

　　9. *Reno Gazette Journal*, 8 July 1990

　　10. Letter Kim Sedway to Bill Raggio, July 1989 (Raggio Collection)

　　11. Dickens, "Personality, Power, and Politics," 230

　　12. *Nevada Appeal*, 26 June 1989

　　13. Letter Brian Mackay to Bill Raggio, June 1989 (Raggio Collection)

## 48. THE SESSION FROM HELL (1991)

　　1. *Reno Gazette Journal*, 2 November 1990

　　2. *Reno Gazette Journal*, 18 January 1989

　　3. *Las Vegas Review Journal*, 18 October 1990

　　4. Sue Wagner won the seat and later was reelected without opposition. In 1990, Wagner ran for lieutenant governor. On the eve of the primary election, she was severely injured in a plane crash when the twin-engine Cessna she was aboard crashed shortly after takeoff from the Fallon Municipal Airport. The pilot, state treasurer candidate Bob Seale was also badly injured, and Seale's wife was killed. Two other occupants, Wagner campaign aide Stephanie Tyler, and Brian Krolicki, Seale's campaign manager, suffered less serious injuries. Krolicki walked about two miles to a ranch house to report the crash.

　　Unable to continue campaigning due to her injuries, she, nonetheless, was elected as lieutenant governor. Wagner served one term and was subsequently appointed to the State Gaming Commission.

　　5. Driggs and Goodall, "Conservatism," xxi.

　　6. *Las Vegas Review Journal*, 7 July 1991

　　7. *Reno Gazette Journal*, 30 June 1991

8. Vargas was one of the oldest and most respected law firms in Nevada, founded in 1934 when Governor Morley Griswold and George Vargas became partners. Vargas would later merge with John Bartlett, who Bill Raggio had replaced as deputy district attorney of Washoe County in August 1952, when Bartlett decided to return to private practice.

9. Rollan Melton letter to Bill Raggio, 7 March 1991 (Raggio Collection)

10. Guy Shipler letter to Bill Raggio, 21 July 1991 (Raggio Collection)

### 49. AMERICAN LEGISLATIVE EXCHANGE COUNCIL

1. This philosophy has its roots in their interpretation of the historical struggle between Jeffersonian and Hamiltonians dating from the post-Revolutionary period. While Hamiltonians sought to use government to protect what the aristocrats had built up, Jeffersonians believed that limiting the federal government would empower all people to fulfill their potential. This, according to the ALEC ideal, creates a choice for voters between "centralist elitists and entrepreneurial populists."

### 50. "A FISCALLY PRUDENT APPROACH" (1993)

1. *Las Vegas Review Journal*, 4 February 1992

2. *Reno Gazette Journal*, 25 October 1992

3. *Reno Gazette Journal*, 3 December 1992

5. In March 1979, the Three Mile Island nuclear power plant in Pennsylvania suffered a serious malfunction endangering the lives of thousands of nearby residents. This brought scrutiny of safety measures for radioactive material across the nation. Though Nevada did not have a nuclear plant, it did have a storage facility for low-level nuclear waste near the town of Beatty. Reports of radioactive waste leaking from trucks while traveling through Nevada to the storage site led the governor to close the facility until more stringent safety measures were assured.

6. While serving a life sentence for murder, without the possibility of parole, Willie Horton became the beneficiary of a Massachusetts prisoner-furlough program. He did not return from his furlough, and eventually committed assault, armed robbery and rape. An effective political advertisement was launched by the 1988 presidential campaign of George H.W. Bush critical of his Democratic opponent, Massachusetts Governor Michael Dukakis, who had supported the furlough program.

### 51. THE PURSE STRINGS (1995)

1. *The Ralston Report*, 16 December 1994, Vol. 2, No. 24

2. *Reno Gazette Journal*, 1 November 1995

3. *Nevada Appeal*, 6 July 1995

4. *Reno Gazette Journal*, 15 April 1996

### 52. MASTER OF THE ENDGAME (1997)

1. Truckee Meadows Human Services 1996 Politician of the Year citation (Raggio Collection)

2. *Las Vegas Review Journal*, 14 April 1996

3. Bill Raggio's only opposition in the 1996 election was Independent American Party candidate Brookes Holcomb.

4. *Las Vegas Review Journal,* 16 May 1997

5. In February 2011, Governor Bob Miller commented on the process to achieve education reform saying it grew out of a bipartisan task force, which included Elaine Wynn, on Standards Assessment and Accountability that he had structured between sessions and was a key part of his State of the State address preceding that session. "Of course," Miller added, "nothing would have passed if not for Bill and I working together to create a mutually acceptable bill."

6. Las Vegas Review Journal, 13 July 1997

7. *The Ralston Report,* 11 July 1997, Vol. 5, EXTRA

8. *Ibid.*

## 53. PAIN AND PARTISANSHIP (1998-1999)

1 *Reno Gazette Journal,* 14 April 1998

2. *Las Vegas Journal Review,* 26 April 1998

3. *Ibid.*

4. In 1998, the attorneys general of 46 states signed the Master Settlement Agreement with the four largest tobacco companies in the United States. In May of that year, the Nevada legislature approved two bills that determined how the tobacco settlement proceeds would be distributed. Approximately 60% of funds would go towards health care programs and 40% to fund the Nevada Millennium Scholarship Program.

5. The primary purpose of the Distributive School Account is to supplement local financial ability to whatever extent necessary and provide the means by which Nevada meets its guaranteed financial support to school districts under the Nevada Plan. Historically, the Class Size Reduction Program had been funded with revenues from estate taxes and state General Fund appropriations.

6. *Reno Gazette Journal,* 18 July 1998

## 54. REDISTRICTING: AN OPPORTUNITY MISSED (2001)

1. During the final hours of the regular session, which was to have ended at midnight, it was decided that since the state constitution had specifically used the term "Standard Time," and the ending date of the session was now under "Daylight Savings Time," the session could be continued until 1:00 a.m. Pending a ruling on the legality of this action, Governor Guinn decided to include, as part of the special session, certain measures passed within that additional hour, just in case they might be later invalidated. The court, however, decided the "extra hour" was appropriate.

2. *The Ralston Report,* 3 July 2001 Vol.9, Nos. 11-12

## 55. CAUCUS REVOLT (2003)

1. *Reno Gazette Journal,* 9 March 2002

2. *Ibid.*

3. As Joe Crowley explained in March 2011: "UNLV also benefited from this as did the

community colleges to a lesser extent. While the UNR people did most of the work on the first two increments, the final 25% was a major system priority that was approved by the legislature [Bill being the driving force] after I had retired."

4. Bowers, *Sagebrush*, 108.

5. Ann O'Connell interviewed by Dana R. Bennett and Dale A.R. Erquiaga, *Nevada Legislature Oral History Project*, March 28, 2008. 31.

6. O'Connell, oral history, 32.

7. *Reno Gazette Journal*, 26 June 2003

8. John W. Marvel interviewed by Dana R. Bennett, *Nevada Legislature Oral History Project*, December 1, 2008. 31.

9. Dale's son, David Joffick, lives in Sydney, Australia with her two grandchildren, Thomas and Harrison Joffick.

10. Harry Reid letter to Bill Raggio, 4 August 2003 (Raggio Collection).

## 56. GOOD COMPROMISES (2005)

1. O'Connell, oral history, 33.

2. Bill had two opponents in the election: Democrat Cameron Crain and Independent American Party candidate Gary Feero.

3. Of the fifteen, Sharron Angle, Bob Beers, John Carpenter, Chad Christensen, Pete Goicoechea, Tom Grady, Don Gustavson, Lynn Hettrick, Ron Knecht, Garn Mabey, Rod Sherer and Valerie Weber were running for re-election. Walter Andonov and David Brown did not run again. John Marvel, the only assembly Republican to cross over and vote for the tax bill, ran again the following year and was reelected, but lost in 2008.

4. In January 2006, despite being denied support from state Republican Party because of her censure, Kathy Augustine announced her candidacy for State Treasurer. In July 2006, she was found unconscious in her Reno, dying four days later without regaining consciousness. In September 2006, her husband, a critical care nurse, was charged with first-degree murder. Toxicology results found Augustine had been administered a paralyzing drug that led to her death. Her spouse was convicted of murder in June 2007.

5. *Las Vegas Review Journal*, 21 May 2005

6. *Las Vegas Sun*, 20 June 2005

8. *Ibid.*

9. After an investigation by the State Ethics Commission, Tiffany ended her $10,000 state contract to sell surplus government vehicles. A state law forbids legislators from holding contracts with state government, unless they are the sole source of a service or product. Tiffany had been designated by the State Purchasing Division as the sole source of Internet auto sales, although many people can sell vehicles. The following year, after a contested primary, Senator Tiffany lost to her Democratic challenger in the general election.

10. *Las Vegas Review Journal*, 20 June 2005

11. *Las Vegas Review Journal*, 26 June 2005

12. Justice Nancy Becker letter to Bill Raggio (Raggio Collection)

13. James E. Rogers letter to Bill Raggio, 16 June 2005 (Raggio Collection)

## 57. AN AIR OF INCIVILITY (2007)

1. Driggs and Goodell, "Conservatism," 6.

2. *Ibid.*

3. *Reno Gazette Journal*, 5 August 2006

4. In 2009, Senator Raggio would remark: "Governor Guinn was also fortunate and wise to have surrounded himself with staff of a similar caliber—competent, bright and with the ability to work with others. Former Assemblyman Pete Ernaut was his first Chief of Staff, followed by the likes of Marybel Batjer and Mike Hillerby, all who served him well and were well respected and received by the legislature."

5. Linda Law and John Trent, "Moving Nevada Into the 21st Century: Governor Kenny C. Guinn 1999-2006—An Executive Summary" (Carson City: Nevada State Printing Office 2006), Introduction.

6. Mrs. Guinn kept the cost of admission to these events relatively low so that he average Nevadan would have a chance to socialize with the First Couple and tour the Governor's Mansion and grounds. When the last Tin Cup Tea was hosted by Dema, in 2006, the event had become so popular that more than 1,300 guests attended, raising over $100,000. In June 19, 2009, the Nevada State Museum honored the First Lady by naming a new building the Dema Guinn Concourse.

7. Jim Gibbons had previously served in the state assembly during the 1989, 1991, and 1993 sessions, with a lapse to serve in the Gulf War. During that period, his wife Dawn was appointed to fill in for him. After Jim Gibbons left the assembly, Dawn was later elected to fill his Assembly District 25 seat and she served in the 1999, 2001 and 2003 sessions, after which she ran unsuccessfully in the Republican primary for Congress.

8. *Reno Gazette Journal*, 23 January 2007

9. *Las Vegas Review Journal*, 6 February 2007

10. Sandra Tiffany note to Bill Raggio, November 2006 (Raggio Collection)

11. *Las Vegas Sun*, 30 May 2007

12. *Reno Gazette Journal*, 15 June 2007

## 58. CHALLENGE FROM THE RIGHT (2008-2009)

1. Dina Titus letter to Bill Raggio, November 2007 (Raggio Collection)

2. *RalstonFlash.com*, 24 June 2005

3. *Reno News & Review*, 3 July 2008

4. *Las Vegas Sun*, 5 August 2008

5. Those who did sign include Governor Jim Gibbons, Lieutenant Governor Brian Krolicki, Congressman Dean Heller, U.S. Senator John Ensign, State Senator Barbara Cegavske, Assemblywoman Sharron Angle, Assemblyman Chad Christensen, Sue Lowden and Danny Tarkanian…among others.

6. *Reno News & Review*, 13 November 2008

7. A young man by the name of Jade Zahreddine visited his office. Jade, a Democrat, informed Bill that he had registered to run against him in the general election. When Raggio asked him why he was running, Zahreddine replied that because of Bill's age, he "needed competition."

"He also said," Bill later deadpanned, "that I had not done enough for education."

8. Steven Horsford was born in Las Vegas in 1973. He attended Edward W. Clark High School and later the University of Nevada, Reno. Horsford currently serves as CEO of the Culinary Training Academy, a joint management and labor partnership between participating gaming companies and the Culinary and Bartenders Unions.

9. Raggio Collection.

10. The "Hardy Case" ruling came not as the result of the 2009 potential conflict of interest issue involving Steven Hill, but rather on a complaint filed with the Ethics Commission

in 2008 alleging Senator Hardy repeatedly broke laws by voting on matters that helped Associated Builders and Contractors. However, the Ethics Commission found sufficient cause to conduct a full hearing on only one of the twelve alleged counts.

Before that hearing began, the legislature filed a lawsuit claiming because the Ethics Commissioners were appointed by the governor; it represented oversight of the legislative branch of government by the executive branch and so violated the principle of "separation of powers." The Supreme Court heard the case in April 2009. The attorney representing the Ethics Commission argued that the legislature's premise was contradictory, since it had been the 1985 legislature that originally granted the Ethics Commission the power to discipline legislators. The Court, however, ruled that the legislature should not have delegated such authority to the Ethics Commission.

Warren Hardy was first elected to the assembly in 1990 and the state senate in 2002. After nearly 20 years of being away from his family and livelihood for long periods of time to attend to his Legislative responsibilities and tired of his family being subjected to offensive news stories about him, he would resign his seat in the senate at the end of the 2009 session.

11. Senator Raggio later spoke of Robert Uithoven's role: "Uithoven came in to see me and was apologetic, saying he had not said that he was going to file an ethics charge against me, and that the rumor was not true. I said, 'Robert, it came out that way because ruining people as to how they're going to vote is extremely inappropriate. Why don't you give us some credit for what we're trying to do to make sure that we provide essential services. Any tax increases will be temporary and we will insist on sunsets. Why not give us some credit for trying to reform the tax and the retirement systems?' He was very apologetic. I really did not understand his posture, though he is very much influenced by [anti-tax political blogger] Chuck Muth."

12. *Las Vegas Sun*, 23 May 2009

13. *Las Vegas Sun*, 24 May 2009.

14. *Ibid.*

### 59. THE PRICE OF CONSCIENCE (2010)

1. The Tea Party is a grassroots political movement that has been sponsoring locally and nationally coordinated protests opposing taxes and spending since early 2009. The name derives from the Boston Tea Party protest by colonists against British taxation policy in 1773. The Tea Party movement has no central leadership; rather it is composed of a loose affiliation of national and local groups that determine their own platforms and agendas. Since it is not a national political party, Tea Party candidates generally run as Republicans.

2. *Reno Gazette Journal*, 8 December 2009

3. A day later, the governor became the subject of a Las Vegas television news story that showed him lying (which he admitted to the following day) while unsuccessfully hiding the fact that was being accompanied back from a national governors' conference in Washington, D.C., by a woman referenced in his wife's divorce papers as one with whom he was having an affair.

4. *RalstonFlash-ralston@vegas.com*, 28 February 2010

5. *Mini-Muth's Truths: April 24, 2010*. Muth's Truths.
http://www.muthstruths.com/2010/04/24/mini-muths-truths-april-24-2010/.

6. *Las Vegas Review Journal*, 8 October 2010

7. *Reno Gazette Journal*, 6 January 2011

8. *Las Vegas Review Journal*, 7 November 2010

# SOURCES AND BIBLIOGRAPHY

## NEWSPAPERS AND PERIODICALS

*Las Vegas Israelite*
*Las Vegas Review Journal*
*Las Vegas Sun*
*Nevada Appeal*
*Nevada State Journal*
*Newsweek*
*Reno Evening Gazette*
*Reno Gazette Journal*
*Reno News & Review*
*San Francisco Chronicle*
*San Francisco Examiner*
*San Francisco News-Call Bulletin*
*Time Magazine*
*Valley Times*

## INTERVIEWS (58)

Alsonso, Michael (Reno) February 19, 2008
Brezny, Joe (Carson City) April 22, 2009
Brinkman, Billie (Carson City) March 18, 2009
Brown, John W. "Web" (Reno) October 27, 2007
Bryan, Richard (Reno) August 21, 2008
Buckley, Barbara (Las Vegas) April 2, 2010
Carano, Don, (Reno) February 10, 2010
Care, Terry (Las Vegas) March 21, 2010
Cashell, Bob (Reno) February 2, 2010
Clift, Claire Jesse (Carson City) October 20, 2009
Crowley, Joe (Reno) March 4, 2008
Davis, Fred (Reno) October 17, 2007
Delanoy, Drake (Incline Village) February 12, 2008
Dickens, Robert, (Reno) June 9, 2008
DiLoreto, Perry (Reno) April 19, 2010
Drendel, John Squire (Phoenix) October 27, 2007
Farr, Bill (Sparks) October 25, 2007
Ferraro, Greg (Reno) March 10, 2011
Francovich, Lillian (Reno) June 30, 2008
Gezelin, Joesphine (Reno) November 8, 2007

Ghiggeri, Gary (Reno) December 21, 2009
Goodman, Oscar (Las Vegas) February 27, 2009
Guinn, Kenny (Reno) September 8, 2009
Hanlon, Bill (Las Vegas) February 17, 2010
James, Mark (Las Vegas) October 25, 2009
King, Tom (Reno) April 3, 2008
Klaich, Dan (Reno) November 17, 2010
Laxalt, Paul (Washington, D.C.) June 10, 2008
Lindell, Michael (Reno) February 2, 2011
Lowden, Paul (Reno) June 10, 2008
Malkiewich, Lorne (Carson City) March 27, 2008
Mathews, Bernice (Reno) September 12, 2009
Melarkey, Betty Avansino (Reno) October 16, 2007
Miles, Dan (Carson City) June 4, 2009
Miller, Bob (Las Vegas) February 28, 2011
Mill, Lila (Perondi) (Carson City) February 19, 2008
Myers, Dennis (Sparks) July 17, 2008
Needham, Jan (Reno) January 27, 2010
Newton, Marilyn (Reno) December 28, 2008 (Email only)
Pappageorge, John (Carson City) March 13, 2009
Raggio, Dale (Carson City) March 18, 2009
Raggio, William J., (18 separate occasions) February 4, 2008—May 13, 2010
Reid, Harry (Washington, D.C.) August 20, 2010
Rhoads, Dean (Carson City), February 14, 2011
Righetti, Leslie (Reno) February 12, 2008
Rose, Bob (Reno) November 7, 2010
Ruvo, Larry (Reno) September 12, 2009
Sande III, John (Reno) February 16, 2010
Scheberle, Ron (Dallas) June 11, 2009
Stewart, Michael (Carson City) March 27, 2008
Streeter, Jack (Reno) October 30, 2007
Swobe, Coe (Reno) March 30, 2010
Thompson, Charles (Las Vegas) February 22, 2008
Titus, Dina (Washington, D.C.) March 4, 2010
Townsend, Randolph (Reno) January 7, 2010
Vucanovich, Barbara (Reno) May 27, 2008
Watson, Jerry (Carson City) March 14, 2009
Williams, Don (Carson City) March 27, 2008
Wilson, Thomas "Spike" (Reno) March 16, 2010
Woodring, Tracy (Reno) July 25, 2008
Wynn, Steve (Las Vegas) March 27, 2010
Young, Cliff (Reno) September 15, 2009

## BOOKS AND ARTICLES

Albert, Alexia, *Brothel*, New York: Random House, 2001

Blum, John Morton, *Years of Discord, American Politics and Society*, 1961-1974, New York: W. Norton and Company

Bowers, Michael W., *The Sagebrush State, Nevada's History, Government and Politics*, Reno: University of Nevada Press, 2002

Davies, Richard O., editor, *The Maverick Spirit, Building the New Nevada*, Reno: University of Nevada Press, 1999

—Balboni, Alan, "Moe Dalitz: Controversial Founding Father of Modern Las Vegas," p. 24

—Douglass, William A., "William F. Harrah: Nevada Gaming Mogul," p. 58

—Edwards, Jerome E., "Grant Sawyer: A Liberal Governor for a Conservative State," p. 134

—Spees, Richard L., "Paul Laxalt: Man of Political Independence," p. 166

—Thompson, William, L. "Steve Wynn: 'I Got the Message,'" p. 194

—Dickens, Robert E., "William Raggio, Personality, Power and Politics," p. 212

—Klos, Patricia Ferraro, "Sue Wagner: Triumph Over Tragedy," p. 234

Demaris, Ovid, *The Last Mafioso: The Treacherous World of Jimmy Fratianno*, Bantam Books, 1981.

Driggs, Don W. and Leonard E. Goodall, *Nevada Politics & Government: Conservatism in an Open Society*, Lincoln: University of Nebraska Press, 1996

Elliott, Russell R., *History of Nevada*, University of Nebraska Press, 1987

Pete Hamill, *Why Sinatra Matters*, (New York: Little, Brown & Company 1998)146.

Highton, Jake, *Nevada Newspaper Days, A History of Journalism in the Silver State*, Stockton: Heritage West Books, 1990

Joyce, Marilee, *The Gentle Giant, How Jim Joyce Helped Shape Nevada Politics for a Generation*, Las Vegas: Nevada Publications, 1994

Kelley, Kitty, *His Way: The Unauthorized Biography of Frank Sinatra*, New York: Bantam Books,1986

Kling, Dwayne, *The Rise of the Biggest Little City*, Reno: University of Nevada Press; 1999

Kling, Dwayne and R.T. King, *Every Light Was On: Bill Harrah and His Clubs Remembered*, Reno: University of Nevada Oral History Program, 1999

Land, Barbara and Myrick Land, *A Short History of Reno*, Reno: University of Nevada Press, 1995

Laxalt, Paul, *Nevada's Paul Laxalt, A Memoir*, Reno: Jack Bacon & Company, 2000

Laxalt, Robert, *Nevada, A History*, Reno: University of Nevada Press, 1977

Marvel, John W., interviewed by Dana R. Bennett, *Nevada Legislature Oral History Project*, December 1, 2008

Neal, Joe M. Jr., interviewed by Dana R. Bennett, *Nevada Legislature Oral History Project*, May 12, 2008

O'Connell, Ann, interviewed by Dana R. Bennett and Dale A.R. Erquiaga, *Nevada Legislature Oral History Project*, March 28, 2008

*Political History of Nevada* (11th edition), Carson City: State Printing Office, 2006

Ralston, Jon. *The Anointed One*, Las Vegas, Huntington Press, 2000

Rawson, Raymond D., interviewed by Dana R. Bennett, *Nevada Legislature Oral History Project*, May 12, 2008

Rowley, William D., *Reno, Hub of the Washoe Country*, Woodland Hills: Windsor Publications, 1984

Sawyer, Grant, Gary Elliott, and R.T. King, *Hang Tough!* Reno: University of Nevada Oral History Program, 1993.

Smith, John L., *Of Rats and Men: Oscar Goodman's Life from Mob Mouthpiece to Mayor of Las Vegas*, Las Vegas: Huntington Press, 2003

Twain, Mark. *Roughing It*, New York: New American Library, 1962

Vernetti, Michael. *Lies Within Lies: The Betrayal of Nevada Judge Harry Claiborne* (Las Vegas: Stephens Press, 2011).

Wagner, Sue and Victoria Ford. *Through the Glass Ceiling*, Reno: University of Nevada Oral History Program, 2005.

Wilson, Thomas R.C. II. Interviewed by Dana R. Bennett, *Nevada Legislature Oral History Project*, May 19, 2008

# INDEX